Fodor's 89

Spain

D0166850

FODOR'S TRAVEL PUBLICATIONS, INC.
New York and London

Fodor's Spain

Editor: Richard Moore
Associate Editor: Thomas Cussans
Area Editor: Hilary Bunce
Contributors: Robert Brown, Harry Eyres, Ailsa Hudson, Pamela Vandyke Price

Drawings: Beryl Sanders
Maps: Swanston Graphics
Cover Photograph: Owen Franken/Stock Boston

Cover Design: Vignelli Associates

MANUFACTURED IN THE UNITED STATES OF AMERICA
10 9 8 7 6 5 4 3 2 1

CONTENTS

CONTENTS

FOREWORD

People have been calling their unattainable dreams "castles in Spain" for nearly six hundred years—since, at least, the days of England's medieval poet Chaucer. But in only the last tiny fraction of that time, around twenty-five years, has the world of romantic mystery that Spain represented become solid reality for hundreds of thousands of holidaymakers. Suddenly holidays in the sun at a price everyone could afford came within everyone's grasp. The fountain-singing courtyards of Moorish Granada, the long somnolent beaches of the Costa del Sol, the twisted flames of El Greco's paintings, the dusty plains where Don Quixote rode to do battle with his vision-enemies—all these found their places in travel agents' brochures, and the rush to enjoy relaxation and romance at bargain-basement prices was on.

But the Spain which vacationers will find today is very far removed from these castled dreams. Since the death of Generalissimo Franco, Spain has been galloping at breakneck speed towards the modern world. Once Franco's steely grip, holding his country back from developments surging through the rest of the world, was broken, the whole structure of Spanish society began to change, and his nation made up with avidity for its lost decades. An ever-growing cosmopolitanism took hold—which received an added boost when Spain entered the European Economic Community in 1986.

A blurring of the traditional national character has been taking place. Harassed businessmen rush to meet tight schedules; long lines of commuter traffic jam the city streets; political graffiti are splashed in abundance on every available wall, bridge and building; Spanish youth sport the most *à la mode* fashions; porno shops, political satire and fast food chains abound—even McDonalds' familiar yellow arches adorn the streets of Spain these days. Most people would be hard put to it to lament the passing of the old restrictions but the speed and enthusiasm with which Spain has embraced its new found freedom has inevitably brought in its wake a few negative aspects. High unemployment, juvenile delinquency, street violence, muggings, and a glaringly apparent drug problem have accompanied this metamorphosis of the traditional Spanish way of life. Service too, especially in hotels, is less willing than it once was, and there are few cafes which keep their doors open till 2 A.M. nowadays. Spanish hours are falling more in line with European ones, the siesta is on the wane and chic plastic cocktail bars have replaced the mahoganied male-only *tertulia* cafes of old. Inflation too is another great bugbear, though fortunately for the American or British tourist the present low value of the peseta has helped Spain regain her place among the budget vacation spots of Europe. The demands of the E.E.C. have already begun to change that situation.

If, however, you look behind the vivacious, shifting modern mask which Spain now wears, you can still find that elusive mystique which enchanted generations of visitors. Away from the hordes thronging out of tour buses and charter planes those castles are still as dreamlike as they ever were.

We would like to thank the many branches of the regional government Tourist Offices throughout Spain who have helped us in updating this edition, and we are especially grateful to Luis de Alba of the Tourist Office in Toledo for his assistance. We would also like to express our thanks to Nicolas Sanguines of the Spanish National Tourist office in London; R.J.M. Garcia, Manager of the Gibraltar Tourist Office in London; Inmaculada Marquez Cera in Seville; and Conchita de los Reyes in Madrid. Robin and Maren Dannhorn have given us considerable help with our material on the Balearics. And, finally, we are once again indebted to Hilary Bunce, our Area Editor, for her care and enthusiasm in preparing the major material for this edition.

*

While every care has been taken to assure the accuracy of the information in this guide, the passage of time will always bring change, and consequently the publisher cannot accept responsibility for errors that may occur.

All prices and opening times quoted in this guide are based on information available to us at press time. Hours and admission fees may change, however, and the prudent traveler will avoid inconvenience by calling ahead.

Fodor's wants to hear about your travel experiences, both pleasant and unpleasant. When a hotel or restaurant fails to live up to its billing, let us know and we will investigate the complaint and revise our entries where the facts warrant it.

Send your letters to the editors of Fodor's Travel Publications, 201 E. 50th Street, New York, NY 10022, or to Fodor's Travel Guides, 30–32 Bedford Square, London WC1B 3SG.

MAP OF SPAIN

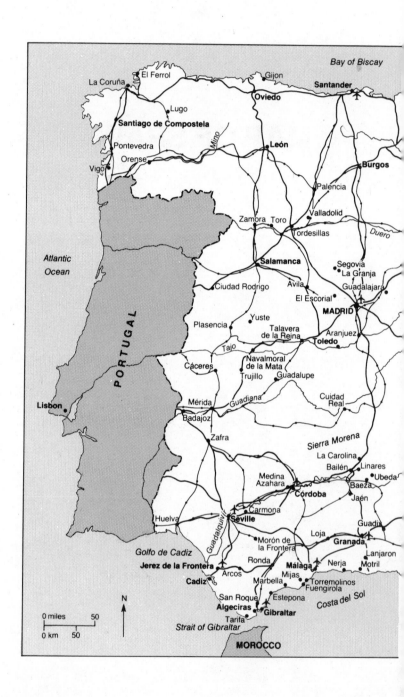

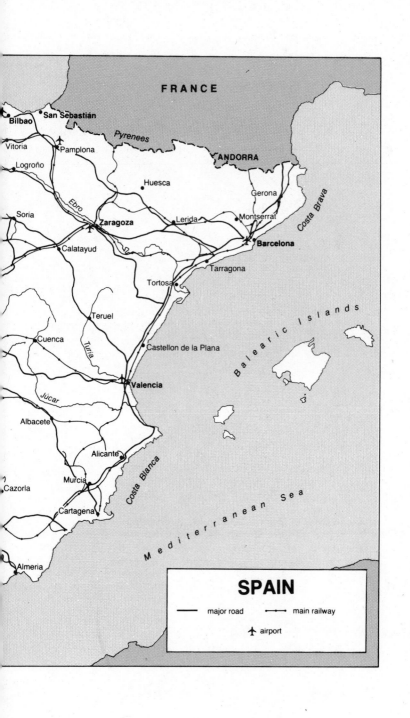

FRANCE

Bilbao
San Sebastián
Pyrenees
Vitoria
Pamplona
Logroño
Huesca
ANDORRA
Gerona
Soria
Ebro
Zaragoza
Lerida
Montserrat
Costa Brava
Calatayud
Barcelona
Tarragona
Tortosa
Teruel
Cuenca
Turia
Castellon de la Plana
Balearic Islands
Júcar
Valencia
Albacete
Alicante
Cazorla
Murcia
Costa Blanca
Cartagena
Mediterranean Sea
Almeria

SPAIN

—— major road   •—•— main railway

✈ airport

FACTS AT YOUR FINGERTIPS

Planning Your Trip

SOURCES OF INFORMATION. The major source of information for anyone planning a vacation to Spain is the Spanish National Tourist Office. They can supply information on all aspects of travel to and around Spain. They also produce a wealth of useful tourist literature, much of it free.

Their addresses are:

In the U.S.: 665 Fifth Ave., New York, NY 10022 (tel. 212–759–8822); Water Tower Place, Suite 915 East, 845 N. Michigan Ave., Chicago, IL 60611 (tel. 312–944–0215); San Vicente Plaza Bldg., 8383 Wilshire Blvd., Suite 960, Beverly Hills, CA 90211 (tel. 213–658–7188). Another office is planned for Miami, Florida.

In Canada: 60 Bloor St. West, Suite 201, Toronto, Ontario M4W 3B8 (tel. 416–961–3131).

In the U.K.: 57 St. James's St., London SW1A 1LD (tel. 01–499 1169).

Within Spain: Tourist information offices are found in all major cities and are run by the government of the local autonomous region or by the City Hall. The former can provide information on a whole region (Andalusia, Catalonia, etc.) and the latter, known as *oficinas municipales de turismo,* on the city in question only. Staff usually speak English and can help with anything from supplying maps, details of sights and museums to obtaining bullfight tickets, bus and train schedules and supplying lists of restaurants and hotels. It should be stressed, however, that the staff of Tourist Offices in Spain are unable to book accommodations, and are not officially supposed to recommend hotels or restaurants.

Most Tourist Offices are found in the city center, close to the main monuments and are often housed in historic buildings. They are rarely found at railroad stations or bus stations though in Madrid and Barcelona both the airports and main railroad stations have small branches of the Tourist Office.

TOUR OPERATORS. Full details of the many operators offering trips to Spain are available from the Spanish National Tourist Office, Iberia Airlines and other airlines and, of course, travel agents. But such is the range of tours available from both North America and the U.K. that a summary of some of the more typical is of interest. Details are as of mid-1988; be sure to check for the latest information.

1

From the U.S. *Globus-Gateway's* first-class package to Spain, Portugal and Tangier is called *Iberian Vacation.* Spend 14 days sightseeing in Madrid, Granada, Seville, Lisbon and El Escorial. Visit Málaga and the Costa del Sol, Mijas, Algeciras, Elvas, Salamanca, Gibraltar and the Costa del Sol. Take a steamer to Tangiers for an overnight stay. The cost ranges from $812 to $841 plus airfare to Madrid.

Maupintour's Mallorca/Spain/Portugal tour for 21 days begins at $3,398 plus airfare. The tour travels by jet between some cities and includes a few days of country drives through Andalusia. The tour runs from Barcelona to the Mediterranean shores of the Costa del Sol, to Gibraltar and Seville, then on to Madrid, Segovia and Portugal's sun coast riviera.

If you're mostly interested in *Madrid and Vicinity, Flag Tours* has a deluxe tour of that area for $1,295 plus airfare. For 8 days visit Madrid, El Escorial, the Valley of the Fallen, Avila, Segovia and Toledo.

Flag Tours also offers hotel packages in Madrid, Barcelona, Marbella, Torremolinos or a combination. They also arrange Fly-Drive vacations in collaboration with Avis.

U.S. operators include: *American Express,* 822 Lexington Ave., New York, N.Y. 10021 (tel. 800–241–1700); 50 Bloor St. West, Toronto, Ontario M4W 1A1 (tel. 416–967–3411).

Caravan Tours, 401 N. Michigan Ave., Chicago IL 60611 (tel. 312–321–9800).

ECI Travel (Viajes El Corte Ingles), 500 Fifth Ave., Suite 940, New York, NY 10036 (tel. 212–944–9400), offer fly-drive parador tours, golfing holidays, packages designed to your own specifications, and a trip that includes the Los Albujeros ranch of the Domecq family at Jerez.

Extra-Value Travel, 683 S. Collier Blvd., Marco Island, FL 33937 (tel. 800–255–2847).

Flag Tours, 5625 FM 1960 W., Houston, TX 77069 (tel. 800–223–8889).

Globus-Gateway/Cosmos, 95–25 Queens Blvd., Rego Park, NY 11374 (tel. 718–268–1700).

GWV International Weekends, 300 First Ave., Needham Heights, MA 02194 (tel. 800–225–5498; 617–449–5450 in MA).

Iberia Air Lines of Spain, 97–77 Queens Blvd., Rego Park, NY (tel. 718–793–3300).

Jacqueline Moss Museum Tours, 131 Davenport Ridge Lane, Stamford, CT 06903 (tel. 203–944–9400), provide tours for those interested in art, sculpture and historical monuments.

Maupintour, 1515 St. Andrews Dr., Lawrence, KS 66046 (tel. 800–255–6162).

Olson Travelworld, Box 92734, Los Angeles, CA 90009 (tel. 213–670–7100).

Petrabax USA, 9745 Queens Blvd., Rego Park, New York, NY 11374 (tel. 800–367–6611 or 718–322–7272) offer lots of Spanish tours (they are a Spanish company) including rail tours on special tourist trains.

TWA Getaway Vacations, 28 So. 6th St., Philadelphia, PA 19106 (tel. 800–GET–AWAY).

Unitours, 60 East 42nd St., New York, NY 10165 (tel. 212–949–9510).

From the U.K. *Swan Hellenic* offer three tours of the art treasures of Spain: *Valley of the Duero* (17 days, £1,645) visiting Bilbao, Logroño, Soria, Valladolid, Zamora, Oporto and Coimbra in Portugal, Salamanca,

Avila, Segovia and Madrid; *Madrid and Andalusia* (14 days, £1,535) visiting Madrid, Toledo, Córdoba, Ronda, and Granada; and *The Pilgrims' Road to Santiago de Compostela* (14 days, £1,365) visiting Pamplona, Burgos, Leon, Santiago de Compostela, Oviedo, Santander, San Sebastián, and Toulouse. All these tours are escorted by a tour manager and a guest lecturer.

Serenissima have a 15-day *Andalusia* tour (£1,325) starting in Gibraltar and visiting Ronda, Cáceres, Granada, the Sierra Nevada, Baeza, Córdoba, Seville, and the Coto Doñana. Their *Pilgrim Route to Santiago* (15 days, £2,250) begins in Toulouse in France and crosses to northern Spain by way of Pamplona, Burgos, León and Santiago de Compostela. *A Walk through Catalonia* (10 days, £965) offers a series of long-distance walks through the Catalan countryside with accommodations in the paradores of Tortosa and Cardona.

Cox and Kings do a *Moors and Murillo* tour (9 days, £1,225) visiting Córdoba, Granada and Seville.

Mundi Color schedule fly/drive holidays, including accommodations in historic and modern paradores; *Cantabrian Coast* (11 days, from £546); *Rioja Wine Trail and Navarra* (10 days, from £427). They are also agents for trips on the luxurious *Al Andalus Express* train that runs between Seville, Córdoba, Granada and Málaga (7 days, from £1,037), and for the *Transcantábrico* narrow-guage train that runs along the north coast between León and El Ferrol in Galicia.

U.K. operators include:

Brittany Ferries, Millbay Docks, Plymouth PL1 3EW (tel. 0752–221321).

Cox and Kings, St. James' Court, 45 Buckingham Gate, London SW1E 6AS (tel. 01–834 7446).

Marsans Travel, 7A Henrietta Pl., London W1M 9AG (tel. 01–493 4934).

Mundi Color, 276 Vauxhall Bridge Rd., London SW1V 1BB (tel. 01–834 3492).

Prospect Art Tours, 10 Barley Mow Passage, London W4 4PH (tel. 01–995 2163).

Serenissima Travel, 21 Dorset Square, London NW1 5PG (tel. 01–730 9841).

Swan Hellenic, 77 New Oxford St., London WC1A 1PP (tel. 01–831 1234).

World Wine Tours, 4 Dorchester Rd., Drayton St. Leonard, Oxon. OX9 8BH (tel. 0865–891919).

WHEN TO GO. The tourist season in Spain runs from the beginning of April to the end of October. If your primary aim is to sightsee, then undoubtedly the best months to visit are May, June and September, when the weather is usually sunny and pleasant without being overbearingly hot. At the height of summer, during July and August, certain parts of Spain may well be too hot for many visitors. At all costs, try and avoid Seville and Córdoba during these months as the heat there can be stifling and many places shut down for the day around 1 P.M. Madrid, too, can be rather unrewarding at this time; not only is it hot and airless but, despite the tourist authorities' efforts to keep the city alive for visitors, you will find many places closed, especially restaurants. If you come to Spain at this season, it is best to head for the coastal resorts or to such mountain regions as the Pyrenees or Picos de Europa.

The northern coast of Spain from Galicia around La Coruña in the west, to the Basque country (Bilbao and San Sebastián) in the east, is the coolest, wettest region of Spain. It is also the greenest, with a climate and landscape often more reminiscent of Wales than of Spain. It is best visited from mid-June through August when there is the least chance of rain. The Costa Brava, Barcelona, Valencia and the Balearics are at their best from mid-May to early September. In southeastern Spain, once around Cape Nao, just north of Alicante, the climate changes dramatically. Here on the Costa Blanca, it can be blazing hot all summer long, and mild balmy weather is not unknown even in January or February. The same is also true of the Costa del Sol on Spain's southern coast. Inland in Andalusia, cities such as Granada and Ronda lying high in the mountains, will be much cooler than the coastal resorts. Nights in Granada can be quite cool even at the height of summer, and in winter, surrounded by the snows of the Sierra Nevada, it is a place to wrap up warmly.

Worth remembering is that the whole of the central tableland of Spain, the Castilian plateau with Madrid as its nucleus surrounded by cities such as Avila, Segovia, Toledo, Cuenca and Burgos, suffers extremes of temperature from summer to winter—by European if not American standards. The keyword to Madrid's climate and to that of much of Spain, is unpredictability. Be warned that rain is not uncommon in *any* part of the country throughout the whole year. Forget *My Fair Lady's* weather report.

Snow in Spain is limited to the occasional powderings on high ground, the exception to this being the four principal skiing areas: the Pyrenees; the Picos de Europa (Cantabrian mountains) in the north; the Guadarrama range to the northwest of Madrid; and the high peaks of the Sierra Nevada just south of Granada.

Climate. Average afternoon temperatures in Fahrenheit and Centigrade for Madrid (top) and Barcelona (below).

	Jan.	Feb.	Mar.	Apr.	May	June	July	Aug.	Sept.	Oct.	Nov.	Dec.
F°	47	51	57	64	71	80	87	86	77	66	54	48
C°	8	11	14	18	22	27	31	30	25	19	12	9
F°	56	57	61	64	71	77	81	82	78	71	62	57
C°	13	14	16	18	22	25	27	28	26	22	17	14

SEASONAL EVENTS. Your decision when to visit Spain may well be determined by a long-cherished desire to witness one of its famous and spectacular fiestas. The best-known fiestas are undoubtedly the fallas of Valencia, held in March; the Holy Week processions, notably in Seville and other Andalusian cities; the Seville Fair around the end of April; and the bull runnings in Pamplona in the second week of July. We should warn you, however, that if you have set your heart on attending any of these, accommodations are extremely hard (though not impossible) to come by, many hotel rooms having been booked as long as 18 months in advance; prices also double or even triple, quite legally, and this affects hotels, taxi fares, public transport and possibly even bar and restaurant prices. So either make your preparations long in advance, or else be prepared to take pot luck; the atmosphere of these great fiestas is so infectious you cannot fail to enjoy yourselves.

Below we list some of the more famous of Spain's many traditional events. The dates given are only an indication, the exact days are often not known until a few weeks before the festival so be sure to check.

January. *Dia de los Reyes,* 5–6. Procession of the Three Kings when children all over Spain receive their Christmas gifts.

La Puebla (Mallorca), 17. Huge bonfires, processions, dancing and the blessing of the herd in honor of St. Anthony. Also lively San Anton celebrations in *Madrid* and *Burgos.*

San Sebastian (Guipúzcoa), 19–20. Tamborrada, drummer processions.

February. *Bocairente* (Valencia), 1–6. Festival of Moors and Christians, fantastic costumes, fireworks.

Cádiz. Carnival festivities in the week leading up to Shrove Tues. Cádiz has the best carnival processions in Spain.

Ciudad Rodrigo (Salamanca). Carnival festivities, bullfights.

Sitges (Barcelona). Sun. after Carnival. The Barcelona–Sitges Antique Car Rally (some years in March).

March. *Valencia,* 12–19. Fallas of San José, bonfires, the burning of effigies, parades and dancing.

Castellón de la Plana. 3rd Sun. in Lent. Romería to St. Mary Magdalene.

April. *Seville,* 3rd or 4th week of month. April Fair. Cavalcades of riders, flamenco dancing and singing, all-night entertainment in fairground tents. Good bullfights.

Andújar (Jaen), 21–24. Romería to the Virgen de la Cabeza at top of Sierra Morena.

Alcoy (Alicante), 22–24. Moors and Christians festival. Spectacular street battles.

Easter. The most famous of Spain's pageants, its Holy Week processions, are seen at their best in Seville, Málaga, Granada, Cuenca and Valladolid.

Chinchón (Madrid), Easter Sat. Passion Play in the ancient Plaza Mayor with 200 actors.

Hijar (Teruel), Holy Thurs.–Easter Day. Beautiful drum processions.

Avilés (Oviedo), Easter Sun. and Mon. Fiesta del Bollo. Variety of events, river races and folklore groups.

Pola de Siero (Oviedo), Easter Tues. Easter egg festival and folklore parade.

Murcia, week beginning Easter Mon. Blessing of the Orchards, Battle of Flowers, Burial of the Sardine.

May. *Córdoba,* 1–2. Las Cruces de Mayo. Processions of floral crosses. Mid-month, festival of decorated patios.

Jerez de la Frontera (Cádiz). Week-long horse fair, flamenco, good bullfights, livestock and agriculture machinery exhibitions.

Santo Domingo de la Calzada (La Rioja), 12. Parade of the Rams, procession of oxen-drawn carts and the Procession of the Wheel.

Almonte (Huelva), 14, Whitsuntide. Romería del Rocío, the most famous pilgrimage in Andalusia.

Madrid, mid-month. San Isidro festivals. Ten days of the best bullfights, fiestas in the Plaza Mayor.

Atienza (Guadalajara) 22. The Caballada. Horse cavalcades and races around the Puerta Caballo in commemoration of the great horse race of 1162.

Corpus Christi celebrations throughout Spain on the second Thurs. after Whitsun (25). Magnificent processions in Toledo; flower-strewn processions in Sitges (Barcelona) and Puenteareas (Pontevedra).

June. *Merida* (Badajoz). Classical Greek and Latin drama performances in the Roman theater throughout the month.

Calella (Barcelona), 1st or 2nd Sunday. Sardana dance and music festival.

Alicante, 20–28. Hogueras de San Juan. Bonfires of effigies, cavalcades and fireworks.

San Pedro Manrique (Soria), 23–24. The Night of St. John. The Passage of the Fire where men walk barefoot across a bed of coals; Procession of the Mondidas, women dressed in white.

Hita (Guadalajara), 30. Medieval theater festivals with bull lancing, archery and falconry in some years.

Granada. Mid-June through mid-July. International music and ballet festival in the gardens of the Alhambra.

July. *San Sebastián* (Guipúzcoa). International Jazz Festival.

San Lorenzo de Sabucedo (Pontevedra). First Sat., Sun. and Mon. A Rapa das Bestas. Round-up in which horses are caught, broken and branded.

Pamplona (Navarra), 6–15. Fiesta de San Fermín. Running of bulls through the streets, parades, fireworks and bullfights.

Olot (Gerona), 2nd Sun. Sardana dance and music festival.

Pontevedra, 11. San Benitiño de Lérez festival. Galician music and song.

San Pedro del Pinatar (Murcia), 16. Festival of the Virgen del Carmen, patroness of sailors and fishermen. The virgin's statue is borne on boats on the Mar Menor.

Torremolinos (Málaga), 16. Also in other Costa del Sol fishing villages. Celebrations in honor of the Virgen del Carmen.

Anguiano (La Rioja), 22. The Dance of the Stilts.

Santiago de Compostela (La Coruña), 25. Pilgrimage to the tomb of St. James the Apostle, with much pomp and ceremony; fireworks.

Cangas de Onis (Oviedo), Festival of the Shepherds.

Villajoyosa (Alicante), 24–31. Moors and Christians Festival, battles on land and sea.

Luarca (Oviedo). Last Sun. Cowherds of Alzada Festival: very colorful.

Jaca (Huesca). Last week in July, first week in August (odd years only). Pyrenees Folklore Festival.

August. *Santander,* all month. International Music and Ballet Festival.

Vitoria (Alava), 4–9. Festivals of the White Virgin. Processions, fireworks, music.

Gijón (Oviedo). First Sun. Asturias Day. Spectacular parade of decorated floats, folk groups and romería.

Arriondas-Ribadesella (Oviedo). Second Sat. Asturias Skull Race Festival.

San Sebastián (Guipúzcoa), mid-month. Semana Grande celebrations. Week-long sports and cultural events, fireworks, and running of cardboard bulls.

Elche (Alicante), 11–15. Famous Mystery Play in honor of the Assumption; also celebrations at many other places.

La Alberca (Salamanca), 15–16. La Loa celebrations for the Feast of the Assumption. Traditional costumes.

Laredo (Cantabria). Last Friday. Battle of Flowers.

Jumilla (Murcia), *Montilla* (Córdoba) and *Requena* (Valencia), end of the month. Grape Harvest Fairs and Festivals.

September. *Almagro* (Ciudad Real). Festival of Spanish Classical Drama.

Villena (Alicante), 4–9. Moors and Christian Festival.

Jerez de la Frontera (Cádiz), Wed. to second Sun. Grape Harvest Festival. Carnival queens, processions, much sherry drinking.

Oviedo, 19. "America Day in Asturias."

Logroño (La Rioja), 18–25. Around St. Matthew's Day, 21st. Rioja Grape Harvest Festival.

San Sebastián (Guipúzcoa). International Film Festival.

October. *Zaragoza,* 12. Fiestas del Pilar in honor of the Virgin of the Pillar. Float parades, jota dance contests and sports.

El Grove (Pontevedra), 2nd Sun. Shellfish Festival. Galician dances, exhibition of live shellfish and shellfish cuisine.

Mondoñedo (Lugo), 18–20. As San Lucas Festival. Important horse, mule and donkey sale.

Consuegra (Toledo). Last weekend. Festival of the Saffron Harvest.

December. *Torrejoncillo* (Cáceres), 7. La Encamisa. Sheet-covered horsemen bearing torches fire volleys of powder in the Plaza Mayor.

Labastida (Alava), 24–25. Nativity parades, midnight Mass celebrations and bonfire.

Madrid, 31. Crowds gather in the Puerta del Sol to see in the New Year, eating grapes on each stroke of midnight.

NATIONAL HOLIDAYS 1989. The following are national holidays when stores, businesses and many museums and monuments will be closed all over Spain. January 1 (New Year's Day); January 6 (Day of the Three Kings, Epiphany); March 19 (St. Joseph); March 23 (Holy Thursday—some cities only); March 24 (Good Friday); May 1 (Labor Day); May 25 Corpus Christi (second Thursday after Whitsun); July 25 (Santiago); August 15 (Feast of the Assumption); October 12 (El Pilar); November 1 (All Saints); December 6 (Constitution); December 8 (Immaculate Conception); December 25 (Christmas Day). In addition to the above, every town and village has its own local fiesta when, with the exception of restaurants, everything will be closed, e.g. May 2 throughout Madrid province; October 9 throughout Valencia region.

WHAT TO PACK. The first principle is to travel light. Flying across the Atlantic, airline baggage allowances are based on size rather than weight and you will be allowed the equivalent of two medium-sized suitcases per person. Bear in mind, however, that if you are making outward connections within Europe, the baggage allowance on European airlines is governed by weight (usually 20 kilos (44 lb.) per person). For your homeward flight, be warned that many Spanish airports are extremely strict about limiting your hand luggage to one small flight bag only. Porters are few and far between at Spanish airports but luggage carts are usually available.

Clothing. The first considerations are the season of the year and the countries you plan to visit. You should also bear in mind the altitude of the places you are visiting. Summer wear may be fine for beach resorts but warmer evening clothes are essential for higher places often only a few miles inland. As a general guideline, if your trip is to be between November and March, you will need only winter wear; if between June and September you need bring only summer clothes; but if you are visiting Spain in April or May or in September or October, it is wise to combine the two. No matter what the season you should always bring an umbrella and a light rain coat. If you are going to the north of Spain, make sure you bring warm sweaters and a jacket.

Another important consideration is footwear. Comfortable low-heeled walking shoes are essential for sightseeing; many of Spain's most picturesque sights involve long walks through dusty, cobbled streets.

Exactly what you choose to take will depend greatly on your type of travel. Generally speaking, dress is informal and unless you are planning to stay in top hotels in a luxury resort such as Marbella, or in some of Madrid's leading 5–star hotels, you are unlikely to need formal evening dress.

On Spanish beaches where not so long ago the bikini was considered scandalous, now anything goes. But, except for beach restaurants, beach wear is not generally accepted in restaurants, shops or hotel lobbies, even those close to the sea, so shirts, shorts and sandals are a must for beach trips.

Miscellaneous. Kleenex are essential when traveling and are expensive in Spain. Toilet rolls never come amiss, especially in country districts. Small tablets of soap are useful too, as few restrooms provide these, nor do some hotels at the lower end of the scale. *Wet Ones,* or similar, are also a good idea, especially for car travelers.

Electrical converters (to 220V) are essential for Americans, and only two-pin round-headed plugs will work in Spanish sockets. Equipment for heating contact lenses should be brought with you as should remedies for headaches, constipation, motion sickness, etc. Medicines are readily available in Spain but are not sold under the brand name you will know them by. Prescriptions for spectacles, special medicines and insulin should always be carried.

SPANISH CURRENCY. The unit of currency in Spain is the peseta. There are bills of 200, 500, 1,000, 2,000, 5,000, and 10,000 ptas. Coins are 1 pta., 5, 25, 50, 100, 200, and 500 ptas. At presstime (mid-1988) the exchange rate was around 110 ptas. to the U.S. dollar and 203 ptas. to the pound sterling. However, these rates will change both before and during 1989.

COSTS IN SPAIN. Prices have soared dramatically over the past decade. Moreover, in January 1986 Spain joined the Common Market which led inevitably to yet another increase in the cost of living. With Spain's E.E.C. membership came the automatic levying of a sales, or value-added, tax, known as I.V.A., which has had a considerable impact on the average tourist's expenditure. I.V.A. has a complicated sliding scale structure, but is usually levied at 6% and this applies to restaurants and most hotels. Luxury, or 5-star, hotels are subject to 12% tax, however, as are car rental charges. The days when Spain was the bargain basement of Europe are now over, and the visitor will most probably find that the cost of living in Spain matches that of its northern European neighbors.

As in most countries, prices vary slightly from region to region and obviously the less visited and more out-of-the-way places will cost less than the more popular destinations. Top of the list for extravagance comes the international resort of Marbella, long the mecca of the rich and famous. Not far behind come the 5-star hotels and top restaurants of Madrid, Barcelona and Seville. As a general rule, hotels on the north coast tend to be higher than average, whereas the little visited but delightful region of Extremadura on Spain's western border with Portugal, offers some of the best value for money. You may well stumble upon some charming bargains in the inland regions such as the little-known provinces of Huesca, Soria, Teruel, Cuenca or Albacete. In the highly developed coastal regions such as the Costa Brava, Costa Blanca or Costa del Sol, there is a proliferation of comfortable 3-star hotels (though many are now beginning to show their cracks) which offer extremely reasonable rates due to their working in close liaison with package tour agencies. For this reason you may find they are totally booked throughout the high season, but that outside of July and August, you have a good chance of finding high standards of accommodations at a reasonable price. Restaurants too, in these coastal regions, are often so numerous that competition between them means an abundance of budget-priced meals.

Despite recent E.E.C. changes in the tax on alcohol, Spanish alcohol is still relatively inexpensive. Where Spain really scores on the budget front is in the field of transport, other that is, than in the cost of gas for motoring.

Finally, for a look at some sample costs, a coffee in 1989 will cost around 100–130 ptas., a beer 80–150 ptas., a soda 120 ptas., a small glass of wine in a bar 60–80 ptas., an American-style cocktail 300–400 ptas.; a cinema ticket 350–500 ptas.; a theater seat 600–1,500 ptas.; a local bus or subway ride 60–80 ptas.; a taxi ride 300–450 ptas.; and an ice cream cone about 80 ptas.

TAKING MONEY ABROAD. Traveler's checks are still the standard and best way to safeguard your travel funds, as most companies will replace them quickly and efficiently if lost. You should always keep a note of the check numbers separate from the checks themselves to help with the replacement process. The best-known checks are those of *American Express, Bank of America, Visa* and *Thomas Cook* though checks issued by all the main American and British banks are readily acceptable in Spain. Take your traveler's checks in dollars rather than pesetas.

You can take in an unlimited amount of Spanish bank notes and it is always a good idea to have *some* local currency upon arrival. Some banks will provide this service; or, in the U.S., contact *Deak International, Ltd.,* 630 Fifth Ave., New York, NY 10111 (tel. 212–757–0100 call for additional branches).

Britons holding a Uniform Eurocheque card and cheque book—apply for them at your bank—can cash cheques for up to £100 a day at banks participating in the scheme *and* write cheques for goods and services—hotels, restaurants, shops, etc.—again up to £100.

Credit Cards. The four most commonly accepted credit cards in Spain are *American Express, Diner's Club, Visa* and *MasterCard* (incorporating *Access* and *Eurocard*). By far the most widely accepted card is Visa. Most hotels and restaurants, department stores and major shops will accept payment by credit card but in smaller stores and inexpensive restaurants, this is unlikely to be the case. In all cases, if you are planning to pay by plastic, you should check first; it is not unknown for an establishment to display a credit card sign and then claim that it does not have the necessary charge forms. We have also had reports of some hotels limiting the amount you can charge to a credit card so again if you are planning several nights' stay, check *first*. Some gas stations in Spain accept payment by credit card, but when you fill up your tank, be prepared to pay cash.

In the Practical Information sections of this book we have included credit card information for as many establishments as we have been able to verify. The initials we use for this information are AE, DC, MC and V—which stand for American Express, Diner's Club, MasterCard (alias Access and Eurocard) and Visa (Barclaycard).

PASSPORTS. Americans. All U.S. citizens require a passport for entry into Spain. In the U.S., apply in person at U.S. Passport Agency Offices, local county courthouses or selected Post Offices. If you have a passport not more than 12 years old you may renew your passport by mail; otherwise you will need:

—proof of citizenship, such as a birth certificate;

—two recent identical photographs, two inches square, in either black and white or color, on non-glossy paper;

—$35 for the passport itself plus a $7 processing fee if you are applying in person (no processing fee when renewing your passport by mail) for those 18 years and older or if you are under 18, $20 for the passport plus a $7 processing fee if you are applying in person (again, no extra fee when applying by mail);

—proof of identity that includes a photo and signature, such as a driver's license, previous passport, any governmental ID card, or a copy of an income tax return.

Adult passports are valid for ten years, others for five years; they are not renewable. Allow four to six weeks for your application to be processed, but in an emergency, Passport Agency offices can have a passport readied within 24–48 hours, and even the postal authorities can indicate "Rush" when necessary.

If you expect to travel extensively, request a 48- or 96-page passport rather than the usual 24-page one. There is no extra charge. When you receive your passport, write down its number, date and place of issue in a separate, secure place. The loss of a valid passport should be reported immediately to the local police and to the Passport Office, Dept. of State 1425 K St., NW, Washington DC 20524. If your passport is lost or stolen while abroad, report it immediately to the local authorities and apply for a replacement at the nearest U.S. embassy or consular office.

Canadians. Canadian citizens apply in person to regional passport offices, post offices or by mail to Bureau of Passports, Complex Guy Favreau, 200 Dorchester West, Montreal, Quebec H2Z 1X4 (tel. 514–283–2152). $25, two photographs, a guarantor and evidence of citizenship are required. Canadian passports are valid for five years and are non-renewable.

Britons. British subjects should apply for passports on special forms obtainable from main post offices or a travel agent. The application should be sent or taken to the Passport Office according to residential area (as indicated on the guidance form) or lodged with them through a travel agent. It is best to apply for the passport 2 or 3 months before it is required, although in some cases it will be issued sooner. The regional Passport Offices are located in London, Liverpool, Peterborough, Glasgow and Newport. The application must be countersigned by your bank manager or by a solicitor, barrister, doctor, clergyman or justice of the peace who knows you personally. You will need two full-face photos. The fee is £15; passport valid for 10 years.

British Visitor's Passport. This simplified form of passport has advantages for the once-in-a-while tourist to most European countries (including Spain). Valid for one year and not renewable, it costs £7.50. Application may be made at main post offices in England, Scotland and Wales, and in Northern Ireland at the Passport Office in Belfast. Birth certificate or medical card for identification and two passport photographs are required—no other formalities.

INSURANCE. The different varieties of travel insurance cover everything from health and accident costs, to lost baggage and trip cancellation. Insurance is available from many sources, however, and many travelers unwittingly end up with duplicate coverage. Before purchasing separate travel insurance of any kind, be sure to check your regular policies carefully. At the same time make sure you don't neglect some eventuality which could end up costing a small fortune.

For example, basic *Blue Cross-Blue Shield* policies do cover health costs incurred while traveling. They will not, however, cover the cost of emergency transportation, which can often add up to several thousand dollars. Emergency transportation is covered, in part at least, by many major medical policies such as those underwritten by *Prudential* and *Metropolitan.* We can't urge you too strongly that in order to be sure you are getting the coverage you need, check any policy carefully before buying. Another important example: most insurance issued specifically for travel will not cover pre-existing conditions, such as a heart condition.

Several organizations offer coverage designed to supplement existing health insurance and to help defray costs not covered by many standard policies. Some of the more prominent are:

Carefree Travel Insurance, c/o ARM Coverage Inc., 120 Mineola Blvd., Box 310, Mineola, NY 11510, underwritten by the Hartford Accident and Indemnity Co., offers a comprehensive benefits package that includes trip cancellation and interruption, medical and accidental death/ dismemberment coverage, as well as medical, legal and economic assistance. Trip cancellation and interruption insurance can be purchased separately. Call 800–654–2424 for additional information.

International SOS Assistance Inc., Box 11568, Philadelphia, PA 19116 has fees from $15 a person for seven days, to $195 for a year (tel. 800–523–8930).

IAMAT (International Association for Medical Assistance to Travelers), 417 Center St., Lewiston, NY 14092, (tel. 716–754–4883) in the U.S.; or 188 Nicklin Rd., Guelph, Ontario, N1H 7L5 (tel. 519–836–0102).

Travel Assistance International, the American arm of *Europ Assistance,* offers a comprehensive program providing medical and personal emergency services and offering immediate, on-the-spot medical, personal and financial help. Trip protection ranges from $35 for an individual for up to eight days to $220 for an entire family for a year. Full details from travel agents or insurance brokers, or from Europ Assistance Worldwide Services, Inc., 1333 F St., N.W., Washington D.C. 20004 (tel. 800–821–2828). In the U.K., contact Europ Assistance Ltd., 252 High St., Croydon, Surrey (tel. 01–680 1234).

Another frequent inconvenience to travelers is the loss of baggage. It is possible, though often a complicated affair, to insure your luggage against loss through theft or negligence. Insurance companies are reluctant to sell such coverage alone, however since it is often a losing proposition for them. Instead, it is most often included as part of a package that would also cover accidents or health. Should you lose your luggage or some other personal possession, be sure to report it to the local police within 24 hours. Without documentation of such a report, your insurance company might be very stingy.

The last major area of traveler's insurance is trip cancellation coverage. This is especially important to travelers on APEX or charter flights. Should you get sick abroad, or for some other reason be unable to continue your trip, you may be stuck having to buy a new one-way fare home, plus paying for space on a charter you're not using. You can guard against this with trip cancellation insurance, usually available from travel agents. Most of these policies will also cover last-minute cancellations.

STUDENT AND YOUTH TRAVEL. All student travelers should obtain an International Student Identity Card, which is usually needed to get student discounts, youth rail passes, and student rates on travel insurance. Apply to *Council On International Educational Exchange,* 205 East 42 St., New York, NY 10017 (tel. 212–661–1414). Canadian students should apply to the *Canadian Federation of Student-Services,* 187 College St., Toronto, Ontario M5S IP7 (tel. 416–979–2406).

The following organizations can also be helpful in finding student flights, educational opportunities and other information. Most deal with international student travel generally, but materials for those listed cover Spain.

American Youth Hostels, Box 37613, Washington, DC 20013 (tel. 202–783–6161).

Institute of International Education, 809 United Nations Plaza, New York, NY 10017 (tel. 212–883–8200).

Educational Travel Center, 438 North Frances, Madison, WI 53703 (tel. 608–256–5551).

HINTS FOR DISABLED TRAVELERS. Unfortunately sightseeing is not made easy for the handicapped visiting Spain. There are no wheelchairs at any of the monuments (except the Prado Museum in Madrid), there are no ramps anywhere and no crutches provided (though these can be bought quite easily at pharmacies and clinics). Most of the well-known sights are not accessible by vehicle and involve lots of walking, often up hills and over cobbles. There are also no toilets for the disabled except at airports.

A major source of information in the U.S. is *Access to the World: A Travel Guide for the Handicapped,* by Louise Weiss, an outstanding book covering all aspects of travel for anyone with health or medical problems; it features extensive listings and suggestions on everything from availability of special diets to wheelchair accessibility. The book is out of print but can be ordered from *Facts on File,* 460 Park Ave. South, New York, NY 10016 ($16.95).

Tours specially designed for the handicapped generally parallel those of the non-handicapped traveler, but at a more leisurely pace. For a complete list of tour operators who arrange such travel write to the *Society for the Advancement of Travel for the Handicapped (SATH),* 26 Court St., Penthouse Suite, Brooklyn, NY 11242 (tel. 718–858–5483). The Travel Information Service at *Moss Rehabilitation Hospital,* 12th St. and Tabor Rd., Philadelphia, PA 19141 (tel. 215–329–5715) answers inquiries regarding facilities in specific countries as well as providing toll-free telephone numbers for airlines with special lines for the hearing-impaired and, again, listings of selected tour operators. International Air Transport Association (IATA) publishes a free pamphlet entitled *Incapacitated Passengers' Air Travel Guide* to explain the various arrangements to be made and how to make them. Write IATA, 2000 Peel St., Montreal, Quebec H3A 2R4 (tel. 514–844–6311).

In the U.K., contact *Mobility International,* 43 Dorset St., London W.1; the *National Society for Mentally Handicapped Children,* 117 Golden Lane, London E.C.1; the *Across Trust,* Crown House, Morden, Surrey (they have an amazing series of "Jumbulances," huge articulated ambulances, staffed by volunteer doctors and nurses, that can whisk even the most seriously handicapped across Europe in comfort and safety). But the main source in Britain for all advice on handicapped travel is the *Royal Association for Disability and Rehabilitation* (RADAR), 25 Mortimer St., London W.1.

Getting to Spain

FROM THE U.S. BY AIR. Airlines specifically serving Spain from major U.S. cities (usually via New York) include *Iberia Air Lines, TWA,* and *Pan Am,* who reopened direct services from the U.S.A. to Spain in 1988. From Canada, Iberia operates regular flights out of Montreal to Madrid.

With air fares in a constant state of flux, the best advice for anyone planning to fly to Spain independently (rather than as part of a package tour, in which case your flight will have been arranged for you) is to check with a travel agent and let him make your reservations for you. Nonetheless, there are a number of points to bear in mind.

The best bet is to buy an APEX ticket. First Class, Business and even the misleadingly named Economy, though giving maximum flexibility on flying dates and cancellations, as well as permitting stopovers, are extremely expensive. APEX by contrast, are reasonably priced and offer the all-important security of fixed return dates (all APEX tickets are round-trip). In addition, you get exactly the same service as when flying Economy. However, there are a number of restrictions: you must book and pay for your ticket 14 days or more in advance; you can stay in Spain for no less than 7 days and no more than 6 months. If you miss your flight, you forfeit the fare. But from the point of view of price and convenience, these tickets certainly represent the best value for money.

Sometimes it is also worth investigating package tours even if you do not wish to use the tours' other services (hotels, meals, etc.); because a packager can block book seats, the price of a package can be less than the cost when the air fare is booked separately.

If you have the flexibility, you can sometimes benefit from last-minute sales tour operators have in order to fill a plane. A number of brokers specializing in such discount sales have also sprung up. All charge an annual membership fee, usually about $35–50. Among these: *Stand-Buys Ltd.,* 311 W. Superior, Suite 414, Chicago, IL 60610 (tel. 312–943–5737); *Moments Notice,* 40 E. 49th St., New York, NY 10017 (tel. 212–486–0503); *Discount Travel Intl.,* 114 Forrest Ave., Suite 205, Narberth, PA 19072 (tel. 215–668–2182); and *Worldwide Discount Travel Club,* 1674 Meridian Ave., Miami Beach, FL 33139 (tel. 305–534–2082). Sometimes, tour and charter flight operators themselves advertise in Sunday travel supplements as well. Do try to find out whether the tour operator is reputable and whether you will have to wait until the operator has a spare seat in order to return.

Fares. Typical round-trip fares as of mid-1988 from New York to Madrid: First class $3,720; Business Class $2,258; Economy $1,364; APEX from $492 to $735 depending on the season. Charter fares are about the same as, or slightly lower than, APEX. Add $23 tax to all fares.

Warning. At peak travel times, in particular flights departing Spain for the U.S. at weekends, both TWA and Iberia flights can be heavily overbooked. We advise earliest reconfirmation of return flights and early arrival at airport of departure to ensure a seat. Be warned that reconfirmation of tickets in no way ensures a seat. Passengers with connecting Iberia internal flights to Madrid should take special care, particularly if flying Málaga–Madrid. These flights can also be so overbooked that passengers risk missing their New York connections, despite reconfirmation. Expect long slow lines at check-in. TWA passengers wishing to reserve seats on return flights from Spain to U.S. should ensure they obtain boarding passes for their return flight *before* leaving U.S. TWA in Spain does not honor reservations made if boarding passes have not been obtained prior to departure from U.S.

FROM THE U.S. BY BOAT. Royal Viking is the only line sailing to Spain from the United States. Its 1988–89 schedule includes Spain on its annual April cruise from Ft. Lauderdale, Florida, to Lisbon. Details from your travel agent or *Royal Viking,* 750 Battery St., San Francisco, CA 94111 (tel. 800–422–8000).

For details on the possibility of freighter travel to or from Spain, consult: *Pearl's Freighter Tips,* Box 188, 16307 Depot Rd., Flushing, NY 11358.

FROM THE U.K. BY AIR. At presstime (mid-1988) air fares had begun to fall, especially off-peak. Also, several new companies had started to operate scheduled flights to Spain. However, there are likely to be further developments in 1989. Check with a good travel agent in March/April when the new schedules and fares have been published. If you book very early you will risk paying too much.

There are three main ways of getting to Spain by air from the U.K. Which one you choose will depend on how flexible you can be in terms of dates, time of travel and how much you wish to spend.

First of all, if the dates of travel are set and time is at a premium, use one of the scheduled services run by the national airlines, *Iberia* or *British Airways.* Between them (mid-1988) they operate up to six flights daily to Madrid, and three to Barcelona from London's Heathrow and Gatwick airports. The flying time is around 2 hours 15 minutes. Other destinations served are Santiago, Valencia, Alicante, Málaga, Seville, Bilbao, the Balearics and Gibraltar. At Madrid and Barcelona you can plug in to Iberia's internal air network. Fares on these premium routes are high, especially over the peak summer weekends (Friday to Sunday inclusive) at around £190 for a Super-Pex return to Barcelona. Midweek flights are much cheaper at around £160 return. To Madrid the return fares work out at around £205 peak and £175 off peak. Demand for seats on these flights is high and it is essential to book well in advance.

Secondly there are the scheduled charter flights run by organizations such as *Monarch, Falcon, Air Europe, Dan Air* and *Aviaco.* These serve both the independent and package traveler. Destinations available include Málaga, Alicante, Gerona, Reus, Palma (Mallorca), Ibiza and Mahon (Menorca). The outward and return dates are usually fixed at seven day intervals with stays of up to 28 nights. For a return to Málaga in peak season allow £165 and early or late season £100. *GB Airways* and *Air Europe* also fly from London and Manchester to Gibraltar.

Thirdly there is the discount flight market for the last-minute booker. Here one can, by brinkmanship, often buy a return flight for as little as £70 in peak season and £55 off peak. Obviously this market is subject to severe fluctuations. The game is to phone around all the reputable flight operators you see in the press (look for the ATOL number or ABTA) about a week before you want to fly. On no account accept the first offer—go through the columns and check them all.

Always ask what the price they are quoting includes—airport tax? fuel surcharge? insurance? The total cost may not be quite as low as the figure in the newspaper. Then look at ads for holidays which include accommodations by companies such as *Portland, Tjaereborg, Cosmos, Global,* etc. who may be selling off left-over holidays (or their own spare seats) at amazingly low prices. For these offers it is essential to be able to pay by credit card (not a charge card) as it protects you if things go wrong.

FROM THE U.K. BY CAR. There is only one direct car ferry service from Britain to Spain, and this is operated by Brittany Ferries. They sail from Plymouth to Santander on the northern coast of Spain.

There are two sailings each way per week throughout the year (except January) and the crossing takes 24 hours. The ferries are heavily loaded in the peak summer season. A car (up to 4.5 meters) and two people, return, will cost around £545 including a cabin. Details from Brittany Ferries, Millbay Docks, Plymouth PL1 3EW (tel. 0752–221321). It is recommended that you book well in advance.

Alternatively, for northern Spain, travel on one of the short sea crossings to Calais/Boulogne, then by way of the A26 to Paris, which is skirted by the Boulevard Périphérique, then on to Spain. However, you may prefer to make use of one of the longer channel crossings to Le Havre, Cherbourg, Caen and St. Malo from Portsmouth with its excellent motorway connections. To give an idea of distance—it is some 980 km. (610 miles) from Cherbourg to the Spanish border, and the drive can be made on good roads. Cost for a car (up to 4.5 meters), driver and passenger (return) with a cabin each way on the ferry works out at around £255, plus petrol/autoroute tolls £115—plus, of course, Spanish Bail Bond, Insurance and any meals and overnight stops en route.

If visiting the eastern coast of Spain, the resorts of the Costa Brava, Costa Dorada, and Costa Blanca, use one of the regularly serviced routes from Dover/Folkestone to Calais/Boulogne and then drive down through France. The quickest road route is by going to Calais/Boulogne then using the A26 to Paris, then down the Rhone Valley on the A6 and along the Mediterranean coast to Perpignan. Using this route it is some 1,130 km. (700 miles) from the coast to the Spanish border. But note that the costs of using the autoroute add up! For the short sea channel crossing (return) allow around £175 for a car (up to 4.5m) driver and passenger, for the French autoroute tolls around £80, for petrol around £140.

If you don't like the idea of these long punishing drives why not consider Motorail? There are services from Calais and Boulogne to Narbonne—some 80 km. (50 miles) from Spain. These trains run several nights a week during the summer, leaving in mid-evening and arriving in Narbonne the following morning. The return fare including the ferry crossing from Dover/Folkestone (any length of car) and couchettes each way for two people works out at around £515. Services also run to Biarritz and these are ideal for northern Spain. For details contact S.N.C.F., 179 Piccadilly, London W1V 0BA (tel. 01–409 3518).

FROM THE U.K. BY TRAIN. The journey has three main stages, London to Paris, Paris to the French/Spanish border and from there to your final destination. Unless you catch a TALGO or the Puerta del Sol it is necessary to change trains at the border because the Spanish railways have a wider gauge. To give an idea of time, the journey from London to Madrid takes around 26 hours.

The fastest and most convenient way to get to Paris is by the Hoverspeed City Sprint combination of rail–hovercraft–rail. There are several departures daily, and the journey takes under 5¾ hours. To reach Madrid from Paris the most comfortable journey is offered by the overnight Paris–Madrid TALGO. This luxury sleeper train, with full restaurant service, leaves Paris Austerlitz station at 8 P.M. and reaches Madrid just after 8.30 next morning. It is advisable to book well in advance. Buy a "Global Ticket" which includes the sleeper and all supplements. On the international TALGO trains there is no tiresome change at the frontier as the wheelsets are automatically re-gauged. The alternative is the "Puerta del Sol," which is cheaper, a little slower, and not quite as comfortable, leaving Paris just before 6 P.M. and arriving in Madrid at 10 A.M. There is also a daytime service to Madrid leaving Paris Austerlitz at 6.51 A.M.; on this you change at Irun, on the frontier, to a connecting TALGO train which reaches Madrid at 9.38 P.M.

The journey to Barcelona can be made most comfortably with an overnight stop in Paris. Then catch one the of superb TGVs (*Train à Grand Vitesse*) from the Gare de Lyon to Avignon; the 742 km. (461 miles) to Avignon are covered in about 3¾ hours. At Avignon board the Catalan TALGO, which will take you right through to Barcelona, arriving at 9.18 P.M. Advance reservations essential on both trains. Or take the Barcelona TALGO which leaves Paris Austerlitz daily at 9 P.M. and arrives in Barcelona at 8.30 A.M. This last is a sleeper, has its wheelsets adjusted at the border, and is by far the best way of getting from Paris to Barcelona. There is a daytime train to Barcelona—frontier change necessary—leaving Paris Austerlitz at 9.39 A.M., but you don't reach your destination until 11.30 P.M.

An ordinary return from London to Barcelona/Madrid will work out at around £180 and break of journey en route is allowed. A *Leisure* return—traveling off peak in France—is around £150 (stay/journey must include a Sunday). Students and young people under 26 should look at the Inter Rail ticket at around £140 for a month's unlimited rail travel throughout Europe. The only condition is that you must have been resident in the U.K. for six months. Otherwise reduced fare tickets are available from *Eurotrain,* 52 Grosvenor Gardens, London SW1W OAG (tel. 01–730 6525) and *Transalpino,* 71–75 Buckingham Palace Rd., London SW1W ORE (tel. 01–834 9656).

For planning your trip the *Thomas Cook Continental Timetable* is indispensable—it gives the times of all the international and long distance trains as well as the main line services in Spain. As scheduling of trains in Europe varies greatly between summer and winter obtain the one nearest to the proposed date of travel. It can be bought over the counter at any branch of Thomas Cook (price around £5), or by post from Thomas Cook Timetable Publishing Office, P.O. Box 36, Peterborough PE3 6SB.

FROM THE U.K. BY BUS. Thanks to the modern motorway networks, bus services are surprisingly quick but their fares are only a little lower than charter flights, and you will have to allow for food on the journey. It is best to use one of the services run by a reliable operator such as *National Express-Eurolines.* National Express-Eurolines is the collective name for a number of services run by several major European bus companies—so don't expect to see the name on the side of the bus! These independent companies also advertise their services using their own names.

National Express-Eurolines, The Coach Travel Centre, 13 Regent St., London SW1Y 4LR (tel. 01–730 0202) have three services from London to Spain. The first is to the east coast calling at Costa Brava resorts, Barcelona, Valencia, Calpe, Benidorm and Alicante. This service runs daily in summer as far as Barcelona and continues on to Alicante four days a week. Return fares at presstime were: Barcelona £99; Alicante £129. The second service is a twice weekly one from London to Madrid and Algeciras, via San Sebastián, Vitoria, Burgos, Córdoba, Torremolinos and Marbella. Return fare to Madrid £110, to Córdoba £119. The third service runs to the north of Spain. There are up to four buses weekly as far as Bilbao. On two days a week the buses carry on, serving Bilbao, Santander, Oviedo, Valladolid, Tordesillas, Pueblo de Sanabria, Orense, Lugo, Santiago and La Coruña. Return fare to Santander is £101 and to Santiago £117. Reductions are available to students.

SSS International, 138 Eversholt St., London NW1 1BL (tel. 01–388 1732) also run three year-round services from London to Spain: to Barcelona, Valencia and Alicante; to Madrid and Algeciras; and to Bilbao, Santander, Oviedo, Valladolid, Orense, Lugo, Santiago and La Coruña. Fares are similar to those of *International Express.*

CUSTOMS ON ARRIVAL. Each person (aged 15 and over) may bring into Spain 200 cigarettes or 50 cigars or 100 cigarillos or 250 grams of tobacco if arriving from European countries, double quantities if you are arriving from elsewhere.

You are also allowed to bring in 1 liter of alcohol over 22° proof, or two liters under 22° proof and two liters of other wines; ¼ liter eau de cologne and 50 grams perfume; gifts to the value of 5,000 ptas. (2,000 ptas. for children under the age of 15).

TIME. During the summer Spain is six hours ahead of Eastern Standard Time, seven hours ahead of Central Time, eight hours ahead of Mountain Time and nine hours ahead of Pacific Time. During the winter, Spain puts her clocks back one hour, but as all America does likewise, the time difference remains the same. Spanish Daylight Saving Time begins at the end of March and ends at the end of September, so there are always a couple of weeks or so in both spring and fall when EST is way out of sync.

Similarly, Spain is one hour ahead of British Summer Time and, during the winter, one hour ahead of Greenwich Mean Time. During October Spain and Britain are on the same time.

Staying in Spain

CHANGING MONEY. All major Spanish banks will cash traveler's checks, as will most hotels, major branches of the *Corte Inglés* department store, and those stores that cater mainly to the tourist bus tour trade. It is advisable to bring your checks in dollars or pounds sterling rather than in Spanish pesetas as Spanish stores and hotels sometimes refuse to change peseta checks. Note also that traveler's checks are not generally regarded as cash in Spain and that making purchases with them in small stores or restaurants is not usually possible.

When cashing traveler's checks in a bank you will always need to show your passport. This applies to some hotels too. Banks also charge a few pesetas tax *(impuestos)* and a considerably larger sum in commission. Generally speaking it is better to cash checks in a bank than in a hotel as the exchange rate is usually more favorable, but as hotels rarely make a commission charge it is well worth taking this into consideration. If you are planning on cashing $100 or more in a bank check what rate of commission that particular bank charges. If it is more than 1½% take your business elsewhere.

If you are planning to cash traveler's checks in your hotel, note that most hotels will only allow their daytime receptionists to provide this service so do not get caught out and find yourself faced with an early morning departure and unable to settle your bill.

On arrival in Spain there are reputable banks or change bureaux in all international airports and ports of entry, and at the main railroad stations in Madrid and Barcelona. But if you arrive in the middle of the night it is unlikely that these will be open. It is always wise to bring around $50 in Spanish currency with you, more if you arrive on a weekend, to take care of taxi fares and other incidentals.

Although not quite in the same class as Italy, Spain's currency needs to be watched. It is very easy to misplace a nought or get a total wrong. Be sure for the first few days to double-check all additions until you get used to handling multi-thousand-peseta deals.

HOTELS. Spanish hotels have raised their rates in leaps and bounds in the last few years, and since as from 1986 all hotels must now charge the I.V.A. sales tax, they are no longer the bargain they once were. Hotels are officially classified from 5-star to 1-star; hostels and pensions are classified from 3-star to 1-star. If an R appears on the hotel plaque, the hotel is classed a *residencia* and does not offer full dining services; breakfast and cafeteria meals may be available. The star-ratings equate roughly with our classifications of Deluxe (L), Expensive (E), Moderate (M), and Inexpensive (I). The number of stars a hotel has is usually—but not always—a guide to its price. Prices charged by each establishment are listed in the *Guía de Hoteles* (published annually and obtainable from bookstores) and should also be on display at the reception desk.

In many hotels rates change according to season and they are always quoted per room and not per person. Sometimes the rate includes breakfast but often this is charged extra. It is also worth checking to make sure you won't be charged for meals you don't take. If you stay more than two nights you have a right to full board terms, which should be the room price plus not more than 85% of the total cost of breakfast, lunch and dinner charged separately.

It is often advisable to inspect your room before you check in; most hotels offer good standards but it is not unknown for an impressive lobby to camouflage shabby rooms upstairs.

Approximate prices for a double room are shown below. A single person in a double room will be charged 80% of the full price. Many of the larger new hotels have double rooms only. If you ask for an additional bed in your room, this should not cost more than 60% of the single room price or 35% of the double room price. Remember that the I.V.A. tax will be added on to your final bill; in the case of 1-star to 4-star hotels I.V.A. is charged at 6%, and in the case of luxury, or 5-star, hotels at the rate of 12%. Remember that if you are planning to pay your bill by credit card, to check beforehand whether your hotel will accept your particular piece of plastic. Finally, should you have a complaint about your hotel, you can enter this in the hotel's complaint book kept for this purpose, report it to the local Tourist Office, or put it in writing to the Complaints Section of the General Directorate of Tourist Activities whose address is: Dirección General de Política Turística, Sección de Reclamaciones, María de Molina 50, 28006 Madrid.

Approximate prices (double room) excluding I.V.A.:

	Major City	*Elsewhere*
5-star: Deluxe (L)	16,000–30,000	14,000–20,000
4-star: Expensive (E)	10,000–15,950	8,000–12,500
3-star: Moderate (M)	6,000–9,950	5,000–7,950
2-star: Inexpensive (I)	3,750–5,950	3,500–4,950

These prices should be taken as indicators only and do not include breakfast. A very few hotels, such as the *Ritz* and *Villa Magna* in Madrid, fall into a super-deluxe category which rates way above our Deluxe (L) rating above. Similarly Marbella's top four hotels far outshine our Deluxe category in price and unadulterated luxury, as do the leading hotels of Barcelona, Seville and San Sebastián.

Credit Cards. The following initials are used to indicate which credit cards are accepted: AE, DC, MC, and V—American Express, Diner's Club, MasterCard (Access and Eurocard), and Visa (Barclaycard).

PARADORES. There are some 70 or so of these state-owned-and-run parador hotels throughout Spain. Many of them are located in superb historic castles or in positions of great natural beauty.

All the paradores are well furnished and equipped and they all have bars and restaurants; many also have swimming pools. We have had many delighted reports from readers and for the most part we would highly recommend these hotels. However, it must also be said that of recent years we have had complaints of indifferent service in some of the establishments. But do not let this deter you overmuch as no tour of Spain would really be complete without a stay in one or two of these magnificent buildings.

All the paradores are listed in the *Practical Information* sections of this book under the towns (or nearest towns in the case of country paradores) where they are to be found. In most cases it is possible to dine in the parador restaurants without actually being an overnight guest; similarly you may go for a coffee or a drink in a parador bar which will also enable you to get a glimpse of the interior of some of these historic buildings.

Occasionally you may come across a parador which is advertised as an *albergue* (meaning "inn"). These are usually modern establishments built in convenient spots for motorists.

Most paradores are classified as 4-star hotels and their prices are often reasonable for the accommodations offered. They are very popular and booking in advance is advisable; in some cases essential. You can make your reservations directly with the parador of your choice, or through the central booking office in Madrid: *Central de Reservas de los Paradores de España,* Velázquez 18, 28001 Madrid (tel. 435 9700); telex no. 44607 RRPP. You can also book through your travel agent or consult your nearest branch of the Spanish National Tourist Office. In Britain, the official parador representative is *Keytel International,* 402 Edgware Rd., London W.2 (tel. 01–402 8182). Once in Spain, any parador you stay in will make free onward reservations for you in another parador.

Various tour companies run special parador tours. In Britain the best of these are *Mundi Color,* 276 Vauxhall Bridge Rd., London SW1V 1BB (tel. 01–834 3492); *Marsans Travel,* 7A Henrietta Pl., London W1M 9AG (tel. 01–493 4934), both of whom do fly-drive holidays to paradores throughout Spain; and *Brittany Ferries,* Millbay Docks, Plymouth PL1 3EW (tel. 0752–221321) who offer go-as-you-please motoring holidays in paradores, in conjunction with their Plymouth-Santander car ferry service.

If you set your heart on spending a night in a particular parador, do check first that it will be open, as many close in January and February for refurbishment, some close in November and December too, and there will always be a few that are closed long-term for extensive restoration.

VILLA RENTAL. Renting a villa or apartment may be pleasant and economical for a long vacation, but do not rely solely on the uniformly glamorous photographs in advertisements. Only use reputable agencies. Among those in the United States, try *Villas International,* 71 W. 23rd St., New York, NY 10010, which has a number of properties along the Mediterranean coast of Spain; or *At Home Abroad Inc.,* 405 E. 56th St., New York, NY 10022, which has rentals in Spain and Portugal.

In the U.K. try: *Casas Cantábricas,* 31 Arbury Rd., Cambridge CB4 2JB (tel. 0223 328721); *Catalan Villas,* Milverton M20, Taunton, Somerset TA4 1NT (tel. 0823 400356); *Continental Villas,* 38 Sloane St., London SW1X 7EE (tel. 01–245 9181); *Halsey Villas,* 22 Boston Pl., Dorset Sq., London NW1 6HZ (tel. 01–723 6043); *Meon Villa Holidays,* Meon House, Petersfield, Hants, GU32 3JN (tel. 0730–68411); *Palmer and Parker Villa Holidays,* 63 Grosvenor St., London W1X OAJ (tel. 01–493 5725); *Starvillas,* 25 High St., Chesterton, Cambridgeshire CB4 1ND (tel. 0223–311990).

YOUTH HOSTELS. Traditionally youth hosteling in Spain has never been as popular with young travelers as it has in many other European countries. This is most likely due to the abundance of shoe-string pensions found in every town and to the fact that many of Spain's hostels are located too far from major centers to be reached on public transport. However, there are some 55 youth hostels in Spain, all of which are listed in the International Youth Hostel Handbook, published annually, and are open to anyone with an International Y.H.A. card.

The Spanish Y.H.A. *(Red Española de Albergues Juveniles, REAJ)* has its headquarters at Ortega y Gasset 71–3A, 28006 Madrid (tel. 401 1300/9460). Open mornings only. Details are also available from Y.H.A. headquarters in your own country: in the U.S.A. from *American Youth Hostels Inc.,* Box 37613, Washington, DC 20013; in Canada from *Canadian Hostelling Association,* 333 River Rd., Tower A, Vanier City, Ottawa, Ontario K1L 8H9; in Britain from *Y.H.A. Headquarters,* Trevelyan House, 8 St. Stephen's Hill, St. Albans, Herts. Youth Hostels in Spain are signposted AJ *(Albergue Juvenil).*

CAMPING. There are about 550 camping sites in Spain. Most have their own mailbox and supermarket and will take both bus tours and caravans. The camping season is April through mid-October and some sites are open all year long. Camping carnets are not essential but are nonetheless recommended, and foreigners must show their passports or identity cards when registering. As might be expected, the heaviest concentration of camps is along the Mediterranean coast, especially the east coast. Booking is not essential but is strongly advised for the most popular sites in the high season.

Spanish National Tourist Offices abroad and local Tourist Offices in Spain will supply you with a free map and a list of camp sites and can answer any queries you may have. An annual publication called the *Guia de Campings* is available from most bookstores in Spain from about March onwards each year, giving full details of sites and fees. Further details can be obtained from the *Camping and Caravan Club Ltd.,* 11 Lower Grosvenor Place, London S.W.1.

RESTAURANTS. As with hotels, all Spanish restaurants are registered with the local provincial delegation and are graded using the same classification system throughout the country. The classification symbol is the fork, as opposed to the star for hotels, and runs from five forks down to one fork. As a general rule five- and four-fork restaurants are rare outside major cities and you will normally find that you get a good meal at a three-fork restaurant. A two-fork restaurant is an average everyday spot but there are nonetheless many delightful restaurants in this category.

Our grading system is slightly simpler: (L) for Deluxe, (E) for Expensive, (M) for Moderate and (I) for Inexpensive. The cost obviously depends on which dishes you choose, but the table below gives an idea of the prices you are likely to pay. These prices are for a 3-course *à la carte* meal for one person without drinks or coffee. Restaurant prices have increased considerably since Spain joined the Common Market in 1986, and unless you stick to the set menus offered by many budget restaurants, dining out can run away with a large portion of your holiday budget. Finding a light, *à la carte* lunch as you would at home is almost impossible, while bread, whether you eat it or not, and mineral water are always charged for. On the plus side, neither a cover not service charge is ever added onto your check.

Approximate prices per person (excluding drinks):

	Major Centers	Other places
Deluxe	6,000 and up	Rare
Expensive	3,500–5,900	3,000–4,500
Moderate	1,500–3,450	1,300–2,950
Inexpensive	800–1,450	600–1,200

Note: Some restaurants include the 6% I.V.A. tax in their menu prices, others do not. It is always wise to check beforehand whether the menu says *IVA incluido* or *IVA no incluido.*

Credit Cards. We use the following initials to indicate which credit cards are accepted: AE, DC, MC, and V—American Express, Diner's Club, MasterCard (Access and Eurocard), and Visa (Barclaycard).

Meal Times. Spanish restaurants do not serve breakfast. (Breakfast, such as it is, is available in cafes). Meal times in Spain are very much later than in any other European country and an important point to bear in mind is that lunch and not dinner is the main meal. At lunchtime, few restaurants open before 1 P.M. and 2–3 is the usual lunch hour, though many diners will linger at their tables till 4 P.M. or even later on Sundays. Most restaurants open their doors for dinner at 8.30 P.M. and stay open till around midnight, with 9.30–10.30 being the usual hour for starting dinner. However, hotel diningrooms serve dinner between 8 and 10 P.M.

Paella. The national dish of paella is one that most visitors to Spain will want to sample. As we frequently receive reports that a restaurant has served a poor paella there are a few points we would like to make. First, few restaurants serve paella in the evening. Since a good paella should always be prepared to order, which takes 20 minutes or more, and is also rather a heavy dish, it is traditionally served at lunchtime only. Secondly, the best paella restaurants will only serve it for a minimum of two people; thirdly, paella is sometimes eaten as an appetizer rather than as a main course, so if you see it being served rather too cheaply or appearing near the top of the menu, do not expect a full-scale paella. Finally, do not choose paella if you are a long way from the coast and outside a major city as the choice of seafood will most likely be limited and its freshness dubious.

BUDGET EATING TIPS. Restaurantes Economicos. These are cheap, unpretentious, usually family-run restaurants found in the back streets of large cities, especially Madrid. The decor is often unexciting, the food fairly basic and they are frequently identified by a T.V. blaring loudly and damp table linen. However, they are usually clean and offer great value for money. Catering largely for workers at lunchtime they usually offer a choice of 3 or 4 *menus del día* (see below) rather than an extensive *à la carte* choice. They are always crowded, often closed at weekends and may be quite hard for the visitor to find—we name a few in our Madrid and Barcelona listings.

Menu del Día. Many restaurants offer a *menu del día* or a tourist menu *(menu turístico)*. This is a fixed-price meal including soup or appetizer, one or two main courses, dessert, bread and sometimes mineral water, wine or beer. Tea or coffee are never included. It is a rather unexciting way to eat, but will work out very much cheaper than choosing *à la carte.* Prices vary, but 700–1,200 ptas. per person is fairly average. Though all restaurants are supposed to offer a *menu del día*, in practice fewer and fewer now do.

Cafeterías. *Cafetería* is the Spanish word for a cafe or coffee house and does not mean the self-service establishment of the United States. They are numerous throughout Spain and serve coffee, tea, alcohol, break-fast, sandwiches, tapas, platos combinados and somewhat expensive cakes and pastries. They are open all day and are ideal for snacks and light meals. Eating at the counter is cheaper than sitting at tables, where there is waitress service.

Fast Food. American fast food has caught on rapidly in Madrid and Barcelona, and is now beginning to take hold of some of the more popular coastal resorts. Though *McDonalds, Burger King,* and *Wendys* have bagged many of the prime sites in Madrid and Barcelona, the hamburger invasion has yet to catch on in other Spanish cities. Takeaway joints do exist but the hamburger chain *Burger Bravos* is the only near-American equivalent to be found outside Madrid and Barcelona. *VIPS* is a smart Spanish chain, very popular with the young.

A few self-service restaurants exist, usually in large cities or close to factory areas, offering typical Spanish food at very reasonable prices.

Platos Combinados. These are served in both cafeterías and cheap restaurants and are a good budget bet. There is usually a choice of six to ten different *platos.* Each consists of a mixture of any of the following: chicken portion, fried squid, fried hake (white fish), omelet, fried egg, sau-sage, *chorizo* (spicy sausage), Russian (potato) salad, asparagus, lettuce and tomato. Prices range from around 400–800 ptas. *Platos combinados* are rarely very good but they do fill the gaps.

Tapas. Tapas are a peculiar and wonderful Spanish invention. They are savory snacks served in cafes and bars as an aperitif. The variety is infinite from every imaginable combination of seafood, through salami, cheese, chunks of *tortilla* (Spanish omelet) down to humble olives. In the evenings many Spaniards go bar hopping trying a different tapa in each bar instead of sitting down to a full meal. A word of warning: tapas are only a budget proposition if you limit your selection—if you are choosing ham, ask how much it is first! Some bars will only serve larger portions known as *raciones* and these can work out quite expensive.

TIPPING. Most Spanish hotel and restaurant bills say "service and tax included" which is misleading; in fact, Spanish hotels are not allowed to include a service charge on their bill, so if you have been satisfied with the service you have received, leave the chambermaid about 500 ptas. a week, tip the porter 50 ptas. a bag, 25 ptas. to the doorman if he calls you a cab, and 50 ptas. or more for room service. If the service in your hotel diningroom has been courteous, leave your waiter around 500 ptas. at the end of your stay, or 200 ptas. if you have only stayed one or two nights. If your hotel has a concierge, and he has been helpful, 500 ptas. would be appreciated.

Similarly, Spanish restaurants are not allowed to add a service charge to their bills, and it is customary to leave a tip if you are satisfied. 10% is the norm in a good restaurant, and less in humbler establishments. In the case of snack meals or inexpensive *menus del día,* round the bill up to the nearest 100 ptas. The old custom of leaving loose change on a saucer in cafes and bars has almost died out, but if the barman or waiter has been friendly, 10–25 ptas. will not go amiss; the waiter in your hotel cocktail bar will definitely appreciate 50 ptas. or so.

Tip taxis 10% when they use the meter, otherwise nothing. Station and airport porters, when you can find them, operate on a fixed rate, usually 60 or 90 ptas. a bag. Cinema and theater ushers get 10 ptas. though this, too, is dying out. At nightclubs or flamenco shows doormen get 50 ptas., coat-check attendants 25 ptas., and waiters 50 ptas. a drink, or more, depending on the kind of establishment. Restroom attendants everywhere get 5 ptas., no matter how humble the facilities; leave it on the saucer as you leave. There is no need to tip service station attendants if you are just buying gas. If they check your tyres for you, or clean your windshield, then 50 ptas. is about right.

MAIL. Airmail rates are as follows: to the U.S., letters up to 15 grams cost 68 ptas., postcards 58 ptas.; to the U.K. and rest of Europe, letters up to 20 grams cost 48 ptas., postcards 40 ptas. Within Spain, letters cost 19 ptas., postcards 14 ptas. If you mail a letter within the same city in Spain, it costs 7 ptas. These rates usually change each year in mid-summer, so check first. Mail boxes *(buzones)* are yellow with red stripes and are plentiful. They usually have two or three slits, one marked *Capital* for the capital of the province you are in, one marked *Provincias* for the rest of Spain, and one marked *Extranjero* for abroad. The word for "post office" is *correos,* and for "stamps," *sellos.*

Hotel delivery is often inefficient and the Spanish mail can be slow. If you are uncertain where you will be staying, you can have mail sent to the *Lista de Correos* (poste restante) at any Spanish post office. Simply have your letters addressed as follows: John Smith, Lista de Correos, Málaga, Spain. To claim your mail, just present your passport or other means of identification.

TELEPHONES. Public pay phones are silver-gray in color and are located on city streets and at stations and airports. They are rarely found in hotel lobbies or in bars and cafes as in some countries. If you want to call from a bar or restaurant, ask the barman and he will usually let you use his phone and charge you afterwards. Pay phones work with 5, 25, 50 and 100 ptas. coins; 10 ptas. is the minimum for a short local call, long distance calls eat up many more coins. Place several coins in the groove at the top of the phone, lift the receiver and dial your number. Coins then fall into the machine as needed. In new-style phones, place your money in the slot and an electronic display will tell you how much money you have left. Area codes work by provinces, each province having its own dialling code beginning with a 9. Any city or village within one province, including the provincial capital, has the same area code. Dialling codes for each province are displayed in telephone booths but there is nothing to tell you which towns belong to which province, so if you are calling outside your own province, you will need to check this first. For calls to another town within the same province, simply dial the number.

International calls to Europe can also be made from pay phones but far and away the best method of making long distance calls abroad, and within Spain if you wish to talk for a long time, is to go to the *telefónica*. There is a telefónica (telephone exchange) in every town of any size and they are usually open from 9 A.M.–9 P.M. in major cities and 9–2 elsewhere. The telephonist dials your call for you and then indicates which cabin you should go to. In many telefónicas, once you have been told which cabin to use, you can dial the call yourself. You then pay the telephonist at the end and you will only be charged the regular rate; there are no supplements or service charges. If your call comes to 500 ptas. or more you can pay with Visa or MasterCard.

Calls from your hotel room phone *always* cost much more than from a pay phone or the telefónica. Be warned that even if you make a collect call home, many Spanish hotels will make a service charge for this, of around 250 ptas. to Europe or 450 ptas. to the U.S. Making a collect call abroad from Spain is not always as simple as it is from the U.S. or Britain. If you are calling collect from Madrid or Barcelona, chances are it can be made immediately, but if you are calling from elsewhere in Spain, you may well have to wait for up to two hours as the call has to be placed through Madrid and lines are frequently busy.

CLOSING TIMES. Shops open in the morning between 9 and 10 to either 1.30 or 2. In the afternoon they open from approximately 4 to 7 in winter, and 5 to 8 in summer. In some cities, especially in summer, they close on Saturday afternoons. Tourist shops in seaside resorts and the *Corte Inglés* and *Galerías Preciados* department stores mostly stay open throughout the siesta. Banks are open 9.30 to 2, Mon.–Fri., and 9.30 to 1 on Saturdays. A few banks open at 9 and in some cities banks close at 12 on Saturdays in summer. Most churches and museums close for the siestas; some museums open mornings only. Post offices normally open 9 to 2, though there are exceptions. They often close early on Saturdays.

Siesta and Paseo Hours. The traditional Spanish siesta is to some extent on the wane. Nevertheless, it is still important to remember that in most places everything—shops, churches, museums, monuments—will be closed between 1.30 or 2 and around 4P.M. in winter and 5 P.M. in summer. If you can't rest or take your time over lunch, as the locals will be doing, plan to do your traveling at this time. The evening *paseo* hour is the real time to witness life in any Spanish town, as citizens don their best clothes and stroll up and down the same street or round and round the plaza major, stopping to greet friends or to take a drink in a sidewalk cafe. This phenomenon occurs around 8.30 P.M. after the last busy shopping hour. Find yourself a cafe with a good view, order yourself a beer or a *cuba libre,* and watch the world stroll by.

ELECTRICITY. Most of Spain has now been converted to 220 volts AC, but some older hotels, hostels and private houses are still on 120 volts.

Be sure to check *before* you plug in. British 240-V. appliances work fine on 220-V. sockets and 110- and 120-V. appliances are also interchangeable. American visitors should bring voltage adaptors with them, as they are very hard to find in Spain, and even luxury hotels won't usually supply them. Bring plug adaptors along too—Spanish plugs are two-pin, round-pin. It's always best to take along a battery-operated razor.

DRINKING WATER. Drinking water is perfectly safe all over Spain except perhaps in a very few out-of-the-way places. However, many Spaniards still tend to drink mineral water in preference to tap water, not least because it is actually much nicer. If you ask a waiter for water, he will bring mineral water unless you specify tap water. Mineral water comes in two types; still *(sin gas)* or fizzy *(con gas)*. It is usual to order mineral water by the half-liter *(media agua sin/con gas)*. If you really want tap water, ask for *agua natural.*

CONVENIENT CONVENIENCES. There are few public facilities in Spain though coin-operated convenience cabins (with music!) are beginning to appear on the streets of Madrid and Barcelona. Restrooms are plentiful in hotels, restaurants, museums, cafes and bars. Department stores such as the *Corte Inglés* or *Galerías Preciados* always have restrooms, usually on the top floor. Ask for *los servicios* or *los aseos,* and then a picture of a man or a woman or the words *Señoras* (ladies) or *Caballeros* (men, lit. knights!) will tell you which way to head.

SPORTS. The range of sporting activities available to visitors is in direct relation to the amount of tourist development in any particular area. Tennis, golf and much more are most easily indulged in where a high density of hotels and villas is found. The farther you get from these centers, the less there is available, until you reach, for example, the wilder mountains, where all you will be able to indulge in is shooting.

Fishing. Spain, with its nearly 3,220 km. (2,000 miles) of coastline and its more than 74,000 km. (46,000 miles) of rivers and streams, together with the many dams and reservoirs scattered around the country, offers magnificent possibilities for those interested in any kind of fishing.

Contact the Spanish National Tourist Office, which will tell you how to go about obtaining a license, where one is needed.

Golf. This has become one of Spain's main attractions and there are over 80 courses most of which have been carefully planned to take account of the best local scenery. Marbella on the Costa del Sol has 14 excellent courses, the Costa Brava has two, and there are several on the Costa Blanca including the two championship 18-hole courses at the superb La Manga complex near Cartagena. Many other courses are located along the Atlantic and Mediterranean coasts as well as inland at Zaragoza, Córdoba, Seville and the well known Puerta de Hierro course in Madrid. In the Balearics, there are four courses on Mallorca, including the Son Vida and Punta Rotja clubs, four on Menorca, and the Rocallisa club at Sta Eulalia del Rio on Ibiza.

Scuba diving. To dive in Spain every foreigner, regardless of whether he is a member of a diving club or not, must have a license and a permit for the relevant area. Details can be obtained from the Spanish Tourist Office. Apply at least two months in advance.

Skiing. Spain has some excellent winter sports areas. By far the best equipped are the Pyrenees resorts from Burguete and Isaba in Navarre, Astun, Candanchú, Cerler, El Formigal, Guarrinza and Panticosa in Aragón, to Espot, La Molina, Nuria, Port del Compte, Salardú and Viella in Catalonia. In the Sierra Nevada, only 35 km. from Granada, is the big Sol y Nieve complex, one of the most fashionable regions. 50 km. from Madrid are the Guadarrama mountains with resorts at Navacerrada, Valcotos and Pinilla; and in the north in the Picos de Europa are the resorts of Pajares, San Isidro, Reinosa and Alto Campóo.

Tennis. Nearly all the large tourist complexes and many major hotels have their own tennis courts. There is Lew Hoad's famous tennis club in Fuengirola on the Costa del Sol and the Puente Romano tennis club in Marbella hosts international championships, while the vast complex at La Manga in Murcia boasts 15 splendid courts.

Pelota. Pelota or more correctly *jai alai* (happy festival) is the Basque national game. Played on large cement courts called *frontones* it is thought to be the world's fastest game, and few people over 30 can play it well. There are frontones in most large Spanish cities but to see it played at its most brilliant, you should visit the frontones of any Basque town. It is sometimes played outdoors but more usually indoors by artificial light between the hours of 5.30 and 9 P.M. The players, usually two on each side, wear a foot-long curving basket *(cesta)* as a kind of extended glove in which they catch the hard ball, and hurl it back above a marked line on the back wall. The ball travels with such speed, the impact is like a machine-gun bullet. Betting is fast and furious and the bookmakers stand with their backs to the game facing the audience. The spectators are protected from the ball by a wire net.

POLLUTION. Approximately one-third of Spanish beaches represent a potential health hazard. Worst affected are those in the Basque province of Guipuzcoa, followed by those around La Coruña, Santander and Valencia, all highly industrialized regions. The regional government of Valencia with help from U.N. funds, has now begun a big program to clean up its waters. Similarly no one who values his health should consider bathing too close to Barcelona; many of its citizens flee as far south as the resort of Sitges before plunging into the Mediterranean. The southern shores of the Costa del Sol are less polluted by industrial waste than by problems of inadequate sewage disposal, though efforts are at last being made to improve this situation. As a general rule the sea and sand of the Costa Blanca resorts tend to be cleaner than those of the Costa del Sol. The cleanest beaches are in Huelva and Murcia provinces.

FAIRS AND FIESTAS. Stumbling unexpectedly upon a local fiesta in a small Spanish town or village can be one of the greatest delights of your trip. The houses will be decked with flags, the main street or central square lined with stalls piled high with candy, coconuts, nuts and *turrones* (nougat), the band playing, the children if not their parents, decked out in party dresses or local costume, and the highlight of the celebration will be the procession with its colorful floats and fancy costumes. More likely than not the inhabitants will be celebrating their local saint's day.

The main fiestas, their locations and times, are already listed under *Seasonal Events* (see p. 4) but here we give brief definitions of the various kinds of celebrations.

Romería. An English dictionary translates this as "a picnic excursion to some shrine or beauty spot" and although it is a pity that in English we have to use nine words instead of one, the translation is fair. These, with their long cavalcades of horsemen, belong essentially to the country districts.

Verbena. Translated in the dictionary as "a night festival on the eve of a religious holiday." These are associated with towns or separate districts in large cities. Being open-air affairs, demanding the still nights of high summer, they reach a peak around August 15, the Feast of the Assumption of the Virgin Mary.

Falla. In medieval times on St. Joseph's Day (March 19) the carpenters' guilds traditionally burnt their accumulated wood shavings on huge bonfires. Today falla means a festival for which effigies, usually of local dignitaries or well-known figures, are built solely for burning. These bonfires are preceded by processions of flower-decked floats, carnival queens and much singing and dancing. Fallas are the specialty (though not exclusively so) of Valencia.

Semana Santa. Holy Week celebrations begin on Palm Sunday when Spaniards all over Spain decorate their balconies with the palm branches they have had blessed in church; to leave them there for a whole year is said to bring good luck. Solemn religious processions take place in many cities throughout the week from Palm Sunday to Holy Saturday. Floats bearing images of Christ or the Virgin Mary are borne through the streets by penitents, often bare-footed, and accompanied by processions of sinister long-robed figures in pointed hoods, to the accompaniment of a single drum beat or wailing *saeta* (religious song). Though solemnity and strength of religious feeling pervades, this spectacle also offers a great occasion to go out on the streets and enjoy oneself way into the small hours. The most famous processions are those of Seville, Valladolid and Cuenca.

Feria. Meaning "fair," a feria was traditionally an event when dealers and gypsies would meet to trade in horses, mules and donkeys. Today, though horses still play an important part in most ferias, you will see little buying or selling of anything other than drinks.

Corpus Christi. The fiesta of Corpus Christi falls on the second Thursday after Whitsun and is a public holiday all over Spain. Celebrations include religious processions though here religion is an excuse for, rather than a restraint upon, the holiday spirit.

Camuñas. Camuñas are Mystery Plays and are performed at Toledo during Corpus Christi and at Elche in Alicante province on August 14 and 15 to celebrate the Feast of the Assumption. The Elche Mystery Play is a particularly interesting and ancient custom. Each role in the play is the property of a particular local family, which must produce a member to play that part or lose this jealously guarded privilege.

Pilgrimages. These are of a purely religious character.

Gigantes y Cabezudos. These "giants" and "bigheads" are pasteboard figures worn by many characters in processions at fiestas all over Spain. Often they symbolize Ferdinand and Isabella (the giants) and the people they ruled over or conquered (the bigheads). When the *cabezudos* have brown faces they symbolize the Moorish invaders who were finally expelled by the Catholic Kings.

La Tuna. The tuna is not normally associated with fiestas but as a colorful Spanish tradition merits a mention here. Traditionally each Spanish university has a minstrel group known as *La Tuna* whose members, wearing costumes of the time of Philip II—black knee-breeches, black stockings and black capes bedecked with colored ribbons presented by lady admirers—serenade diners in restaurants or move from bar to bar singing their traditional songs to guitar and accordian accompaniments. Though it can no longer be said that all *tuna* members are university students and in most cases they now spend more time serenading tourists than they do their lady loves of old, the *tuna* is still a delightful tradition.

BULLFIGHTS. The bullfighting season starts officially with the Valencia *fallas* in March and ends with the El Pilar celebrations in Zaragoza in October. The best bullfights usually take place at the biggest fiestas and for times and places see our chapter on bullfighting and under *Seasonal Events.*

If you are hoping to attend a *corrida* during the Seville April Fair or the Pamplona San Fermines, it is wise to buy your ticket as early as possible. Some cities, such as Madrid, have central ticket offices known as *despachos de toros,* in others you buy your tickets at the ring. Wherever you are the local tourist office should be able to advise you where to obtain tickets. Try and buy your tickets from official ticket booths *(despacho oficial);* many other despachos sell tickets quite legally but if they are not "official" they will impose a surcharge of around 20% on the price of a ticket. If a ticket booth displays a sign *no quedan localidades* it means there are no seats left; and if it continues *ni entradas* there is no standing room either. Try another ticket office which may not have sold out yet.

Prices are determined by the proximity of the seat to the ring and by its position in the stand. Ringside seats are known as *barreras* and are naturally the most expensive; the cheapest seats are those known as *gradas* which are high up at the back of the ring. You will also have a choice of *sol* (sun), *sombra* (shade), or *sol y sombra* where you start off with the sun in your eyes but as the fight progresses the sun will dip down behind the edge of the ring. *Sombra* are the most expensive but in high summer are well worth the extra pesetas to avoid sweltering or being blinded by the relentless sun.

Always ask the starting time when you buy your tickets. This varies between 4.30 and 7 P.M. depending on the place and month of the year. Be punctual—there is an old saying that the only things that start on time in Spain are bullfights and Mass—for once the corrida begins, you are not allowed in. Allow plenty of time to find your seat which is not always easy in a large ring. Look closely at the numbers on your ticket, *tendido* is usually the gate through which you will enter the ring, and *fila* the row in which your seat is located. Cushions to sit on can be rented for a small fee and are a must unless you like sitting on hard stone benches with no back support. Most corridas last 2½–3 hours and there is usually a break between the third and fourth bulls which, if you have had enough, is the best time to leave.

PLACES OF INTEREST. Museums and Art Galleries. The Spanish do not distinguish between museums and art galleries, the word for both being *museo*. Many museums belong to the *Patrimonio Nacional,* that is, they are state-owned and run. These museums are free to Spaniards but there is an entrance fee for foreigners. (Holders of I.S.I. cards and teachers should in theory get in free—it's always worth asking). Most other museums make a charge of anything from 35 ptas. to 350 ptas., though you will find the most famous places charge considerably more.

Opening times change constantly. As a rough guide, most museums are open in the mornings between 9.30 and 1, and some of them open again in the afternoon between 4 and 7 or 5 and 8. Most museums shut one day a week, usually Sunday or Monday.

Cathedrals and Churches. Cathedrals are open to sightseers during much the same hours as museums. Most cathedrals are free to visit though there is usually a nominal charge to see their treasures or visit their cloisters. The exceptions to this rule are the two most visited cathedrals, Toledo and Seville, both of which make an entry charge. Churches tend to open and close at whim but generally they open around 7.30 A.M., close for the siesta and open again in the late afternoon till early evening. Some, such as those in Segovia, are open during Mass only. You should avoid wearing shorts or revealing clothing in Spanish churches, but there is no longer any need to cover your head or arms. In a few places bare shoulders may still be frowned on.

Roman Remains. Spain boasts its fair share of Roman ruins. The greatest sites are the aqueducts of Segovia and Tarragona, the Itálica excavations near Seville, and the outstanding Roman theater and forum of Mérida. Numerous mosaics, bridges and Roman arches are to be found throughout Spain.

Moorish Inheritance. Spain is unique in Europe in having a great wealth of Moorish architecture and nowhere is this seen better than in Andalusia where the Moors lingered longest.

Alcázares. The word *alcázar* and its derivatives *alcazaba* and *alcazabilla* is a Moorish word meaning "fortified high ground." Spanish cities are dotted with alcázares, many of them now in ruins, some of them spectacular sights in themselves, others offering magnificent views over the surrounding countryside.

Medieval castles and walled cities. Spain has long been known as the land of castles, and Castile, whose very name is derived from the word "castle" is the place to see them. All are steeped in history and some can be visited; for details of visiting times it is best to check with the local tourist office. Avila is Spain's best example of a medieval walled city.

Getting Around Spain

BY AIR. There are daily flights between Madrid and all the major cities and between Barcelona and most cities. Flights connecting other Spanish cities are usually twice or thrice weekly or Mon. to Fri. only. There are frequent flights between the mainland and the Balearics where each island has its own airport. There are also regular flights to Spain's other outlying possessions, Melilla in North Africa and the Canary Islands. At presstime there were as yet no flights between Spanish airports and Gibraltar though by 1989 it is very possible that *Iberia* will have inaugurated some. Distances in Spain are great and as both road and train travel can be slow, domestic flights are often the solution for those with limited time. Fares on domestic routes are reasonable too. Madrid–Barcelona is approx. 10,820 ptas; Madrid–Málaga 10,615 ptas; Barcelona–Málaga 14,480 ptas.

Between Madrid and Barcelona, Iberia operates a shuttle service known as *puente aéreo.* There are hourly, or in some cases half-hourly, flights in both directions.

At Madrid and Málaga airports the national and international terminals are in different buildings so you need to specify which one you want to your cab driver, the Spanish being *terminal nacional* and *terminal internacional.* Elsewhere a direction to *vuelos nacionales* (domestic flights) or *vuelos internacionales* (international flights) should end you up in the right place. Arrivals are *llegadas* and departures *salidas* and at Madrid these are on different levels so instruct your cab driver accordingly.

BY TRAIN. Extensive electrification, the construction of new lines and the upgrading of others, the provision of new rolling stock and locomotives and the modernization of many stations as well as the installation of a more efficient booking system have all helped the Spanish State Railroads *(Red Nacional de Ferrocarriles Españoles* or *RENFE)* to reach those standards of efficiency found in most other west European countries.

The main routes radiate from Madrid which is linked by fast trains to practically all the principal Spanish cities. Journeys between other cities, which may look perfectly straightforward on a map, often involve surprising changes of train.

The first thing to understand about Spanish rail fares is that they are determined both by the kind of train you travel on and by the distance covered. Generally speaking they are moderate in comparison to those of other countries and the *rápido* and *expreso* fares are extremely cheap. Basically there are three types of express in Spain. The first and most expensive is the *TALGO,* a unique deluxe train. Next there is the *electrotrén* or ELT which, as its name implies, is electric, and the third type of train is the TER. 1st and 2nd class seats and various catering facilities from full dining cars to mini-buffets are available on all of these. Seat reservation is almost always obligatory, though tickets for remaining unreserved seats are sold off from two hours before the train's departure. These trains together with *Corail* and *InterCity,* all require fare supplements but are well worth the extra cost. Other trains are confusingly known as *rápidos* or *expresos* (rarely the case) and again carry both 1st and 2nd class. Rápidos and expresos are usually too slow and crowded to be recommended for long daytime journeys though at night, with a couchette reservation, they provide perfectly adequate budget transport.

It is more usual in Spain to buy your ticket and make your advance bookings in the RENFE office in the center of town than to buy your ticket from railroad stations, though tickets are readily available at both. To buy your ticket in advance you must be traveling a minimum of 250 km. on a TALGO, 200 km. on a TER or electrotrén, or 100 km. on a rápido or expreso. Seat reservation can be made up to 60 days in advance. Buy your advance tickets from the window marked *Largo Recorrido, Venta Antici- pada* (Long Distance, Advance Sales). Expect to stand in line for a long time whether at a RENFE office or a station. An electronic network con- nects the reservation offices of RENFE all over the country. This enables you to buy a ticket for any journey within Spain even if you are not in the city where you will begin your journey. For example, in Seville, you can buy a ticket with a reserved seat for a journey from Madrid to Barcelo- na.

A useful tip to avoid the excessive high-season delays at stations and RENFE offices is to buy your tickets from travel agents displaying the blue and yellow RENFE sign; they charge no commission, may well speak English and are much swifter, though you may have to return later in the day to collect your ticket.

Spanish National Railways introduced a Tourist Card in 1987 giving unlimited travel on the RENFE network. The card can be bought throughout the year for periods of 8, 15 and 22 days in first class for £70, £115 and £130 respectively; in second class for £50, £80, £105 (1988 prices). Unfortunately, the card can be difficult to get hold of. In Europe contact RENFE, 1–3 Av. Marceau, 75116, Paris, France. The card may also be bought at the border stations of Irun and Port Bou, or in Barcelona or Madrid. The card does not cover travel on the extensive narrow gauge system running along the north coast of Spain.

Fares. As already mentioned, Spanish rail fares are very reasonable. Couchettes *(literas)* are available on most overnight services on rápidos or expresos to holders of 2nd-class tickets for a supplement of 1,090 ptas. in a non-airconditioned car, 1,500 ptas. airconditioned. Sleepers are also available on many overnight trains and these have a two-tiered price sys- tem depending on whether your journey is over or under 550 km. All beds cost a little more if the train is airconditioned.

Auto-Expreso. If you want to put your car on the train, the *Auto- Expreso* service is available on most long-distance routes. Your car can travel on the same overnight train as you do, or alternatively, you can send it on ahead or it can come later.

Non-smoking compartments. Non-smoking cars are now available on all long distance services, though Spaniards are not always the most obedi- ent of travelers in obeying these restrictions. When buying your ticket it is important to specify smoking or non-smoking as seat reservation is auto- matic with most tickets. This is particularly important when making cou- chette reservations as many Spaniards will happily smoke all night long.

Left Luggage. Left luggage facilities have been withdrawn from most Spanish stations.

Budget Rail Fares. Blue Days. "Blue Days" *(Días Azules)* leaflets are available from any RENFE office or station and show those days of the year when you can travel at reduced rates—there are approximately 270 Blue Days a year. There is a 25% discount on journeys made on Blue Days and there are frequently cheap rates for such things as round trip fares, Madrid–Barcelona journeys, or for taking your car on *Auto-Expreso.* Be warned though, that some of the Blue Day bargains, such as the pension- ers' 50% discount or reduced rates for family groups, apply only to Spaniards or to foreigners who have lived in Spain and held a *residencia* permit for at least six months.

Chequetrén. This is a book of coupons that allows you 15% discount on normal fares. It can be used on any train, and in both 1st and 2nd class, and by up to six people at once. Available from major stations and RENFE offices.

BY BUS. The public bus network in Spain is extensive and many places not served by the railroad can be reached by bus. There is little difference between bus and train fares, generally speaking, but as a rough guide, the luxury bus services may prove rather dearer than all trains except the TALGO, and the regular, older buses usually work out rather cheaper. Advance reservation is usually only necessary for the luxury long distance services, such as Valencia–Seville or Madrid–Málaga. Some cities have modern bus depots but in others, and this surprisingly includes Madrid and Barcelona, buses leave from different places all over town depending on their destination; your best bet is to ask at the local tourist office. Bus travel has some advantages over train travel: first, you often see more, as in the most picturesque parts of Spain trains frequently spend long times in tunnels; secondly, buses usually drop you off in the center of town whereas many railroad stations are located right on the edge of town; thirdly, left luggage facilities are still available at most bus depots.

When you are looking at timetables it is useful to know that *dias laborales* means Mon.–Sat., and *dias festivos* are Sundays and public holidays, though in the case of a fiesta it is always wise to double check times.

Tours. Bus tours are a very popular means of travel in Spain, both with Spaniards and visitors from abroad. There are hundreds of different tour operators and tours are run to all regions of sightseeing interest, the most popular run being to the Andalusian cities of Seville, Córdoba and Granada usually combined with a stay in one of the Costa del Sol resorts and a visit to maybe Ronda or Jerez. Other tours go to Extremadura and Portugal, the cities and paradores of Old Castile, the Rioja wine growing district and to Galicia and Asturias. All tours are accompanied by multilingual tour escorts who take charge of all arrangements.

The following are some of the largest and most reputable operators with offices throughout Spain: *Juliá Tours,* Gran Vía 68, Madrid (tel. 270 4600); *Pullmantur,* Plaza de Oriente 8, Madrid (tel. 241 1805); *Trapsatur,* San Bernardo 23, Madrid (tel. 266 9900); *Marsans,* Gran Vía 59, Madrid (tel. 247 7300). Tours can be booked either through the head offices or through most travel agencies; in many cases your hotel will be able to book them for you.

BY CAR. To take a car into Spain, your home driving license is essential, and non-E.E.C. nationals must also have a Green Card and International Driving License; these are also advisable, though not essential, for British subjects. In addition, it is prudent to purchase bail bonds to keep you out of jail if arrested for a motoring offense or after an accident. Spanish law also requires you to carry a spare set of bulbs for every light on your car and to have your driving license and car registration document on you whenever you are driving.

Spanish roads are classified A for *autopista* (toll freeway or motorway), N for *nacional* or main road, and C for the small roads that can be found all over the country. Those that have neither number nor letter are best avoided by all but the bravest of motorists. Autopistas are few and far between except in the north from the French Atlantic border to around Bilbao and on the Mediterranean coast from the French frontier down as far as Alicante. If you are in a hurry, these are worth every peseta of the tolls you'll pay as the traffic on the alternative N roads is dictated by slow moving trucks heading immense columns of cars in permanent traffic jams. A massive road improvement project is underway throughout the country, but especially on the main routes of Andalusia and on the highway along the north coast. Be prepared for many major road works therefore, and for some lengthy delays. The project will result in the construction of some much needed *autovías*, or expressways.

Driving is on the right and horns may not be used in cities, nor dipped headlights. Children may not ride in the front seats. City speed limits are 60 km.p.h. (37 m.p.h.), other limits are 120 km.p.h. (74 m.p.h.) on autopistas, 100 km.p.h. (62 m.p.h.) on N roads, and 90 km.p.h. (56 m.p.h.) on other roads unless otherwise signed. The wearing of front seat belts is compulsory on the highway but not in cities (except on the M30 Madrid ringroad). A single white line in the center of a road means you are not allowed to cross it; a dotted line means you may cross, i.e. overtake. Red and white stripes on the sidewalk curb mean parking is not permitted.

Road signs. The most common road signs that may present difficulty are: *ceda el paso*—give way; *carretera cortada*—road closed; *obras*—road works; *desvío*—detour; *encender las luces* or *luces de cruce*—lights on (when going through a tunnel); *apagar las luces*—lights off.

Gasoline prices. Gasoline (petrol) prices at presstime were 78 ptas. a liter for *super* (97 octane) and 72 ptas. a liter for *normal* (92 octane). *Super* was the most commonly used gas. On the remoter country roads, gas stations are few and far between. They rarely accept payment by credit card.

Car hire. *Avis* and *Hertz* are well represented at all Spanish airports and in most major cities; so too are *Godfrey Davies/Europcar* and *Budget*. *Ital* is a reputable Spanish car hire firm with branches in many cities and *Atesa* is probably the most upmarket of car rental firms offering self-drive or chauffeur-driven services. Many smaller local firms have special deals with hotels whereby guests can benefit from advantageous rates. If you are booking from abroad, *Iberia* airlines do fly-drive holidays in conjunction with Atesa cars, and *British Airways* will reserve an Avis car for you if you fly with them. The rates they offer may well be more favorable than those you can obtain by hiring a car yourself in Spain. Cars must be hired for a minimum of seven days if you want to get unlimited kilometer rates; otherwise you pay by the day plus so many pesetas per km. *Semana comercial* (Mon.–Fri.) rates are a little more advantageous than ordinary daily rates. You pay extra for insurance, and collision waiver. I.V.A. will be levied at 12% of your total bill, so remember to budget for this. In theory you need an International Driving Permit or an official translation of your home country's license to hire a car in Spain; in practise, most firms only ask for your ordinary license.

Vital Warning. The theft situation, especially break-ins to cars, is now so bad in Spain that you should *never* leave anything visible inside your car; not even maps, books or food purchases in the case of big cities. Lock everything in the trunk out of sight when you make daytime stops and always take purses, cameras and valuables with you. At night everything should be removed to your hotel. If you are traveling in your own car, we would advise paying for it to go in a supervised *parking* at night; many of these are underground, often beneath city squares. Parking fees are low by British or American standards and well worth the peace of mind they bring. Parking places are signed by a "P" usually on a blue background.

Leaving Spain

CUSTOMS. If you propose to take on your holiday any *foreign-made* articles, such as cameras, binoculars, expensive time-pieces and the like it is wise to put with your travel documents the receipt from the retailer or some other evidence that the item was bought in your home country. If you bought the article on a previous holiday abroad and have already paid duty on it, carry with you the receipt for this. Otherwise, on returning, you may be charged duty (for British residents, VAT as well).

Leaving Spain. Tourists leaving Spain rarely have to go through a customs check, though it is just possible that you will be asked how much Spanish currency you have on you. Officially, you are not allowed to leave Spain with more than 100,000 ptas. in cash.

U.S. Residents. You may bring in $400 worth of foreign merchandise as gifts or for personal use without having to pay duty, provided you have been out of the country more than 48 hours and provided you have not claimed a similar exemption within the previous 30 days. Every member of a family is entitled to the same exemption, regardless of age, and the exemptions can be pooled. For the next $1,000 worth of goods a flat 10% rate is assessed.

Included in the $400 allowance for travelers over the age of 21 are one liter of alcohol, 100 non-Cuban cigars and 200 cigarettes. Only one bottle of perfume trademarked in the U.S. may be brought in. However, there is no duty on antiques or art over 100 years old. You may not bring home meats, fruits, plants, soil or other agricultural products.

Gifts valued at under $50 may be mailed to friends or relatives at home, but not more than one per day of receipt to any one addressee. These gifts must not include perfumes costing more than $5, tobacco or liquor.

Canadian residents. In addition to personal effects, and over and above the regular exemption of $300 per year, the following may be brought into Canada duty-free: a maximum of 50 cigars, 200 cigarettes, 2 pounds of tobacco and 40 ounces of liquor, provided these are declared in writing to customs on arrival. Canadian Customs regulations are strictly enforced; you are recommended to check what your allowances are and to make sure you have kept receipts for whatever you may have bought abroad. Small gifts can be mailed and should be marked "Unsolicited gift, (nature of gift), value under $40 in Canadian funds." For other details, ask for a Canadian Customs brochure, *I Declare.*

British residents. There are two levels of duty free allowance for people entering the U.K.; one, for goods bought outside the E.E.C. or for goods bought in a duty free shop within the E.E.C.; two, for goods bought in an E.E.C. country but not in a duty free shop.

In the first category you may import duty free: 200 cigarettes or 100 cigarillos or 50 cigars or 250 grammes of tobacco *(Note* if you live outside Europe, these allowances are doubled*);* plus one liter of alcoholic drinks over 22% vol. (38.8% proof) or two liters of alcoholic drinks not over 22% vol. or fortified, still or sparkling wine; plus two liters of still table wine; plus 50 grammes of perfume; plus nine fluid ounces of toilet water; plus other goods to the value of £32.

In the second category you may import duty free: 300 cigarettes or 150 cigarillos or 75 cigars or 400 grammes of tobacco; plus 1½ liters of alcoholic drinks over 22% vol. (38.8% proof) or three liters of alcoholic drinks not over 22% vol. or fortified, still or sparkling wine; plus five liters of still table wine; plus 75 grammes of perfume; plus 13 fluid ounces of toilet water; plus other goods to the value of £250. (*Note* though it is not classified as an alcoholic drink by E.E.C. countries for Customs' purposes and is thus considered part of the "other goods" allowance, you may not import more than 50 liters of beer.)

In addition, no animals or pets of any kind may be brought into the U.K. without a license. The penalties for doing so are severe and are strictly enforced; there are *no* exceptions. Similarly, fresh meats, plants and vegetables, controlled drugs and firearms and ammunition may not be brought into the U.K. There are no restrictions on the import or export of British and foreign currencies.

SPAIN AND THE SPANIARDS

A Changing Image

by
HARRY EYRES

Harry Eyres has lived, and traveled extensively, in Spain, both as a student and as the Spanish correspondent of the London Spectator, *for which he still writes on Spanish affairs.*

Spain—to risk one of the few generalizations that can be made about a land of such diversity—is the most individual country in Europe, and the Spanish are the most individualistic people. In fact, they are so individualistic that they find it difficult to accept the existence of anything as totalitarian as the Spanish nation. Spain has preserved its regional differences and identities better than other European nations, which gives it both the advantage of variety and the danger of disunity. It is a land of nationalisms rather than nationalism. The most violent, of course, is that of the Basques, with their strange prehistoric language and their terrorist independence movement, E.T.A. But the Basques are not the only Spaniards with their own language and pretensions to independence. Six million people on the east coast and in the Balearic islands speak Catalan, a language related to old Provencal, quite separate from Spanish, (which incidentally is known in Spain as Castilian), and equally rich in culture, history and tradition. Away in the wet northwest corner of the peninsula, the Galicians speak Gallego, which is related to Portuguese, and nurture their less vigorous dreams of an independent Galicia.

These complications should intrigue rather than disturb the visitor. Catalan street signs in Barcelona may be hard to decipher at first, but Catalans will speak Castilian if you ask them politely. Though E.T.A. have taken to planting bombs on beaches, they have so far confined their killing to the National Police and the Civil Guard.

Galloping Modernity

Indeed some visitors may prefer to forget altogether about political problems, relying on traditional images of bullfights and castanets, or beaches and sangría. Such things can be found, though the romantic idea of Spain is very much based on the South, and Andalusia in particular. Young Spaniards will not thank you for expecting them to conform to stereotypes of the torero or the haughty señorita. Among the more educated people there is a very strong wish to get away from all that paraphernalia, partly because it was promoted so strongly during the long repressive regime of Franco, whose belief in the immortal essence of Spain involved much artificial preservation of tradition. Most Spaniards now want to be modern and West European, not, as the Spanish Tourist Board used to say, "different."

There can be no denying that they have moved a very long way to that end in an extremely short space of time. What was still in the 1930s a rural and agricultural society has become predominantly urban and industrial, or even post-industrial. Ten years after the death of Europe's second last surviving Fascist dictator, Spain has a democratic system headed by a sane and tactful constitutional monarch, and a socialist government—voted in by an enormous majority—for the first time since the short-lived Second Republic of 1931–36.

That earlier period of democracy ended in the carnage of the Civil War, which seemed for a long time (its memory was fostered by Franco) to have reaffirmed the Black Legend of Spain's tragic destiny. Spaniards now do not like to talk about it, but more out of a wish to forget a time of appalling waste than because of unhealed wounds. When Lt. Col. Tejero of the Guardia Civil walked into the Cortes (Parliament) brandishing a pistol on 23 February 1981, it appeared for a short time as if Spain's renascent democracy had been ended once again by a military coup. When this attempt failed, however, almost entirely because of King Juan Carlos's firm and immediate appeal to the army to remain loyal to him as its commander-in-chief, it proved instead that the new democracy in Spain had been strengthened by its first serious ordeal. Future threats from the Armed Forces, the only real danger to the democratic system, had become suddenly less credible.

The final confirmation, for most Spaniards, that their country has shrugged off its persistent image of backwardness, is Spain's acceptance into the European club, the E.E.C. What benefits this will bring remain to be seen—and there are some who even dare to doubt that it *will* bring substantial benefits—but its psychological importance cannot be doubted. Fernando Morán, then Spanish Foreign Minister, summed it up when he said after terms had been agreed in March 1985: "now at last Spain can hold her head high once more in international relations."

Perhaps even more important than this political modernization is the drastic liberalization which has occurred in Spanish society. From being one of the most conservative countries in Western Europe, Spain has suddenly become, in certain respects, one of the most liberal. The taking of some soft drugs, for example, is now permitted, even if their sale is not (though the vendors of so-called "chocolate" at the entrance to the arcaded Plaça Reial in Barcelona do not seem to be aware of this). It must be said that many people are linking the rise in crime on the streets with the availability of drugs, and there are signs of the government backpedalling on this issue. Abortion is now legal, though only for medical reasons or after rape—and here too there are signs of a conservative backlash, because the Constitutional Court recently (1985) ruled against the Socialist government's pro-abortion legislation—though only on a technicality. Pornography, banned for so long under the "muy católico" Generalissimo Franco, is back on the streets, and it seems to be making up for lost time. Pornographic comics, strangely combining strip (in both senses) cartoons with radical politics are popular with the student generation, who have been going through all the styles, fashions and movements which Spain missed out on from the '50s to the '80s, rock'n'roll to punk, in an accelerated rampage. Toplessness is rife on the crowded beaches, despite the disapproval of the Catholic organization Opus Dei and the right-wing daily paper *A.B.C.*

The Spanish Landscape

Despite all this evidence of Spain's modernity, however, it may still be that it is the anachronistic and, dare one say, "different" elements of the country which will interest and attract the visitor most. Under this heading come history, culture and many aspects of the way of life in Spain which still contrast (and we at least may be grateful for it) with the increasingly homogenized world outside. One thing not much affected by modernization is the landscape, or at least its more permanent features, the mountains, the light, the sea—if we forget for the moment the ghastly ribbon development which has spoilt so much of what Rose Macaulay in the 1950s could still call its "fabled shore."

Spain is a large country by European standards, only slightly smaller than France, twice the size of Britain, and it contains an extraordinary variety of geography and, above all, climate, which goes far towards explaining the strength of regional character and identity noted earlier. It might be better to think of Spain as a subcontinent than a country. Certainly the idea of a uniformly "sunny Spain" is misleading, but not as misleading as the English ditty "The rain in Spain falls mainly on the plain," which, if you take the plain to mean the central tableland or meseta, is precisely the opposite of the truth. This plateau (about 2,000 feet high) which covers two-fifths of the peninsula is parchingly arid for most of the year, as are large stretches of the eastern coastal region and the southwestern region of Extremadura. The northwestern "nationality" of Galicia, on the other hand, is wetter than Ireland, with which it has much in common. This excess of humidity is very much the exception in Spain, and it is a costly irony of fate that rainfall should be highest in areas where the soil is poorest. Aridity is the keynote, and nowhere is this brought home more vividly than at the historic pass of Roncesvalles, where Roland made his last stand, which connects the French *département des Pyrenées Occidentales* with the little Spanish kingdom of Navarre. In summer, looking from the Spanish side, you see a bank of cloud like smoke rolling through the defile from the damp deciduous forests of beech and chestnut which cover the French western Pyrenees, then dissolving into blue sky as it reaches the great golden-tawny expanse of the Navarrese plain.

Such a color can only be produced by long hours of burning sun. The summer sun in Spain is often more awesome than, as the tourist brochures stupidly reiterate, pleasant and sexy. It is capable of obliterating all activity and reducing one to utter torpor. Unlike that of northern countries, Spanish sun can have a negative or destructive value. It ages people prematurely and etches bitter lines in those faces which we picturesquely associate with Picasso peasants. On the other hand, it relaxes the muscles and dissolves away many of the neuroses which afflict people from sunless lands. A Spanish Edvard Munch is inconceivable. In winter, spring and autumn the extra light and heat which the northerner will experience can only be a bonus. I have breakfasted outside under the lemon tree on my patio in Barcelona on Christmas Eve with the thermometer standing at 70°, and throughout November and December there will be days, in the low-lying areas at least, when it is as warm as high summer in England. Even in January and February, when the temperature often falls below zero in Madrid, the weather is frequently bright and cloudless, and the crystalline light of Castile exhilarating, however cold the air.

Apart from the sun-baked dryness, the most striking feature of the Spanish landscape is its ruggedness. This is, after Switzerland, the second most mountainous country in Europe, containing its highest roads and villages. This means ample opportunities for skiing in ranges like the Pyrenees, the Sierra Nevada, the Guadarrama and the Picos de Europa. It also means innumerable remote and lovely valleys, often deserted by nearly all their former inhabitants in the drift towards the towns, where those who favor adventurous holidays can hunt, fish, walk, or just find an almost overwhelming peace camping in the open or sleeping in derelict farmhouses. Such relics of paradise exist, for example, three hours drive from Barcelona in the Catalan hinterland, where you can find yourself quite literally in another world. The experience can be disorientating, but will not be easily forgotten.

Early History

To some people this romantic notion of getting away from it all and communing with nature will seem nostalgic, unrealistic, or simply boring. Human activity, which in its more memorable forms means culture and history, will be the focus of their attention. Spanish culture and history have of course been decisively influenced by geography. The three features of that geography to note here are the barrier of the Pyrenees, neatly isolating Spain from the rest of Europe, the proximity to Africa (indeed W.H. Auden described Spain as "that fragment nipped off from hot Africa soldered so crudely to inventive Europe"), and the outlook westwards to the Americas.

Not that the Pyrenees have ever been an impassable barrier—first the Carthaginians, to attack the Romans, then the Romans, to defeat the Carthaginians, found it possible to cross them repeatedly. In the end Spain, or rather two Spains, Hispania Citerior and Hispania Ulterior (and the plurality may be significant) became part of the Roman empire: they produced four emperors as well as literary figures as distinguished as the Senecas, Martial and Lucan. The most important evidence of Roman dominion is the language, or languages (again plural)—Castilian, Catalan and Gallego, but not of course Basque, are all members of the Romance family—but there are also imposing physical remains like the aqueduct at Segovia and the theater and other ruins in the Extremaduran city of Mérida. No question then that Spain was very much part of Western Europe.

The Moorish Inheritance

It did not stay that way. In 711 the troubled period of Visigothic rule ended when Spain was invaded by Arabs from North Africa, who overran the country in an astonishingly short space of time. The Moorish rule which prevailed throughout much of the peninsula for the next seven-and-a-half centuries was generally tolerant—far more tolerant, most historians consider, than the Christian rule which followed—and it produced peaks of civilization which Spain has since rarely, if ever, surpassed.

The influence of the Moors on Spain is a huge subject which can only be touched on here. It is certainly not confined to the 4,000 odd Arabic words (including nearly all those beginning "al," like "alcalde," "alcázar," "albañil" and so on), or the beautiful remains of Moorish architecture, but persists in ethnic and, more interestingly, social characteristics which are the legacy of those 750 years of intermingling. Still, the architecture is what most tourists will want to see. It is difficult to say anything new about the Alhambra at Granada, but it *is* delicate and superbly civilized and one of the few wonders of the world in which you could want to live. Personally I prefer the Generalife, with its famous gardens but also less restored and therefore more evocative buildings. Manuel de Falla's *Nights in the Gardens of Spain* (one of the few great pieces of Spanish music not written by a Frenchman) is a wonderful recreation of its atmosphere of delicate and sensual beauty.

The most amazing Moorish building in Spain is not of course in Granada, but in Córdoba: the grand mosque or Mezquita, whose vast interior supported by over 800 columns, as Richard Ford rightly and simply said in the first handbook to Spain, "cannot be described, it must be seen." Hidden away in this forest or labyrinth of striped marble is a fair-sized Christian cathedral. It was ordered to be built by the Emperor Charles V, who also knocked down part of the Alhambra to construct a Renaissance palace, vilified by most guide writers, but to me a telling contrast to its surroundings. Charles however was not pleased when he saw how his orders had been carried out in Córdoba, and he rebuked the clerical authorities in resonant words which convey his generous appreciation of the culture he was annihilating: "You have built here what you, or anyone, might have built anywhere else; but you have destroyed what was unique in the world."

He and his successors did not take this message to heart. Andalusia has never recovered the prosperity it enjoyed at the height of Moorish rule.

The Conquest of the Americas

Having rooted out the cultured Moors and the rich and industrious Jews from their own land, the Catholic Kings turned their attention overseas. The colonization of Central, South and parts of North America was an astonishing feat, carried out, like the unification of Spain itself, in just one generation. Whether it had an altogether positive value, either for the colonies or for Spain itself, is debatable: in our post-colonial, post-imperial age the destruction of the Aztec, Maya and Inca cultures is likely to seem more shameful than heroic, especially when the Spanish administrations which replaced them have become the byword for seediness and corruption. However, Hispano-America still exists, and forms a kind of cultural commonwealth with Spain of which Spaniards at least feel proud, and is now showing signs of sloughing off its centuries-old apathy and emerging into the modern world. Its literary culture, revived by such figures as Borges, García Márquez and Vargas Llosa, is at the moment second to none.

For Spain herself, the colonization of the Americas was both her greatest achievement and the cause of her long decline. Instead of stimulating the economy, Peruvian gold and Bolivian silver encouraged indolence and produced inflation. At the same time religious dogmatism and at times fanaticism (the Inquisition is not entirely a legend) gave rise to costly religious wars, and then isolation from Protestant Europe. The first centralized state in Europe put unity above everything else, and kept itself together, just, at the cost of the prosperity which the rising capitalist system was bringing to other parts of Europe. The naturally bourgeois, trading, capitalist Catalans resented this, tried to break away, and were crushed in two bloody wars which have not been forgotten to this day. The Catalans' heyday had been in the 13th, 14th and 15th centuries when their mercantile empire extended as far as Athens and they produced literature, art and architecture to match any in Europe. The *barrio gótico* (including the cathedral with its idyllic cloister full of trees and geese) and the church of Santa Maria del Mar in Barcelona, as well as the majestic cathedrals of Palma and Gerona, still bear ample witness to the glories of Catalan Gothic.

Art and Culture

From the late 16th century onwards, Spain, ruled by introverted monarchs like Philip II, turned in on herself. Her architecture, after the rich Plateresque period when stone was treated like gold or silver, acquired a somber austerity, epitomized by Philip's grey granite monastery, which looks more like a Ministry, the Escorial. In painting, as well as fine devotional artists of widely different character like the ascetic Zurbarán and the gentle Murillo, Spain in the 17th century produced the first of her indigenous, isolated universal geniuses in Velázquez. The Velázquez rooms in the Prado are a must for anyone interested not just in Spain but in European culture, and in themselves make a nonsense of Kenneth Clark's omission of Spain from his personal view of civilization.

The next great Spanish pictorial genius was Goya, and it would not be much of an exaggeration to say that he was the next thing of any real interest to happen in Spain after Velázquez's death in 1660. Once again the

Prado is the place to appreciate the full range of this extraordinary artist who managed to combine vitality and grace with horror and despair.

Goya ended his days in Bordeaux, and exile or emigration became a familiar fate of Spanish artists and intellectuals from his day until very recent times. The rest of the 19th century was not a happy time for Spain (though it produced two great novelists in Pérez Galdós and Leopoldo Alas), and the century ended, symbolically, with the loss of her remaining colonies in the disastrous wars of 1898. In fact, the annus terribilis of 1898 became a symbol not just of military defeat but also of intellectual regeneration. Chastened by the events of that year, which seemed to indicate a near-terminal decline from the days of national greatness, a group of writers, of whom Unamuno and Ortega y Gasset are the most famous, set about examining the state of the nation's soul.

The first three decades of this century were altogether an astonishingly vital creative period in Spain. Apart from the poets there were the painters Picasso, Gris and the Catalans Miró and Dalí, and Dalí's friend and Surrealist collaborator the film director Luis Buñuel. Picasso and Miró have their own museums, both beautifully housed, in Barcelona, and Dalí has his idiosyncratic one in his native town of Figueras. These men were experimenters at the forefront of the avant-garde impetus of European art at that time, which went so far beyond the present that looking at it now one feels passé. Equally modern, but in a different, highly religious spirit, is the work of the Catalan architect Antoni Gaudí. His church of the Holy Family (Sagrada Familia) in Barcelona, which looks like a cross between a Gothic cathedral and a flight of rockets, is still not finished, and will not be for a century or two, but it is still one of the world's most impressive buildings. How tragic then that all this creative exuberance, fostered by the relatively benign dictatorship of Primo de Rivera in the 1920s, then the Republic of the 1930s, was dissipated by the Civil War. It is only now, after 40 years of stifling repression under Franco, that culture can breathe again in Spain. Some exciting work is certainly being done—filmmakers like Victor Erice and Carlos Saura have at last provided a worthy succession to Buñuel—and Madrid now considers itself to be the cultural capital of Europe.

The Art of Living

There is a sense in which all this talk of culture and history is beside the point—the point being that Spain's special strength has always been in popular culture rather than high culture, the art of living rather than fine art. Spain's ultimate art-form is the fiesta, a popular religious celebration which turns into a street party, and embraces dance, processions, masquerade and bullfight. The fiesta is not a piece of phoney folklore artificially preserved for tourists, but an integral part of Spanish life. Fiesta is also the ordinary Spanish word for party. The biggest one of all takes place every July in Pamplona—ten solid days of drinking, dancing, bull-running and bullfighting, called the Sanfermines after the town's patron saint (who may never have existed). The whole affair, despite the religious processions, is profoundly pagan and bacchanalian. Many tourists take part in it, but they are easily absorbed into the mass of Spaniards who come from all parts of the peninsula, thieves and beggars as well as aficionados, swelling the population of Pamplona to twice its normal size of 150,000. It is a joyful, liberating and totally exhausting experience (not to go to bed, at night anyway, for the duration of the fiesta is a point of honor), and the real heroes are the waiters who maintain an incredibly professional 24-hour service against all odds. The would-be heroes are those who run with the bulls every morning through the narrow Calle Estafeta to the bullring armed only with a rolled-up newspaper. As several people get gored every year, and fatalities are not uncommon, this is a sport best left to the local lads, who know what they are doing. As for the bullfights themselves, by all means go to one, with Hemingway at your side (though you will find queueing for seats in Pamplona a frustrating exercise), for they are a genuine and unique part of Spanish popular culture, but if you are like me you will find them not so much revolting as ultimately boring.

Every night of the Sanfermines a band plays in the Plaza del Castillo until four A.M., and the locals, dressed in white with red sashes, dance with a grace which makes the foreigner feel ashamed and envious. All Spanish people seem able to dance well, no matter what age they are, and every part of the country has preserved its indigenous traditional dances. These range from the statuesque Sardana of Catalonia, with its strong nationalistic overtones, to the passionate, very unEuropean flamenco of Andalusia.

Eating Well

I described the waiters as the heroes of the Sanfermines, and waiters are perhaps the most important professional group in Spain. The enormous success of tourism in Spain must be largely owing to them, and the fact that there is no other country in Europe at least where one can eat and drink in so civilized a manner at so modest a cost. The sheer number of bars and restaurants is staggering, but even more important is the flexibility they offer in terms of one's being able to eat or drink anything one wants from eight in the morning until two the next, and above all the ease of atmosphere which makes eating and drinking out seem the most natural thing in the world.

As for the food and drink themselves, I have never understood why Spanish cuisine has such a dubious reputation. The abundance of good ingredients, fresh fish (available everywhere), olive oil, tomatoes, cheese from La Mancha, and the very limited encroachment of fast food, make eating a constant pleasure even at a simple level. In the smart restaurants of Madrid and Barcelona, you can enjoy genuine haute cuisine at a fraction of what it costs in France. Spanish wine, even if it cannot reach the heights of the finest from France and Germany, offers the best value in Europe. I lived happily for months on a mellow Valdepeñas which cost 70 pesetas a bottle; excellent Riojas and Penedes wines can be had for only three or four times that amount, as can sherry and delicious bubbly (now that Spain is in the E.E.C. it can no longer be called champagne) from San Sadurní de Noia. Brandy is perhaps too cheap, and if it wants to tackle the problem of alcoholism, the Spanish government should consider raising the duty on hard liquor, which until recently stood at 1 peseta a bottle.

I have left until last what I consider the best thing Spain can offer, and that is an evening spent going round bars or "tascas" eating tapas. Tapas are small dishes, usually eaten to the accompaniment of equally small glasses of wine or sherry, and they consist of things like fried fish or shell-

SPAIN'S HISTORY AND ART

Land of Contrast

by
AILSA HUDSON

Spain, the crossroads between Africa and Europe, the Atlantic and the Mediterranean, is a country of striking contrasts. On the one hand, this gigantic peninsula offers a welcoming coastline of natural harbors and fertile foreshores, but on the other, for those who penetrate it more deeply, it throws up barriers of high sierras and plateaux, with a rude climate and sparse resources. The coastal fringe seems to turn its back on the central mesetas, and mirrors the history of Spain—a ceaseless struggle between the will to unite and the tendency to dispersion and isolation, still seen today in the struggle of the Catalans and the Basque separatists.

The history you see in the coastal Greek and Roman remains at Ampurias, the Moorish palaces and mosques of Granada and Toledo in the south, and the splendid royal residences of the interior, has been largely determined by the diverse physical background of the country.

To grasp some understanding of the peoples and culture which greet you today, it is essential to know something of the colorful and often turbulent past which has shaped them.

47

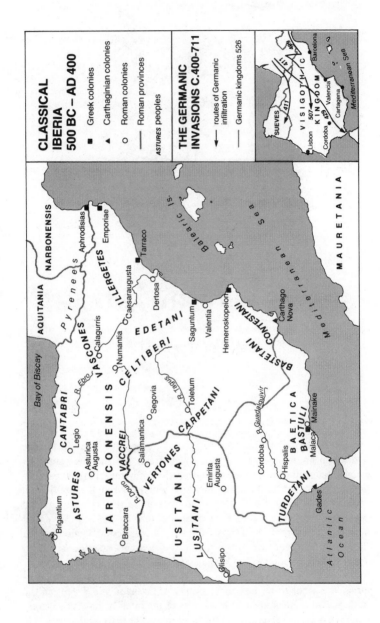

CLASSICAL IBERIA 500 BC – AD 400

■ Greek colonies
▲ Carthaginian colonies
○ Roman colonies
— Roman provinces
ASTURES peoples

THE GERMANIC INVASIONS C.400-711

→ routes of Germanic infiltration
— Germanic kingdoms 526

SUEVES
VISIGOTHIC KINGDOM
507
429
411
Lisbon
Córdoba
Cartagena
Valencia
Barcelona
Mediterranean Sea

NARBONENSIS
NARBONENSIS
AQUITANIA
Pyrenees
Bay of Biscay
Aphrodisias
Emporiae
ILLERGETES
Tarraco
VASCONES
Calagurris
Caesaraugusta
Dertosa
R. Ebro
EDETANI
Numantia
CELTIBERI
Saguntum
Valentia
Hemeroskopeion
CONTESTANI
CANTABRI
Legio
Asturica Augusta
ASTURES
Segovia
R. Tagus
Toletum
CARPETANI
BASTETANI
Carthago Nova
Mediterranean Sea
MAURETANIA
Balearic Is.
Balearic Sea
TARRACONENSIS
VACCREI
Salamantica
VERTONES
Emirita Augusta
LUSITANIA
R. Douro
Brigantium
Braccara
LUSITANI
Olisipo
BAETICA
BASTULI
Córdoba
R. Guadalquivir
Hispalis
Malaca
Mainake
TURDETANI
Gades
Atlantic Ocean

From the Phoenicians to the Visigoths

c. 1100 B.C.   Earliest Phoenician colonies, including Cádiz, Villaricos, Al-
               muñécar and Málaga
c. 650   Beginning of Greek colonization of the eastern seaboard
237–206   *Carthage v. Rome*—237 Carthaginians land in Spain; c. 225
               Cartagena founded by Hasdrubal as capital of the Cartha-
               ginian colony; 219 Hannibal's successful siege of Sagunto,
               a Roman ally, precipitates the Second Punic War; 218 The
               Romans under Scipio Calvus land at Ampurias to assault
               Carthaginian supply lines in Spain; 212 Romans capture
               Sagunto; 209 Scipio Africanus captures Cartagena and
               uses it as his base for the defeat of the Carthaginians in
               Spain; 206 Carthaginians expelled from Spain
138   Roman conquest of Galicia
121   Roman conquest of the Balearic Islands
29–19   The Cantabrian War brings the whole of Spain under Roman
               domination
A.D. 67   St. Paul is said to have visited Spain
74   The Edict of Vespasian extends rights of Roman citizenship
               to all Spaniards
200s   Christian communities established throughout Spain
380   Emperor Theodosius I, a Spaniard, proclaims Christianity
               the only tolerated religion throughout the empire
409   The first wave of Germanic invaders, the Sueves and the
               Vandals, reach Spain, signalling the end of the period of
               classical culture. Settling in Iberia by treaty with Rome,
               they set up a series of kingdoms broadly based on the old
               Roman colonies

The settlement of Spain dates from an early age. Paleolithic remains
have been found in abundance at many sites, including the famous caves
at Altamira painted with animals and hunting scenes, the "Sistine Chapel
of Prehistoric art." During the second millennium B.C. the northern, western and southern parts of the Iberian peninsula shared a copper age culture
with much of northwest Europe, characterized by megalithic structures,
passage graves and extensive mineral exploitation. Mineral wealth led to
Spain's early emergence as a trading and exporting centre, and during the
first millennium B.C. it attracted Phoenician, Greek and eventually Carthaginian traders and settlers. The remains of their towns and cities still
scatter the eastern seaboard.

By this time the native inhabitants can be broadly divided into the Iberians in the south, the Basques in the western Pyrenees, and the Celts who
had colonized much of northern Iberia.

The influence of the Mediterranean colonists upon the native peoples
was limited to the coastal zones, but some fine examples exist of hybrid
sculpture, such as the *Lady of Elche* (Archeological Museum, Madrid).

Carthaginian aggression finally provided their rivals, the Romans, with
a pretext for resuming open warfare. During the Second Punic War
(219–202 B.C.), despite Hannibal's successes in Italy, Rome thrust out at

Spain. By the end of the war Carthaginian forces had been totally expelled from Spain, and Rome with its usual ruthless efficiency proceeded to conquer the interior and the west.

The coastal regions of Spain were quickly Romanized, but resistance elsewhere was fierce and the invasion took over 75 years to complete. The Romans brought with them their institutions, their language, law and order, tailor-made local government, roads and, in later years, Roman citizenship and Christianity, all of which left an indelible mark. They rapidly exploited Spain's natural resources, lead, silver, iron ore, tin and gold being mined unceasingly during the first two centuries A.D. Andalusia became Rome's granary, and wine, olive oil and horses were other major exports. The peninsula soon became the pre-eminent colony outside Italy, and indeed a number of outstanding Roman figures were born in Spain, including the emperors Trajan and Hadrian, and the writers Seneca, Martial and Quintilian.

The extent and permanence of Roman colonization is demonstrated by the wealth of remains which are still visible throughout Spain today. These include many towns and cities, such as Tarragona, Sagunto (near Valencia), Itálica (near Seville) and Mérida (near Badajoz), and remarkable civil engineering feats, such as the 128-arch aqueduct at Segovia and the bridge at Alcántara. Ampurias has Greek and Roman remains side by side.

The beginning of the fifth century A.D. brought the gradual decline of Roman dominance in Spain, as the infiltration of Germanic peoples which had occurred elsewhere in the empire finally reached the Iberian peninsula. The Sueves, Alans and Vandals crossed the Pyrenees in 409 and within two years had established themselves in separate kingdoms, ending the endurance and continuity of the classical era.

Christians and Muslims

419	Visigoths establish themselves in northern Spain, creating a large kingdom with its capital at Toulouse
507	Toledo becomes Visigothic capital
558	Extension of Visigothic rule to include much of the south, and the kingdom of the Sueves in the west
587	Visigothic king Reccared embraces Catholicism: enforced baptism of Jews follows
711	Invasion from North Africa by Muslim Berber armies. King Roderick defeated and Visigothic kingdom destroyed
712	Muslim invasion completed, Visigothic resistance isolated in a strip of Christian states across the north of Spain. Muslim capital established at Córdoba, and the territory administered as an emirate of the Ummayad Caliphate of Damascus
718	Pelayo, successor of Roderick, creates the kingdom of Asturias; the Christian reconquest of Spain is launched
732	Muslim expansion north of the Pyrenees halted by the Franks at Poitiers; Muslims withdraw to Iberia
756	Abd al-Rahman I establishes semi-independent Ummayad dynasty in Spain

777	Frankish invasion of Spain under Charlemagne checked at Zaragoza
778	Charlemagne's retreat shattered at Roncesvalles, but Franks establish rule over Spain north of the Ebro
837	Muslim suppression of Christian and Jewish revolts
899	Miraculous discovery of remains of St. James the Greater, foundation of the church of Santiago de Compostela
912–961	Reign of Abd al-Rahman III, the apogee of Ummayad culture. Reorganization of government, navy, agriculture and industry
c.930–970	Rise of Count Fernán González of Burgos, establishing Castile as autonomous Christian power
970–1035	Sancho the Great unites Castile and Navarre and begins the conquest of León
976–1009	Reign of Hisham II, effectively deposed by Hajib al-Mansur whose brilliant administrative reforms and successful campaigns against the Christian kingdoms briefly revives flagging Ummayad power
1002	Death of al-Mansur, followed by power struggles, civil war and the disintegration of centralized Ummayad authority

Despite the barbarian name-tag, the peoples who settled in the northern and western regions of the later Roman empire saw themselves for the most part as successors to and preservers of Roman culture and the resident Hispano-Romans (who out-numbered the Visigoths five to one) continued to exist much as before. Prior to the baptism of Reccared and the reforms of Receswinth, the Visigoths maintained their own religion and civil code, but with the extension of their territory throughout the peninsula a centralized system of law, religion and government became necessary. Something of the classical heritage was revived and preserved, reflected in the encyclopedic works of Isidore of Seville, and in the Visigothic architectural decoration in Córdoba cathedral and the church of San Juan de Baños de Cerrato, near Palencia, built by Receswinth.

However, the economic and strategic importance of Spain encouraged attempts at invasion by the Franks and the Byzantines. The third such attempt, by the Islamic Berbers, was successful. Within seven years Iberia was conquered, and Christian resistance limited to pockets in the north. Islamic expansion was finally checked by Charlemagne, but with the Ummayad dynasty in firm control of Spain south of the Ebro a period of cultural blossoming began. In many ways the Arabs were the heirs to classical culture. They were largely tolerant of Christians and Jews living in their realm. They embellished and improved much of the legacy of Roman civilization, introducing new plants and agricultural techniques, reinvigorating manufacturing and trade and introducing distinctive styles and motifs still traceable in modern ceramics, carpets and folk music. They built palaces, mosques, libraries and schools; many of those buildings which survive in Andalusia were built much later, but the 850 columns elaborating the mosque at Córdoba and the smaller mosque at Toledo testify to the magnificence of early Moorish architecture. The distinctive characteristics of this style are the horseshoe arches and extensive geometric and floral patterns intermingled with Kufic script.

The polyglot nature of Moorish society permitted the fertile intermingling of many groups and factions—there was exchange and respect between the localised groups of each faith, as well as intermittent revolts and power struggles. It was against this backdrop, in the first half of the eighth century, that a substantial Christian state developed in Asturias. The moral strength of the Christian north was boosted considerably by the apparent discovery of the remains of St. James the Greater, and the foundation of the cathedral of Santiago de Compostela, which has remained an important pilgrimage centre. By the tenth century, mainly under the leadership of Castile, the Christian states rallied sufficiently to begin the long task of reconquest.

The Reconquest

1065–1109	*Reign of Alfonso VI of Castile* who led the revival of the Christian reconquest of Spain; 1085 Toledo captured by Alfonso VI; 1086 The Almoravids enter Spain to help combat the Christians. Alfonso VI defeated at Zallaka; c.1091 Muslim Spain integrated with the Almoravid empire; 1087–88 Rodrigo Díaz de Bivar, known as El Cid (Lord), re-enters the service of Alfonso VI. A knight of Burgos (in whose cathedral he and his wife are buried), he served under Sancho II of Castile. Exiled in 1081 he returned to help the Christian assault, but subsequently served the Muslim ruler of Zaragoza. He eventually ruled Valencia. After his death (1099) Valencia was regained by the Almoravids
1126–57	*Alfonso VII of Castile* takes the Christian offensive; 1137 Aragón unites with Catalonia, forming a new Christian power centered on Zaragoza; 1144 Christian attacks on Andalusia; 1146 The Almohades come to the defence of Moorish Spain, eventually taking complete control
1158–1214	*Reign of Alfonso VIII of Castile* who leads a series of successful campaigns against the Moors; 1195 Alfonso VIII defeated by the Moors at Alarcos, but, supported by Pope Innocent III he prepares for a major assault; 1212 Victory at Las Navas de Tolosa by united Christian armies. Almohades expelled from Spain and Moorish power limited to the kingdom of Granada; 1214 Catalonia secured from the Franks by the Aragonese at Muret
1213–76	Reign of Jaime I the Conqueror of Aragón who regained the Balearics (1229–35), Valencia (1238) and Murcia, which he ceded to Castile
1230–52	Reign of Ferdinand III (St. Ferdinand) of Castile and León, who conquered Córdoba (1236) and Seville (1248)
1252–84	Reign of Alfonso X the Wise of Castile, scholar, astronomer, poet, historian and codifier of the law
1270	End of the main period of the Reconquest, as Portugal concentrates on control of the Atlantic coast, Aragón seeks power in the Mediterranean, and Castile enters a period of dynastic power struggles

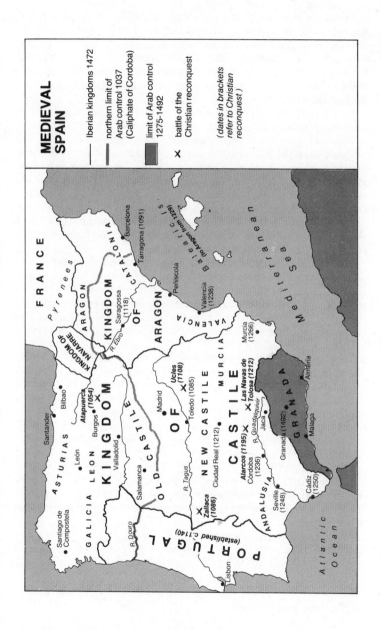

MEDIEVAL SPAIN

—— Iberian kingdoms 1472

—— northern limit of Arab control 1037 (Caliphate of Cordoba)

limit of Arab control 1275-1492

X battle of the Christian reconquest

(dates in brackets refer to Christian reconquest)

FRANCE

Pyrenees

KINGDOM OF NAVARRE

KINGDOM OF ARAGON

ARAGON

CATALONIA

Barcelona

Tarragona (1091)

Saragossa (1118)

R. Ebro

Peñiscola

Valencia (1238)

VALENCIA

Balearic Islands (c.1229)

Mediterranean Sea

Santander

Bilbao

ASTURIAS

León

GALICIA

Santiago de Compostela

LEON

Burgos

Atapuerca (1054)

OLD CASTILE

KINGDOM OF CASTILE

Valladolid

Salamanca

R. Douro

PORTUGAL (established c.1140)

Lisbon

Madrid

NEW CASTILE

Ucles (1108) X

Toledo (1085)

R. Tagus

Zallaca (1086) X

Ciudad Real (1212)

Alarcos (1195) X

Córdoba (1236)

R. Guadalquivir

Seville (1248)

ANDALUSIA

MURCIA

Murcia (1266)

Las Navas de Tolosa (1212) X

Jaca

Granada (1492)

GRANADA

Almería

Malaga

Cádiz (1250)

Atlantic Ocean

Although this period saw the gradual decline of Moorish power and the establishment of three increasingly distinct and secure Christian states in Portugal, Castile and Aragón, the Christian states remained almost continually under arms, while the Muslims saw the establishment of two powerful dynasties, the Almoravids and Almohades, both marked by considerable cultural achievements. The Alcázar and the Giralda still dominate Seville today and, with the Alhambra at Granada (completed in the 14th century), are unique in Islamic architecture, a true fusion of Moorish and local styles.

Arabic scholasticism continued to advance, with the first major universities being founded at Valencia (1209) and Salamanca (1242). The work of outstanding Arabic scholars provided a direct link with the classical past long after the Reconquest was complete. Idrisi the geographer and the philosopher Averroes were both active in the 12th century. So too was the great Jewish philosopher Maimónides who translated Arabic medical texts and Sarasorda who introduced Muslim mathematics to the West. One aspect of the intermingling of Islamic and Christian cultures was the development of lyrical poetry and the art of the troubadour. The exploits of El Cid were a popular subject and probably first recorded in the 12th century in the *Cantar de Mio Cid*.

Throughout the period the strength of the Church remained stable. Carolingian and then Romanesque architecture, derived from southern French models, was developed most spectacularly at Santiago de Compostela. Later, the High Gothic style made its appearance in the building of the cathedrals of Toledo (c.1230), Burgos (1126) and León (c.1230). Catalan Gothic can be seen in the cathedrals of Barcelona (1298) and Gerona (1312).

The Reconquest also had a lasting effect on the social structure of Spain. The Christian kingdoms developed a nobility based on military achievement and as the Reconquest proceeded south such figures were granted substantial domains—some still owned by their descendants. At a slightly lower level were the wealthy knights—*infanzones* and *hidalgos*—a class which was created by and lived for force of arms. It was this chivalric brotherhood which carried Spanish might overseas to Holland, the Americas and the Indies after the Reconquest—but which also provided the model for Don Quixote.

However, the gradual process of Reconquest also held back the development of feudalism, and the long tradition of guerrilla warfare in Castile led to a concentration of the population in towns, and an impoverishment of agriculture which still exists today.

Minority groups, including Jews and non-belligerent Muslims, continued to live unhampered in the Christian states. The piecemeal granting of communal sovereignty still influences local politics, and forms the spine of the arguments for separatism voiced today.

The High Middle Ages

1282   Peter (Pedro) III adds Sicily to the Aragonese kingdom; Aragón becomes the principle power in the western Mediterranean

1295	Frederick I of Sicily establishes dynasty independent of Aragón
1340	Alfonso XI of Castile ends the threat of the Moroccan Muslims at Rio Salado
1374	Peace of Almazan between Castile, and Portugal and Aragón
1409	Martin of Aragón reunites Aragón and Sicily, ending a period of dynastic struggle
1435	Alfonso V of Aragón and Sicily conquers Naples and southern Italy, transferring the center of power away from the Spanish mainland to Italy
1454–74	Reign of Henry IV of Castile, during which the rivalry and anarchic power of the nobility reaches its height
1469	Marriage of Isabella, princess of Castile, to Ferdinand, heir to the throne of Aragón; this marriage becomes the key to Spanish unity
1474	Isabella succeeds to the Castilian throne
1478	Establishment of the Inquisition
1479	Ferdinand succeeds to the throne of Aragón, Catalonia and Valencia. The rule of the combined Catholic crowns restores royal power in Castile
1492	Conquest of the last Moorish outpost of Granada makes Ferdinand and Isabella rulers of all Spain. Attempted conversion of Muslims and Jews follows; subsequent expulsion of all Jews; first voyage of Christopher Columbus, under the patronage of Isabella, discovers the West Indies. Further voyages (1493, 1498 and 1502) establish the existence of the Americas
1494	Treaty of Tordesillas whereby Portugal and Spain divide the non-European world into two spheres of influence. Almost all of the known Americas and the Philippines fell under Spanish rule in the 16th century
1502	Uprising of Moors in Castile leads to forcible conversion on pain of expulsion for all Muslims
1504	Death of Isabella; her daughter Joanna with her husband Philip try in vain to claim Castilian inheritance. Philip dies and Joanna is locked away, insane
1509–11	A series of military expeditions under Cardinal Cisneros in North Africa conquer Oran, Bougie and Tripoli
1512	Conquest of Navarre by Ferdinand
1516	Death of Ferdinand. Cardinal Cisneros becomes regent until the legal heir, Charles I (son of Joanna and Philip) arrives from Flanders

Played against the backcloth of the later stages of the Reconquest was the drama of the struggle for political maturity of the great kingdoms of Castile and Aragón.

Aragón largely abandoned the fight against Islam, and turned instead to the development of a west Mediterranean empire to rival the Holy Roman Empire of central Europe. In this it was largely successful, acquiring Sicily and the southern part of the Italian peninsula. However, rapid population growth, the overworking of the land, plague and an unstable economy led to widespread agrarian revolts and eventually to open civil war (1462–72), dominated by a nobility dissatisfied with the monarchy and yet unwilling to relinquish its historical rights.

A greater stability marked the development of Castile. The effects of the Great Plague (1347) were less devastating than in Aragón and a major economic advance was the granting of privileges to the Mesta, a guild of cattle and sheep herders, who were permitted almost unrestricted access to seasonal pasture. Not only the massive increase in wool production, but also the regular annual movement around the kingdom of an increasingly prosperous group stimulated economic growth, although uncontrolled grazing of the mesetas eventually proved destructive. Castile also developed on two maritime fronts: to the north on the Atlantic seaboard centered on Cádiz, and in the south building up a trading zone on the northern and Atlantic coasts of Africa.

With the unification of the kingdoms of Aragón and Castile by the marriage of Ferdinand and Isabella the monarchy assumed firm political control. The powers of the nobility and the clergy were contained, and the Catholic kings found their most extreme voice in the creation of the Inquisition and the subsequent conversion or expulsion of Muslims and Jews.

During this period Spanish Gothic architecture reached its peak, producing the most ornate and decorated examples of the style in Europe. A fine example is the cathedral at Seville. The intensely decorative element of Spanish Gothic was to persist for some centuries, being applied to the Italian Renaissance style which appears at the end of the 15th century, and evolving into a hybrid mannerist form known as Plateresque.

Similarly, Moorish architecture reached an apogee of stylistic refinement and decorative elaboration in Granada with the completion of the Alhambra, while the combination of three styles—Moorish, Gothic and Renaissance in the cathedral at Granada reflects the exact historical moment of the completion of the Reconquest. As the Reconquest proceeded, and the Moorish urban craft populations became absorbed by the Christians, a unique hybrid style came into being, known as *mudéjar*. Intricate working in wood, ivory, enamel, silver and gold as well as mosaics, leatherwork and ceramics reached a peak in Toledo, especially in the art of damascening—inlaying steel with gold and silver. Examples of this work are still produced in the region today. Mudéjar architecture extended this tradition on a large scale, finding expression in elaborate brickwork in towers and apses and ornately carved wooden *(artesonado)* ceilings.

The development of Castilian ecclesiastical painting underwent two distinct foreign influences—firstly that of the Italian school of Giotto and then, with the visit of Jan van Eyck (1428), that of the Flemish school.

By the end of the 15th century Castile had entered the mainstream of European culture and had a thriving literary tradition of its own. Outstanding in this period were: Juan Manuel (1282–1348) who collected fables in *El Conde Lucanor;* Juan Ruiz, who wrote the *Libro de Buen Amor;* and later the popular dramatist Juan del Encina (c.1469–1529). The advent of printing in 1474 led to the wide circulation of contemporary literary works and among these was the first Spanish novel, *La Celestina,* (c.1499) a novel in dialogue attributed to Fernando de Rojas.

The crusading energy of the Reconquest found its vocation after the fall of Granada during the reign of Ferdinand and Isabella when the Spanish attempted to find a westward route to Asia. By the time of Magellan's successful discovery of such a route, Spain had established firm control of the Caribbean and was poised to take hold of the greatest treasure hoard in man's history—the Americas.

The Habsburgs

1519	Charles I, the founder of the Spanish Habsburg dynasty, elected as Holy Roman Emperor, thereby becoming Charles V. He inherits the Spanish Netherlands and Franche-Comté from his father; Cortés conquers the Aztec empire in Mexico
1519–22	Magellan rounds Cape Horn, traverses the Pacific and claims the Philippines for Spain, dying there. The first circumnavigation completed by his lieutenant Elcano
1521	War with France; decisive victory for Charles at Pavia (1525)
1531	Pizarro conquers the Inca empire in Peru
1535–51	Territorial wars with France
1554	Charles' heir, Philip, marries Queen Mary of England
1556	Charles abdicates in favour of his son Philip II, who inherits Spain, Sicily and the Netherlands; the Holy Roman Empire is conferred on Charles' brother Ferdinand
1560	Capital established at Madrid
1563	Construction of El Escorial begins
1567	The beginning of the Dutch Revolt, a prolonged struggle for an independent Protestant Netherlands
1569	Revolt of the Moriscos (supposedly converted Muslims): brutally suppressed
1571	Battle of Lepanto, the climax of naval rivalry between Spain and the Ottomans. Spain, with the aid of Venice, destroys the Ottoman fleet
1580	Philip inherits the Portuguese throne
1587	Spanish fleet destroyed by the English fleet at Cádiz
1588	The Spanish Armada. The Reformation, English aid to the Dutch rebels, rivalry in the Atlantic and Caribbean and finally the execution of Mary Stuart provoke Philip to attempt to destroy Protestant rule in England. The fleet meets with disaster, and Anglo-Spanish hostility continues until 1603
1589–1600	Involvement in French religious wars
1598	Philip II dies; Philip III's shyness and piety lead to an increase in nobility and church power and estates, and a marked agricultural and economic decline
1609	Expulsion of the Moriscos
1618	Spain's Habsburg interests draw her into the Thirty Years' War
1621–65	Reign of Philip IV whose minister, Count-Duke Olivares, attempts to modernize government by centralization and increased royal power
1622	Beginning of lengthy territorial war with France
1640–59	Catalonian revolt; Republic declared and recognized by France, lasting 12 years

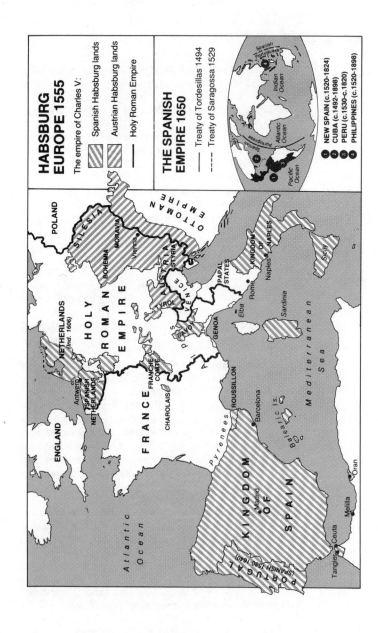

HABSBURG EUROPE 1555

The empire of Charles V:

Spanish Habsburg lands
Austrian Habsburg lands
—— Holy Roman Empire

THE SPANISH EMPIRE 1650

—— Treaty of Tordesillas 1494
----- Treaty of Saragossa 1529

① NEW SPAIN (c.1520–1824)
② CUBA (c.1492–1898)
③ PERU (c.1530–c.1820)
④ PHILIPPINES (c.1520–1898)

POLAND

SILESIA

MORAVIA

BOHEMIA
Vienna

AUSTRIA
STYRIA

OTTOMAN EMPIRE

HOLY ROMAN EMPIRE

NETHERLANDS

TYROL

VENICE

PAPAL STATES

Rome

KINGDOM OF NAPLES

Naples

Sicily

Antwerp

SPANISH NETHERLANDS (Ind. 1606)

FRANCHE COMTÉ

GENOA

Elba

Sardinia

Mediterranean Sea

CHAROLAIS

FRANCE

ENGLAND

Pyrenees

ROUSSILLON

Barcelona

Balearic Is.

Atlantic Ocean

KINGDOM OF SPAIN

Madrid

Oran

PORTUGAL (SPANISH 1580–1640)

Tangier Ceuta

Melilla

Spanish
Portuguese

Indian Ocean

Atlantic Ocean

Pacific Ocean

1648	Peace of Westphalia, ending the Thirty Years' War, brings independence to Holland
1659	Treaty of the Pyrenees ends both the war with France and Spanish ascendancy in Europe
1665–1700	Reign of Charles II; last of the Spanish Habsburgs
1674	Spain joins coalition against France
1678	Treaty of Nimwegen; Spain cedes further European territories to France
1698	First partition treaty between England, Holland and France; an attempt to resolve in advance the problem of the succession to Spain and her empire
1700	Charles names Philip of Anjou, Louis XIV's grandson, as his heir

The accession to the Spanish throne of Charles I, bringing the Netherlands which he inherited from his mother, and his subsequent (partly rigged) election as Holy Roman Emperor made Spain the most powerful country in Europe.

Another factor also altered the balance of European power in Spain's favor; with the rapid exploration and exploitation of new lands overseas the axis of European power swiftly moved from the central Mediterranean to the Atlantic seaboard, dominated by Portugal, Spain and the Netherlands. The simultaneous rise of France and England made them fractious contenders for Atlantic honors, and their skirmishes punctuate the period of Habsburg ascendancy.

Thus Spain accrued great wealth, and an economy underwritten by global trade, overseas plantations (using native slave labor) and silver looted and mined by the Conquistadores in the Americas.

The Reformation had little effect on Spain; it remained part of the Catholic core, and during Philip II's reign played a great part in the Counter-Reformation, assuming an ideological offensive against the Dutch separatists and the English. The blood shed in the Netherlands and during the heyday of the Inquisition is notorious, and the crusade was carried overseas (often forcibly) by the Jesuit Order, created by the Spanish soldier Ignatius de Loyola (1491–1556). Another great figure of the period was St. Teresa of Avila (1515–82) who reformed the Carmelite nunneries, but whose great contributions were her autobiography (which includes descriptions of divine visions) and her *Castillo interior* which greatly influenced Catholic mysticism.

The Habsburg monarchs could afford to exercise patronage on a grand scale, and the 16th and 17th centuries were the Golden Age of Spanish culture. El Escorial, the royal residence and monastery near Madrid, is their greatest monument, but reflects the somber religious tastes of Philip II. The Counter-Reformation throughout the Catholic countries produced a reinvigoration of devotional art. One of the most distinctive painters of the period lived and worked in Toledo—the Cretan-born El Greco (1541–1614). His unique fluency in both line and color created an ecstatic visionary world—a realization in paint similar to the revelations of St. Teresa. However, the Spanish Baroque school was principally created by the work of a group of painters who had studied in Italy: Navarrete (c.1526–79), Ribalta (1565–1628) and the morbid Ribera (1588–1652).

The handling of devotional subjects in the 17th century was to become softer and more Italianate in the works of Murillo (1617–82) and Zurbarán (1598–1664). But the master of Spanish painting at that time was Velázquez (1599–1660) whose work was predominantly concerned with contemporary life—genre scenes and portraits—and found its fullest expression in his work as court painter to Philip IV. His careful compositions, unique handling of form and light and in later years his color sense imbue his subjects with a heroic but immediate stature.

It was, however, in literature that Spain took the cultural lead in Europe. Poets thrived in the age of humanism inaugurated by Ferdinand and Isabella, including Garcilaso de la Vega (1503–36), the mystical poet Juan de la Cruz (1542–91) and the theologian Luis Ponce de Léon (b.1528). Later outstanding poets were Quevedo (1580–1645) and Góngora (1561–1627). Lope de Vega (1562–1635), responsible for over 2,000 plays, is regarded as the father of modern drama; however, the dramatic tradition was brought to its highest point in the work of Calderón (1600–81) whose most famous play *La Vida es Sueño* ("Life is a Dream") is still performed today throughout Europe. The other towering literary figure of the period is Miguel de Cervantes (1547–1616) whose *Don Quijote* is an unsurpassed ironical portrait of contemporary Spain. An elegaic view of the lost cause of Spanish chivalry, it is one of the world's greatest novels.

Cervantes had been wounded at the battle of Lepanto, one of Spain's last significant victories in Europe. The weakening of the Spanish monarchy after Philip II's reign was due to a number of factors, not least the ascendancy of France and the Protestant states of the north. Economically Spain was unable to compete with the latter; its creative medieval mercantile classes—Jews and Muslims—had been expelled, and the nobility were reluctant to invest their substantial wealth in anything but property. By the end of the Habsburg period Spain and its empire were increasingly viewed by the rest of Europe as a glittering cadaver ripe for profitable dismemberment.

The Bourbons

1701–14	*The War of the Spanish Succession*—three legal claimants exist—Louis XIV; Leopold I, a German Habsburg and the electoral prince of Bavaria; and Philip of Anjou who is supported in Spain and becomes the first Bourbon ruler as Philip V; 1704 Gibraltar captured by the British; 1709 Menorca captured by the British; 1713 Treaty of Utrecht whereby Philip is recognized as the king of Spain on condition that France and Spain remain separate; 1714 Treaty of Rastatt in which Spain cedes Flanders, Luxembourg and Italy to the Austrian Habsburgs. The special privileges of Catalonia and Valencia are abolished
1717–18	Spanish seize Sardinia and Sicily
1720	Treaty of the Hague settles Habsburg and Bourbon claims in Italy
1727–29	War with Britain and France
1733–35	Spanish invasion of Habsburg Naples and Sicily
1739–41	War of Jenkins' Ear against the British

1756	Spanish recovery of Menorca during the Seven Years' War
1759–88	*Reign of Charles III* who promotes economic and administrative reform—1761 War with France against Britain; 1762 Treaty of Paris; Spain cedes Menorca and Florida to Britain, and in compensation receives Louisiana from France; 1779 Spanish support for the Americans in the War of Independence; regains Florida and Menorca
1788–1808	*Reign of Charles IV*—1793 Revolutionary France declares war on Spain; 1795 Treaty of Basel ends the Franco-Spanish war. Spain now allies with France against Britain; 1797 Franco-Spanish fleet defeated by the British at Cape St. Vincent; 1805 Spain and France defeated by the British at Trafalgar; 1807 Treaty of Fontainebleau; Napoleon's influence becomes manifest. Spanish invasion of Portugal with French support; 1808 Abdication of Charles IV in favor of Joseph, Napoleon's brother. Portugal invaded by the British. Napoleon personally leads a French invasion, defeating the Spanish at Burgos and Espinosa, taking Madrid in December. The British invade northwest Spain
1809	Defeat of the British at Corunna
1809–14	Gradual conquest of Spain by the British forces, and restoration of the Bourbons under Ferdinand VII (reigned 1814–33)
1833	Ferdinand deprives his brother Don Carlos of direct succession to the throne in favour of his infant daughter Isabella (reigned 1833–68), her mother María Cristina becoming regent upon Ferdinand's death
1834–39	First Carlist War: Don Carlos, with conservative and regional separatist support, contests the crown
1836	*Progresista* revolt in Andalusia, Aragón, Catalonia and Madrid. Restoration of the 1812 constitution
1840	María Cristina forced into exile by the rebellion of General Baldomero Espartero, who becomes dictator
1842	Republican separatist revolt in Barcelona bloodily suppressed
1843	Coalition of moderates and *progresistas* ousts Espartero and declares Isabella of age. General Narváez creates the Guardia Civil
1854	Revolution led by General Leopoldo O'Donnell and Espartero; Liberal alliance formed
1864	Narváez becomes premier; period of reactionary policy
1868	Death of Narváez places absolutist regime in jeopardy. Admiral Juan Topete, supported by liberals, topples the crown. Provisional government formed under Marshal Serrano
1873	First Spanish Republic declared in the midst of Carlist uprisings
1875	Alfonso XII, son of Isabella, restored to the throne. Continuation of the Carlist War
1885	Regency of Alfonso's widow María Cristina
1890	Universal suffrage introduced

1895   Cuban revolution
1898   Spanish-American war results in the loss of the remaining
                Spanish empire in Cuba and the Philippines.

The succession to the Spanish throne of Philip of Anjou brought European tensions and rivalries to a head; the War of the Spanish Succession affected the whole of Europe, and although Philip finally won, Spain lost further territories and the promise of a future union with France.

During the 18th century there was considerable growth and expansion within Spain and by the turn of the century the growing economy and weak monarchy seemed to make Spain an attractive and relatively easily acquired property within Napoleon's scheme for a new Europe. Napoleon effected the abdication of Charles IV and invaded the peninsula. He had correctly identified a historical moment in Spain's cultural development—a clash between a modern vitality and the lingering ghosts of the past represented by the Church (and the Inquisition) and the Crown. This moment is most brilliantly captured in the work of the Aragonese artist Francisco de Goya (1746–1828); on the one hand he portrayed the joy and vitality of everyday Spanish life—the *fiestas, majas* and bull fighting; on the other he was a passionate satirist of the Inquisition and the futility of war. Even his royal portraits betray a knowing recognition of a doomed family. Late in life the darker side of his preoccupations rose to the surface in the *Caprichos* and the horrific murals in his house of black sabbaths and abominations—echoes of Spain's medieval heritage.

A prerequisite of the Bourbon restoration in 1814 was a constitution carefully constructed to limit the powers of the Crown. Ferdinand immediately rode roughshod over it, setting an example to his nominated successor, Isabella, selected in illegal preference to the heir, his brother Don Carlos. The monarchy was irrevocably split, and the way open for ambitious statesmen—such as Espartero, Narváez and O'Donnell—to seize power. The age of the *pronunciamiento*—of successive coups and changes of government—had arrived. It reached its climax in 1898; Spain's attempt violently to suppress independence movements in Cuba and the Philippines provoked American intervention and outbursts from intellectuals and Basque and Catalan separatists at home. The eventual loss of the colonies undermined royal power for good.

A century of such vigorous polemic breeds fine literature. The Romantic movement in drama was led by José Zorrilla (1817–93), best known for his play *Don Juan Tenorio,* which is still performed today. The epic quality of Byron can be traced in the work of the poet José de Espronceda (1808–42) and the melancholy vein of Romantic poetry was developed by Gustavo Adolfo Bécquer (1836–70). The later radical development of Romanticism—Realism—was most fully realised by Benito Pérez Galdós (1843–1920), Spain's Dickens, whose novels include *Doña Perfecta* and *Fortunata y Jacinta;* he also wrote an impressive cycle of historical novels, the *Episodios Nacionales.* Vicente Blasco Ibáñez (1867–1928) took realism a step further in his powerful social novels, the best known being *La Barraca,* and the original which became the film *Blood and Sand.*

The leading composers of the 19th century, Isaac Albéniz (1860–1909) and Enrique Granados (1867–1916) also worked in the Romantic style. But by 1898 social and cultural differences had crystallized, and a more politicized consciousness accompanied Spain's entry into the 20th century.

Republicanism and the Right

1902–31   *Reign of Alfonso XIII*—1909 Conscription of troops for Mo-
            rocco provokes a general strike in Barcelona. Uprising
            spreads to other Catalonian cities, convents are burned
            and clergy massacred before it is violently suppressed. The
            king calls a Liberal ministry and invites the participation
            of all political parties; 1910 Liberals in power; 1912 Assas-
            sination of anti-clerical Liberal premier José Canalejas;
            1913 Conservatives return to power; 1914 Spain declares
            neutrality in the First World War; 1921 Massive defeat
            of Spanish forces in Morocco during the Rif revolt; 1923
            Army mutiny at Barcelona precipitates the military coup
            of General Manuel Primo de Rivera who, with royal sup-
            port, proclaims national martial law; 1925 Primo de Rive-
            ra becomes prime minister of a largely military cabinet,
            ending his dictatorship; 1927 End of campaign in Moroc-
            co; 1930 Resignation of Primo de Rivera; 1931 Restora-
            tion of the constitution leads to municipal elections and
            an overwhelming victory for the Republicans led by Nice-
            to Alcalá Zamora. Alfonso XIII leaves Spain. Royal prop-
            erty is confiscated and Zamora elected first president, im-
            mediately succeeded by Manuel Azaña

1932   Conservative revolt under General José Sanjurjo suppressed.
            Catalan charter of autonomy approved in principle by the
            Republican government

1933   Two radical uprisings of anarchists and syndicalists; both
            suppressed by the government. The Associations Law
            strips the Church of its property and traditional rights.
            Regular elections show a swing to the Right. Foundation
            of the Falange—a nationalist anti-Marxist youth move-
            ment—by José Antonio Primo de Rivera, son of the for-
            mer dictator

1934   Victory for the moderate Left in Catalonia. Strike in Barcelo-
            na. Formation of a cabinet under Alejandro Lerroux,
            broadly aligned with the Right. President Luis Companys
            of Catalonia declares independence but is suppressed by
            government troops, as is the Communist uprising in Astu-
            rias

1936   Popular Front (Republicans, Socialists, Syndicalists and
            Communists) wins a decisive electoral victory over the
            Right. Revolt of military garrison led by Generals Francis-
            co Franco and Emilio Mola at Melilla in Spanish Morocco
            spreads to mainland garrisons at Cádiz, Seville, Zaragoza
            and Burgos. The government retains control in Madrid
            and Barcelona and declares the confiscation of all clerical
            property. Military leaders declare a state of war. Rebels
            capture Badajoz, Toledo, (later relieved), Irún and San Se-
            bastián, establishing themselves in the north, west and
            south. General Franco is declared Chief of State by the

rebels. Popular Front government grants the Basques home rule. Siege of Madrid begins

1937   The rebels capture Málaga, but fail to encircle Madrid. Loyalists win battle at Brihuega. New socialist government formed (excluding the Anarchists and Syndicalists). German warships bombard Almería. Rebels capture Bilbao and, as Basque resistance collapses, Santander. Gijón and the whole of Asturias falls to the rebels. Government moves from Valencia to Barcelona. Franco establishes complete naval blockade of the Spanish coast

1938   The rebels capture Teruel and begin drive to the sea, taking Viñaroz on the coast, dividing the Loyalist centers in Castile and Catalonia. Pitched battles along the Ebro

1939   Barcelona taken by rebels. Over 200,000 loyalist refugees escape to France. Franco's government is recognized by Britain and France. Radical government replaced by a new National Defence Council under General José Miaja. Republican fleet flees Cartagena for French North Africa. Madrid government crushes Communist insurgency and sues for peace with honor, but Franco insists on unconditional surrender, the end of the Civil War coming with the surrender of Madrid. Franco institutes a massive purge of the Left wing at home, and joins the German-Italian-Japanese anti-Communist pact. German and Italian troops withdraw from Spain. Spain declares her neutrality in World War II

1942   The Cortes, the national representative body, is re-established along Fascist lines

1945   Don Juan, the Bourbon claimant to the throne, calls for Franco's resignation. Despite the severing of diplomatic relations with Germany, Spain gives refuge to many Germans. Spain excluded from membership of the United Nations. Franco introduces nominal royalists to the cabinet and promises the restoration of the monarchy

1946   U.S.A., U.K. and France urge the removal of Franco and the restoration of democratic elections

1950   Spain joins the United Nations

1953   Spain agrees to the establishment of N.A.T.O. naval and air bases on its territory in return for economic and military aid

1956   Moroccan protectorate terminated

1968   Spain closes the frontier with Gibraltar

1969   Prince Juan Carlos de Bourbon named by Franco as his successor. President Nixon visits Spain, reaffirming U.S. defence interests there and continuing economic aid

1970   Eruption of the Basque problem. The court martial of 15 Basque nationalists for the assassination of a police official leads to widespread protest: state of emergency declared. Death and gaol sentences passed by the court martial are commuted and reduced in response to great unrest

1973   Franco's first prime minister, Admiral Carrero Blanco, as-
              sassinated by Basque terrorists
1975   Spanish Sahara crisis. Under pressure Spain cedes the miner-
              al-rich province to Morocco. Franco dies and is succeeded
              by Prince Juan Carlos

The events of 1898 led to an increase in Liberal power and a decrease in the ability of the monarchy to control internal affairs. Waiting in the wings, as always, was the extreme Right, represented principally by the army. They were balanced by the increasingly politicized separatists, who devolved by degrees to the Left.

Spain's decline and loss of empire gave rise to a great deal of soul-searching which found an outlet in the literature of the day. The best known member of the literary "Generation of '98" was the novelist, essayist, philosopher and poet Miguel de Unamuno (1864–1937) whose many works include *The Tragic Sense of Life*. Other influential members included the philosopher and essayist José Ortega y Gasset (1883–1955), the novelist Pío Baroja (1872–1956) and the eccentric modernist writer and dramatist Ramón del Valle-Inclán (1866–1936).

For some it was time to leave Spain for better climes, not least for Spain's greatest modern painter, Pablo Picasso (1881–1973) who lived and worked largely in Paris. An innovator and stylist, his contribution to the development of Cubism and modern art in general was due to a profound knowledge of classical and primitive art and great technical facility. The modernist painter Juan Gris (1887–1927) was only one of a number who followed Picasso to Paris.

But such cultural dissatisfaction was only the tip of the iceberg. During the 19th century the economy had failed to keep up with either the rest of Europe or with a rapidly growing population. By the beginning of this century it was clear to both the monarchy and the Right that popular support was the key to power. The Left already knew this, but was plagued by factionalism; however, it made its presence felt in the industrial north and in Catalonia through widespread strikes, attacks on the clergy, repeated demands for autonomy, and resistance to conscription.

The government of General Primo de Rivera violently suppressed all dissidence in Spain and Morocco, and increasingly modeled itself on Italian Fascism, most notably in the creation of the right-wing youth movement, the Falange. Meanwhile, the Left rallied to present a popular united front, won a general election in 1936 and established the Second Republic. An ambitious program of social and political reforms was placed in hand—not least Catalonian autonomy—but the government was seen to be aligned with vociferous extremists—Communists, Anarchists and Syndicalists. The Church and the landowners were dangerously alienated, and it only needed a spark to unleash a vortex of destruction. This came with the arrest of Primo de Rivera's son and the murder of an Opposition politician, José Calvo Sotelo, apparently connived at by the government.

The army was secretly briefed, and on July 17, 1936, a military mutiny erupted in Spanish-occupied Morocco. It spread rapidly, coalescing into a Nationalist Front backed by the Church and the landowners, and General Franco swiftly emerged as its leader. Within the first few months Spain became a battleground for European ideologies, the Fascist regimes in

Germany and Italy sending arms, supplies, advisers and finally over 85,000 troops to support Franco. The U.S.S.R. sent food and arms to the beleaguered government, and radical sympathizers from all over Europe and North America—among them George Orwell—rallied to form the International Brigades. The struggle was particularly vicious; atrocities were perpetrated by both sides—the massacre of the clergy by Republicans in Catalonia and the saturation bombing of Guernica by the Right (using German planes) were only two examples which provoked international protest. As usual it was the common people who bore the brunt of the casualties which totalled over a million by 1939. The military discipline and experience of the Nationalist rebels, their single-mindedness and superior hardware, gave them the upper hand, finally overwhelming the last Republican outposts in Catalonia and Valencia in a crucible of blood and fire. The Republicans, where possible, fled to avoid the inevitable repression and recriminations which would follow. Those who remained faced trial and execution or internment in concentration camps.

The neutrality of Franco's government during World War II placed it in an ambiguous situation—then and in the post-war years. The economy was in ruins and fear of complete collapse forced the Western powers to provide economic support for Franco's regime, while quietly condemning it. Consciences were soothed by Franco's promise of a restoration of a constitutional monarchy. Franco himself, always afraid of loosening his steel grip on the country, lived long enough to see Spain becoming increasingly anachronistic in the democratic and industrial framework of modern Europe.

Culturally Spain contributed to many of the outstanding European movements between the wars. The work of Spanish artists—even when living abroad as many did during the Civil War—reflects the violence and paradox of their country's contemporary history. The most famous monument to the catastrophe of the Civil War remains Picasso's *Guernica* (1937). Joan Miró (1893–1983) and Salvador Dalí (b.1904) both developed unique and instantly identifiable Surrealist styles and became the old masters of the movement. The sculptor Julio González (1876–1942) developed plastic cubism (he taught Picasso to weld) and his work remains a seminal influence on modern sculpture. Non-representational painting and collage dominates the work of Antonio Tàpies (b.1923).

Another member of the Surrealist movement, Luis Buñuel (1900–83), became Spain's foremost filmmaker. Produced mainly abroad, his many works, from the early Surrealist essay *Un Chien Andalou* (made with Dalí, 1928) to the ferocious absurdity of *The Discreet Charm of the Bourgeoisie* (1972), consistently attacked the clergy and the obsessive hypocrisy of the rich middle classes.

The most significant Spanish composer of this period was Manuel de Falla (1876–1946), whose work, including the Ritual Fire Dance from *El Amor Brujo,* was inspired by native folkloric melody and rhythms.

Literary accounts of the Civil War were produced by foreign Republican sympathizers—notably Orwell, Hemingway and Eric Mottram—but the most famous figure of the time was the poet Federico García Lorca (1898–1936) who was himself a victim of the Nationalist partisans. He was shot early on in the Civil War, but not before he had completed stunning dramatic and poetic masterpieces. His best known plays are *Bodas de Sangre* (Blood Wedding), *La Casa de Bernarda Alba* and *Yerma,* whilst his *Romancero Gitano* (Gypsy Ballads) and *Poeta en Nueva York* (A Poet in New York) are his most outstanding collections of poetry. Other poets of the Civil War period include Miguel Hernández (1910–42), who died in gaol, and Rafael Alberti (b.1902) who was elected to the Spanish Parliament in 1977—both of them Republicans. Other outstanding poets of the period were the brothers Antonio (1875–1939) and Manuel Machado (1874–1936), and the 1956 Nobel Prize-winner Juan Ramón Jiménez.

The years immediately following the Civil War were grim—censorship was severe and arbitrary and there was a sharp break in literary continuity; Unamuno, Valle-Inclán, Antonio Machado and Lorca were dead and the great majority of the best writers had disappeared. The '40s were lean years for Spanish literature, and although the '50s saw a slight relaxation and change of mood as Spain's links with Europe were re-established, total freedom of expression was still not available to writers. Nevertheless, certain writers did contribute to a minor renaissance of the Spanish novel, notably Camilo José Cela (b.1916), one of the few truly experimentalist novelists in post-war Spain, and Miguel Delibes (b.1920), as well as the excellent novelists Sánchez Ferlosio, Juan Goytisolo and Daniel Sueiro.

After Franco

1977	First General Election for 40 years, won by the Center Democratic Union under Adolfo Suárez. The Movimiento Nacional, the only political organization permitted under Franco, is disbanded. The Communist Party, trade unions and the right to strike are all legalized
1978	Relaxation of censorship. New constitution promulgated restoring civil liberties
1979	Suárez government returned, but the Socialist Party makes major gains, especially in urban areas. Statutes of Autonomy for Catalonia and the Basque country successfully introduced. Resurgence of Basque terrorist (E.T.A.) activity
1981	Suárez resigns. Attempted military coup led by Colonel Antonio Tejero fails. Leopoldo Calvo Sotelo becomes Prime Minister. New anti-terrorist measures introduced
1982	Spain becomes a full member of N.A.T.O. Sotelo dissolves his parliament and loses the election to a Socialist landslide victory led by Felipe González
1985	Frontier with Gibraltar opened
1986	Spain becomes a full member of the E.E.C. Nationwide referendum votes for Spain to stay in N.A.T.O. Felipe Gonzalez's Socialist Party wins General Election with overall majority for second time.

King Juan Carlos' commitment to the restoration and protection of democracy has proved successful, and the reconstruction of Spain has proceeded apace. But old divisions still linger, especially in the Basque country where armed separatist activity by E.T.A., the minority Basque terrorist organization, is directed against the police and army, who are still regarded by many Basques as bastions or right-wing reaction. The fragility of Spain's fledgling democracy was demonstrated in Tejero's attempted coup of February 1981, but the government nevertheless went ahead with the granting of autonomy to Catalonia and the Basque country, followed in the mid-1980s by the division of the entire country into 16 autonomous regions. The establishment of these self-governing communities, albeit an often arbitrary and very costly process, has played a major part in furthering the cause of democracy in Spain. The considerable authority conceded by the government to the various autonomous communities has generally satisfied the desire of most Spaniards to be rid of the overcentralized power of Madrid that was the hallmark of the old Franco regime. Though guerrilla activity in the name of separatism continues today, only a tiny minority of Spaniards now sympathizes with such extremism.

The devaluation of the peseta boosted the economy immensely, increasing exports and providing a huge source of foreign income from tourism, which in turn has meant that many people have had first-hand experience of Spanish life and culture. For many, music and its performance has provided the most immediate experience of this. Andrés Segovia remained, until his death in 1987, the grand master of the guitar, and flamenco guitarists such as Carlos Montoya, Narciso Yepes, Paco Peña and Paco de Lucía are internationally famous, as is dancer and choreographer Antonio Gades. Virtuoso singers on the international circuit include Victoria de los Angeles, Montserrat Caballé, Teresa Berganza, Pilar Lorengar, José Carreras and, of course, Plácido Domingo. Popular music remains derivative of mainstream developments, although Rock Andaluz is an interesting variation, and there are thriving annual jazz festivals at Barcelona, Sitges and San Sebastián.

With the lifting of censorship the Spanish film industry has enjoyed a period of intense activity and creativity, with directors such as Carlos Saura *(Raise Ravens, Blood Wedding, Carmen, A Love Bewitched)*, Victor Erice *(Spirit of the Beehive, The South)*, and Manuel Gutierrez Aragón *(La Mitad del Cielo)* winning major prizes at international festivals and gaining substantial audiences overseas. However, the wave of excessive enthusiasm which greeted the abolition of censorship has now abated somewhat, though Spain still shares with other liberal countries the problem of controlling pornography and drug abuse.

The present Socialist government, faced with the unenviable task of alienating neither right nor left, has been forced to institute a tough line to deal with terrorism. But it at the same time has undertaken a thorough reform and modernization of the armed forces and police in an attempt to purge Spain once and for all of the vestiges of Francoism. The control of drug abuse, youth delinquency, and ever-increasing street crime—all arguably the result of Spain's horrendously high levels of unemployment—are, together with the Basque terrorist situation, the greatest problems facing the moderate Socialist government of Felipe González today.

However, the eventual fulfillment in 1986 of Spain's quest to join the European Economic Community, coupled with her decision to remain in N.A.T.O, has signified the end of her alienation from the rest of Europe and of her long 50-year struggle for recovery from the devastation and isolation caused by the Civil War. Now Spain is looking to the future with a new sense of vigor and European identity. In 1992 Barcelona will host the Olympic Games; Seville a world fair to commemorate Columbus' discovery of America—most probably the last great international gathering of the 20th century; and Salamanca and Madrid have both put in bids for nominations as European City of Culture.

WINES OF SPAIN

A Bright Future

by
PAMELA VANDYKE PRICE

Pamela Vandyke Price is a noted British writer on wine. She has published 21 books on the subject, her latest being The Penguin Wine Book. *Her writing, broadcasting and lecturing on wine and wine-related subjects have won her several awards, both French and British.*

Although it has been one of the world's most important wine producing countries since Roman times, Spain, apart from a few prestigious areas like Jerez and the Rioja, has never had a very good reputation for her wine. Spanish wines have been used for blending, thought of simply as basic carafe filler, or at best marketed as imitations of classic French wines like Chablis, claret or Burgundy. Things are changing now, and not before time. The visitor prepared to try the local wines will find that Spain has very little to apologise for. Her varied regions, which have remained strongly independent in spirit, produce wines of distinctive character and often surprising quality. New wine-making technology has helped enormously, particularly the use of cool fermentation to produce fresh, crisp white wines in Penedés and the Rioja which are very much to the modern taste, and quite different from the flat, heavy, sweetish Spanish whites of the bad old days.

The Spaniards accept and enjoy the wines of their country without making much fuss about them. Rioja and sherry are available everywhere, but otherwise you may find that people in a particular region have little awareness of wines from elsewhere in the country. They may even be surprised if you show interest and enthusiasm for wines which they have always taken for granted. But here also things are changing. A new more sophisticated generation has grown up in Spain and begun to develop a connoisseur's taste for fine wines. At the same time wine makers of international caliber like Miguel Torres Jr. in Penedés have come to the fore to cater to their needs. The process is continuing apace, and spreading to previously unknown areas like Rueda near Valladolid. The future for Spanish wines looks very bright indeed.

History

Wine probably first came to Spain when the Romans imported vines to supply their armies with wine, and many of the regions where they settled are still wine centers: Cádiz, Málaga, Alella and many more. Invasions by the northern tribes and, subsequently, the Moors who of course were forbidden to drink alcohol, was a serious setback, but it is possible that, even under Moorish occupation, vine cultivation and wine making were not totally abandoned.

After Spain became Christian again, wine production flourished, especially as an adjunct to the great religious houses, and in addition to the home market, the vine was taken across the Atlantic to the New World. Columbus had a man from Rioja in his crew in the famous voyage of 1492 and, it is thought, some Rioja wine as well. "Stout Cortes," conqueror of Mexico, required the settlers to plant ten vines for every native on their property. As missionaries followed the Spanish armies, they planted vines in various regions in the New World, so that the resulting wines could be used for both religious purposes and medicinal ones—tonic, sedative, analgesic, digestive, as well as a disinfectant for doubtful water supplies. So the California vineyards of today have close historical associations with those of Spain.

Spanish wines were also famous in other export markets. Geoffrey Chaucer, son of a vintner, refers in the 14th century to a wine that "creepeth subtilly" and gives the drinker the impression of actually being in Spain! In Shakespeare's *Henry IV*, Falstaff's famous eulogy of sack (a type of sherry) is well known; it is now thought that this word came from the Spanish word *sacar*—to take out or export. When, in 1587, Sir Francis Drake "singed the King of Spain's beard" in his raid on Cádiz, the English went off with 2,900 pipes (i.e. barrels) of wine that were awaiting shipment on the quayside. In the next century, diarist Samuel Pepys recorded mixing sherry with Málaga. From the 18th century onwards, many settlers from England, Scotland and Ireland arrived in Spain to do business in wine and some of the names famous in the sherry world today date from that time—such as Osborne, now pronounced in the Spanish way and advertised by a huge black bull beside many Spanish highways.

From very early times the Spanish authorities have been keen to exercise controls to maintain the quality of their wines. In the medieval period, wheeled traffic was prohibited in the streets of Logroño in the Rioja, so as not to disturb the casks of wine stored beneath. In the 13th century, the King introduced legislation concerning the wines of Jerez: progressively, other regions began to define the exact areas where wines could be grown for wine making and restricted the bringing in of wines from other areas.

Until recently huge quantities of Spanish wine went for blending—sometimes even "helping" some of the famous French classic wines—but, since World War II, controls have become strict and now increasing efforts are made to popularise Spanish wines under their own names in export markets. Both the U.S. and the U.K. wine-loving public now pay serious attention to quality Spanish wines.

Wines bearing a label indicating they possess the Denominación de Origen are subject to the same sort of controls as regards exact areas, vines, methods of cultivation and wine making as the French Appellation d'Origine Controlée wines. Each region has its own particular controls. The sparkling wines are subject to controls that apply throughout Spain. You'll notice the special paper seals indicating exact origin, on many Spanish wines, such as those of Rioja, La Mancha, Navarra, Penedés. Now that Spain is a member of the E.E.C. Spanish wines will also be subject to regulations applying within the European community.

The Wine Regions

Sherry. Sherry is one of the most famous and oldest wines in the world. It is also associated with longevity—if anyone in the sherry world dies before reaching 80 or 90 years of age, they are lamented as being cut off in the prime of life! Remember that wines made according to the sherry procedure, but in countries other than Spain, must bear clear labelling to indicate that they are not Spanish; in fact, nowadays many sherry-type wines bear purely local or national names, a system parallel to that which operates with Champagne to protect it from Spanish competition!

Sherry comes from a defined area around the town of Jerez (pronounced "Hayreth") de la Frontera, near the southern tip of Spain in the province of Andalusia: the other two important towns in the region are Puerto de Santa Maria and Sanlúcar de Barrameda, near Cadiz, on the coast. The finest wines come from vineyards with the startlingly white soil known as *albariza* and throughout the vineyards you'll notice lookouts, which are called *Bienteveo* ("I've got my eye on you") to shelter those guarding the grapes.

In former times, sherry grapes were crushed by treaders wearing special boots, the soles studded with nails, so that the pips of the grapes could be caught between the nails and not crushed, which would have made the wine bitter. These days, modern presses are used. After the wine is made, it goes into casks, known as butts, which are assembled in the bodegas (wineries); these are often likened to cathedrals, and certainly the long lines of butts ranged in tiers sometimes three or four high, in the dim light from the high windows, curtained to keep the atmosphere cool, create a majestic effect.

The groupings of wines in the great installations are known as *soleras:* the solera system by which sherry is made works in the following rather complex way. The wine goes through a series of stages, each consisting of a number of butts. The fully matured blend which will be bottled is drawn off from the last stage, which is then topped up from the next-but-

SPANISH WINE REGIONS

Denominaciónes de Origen

1 Alella
2 Almansa
3 Alicante
4 Ampurdan-Costa Brava
5 Campo de Borja
6 Cariñena
7 Condado de Huelva
8 Jerez-Xeres-Sherry-y-
   Manzanilla-Sanlúcar
   de Barrameda
9 Jumilla
10 La Mancha
11 Malaga
12 Mentrida
13 Montilla-Moriles
14 Navarra
15 Penedés
16 Priorato
17 Ribeiro
18 Ribera del Duero
19 Rioja
20 Rueda
21 Tarragona
22 Utiel-Requena
23 Valdeorras
24 Valdepeñas
25 Valencia
26 Yecla

last one, and so on back to the first stage consisting of new, recently fermented wine. A top class solera will have from seven to 15 stages and the wine will pass through them at intervals of about six months to a year or more. The effect of the system is one of progressive evolution—the wine acquires new characteristics at each stage, rather like a pupil learning new knowledge and skills in a good school.

Samples are drawn through the bungholes of the butts by an instrument called a *venencia;* this has a flexible whalebone handle, on one end of which is a deep metal cup, which is plunged into the wine and will not disturb any *flor* that may have formed on the surface. On the other end is a hook so that, if the venenciador lets the instrument slip, it will catch on to the side of the bunghole. The *capataz* or head cellarman will often display great skill by whirling the venencia around his head before pouring the wine unerringly into a number of glasses—up to 13!—in one hand, without letting a drop of wine fall to the floor.

Although sherry bodegas usually produce a range of several different sherries, there are three main types: fino, amontillado and oloroso. Fino, very light and dry, at certain times in its development displays a *flor* or coating of yeast working on its surface, endowing this wine with a special character. The fino of Sanlucar de Barrameda is called manzanilla and is notably tangy—some people even detect the saltiness of the sea of its homeland in tasting it. The venencia used here is made of bamboo instead of whalebone and silver. All fino sherries should be drunk as fresh as possible—if you see only a little wine in a nearly-empty bottle, try to get your helping from an unopened bottle. Fino should also be cool and, ideally, the bottle should be chilled: otherwise, you can put some ice in your wine on a stuffy day, even though this is rather a pity.

Amontillado is a beautiful wine that is really a matured fino. The flavour reminds some people of hazelnuts. The cheap amontillados, however, are made by blending wines instead of allowing the fino to mature gradually.

Oloroso is a sherry that never grows any flor. It is deep in colour and—surprise!—is originally bone dry although full in style. In its homeland oloroso is never a sweet wine, although it is often drunk towards the end of a meal. Olorosos for export markets, where the climate may be chilly, are made by adding a little sweet wine and some colouring—hence the sort of dark sherry many people know by this name. Each sherry establishment will make a range of different wines—different in price as well as style—but you won't find the famous cream and milk sherries in Spain, as they are specifically made for export. If you do want a truly sweet sherry, then ask for *Jerez dulce.*

A "tonic" type of wine is also made, using quinine; *Jerez-Quina* is a well-known name. Visitors may find it difficult to like this sort of thing, although a range of *vinos quinados,* using quinine from South America, are popular with the locals.

Two things visitors may not always realize: first, all sherry is fortified, that is, it is made slightly higher in alcohol than table wine, by the addition of brandy during its production. In Spain itself, however, sherry will be less high in alcohol than in export markets, because the brandy prepares it for shipping and makes it resistant to the various possible hazards en route. Also it should be remembered that there's no such thing as a vintage sherry; it's all a carefully crafted blend of wines. If you do see a date on a label, this may refer to when the particular solera was first laid down, or to when the firm was founded. The same applies to dates on casks which, in some bodegas, may bear the signatures of distinguished guests—royalty, bullfighters and world-famous personalities.

Montilla. Here, near Córdoba, wines somewhat similar to those of Jerez are made—the name "amontillado" actually comes from Montilla. Traditionally, the wine is fermented in huge jars, called *tinajas,* although today modern vats are seen in many bodegas. The best wines are produced in soleras but, unlike sherry, they are not fortified with brandy at all, which makes them easier to drink in quantity.

Montilla wines can be elegant and agreeable; the main types are usually labelled as fino, medium dry and cream. (The word "amontillado" can't be used for them because of legal action by the sherry firms). These wines are remarkably good value.

Málaga and Tarragona. Very fashionable in the past, these wines have declined in favor. They are not all sweet; there are some Málagas dry enough to be drunk as aperitifs and the full, dryish versions are excellent after-dinner drinks. The word "lagrima" on a label signifies a luscious wine, made by the pressure of the piled up grapes squeezing out the juice like tears—"lagrima" is Spanish for a tear.

Rioja. This is one of the most important Spanish wine regions for the production of fine table wines, especially reds. It came into its own in the late 19th century when the phylloxera plague struck the French vineyards, and many growers from Bordeaux emigrated to this part of north-central Spain on either side of the upper Ebro river. This, and the fact that Bordeaux-shaped bottles are used for the lighter, *clarete* style of red Rioja, leads some people to think of it as the claret of Spain. Red Rioja is certainly more elegant than most Spanish red wine, though its oaky flavour is quite distinctive.

The region is divided into three sub-regions—Rioja Alta, Rioja Alvesa and Rioja Baja, each making individual wines. The two centers are Haro and Logroño; the bodegas based there vary from the ultra-modern to the dyed-in-the-wool traditional. The old-style wines, aged in oak, are aromatic and assertive. Most bodegas produce a range of wines, vintage and non-vintage, whites from dry to sweet and a rosado. Try as many different Riojas as you can.

Catalonia. Five areas here possess a Denominación de Origen: the Penedés, Priorato, Alella, Tarragona and Ampurdan-Costa Brava. A huge variety of table wines is made—sample as many as you can.

The Penedés region is the most important for fine wines and at Vilafranca del Penedés, a charming old town, there is a fine wine museum and a bar where you can sample wines and buy souvenirs. There are also presses and wine making equipment on show at *Torres,* the world-famous firm, who can arrange tours. The countryside is delightful and the wines of all establishments merit trying—they are becoming well known in export markets.

Navarra. This region, on the frontier with France, is becoming known for several wines generally similar to Rioja, including those of the Senorio

de Sarria and Chivite. Many skilled makers are working here so, even if
you don't visit the area, look out for the wines on the wine lists.

Galicia. This region is notable above all for its light, fresh aromatic
white wines, sometimes slightly petillant, reminiscent of the Vinho Verde
of neighboring northern Portugal. You may see the locals drinking the
assertive reds from white drinking vessels, the better to see the deep color.
Remember the names of Monterrey, Valdeorras, Albariño, Ribeiro, and
Godello when you look down a wine list.

Vega Sicilia. This is one of the most extraordinary wines of Spain,
made in a bodega 40 km. (25 miles) east of Valladolid, near Valbuena del
Duero in the Ribera del Duero region. The name comes from Saint Cecilia,
patron of music—and Vega Sicilia wines, all red, have inspired much musical prose. They are kept in cask for ten years, those sold as Valbuena are
bottled after three or five years. Difficult to find, invariably expensive,
these are wines for very special occasions indeed: if you do have the chance
of trying them, make sure that either you or the restaurant serving them
have the time to let the wine breathe three or four hours before drinking.

Other Regions in the North. Note the wines of Rueda, Toro, Leon
and Cariñena. Some may be rather "peasanty" for modern tastes, but all
are of interest. The red and white Chacoli wines of the Spanish Basque
country are petillant (semi-sparkling), very dry and traditional with the
region's shellfish, or for aperitifs.

The Central Region. Much of the wine made here was, until recently,
sold for blending or distilling. Today, some regional names are becoming
known, thanks to modern methods of wine making and the influence of
foreign shippers. Wines having a Denominación de Origen are: Almansa,
La Mancha, Mentrida and Valdepenas. This is Don Quixote country and
many of the wines, although modest, are pleasant drinks.

The Levante. Another region formerly mainly making bulk wines, as
it produced deep-toned, buxom beverages, useful for "helping" more fragile wines elsewhere. Names to bear in mind today are: Valencia, Utiel-
Requena, Alicante, Yecla, Jumilla.

The Balearic Islands and the Canaries. Wine is made in fair quantities on Mallorca, both red and white and that produced on the Benisalem
estate is well reputed. But these holiday islands cater for holiday drinkers
and only modest quality seems to have been achieved. Although Canary
wine enjoyed a high reputation in the past and was referred to by Shakespeare (it then seems to have been mostly sweet), today the wines there
are made for local everyday requirements.

Sparkling Wines

Vast amounts of sparkling wine are made, the main production coming
from the Penedés region in the northeast. The so-called *Cava* wines are
made by the Champagne method: when one sees the huge installations,
it's hard to realise that it was as recently as 1872 that the family firm of

Codorniu, established in the 16th century, went in for sparkling wines. Today, this enormous winery at San Sadurni de Noya is bigger than any Champagne establishment. There's a wine museum here and well-organised tours can be arranged, with multi-lingual guides. Freixenet is the other giant, but there are many other firms. Most produce a range, from the very dry *brut,* through *seco* and *semiseco* to the *semidulce* and *dulce,* also some luxury blends. At the Castle of Perelada, to the north, there's also a wine museum, but this region is best known for Perelada sparkling wines, made by the *cuve close* or sealed vat method; the wine must be kept quite apart from *Cava* wines and the corks have a black oval on their bases, whereas *Cava* corks have a star.

Relevant Words and some Label Terms

If you want ordinary everyday wine, ask for *Vino corriente.* A *copa* is a glass, a *copita* is the tulip-shaped glass used for sherry. *Tinto* is red, *blanco* is white, *rosado* is rosé, *clarete* means a light-bodied red wine. *Reserva* implies a wine of some quality and maturity. *Seco* is dry, *dulce* is sweet, *brut* is very dry, *abocado* is medium-sweet. *Vino de mesa* and *vino de pasta* are both terms meaning table wine—and don't forget that, in the sherry region, a sherry may also be a *vino de pasta. Espumosa* is sparkling wine and one labelled *Cava* means it will have been made according to the Champagne method. In fact it's illegal to refer to such wines as *champán,* but Spanish waiters continue to do so!

Rancio doesn't mean rancid, but is a term used to describe the taste of a white wine that has been matured long-term in a cask, thereby being exposed to some air, which gives it a somewhat different flavor from the very fresh, light white wines made everywhere these days. A *porrón* is the curious flask with a long projecting spout, from which the wine can be poured directly into the mouth without the flask touching the lips—very hygienic when several are sharing the wine. Sometimes the experienced show off by sending the wine down their noses or pouring from the porrón held high above their heads.

The words *cosecha* and *vendimia* both mean vintage, and now that Spain has joined the E.E.C. use of these terms must comply with E.E.C. regulations. In former years wines labeled vintage did not necessarily come solely from one year—in some of the classic wines of Spain the casks were topped up or "refreshed" with other wine. Regulations were tightened in 1976, and now labeling is subject to the same controls as the rest of Europe.

A *bodega* really has two meanings: it's a term used to signify a wine shop, but is also applied to a winery, and therefore the word is often used in conjunction with the name of a particular firm.

Drinking Traditions

As you probably know, the mid-day and evening meals tend to be taken later in Spain than in other countries. This means that people can take their siesta during the hottest time of the day and then can enjoy a long evening.

You can usually get wine by the glass in any bar or café (though not in restaurants), and in the sherry region you'll see sherry served throughout a meal, often in half bottles.

Traditionally, any aperitif will be accompanied by something to nibble, even if merely biscuits, olives and nuts. This is all part of the Mediterranean concept of not drinking without eating and these refreshments, known as *tapas*, can be quite elaborate, sometimes even sufficient for a mini-meal. *Sangria* is a refreshing mixture of wine and fruit juice, often red wine with citrus, but it can be based on white wine. It comes in a large jug, useful for sharing between several people.

A great deal of Spanish brandy is made, sweeter, heavier, and darker than Cognac. There is also a wide range of liqueurs—some of the world famous ones are made under license in Spain—and in most wine regions there are some sweet wines, suitable for drinking after meals.

In small bars and country restaurants, wine may often be served in large jugs, which are used to draw it straight from the casks. Here, you may be provided with tumblers rather than glasses with stems.

Visiting Wineries

In the sherry region of Andalusia, in parts of the Rioja area and in the Penedés, including the installations where sparkling wines are made, there are various good facilities for visiting wineries, plus English-speaking guides. The larger firms like to show interested travelers around, although sometimes they may seem to spend more time displaying modern vats, bottling and despatch departments rather than anything more obviously picturesque. Still, be polite and don't try to hurry a tour!

Elsewhere, and in smaller installations, you may find it harder to fix a visit, especially if you do not speak any Spanish. However, your hotel or the local tourist office may be able to arrange something.

Remember that at vintage time (September and October) installations tend to be hard at work and cannot receive visitors easily. During vintage festivities bodegas may also be shut, so ask before you try to get in. Also, and this applies for most of the year, wineries usually shut from about 1 P.M. for three hours.

Many of the larger wine firms have collections of exhibits to do with wine, often dignified as "Museums" and, of course, many general museums have sections devoted to local traditions, including wine making.

Wear walking shoes, for many installations are extensive, and take a jacket because cellars can be cool; those making sparkling wines are definitely cold. If a member of a firm shows you round, there is no need to do more than express thanks at the end of a tour, but an official guide may expect a tip—this is usually made obvious.

Further Information

The following are sources of information for anyone seriously interested in Spanish wines: I.N.F.E., Pasco de la Castellana, 14, Madrid - 1, Spain; Wines of Spain, Commercial Office of Spain, 405 Lexington Ave., New York, NY 10017, U.S.A.; Vinos de Espana, Commercial Office of Spain, 55 Bloor St. W., Suite 1204, Toronto, Ontario M4W 1A5, Canada; Spanish Promotion Centre, 22 Manchester Square, London W1M 5AP, England.

Also recommended are Jan Read's books, *The Simon and Schuster Pocket Guide to Spanish Wines* (U.S.); *The Century Companion to the Wines of Spain and Portugal* (U.K.); the detailed and scholarly *Wines of Spain* (Faber and Faber); and Julian Jeffs' *Sherry* (Faber and Faber).

EATING IN SPAIN

Gazpacho and Garlic, Shellfish and Squid

Eating in Spain can be a delightful adventure or a sad disappointment. The traveler who has the good sense to hunt out local specialties and to choose carefully the restaurants where he eats can enjoy his trip to Spain for the food alone. But many hotels, particularly in the popular coastal areas, put on their version of an Anglo-Saxon meal, which is usually disastrous.

Spanish cuisine is neither so dainty nor so varied as the French or, perhaps, the Italian, but it has virtues of its own. It is substantial and plentifully served and still has its light and delicate dishes for hot weather. One virtue for the traveler is that restaurant prices are still very reasonable, though for how much longer remains to be seen.

The Spanish, as a nation, eat out a lot, hence the huge number of restaurants, many of them colorful and full of local atmosphere. Service, for the most part, is courteous and highly professional but don't expect it to be swift; that is not the Spanish way.

Spaniards do not like their food very hot. They say it has no taste that way. Those who like their food piping hot should insist with the waiter that it be served *muy caliente*. Nor is Spanish food highly seasoned, as many visitors expect it to be. In fact, cooking with chilli is almost unknown in Spain, and pepper pots are not commonly placed on tables. Olive oil is the basis of all cooking, and when well used you will hardly notice it. The same cannot be said, however, for the liberal use of garlic which dominates many Spanish dishes. If you really don't like garlic, avoid any dishes that are served *al ajillo.*

Meat is generally good though not outstanding. Pork *(cerdo)* and veal *(ternera)* predominate along with the ubiquitous *biftec,* generally a thin piece of beef rather than the steak you might expect. In fact, ordering steak is not usually the wisest choice. Roasts tend to be good in Castile and game, particularly pheasant *(faisán),* partridge *(perdiz),* and quail *(cordonices)* are quite common when in season.

Vegetables and salads are plentiful. It is customary to order vegetables as a first course, usually lightly fried *(salteados)* and mixed with oil, tomato or diced ham making a very tasty starter. Examples are *judías verdes con tomate* (green beans in tomato sauce), *champiñones al ajillo* (mushrooms sautéed in garlic), and *alcachofas con jamon* (artichoke hearts and ham). Cold vegetable starters include *espárragos con mahonesa,* canned asparagus tips which in Spain are traditionally eaten with mayonnaise rather than butter, endives and palm hearts. Spaniards usually order a mixed salad to accompany their main course and this is served on a communal dish into which everyone dips at will. The salad is rarely served with dressing already on it; instead you mix your own dressing with the oil and vinegar on the table.

Where Spain scores best on the gastronomic front is in the sheer variety and abundance of fresh fish and seafood *(mariscos)* on offer in almost every region of the country. The rapid and efficient transportation of freshly caught fish to all but the farthest flung reaches of the nation is one of the country's better organized features.

Merluza (hake) is found all over Spain, and when served well can be quite tasty though it is not the most interesting of fish. *Rape* (angler or monkfish) is another popular whitefish and with its slightly chewy texture makes good fish kebabs. Other commonly found fish are swordfish *(pez espada)* with its delicate taste and close texture rather like meat, and sole *(lenguado)* which is especially delicious served in an orange sauce. Tuna fish *(bonito* or *atún)* is served fresh in the north, cut into steaks and cooked in a rich tomato and onion sauce. It is even more plentiful on the Atlantic coast between Gibraltar and Cádiz. Fresh trout and salmon can also be had in season though be careful not to confuse *salmón* (salmon) with *salmonete* (mullet). *Trucha a la navarra* is a popular way of serving trout, when it is fried and stuffed with a salt cured ham similar to bacon. In San Sebastián, Bilbao, Málaga and other fishing ports, fresh sardines, grilled or fried, are popular. A dish likely to be strange to Anglo-Saxon visitors is squid, or cuttlefish, and it is well worth sampling. Known as *calamares,* or if small, *pulpitos* or *chipirones,* it is at its best in the Basque country and Catalonia. It is served either in its own ink, in a dark sauce, or cut up and deep fried in batter rings *(calamares fritos)* and in this case should be served piping hot and with lemon wedges. Another popular shellfish dish is *almejas a la marinera,* small clams steamed in their shells and served in a delicious sauce of garlic, olive oil and finely chopped parsley. Lobster *(langosta),* crayfish *(langostinas)* and shrimp *(gambas)* are plentiful and very good. *Sopa de pescado* is a fish soup not inferior to French *bouillabaisse,* though less complicated. Traditionally the staple food of fishermen, it is made with shrimps, clams and chunks of *merluza* and other dainties, and is to be recommended in most restaurants. *Zarzuela de mariscos* is another Spanish delicacy, if this is the right word for such a robust dish. Here a great variety of shellfish and white fish are first fried, then cooked in a sauce made up of onions, garlic, tomatoes, wine and laurel. It is served in many of the better restaurants.

One of the basic elements of Spanish diet is pulses—dried beans, lentils and chick peas. They are cooked in all sorts of ways and the dishes have different names in each part of the country. The Basques like white or red beans stewed with *chorizo*—a peppery red sausage—and blood sausage. Farther west, Asturias is famous for *fabada,* a sort of simplified cassoulet of white beans with salt pork and sausage. Each region has its bean dish. Madrid's specialty is *cocido,* made with big yellow chick peas. Boiled beef, boiled chicken, boiled bacon and other choice bits are served with a great dish of peas, preceded by a broth made with the water they have been cooked in. It is a meal all by itself. *Garbanzos* are chick peas served in an earthenware casserole with olive oil, tomatoes and chorizo. These pulse dishes tend to be filling and are best ordered only when you feel like something warm and very satisfying.

Spanish desserts *(postres)* are something of a let-down. The patisserie is a far cry from what Central Europe has to offer. The Moorish-inspired dry cakes, like *polvorones (polvo* means "dust" to give you an idea), *manoletes, yemas* or *roscas* are far too sweet for most Anglo-American palates. More often than not you will be forced to fall back on the ubiquitous *flan* (creme caramel). There is no need to despair however: Valencia oranges, melons, strawberries, Almería grapes, Alicante dates and wonderful peaches from Aragón can usually make up for this gap in Spanish gastronomy. But don't be tempted to choose fruit dishes served *en almibar* as this is the Spanish way of saying "canned."

Finally we come to cheese. The best known one is *manchego,* from La Mancha. It comes in various shapes, sizes and tastes but the best should be slightly moist and with a taste that stops just short of being sharp. Roquefort is also becoming popular, but by far and away the best blue cheese is a delicacy usually found in the north, where it is made in the Picos de Europa mountains. This is the famous *queso cabrales* made from a blend of sheep, goat and cows' milk and left to mature wrapped in a large leaf. It is also on sale in Madrid and Barcelona and if you have an opportunity to try it, is a real treat.

Regional Specialties

Most of the dishes mentioned above can be found throughout Spain, but in addition, each region has numerous local specialties. The parador hotels are good places to sample these, as they have a special brief to concentrate on their regional cooking. Here are just a few of the things to look out for.

Galicia. Galicia in the far northwest of Spain offers an outstanding variety of fish and shellfish caught fresh from its shores. Especially typical are *centollas,* a large crab stuffed with its own minced meat. *Empanadas* are a kind of pie, half way between a pizza and a Cornish pasty and may be filled with either meat or fish mixtures. *Caldo gallego* is a typical Galician broth and *lacón con grelos* a regional meat dish consisting of ham and turnip tops and generally much better than it sounds. Make sure you sample some of the rich Ribeiro wines traditionally drunk out of white china bowls rather than glasses, and a *queimada* or two, a glass of the local *aguadiente* set alight (its name means "burning").

Asturias and Cantabria. The verdant provinces of Oviedo and Santander are famous throughout Spain for their dairy cattle and milk products. Here is your chance to sample the superb *cabrales* cheese, or maybe a creamy *cuajada*, a thick set yogurt flavored with honey. Recommended in Santander is the dessert of "fried milk," *leche frita,* a delicious caramelized custard. Asturias is known for its bean stew, *fabada asturiana,* and for its cider *(sidra).* Besides being the only region in Spain where cider is produced and drunk, the Asturians have an amazing manner of pouring their local drink. Holding the pitcher above one shoulder, they pour it over the other shoulder into a glass held almost at ground level, all of which is no doubt intended to improve the sparkle. Good in Santander are *percebes* (barnacles) and some tiny prawns said to be unique to this city. *Cocido montañés* is a bean, cabbage and pork stew.

Basque Country. The Basques have the reputation of being great eaters, and the food of the Basque country is among the best in Spain. It is one of the few regions where good beef can usually be found, though the traveler who insists on steaks may be disappointed as veal is the Basques' own preference. They like hearty dishes and usually eat several at a meal. One of their specialties that has spread all through Spain is salt codfish cooked with fresh tomatoes—*bacalao a la Vizcaina*—and another is the same fish cooked slowly *(pil-pil)* in olive oil. *Merluza a la vasca* too is best served on its home ground. This consists of baked hake served in a casserole in a sauce of clams and shrimps, and garnished with hard boiled egg, asparagus shoots and peas. *Xangurro* a crab shell stuffed with its own meat and baked with rum and coñac is sometimes a little over-rated but is delicious when well done.

In winter their great luxury is *anguilas,* baby eels, cooked whole and served in sizzling hot olive oil with garlic and pieces of red-hot peppers. It takes nerve to try them the first time and it remains an acquired taste.

Following the vogue for *nouvelle cuisine* in France, *Basque nouvelle cuisine* has taken off in a big way and can be sampled not only in the Basque region but in many top restaurants in other parts of Spain.

Aragón. Aragonese cooking tends to be reliable and basic and notable mainly for the quality of its fruit and vegetables.

Catalonia. Catalan cooking is notable for its liberal use of garlic, and tomatoes and peppers are also used lavishly. Spaniards, or rather Catalans, say that many of the dishes served in France *à la Provençal* are Catalan dishes introduced by the Spanish-born Empress Eugénie and baptized with French names to avoid offending national susceptibility. For real garlic lovers, they have a relish made principally of garlic, on the style of the French *aioli,* but it is a little powerful for many foreigners. *Pan tomate* is something you will see in many typical restaurants. This is slices of bread spread with olive oil and puréed tomatoes and eaten as an accompaniment to many dishes, especially seafood.

Pasta dishes tend to be more popular in Catalonia than elsewhere in Spain, and cannelloni and maccaroni appear on many menus as starters.

Snails too, are typical of this region, though you won't find them much anywhere else in Spain.

One of Catalonia's boasts is that its meat is usually better than other parts of Spain, because, in the foothills of the Pyrenees, there is good grazing. A local meat specialty is *butifarra,* a Catalan sausage.

Valencia and Alicante. Paella is now so universally popular that it is often thought of as Spain's national dish, but originally it came from Valencia and many of the best paellas are still to be found there and in the neighboring province of Alicante. Paella is based on rice, flavored with saffron, and embellished with many tidbits of seafood: shrimps, calamares, clams, mussels and anything else that takes the chef's fancy. Small pieces of meat and chicken are also included and the top is decorated with strips of sweet red pimento, green peas and succulent crayfish. It should be served in the shallow iron pan in which it has been cooked. Paella is made to order and will take at least 20 minutes to prepare so it is not a dish for those in a hurry. Traditionally it is eaten at lunchtime and not in the evening.

Valencia is also the orange growing area of Spain and its large succulent fruits are at their best around March. Alicante and Jijona are famous for their *turrones,* a kind of nougat made with almonds and other nuts and flavored with honey. The palm groves of Alicante province are also well known for their dates.

Castile. Castile is associated above all with roast meats *(asados).* Segovia is one of its prime culinary centers and all its restaurants serve the specialties *cochinillo* (suckling pig) and *cordero asado* (roast lamb). *Sopa castellana* is also much served and is a clear broth with chunks of ham, hard boiled eggs and a liberal scattering of vegetables. The dessert *ponche segoviano* will appeal to those with a sweet tooth.

Toledo is known for its game dishes, especially partridge *(perdiz).* Further south the region of La Mancha has a peasant cuisine of its own. *Migas,* a mixture of croutons, ham and chorizo, and *pisto manchego,* a strong tasting casserole of vegetables based on green peppers and olive oil, may not appeal to every palate, but you should not miss sampling the famous cheese *queso manchego,* here on its home ground, nor the delicate *flores manchegas,* a petal-shaped cookie.

Extremadura. This region, together perhaps with La Mancha, is one of the few in Spain where you are better off sticking to meat rather than fish. Sausages, hams and *chorizos* (a highly spiced and fatty salami-like sausage) have long been the livelihood of the region.

Andalusia. Seafood here is excellent especially in and around Málaga. One thing that deserves special mention is *gazpacho andaluz* whose popularity throughout Spain has ranked it second only to *paella* as the national dish. *Gazpacho* is a chilled warm-weather soup. Made with olive oil, vinegar and strained tomatoes, its predominant taste is of garlic. Diced cucumber, green pepper, egg, tomatoes and croutons are served as garnishes.

Almería is famous for its grapes and Málaga for its sweet muscatel raisins which are used in the making of *Málaga Virgen,* a sweet muscatel wine. In Granada the *tortilla sacromonte* is typical, a potato omelet filled with diced ham and mixed vegetables. *Tortillas,* by the way, are omelets in Spain and not unleavened bread as in Mexico. *Tortilla española* is a thick, chunky potato omelet and *tortilla francesa,* a regular thin omelet. Loja is known for its *sopa sevillana,* a fish soup flavored with mayonnaise and containing *merluza,* clams and sometimes shrimp, and garnished with hard boiled egg. Trout is also common here due to the nearby trout farms. Avocados are farmed around Almuñecar, and strawberries are grown around Huelva.

Breakfast and Other Snacks

No matter how well you have prepared yourself for continental breakfasts, the meager Spanish breakfast will almost certainly be a disappointment. A few of the better hotels now make an effort to serve something like an English breakfast, otherwise you had better brace yourself to be confronted by a plate of stodgy buns, known as *croissants, ensaimadas, suizos* or *madalenas,* usually dry and tasteless. The accompanying orange juice is often a disgrace to a country which grows good oranges. There will be a choice of tea or coffee, and hot chocolate may also be on offer. Many Spaniards skip breakfast altogether, making do with a coffee till they stop work for a mid-morning snack.

Chocolate and Churros. Churros are a kind of fritter deep fried usually in rings. They are eaten sprinkled with sugar, and are very popular at fiesta time. Some cafes serve them for breakfast but they are best when eaten piping hot from a *churrería* or a roadside stall, though the latter can cause digestive upsets if the oil is not too fresh. Churros are traditionally eaten with cups or tall glasses of hot chocolate.

Tea and Coffee. Tea is usually made with tea bags and served weak and on its own in the American style. If you want it with milk or lemon, ask for *un té con leche* or un *té con limón.* Coffee is served either black and very strong in a small cup *(café solo)* or with milk *(café con leche)* in a larger cup cappuccino style. If you want your coffee black but longer and weaker, ask for *un café americano.*

Ice Cream and Iced Drinks. Spanish ice cream is varied and delicious. A few particularly Spanish flavors are *almendra* (almond), *avellana* (hazlenut), *turrón* (nougat), *Málaga* (rum and raisin), *nata* (cream) and *mantecado* which is extra rich and creamy, similar to Cornish ice cream. Well worth trying in summer are the refreshing *granizado de limón* and *granizado de café.* Served only in ice cream parlors, these are lemon juice or cold coffee poured over crushed ice. *Blanco y negro* is cold black coffee with vanilla ice cream. *Horchata* is a delicious and exclusively Spanish drink. Served ice cold it looks but doesn't taste like milk. Instead it has a sweet and distinctive nutty taste for it is made from nuts. Look out for shops displaying the *Hay horchata* signs but beware the bottled variety.

Tapas and Raciones. Finally that most fascinating of all Spanish customs, tapas, those savory tidbits that you will see piled high on the counters of any bar or cafeteria. The variety of tapas on offer is immense: chunks of *tortilla, patatas bravas* (potato chunks in a spicy sauce), salamis, *chorizo,* cubes of marinated beef, squid, clams, mussels, shrimp, octopus, whitebait, fish roes, all served either plain or concocted into an elaborate salad. Ham is a delicacy—and often an expensive one. You can choose from either *jamón de York,* cooked ham, or the delicious and extremely rich *jamón serrano,* mountain ham, that has been laid out in the sun on the snow of the mountains, for the sun to cure it, while the snow keeps it from spoiling. It is a fine dark red in color, and when sliced thin, is translucent. Tapas are also served in larger portions called *raciones* and if you share three or four of these, they make a very adequate supper.

Worth observing is the "tapas and pastries ritual." Cafes and bars begin the day with their counters heaped with pastries. Around midday these are removed and replaced by the tapas for pre-lunch snackers. After lunch, at around 3 P.M., off go the tapas and back come the pastries which prove popular from 6–7 P.M. with afternoon shoppers. Finally, at about 8 P.M. out go the pastries for the last time and back come the tapas as the evening paseo and aperitif hour approaches. So, whichever of the two you wish to sample, make sure you get the timing right!

Bull fight in a Village by Goya

BULLFIGHTING FOR BEGINNERS

Art, Not Sport

Mention Spain to any non-Spaniard and one of the first things that springs to mind is the bullfight. However, although bullfighting may seem to be the national spectacle, you would be wrong to assume that every Spaniard regularly attends a bullfight or is even knowledgeable on the subject.

Far and away more popular is the national game of soccer (football to British readers) which the Spanish call *fútbol*. Spaniards pack the soccer stadiums of large cities during the season and are regularly to be found glued to their T.V. sets for a mid-week game. Soccer matches and bullfights both take place on Sunday afternoons but don't make the mistake of considering them rival sports, for the Spanish do not consider bullfighting to be a sport, rather it is an art form.

For the last 20 years the general popularity of bullfighting has waned considerably, at least among Spain's native population. But the spectacle continues to flourish, boosted largely by the ever-increasing number of tourists for whom a *corrida* is an obligatory outing. In many cases the quality of the bullfights has waned too, for many of the regular Sunday afternoon fights are now little more than performances put on for the benefit of tourists. However, that is not to say that there are not still some excellent bullfights, most of which are held at times of major fiestas such as

Valencia's fallas in March, Seville's April Fair, Jerez de la Frontera's May Fair, and the San Fermines bull runnings in Pamplona in July. In Madrid around May 15 the festivities for San Isidro see some of the best bullfights in the country. At all of these times the fights are televised on nationwide T.V. and it is not unusual to see Spaniards all over the country crowding into bars or hotel lounges to watch the coverage. Good toreros are still held in great esteem and frequently make news headlines.

The ritual slaughter in the ring may no longer be every Spaniard's idea of a Sunday afternoon's fun but it is still big business, employing some 158,000 workers and grossing around $275 million on ticket sales. A top matador can earn up to $18,000 for one fight alone, spectators will pay up to $180 for a ticket for one of the top fights, and each year the Spanish government earns some $35 million in revenue from bullfights. In 1985 "toro pools" were introduced, whereby competitors bet on the outcome of fights by guessing how many ears will be awarded. Half of the takings are returned in prize money, the other half, after deductions for expenses, are reinvested in bullfighting. As Spanish *fútbol* pools bring in some 2,000 million ptas. a year, the boost to the bullring was calculated to be spectacular. In the same year a record 31.6 million spectators attended a bullfight. Another proof that the popularity of the bullfight is far from dead came with Spain's negotiations to enter the Common Market, for no matter how hard the E.E.C. officials in Brussels insisted there should be an end to it, the Spanish were adamant: the bullfight would remain.

If you are dead set against bullfighting, there is no pressure to attend and you may be encouraged to know that there are anti-bullfight movements within Spain as well as outside the country; it is a debate which is given free rein these days. And Spain's anti-bullfight movement, the *Comite Antitaurina,* formed in 1986, is becoming ever more adept at making its protest heard. If you do decide to attend, you are quite frankly more likely to be bored during your first fight than you are to be revolted or deeply shocked, for appreciating a bullfight is a skill that can only be acquired with practice. The untrained eye will take in little at first and may quickly tire of the spectacle. So to help you understand something of what you will see, we offer the following pointers.

How to Watch a Bullfight

Anglo-Saxons, on their first introduction to bullfighting customarily voice an objection to it that indicates their lack of understanding of its basic nature. They consider that it is unfair. It is a contest between a man and a bull, in which the bull always dies. There is something wrong, they feel, in a sport in which the identity of the winner is fixed in advance.

So there would be, if bullfighting were a sport. But bullfighting is not a sport. Bullfighting is a spectacle. In a sense it is a play, with a plot. The plot calls for the bull to die. To object to that is as pointless as to object that the plot of *Julius Caesar* calls for Caesar to die. In another sense, it is a ballet. One of its essential features is the performance of stylized traditional movements, and a byproduct of their accurate performance is grace. In still another sense, it is an exhibition of physical dexterity, with the risk of injury or death accepted as the penalty for clumsiness, like the art of a trapeze performer. But in its essence, it is a demonstration of the mastery of a human over two living organisms—over the bull, for the point of the torero's art is to maneuver a thousand pounds of recalcitrant, malevolent armed muscle according to his will—and over himself, for perhaps the basic meaning of the bullfight is that it is an ordeal of the quality most prized by Spaniards, courage. The bullfighter must master his own fear before he can master the bull.

The brave man is not the one who does not feel fear; he is the man who feels fear and still faces the danger that frightens him. Bullfighters are invariably afraid when they enter the ring. Make no mistake about that. They are afraid, and they are right to be afraid. They know that their chance of dying in the ring is one in ten. They know that their chance of being crippled is about one in four. They know, usually, what the horn ripping through the flesh feels like; no bullfighters finish their careers completely unscathed.

The bull may always die (he can avoid that fate by refusing to fight, but this is rare), but he does not always lose. In that sense, bullfighting *is* a sport. But you will understand it better if you cease to regard it as a sport and look upon it instead as a spectacle—a spectacle to which death does not put an end, but is itself an intrinsic element.

The Plot

Bullfighting is a highly ritualized affair. All its details have been developed over a long period into a pattern that now never varies, each one ticketed with its own label in the extensive vocabulary of bullfighting. To begin with, the bullfight is not a fight—it is a *corrida,* a "running" of the bull. It is divided, like most plays, into three acts, the *tercios*—the act of the picadors, the act of the banderillas, and the act of death. There is also a curtain-raiser, the parade across the ring, in which all the participants in the coming spectacle take part, even to the men who will drag the dead bulls out of the arena.

The act of the picadors has scenes—the *doblando,* the first luring of the bull with the capes; the matador's first playing of the bull; the arrival of the mounted picadors to attack the bull with their lances; and the *quites*—which is the work of the matadors in luring the bull away from the picador. The fine points of these maneuvers will be explained in a moment.

The act of the banderillas also usually has three scenes, in the sense that three pairs of gaily decorated darts are ordinarily thrust into the bull's shoulders, but each of these scenes is the same.

The act of death, the *faena,* has two scenes—first, the playing of the bull with the small red flannel *muleta,* which replaces the billowing capes at this stage of the fight—and the killing with the sword—the moment of truth.

All of this you will see in every bullfight, good, bad or indifferent. How is a novice to know whether the manner in which it is performed is skillful or clumsy?

You may be surprised, at your first bullfight, to hear the crowd roar its approval for a maneuver that, to you, looks no different from those that preceded it, and were allowed to pass in silence. You may be baffled when seat cushions start flying into the ring, hurled by an angry crowd whose method of showing its ire is to attempt to trip up the matador and give the bull a chance at him. The fine points that arouse the admiration or the contempt of the crowd (and the crowd, at a Spanish bullfight, provides a spectacle second only to what is going on in the ring) cannot be expected to be obvious to a newcomer. You will undoubtedly know whether the performance you are watching is, in general, skillful or clumsy, for deft movements are graceful and awkward ones are not and it takes no expert to appreciate the difference between the single clean thrust of the sword that sends the bull down as though he had been struck by lightning and the blundering butchery marked by thrust after thrust, with the sword spinning into the air as it strikes the shoulder-blade of the bull instead of piercing through the opening that leads to the heart. But in order to know why a performance is good or bad, you will need some coaching.

What to Look For

The three elements by which the critics judge bullfighters (and the bullfight critic, in Spain, is a highly respected individual, whose verdicts can make or break a matador's career) are *parar, mandar* and *templar.* Parar is style, and consists in standing straight firmly planted, unyielding, bringing the bull past in a thundering rush with a gracefulness that gives no ground. Mandar is mastery of the bull, controlling his every move and spinning him about like a puppet. Templar is timing, and the acme of skill in this respect is to perform the maneuvers of the fight in slow motion. The more slowly the bull is moving as he passes the matador, the longer the time of dangerous propinquity lasts, and the more opportunity is granted to the animal to change tactics and go for the man instead of the cape.

Watch the matador's feet. He should not move them as the bull thunders past. If he really has control of the animal, he will make it avoid him; he will not have to move to avoid it. Watch how closely he works to the bull. Obviously his mastery of the beast must be more exact if he lets the horn graze his chest than if he pulls it by a foot away. Closeness can be faked. If the torero holds his arms with the cape far out from his body, if he leans well forward so that, without moving his feet, he can still bring the upper part of his body back when the bull reaches him, then he is not showing the same skill as the man who stands ramrod straight and maneuvers the bull without budging himself.

Some grandstand plays are really dangerous. Some aren't. Kneeling really is, because it reduces the mobility of the bullfighter. Passes in which the cape swings over the head of the torero are dangerous because it makes him lose sight of the bull at a critical moment. Passes in which the cape is held behind the bullfighter's body are also dangerous, obviously. Passes in which the bull, charging towards one side of the torero, is drawn across his body to pass on the other side are dangerous.

Psychology of the Bull

On the other hand, standing with one's back against the fence, which looks dangerous, often isn't. It depends on the bull. Most bulls have no desire to bang their heads against a hard wooden wall. It is often more dangerous, close to the fence, to allow the bull to pass between it and the bullfighter; bulls have a tendency to swerve outward from the fence. If you notice that the bull returns habitually to a certain spot in the arena after his various charges, it is more dangerous to fight him in that part of the ring than elsewhere; he has elected it, by some mysterious instinct, as his home ground, and he is fiercer on it. It is more dangerous for the matador to taunt him into charging outward from this territory than into it. When he is returning to his base, he is intent upon getting back "home." He is paying no attention to the man who may happen to be standing on the edge of the path he is following. Bullfighters know that and sometimes take advantage of the bull's rush past to draw applause from spectators who haven't grasped the situation.

Paradoxically, the bull who looks most dangerous to you is the one who looks least dangerous to the torero—the one who comes charging into the ring full of fight and makes a vicious dash for the first bullfighter he sees. The type of bull that is out to kill is the type of bull the torero can handle. He has a one-track mind; and a bull with a one-track mind is predictable. You can tell what he will do. Therefore you can control him. Bullfighters like a fighting animal, one that is going to charge hard—and straight.

The Opening Scene

First of all you will need to identify the matadors. They will be the men walking in front of the opening procession into the arena, just behind the mounted escort. The senior will be on the right and he will kill the first and fourth bulls. The youngest will be in the center and he will kill the third and sixth bulls.

As each of the six bulls makes its entrance, its weight in kilos is posted at the edge of the ring.

When the bull first charges into the arena, one of the bullfighters will wave his cape at him and very probably, at the bull's rush, will dart behind one of the bulwarks that guard the openings into the corridor behind the barrier. Don't mark him down as a coward for that. It is all part of the ritual. The bull is not yet actually being played. He is being studied. Perhaps the first cape will be waved by the man closest to him, to find out if his near vision is good. Then a man on the other side of the ring will try, to test his vision at a distance. The matador is watching how he charges, and whether he has a tendency to hook to the left or the right. Upon his correct interpretation of the bull's reaction to these preliminary flaggings will depend his success in the rest of the fight.

After these opening evolutions, the matador comes out to demonstrate his skill with the cape. This is your first real chance to witness the art of the bullfighter. If, in reading bullfight stories, you have come across the term *verónica,* and wondered what it meant, it is probably what you are watching now. The verónica is the simplest and most basic of the various passes *(pases),* and it is almost always the one with which the matador begins. Its name, by the way, derives from the way St. Veronica is said to have held the cloth with which she wiped Christ's face. The torero holds the cape before him, more or less gathered into folds, his profile towards the bull, and as the animal charges, he spreads the cloth before the animal's snout, swings it by his body, and the bull follows it past. Ordinarily, as the bewildered bull turns, he swings him by again, then perhaps a third time, each time a little closer, as he becomes acquainted with the animal's reactions and acquires *mandar,* and perhaps finishes by gathering the cape in against his body in a half verónica as the bull passes. This usually stops the bull short, and the matador can turn his back disdainfully on the horns and walk away, a display of mastery over the bull that always brings a roar of *"Olé."*

The Picador

With the end of this scene, the picadors appear—the mounted bullfighters with lances. The object of this part of the fight is to launch an offensive against that tremendous hump of flesh on the top of the bull's neck, the tossing muscle. Until that has been tired, so that the bull will drop his head, he cannot be killed with the sword. The way to the animal's heart is opened only when the front feet are together and the head dropped.

The picador attacks the tossing muscle by meeting the bull's charge with his lance, which he digs into it. The role of the horse is to be tossed—not to be gored. He wears a mattress to protect him from goring and the management, which has to pay for the horses, sincerely hopes that it will succeed. But the bullfighters want the horse to be tossed. A bull whose tossing muscle has hoisted three heavy horses into the air is a bull beginning to be tired. There is also a second motive, to maintain the bull's combativity. He will not go on indefinitely charging into yielding cloth and empty air. He has to be allowed to hit something solid or he won't play.

There is perhaps one exception to the statement that the bullfighters want the horse to be tossed. The picador, though it is part of his job, isn't happy about it. When his horse is tossed, he goes down. The picador, unlike the horse, has no mattress. He does have a heavy piece of armor on the leg which is going to be on the side from which the bull will charge, and it is so heavy that when he goes down he can't easily get up unaided. He depends on his colleagues to draw the bull away.

Years ago, of course, the picador was even more vulnerable, because his horse had no protection at all against the bull. Everything depended on the picador's skill at holding off the bull with his lance. So many horses were gored, however, that the *peto* or mattress was prescribed. This last grew longer and longer until finally it began to scrape the ground. Picadors grew careless and sometimes jabbed away at a bull until he was half-dead from lance wounds alone. For this reason the size of the *peto* is now limited to about 60 pounds (instead of 90 or more), thus making the horse somewhat vulnerable and restoring a certain degree of skill to the picador's task. Horses are sometimes gored and this is often one of the nastier aspects of the fight.

Watch closely now, for here it is probable that you will have an opportunity to see some dexterous capework. The usual bullfight program calls for the killing of six bulls by three matadors. Although each matador has two bulls definitely assigned to him for the kill, at this stage of the fight all three will probably intervene. It is usual for the picadors to appear three times. The three matadors take turns in drawing the bull off, and in demonstrating their mastery of the animal. Thus this portion of the fight takes on the aspect of a competition among the three, and you may see exceptional brilliance displayed at this juncture.

Now you are likely to see some of the most intricate passes—though the chances are that at your first fight they will all look much alike. One pretty effect is to end a series of verónicas by holding the cloth of the cape to the waist and twirling as the bull passes, so that it stands up like the skirt of a pirouetting dancer. This is called a *rebolera*. In the *chicuelina,* a rather dangerous pass, the matador gathers in the cloth just as the bull is passing, wrapping it around his own body. He hopes the bull's rush will carry him past, in spite of the sudden removal of his target. Usually it does. This pass is named for the bullfighter who first used it. So is the *gaenera,* which starts like a verónica, but in which the cape is thrown up over the head as the bull is passing. So is the *manoletina,* in which the cape or muleta is held behind the matador's back while the bull is invited to charge only an arm's length away.

The Banderillas

The planting of the banderillas—the pairs of decorated darts that are thrust into the bull's shoulders—comes next. This is a spectacular feat to the uninitiated, but it is in fact one of the least dangerous parts of the fight. Watch closely, however, if you see the matador himself preparing to perform this maneuver, instead of entrusting it to the banderilleros, which is the normal course. That means he is particularly expert with the darts, and you may see an extra twist added.

The Climax

The last stage of the fight, the *faena,* is the final playing of the bull and his killing. This is when the matador, at least if he feels he had a good bull, a responsive animal, bold and aggressive, will put on his best show. If, before advancing into the ring, he holds his hat aloft and turns slowly round, to salute the whole audience, it is your cue to miss nothing. It means that he is dedicating the bull to everyone, and that is done only when the torero believes he has an opportunity to give a particularly fine performance with all the extra, spectacular flourishes.

This is also the most dangerous part of the fight. For the large cape, the muleta is now substituted, a small piece of red cloth that offers a much less conspicuous target for the bull's attention than the matador's body. It is now that his skill will be exerted to its utmost and now that you will want to follow more closely every movement of the torero until at last the great black bulk of the bull goes crashing down onto the sand.

You may think that the quality of the bullfighting has suddenly decreased at the beginning of the faena, for there may not be much grace in the opening passes. That is because their object is to attain complete mastery over the bull. His will to fight is being broken, and it is done by violence rather than by grace. It is at this stage that you will see the faena's counterpart of the opening act's verónica, that is to say the most simple pass of this part of the fight, the *natural.* This consists in presenting the muleta, held out in one hand to the left side of the matador, and swinging it before the bull's muzzle as he charges. This is more dangerous when done with the right hand *(un natural con derechazo).*

Once the bull has been shown again who is master, however, you may see some of the most daring and elegant passes of the whole corrida. Passes in which the matador stands erect holding the muleta with both hands, as though flagging the animal by, are called 'statues'—*estatuarios.* It is at this stage that you may see the *manoletina,* mentioned above, and some overhead passes *(pases por alto).* The most dangerous pass you are likely to see now is the *arrucina,* in which the muleta is held behind the body.

Also risky is the *pendulo,* in which the cloth is swung back and forth behind the matador's legs.

At the end of this demonstration, the time comes for the kill. First, it is necessary to square *(cuadrar)* the bull—that is, to maneuver him into a head-on position with the two front feet together. To judge this perfectly is an essential part of the matador's skill. For if he attempts to strike when the bull's feet are not perfectly together, or if its head is not lowered at just the right angle, or even if the bull moves his feet as the matador lunges forward with his sword, he will not make a clean kill. Instead the blade may strike bone and be sent flying high into the air leaving the bull writhing in agony and the matador needing to make another attempt. Such a misjudgement invariably elicits the wrath of the crowd who will start booing and jeering and possibly throwing cushions into the ring.

The Kill

With the bull fixed, the matador drives the sword in over the horns with his right hand, while his left, with the muleta, sweeps under his eyes and pulls his head down. It is a moment as dangerous for the man as for the bull; if the swing of the muleta fails to hold that head down, instead of sword into bull it will be horn into man. But if the matador has judged correctly, the bull crumples to the ground after a few moments' agony.

What the president of the fight, whose judgment is usually much influenced by the reaction of the crowd, thinks of the bullfighter's performance will be indicated now. If the matador did well, he is awarded an ear; exceptionally well, both ears; and for a really superlative performance, the ears and the tail. This is ordinarily as far as recognition goes, but there have been occasions on which a hoof or two has been added, and the all-time record is probably held by Carlos Arruza, who in Málaga was awarded the whole animal, at the end of a fight in which he had once been tossed. The dead bull may be dragged around the ring and cheered in tribute to his courage. This in no way reflects upon the performance of the matador—indeed, quite the contrary.

A few final points to bear in mind. A bullfighter is a *torero* (never, except in *Carmen,* a *toreador*) and only the star who kills the bull is a *matador (matar* meaning "to kill"). *Novilladas* are fights with young bulls and aspirant matadors, and for this reason, tickets are usually cheaper than for regular *corridas.* Should you come across a *rejoneador,* this is the revival of the old and spectacular style of bullfighting in which each phase of the contest is performed by the rejoneador mounted on a beautiful Arab horse which, needless to say, is kept out of contact with the bull's horns. It is closer to the Portuguese style of bullfighting than to the traditional Spanish style.

For information on purchasing tickets and tips on which seats to choose, see under *Bullfights* in *Facts at your Fingertips.*

Velasquez

MADRID

Hub of a Nation

Madrileños, as the citizens of Madrid are called, are fond of claiming that the only better place to be is Heaven. Certainly Madrid is unique, a Mediterranean city nearly 480 km. (300 miles) from the sea, graced most days of the year by a flawless intensely blue sky. Given this piercing light and lack of rain, it is little wonder that Madrid has developed into a city where work tends to be seen as the interlude between bouts of pleasure. Madrid and its inhabitants exude a warmth unique in Spain. The stranger feels irresistibly buoyed up by the vivacity of the people, their friendliness and quick humor. The streets are charged with energy. Madrid is a city that turns foreign visitors into residents.

By European standards Madrid is a relatively recent capital. It was only in 1561 that Philip II decided to fix the court in Madrid, then a small, inconsequential town of some 30,000, mainly very poor, inhabitants. His decision was governed by the fact that Madrid lies at the geographical center of the Iberian peninsula. Today its central position is often compared to the hub of a wheel from which all the main road and railroad lines radiate outwards like spokes to the farthest corners of Iberia.

Yet Madrid remains an odd place for a town, a plateau protruding 600 meters (2,000 feet) up out of the Castilian tableland and the highest capital in Europe. Although Philip II's court had been a byword for austerity, by the second half of the 18th century Madrid was famous among voluptuaries. Casanova came to Madrid for its renowned pre-Lent Carnival and returned to Italy with rapturous reports of its carnal delights. Franco closed down the brothels in 1956 but the enthusiasm with which Madrid has now embraced sexual freedom must cause the old dictator to twirl in his grave.

Madrid city center scores over Berlin, London and Paris by its size. Despite the fact that the city's population has doubled since 1960 and is now around four million, the central area is the same size as 50 years ago. Much of Madrid's charm resides in the fact that it is possible to walk about downtown, with no need to use transport. Turn off any main thoroughfare and you will most likely find yourself in a street of old bars and small artesans, plumbers or carpenters, old-fashioned grocers with shutters fighting the newer supermarkets, with perhaps a Chinese restaurant or a sex shop adding a contemporary flourish. Ambling around the center of Madrid is a pleasure that never cloys.

The rush hours in Madrid are as horrendous as those in any capital of an industrialized country. Madrid lacks the suburban rail and subway links of Barcelona, so many Madrileños insist on driving to work despite the hold-ups and parking problems involved.

The lack of rain in Madrid means that the city's pollution problem is one of the worst in the world, though of late the government has taken steps to counteract it. It is to be hoped that the cleaned-up Manzanares river is only the first in a series of such measures.

Life in Madrid is lived largely on its streets and in its bars and cafes, and there is no better way of sampling the flavor of this most vivacious of cities than by joining in the ritual of twice-daily visits to the city's packed taverns. The morning is interrupted by a coffee break, often a late breakfast. Twelve-thirty is too early for lunch but it is a popular time for the bars to fill with pre-lunch drinkers and those in search of a snack. Restaurants fill up quickly after 1 P.M., their opening time, with those who have only an hour for lunch.

Madrid is not only a Mediterranean city because of the light and the atmosphere but because it also has some of the best seafood in Spain. Every day the pick of the catch is flown to the capital. Some of the most delightful summertime restaurants are a few kilometers out of the city on the roads to Guadalajara, Burgos and La Coruña, where you can eat out of doors: shellfish followed by steak or charcoal-grilled baby-lamb chops, their taste unique in the world.

Instead of sitting down to dinner many Madrileños prefer to go *tasca*-crawling. *Tascas* are small taverns serving tantalizing *tapas,* perhaps black pudding or squid fried in batter, pigs' ears or *mollejas,* bulls' testicles sliced wafer-thin and fried with garlic, a dish for the gods. All bars have tapas, but the tascas concentrate on them and so have a wider range. The tascas are located around the Puerta del Sol, on the Calle de la Victoria and Calle de la Cruz, in Echegaray and on the narrow side streets around the Plaza Santa Ana, home of the *Cervecería Alemana* that Hemingway used to patronize, and on the streets around the Plaza Mayor. In the latter you may chance upon the *tuna,* students playing guitars and clad in the gear of the Inquisition. The tradition is 400 years old and it is worth tipping generously to help keep it alive; as well as their traditional songs they will also play requests.

Madrid's Holy Week processions are not as spectacular as those of more religious cities like Valladolid, Avila or Zamora, but the *Procession del Silencio* on Good Friday night is nevertheless impressive.

In May the flowers are in bloom and the *económicos* are serving fresh asparagus and strawberries. May 15 is the fiesta of San Isidro, the patron saint of Madrid, an excuse for two weeks of bullfights, fireworks, street festivals and open-air dances. On May 15 it is traditional to drink from the spring at the saint's hermitage just across the Manzanares, where there is an attendant funfair and stalls. This is the authentic San Isidro celebration as portrayed by Goya.

Most Madrileños take their vacation in July or August, and escape to the mountains or the coast. Ten years ago Madrid was deserted in August but gradually as more and more of its citizens have awoken to the charm of scant traffic, cinemas and shops open, and a full program of open-air evening events including opera, operetta, drama and variety performances is organized by the City Council.

Discovering Madrid

To do Madrid ample justice, you need to stay a minimum of three days, after which at least another couple of days or so can be dedicated to excursions to Toledo, Aranjuez, Segovia, Avila, the Escorial and the Valley of the Fallen.

With the exception of the northern reaches of the city around the upper part of the Castellana, Madrid is still a fairly compact capital and you can usually walk from one tourist attraction to another and be assured that enough sights will line your way to reward your efforts. If you get tired, simply take a bus or one of the numerous cabs, still quite cheap, back to your hotel. Or you can relax in one of the many sidewalk cafes and renew your strength for further sightseeing.

The Prado as a Starting Point

Since the attraction most tourists head for first upon arrival in Madrid is the Prado Museum, we will start our tour of the city from this world-famous art gallery, one of the great storehouses not only of Spanish art, but of Flemish and Italian masterpieces.

Located on the main north–south axis, the Castellana (here called the Paseo del Prado), the Prado is best entered through its main entrance on its northern side opposite the Hotel Ritz. Here there is a statue of the artist Francisco Goya. The Prado's other door facing onto the Paseo del Prado, behind a statue of the painter Diego Velázquez, is used mainly as an exit.

The Prado was originally opened in 1823 and has since been superbly stocked with the works of Velázquez, Murillo, Zurbarán, Ribera, Valdés Leal, Alonso Cano, El Greco, Berruguete and Goya as well as with a fine collection of Titian, Rubens, Raphael, Botticelli, Correggio, Mantegna and Bosch which were transferred from the Escorial Monastery outside Madrid where King Philip II had originally housed them. Both he and his father, Emperor Charles V, were avid collectors and brought many art treasures from southern Italy and the Netherlands, both at that time part of the Spanish empire.

To view the Prado's vast collection of paintings and treasures properly would take weeks. But the highpoints most popular with tourists are usually the El Greco, Velázquez, Goya, and Bosch galleries. Explanatory notes on the major artists are available in the relevant galleries at a small charge.

The greatest treasures are on the upper floor and a visit is best begun at the Goya (north) entrance end. The main gallery and adjoining rooms contain El Grecos, Riberas, Titians, Murillos, and, of course, the works of Diego Velázquez. Be sure to see the *Surrender of Breda,* one of his most impressive paintings, *The Drunkards,* and his series of four dwarfs. *Las Meninas,* perhaps his best known canvas, has been placed in a room by itself, with a strategic mirror to help you appreciate its extraordinary complexities.

The Prado provides a unique opportunity to see the full diversity of Goya's styles in several adjacent rooms at the far end of the upper gallery. Among highlights are portraits of the royal family, including the superb *Family of Carlos IV,* and the beautiful *Marquesa de Santa Cruz* purchased from Britain in 1986 amid much controversy. In a nearby room hang the *Naked Maja* and the *Clothed Maja,* and next door two of the artist's most celebrated works, the *2nd of May,* showing the uprising of the Spaniards in 1808 against the French Mamelukes in the Puerta del Sol, and the *Fusillade of Moncloa,* or *3rd of May,* which depicts the execution of patriots by a French firing squad with the same intensity of reaction to its subject as the later *Guernica* by Picasso.

Downstairs on the ground floor are the paintings of Goya's "Black Period," when he was already deaf and living outside the city. The most startling are *The Pilgrimage to San Isidro, Meeting of Witches,* and *Saturn.* Most of the ground floor is given over to the Flemish school, notably to Rubens, Van Dyck, and Brueghel, and to a sizable collection of late medieval religious paintings, mostly by Spanish artists including Luis de Morales. But before you leave, be sure not to miss the astounding collection of Hieronymus Bosch paintings displayed to the side of the Goya entrance, which includes his *Garden of Earthly Delights,* and the triptych *The Hay Wagon.*

In the fall of 1981 Picasso's *Guernica* was brought to Spain after its years of exile in New York. Its arrival in Madrid was the highlight of that year's celebrations of the centenary of the artist's birth. It is now housed permanently in the Casón del Buen Retiro, an annex to the Prado Museum which stands nearby at the end of the Calle de Felipe IV. The Casón del Buen Retiro is also the home of 19th-century Spanish painting and can be visited on the same ticket as the Prado. On one side of the small square in front of it rises the Royal Academy of the Spanish Language, the learned body charged with safeguarding the Castilian language. It re-edits its monumental dictionary every ten years or so.

In the vicinity of the Prado are three other museums of lesser interest to the tourist on a short stay but nonetheless worthwhile for those with more time to spare. Adjacent to the Post Office on the Calle Montalban is the Navy Museum, small but well-furnished, with ship models, nautical instruments, and Juan de la Cosa's famous map of the New World. At the end of the same street heading towards the Retiro Park is the Decorative Arts Museum, and close to the Cason del Buen Retiro is the Army Museum, fronted by a terrace covered with vintage cannons and mortars. The museum has a good collection of weapons, armor, flags, maps and paintings.

MADRID

0 Miles   ¼

0 Kilometers   ¼

Points of Interest

1   Atheneum
2   Biblioteca Nacional
3   Casa Cisneros
4   Casa de Lope de Vega
5   Casa de la Villa (City Hall)
6   Casón del Buen Retiró
7   Centro de Arte Reina Sofía
    (Queen Sofia Arts Center)
8   Fuente de la Cibeles
    (Cibeles Fountain)
9   Monasterio de la Descalzas Reales
10 Monasterio de Ja Encarnación
11 Municipal Museum
12 Museo Arqueológico
13 Museo des Artes Decorativas
14 Museo Carruajes (Coach Museum)
15 Museo de Cera (Wax Museum)
16 Museo Cerralbo
17 Museo del Ejército (Army Museum)
18 Museo Etnología
19 Museo Lázaro Galdiano
20 Museo Naval
21 Museo del Prado
22 Museo Romántico
23 Museo Sorolla
24 Palacio de Liria
25 Palacio Real
26 Puerta de Alcalá
27 Puerta del Sol
28 Real Academia de Bellas Artes de
    San Fernando
29 Real Fábrica de Tapices (Royal
    Tapestry Workshops)
30 San Antonio de la Florida
31 San Francisco el Grande
32 San Ginés
33 San Jerónimo el Real
34 San José
35 Teatro Español
36 Teatro Real (Opera House)
37 Teatro Zarzuela
38 Templo de Debod
39 Torre de Lujanes
40 Torre de Madrid

ℹ️ Information
✉️ Post Office
Ⓜ️ Metro Station

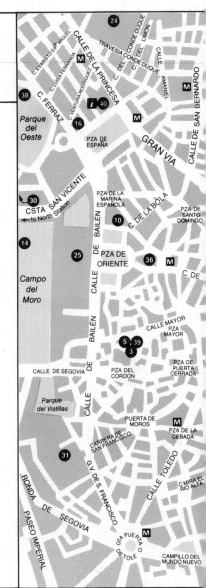

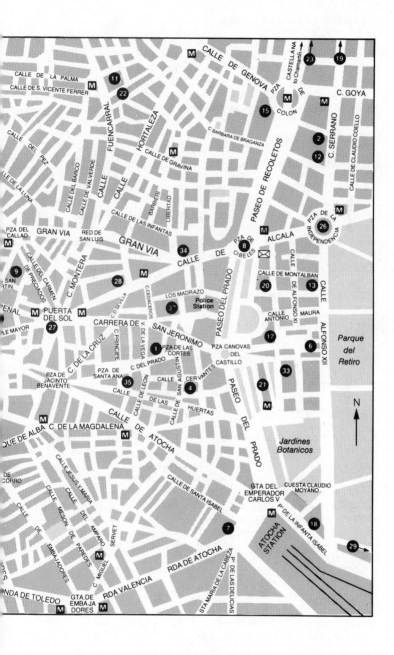

From the Prado to Atocha

After visiting the Prado you could take a stroll through the adjacent Botanical Gardens, opened in 1774 in the reign of Charles III, and come out upon the Cuesta Claudio Moyano, the site of a fascinating second-hand-book market whose stalls offer hours of splendid browsing. A little further on at the corner of Alfonso XII and the Paseo de la Infanta Isabel you come to the Ethnological Museum, of minor interest except to the most dedicated of museum goers. The Plaza Atocha, or to give it its full name, the Glorieta del Emperador Carlos V, has recently undergone a huge transformation. In 1986 an ugly overpass was demolished and an underground tunnel constructed to alleviate the considerable traffic problems of this southern end of the Castellana. The demolition of the overpass has revealed the imposing 19th-century glass-and-steel structure of the old Atocha Railroad Station, designed by Eiffel of Eiffel Tower fame. Though sadly dilapidated at the moment, this old building should shortly undergo a facelift when it is incorporated into the new adjacent station, currently under construction. The large building opposite is the Centro de Arte Reina Sofia which opened in 1986 in a former hospital and now houses some of Madrid's most exciting art exhibitions. If from here you proceed up the Calle de Atocha, you will enter an old working-class area, well worth a stroll for those seeking offbeat neighborhoods and local color.

From the Retiro to Cibeles

By far the best plan after a bout in the ever-crowded Prado is to take a stroll in the Retiro Park just a couple of streets away. Madrid's prettiest and most popular park, the Retiro dates back to the 15th century, though it was not opened to the public until 1876. Among the park's attractions are several outdoor cafes, Florida Park, a leading nightclub, a lake for rowing, playgrounds for children and shady lanes, often decorated with statues and monuments and fountains, ideal for strolling. In spring and summer, band concerts are held on Sunday mornings, and members of the Catalan colony in Madrid meet and solemnly dance the sardana. The Retiro plays host annually to a dog show, art exhibitions in the 19th-century glass-and-iron Crystal Palace and in summer, puppet shows and outdoor theatrical performances.

In addition to the large lake with its huge monument to Alfonso XII, there are two smaller ones, stocked with ducks and swans and surrounded by weeping willows. Fountains, statues and busts, beautiful flower arrangements and a delightful rose garden all help to make the Retiro a welcome haven from the city's bustle.

Leaving the Retiro at its main exit, the Plaza de la Independencia, you'll see a large arch, the Puerta de Alcalá, built in 1778 by Sabatini in Charles III's reign. The arch was formerly one of the gates to the city, with an adjoining customs' station; beside it stood the old bullring, which was later moved to its present location on the Calle de Alcalá at Ventas.

If at the Plaza de la Independencia you turn down the Calle de Alcalá, you will come to the Plaza de Cibeles, named after the Greek goddess Cybele (daughter of Uranus) who sits mounted on a chariot. The fountain has become the unofficial emblem of the city. Cibeles, as the square is known to Madrileños, is the great crossroads of the city, the intersection of the Calle de Alcalá and the Castellana. The cafes in the central promenade on the southern side are perennial favorites and here also a small playground, trees and benches make the area between Cibeles and the Neptune fountain an especially inviting place to rest after sightseeing.

The Salamanca Neighborhood and Beyond

The area northeast of Cibeles, the Salamanca neighborhood, is named after the financier José Salamanca who started building this then-new residential area in the 1870s. The *barrio* or neighborhood is bounded on the south by the Calle de Alcalá and the Calle Goya, the latter a busy shopping street lined with shops and branches of the two leading department stores, the Corte Inglés and Galerías Preciados.

You can now proceed north along either the Castellana or the Calle Serrano, the latter being the most elegant and expensive shopping street in the city. The surrounding streets parallel and perpendicular to Serrano are the domain of elegant shops and boutiques as well.

Going up Serrano from the Plaza de la Independencia (Puerta de Alcalá) you come first on the left to the Archeological Museum, a large, sprawling building with sections dedicated to Greek, Roman, prehistoric and Christian and Moorish cultures. Here you can see a reproduction of the Altamira prehistoric caves in Santander, a worthwhile visit since visits to the caves themselves are limited. Beside the museum once stood the old Mint, which has now been torn down to make room for a huge esplanade decorated with olive trees, sculptures by Vaqueros Turcios, allegorical of the Discovery of America, and the statue of Columbus high up on a pillar, which formerly stood in the center of the Plaza de Colón (Columbus Square). Underneath is the airport bus depot, as well as arcades, shops, and the Villa de Madrid theater, a leading cultural center and experimental theater.

Crossing the Calle Goya, you come on the right to the Celso García department store and then on the left to another branch of the Galerías Preciados department store. After passing many sidewalk cafes and art galleries, as well as the American Embassy and the British ambassadorial residence and dozens of boutiques, you finally reach the Lázaro Galdiano Museum on the corner of María de Molina.

Housed in what was formerly the luxurious private villa of José Lázaro Galdiano, writer, journalist and antique collector of the early 20th century, the museum contains a magnificent collection of *objets d'art,* all tastefully displayed, which ranges over clocks, paintings from Spanish and foreign masters, armor, furniture, tapestries, enamels and jewels—in all a really splendid array which is well worth a visit.

If you have walked as far as the Lázaro Galdiano Museum, you may well opt for a bus or cab ride back down the Castellana to Cibeles. If, on the other hand, you decide to brave the streams of fast-flowing traffic and the accompanying exhaust fumes, there are many sights to reward your efforts on this impressive modern avenue. Few of the noble palaces of old remain, but just every now and again, tucked away between glass and concrete structures, you will catch a glimpse of these splendors of yesteryear. Heading south down the Castellana from the Glorieta de Emilio Castelar, you will come to the overpass linking the Paseo de Eduardo Dato to the

Calle Juan Bravo. Underneath this is a pleasant garden adorned with several sculptures forming the outdoor sculpture museum, an agreeable place to sit for a while. The Castellana at this point is lined with the embassies of several countries, Finland, Germany and Belgium among them, before reaching the Plaza de Colón. Here in the northwest corner on your right are two large office buildings, the Torres de Jerez, much criticized for their graceless obtrusiveness and architectural non-style. Curiously enough, they were built from the top downwards, using a narrow central tower as a support. Inside one of them is the famous Chicote's bottle museum with its 10,500 bottles formerly housed in the basement of Chicote's bar on the Gran Vía. Across the street in the Centro Colón office complex is the Museo de Cera, one of Europe's more worthwhile wax museums. On the other side of the square are the Gardens of the Discovery of America and the monument to Columbus which you will have already seen on your walk up the Calle Serrano.

Continuing on down the Paseo de Recoletos, the first building on the left is the impressive National Library which often features exhibits and art shows in its salons. Next, also on the left-hand side, comes the sumptuous Banco Hipotecario, formerly the home of the Marquis of Salamanca. Then on the right comes the famous old Cafe Gijón, full of nostalgic atmosphere for the time when it hosted some of the greatest *tertulias* (political, literary or artistic discussions) of the capital. It is still worth a visit for those in search of shades of a more romantic past, and in summer tables and chairs are set outside on the avenue's sidewalk in front of the cafe.

Arriving back at the Plaza Cibeles, the building on the northwest corner is the Palacio de Buenavista, built originally for the Duke of Alba in 1769. Today, surrounded by lush gardens and guarded by soldiers, it serves as the Ministry of the Army. Opposite, on the northeast corner, is a palace built at the turn of the century for the Marquis of Linares. During the Franco era it was slated to be torn down, like so many other palaces lining the Castellana, but, in 1976, a reprieve came from the new government, which recognized the palace's historical worth. The City Hall is currently negotiating to purchase it and convert it into a museum.

Cibeles to Gran Vía

On the southeast corner of Cibeles rises the huge, cathedral-like Palacio de Comunicaciones which the people of Madrid often jokingly refer to as Nuestra Señora de Comunicaciones—Our Lady of Communications. It is, in fact, the Main Post Office, built in 1918, and one of the landmarks of the city.

On the southwest corner of Cibeles is the Banco de España (1891), analogous to the Federal Reserve Bank in the U.S. In the bank's underground vaults are stored the gold reserves of Spain.

Progressing along the Calle de Alcalá, on the right is the Church of San José, completed in 1742. Just past the church, branch right onto the Gran Vía, lined with shops, cafes, newsstands and numerous movie theaters. On the left side you will see the elegant Grassy jewelry store, and on the right Loewe, Spain's leading leather store, and then the Museo de Chicote, now a restaurant but formerly Chicote's bar, a favorite meeting place during pre-war days and much frequented by Hemingway and other writers.

The small traffic circle you come to next is the Red de San Luis. You can here branch left down the Calle Montera which will take you to the Puerta del Sol, or go toward the right up the rather dismal Calle Hortaleza or the Calle Fuencarral. The latter is lined with inexpensive shoe shops, and ultimately links up with the "boulevards," a network of avenues skirting the center, which start at Colón and end at the Parque del Oeste. On the way notice the impressive Churrigueresque façade sculpted by Pedro de Ribera in 1722 on what was formerly a hospital. Today the building houses the city's Municipal Museum and close by is the 19th-century Romantic Museum. Off to the left in the streets around the Plaza Dos de Mayo is the area known as Malasaña, whose narrow streets are packed with music bars very popular at night with the young of Madrid. However, it is an area best avoided by the visitor as it has become the center of Madrid's drug scene, and violence and unpleasant incidents are not infrequent. If you continue as far as the Glorieta de Bilbao, the crowded Café Comercial, another of the famous cafes of old, is well worth a visit.

Back on the corner of Fuencarral and Gran Vía stands the old Telephone Building (La Telefónica), at one time the highest structure in the city. During the Civil War of 1936–39, when Madrid remained loyal to the Republic, the Telefónica was the main observation point for Republicans surveying the battleground around the university campus and the Casa del Campo Park, when it was piled stories-high with sandbags. Walking on past the movie theaters with their large canopies, you come on the left to the Plaza del Callao. The main building of the Galerías Preciados department store, together with its annex, takes up most of the square. Two pleasant shopping streets, which are closed to traffic and where benches and flowers have been installed, the Calle de Preciados and the Calle del Carmen, both lead down to the Puerta del Sol. At the lower end of Preciados is the original Corte Inglés department store, which now has branches all over Madrid. If instead you branch right, down the Calle Preciados toward the Plaza de Santo Domingo, you come to several excellent restaurants.

The Plaza de España to the Victory Arch

Continuing down the Gran Vía past Callao, you pass on the right the Sepu budget store as well as numerous cafeterias, movie theaters, airline offices, hotels, travel agencies and shops. Cross the Calle de San Bernardo (which toward the right takes you to the old university building, the Music Conservatory and then links up with the boulevards) and a few streets on you come to the large, spacious Plaza de España, flanked by two highrise towers, the Torre de Madrid, with 37 floors and the highest building in Madrid, and the Torre de España, the second-highest building with 25 floors. On the ground floor of the former is the Tourist Office, which supplies handy maps and other useful information; the latter houses the elegant Hotel Plaza, long a favorite with American visitors.

A large, three-story garage was built under most of the Plaza de España, but the square, as all others where similar facilities were built, was then tastefully redone. Now the Plaza is a delightful place for reading, relaxing or refreshment. Around the fountain, tourists sun themselves and hippies strum guitars. In the middle of the park stands a monument to Cervantes surrounded by his best loved characters, Don Quixote and Sancho Panza.

From this square, should you proceed straight ahead up the Calle
Princesa, you'll first see on the left a conglomerate of shops and restaurants
huddling in the large courtyard of an office building, which has become
a popular meeting place for young Madrileños.

On the right of the Calle Princesa stands the Palacio de Liria, privately
owned by the Duchess of Alba and open to the public by arrangement
only. It is one of the few palaces which still belong to an aristocratic family,
and is actually lived in by the much-titled Duchess. Work on it began in
1770. After being badly damaged during the Civil War, it was subsequently rebuilt. A pleasant cafe and a mesón-restaurant in the small park in
front make ideal stopping-off places.

Continuing up the street on the left is the Hotel Meliá Madrid. Further
up you come first on the right to the Hotel Princesa Plaza, then on the
corner of the boulevards another Corte Inglés department store; there are
shopping arcades on either side of the street. Beyond, as far as the Triumphal Arch, is an area known as Argüelles, popular with students from the
university of Madrid who come here to drink *cañas* (small draft beers)
and eat plates of squid. At the top of Princesa on the left is the Airforce
Ministry building, a copy of Juan de Herrera's Escorial, and in front the
Victory Arch built by Franco in 1956 to commemorate his triumphal
entry into Madrid at the end of the Civil War.

The University City and Moncloa

Beyond the Victory Arch lies the University City, an area with several
points of interest but too spread-out to visit on foot. However, it can be
reached on city bus routes or by a short cab ride, and its main places of
interest can be glimpsed from tour buses on excursions to the Escorial.

The University City was begun in 1927 but was mostly destroyed during
the Civil War when it was the battleground for the Nationalist troops besieging Madrid. However, it was rebuilt, though generally in undistin-
guished style, and is today one of Spain's most prestigious universities,
with over 100,000 students, many of whom come from Latin America.

Just off to the right of the Avenida de la Victoria is the Museum of the
Americas and, further on, on the left, at the beginning of the Avenida
Puerta de Hierro, you will come to the Museum of Contemporary Spanish
Art. The word "contemporary" may seem to be something of a misnomer,
but it is nevertheless a worthwhile museum. Beyond lies the Moncloa Palace, home of Spain's Prime Minister. At the end of this avenue, Madrid's
western limit is marked by the Puerta de Hierro, an iron gateway built
in 1753 by the Bourbon monarchs who used to come hunting around El
Pardo. The road which branches off to the right here leads to the Zarzuela
Palace, home of King Juan Carlos, and eventually to Franco's former
home, the palace of El Pardo, now a museum.

From the Plaza de España to the Casa de Campo

At the Plaza de España you can take an alternative route. Walk to the
other side of the square, cross the Calle Ferraz, and enter the Parque del
Oeste (West Park), formerly the Cuartel de la Montaña (a barracks), and
you'll come to the Temple of Debod, an authentic Egyptian temple which
formerly stood in the Aswan area of the Nile. It was transported stone

by stone to Madrid from Egypt when the Aswan area was flooded. The temple and its pleasant surroundings and palm-tree landscaping are well worth a visit.

Crossing over Ferraz, you come to the Cerralbo Museum, formerly the private mansion of the Marquis of Cerralbo. The building is crammed full of paintings, furniture and personal mementos, and is rather less museum-like than the Lázaro Galdiano Museum. Visiting it is akin to paying a call on a nobleman's private quarters at the turn of the century. The mansion was built by the traditional-minded marquis in 1876.

Returning to the Parque del Oeste across the street, you continue up the Paseo de Rosales (named after a 19th-century bohemian painter from Madrid). Lining the paseo are countless outdoor cafes, delightful in fine weather. The park is well cared for. Especially beautiful is a large rose garden, with bowers, a fountain and benches.

At the corner of Rosales and Marqués de Urquijo (the end of the boulevards) is an excellent ice-cream parlor with dozens of exotic flavors. Across, at the corner beside the children's playground, is the end station of the cablecar (teleférico) which takes you over the Manzanares river to the Casa de Campo Park, popular with Madrileño families. It is a trip well worth making, for it affords some breathtaking views of the city and the Royal Palace. At either end of the cablecar are restaurants—the one on the Casa de Campo side with outdoor self-service facilities. Buses run regularly from the cablecar station to the zoo and the amusement park.

From near the cablecar entrance in the Parque del Oeste, it is possible to make your way down to the Hermitage of San Antonio de la Florida where the church is decorated with Goya frescos revealing the artist's somewhat sarcastic attitude to the Church. Beneath the crypt of the church lies Goya's headless body, brought back to Spain from France in 1888.

Old Madrid

A tour of Old Madrid can best be started from the Plaza Mayor, a few streets down from the Puerta del Sol. This, the oldest section of the city, was built during the rule of the Habsburg dynasty prior to the mid-18th century. Old Madrid is a warren of narrow streets, silent churches and small squares, a welcome respite from the hectic pace and fumes of the city, an area ideal for the cursory wanderer who will let whim dictate his steps and so encounter charming vistas, streets and buildings at each turn. Getting lost here is part of the fun, for you are sure to come out eventually at some imposing monument or church which will act as a landmark. Much of the area around Calle Segovia is now coming back into fashion with many old buildings being restored and several good restaurants flourishing in hidden nooks and corners.

The Plaza Mayor

The Plaza Mayor measures approximately 110 by 90 meters (360 by 300 feet) in length and width and is one of the most beautiful and also one of the most representative squares in the city. Work on it was begun by Juan Gómez de Mora in 1617 in Philip III's reign and when it was completed in 1620 eight days of merrymaking followed. Fires gutted parts of the structure in 1631, 1672 and 1790; complete restoration was not undertaken till 1853.

In the 17th century the square was used for bullfights and also once for an *auto da fé,* the burning of a heretic, with the king watching from the section called the Panadería (Bakery) in the center of the northern side, while the 476 balconies were full of nobles and dignitaries enjoying the fun. The square was also used for the canonization of San Isidro, San Ignacio de Loyola, San Francisco Xavier, Santa Teresa de Jesús and San Felipe Neri. In it were held masked balls, firework displays and plays, among them those of Lope de Vega.

In 1629 the square was lavishly decorated for 42 days to celebrate the marriage of the Infanta María and the King of Hungary. Here also was celebrated the arrival in 1623 of the Prince of Wales, the future Charles I of England. During his reign, King Philip V turned the square into a market; and in 1810 triumphal arches were raised to receive the Duke of Wellington; later, in 1812 the square's name was changed to the Plaza de la Constitución. And in 1847 the last bullfights were held here to commemorate the marriage of Queen Isabel II.

Until the late '60s the Plaza Mayor was a bustling, commercial square, with buses and trolley cars and traffic noisily clanking through it. But with the crush of tourists invading Madrid, the city decided to close it to traffic. Around 1970 a large parking lot was built under the square, but the cobblestones and the equestrian statue of Philip III by Juan de Bolonia, made in 1616, were dutifully replaced.

Though the day-to-day vitality of the Plaza Mayor is gone, it is still lined with old shops and taverns; the most famous of the former are the hat and uniform shops where an extraordinary selection of head-gear can be bought—anything from a pith helmet to a cabby's tweed cap. Three good restaurants with tables and chairs placed outdoors provide a pleasant opportunity for outdoor lunching or dining. In summer, theatrical performances and the Festivales de España are sometimes held here; before Christmas the square fills with stands selling decorations, noisemakers and Nativity scenes, while all around fir and pine trees are placed on sale. On Sunday mornings the square fills with stamp and coin collectors who cluster on the sidewalks and cobblestones as they buy, sell and swap parts of their collections. Though the plaza is always bustling in summer, you should take care here if you're visiting in winter, especially at night, when it's often deserted except for groups of dropouts and drug addicts.

Researching the Mesones

Walking down the time-worn steps under the Arco de Cuchilleros, in the southwest corner of the square, you come to one of the most picturesque tourist areas in the city. The two streets leading from the Calle Mayor down to the Plaza de Puerta Cerrada (marked by a stone cross), the Cava de San Miguel and the Calle Cuchilleros, are lined with taverns and mesones which at night are a-bustle with a merry crowd spearing tapas and drinking beer and wine. To make the taverns still more enticing, many owners hire guitarists and accordion-players to liven things up. Especially on Saturday nights, the area has a touch of carnival about it as tourists and locals spill out onto the streets and the noise reaches a boisterous pitch.

The Cuevas de Luis Candelas, one of the oldest of the mesones, has an old barrel-organ to provide the music. The Cuevas is named after a famous bandit (1806–37) whose exploits passed into the realm of folklore over the years. In an effort to prove its authenticity, the tavern has hired a doorman and dressed him up in a bandit's costume. Some wags feel that it is the tourists instead of the coach travelers who are now being fleeced; but apocryphal or not, the Cuevas is always a fun spot for roving visitors.

From Luis Candelas' you can proceed to the Mesón del Toro, the Mesón de la Tortilla, or a half-dozen other mesones, each specializing in local foods, which are usually recognizable in their windows where you may see mushrooms frying in oil or omelets being flipped into the air. Most of the taverns are more suited for a drink or a tapa than a full-course Spanish meal. For that, you can go to El Cuchi, a fun-packed restaurant at the foot of the Cuchilleros steps, or to Botin's, one of the quaintest old restaurants in town which makes a determined effort at being picturesque on its three stories crammed with wooden furniture and Castilian knick-knacks. The prices are moderate, the rooms oozing with charm, and the crowd of tourists usually impenetrable.

Around the corner at the Puerta Cerrada lurks another oldtime haunt, Casa Paco, unbeatable for its thick, juicy steaks served on sizzling plates. This atmospheric and always crowded restaurant began life as a tavern over 50 years ago. If you haven't reserved a table, you will most likely have to wait a while in the bar up front, a not altogether unpleasant fate.

The Royal Palace

Bearing right, the narrow, curvy Calle de San Justo takes you to the Plaza del Cordón and the Casa de Cisneros, originally built in 1537 and restored in 1915. The house once belonged to the nephew of Cardinal Gonzalo Ximenez de Cisneros, Primate of Spain and Inquisitor General, much maligned abroad for his role in the Inquisition.

A sharp right takes you up the Calle del Cordón to the Plaza de la Villa, the site of Madrid's City Hall (Ayuntamiento) and the Torre de los Lujanes, where King Charles V supposedly kept his main European rival, François I of France, prisoner for a while after winning the Battle of Pavia.

Continuing down the Calle Mayor, past the Consejo de Estado y Capitanía (Council of State and Captaincy), you come to the Calle de Bailén where, on turning right, you come across the Royal Palace, second only to the Prado as one of Madrid's greatest sights. Beside it stands the stark Cathedral of La Almudena, a modern afterthought which has been ignominiously shrugged off by the Madrileños, who consider it an intrusive pastiche. Construction remains incomplete though work is once again in progress.

The Royal Palace, a magnificent Bourbon structure, stands on the site of the former Alcázar, or fortress, which burned down in 1734. The first stone of the palace was laid in 1737 in Philip V's reign using plans drawn up by Juan Bautista Sacchetti, but it wasn't completed until 1764, under Charles III's rule. The palace provided a stylish abode for Spanish monarchs for almost 200 years. Even Napoleon's brother, Joseph, was sumptuously housed in it in the early 19th century. After the French were ousted, King Ferdinand VII moved into the palace. The building remained a royal residence until the coming of the Second Republic in 1931 when King Alfonso XIII left it for exile in Italy.

Though General Franco sometimes used the palace for official state receptions and audiences, he lived in the El Pardo Palace just outside the city, leaving most of the Royal Palace as a museum. King Juan Carlos presently lives in the less ostentatious Zarzuela Palace, also outside the city.

A tour of the Royal Palace could easily take several hours, especially if you really want to appreciate the sumptuous salons with their precious carpets, porcelain, clocks, and chandeliers, and include visits to the Pharmaceutical Museum, the Royal Armory, and the Library. But guided tours are now obligatory and most of the guides will whisk you round the main highlights of the Royal Apartments in about 1½ hours. The Coach Museum is at the other end of the gardens and must be entered from that side, a five-block walk away.

Outside the palace is the spacious Plaza de Oriente, enhanced by large stone statues of pre-unification kings and warriors. Originally 108 of them were intended to adorn the roof, but their weight was so great it was considered more prudent to place them in this park and in the Retiro. The Plaza de Oriente has traditionally been used for demonstrations for and against the regimes in power. Across from the palace stands the old Opera House, which now serves as Madrid's main concert venue, though a new concert hall is due to open shortly in the northern reaches of the Castellana.

San Francisco el Grande

If, on reaching the bottom of the Calle Mayor, you turn left onto the Calle Bailen and walk southward over the viaduct bridge, you pass the pleasant Vistillas Park on the right, and the nearby Plaza de Gabriel Miró commanding some good views, and the studio of the painter Ignacio Zuloaga, before coming to the most important church in Madrid, the basilica of San Francisco el Grande, begun in 1761 by Fray Francisco de las Cabezas and completed in 1784 by Francisco de Sabatini.

The inside decorations date from 1881. Outstanding is the large dome which can be seen from many points in the city. It measures 29 meters (96 feet) in diameter, larger than St. Paul's in London. Paintings in the chapels include works by Goya, Claudio Coello and Lucas Jordán. The 50 splendidly-carved choir stalls originally stood in El Paular Monastery outside Madrid. The fine English organ dates from 1882.

A few streets ahead along a rather bleak section takes you to the Puerta de Toledo, an arch built in 1827 under Ferdinand VII's rule by Antonio Aguado.

Double back up the Calle Bailén and then right to the Carrera de San Francisco, formerly the scene of lively summer verbenas or street festivals during the celebrations in honor of La Paloma, which takes you to the Puerta de Moros square, opposite the Cebada market. The present "barley market" is a relatively new structure and replaced the steel-and-glass one long a landmark of the city. Beyond the Plaza de la Cebada and crossing the Calle de Toledo, go down the Calle de Maldonadas and you come out at the Plaza de Cascorro, the threshold of the Rastro.

The Flea Market

The Rastro, or Flea Market, has long been one of Madrid's main tourist sights, especially on Sunday mornings, but beware, for it is also a haven for pickpockets who fare well among the jostling crowds. It is a sprawling indoor and outdoor emporium that attracts gypsies and art connoisseurs, tourists and dropouts, where you can find anything from a rusty flintlock rifle to a new puppy dog. Despite the fact that decades of bargain-hunters and professional antique dealers have raided the Rastro, new objects turn up constantly, and bargains are still occasionally found if you know what you're after. Some of the wares are wildly overpriced, so watch your step. It really takes repeated visits before you get the hang of it and know which sections to hunt in. Though the most active time is Sunday mornings, the better antique shops are open every day of the week, but not the street stands.

The main thoroughfare of the Rastro is the steep hill of the Ribera de Curtidores, which on Sundays is jammed full with pushcarts, stands and hawkers and gypsies selling trinkets, plastic toys, records, camping equipment, new furniture and foam rubber mattresses. The better wares are usually kept inside the stores on either side of the street.

Those seeking antiques, though hardly at bargain prices, might enter the two sections off the Ribera de Curtidores, about halfway down the length of the street. On the left, the Galerías Piquer is renowned for its choice art pieces, and on the right another Galería is equally reputable. The Galerías each consist of a large courtyard surrounded by a dozen or so antique stores on two levels. To pick through the Galerías carefully takes hours.

Also leading off from the Ribera de Curtidores on the left are two narrow streets, one specializing in the sale of modern paintings and the other selling birds, fish, puppies and other pets.

At the bottom of the Ribera, where the iron junk market starts, you turn right down the Calle Mira el Sol one block and come out on the Campillo del Mundo Nuevo, a square with a park in its center, where among other stands and items spread on tables and blankets, you'll find a book and record fair where bargains can occasionally be found. The Rastro sprawls across the Ronda de Toledo, to the other side of the road, but that section of it is mostly reserved for electrical appliances, old bicycles and spare machinery parts.

Instead walk back up one of the steep narrow streets such as the Calle Carlos Arniches or the Calle Mira el Rio Baja, lined with junk shops and stands, a good bargain-hunting area. Wind up at the Plaza General Vara del Rey, another recommended area surrounded by antique shops and jammed on Sundays with stands of every description.

Vendors start putting away their wares and locking their shops around 2 P.M. at which time you can dip into some tapas at one of the taverns on the Plaza del Cascorro.

Another Stroll from the Prado

Back at the starting point at the Prado Museum, another itinerary takes you across the Paseo del Prado, up past the Palace Hotel to the Carrera de San Jerónimo; on the right stands the Congreso de los Diputados or the Palacio del Congreso, the Spanish Parliament, opened in 1850 and in front of which crouch two lions cast from the molten metal of cannons captured in the war with the Moroccans in 1860. At the back of the Parliament building is the delightful and superbly restored Teatro de la Zarzuela where operas and colorful musicals, known as *zarzuelas,* are staged.

Crossing over the street in front of the parliament, and going down the Calle de San Agustín, you come to the Calle Cervantes, on which, at no. 15, stands the house where Spain's famous playwright, Lope de Vega, lived from 1610 until his death in 1635. Close by, on the corner of Cervantes and the Calle León, stood the house in which Cervantes died in 1616. Turn right on León and walk to the Calle del Prado, where in front of you stands the Atheneum, an influential club and cultural center.

Turning left up the Calle del Prado, you'll come out on the Plaza Santa Ana, where on one side of the square you'll see the Teatro Español, one of Madrid's leading theaters, which specializes in Spanish classical drama. Across the square is the old-world Hotel Victoria, much favored by bullfighters in the days when Hemingway was in Madrid. The wood-paneled Cervecería Alemana on one side of the square used to be a popular rendezvous for literati, and in recent years became for a while a bohemian haunt. Today it is a favorite with tourists.

A short walk down the Calle Príncipe, or the Calle de la Cruz, past Seseña, the store specializing in capes, takes you to the Carrera de San Jerónimo, where some refreshment at the Museo del Jamón or the old-world Lhardys delicatessen may now be in order. Not far away up Calle Sevilla on Alcalá is the recently refurbished Real Academia de Bellas Artes, whose fine display of Spanish masters—Velázquez, El Greco, Murillo, and Goya among them—is second only to the Prado's magnificent collection.

The Puerta del Sol

A few more steps lead you into the Puerta del Sol (Gate of the Sun), among the major crossroads of Madrid and, indeed, of all of Spain. Kilometer distances in the country are still measured from this zero point. In 1986 the Puerta del Sol underwent an impressive remodelling to improve traffic flow and accommodate the revamped metro station beneath. The facades of its old houses were cleaned and repainted an attractive buff-pink, La Mariblanca, a copy of the statue which 250 years ago adorned a fountain in the square, is now back on an island in the center, and the much loved bear and *madroño* (strawberry tree) statue, symbol of the city, moved to the bottom of Calle Carmen. Formerly, the Puerta del Sol was famous for its bustling, all-night cafes and hectic traffic. Around it on the Calle de Alcalá and the Calle Arenal a generation of artists and intellectuals thrashed out the problems and theories of an as-yet non-industrial Spain in endless *tertulias* and talk-sessions. Unfortunately none of the cafes remain, and much of the action has moved on to other parts of town. However, the square is still a very lively intersection, as can be seen any evening around 8 o'clock, when the citizens of Madrid begin their ritual evening stroll, the *paseo.* On December 31 it fills with people cheering in the New Year as they watch the golden ball on top of the Dirección General de Seguridad building descending at midnight. Most still follow the old custom of trying to swallow one grape at each stroke of the clock. The large ministry building is now police headquarters. On one corner, the old Hotel París overlooking the square still keeps its vigil. On another is the perennially popular La Mallorquina bakery to which Madrileños with a sweet tooth have been flocking for pastries and sweets for decades. The tearoom upstairs commands a good view of the square.

The Puerta del Sol has been the scene of many stirring events and its history is closely linked to that of the country. The most famous incident that occurred here was the uprising in 1808 against the French, depicted in Goya's painting, *El Dos de Mayo*.

Arenal to the Opera and Calle Mayor

Proceeding on the Calle Arenal, you come on the left to the old Teatro Eslava, now one of the city's leading discos, and next to it the Church of San Ginés. Branching to the right off the Calle Arenal, along the Calle San Martin, you come to the Convent of the Descalzas Reales, founded in the 16th century by Princess Joan of Austria, daughter of Charles V and the Queen of Portugal. In 1559, the Franciscan sisters of Santa Clara moved into the building. Since then it has been lived in by many famous scions of royalty and to this day contains cloistered nuns in one part of the convent. Tours through other sections of the building are provided so that tourists can now admire the superb tapestries and assorted paintings by El Greco, Velázquez, Titian and Breughel the Elder that decorate its historical walls.

The building across the refurbished square (again with an underground garage) houses the Montepío, or Government Pawnbrokers Office; on another side of the Plaza de las Descalzas is a Portuguese fado restaurant and an excellent antiquarian bookshop, Luis Bardón.

Leaving the square at another exit, along the Calle de Trujillos, you come out eventually on the Plaza de Santo Domingo. Turn left down the Calle de la Bola at the far side, then right at the third street and you will emerge at the Plaza de la Marina Española, where you'll see a large building which was the Spanish Parliament in 1820. Originally it housed the Colegio de Doña María de Aragón, one of the earliest university-type institutions in Madrid. Under Franco it was the headquarters of the Falangist Movement, and today the building houses the Palace of the Senate.

You can then continue on to the Plaza de España, or down to the Plaza de Oriente facing the Royal Palace and back around the Opera into the Calle Arenal. Finally, you might like to cut up through one of the old narrow streets linking Arenal with the Calle Mayor, the "Main Street" of old Madrid. As you wander down this historic street, lined with old-fashioned shops selling books, curios and religious objects, look out for no. 50 where Lope de Vega was born in 1562, no. 75 the home of the the 17th-century playwright Calderón de la Barca, and no. 53 glorying in the name of *El Palacio de los Quesos* (Cheese Palace), a shop selling cheeses from all over Spain. Leaving the past behind you, this route brings you out once more in the bustling hub of Madrid, the Puerta del Sol.

Excursions from Madrid

Madrid is ideally situated for side trips as there are several towns and cities of outstanding interest lying within easy reach of the capital. Should you decide to keep your hotel base in Madrid, such places as Toledo, Aranjuez, Chinchón and Alcalá de Henares in New Castile, Avila and Segovia in Old Castile, and the nearby Monastery of El Escorial and the Valley of the Fallen in Madrid province, all lie within 100 km. (60 miles) of Madrid and are easily reached on day trips by private car, on public transport or, in the case of the larger cities, on tour buses which make regular excursions from the capital.

PRACTICAL INFORMATION FOR MADRID

GETTING TO TOWN FROM THE AIRPORT. The least expensive way to travel from the airport to the city center is to take the yellow airport bus to the Plaza Colon terminal on the Castellana. The journey takes around 20–30 mins. These buses leave the national and international termini at Barajas airport about every quarter hour from 5.15 A.M. to 12.45 A.M., and the fare, including baggage, is around 200 ptas. The Colon terminal is underground, taxis meet the buses, and it is only a short ride then to most of Madrid's hotels. Left luggage lockers are available at the terminal.

Taxi fares into central Madrid are not prohibitive. The average ride will cost what is on the meter (800–1,200 ptas.) plus surcharges (see *Getting Around* below). If your hotel is in northeast Madrid, on the airport side of town, best take a cab straight away; it will cost only a little more than the combined airport bus and cab ride.

TOURIST OFFICES. The main *Madrid Tourist Office* is on the ground floor of the Torre de Madrid on Plaza de España, near the beginning of Calle Princesa. It is open Mon. to Fri. 9–7, Sat. 10–2, closed Sun. There is another branch in the arrivals hall of the international terminal at Barajas airport, open Mon. to Fri. 8–8, Sat. 8–1, closed Sun. The *Municipal Tourist Office* is at Pza. Mayor 3 and is open 10–1.30 and 4–7; closed Sat. P.M. and Sun.

TELEPHONE CODE. The area code for the city of Madrid and for anywhere within Madrid province is (91). This should only be used when calling from outside Madrid province.

GETTING AROUND. By Metro. The subway is the easiest and quickest way of traveling around Madrid. There are ten lines and over 100 stations. The metro runs from 6 A.M. to about 1.30 A.M. Fares are 60 ptas., whatever distance you travel. Subway maps are available from ticket offices, hotel receptions, and the tourist offices at Barajas airport and on Pza. España. Plans of the metro are displayed in every station and in the trains themselves. Many ticket windows close at 10 P.M., so you will need change for the automatic machines at night or to be in possession of a *taco*.

Savings can be made by buying a *taco* of ten tickets with costs 410 ptas., or by buying a tourist card called *Metrotour* which allows you unlimited metro travel for 3 days at 675 ptas., or 5 consecutive days at 975 ptas.

By Bus. City buses are red and run between 6 A.M. and midnight. The fare is 60 ptas., or 85 ptas. for a transfer. The yellow microbuses, which are airconditioned, cost 70 ptas. Plans of the route followed are displayed at bus stops, and a map of all city bus routes is available free from EMT kiosks on Pza. Cibeles or Puerta del Sol. A *bono-bus,* good for ten rides, costs 370 ptas. and can be bought from an EMT (Empresa Municipal de Transportes) kiosk or any branch of the *Caja de Ahorros de Madrid.* Books of 20 tickets valid for microbuses are available from the kiosk on Plaza Cibeles, cost approximately 1,325 ptas. *Note:* These fares may well increase before 1989.

A good way to get acquainted with the city is to ride the *Circular* bus, marked with a red C. Its route passes several monuments and a number of the main streets, and a ride will cost you only one ticket. Another good ride is on bus 27 along Paseo del Prado, Paseo Recoletos and the Castellana.

By Taxi. Taxi meters start at 90 ptas., and the rate is 40 ptas. per kilometer. Supplements are 50 ptas. Sun. and holidays, 50 ptas. between 11 P.M. and 6 A.M., 50 ptas. when leaving bus or railroad stations, 50 ptas. to or from a bullring or soccer stadium on days when there is a fight or match, 75 ptas. to sporting facilities on the edge of Madrid, 150 ptas. to or from the airport, and 25 ptas. per suitcase. Taxis available for hire display a *Libre* sign during the day and a green light at night. Taxi stands are numerous or you can flag them down in the street. Taxis hold three or four passengers. Always check the driver puts his meter on when you start your ride. Tip 10% of the fare. To call a radio cab, call 247 8200/8500/8600.

RAILROAD STATIONS. There are three main stations. Chamartín in the north of the city is the departure point of most trains to the northwest, north and northeast (including Barcelona), and more and more trains to Valencia, Alicante, and Andalusia now leave from here too. Atocha at the far end of Paseo del Prado is the departure point for some trains to the Valencia region and Andalusia, and for most to Extremadura and Lisbon. Always be sure to check which station your train leaves from. An underground line connects Atocha with Chamartín. Trains to local destinations such as El Escorial, Avila, Segovia, Guadalajara, and Alcalá de Henares, can be boarded at either Atocha Apeadero or Chamartín Cercanías.

The other main station is Estacíon del Norte (North station, or Príncipe Pío), just off Cuesta de San Vicente. There you can get trains to Salamanca, Fuentes de Oñoro, Santiago de Compostela and La Coruña—and all other destinations in Galicia.

For train information and tickets in advance, go to the RENFE office at Alcalá 44, any of the main stations (Norte is the least crowded), or call 733 3000. The RENFE office is open Mon. to Fri. 8.30–2.30 and 4–5, and Sat. 8.30–1.30. The advance ticket offices at Chamartín and Atocha stations are open daily 9–9, and at Norte daily 9–7. There is also a RENFE office in the international arrivals hall at Barajas airport, open Mon. to Sat. 8–8, Sun. and fiestas 8–2. Travel agents displaying the blue and yellow RENFE sign also sell rail tickets, at no extra charge, and are a good bet in the crowded summer months.

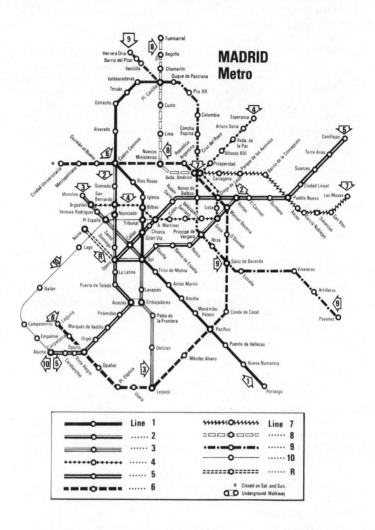

MADRID Metro

BUS STATIONS. Madrid has no central bus depot. There are two main bus stations, the Estación del Sur, Canarias 17 (tel. 468 4200), and Auto-Res, Pza. Conde de Casal 6 (tel. 251 6644). Buses to Aranjuez and Toledo, Alicante and many destinations in the south leave from the Estación del Sur; to Cuenca, Valencia, Extremadura and Salamanca from Auto-Res. Auto-Res has a central ticket and reservations office at Salud 19 just off Gran Vía. To other destinations, they leave from all over the city and it is best to enquire at the Tourist Offices.

As a guide to some of the more popular destinations, buses to Avila, Segovia, and La Granja are run by *La Sepulvedana* (tel. 247 5261) and leave from Paseo de la Florida 1; to Escorial and Valle de los Caidos by *Empresa Herranz* (tel. 243 8167) leaving from Isaac Peral 10; to Chinchón by *La Veloz* (tel. 227 2018) from Sánchez Bustillo 7.

HOTELS. Madrid offers a wide range of hotels, all the way from the millionaire *Ritz* to modest little pensions where you can get a room for around 2,000 ptas. a day. Many hotels are fully booked at Easter and around July and August. There are hotel accommodations services at Chamartín and Atocha stations, and at both the national and international airport termini. Or you can contact *La Brùjula* hotel agency (tel. 248 9705) at Torre de Madrid, 6th floor, in the Pza. de España; open 9 A.M.–9 P.M. All hotels have all rooms with bath unless stated otherwise. For a guide to prices, see *Hotels* in *Facts at Your Fingertips*.

Super Deluxe

Ritz, Plaza de la Lealtad 5 (tel. 521 2857). 156 rooms. Elegant and aristocratic with beautiful rooms, large suites and a justly famous dining room; Spain's most exclusive hotel. AE, DC, MC, V.

Villa Magna, Paseo de la Castellana 22 (tel. 261 4900). 194 rooms. The most luxurious of hotels and Madrid's international rendezvous. With restaurant, bars, banquet rooms and garage. Decor is elegant and tasteful; pleasant garden. AE, DC.

Deluxe

Barajas, Avda. de Logroño 305 (tel. 747 7700). 230 rooms. Luxurious airport hotel with pool; 24-hour courtesy bus service from airport. AE, DC, MC, V.

Castellana, Castellana 49 (tel. 410 0200). 311 rooms. Elegant hotel right on the Castellana, just above Plaza Emilio Castelar. AE, DC, MC, V.

Eurobuilding, Padre Damián 23 (tel. 457 1700). 420 rooms. An enormous hotel with two entrances, one on Padre Damían and one on Juan Ramón Jiménez. With a pool, gardens, several bars, nightclub; *Balthasar* restaurant and *Le Relais* coffeeshop. Popular with Americans and businessmen. AE, DC, MC, V.

Fenix, Hermosilla 2 (tel. 431 6700). 216 rooms. A new 4-star hotel located near Plaza Colón between the Castellana and Serrano.

Holiday Inn, in the Azca Center off Calle Orense (tel. 456 7014). 313 rooms. Part of the big shopping and entertainment complex close to the Castellana in the north of the city; decor is luxurious, and there is a pool, sauna and gymnasium, executive suites, banqueting salons, conference rooms, underground garage, an Italian-style cafeteria, and a steak house. AE, DC, MC, V.

Meliá Castilla, Capitán Haya 43 (tel. 571 2211). 936 rooms. Madrid's largest hotel in the increasingly fashionable and gourmet area in the north of the city. It has a pool, and also boasts the *Scala* nightclub, one of Madrid's leading nightspots. AE, DC, MC, V.

Meliá Madrid, Princesa 27 (tel. 241 8200). 266 rooms on 25 floors. Well-appointed hotel just up from Plaza España. AE, DC, MC, V.

Miguel Angel, Miguel Angel 31 (tel. 442 8199). 305 rooms. Luxurious hotel with elegantly appointed public and private rooms. Conveniently located in smart area, it has fast become a favorite. Pool. AE, DC, MC, V.

Mindanao, San Francisco de Sales 15 (tel. 449 5500). 289 rooms. In residential area close to the University City in the northwest of the city. With pools and sauna. *Domayo* restaurant offers regional Spanish dishes and French cuisine, while the *Keynes* bar is a favorite spot for Spanish society. AE, DC, MC, V.

Monte Real, Arroyo Fresno 17 (tel. 216 2140). 77 rooms. In the Puerta de Hierro section out of town, and the last word in ritzy elegance, quiet and dignified. With pool and large gardens, and just 1 km. from Puerta de Hierro golf club. AE, DC, MC, V.

Palace, Plaza de las Cortes 7 (tel. 429 7551). 518 rooms. Dignified turn-of-the-century hotel, a slightly down-market step-sister of the nearby *Ritz* and long a favorite of politicians and journalists. Its *belle époque* decor—especially the glass dome over the lounge—is superb, if now somewhat faded in parts—some of the rooms are in need of refurbishing. Very central, opposite parliament and close to the Prado Museum. AE, V.

Princesa Plaza, Serrano Jover 3 (tel. 242 3500). 406 rooms. Modern hotel on corner of Princesa, a focal point for Madrid businessmen. AE, DC, MC, V.

Tryp Palacio, Paseo de la Castellana 57 (tel. 442 5100). 182 rooms. Totally renovated in 1988 to high standards of luxury and comfort; now the flagship of the big Tryp chain. AE, DC, V.

Wellington, Velázquez 8 (tel. 275 4400). 257 rooms. An old favorite in the Salamanca district close to Retiro Park, attracting a solid, conservative clientele. It has long been a focal point of the bull-fighting world, and in the May San Isidro festivals plays host to famous toreros, breeders and bullring critics. AE, DC, MC, V.

Expensive

Aitana, Castellana 152 (tel. 250 7107). 111 rooms. A comfortable, modern hotel much favored by businessmen, on the northern reaches of the Castellana close to the Azca Center and the Bernabeu soccer stadium. AE, DC, V.

Alcalá, Alcalá 66 (tel. 435 1060). 153 rooms. Convenient for Retiro Park and Goya shopping area. Good value. AE, DC, MC, V.

Arosa, Calle de la Salud 21 (tel. 232 1600). 126 rooms. Elegant older hotel between the Gran Vía and Plaza del Carmen. Helpful, friendly service. AE, DC, MC, V.

Calatrava, Tutor 1 (tel. 241 9880). 99 rooms With disco, private garage. Close to Plaza de España. AE, DC, MC, V.

Chamartín, above Chamartín station (tel. 733 7001). 378 rooms. Large, modern hotel, part of the huge government-financed Chamartín complex. Its size makes it rather impersonal, and it is a long way from the center, though convenient for the station. AE, DC, MC, V.

El Coloso, Leganitos 13 (tel. 248 7600). 84 rooms. Modern, well-appointed hotel, centrally located just off Gran Vía and Plaza España. AE, DC, MC, V.

Convención, O'Donnell 53 (tel. 274 6800). 790 rooms. A huge hotel, opened in 1978 near Goya shopping area. Caters largely for business travelers and international conventions. AE, DC, MC, V.

Cuzco, Castellana 133 (tel. 456 0600). 330 rooms. Modern and pleasant, close to the Bernabeu stadium. AE, DC, MC, V.

Emperador, Gran Vía 53 (tel. 247 2800). 231 rooms. Popular, comfortable, older hotel on corner of San Bernardo. Rooftop pool and terrace with good views. AE, DC, MC, V.

Emperatriz, Lopez de Hoyos 4 (tel. 413 6511). 170 rooms. Attractive, stylish hotel just off the Castellana. Good service; recommended. AE, DC, MC, V.

Florida Norte, Paseo de la Florida 5 (tel. 241 6190). 399 rooms. Pleasant modern hotel in west of town close to North Station; a little geared to tour groups. AE, DC, MC, V.

Los Galgos, Claudio Coello 139 (tel. 262 4227). 359 rooms. Comfortable; rooms well-appointed and most with balcony. Near Serrano shopping area. One of the most expensive in this category. AE, DC, MC, V.

Gran Atlanta, Comandante Zorita 34 (tel. 253 5900). 180 rooms. Recent, functional hotel close to the Azca Center on Orense. Decor is dark and gloomy in typically Spanish style, but the hotel is comfortable and the service friendly. AE, DC, MC, V.

Gran Hotel Velázquez, Velázquez 62 (tel. 275 2800). 130 rooms. Oldish, but comfortable and spacious with some style, though it has begun to take tour groups. It is a regular venue for Madrileños, who favor its banqueting rooms for their weddings, while its bar frequently hosts one of the few remaining teatime *tertulias.* AE, DC, MC, V.

Gran Hotel Versalles, Covarrubias 4 (tel. 447 5700). 145 rooms. Functional but pleasant hotel with regular clientele, located in the Alonso Martínez area. AE, DC, V.

Mayorazgo, Flor Baja 3 (tel. 247 2600). 200 rooms. Pleasant hotel tucked away in a side street off Gran Vía. AE, DC, MC, V.

Plaza, Plaza de España (tel. 247 1200). 306 rooms. Elegant, central hotel very popular with Americans. Rooftop pool, with superb views. One of the most expensive in this category. AE, DC, MC, V.

El Prado, Calle del Prado 11 (tel. 429 3568). 45 rooms. Modern comfortable hotel in an old part of town close to Plaza Santa Ana. AE, DC, V.

Sanvy, Goya 3 (tel. 276 0800). 141 rooms. Recently renovated hotel just off Castellana. AE, DC, MC, V.

Suecia, Marqués de Casa Riera 4 (tel. 231 6900). 64 rooms. Once patronized by Hemingway, this hotel boasts a good Scandinavian restaurant. Close to Cibeles and next to the Teatro Bellas Artes just off Alcalá. AE, DC, MC, V.

Moderate

Anaco, Tres Cruces 3 (tel. 222 4604). 37 rooms. Small, modern and comfortable hotel just off Plaza del Carmen. Very central. AE, DC, MC, V.

Carlos V, Maestro Vitoria 5 (tel. 231 4100). 67 rooms. Pleasant old hotel, centrally located just off main shopping street. AE, DC, MC, V.

Colón, Dr. Esquerdo 117 (tel. 273 5900). 385 rooms. Large 4-star hotel with good rates, though a little out of the center. AE, DC, MC, V.

Liabeny, Salud 3 (tel. 232 5306). 209 rooms. Comfortable, functional 4-star hotel, centrally located near Pza. del Carmen and main shopping area. AE, MC, V.

Opera, Cuesta Santo Domingo 2 (tel. 241 2800). 81 rooms. Modern and very comfortable, centrally located in the old part of the city close to the Opera and only a short walk from the Royal Palace.

Principe Pío, Cuesta San Vicente 14 (tel. 247 8000). 157 rooms. Pleasant hotel near the Royal Palace and North station. Good service. AE, MC, V.

Regina, Alcalá 19 (tel. 521 4725). 142 rooms. Elegant, older hotel, recently renovated. Overlooks Calle Sevilla and close to Puerta del Sol.

Rex, Gran Vía 43 (tel. 247 4800). 146 rooms. Good, smallish hotel on corner of Silva, just down from Callao. AE, DC, V.

Serrano, Marqués de Villamejor 8 (tel. 435 5200). 34 rooms. Small hotel in smart area between Calle Serrano and the Castellana.

Victoria, Plaza del Angel 7 (tel. 231 4500). 110 rooms. Stylish old hotel with stained-glass windows and decorative cupola, pleasantly located between Plaza Santa Ana and Plaza del Angel. Long a favorite of bullfighters and aficionados. It will appeal more to those who are seeking old world charm rather than modern comforts. AE, DC, MC, V.

Zurbano, Zurbano 81 (tel. 441 5500). 262 rooms. Modern, elegant hotel in a fashionable area. High standards. AE, MC, V.

Inexpensive

Asturias, Sevilla 2 (tel. 429 6676). 175 rooms. Old-world charm, but on a rather busy intersection overlooking Plaza Canalejas, just up from Puerta del Sol. Much-needed renovations are underway—check your room is one of those already refurbished before booking. AE, DC, V.

Clíper, Chinchilla 6 (tel. 231 1700). 52 rooms. Good-value hotel on a narrow street off the central part of Gran Vía, between Callao and Red de San Luis. AE, MC, V.

Francisco I, Arenal 15 (tel. 248 0204). 58 rooms. Old hotel with modernized decor, halfway between Puerta del Sol and the Opera. Top-floor restaurant is recommended.

Inglés, Echegaray 10 (tel. 429 6551). 58 rooms. An old budget favorite. Location is somewhat shabby but convenient, close to (I) restaurants and Puerta del Sol. AE, DC, MC, V.

Metropol, Montera 47 (tel. 521 2935). 72 rooms. Well renovated hostel with high standards on corner of Gran Vía.

Moderno, Arenal 2 (tel. 231 0900). 98 rooms. Renovated old hotel in a very central position just off Puerta del Sol. Traffic can be noisy. AE, V.

Mora, Paseo del Prado 32 (tel. 239 7407). 42 rooms. Convenient to Prado and not far from Atocha Station.

París, Alcalá 2 (tel. 521 6496). 114 rooms. A delightful hotel full of stylish, old-fashioned appeal; currently being renovated. Right on Puerta del Sol. DC, V.

Regente, Mesonero Romanos 9 (tel. 521 2941). 124 rooms. Simple, old-fashioned hotel close to Gran Vía and the pedestrian shopping streets of Callao. Low rates and reasonable value for the price. AE, MC, V.

Motels

Los Angeles (M), on the N-IV to Andalusia (tel. 696 3815). 46 rooms. 14 km. from town. With pool and tennis.

Avion (M), Avda. Aragón 345 (tel. 747 6222). 64 rooms, pool. 14 km. out on N-II. Convenient for those driving in from Barcelona.

Los Olivos (I), on the N-IV to Andalusia (tel. 695 6700). 100 rooms. 12 km. out of town. With pool.

Youth Hostels. There are two youth hostels in Madrid: the biggest is **Richard Schirrmann,** in Casa del Campo park (tel. 463 5699), with 120 beds; the other, more central, one is **Santa Cruz de Marcenado,** at No. 28 on the street of the same name (tel. 247 4532), with 78 beds. The nearest metro to the former is Lago, to the latter it's Argüelles, San Bernardo or Ventura Rodriguez.

RESTAURANTS. If Madrid is your first stop in Spain, you may feel ravenous before you see any signs of food on the way. Normal meal hours in the capital are even later than in the rest of Spain—where they are already later than elsewhere in Europe! Few people think of eating lunch in the capital before 2 P.M., 3 P.M. is quite normal, and 3.30 not at all unusual; and while most Spanish diners begin to eat at 9.30 or 10, 10.30 is more usual for Madrileños. However, if you just can't wait, a few restaurants and most hotels open their dining rooms earlier for the benefit of foreigners, or you can get a snack in any of the numerous cafeterias around town.

Madrid is plentifully provided with restaurants of all classes and of all types. The truly cosmopolitan mix includes French, German, Italian, Chinese, Mexican, Latin American, Japanese, Moroccan, Polish, Russian and American cuisine—not to mention Asturian, Basque, Galician, Valencian, Catalan, as well, of course, as Castilian.

All restaurants, except those in the top 4– and 5–fork classifications, are theoretically required to offer a *menu del día* (although not all of them do, and the practice is becoming less and less common), comprising a 3-course, fixed-price set meal, including bread, wine and dessert. Though there is often a choice, unless the fixed meal happens to be exactly what you want, you may well prefer to compound your own *menu*—though this is almost certain to prove more expensive.

A word of warning: many of the best-known restaurants close for a month in summer, and some are also closed in Easter week. Many close on Sundays, and some also on one other day during the week; be sure to check.

For an approximate guide to prices, see *Restaurants* in *Facts at Your Fingertips.*

Deluxe

El Amparo, Puigcerdá 8 (entrance Jorge Juan 10) (tel. 431 6456). Elegant restaurant with the emphasis on Basque traditional and *nouvelle cuisine.* Imaginative dishes and pleasing decor. Closed Sat. lunch, Sun., Easter week and Aug. AE, V.

Clara's, Arrieta 2 (tel. 542 0071). Superb food in the classic setting of a fine old building on the corner of Plaza Isabel II. Is considered one of the very best gourmet attractions in town. Closed Sat. lunch and Sun. AE, MC, V.

Club 31, Alcalá 58 (tel. 231 0092). International cuisine and Spanish regional dishes. Under same management as *Jockey* and with same high standards. Ideal for late diners as orders are taken uptil midnight. Closed Aug. AE, DC, MC, V.

Horcher, Alfonso XII 6 (tel. 522 0731). One of Madrid's most famous—and expensive—restaurants. Service is excellent, ladies are even brought a cushion to rest their feet on! Specialties are Central European dishes and game. Closed Sun. AE, DC.

Jockey, Amador de los Ríos 6 (tel. 419 1003). A long-standing favorite and one of the best. Closed Sun. and Aug. AE, DC, MC, V.

Ritz Hotel, Plaza de la Lealtad 5 (tel. 521 2857). A considerable part of the six million dollars recently spent on renovating the Ritz went on refurbishing the dining room, which is now resplendent with silk curtains and marble columns. The hotel garden is probably the most attractive place to dine in summer. AE, DC, MC, V.

Zalacaín, Alvarez de Baena 4 (tel. 261 4840). Considered Spain's best restaurant by gourmets. In a private villa with elegant decor and topnotch food; highest recommendations. Closed Sat. lunch, Sun., Easter week and Aug. AE.

Expensive

Al-Mounia, Recoletos 5 (tel. 435 0828). Outstanding Moroccan restaurant specializing in North African cuisine, Moroccan pastries and mint tea. Closed Sun., Mon. and in Aug. AE, DC, MC, V.

Annapurna, Zurbano 5 (tel. 410 7727). One of Madrid's top Indian restaurants. Superb cuisine and atmosphere. Closed Sun. AE, DC, MC, V.

Bajamar, Gran Vía 78 (tel. 248 5903). Offers some of the best seafood in town in its downstairs dining room. AE, DC, MC, V.

El Bodegón, Pinar 15 (tel. 262 8844). Small restaurant with outstanding food and a regular, faithful clientele. Closed Sun. and in Aug. AE, DC, MC, V.

Cabo Mayor, Juan Hurtado de Mendoza 11 (tel. 250 8776). Imaginative cuisine. Closed Sun., and last 2 weeks of Aug. AE, DC, V.

Café de Oriente, Plaza de Oriente 2 (tel. 241 3974). Stylish restaurant. In summer, you can dine on a terrace overlooking the Teatro Real and the Royal Palace. Closed Sat. lunch, Sun. and Aug. AE, DC, V.

El Cenador del Prado, Calle del Prado 4 (tel. 429 1549). Imaginative cuisine and beautiful decor. Closed Sat. lunch, Sun. and Aug. AE, DC, MC, V.

Combarro, Reina Mercedes 12 (tel. 254 7784). Outstanding Galician restaurant with superb fish and seafood though meat dishes are also excellent. Closed Sun. and Aug. AE, MC, V.

Las Cuatro Estaciones, General Ibáñez Ibero 5 (tel. 253 6305). Decor and menu to match the four seasons. A novel and attractive restaurant but the prices are high. Closed Sat. and Sun., and in Aug. AE, DC, V.

La Dorada, Orense 64 (tel. 270 2004). Outstanding seafood restaurant serving fish flown in daily from Costa del Sol. Closed Sun. and Aug. AE, DC, V.

La Gabarra, Sto Domingo de Silos 6 (tel. 458 7897). Currently very fashionable, with superb Basque cuisine and outstanding service. Closed Sat. lunch, Sun. and Aug. AE, DC, MC, V.

Gure Etxea, Plaza de la Paja 12 (tel. 265 6149). An excellent Basque restaurant, much praised by readers. Closed Sun. and Aug. AE, DC, V.

Irízar, Jovellanos 3 (tel. 231 4569). A renowned and luxurious restaurant serving Basque cuisine with some French and Navarre nouvelle influence; a good place to go for a treat. Closed Sat. lunch and Sun. dinner. AE, DC, V.

Itxaso, Capitán Haya 58 (tel. 450 6412). Basque restaurant with elegant, somber decor, close to Hotel Meliá Castilla. Its fish and seafood dishes are outstanding. Closed Sun. and Aug. AE, DC, MC, V.

Korynto, Preciados 36 (tel. 521 5965). A long-established seafood restaurant in the heart of Madrid. Prices are high but the freshness and quality are tops. AE, DC, MC, V.

Lhardy, San Jerónimo 8 (tel. 522 2207). A veritable old Madrid institution. Worth a visit as much for its old-world decor as for its long-famed cuisine. Closed Sun. and in Aug. AE, DC, V.

El Mentidero de la Villa, Sto Tomé 7 (tel. 419 5506). Stylish restaurant whose cuisine shows Japanese and French influences. Well recommended. Closed Sat. lunch, Sun., and 2 weeks in Aug. V.

New Yorker, Amador de los Ríos 1 (tel. 410 1522). Fashionable restaurant with an international menu and a fine collection of modern Spanish art. Very popular with businessmen. Closed Sat. lunch, Sun., and mid-Aug. to mid-Sept. AE, DC, MC, V.

Nicolasa, Velázquez 150 (tel. 261 9985). Top Basque dishes served by owners of its namesake in San Sebastián. The decor is most attractive and the waitresses wear Basque costume. Closed Sun. and Aug. AE, DC, MC, V.

O'Pazo, Reina Mercedes 20 (tel. 253 2333). An elegant Galician restaurant with a reputation for some of the best seafood in Madrid. Closed Sun. and Aug. AE, DC, MC, V.

El Pescador, José Ortega y Gasset 75 (tel. 402 1290). Prime-quality fish dishes and good service. Closed Sun. and mid-Aug. through mid-Sept.

Platerías, Plaza Santa Ana 11 (tel. 522 6334). Good menu based on fresh market produce. Daily specials are recommended. Closed Sun. and Aug. AE, DC, MC, V.

Príncipe de Viana, Manuel de Falla 5 (tel. 259 1448). Fashionable restaurant with Basque, Navarre and international dishes. Closed Sat. lunch, Sun., Easter week and Aug. AE, DC, MC, V.

Sacha, Juan Hurtado de Mendoza 11 (tel. 457 7200). Cozy, with exquisite decor; outdoor dining in summer. Closed Sun., Easter week and Aug. AE, DC, MC, V.

Señorío de Bértiz, Comandante Zorita 6 (tel. 233 2757). Managed by former members of *Zalacaín* team, it offers outstanding cuisine, service and decor. Closed Sat. lunch, Sun. and Aug. AE, DC, V.

Solchaga, Plaza de Alonso Martínez 2 (tel. 447 1496). Several charming diningrooms of distinctive character resembling an old-fashioned private house rather than a restaurant. Closed Sat. lunch and Sun. AE, DC, MC, V.

La Trainera, Lagasca 60 (tel. 276 8035). A good, reliable fish and seafood restaurant with a regular clientele. Closed Sun. and Aug. V.

Moderate

Alkalde, Jorge Juan 10 (tel. 276 3359). Cave-like rooms, pleasant atmosphere, excellent food and service. One of Madrid's most consistently good restaurants. Closed Sat. night, and Sun. in July and Aug. AE, DC, V.

Apriori, Argensola 7 (tel. 410 3671). Inventive dishes in relaxed informal setting; pleasant decor, English spoken. Closed Sat. lunch and Sun.

Armstrong's, Jovellanos 5 (tel. 522 4230). Charming English-owned restaurant opposite Teatro Zarzuela. Imaginative cuisine includes good choice of salads, brunch on weekends and teatime. Opens for dinner at 6 P.M. Closed Sun. evening and Mon. AE, DC, MC, V.

Balzac, Moreto 7 (tel. 239 1922). Serves its own original style of Basque cuisine, and is especially well-known for its desserts. Closed Sat. lunch and Sun. AE, DC, V.

La Barraca, Reina 29 (tel. 232 7154). A cheerful Valencian restaurant just behind the Loewe leather store on Gran Vía; it's *the* place for *paella* other than Valencia itself. AE, DC, MC, V.

El Callejón, Ternera 6 (tel. 522 5401). An old Hemingway favorite just off Preciados. Closed Sat. AE, DC, MC, V.

Carmencita, Libertad 16 (tel. 231 6612). Charming old Madrid favorite serving mixture of nouvelle and traditional dishes. Well worth a visit. Closed Sun. V.

Casablanca, Barquillo 29 (tel. 521 1568). Popular and original restaurant; well recommended. Closed Sun. and Aug. AE, DC, MC, V.

Casa Botín, Cuchilleros 17 (tel. 266 4217). Just off Plaza Mayor, this is Madrid's oldest restaurant, having been catering to diners since 1725. It was a great favorite with Hemingway, and though popular with Spaniards, too, it is definitely aimed at tourists. Service is pleasant and efficient, the food reasonably good—and, though it has become a tourist mecca, it is still worth a visit. Two sittings for dinner, at 8 and at 10.30; booking essential. AE, DC, MC, V.

Casa Lucio, Cava Baja 35 (tel. 265 3252). Characterful restaurant near Plaza Mayor, serving topnotch Spanish fare (steaks, lamb, eel, etc.) in mesón setting in a maze of small rooms. Personalized service, excellent value. Closed Sat. lunch and Aug. AE, DC, V.

Casa Paco, Puerta Cerrada 11 (tel. 266 3166). This atmospheric old tavern is a perennial favorite and renowned for its steaks. Limited space and there is nearly always a line. Closed Sun. and Aug. DC, V.

El Cuchi, Cuchilleros 3 (tel. 266 4424). A colorful dinner awaits you in this fun-packed mesón with more than just a hint of Mexico to it; just off the Plaza Mayor, and the one place "where Hemingway *didn't* eat." AE, DC, MC, V.

Fuente Real, Fuentes 1 (tel. 248 6613). This stylish restaurant, tucked away between Mayor and Arenal, offers imaginative cuisine and original decor—it's half way between a turn-of-the-century private house and a museum packed with personal mementoes such as antique dolls, Indian figures, and Mexican Christmas decorations.

Hogar Gallego, Plaza Com. Morenas 3 just off Calle Mayor (tel. 248 6404). Galician restaurant specializing in seafood. Outdoor dining in summer. Closed Sun. evening and most of Aug.

Horno de Santa Teresa, Sta. Teresa 12 (tel. 419 0245). Traditional old-style restaurant famous for good service and classic cuisine. Closed Sat. and Aug. AE, DC, V.

House of Ming, Castellana 74 (tel. 261 9827). Excellent Chinese delicacies served up in a luxurious setting. Closed Aug. AE, DC, V.

Mesón San Javier, Conde 3 (tel. 248 0925). Traditional old favorite tucked away behind City Hall. AE, DC, V.

La Taberna del Alabardero, Felipe V 6 (tel. 247 2577). Alongside the Teatro Real with atmospheric bar and several small dining rooms specializing in Basque and French dishes. Closed late-Aug. AE, DC, MC, V.

La Toja, Siete de Julio 3 (tel. 266 4664). Just off Plaza Mayor and specializing in seafood. A good place to try paella. Opens for dinner at 8. AE, DC, V.

Valentín, San Alberto 3 (tel. 521 1638). Longtime rendezvous of the influential and the famous, from bullfighters to literati. Intimate decor, good service, standard Spanish dishes. Close to Puerta del Sol. AE, DC, MC, V.

Inexpensive

La Bola, Bola 5 (tel. 247 6930). Plenty of old-world charm in this atmospheric restaurant that has been in the same family since the early 1800s. Closed Sun.

El Buda Feliz, Tudescos 5 (tel. 232 4475). Excellent Chinese restaurant near Plaza Callao. AE, DC, MC, V.

Casa Ciriaco, Mayor 84 (tel. 248 0620). An atmospheric old standby where the Madrid of 50 years ago lives on. Closed Wed. and in Aug.

Casa Ricardo, Fernando el Católico 31 (tel. 447 6119). One of Madrid's oldest *tabernas,* boasting bullfighting decor and excellent home-cooking. Closed Sun.

El Granero de Lavapies, on Calle Argumosa, near Lavapies metro. Vegetarian restaurant, open for lunch only; closed Sun.

El Luarqués, Ventura de la Vega 16 (tel. 429 6174). Decorated with photos of the picturesque port of Luarca on the north coast, this popular restaurant is always packed with Madrileños who recognize its sheer good value. *Fabada asturiana* and *arroz con leche* among the Asturian specialties on the menu. Closed Sun. evening, Mon., and in Aug.

La Quinta del Sordo, Sacramento 10 (tel. 248 1852). An old favorite just off Calle Mayor, though it's rather overpatronized by budget tour groups. AE, DC.

Terra a Nosa, Cava San Miguel 3 (tel. 247 1175). Typical Galician bistro near Plaza Mayor. Popular and crowded, with bags of atmosphere.

Outside Madrid

The following are all (E) and ideally suited for dinner on a summer's evening:

El Mesón, 13 km. (eight miles) out on C607, the road to Colmenar Viejo (tel. 734 1019). In an attractive rustic setting. AE, DC, MC, V.

Porto Novo, on the N-VI to Galicia, about ten km. (six miles) from Madrid (tel. 207 0173). Closed Sun. night. AE, DC, V.

Rancho Texano, on the N-II to Barcelona at km. 12 (tel. 747 4736). Very popular American steakhouse specializing in charcoal-grilled steaks and Baked Alaska. Closed Sun. evening. AE, DC, MC, V.

Los Remos, on the N-VI to Galicia, at km. 13 (tel. 207 7230). A longtime favorite with Madrileños. Superb fish and seafood, and some meat dishes too. This one is the best. Closed Sun. evening and last 2 weeks in Aug. AE, DC, V.

CAFETERIAS. For snacks a good place to go is one of the numerous cafeterias—by which we do not mean the self-service type of establishment found in the United States and Britain, but rather, smart cafes with table service. Here, you can order sandwiches, pastries, even simple meals, *platos combinados,* etc., and drink from a choice of fruit juices and other soft drinks, coffee—as well as beer, wine and liquor. Cafeterias are open from early in the morning until at least midnight. They are the best place for breakfast and mid-morning coffee, or for a meal outside restaurant hours. Reliable chains with branches all over Madrid are **California, Manila, Morrison** and **Nebraska.**

TRADITIONAL CAFES. Cafe Comercial, Glorieta de Bilbao 7. An old-time cafe that has not changed much over the last three decades; always crowded.

Café Gijón. Paseo de Recoletos 21. The best and most famous of the remaining cafes of old. It is still a hangout for writers and artists, carrying on a tradition dating back to the turn of the century, when the cafe was a meeting place of the literati. Tables outside on the main avenue in summer.

Cafe Lyon, Alcalá 57. Charming, old-fashioned decor; just up from Cibeles.

Cafe Metropolitano, Glorieta de Cuatro Caminos. Student atmosphere.

Cafe Viena, Luisa Fernanda 23. Done out like an old-time cafe, you can dine here evenings to the accompaniment of piano music.

The Embassy, corner of Castellana and Ayala. Elegant pastry shop and tearoom with a vast assortment of sandwiches, canapés and pastries.

La Mallorquina, on Puerta del Sol between Mayor and Arenal. An old-world pastry shop with a tea salon, where the incredible, probably doomed, tea ritual is enacted between 6 and 7 P.M.

FAST FOOD. American hamburger joints such as **McDonalds, Burger King** and **Wendy's** have mushroomed in Madrid over the last few years, and can now be found all over the city. In some cases, they have been obliged to keep to the traditional Spanish decor, which makes for some interesting not to say bizarre juxtapositions—the McDonalds on the corner of Montera and Gran Vía, and the Burger King on Arenal just off Puerta del Sol, are especially worth seeing. **Pizza Hut** also has a couple of branches, at Orense 11 and Plaza Santa Barbara 8. **VIPS** is a popular chain of cafes, much patronized by the young of Madrid, that serves hamburgers, club sandwiches, and ice cream into the small hours of the morning. It's Madrid's answer to the drugstore, and branches can be found all over town.

BARS AND CAFES. If you want to spend an enjoyable, typically Spanish, evening, then go bar-hopping in any of the following areas. You'll find many bars and cafes where you can sample the local wine, or have a glass of beer, and choose from any number of tapas. Stylish cafes with old-time piano music or chamber music are also very much in vogue, as are jazz cafes.

The **Plaza Santa Bárbara** area just off Alonso Martínez is currently one of the liveliest nighttime areas. Begin in the plaza itself, then stroll along any of the adjacent streets such as Santa Teresa, Orellana, Campoamor, Fernando VI or Regueros, and you will not be disappointed by the vast range of bars on offer. To mention just a few:

Café de Paris, Sta. Teresa 12. Stylish loud music bar currently very much in vogue.

Café Universal, Fernando VI 13. Very fashionable, serving good cocktails.

Cervecería Internacional, Regueros 8. A must for beer-lovers. A great selection of foreign beers and even a souvenir shop.

Cervecería Santa Bárbara, Plaza Sta. Bárbara 8. Atmospheric and very popular beerhall with a good range of tapas.

Bar Haddok, Orellana 14. Lively modern bar, very crowded at night.

Nicandra, Orellana 1. Smart bar ideal for a pre-dinner drink.

Rebote, Campoamor 13. One of the most popular in the area.

The **Malasaña** area around Bilbao and Fuencarral was the "in" place in the early '80s for Madrid's youth and it still boasts countless interesting cafes and bars open till the small hours around Plaza Dos de Mayo and Calles Ruiz, San Andrés and Vicente Ferrer. However, the area has become the center for Madrid's drug dealers and heroin addicts, and for this reason its popularity is now on the wane and it is best avoided, especially at night.

Not far away on the opposite side of the Glorieta de Bilbao, much of the action has now moved to the **Calle Cardenal Cisneros** which is packed with atmospheric tapa bars; the nighttime scene here is lively and much safer.

The **Huertas** area around Calle de las Huertas, leading from Paseo del Prado to Plaza del Angel, is another lively nighttime locale chockablock with cafes offering folk or chamber music and several colorful tapa bars.

El Elhecho, Huertas 56. Very popular. Turn-of-the-century decor with potted ferns *(elhechos);* evenings there's chamber or piano music.

La Fídula, Huertas 57. Another stylish cafe with (usually chamber) music nightly at 11.

The nearby **Calle Santa María** also has good bars such as **Café Ombu** at no. 3, **Harpo's** at no. 36, and **El Ratón** at no. 42.

The **Orense** development around the Azca Center has proved a magnet for the teenagers and the young of Madrid, who congregate here in the evenings in the many fast-food joints, discos, *whiskerías* and *coctelerías.* It is perhaps not worth making a special trip to, but if your hotel happens to be in the area, and you are young—or young at heart—then you could do worse than take a look.

The traditional mesones area just off **Plaza Mayor** on Cava San Miguel and Calle Cuchilleros has long been famous. Do the rounds of the mesones with names like the **Tortilla, Champiñón, Boquerón, Huevo,** etc., most of them named after their particular specialty, and on a busy night you may well come across someone playing the guitar and singing, or be serenaded by the wandering *tuna* minstrels.

For some of the oldest bars in Madrid, try the streets around the **Rastro.** Here you'll find such durable retreats as the **Mesón de Paredes, Jesús y María, Magdalena, Cascorro,** and **La Esquinita**—the latter, a bar with magnificent tapas, beer served in mugs, and roast chicken. The **Taverna de Antonio Sánchez,** at Mesón de Paredes 13, is an old mesón just off Plaza de Tirso de Molina, that first opened its doors in 1850 and was once a hangout for bullfighters. Its decor includes the head of the bull that killed Antonio Sánchez, son of the owner, and some drawings by Zuloaga.

The old, narrow streets between **Puerta del Sol** and **Plaza Santa Ana** are packed with crowded, colorful tapa bars. Wander along Espoz y Mina, Victoria, Cruz, Núñez de Arce, and Echegaray, and enter any bar that takes your fancy. Don't miss out on the alleyway, Pasaje Matheu, between

Victoria and Espoz y Mina, where there are several favorites. Here are but a handful of the many places on offer:

Cafe Central, Plaza del Angel 10. Atmospheric, old-style cafe with jazz, folk and classical music. Often has live jazz between 10 and midnight.

Cervecería Alemana, Plaza Santa Ana 6. Popular beer hall over 100 years old, originally founded by Germans. Once patronized by (who else?!) Hemingway, and now by tourists.

Cuevas de Sésamo, Príncipe 7. Popular basement piano bar.

Los Gabrieles, Echegaray 17. Magnificent old *bodega* with four bars whose superb ceramic decor has been expertly restored.

La Trucha, Manuel Fernández y González 3. Colorful and atmospheric, with strings of garlic and giant hams hanging from the ceiling. Specialties are *trucha navarra,* trout stuffed with ham and garlic, and *rabo del toro,* bull's tail.

Viva Madrid, Manuel Fernández y González 7. Beautiful old bar, currently one of Madrid's most popular meeting places.

NIGHTLIFE. Since Franco's death, the nightclub scene in Madrid has flung off all restraint and the city now throbs with shows featuring striptease, topless dancers, drag and every kind of no-holds-barred entertainment. Pick-up bars, ranging from the old-time standbys to flashy, elegant new places in the northern Castellana area, have multiplied enormously over recent years. Travelers who knew the tame Spain of a few years ago will be amazed by the change—all censorship has been discarded.

Florida Park, in Retiro Park (tel. 273 7804). Entrance opposite Calle Ibiza. You can have dinner here, and the shows often feature ballet or Spanish dance. Open from 9.30 to 3.30 in the morning, daily except Sun., with shows at 11.

Lola, Costanilla de San Pedro 11 (tel. 265 8801). The newest arrival on the Madrid night scene. Dinner at 9.30 followed by cabaret and dancing till around 4 A.M. The food is vastly superior to most nightclubs and the show has proved very popular.

Madrid's Casino, 28 km. (17 miles) out, on the N-VI road to La Coruña, at Torrelodones (tel. 859 0312). One of the largest casinos in Europe and offering French and American roulette, chemin de fer, baccarat, and blackjack. Three restaurants, six bars, and a nightclub with cabaret. Open 5 P.M. to 4 A.M. Free transportation service from Plaza de España 6.

La Scala, Rosario Pino 7, in Hotel Meliá Castilla (tel. 450 4400). Madrid's top nightclub, with dinner, dancing and cabaret at 8.30, and a second, less expensive, around midnight. Open till 4 A.M.

Discos. These are numerous and very popular in Madrid. Some charge an entrance fee, usually starting around 1,000 ptas., which includes your first drink; others just charge for your drinks. Most have two sessions: *tarde* from around 7.30–10.30, and *noche* from 11.30 onwards. Gay discos and transvestite clubs are also thick on the ground. For a complete listing, read the weekly *Guía del Ocio.* The following are just a few of the better-known ones:

Boccacio, Marqués de la Enseñada 16. A long-standing favorite and still very popular.

Joy Eslava, Arenal 11. Located in the old Teatro Eslava, and one of the liveliest and most popular discos in Madrid. AE, DC, V.

Keeper, Juan Bravo 39. Fashionable discothèque on three floors with all the latest in ultra-modern equipment.

Mau Mau, Padre Damián 23. In the *Hotel Eurobuilding* this is one of Madrid's smartest, and most expensive, discos.

Oh Madrid, Ctra. de la Coruña. Nine km. (five miles) out on the N-VI, this long-popular disco also offers a swimming pool and barbecue; very pleasant on a summer evening.

Pacha, Barceló 11. Another leading contender on the disco scene. Opened in 1980 in the old Teatro Barcelo; decorated like Studio 54 in New York. Open Wed. to Sun. only. AE, V.

Flamenco. Madrid offers the widest choice of flamenco shows in Spain and some of them are very good. While those uninitiated in the art of flamenco will most likely enjoy all the *tablaos,* the connoisseur will be disappointed at the extent to which shows are aimed right at the tourist market. Many clubs employ visiting rather than permanent artistes so quality can be variable. Dining is mostly mediocre, and very overpriced at 4,800–6,500 ptas. a head, but it ensures the best seats. If you are not dining, entrance including one drink varies between 2,000–3,500 ptas. Clubs serving dinner usually open around 9 or 9.30, those offering show only at around 11 P.M. Most clubs stay open until 2 or 3 A.M. Be sure to reserve.

Arco de Cuchilleros, Cuchilleros 7 (tel. 266 5867). Small, intimate club in the heart of old Madrid, just off Plaza Mayor. One of the cheapest and the show is good. No dining. Open 10.30–2.30 with two shows nightly.

Café de Chinitas, Torija 7 (tel. 248 5135). Well-known throughout Spain and abroad with some famous *cuadros.* The show is good, one of the best, and the dinner average. Open 9.30–3.

Los Canasteros, Barbieri 10 (tel. 231 8163). Show and drinks only, no dinner. Open 11–3.30.

Corral de la Morería, Morería 17 (tel. 265 8446). One of the best, owned by the famous Lucero Tena. Serves dinner. Open 9–3.

Corral de la Pacheca, Juan Ramón Jiménez 26 (tel. 458 1113). Right up in the northern part of town. A bit touristy but fun. Folk dancing and *sevillanas* as well as flamenco. Serves dinner. Open 9.30–2.

Torres Bermejas, Mesonero Romanos 11 (tel. 232 3322). Two shows nightly, the first with dinner which is expensive. Performances vary and some flamenco interpretations are not always too authentic. Open 9.30–2.30.

Venta del Gato, Avda. de Burgos 214 (tel. 202 3427). Seven km. (four miles) north on the road to Burgos. Authentic flamenco, and other flamenco dancers among the audience. The show begins at 11.30.

Zambra, Velázquez 8 (tel. 435 5164). A new club opened in 1987 in the Hotel Wellington by the former manager of *Las Brujas.* Smart ambience, jacket and tie are essential, and good show. Dinner is served from 10 P.M. to 4 A.M.

CITY TOURS. Tours of Madrid are run by the following three tour operators: *Pullmantur,* Plaza de Oriente 8 (tel. 241 1807); *Trapsatur,* San Bernardo 23 (tel. 266 9900); and *Juliá Tours,* Gran Vía 68 (tel. 270 4600). All three offer the same tours at the same prices and there is little to choose between them. In high season all tours (except bullfights) operate daily, but in low season the tours may be shared out among the three operators.

Tours are conducted in English as well as Spanish, and if need be, in French and other languages too. You can book your tours direct with the operators at the addresses above, or through any travel agency, or, in most cases, through your hotel. Departure points are from the above addresses, though in some cases you can be collected from your hotel.

Madrid Artístico. Morning tour of Madrid including visits to the Royal Palace and Prado Museum. Entrances included.

Madrid Panorámico. A panoramic drive around the city seeing all the main sights as well as some of the more outlying ones such as the University City, Casa del Campo Park, northern reaches of the Castellana and the Bernabeu soccer stadium. This is an ideal orientation drive for the first-time visitor to Madrid. It is a half-day tour, usually in the afternoons.

Madrid de Noche. This night tour of Madrid is available in various combinations. All begin with a drive through the city to see the illuminations of its monuments and fountains, followed either by dinner in a restaurant and a visit to a flamenco club; or by dinner and cabaret at Madrid's leading nightclub, *La Scala;* or by a visit to both a flamenco show and a nightclub.

Panorámica y Toros. Departures on days when there are bullfights (usually Sundays) 1½ hours before the fight begins. Panoramic tour of the city seeing the most important sights and an explanation of bullfighting before you arrive at the Ventas bullring to watch the *corrida.*

WALKING TOURS. Detailed walking tours of Madrid are run by the city hall but are conducted in Spanish only. For details, pick up a copy of the *Conozcamos Madrid* leaflet from the Municipal Tourist Office at Plaza Mayor 3, or contact the Tourist Office at Señores de Luzón 10 (tel. 248 7426), off Calle Mayor opposite the City Hall. Open Mon. to Sat. 9–1.

EXCURSIONS. Whole- or half-day excursions from Madrid to the places listed below are run by *Pullmantur, Trapsatur* and *Juliá Tours.* (For addresses and points of departure, see above under *City Tours.*) Tours can be booked through your hotel, travel agencies or at the tour operators' headquarters. Below we list only those tours which return to Madrid on the same day. Excursions to places further afield or involving overnight stays are also available; apply to any of the three operators for details.

Aranjuez. Half-day excursion in the afternoon, daily except Tues., Apr. to Oct. only, visiting the Royal Palace, gardens and the Casita del Labrador.

Avila, Segovia, La Granja. Full-day tour driving to Avila to see the medieval city walls, the cathedral and the Convent of Santa Teresa, birthplace of the saint. On to Segovia to see the 2,000-year-old Roman aqueduct, to visit either the cathedral or the alcázar castle, and lunch in a typical restaurant. Return via La Granja, once the summer residence of Spanish kings, to visit the palace and gardens modeled on Versailles. On Mon. the palace of Riofrío will be substituted for La Granja.

Cuenca. Full-day tour, Tues., Thurs. and Sat., May through Oct. Visits to the Enchanted City with its strange rock formations, and to the picturesque city of Cuenca, famous for its hanging houses, and where you will see Plaza Mayor, the cathedral, and the Museums of Archeology and Abstract Art. Lunch included. Book in advance.

Escorial and Valley of the Fallen. Half-day excursion, daily except Mon., visiting the Monastery of the Escorial, including the mausoleum of the Spanish kings since Charles V, and the Valley of the Fallen built to commemorate those who died in Spain's Civil War of 1936–39 and whose basilica houses the tomb of the dictator General Franco.

Rutas Verdes de Madrid. Tours through Madrid's countryside organized by the Madrid tourist authority and run by *Juliá Tours* and *Trapsatur.* Two itineraries operate on alternate Sat. The first route takes in the Sierra de Buitrago, the reservoir of Atazar and Torrelaguna, with a lunch stop in Buitrago. The second one covers La Cabrera, Valle de Lozoya, lunch in Rascafria, Puerto de Cotos and Villalba. Buses leave from outside the Tourist Office on Duque de Medinaceli, just off Plaza de las Cortes. Check availability with the Plaza de España Tourist Office first.

Salamanca and Alba de Tormes. Full-day tour, Mon., Wed. and Fri., May through Sept. Drive via the medieval walls of Avila to Salamanca where you will visit the ancient and prestigious university, the old and new cathedrals, the convents of San Esteban and Las Dueñas, and Spain's most beautiful Plaza Mayor. Then on to Alba de Tormes to visit the Carmelite Convent, which houses the remains of Santa Teresa of Avila. The trip includes lunch; book in advance.

Toledo. Whole- or half-day excursions (morning or afternoon) to this historic city visiting the cathedral, the Chapel of Santo Tomé to see El Greco's *Burial of the Count of Orgaz,* one of the old synagogues, the Church of San Juan de los Reyes, and a sword factory for a demonstration of the typical Toledo damascene work. The full-day tour also includes lunch in a restaurant and a visit to the Hospital de Tavera.

Toledo and Aranjuez. Daily except Tues. Full-day excursion to Toledo visiting places mentioned above (except Tavera), lunch, and on to Aranjuez on the banks of the Tagus, to visit the Royal Palace and the Casita del Labrador, "the laborer's cottage" modeled on the Trianon at Versailles.

Toledo, Escorial and Valley of the Fallen. Full-day excursion, daily except Mon., visiting Toledo (as above), lunch, the monastery of the Escorial and the basilica of the Valley of the Fallen. *Juliá Tours* and *Trapsatur* only.

EXCURSIONS BY RAIL. RENFE runs a popular series of rail trips at weekends in summer, from April through October. One-day excursions, mostly on Sundays and fiestas, include the *Tren de la Fresa* (Strawberry Train) to Aranjuez, the *Tren Murallas de Avila,* and the *Tren Doncel de Sigüenza.* Two-day excursions with departures on Saturdays and one night in a hotel included, are the *Tren de la Mancha, Tren Catedral de Burgos, Tren Plaza Mayor de Salamanca, Tren Ciudad Monumental de Cáceres,* and the *Tren Ciudad Encantada de Cuenca.* They cost 1,350 ptas. for a one-day trip and 10,000 ptas. for 2-day trips (1988 prices). Details from RENFE offices (p. 113) and stations, or call 228 3835 or 227 7058.

MUSEUMS. The opening times given below hold good at time of writing, but are subject to frequent change, so do check before making a journey. Most Madrid museums have different schedules for winter and summer months. *Patrimonio Nacional* (i.e. state-owned) museums are free to Spaniards with I.D., but make an entrance charge to visitors from abroad.

Museo del Aire (Air Museum), ten km. (six miles) out, on Paseo de Extremadura. Collection of planes and mementos illustrating the history of aviation and housed in Escuela de Transmisiones. Open Tues. to Sun. 10–2; closed Mon.

Museo de América (Americas Museum), Reyes Católicos 6. Excellent displays of Inca and Quinbaya treasures. Open Tues. to Sun. 10–7; closed Mon.

Museo Arqueológico Nacional (Archeology Museum), Serrano 13. Admirable collection including some particularly fine Greek vases and Roman artifacts, 180,000 coins, a good ceramics collection, the treasures of Iberian Spain—among them, the famous Dama de Elche and the Dama Ofrente del Cerro de los Santos—and a large display of medieval art and furniture. In its gardens you can visit a replica of the Altamira Caves, of particular interest now that exploration of the original is strictly limited. Open Tues. to Sun. 9–1.30; closed Mon.

Museo de Carruajes (Royal Coach Museum), Paseo Vírgen del Puerto. Can be visited on an individual ticket or on an all-inclusive ticket to the Royal Palace. Open Tues. to Sat., 10–12.45 and 3.30–5.15 in winter, 10–12.45 and 4–5.45 in summer; Sun. and fiestas 10–1.30 only. Closed Mon. and when official functions taking place in the Royal Palace.

Museo de Cera (Wax Museum), Paseo de Recoletos 41. One of the better examples of this specialized genre, with panels of scenes and personages out of Spanish history, as well as personalities ranging from Gary Cooper to President Kennedy. Open Mon. to Sun. 10.30–2 and 4–9.

Museo Cerralbo, Ventura Rodríguez 17. Tapestries, paintings, and some of the loveliest old porcelain to be seen anywhere, housed in the Cerralbo mansion. A good place to see the aristocratic setting of a turn-of-the-century villa. Open Tues. to Sat. 10–2 and 4–7, Sun. 10–2; closed Mon. and in Aug.

Museo de Ciencias Naturales (Natural Science Museum), Paseo de la Castellana 80. Zoological, geological and entomological collections. Open daily 9–2; closed Aug.

Museo del Ejército (Army Museum), Méndez Núñez 1. Vast but well-labeled collection of trophies, weapons and documents from wars in Europe and America, with a special section dedicated to the Civil War. Open Tues. to Sun. 10–2; closed Mon.

Museo de Escultura al Aire Libre (Openair Sculpture Museum). Situated beneath the overpass where Juan Bravo meets the Castellana. Contains the well-known *Sirena Varada* by Chillida.

Museo Español de Arte Contemporáneo (Museum of Contemporary Spanish Art), Avda. Juan de Herrera in the University City. Modern art and sculpture, with 375 paintings and 200 sculptures—including works by Picasso and Miró—set in pleasant gardens. Open Tues. to Sat. 10–6, Sun. 10–3; closed Mon.

Museo del Ferrocarril (Railroad Museum), Paseo de las Delicias 61 in the old Delicias station. Open Tues. to Sat. 10–5; Sun. and fiestas 10–2; closed Mon.

Museo Lázaro Galdiano, Serrano 122. One of the "musts" of Madrid, this museum is housed in an old, aristocratic mansion, and—besides containing a magnificent collection of paintings, furniture, clocks, armor, weapons, jewels, and artifacts—is a delight thanks to the tasteful arrangement of its treasures. There is a sizable collection of English paintings and the best display in Europe of ivory and enamel, as well as works by El

Greco, Zurbarán, Velázquez and Goya. Open Tues. to Sun. 10–2; closed Mon.

Museo Municipal (Municipal Museum), Fuencarral 78. Several rooms depicting Madrid's past, including a model of the city as it was in 1830. Open Tues. to Sat. 10–2 and 5–9; Sun. 10–2.30; closed Mon. and fiestas.

Museo Nacional de Artes Decorativas (National Museum of Decorative Art), Montalbán 12. Interesting collection of Spanish ceramics, gold and silver ornaments, glass, textiles, embroidery, furniture, and domestic utensils. Open Tues. to Fri. 10–3; Sat., Sun. and fiestas 10–2; closed Mon. and July through Sept.

Museo Nacional de Etnología (Ethnological Museum), Alfonso XII 68. Primitive artifacts and weapons from the Philippines, Africa, Asia and America, with several interesting mummies. Open Tues. to Sat. 10–2 and 4–7; Sun. 10–2; closed Mon. and Aug.

Museo Naval (Navy Museum), Montalbán 2. Ship models, nautical instruments, etc., with two rooms dedicated to the Battle of Lepanto and to the Discovery of America. The most famous exhibit is Juan de Cosa's original map, used by Columbus on his first voyage to the New World. Open Tues. to Sun. 10.30–1.30; closed Mon.

Museo del Prado, Paseo del Prado. The Prado is one of the world's greatest art collections. If your time is limited, the most priceless treasures—Velázquez, El Greco, Murillo, Zurbarán, and most Goyas—are one floor up and can be reached directly by a flight of steps from the outside, thus bypassing the ground floor and, incidentally, the long lines that often form at the lower entrance. Once inside, you have access to both floors, though not necessarily to special exhibitions which are charged separately. The Prado is always unbearably crowded, especially at weekends. Its modernization program involving the installation of airconditioning and better lighting is now well under way, but until it is completed some works are not on show while others have been moved to temporary locations and may be difficult to find. Open Tues. to Sat. 9–7, Sun. 9–2; closed Mon.

Admission to the Prado also includes entrance to the **Cason del Buen Retiro** annex, home of 19th-century Spanish painting and of Picasso's *Guernica* (entrance to latter is round the back in Alfonso XII). If you can't visit both on the same day, hang on to your ticket as it will still be valid for the part you haven't seen. Open same hours as Prado.

Another Prado annex, the **Palacio de Villahermosa,** Pza. de las Cortes 6, diagonally opposite the Prado across Pza. Cánovas del Castillo, is the new home of the great art collection of Baron Thyssen-Bornemisza, which the Baron loaned to Spain in 1988. Open same hours as Prado.

Museo Romántico (Romantic Museum), San Mateo 13. Designed and decorated like a 19th-century palace with paintings, furnishings and *objets d'art* from 1830–68. Open Tues. to Sat. 10–6, Sun. 10–2; closed Mon. and Aug.

Museo Sorolla, General Martínez Campos 37. The famous painter's house with a number of his works, as well as a good collection of popular art and sculpture. Open Tues. to Sun. 10–2; closed Mon.

Museo Taurino (Bullfighting Museum), Ventas Bullring at the end of Calle Alcalá. Bullfighting paraphernalia. Open Tues. to Sun. 9–3; closed Mon.

Real Academia de Bellas Artes de San Fernando (Fine Arts Academy), Alcalá 13. Splendid collection of works by great Spanish masters— Velázquez, El Greco, Murillo, Zurbarán, Ribera, and Goya. Open Tues. to Sat. 9–7; Sun. and Mon. 9–2.

PLACES OF INTEREST. Casa de Lope de Vega, Cervantes 11. The great playwright's house and garden, skilfully restored. Open Tues. and Thurs. 10–2; closed mid-July through mid-Sept.

Centro de Arte de Reina Sofía, Santa Isabel 52, off the Plaza Atocha. Huge art center in a converted 18th-century hospital. Leading art and sculpture exhibitions. Open daily, except Tues., 10 A.M.–9 P.M.

Ermita de San Antonio de la Florida and Goya Pantheon, Glorieta de San Antonio de la Florida. The hermitage dates from the end of the 18th century and was built by order of Charles IV. The ceiling of the church is covered in frescos by Goya of respectable court officials hobnobbing with less respectable ladies, though they are dimly lit. The church is now a kind of museum to Goya, and the artist's headless body is buried here. He died in France in 1828 and 60 years later his body, minus its head, was exhumed and brought to rest in Spain. Open 10–1 and 4–7 in summer; 11–1.30 and 3–6 in winter; closed Wed. and Sun. P.M.

Monasterio de las Descalzas Reales, Plaza de las Descalzas Reales 3. A 16th-century convent with superb and lavish ornamentation and a veritable wealth of jewels and religious ornaments, paintings including one by Zurbarán, and famous Flemish tapestries based on designs by Rubens. It won the European Museum of the Year award in 1988. Part of the building is still used as a convent. The entrance ticket (free to E.E.C. nationals) also includes a visit to the Monastery of the Incarnation not far away (see below). Open Tues. to Thurs. and Sat. 10.30–12.30 and 4–5.15; Fri. 10.30–12.30; Sun. and fiestas 11–1.15; closed Mon.

Monasterio de la Encarnación, Plaza de la Encarnación. Begun in 1611, this convent contains hundreds of paintings and frescos, but is in fact less interesting than the Descalzas Reales. Open Tues., Wed., Thurs. and Sat. 10.30–12.45 and 4–5.30; Fri. 10.30–12.45 only; Sun. and fiestas 11–1.15; closed Mon. Can only be visited on guided tours; free to E.E.C. nationals, and to everyone on Wed.

Palacio de Liria, Princesa 20. Contains an immense wealth of paintings by many great European masters, including Titian and Rembrandt, and a portrait by Goya of the 13th Duchess of Alba, believed to have been the model for his famous paintings in the Prado of *La Maja Vestida* and *La Maja Desnuda.* The palace can be visited by applying in writing in advance. Twelve of its rooms are open to the public. The guide who takes visitors round, though very informative, speaks only Spanish. Open Sat. only; closed Aug.

Palacio de El Pardo, in the village of El Pardo, 15 km. (nine miles) from Madrid. El Pardo is surrounded by woods which were much favored by the kings of Spain as hunting grounds. The palace was begun originally in the 15th century, but was mostly built by Sabatini during the reign of Charles III. It contains works by Titian, Bosch and Coello. The home of Franco from 1940 until his death in 1975, much of it now stands as a museum to that period of Spanish history. Open Mon. to Sat. 10–1 and 4–7, Sun. 10–1.

Palacio Real, Plaza de Oriente. The Royal Palace was begun in the reign of Charles III. Entrance is through the vast courtyard on the left of the palace, and then through the door to the right of the courtyard. Guided tours are compulsory. Admission varies depending on how much you want to see; you can visit just the State Apartments—or buy an all-inclusive ticket that includes the Royal Armory, Royal Library, Royal Pharmaceutical Dispensary and Coach Museum. Open Mon. to Sat., 9.30–12.45 and 3.30–5.15 in winter, 9.30–12.45 and 4–6 in summer; Sun. and fiestas 9.30–1.30. The palace is closed to the public when in use for official functions.

Real Basilica de San Francisco el Grande, Plaza de San Francisco. Madrid's most outstanding church. Open daily 11–1 and 4–7.

Real Fábrica de Tapices, Fuenterrabiá 2. A visit to the workshops of the Royal Tapestry Factory is recommended, and includes entrance to their exhibition of tapestries. Open Mon. to Fri. 9.30–12.30; closed Sat., Sun., fiestas and Aug.

Temple of Debod, in the Parque del Oeste. An ancient Egyptian temple given by the Egyptian government to Spain when its original site was flooded by the construction of the Aswan Dam. Open Mon. to Sat. 10–1 and 5–8, Sun. and fiestas 10–3.

PARKS AND GARDENS. Jardín Botánico, to the south of the Prado, between Paseo del Prado and Retiro Park. First opened in 1781. Over 30,000 different species from all over the world. Open daily 10–8.

Casa del Campo, across the Manzanares from the Royal Palace. Formerly the royal hunting grounds, the land was first acquired by Philip II in 1599. Shady walks, lakeside cafe, rowing boats on the lake, sports center (with pool), jogging track, zoo and amusement park, among the attractions. To reach the park, take subway to El Lago or Batan, or bus 33 from Plaza de Isabel II, or—the best idea—cablecar from Paseo Rosales.

Parque del Oeste, on western edge of Madrid, off Paseo del Pintor Rosales. A pleasant park containing the Temple of Debod and a pretty rose garden.

Parque del Retiro. This shady, once-Royal, retreat *(retiro)* makes the perfect refuge from Madrid's relentless heat. Embellished with statues and fountains, and a beautiful rose garden, the park is at its liveliest Sunday mornings with buskers, puppet theaters, and much of Madrid out strolling. You can hire a boat on the lagoon known as El Estanque or visit the temporary exhibitions held in the Crystal Palace or the Palacio de Velázquez.

MUSIC, MOVIES AND THEATERS. Music. The main concert hall is the old *Opera,* or *Teatro Real* as it is also known, located opposite the Royal Palace. Weekly concerts are given here, Oct. through Apr., by the Spanish National Orchestra and the National Radio and TV Orchestra, often under visiting conductors. Opera and ballet are also performed here Oct. to July.

The other main concert hall is the restored *Teatro Lírico Nacional de la Zarzuela* whose ground plan is identical to that of *La Scala* in Milan. An annual opera season is held here, so too are zarzuela performances, a colorful combination of operetta and folk dance.

Other concert venues include the *Sala Fenix,* Castellana 33, the *Salón del Ateneo,* Prado 21, and the *Fundación Juan March,* Castelló 77.

For program details, starting times and ticket prices, see the daily paper, *El País,* or the weekly leisure magazine, *Guía del Ocio,* available from newsstands all over Madrid.

Movies. Most foreign films shown in Spain are dubbed into Spanish, but there are about half a dozen cinemas in Madrid showing films in their original language with Spanish subtitles. Consult the local press, *El País* or *Guía del Ocio,* where these films will be marked "v.o." for *version original. El País* also lists cinemas showing subtitled films. A good cinema to try for films in English is the *Alphaville* (with four screens, entrance on Martín de los Heros) just off Plaza España. The official *Filmoteca* showing different films each day, always in their original language with Spanish subtitles, is in the Cine Torre, Princesa 1 just off the Plaza de España. Most movie houses have three performances a day at roughly 4.30, 7.30 and 10.30. Tickets cost 400–500 ptas. Madrid's International Cinema Festival, IMAGFIC, is held each year in March or April; details from the IMAG-FIC office, Gran Vía 62 (tel. 241 5545).

Theaters. If your Spanish is not very good, the legitimate theater is likely to be a complete loss to you. However, you won't need Spanish to enjoy a *zarzuela* or a musical revue. They're good fun. The best bet for non-Spanish-speaking visitors is the *Zarzuela,* Jovellanos 4, where you may see the top dance groups, operas, operetta and, of course, *zarzuela,* if it's the season. The *Teatro Español* at Príncipe 25, on Plaza Santa Ana, shows Spanish classics, and the *Teatro María Guerrero,* Tamayo y Baus 4, the home of the state-sponsored *Centro Dramático Nacional,* regularly shows interesting plays. The *Centro Cultural de la Villa de Madrid,* the underground theater on Plaza Colón, is an exciting contemporary theater.

Most theaters in Madrid have two curtains, at 7 and 10.30 P.M. They close one day during the week, usually Mon. Tickets are inexpensive and on the whole easy to obtain. With a few exceptions it is not at all unusual to buy tickets on the night of the performance. Details of plays are listed in *El País* and in *Guía del Ocio.*

SPORTS. Bullfighting comes first to mind, though most Spaniards would not wish to see it classified as a sport. Madrid has two main rings, so be careful you get the right one. If you have the opportunity during your stay, try to visit the big Ventas bullring, which seats 25,000. A smaller bullring is the Vista Alegre in the Carabanchel Bajo region across the Manzanares river. The bullfighting season in Madrid runs from April through October. There's almost always a fight Sundays, and often on Thursdays, too. Tickets can be bought in advance from Calle de la Victoria, off Carrera San Jerónimo, or at the bullring itself on the afternoon of the fight. The average Sunday *corridas* are now little more than a tourist spectacle—and not very good at that—but if you are intent on seeing a really good fight, try to be in Madrid around the middle of May during the San Isidro festivals; this will be your chance to witness some of the best fights in Spain, and tickets may well be hard to obtain.

Pelota is a peculiarly Spanish game. It is the hardest, fastest ball game in the world. It is also a betting game, in which you get fast action for your money. If you want to try your luck, place your bet on Red or Blue and trust to luck. The handiest pelota court in Madrid is the Frontón Madrid, at Dr Cortezo 10, though it was closed for renovation at presstime.

Football (soccer) is Spain's number one sport and has far surpassed pelota or even bullfighting in popularity. It may be seen between September and May in the huge Santiago Bernabéu Stadium on the Castellana, home of Real Madrid, which holds 130,000 spectators, or in the Vicente Calderón Stadium, home of Madrid Atlético, near the Manzanares river. If you want to see **basketball** or even **baseball** (it's not unknown in Spain), check with your hotel porter on games that may be scheduled—depending of course, on the season. **Horse races** take place at the Hipodromo de la Zarzuela, on the Ctra de La Coruña, except in the summer months. **Car racing** at the Jarama Track, on the road to Burgos.

If you want exercise yourself, there is a fashionable and luxurious **golf** club, the Real Club de la Puerta de Hierro, on the Carretera de El Pardo. (Membership fees are prohibitively high, however.) Golf de Somosaguas, beside the Casa del Campo park, tel. 212 1647. Also Nuevo Club de Golf, at Las Matas at km. 26 on the Coruña highway, tel. 630 0820. For latter, membership not required, only a club card made out by your hotel. Club has pick-up service. There are plenty of places to **swim**—several of the 4- and 5-star hotels have pools, or you could try the Piscina El Lago, Avda. de Valladolid 37 or the Piscina Municipal, Avda. del Angel in Casa de Campo. You can play **tennis** also at the golf club, or at Casa del Campo, which has 15 all-weather courts.

Ice skating is at the Real Club in the Ciudad Deportiva, Paseo de la Castellana 259. There are two sessions daily, 11–1.45 and 5–11.45, and skates can be hired.

Greyhound racing is at the Canódromo Madrileño; buses leave from the Plaza Ramales. For **rowing,** there is the lake in the Retiro Park and the lake in the Casa de Campo, a much larger park across the Manzanares. In the winter, there is **skiing** in the sierra at Navacerrada. For **flying** enthusiasts, there exists the Royal Aero Club, with its airport at Cuatro Vientos; offices are at Carrera San Jerónimo 19.

SHOPPING. The large number of well-stocked stores sell everything imaginable. The glittering curio shops with their wares piled helter-skelter on dusty shelves, the richness and abundance of authentic works of art and, above all, the love and pride with which local goods are manufactured, make shopping in Madrid one of the chief attractions for anyone visiting this booming capital. Prices for clothes and shoes are generally higher than in the U.S. or Britain.

Main Shopping Areas. Madrid has two main shopping areas. The first is in the center of town where the principal shopping streets are Gran Vía, the Calles de Preciados, del Carmen and Montera and Puerta del Sol. The second, and more elegant area—and naturally more expensive—is in the Salamanca district bounded by Serrano, Goya and Conde de Peñalver. A fashionable boutique area is growing up around Calle Argensola off Calle de Génova. In the north of town the Azca Center betwen Calle Orense and the Castellana is a recent shopping development. The latest shopping center is *La Vaguada* or *Madrid 2,* in the northern suburbs. With 350 shops, two department stores, several cinemas, restaurants and cafes, it is well worth a visit and can be reached on the metro to Barrio del Pilar.

Department Stores. On the whole, visitors will generally find the best bargains in the department stores, in anything from souvenirs to furniture. Moreover, chances are you'll feel more at ease picking through the counters at your own speed than struggling to make yourself understood with the small shopkeepers. The department stores listed below all provide interpreter service for foreign clients, currency exchange desks (open when banks are closed), shipping services, and they operate tax refund plans for foreigners, though you'll need to spend 48,000 ptas. on any one item before refunds can apply.

Galerías Preciados is the longest-established department store in Madrid. Ask for its *Passport Service Card* at the Client Service Department which entitles foreign visitors to 10% discount on most purchases. Its main building is on Plaza Callao, right off the Gran Vía. Within the two seven-story buildings you'll find almost anything you may need. Another *Galerías* branch is located on Calle Arapiles near the Glorieta de Quevedo, and still another on Calle Goya, corner Conde de Peñalver. A few years ago *Galerías Preciados* took over the old *Sear's* department store on Calle Serrano, corner of Ortega y Gasset, and a brand new store is now open at La Vaguada. The Callao branch of *Galerías* is highly recommended for tourist souvenirs. Also outstanding are the Spanish ceramics, rugs, glassware and other handicrafts. Remains open throughout lunchtime.

El Corte Inglés in many ways is similar to *Galerías* and is its main competitor. There are four *Corte Ingleses* in Madrid: Calle Preciados, right near the Puerta del Sol; another one at the corner of Goya and Alcalá (also near the Goya *Galerías*); a third in the Urbanización Azca between the Castellana and Orense; and the fourth on the corner of Calle Princesa and Calle Alberto Aguilera. All have cafeterias. Quality of wares at the *Corte Inglés* is somewhat higher than that of *Galerías*. Best bet here, perhaps, are their leather goods. Remains open throughout lunchtime. The Preciados branch is probably the best. The Client Service Department for tax refunds and tourist discounts is on the 3rd floor.

Celso Garcia is a smaller, more intimate department store on Calle Serrano, corner of Ayala. Its goods tend to be of a higher quality and more exclusive taste. There is a huge new branch in the Azca shopping center on the Castellana.

Special Shopping Areas. One of the most interesting and colorful of the Madrid shopping areas is one you should save for a Sunday morning. It's the **Rastro** or Flea Market, which stretches down Ribera de Curtidores from El Cascorro statue, and extends over a maze of little side streets branching out from either side. Here, on a Sunday morning, you'll see an incredible display of secondhand odds and ends, spread out on blankets on the ground.

The central area, Curtidores, is more traditional. Here canvas booths have been set up to sell everything under the sun. Most of these, though, are cheap articles which are of little interest to the tourist, except for picture-taking.

If you want to try your hand at bargaining (which is a must here), there are booths selling everything conceivable. Buy with care, though, and don't carry money exposed. *Serious warning:* This place is an infamous hangout for pickpockets, who take advantage of the crowd's pushing and jostling. Women should leave pocketbooks behind and no one should take their passports or more money than they would mind losing.

From a buyer's viewpoint, the most interesting part of the Rastro is a series of galleries which line the street behind the booths. In dark shops built around picturesque patios, you can find all the antique dealers of Madrid represented. These shops, unlike the booths, are open all week during regular shopping hours, as well as on Sunday mornings. Here you can find old paintings and wood carvings, porcelain, furniture and jewelry. Also, in the *Nuevas Galerías,* Shop 45, you'll find a lapidary with unset precious, semi-precious and imitation gems which are well worth a look.

If you are a **stamp collector,** don't miss the *Stamp Fair,* held each Sunday and holiday morning from about 10 to 2 under the archways of Plaza Mayor.

Secondhand books can be bought all year round from the bookstalls on Cuesta Claudio Moyano, near Atocha railroad station. With a little browsing, you'll find curiosities and first editions. And if you're in Madrid at the end of May and the beginning of June, you can visit the National Book Fair, held in the Retiro Park from 10 A.M. to 10 P.M. daily. Here, Spanish booksellers offer both their newest releases and old standards—all at a 10% discount.

For **handicrafts** and **Toledo ware,** you will find literally hundreds of shops all over Madrid, many of which are reliable, some less so. Try the department stores first, particularly the *Corte Inglés* and *Galerías Preciados.* Then you might try *Artespaña,* the official Spanish government handicraft shop. They have branches at Gran Vía 32, Hermosilla 14 and Plaza de las Cortes 3. They have a wonderful assortment of all things Spanish—wood carvings, handwoven rugs, embroidered tablecloths, Majorcan glassware, attractive stone ornaments for gardens and rustic Spanish furniture. *Artespaña* will ship goods throughout the world, but be prepared for some high prices.

Toledo wares are particularly good at *Artesanía Toledana,* Paseo del Prado, and at *El Escudo de Toledo,* next door on Plaza Cánovas del Castillo. In both these stores you'll find a large selection of daggers, swords, chess boards, paintings, fans, Lladró porcelain, guns and leather wine bottles. For **Granada wares,** marquetry, inlaid mother of pearl and so on, try *Artesanía Granadina,* Marqués de Casa Riera.

Ceramics are a time-honored Spanish craft. Among the best examples are the exquisitely colored Manises lustrous glaze from Valencia, the blue and green designs from Granada, and the blue and yellow Talavera pottery and pretty greens from Puente del Arzobispo. They can be found in most of the large department stores where you can also find the famous Lladró porcelain. These delicate figures are made in the Lladró factory at Tabernes Blanches just to the north of Valencia. Below are just one or two of the many shops you might try:

Original Hispana (O.H.1), Maestro Guerrero 1 behind the Hotel Plaza in Plaza de España. A vast and excellent display of Lladró.

Cántaro, Flor Baja 8 just off Gran Vía, specializes in ceramics from all over Spain and ironwork.

The following areas are good for **antiques:** the Rastro, Calle del Prado, Carrera de San Jerónimo, Plaza de las Cortes, Plaza de Santa Ana.

For **fans,** try either the department stores or, for really superb examples, try the long-established *Casa de Diego* Puerta del Sol.

Shoes. A chapter apart are Spanish shoes for both men and women. You'll find them made of sturdy yet flexible leather, handcrafted in the latest styles and colors. The Spanish last is long and narrow so be very sure of trying your choice on carefully. Prices have gone up considerably, so unless shoes are very comfortable, don't buy them. Take a stroll along Gran Vía, San Jerónimo or Calle Serrano, where numerous shoe shops vie for attention.

Books. An excellent bookshop for maps and guidebooks is the *Librería Franco Española,* Gran Vía 54. For books in English, go to *Booksellers, S.A.,* José Abascal 48 (tel. 442 7959) or *Turner's English Bookshop,* Génova 3 (tel. 410 2915).

USEFUL ADDRESSES. Embassies. *American Embassy,* Serrano 75 (tel. 276 3600). *British Embassy,* Fernando el Santo 16 (tel. 419 1528/0208).

Police station. To report lost passports, stolen purses, etc., go to the police station at Calle de los Madrazo 9 (tel. 221 9350).

Main post office. Plaza de Cibeles. Open *for stamps:* Mon. to Fri. 9–10; Sat. 9–8; Sun. 10–1. *Telephones, telex, telegrams:* Mon. to Fri. 8–midnight, Sat., Sun. 8 A.M.–10 P.M.

Main telephone office. Gran Vía 30 on the corner of Valverde. Open 24 hours.

Car hire. The most central offices of the main car-hire firms are: *Avis,* Gran Vía 60 (tel. 248 4203); *Europcar,* San Leonardo 8 (tel. 241 8892); *Hertz,* San Leonardo, corner of Maestro Guerrero just off Plaza de España (tel. 248 5803); *Ital,* Princesa 1 (tel. 241 2290). Central reservation numbers are *Atesa* (450 2062); *Avis* (457 9706); *Budget* (279 3400); *Europcar* (456 6013); *Hertz* (242 1000); *Ital* (402 1034).

Laundromats. *Lavomatic,* Bernardo López García 9 (tel. 241 5569), and *Lavomatic Electrodom,* Canillas 68 (tel. 416 1047), are both self-service coin-operated launderettes. *Yulienka,* on Calle Conde Duque, will do your washing and ironing for you.

Left-luggage facilities. *Estación Sur de Autobuses,* Canarias 17. There are coin-operated luggage lockers at Chamartín station and the underground Plaza Colón air terminal. Colón has the largest lockers.

Lost property. For items lost in city buses, Alcántara 26; in taxis, Alberto Aguilera 20; in the metro, the lost and found at Cuatro Caminos station.

American Express, Plaza de las Cortes 2 (tel. 429 7943/5775). Open Mon. to Fri. 9–5.30 and Sat. 9–12. American Express cash machine outside. Emergency numbers: 279 6200 or 459 9009.

Emergency phone numbers. Police 091; fire brigade 080; ambulances 230 7145 or 734 4794 (Red Cross).

Airline offices. *Iberia* has several offices around the city, the main ones being at Velázquez 130 (tel. 261 9100), Princesa 2 (tel. 248 6683) and Plaza de Cánovas del Castillo 5 (tel. 429 7443). The latter is perhaps the principal office and is the one you should go to if you are having problems with luggage lost on an Iberian flight. It is open Mon. to Fri. 9–7, Sat. 9–2. Ticket purchases on Sun. must be made at the airport. For 24-hour flight arrival and departure information, call *Inforiberia* on 411 2545. For international reservations, call 411 2011 (30 lines), and for national reservations call 411 1011, 8 A.M.–10 P.M. Iberia's general switchboard number is 585 8585.

British Airways is at Avda. Palma de Mallorca 43, 1st floor (tel. 431 7575), and Princesa 1 in the Torre de Madrid (tel. 248 7544/9574/2065). Open Mon. to Fri. 9–5 only. The B.A. sales office at Barajas is open daily 9–7. *TWA* is at Pza. Colón 2 (tel. 410 6012/6512/6007,8,9). Open Mon. to Fri. 9–5.30. TWA ticket sales office at airport is open daily 8–4. *Pan Am* is at Gran Vía 88 (tel. 241 4200/248 8535) beside the Plaza Hotel.

Toledo · El Greco.

NEW CASTILE

Don Quijote's Tiltyard

New Castile, a vast tableland watered by the large rivers of the Tagus and Guadiana, is flatter than Old Castile, though both lie on the Meseta plateau, and stand at heights of 500–1,000 meters (1,640–3,280 feet). The area is sparsely populated and arid, though vast acreages of wheat stretch to the horizon, and fields of saffron bloom purple in the fall. Only near the forested mountains in the northwest are there leaping torrents and lakes, and the slopes are good only for sheep raising.

In the north the Guadarrama mountains offer excellent winter sports or a refreshing break from Madrid's stifling summer heat. The air is clear and the setting is ideal for mountain sports, a summer picnic or even a rest cure. Dormitory suburbs for the capital are now beginning to encroach on much of the Guadarrama's natural beauty but once above the lower slopes with their sprawl of urban chalets and weekend homes, the vast mountain vistas and forested slopes are still a lovely sight.

In stark contrast to the verdant Guadarrama are the limitless tawny horizons of La Mancha in the south of New Castile. La Mancha is a name derived from the Arabic word *manxu* meaning "dry and arid" and here, though in a few places the earth is green with verdure, in others the ground has cracked and sunk, and is only cultivated by dint of constant irrigation. The La Mancha region centers on the province of Ciudad Real but stretches eastwards too, into parts of Cuenca and Albacete. Its skies are vast and luminous and the flat terrain, though still on the high central plateau and averaging over 450 meters (1,500 feet) above sea level, is dotted with rounded hills and crumbling windmills, and bordered in the far west and south by the ranges of the Montes de Toledo and the Sierra Morena. Fields of saffron line the road to Consuegra and acre upon acre of vineyards mark the approach to Valdepeñas through one of Spain's principal wine growing regions. In the east, the rocky crags, peaks and gorges of Cuenca provide a vivid contrast with the flat tablelands of La Mancha.

New Castile, lying to the south of Old Castile, was for long a buffer zone between Christian and Moor. In the early years of the Reconquest the defense of this region lay in the hands of the three great military orders of Calatrava, Santiago and San Juan, and many traces and relics of these three great orders of the past are to be found today in the scattered villages of La Mancha. Fortress castles dotted the landscape and it is the Spanish word *castillo,* meaning castle, that gave rise to the name of Castile. Chains of fortresses, among them the castles of Sigüenza, Belmonte, Alarcón and Oropesa, were built to defend the borders of the old Christian kingdoms, and were later granted to powerful noble families to help man the chain of defense against the Infidel enemy to the south.

Exploring New Castile

Five provinces make up the historic entity of New Castile, the province of Madrid, and surrounding it to the south and east, the provinces of Toledo, Ciudad Real, Cuenca and Guadalajara. Recently, in keeping with the move towards regional government throughout Spain, the region has been officially renamed Castilla-La Mancha with the province of Madrid standing as a separate autonomous region known as La Comunidad de Madrid and independent of the other four provinces.

Many visitors will base their exploration of New Castile in Madrid, most likely beginning with day trips to the more notable sights around the capital, and then perhaps venturing further afield en route to Extremadura, Andalusia or eastwards to the Valencian coast.

Excursions from Madrid

El Pardo, about 14 km. (nine miles) from Madrid, is notable for its royal palace. Built in the 15th century, it was, like so many of Spain's palaces, destroyed by fire and then rebuilt. It now contains tapestries, frescos and paintings of great worth. The palace was the residence of General Franco and is now open to the public.

Northwest: El Escorial and the Valley of the Fallen

Fifty km. (31 miles) from Madrid, on the slopes of the Guadarrama foothills, lies the village of San Lorenzo de El Escorial. Its austere monastery, the Escorial, burial place of Spanish kings and queens, was erected in a barren and severe setting by Philip II as a memorial to his father, Charles V, "to offer respect and honor to death," and to commemorate Spain's victory at Saint Quentin in 1557.

The building was begun by Juan Bautista de Toledo and finished by Juan de Herrera, making him one of Spain's best-known architects and establishing a new architectural trend. Everything is on such a large scale that the edifice seems cold and drab from a distance; it is only when it is studied at close range that the beauty of the classical ornamentation and of its gardens and pools is seen. You may wander freely about the courts and patios, but tickets must be purchased for the endless suite of rooms and other buildings.

This monastery-palace is eloquent testimony to the acute religious mania that clouded Philip's brain during the years before his death in 1598. The building is a vast rectangle 206 meters (676 feet) long by 160 meters (526 feet) wide, containing no less than 16 courts, 88 fountains, three chapels, 15 cloisters, 86 staircases, 300 rooms, 1,200 doors and 2,673 windows.

The combination of truly royal grandeur with monastic austerity has resulted in something unique in the world, from the small, bare and poorly furnished cell in which Philip chose to die, to the beautiful carpets, porcelain and tapestries (all specially made by the Royal Factory at Madrid) with which his less austere successors decorated the rest of the building.

The church is in the shape of a Greek cross; large, with many chapels. On either side of the main chapel are statues of Charles V and Philip II with their wives. The choir rests on a vault without apparent support, a masterpiece of Herrera, who also designed the stalls. In the trans-choir is a famous cross by Benvenuto Cellini. The museum and vestry contain paintings by Velázquez, Ribera, El Greco, and Flemish artists. The library is a gold mine for book lovers, with its 40,000 rare volumes, frescos and rich wood-carvings. Among the treasures are Teresa of Avila's diary, illuminated manuscripts including the *Codex Aureus* with its gold lettering, and a great globe which once belonged to Philip II.

Hidden away, and reached by long winding halls, is the private apartment of Philip, remaining as it was when he was alive. Here is no luxury, but rather Spartan surroundings. His bed was so placed, above and to one side of the high altar, with a small window overlooking it, that he could take part in the mass without rising from his pillow when ill.

The Pantheon is reached by a stairway leading to the crypt, which is divided into several chambers. The Royal Pantheon is of black marble and bronze, with an altar in the center, its walls are lined with urns of uniform design containing the remains of the kings of Spain from Charles V to Alfonso XIII. Only two are buried in other places—Philip V and Ferdinand VI. The body of Alfonso XIII who died in Rome in 1941 was finally brought to rest in the Escorial in January 1980, and that of his English queen, Victoria Eugenia, was brought here in 1985.

As an antidote to a cold and eerie experience, climb up the mountains to "Philip's Chair" and sit on the rocky steps, walk out to the Prince's Lodge, built in the 18th century, and then come back to stroll in the Jardín de los Frailes (Friars' Garden) amid the cut boxwood, rose bushes and shrubs.

The Valle de los Caídos can be included in your trip to the Escorial, as it's only a few miles further on. Set in a state park, with magnificent views, it is an extraordinary architectural concept which serves as a memorial to Spain's Civil War dead. It is also the last resting-place of General Franco. Like a modern-day Valhalla, the crypt is cut through 260 meters (853 feet) of living rock and surmounted by a 150-meter (429-foot) cross of reinforced concrete faced with stone (with a funicular that rarely works to the top). A Benedictine monastery and school complete the memorial.

East: Alcalá

Alcalá de Henares, 34 km. (21 miles) from Madrid, is a birthplace of learning and of famous people. It was here that Cardinal Cisneros founded, in 1498, the Colegio Mayor de San Ildefonso, which was the origin of the University of Madrid. Moved to the nation's capital in 1836 Alcalá University has now been restored and houses, among other institutions, a Civil Servants Training Center. Among those who first saw the light of day in Alcalá are Cervantes, Catherine of Aragón, and Emperor Ferdinand, brother of Charles V.

You can visit the Archbishop's Palace (now an archive), with its Renaissance facade and Plateresque stairway, and the reconstructed house (now a museum) where the author of *Don Quijote* was born. He was baptized in the church of Santa María la Mayor, destroyed, like all Alcalá's religious buildings, between 1931 and 1939. The Casa Consistorial (Old Courtroom), formerly part of the University, then the City Hall (from 1870), has an edition of the first Polyglot Bible, editions of *Don Quijote*, and the baptismal certificate of Cervantes. The Church of San Justo is late 16th-century, heavily reconstructed after the Civil War, and stands on the legendary site where the child saints, San Justo and San Pastor, were murdered. An urn on the high altar contains the relics of San Diego de Alcalá.

South: Aranjuez

The Palace of Aranjuez, only 48 km. (30 miles) from Madrid (main road south), was begun by Philip II, but the garden and the cascade that fall into the Tagus river date from the 18th century. Here in 1808, the meeting took place that saw the overthrow of Godoy, adviser to Queen María Luisa.

First see the palace, with its lavishly furnished rooms filled with priceless art treasures, and then lunch at one of the outdoor restaurants that border the river. When the sun is low, visit the *Casa del Labrador* (farm house), built by Charles IV in imitation of Versailles' Trianon, and walk through the *Jardín del Príncipe*. There's a miniature train which will take you to the Casa del Labrador, a picturesque ride for those short on time.

The palace is notable for its harmonious extension into the town by way of graceful arcades round the huge square, and especially for its gardens. The Queen's Garden and the Island Garden, both filled with valuable statuary, are the last word in the forgotten art of formal landscape designing, though somewhat neglected. The ornate Casa del Labrador here is a perfect example of the artificial elegance associated with that period.

Southeast: Chinchón

Forty-five km. (28 miles) from Madrid, turning right off the N-III towards Valencia, lies the picturesque village of Chinchón with just 4,000 inhabitants. It is a popular spot with Madrileños who drive out here at weekends to sample the *anís* for which Chinchón is famous. Chinchón these days is synonymous with this popular aniseed liquor but its other claim to fame rests with the fact that it gave its name to quinine—the Marquesa de Chinchón, wife of a 17th-century Viceroy of Peru, having been cured of a fever by quinine, brought the remedy back to Europe where it was subsequently named "chinchona." There is a parador here and up above the town its old castle now serves as an *anís* distillery. But *anís* and quinine apart, the outstanding attraction of Chinchón is its picturesque Plaza Mayor, irregularly shaped and flanked by ancient wooden houses. Bullfights are still held in the plaza during the town's fiesta and should you not feel like braving the spectacle from an arena-side seat, you can do so more safely from any of the numerous atmospheric *mesones* that overlook the plaza, peering out from the strings of garlic that festoon the doorways and sampling any of a dozen different varieties of the potent liquid. You may be only 45 km. (28 miles) from the hurlyburly of 20th-century Madrid but here in Chinchón's plaza things look little different from the Spain of four centuries ago.

Toledo—the National Monument

Of all the names of the provinces that make up the region of New Castile, Madrid, Toledo, Ciudad Real, Cuenca and Guadalajara, the name that rings with the clash of tempered steel is Toledo, and in the province of Toledo, the city of Toledo overshadows all the rest.

Toledo is like a huge tapestry that depicts all the elements that have contributed to the development of the civilization of Spain. It is history recorded in stone by those who could not read or write, but history more eloquent than anything inscribed in books and, unlike words, never to be misunderstood by posterity. Architects made the plans, but it is the hand of the workman and the craftsman-artist, carving his imagination into the stones, that tells the story. It is a story that the buildings of Toledo proclaim with voices that echo the pride and simple beliefs of the original master masons, their skilful workmanship inspired by a deep religious fervor and founded on an unshakeable reliance in their God and his saints.

The exceptional situation of Toledo adds to its beauty considerably. The surrounding landscape offers a direct contrast to the austerity of the city. The earth, of a reddish shade, is rolling and steep in some places; and the country homes, known locally as *cigarrales,* are surrounded by broad cultivated fields and fruit orchards.

The first impression of the city itself is one of austerity, silence, and absence of human life, for it remains as the Moors built it—houses rising straight up (many without windows on the street), barred gates presenting an appearance of prisons. It is only after investigation that you find agreeable lived-in patios behind those formidable walled homes and realize the barriers are a necessary protection from the elements. The whole city is a tortuous network of cobbled alleys, designed, it would seem, more for a patient donkey than for the myriad of tiresome cars that compete precariously with today's sightseers.

The best time to visit Toledo is in the spring or fall, because in summer it is scorched by the sun and in winter it is swept by icy winds. The most important festivals take place during Easter week and Corpus Christi (Thursday after Trinity Sunday), when beautiful damasks and tapestries drape the balconies and windows of the town while a stately procession of priceless works of religious art, taken from the churches, wends its way through the city streets. Here the pasos, those exquisitely carved and brilliantly colored religious statues, so characteristic of Spain, are seen in an appropriate setting.

Most visitors make Toledo, an hour and a half by bus southwest from Madrid, a one-day excursion from the capital, which is a pity. It is true that you can get a telescopic view of Toledo in one day and visit its main points of interest; but a longer stay opens up rewarding glimpses of nooks and corners typically Moorish in their atmosphere, evoking the spirit of the ancient city. Besides which, a more leisurely trip gives you a chance of stopping halfway between Madrid and Toledo at the village of Illescas, to see the five remarkable El Grecos in the church of the Hospital de la Caridad. If you are able to stay overnight, you will also find that, when the tide of visitors subsides (and the streets of Toledo are swamped from March till October) the city regains its ancient character—you will also be able to enjoy the floodlighting that turns the city into a place of nocturnal magic.

History and Architecture

As the Roman Toletum, Toledo was already a municipality in the year 192. In 418, it was occupied by the Visigoths, who transferred their court here in 567 and held the city until they were defeated by the Moors in 711. For 373 years (712–1085), the city was under Moslem rule, and the inhabitants adopted the speech and habits of their conquerors, although keeping their Christian religion, thus becoming Mozárabes. In 1085, Alfonso VI reconquered the city.

Under Alfonso X, the famous School of Translations was created, which made Toledo one of the leading centers of medieval learning. The Moors, Mozárabes, Christians and Jews combined to create the richest commercial and industrial city of those times. During the first years of the 16th century, Toledo was the head of the Castilian Comuneros movement against Charles V, and the city was defended nobly by Juan de Padilla and his wife, María de Pacheco, who continued to fight after his death. Although Toledo remained the capital of the monarchy, the kings spent much time away from the city and, in 1561, Philip II established the court at Madrid. However, Toledo has always kept the title *Ciudad Imperial y Coronada* (Imperial and Crowned City) and in 1987 was further endowed with the lofty title of *Patrimonio de la Humanidad.* Small wonder that Toledo has long been declared a National Monument.

The church became all-powerful in Toledo and many of the most important events in Spanish history of the 16th century are connected with the cardinals of Toledo, who are still the primates of Spain.

The two great influences that characterize the Spanish scene, Christian and Moorish, are expressed in the architecture and art of Toledo. It is especially rich in buildings of the late 15th and 16th centuries. While Christian and Moorish styles overlap in many cases in the hybrid style called Mudéjar, in others they emerge as fairly pure examples of their types. There is little of the Moor in the cathedral and it is difficult to trace any Christian influence in the mosque, now called El Cristo de la Luz which is one of the earliest examples of Moorish architecture in Spain. The Sinagoga del Tránsito reveals Christian, Moorish and of course, Jewish influences. The interiors of most of the buildings are full of peerless works of art. The tombs, so wonderfully preserved, cannot be matched in their conception and exquisite detail. Particularly notable is the fine wrought ironwork. The old blacksmiths were artists, but did not allow their imaginations to run riot. The results show harmony and boldness, but also great restraint.

Exploring Toledo

Toledo is as much a museum of the Spanish spirit out-of-doors, as it is behind the often forbidding walls that rise on every side. One of the best ways to encompass this unique city is to wander its streets, dipping into the treasures of art and religion at will. The walk around the old city that we describe here is easily divided into segments and should help to reveal some of the secrets of Toledo. Start outside the old city walls on the road from Madrid. Looking south, toward the city that is, the remains of the Circo Romano (Roman amphitheater) are away to the right and, on the road itself, you'll see the vast Hospital de San Juan Bautista, founded by Cardinal Tavera in 1541. Known as both the Hospital de Tavera and the Hospital de Afuera, this is an excellent museum to take as a starting point, as it will introduce you to many Toledo themes.

Part of the building is made up of the private apartments of its last owner, the Duchess of Lerma—the bedroom, study, reception room and library. The pictures are few by Toledo standards, but of exceptional quality. Some El Grecos, including a portrait of the cardinal and a superb *Baptism of Christ,* works by Tintoretto, Ribera (a bizarre *Bearded Woman*), Zurbarán and Moro among them. If these are the first El Grecos you see in Toledo, brace yourself—a flood awaits. The library has shelves of neatly filed archives, all interestingly labeled, another El Greco (this time one of his very finest, *The Holy Family*) and a death mask of the cardinal from which El Greco probably painted the portrait. Elsewhere in the complex are wide, elegant Renaissance courtyards, a chapel with Tavera's tomb—a lovely piece of funerary-marble carving by Berruguete—and a reconstructed 16th-century pharmacy.

Turning back towards the town you will see the restored Moorish city walls, pierced by a ninth-century Moorish gate, the Puerta Vieja de Bisagra and beyond that the Renaissance Puerta Nueva de Bisagra, dating from 1550. Just past the gate and a little to the right is the brick 13th-century church of Santiago del Arrabal. Its tower, however, is a little older and is Moorish. Beyond the church is the Puerta del Sol. Though rebuilt by the Crusaders in the 14th century, its original Mudéjar gatehouse dates from the 12th century. Just to one side of the Puerta del Sol is the little Ermita del Cristo de la Luz. It was built by the Arabs as a mosque in the 10th century and the date 980 can still be seen on the facade. It was converted into a church in the 12th century.

The main road from the Puerta del Sol bears right and leads to the Plaza de Zocodover, once a Moorish *souk,* now a pretty triangular square with trees, cafés and arcades that is the center of city life. It was damaged in the Civil War but subsequently restored and its original character carefully preserved.

At the southeastern corner of the square, the Cuesta del Alcázar leads, as its name suggests, to the fort of the Alcázar, a massive square building that stands resolutely on the highest point in the town. The first fort was built on this site in 1085 and was enlarged almost continuously until Charles V entirely rebuilt it in the 16th century. It was severely damaged

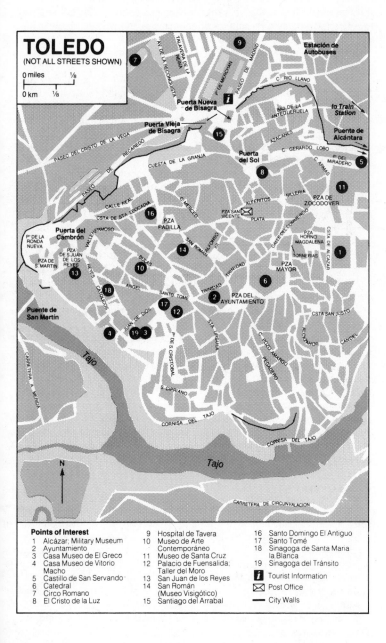

TOLEDO
(NOT ALL STREETS SHOWN)

0 miles   ⅛
0 km   ⅛

Points of Interest

1   Alcázar; Military Museum
2   Ayuntamiento
3   Casa Museo de El Greco
4   Casa Museo de Vitorio Macho
5   Castillo de San Servando
6   Catedral
7   Circo Romano
8   El Cristo de la Luz

9   Hospital de Tavera
10 Museo de Arte Contemporáneo
11 Museo de Santa Cruz
12 Palacio de Fuensalida; Taller del Moro
13 San Juan de los Reyes
14 San Román (Museo Visigótico)
15 Santiago del Arrabal

16 Santo Domingo El Antiguo
17 Santo Tomé
18 Sinagoga de Santa María la Blanca
19 Sinagoga del Tránsito

🛈 Tourist Information
✉ Post Office
── City Walls

in the Civil War when, defended by the Nationalist Colonel Moscardó, it was besieged by the Republicans for over two months. The holding for ransom of Moscardó's son and his subsequent shooting by the Republicans has passed into Spanish legend. Moscardó's famous telephone conversation with his son is recalled in the colonel's room of the Alcázar now faithfully restored as a museum and shrine of the Civil War.

Retracing your steps back to the Plaza de Zocodover, you'll find the Arco de Sangre about half way along on the right hand (eastern) side, a Moorish gate badly damaged in the Civil War and subsequently heavily restored. Beyond it is the Hospital de Santa Cruz, a magnificent Renaissance building. It was built between 1494 and 1515—first for Cardinal Mendoza then, after his death for Queen Isabella, who completed his charitable concept. Designed as a hospital, the huge cross shape makes a spacious setting for the art it now houses instead of the sick. Downstairs there are tapestries, carvings and some pictures, with a few of the pieces being of quite outstanding beauty, while on the upper floor, one whole arm of the cross contains 22 El Grecos. Several of them (*The Assumption of the Virgin* being the best) exist elsewhere in other versions, but to be able to see so many together in one place and compare their extraordinary combination of vision and technique is a rare treat for the art lover. These galleries also contain pictures by Luis Tristán, a pupil of El Greco, Ribera, Goya (an odd *Crucifixion*), but they are totally overshadowed by the soaring imagination of the Cretan master. The Santa Cruz Museum extends beyond the cruciform galleries to an attractive cloister, beside which is an archeological collection.

Below the Hospital and to the northeast is the Puente de Alcántara, which spans the rocky banks of the Tagus. There has been a bridge on this site since Roman days, though the original Roman structure was destroyed by the Moors in the 9th century. The present bridge replaced that built by the Moors *(al kantara* is the Arabic for "bridge") and dates from 1259, though it was substantially rebuilt in the late 15th century. The square tower at its west end contains a statue of San Ildefonso by Berruguete. At the far end of the bridge is the rather stern Castillo de San Servando. This was fortified especially for the defense of the bridge in the 11th century.

The Cathedral

Back in the Zocodover, take the Calle del Comercio down to the most splendid and conspicuous of all Toledo's treasures, the glowering golden mass of the Cathedral. Its magnificence is difficult to express in words. Originally the site of a Christian church, then a mosque, the first stone was laid by San Fernando in 1227 and it was completed in 1493. It is pure 13th-century Gothic with the usual Spanish variations. Gloom, vastness and energy are its predominant characteristics, but it is full of medieval romance and overflowing with art treasures.

The exterior is dominated by a tower 91 meters (300 feet) high and the flying buttresses, finials, great rose windows, and huge doors add to the impression of its immense size. Of the eight doors, those called *Reloj* (clock), 13th century, and *Los Leones* (lions), end of 15th century, are Gothic, *Presentación* is Renaissance and *Llana* (plain) is Neoclassical.

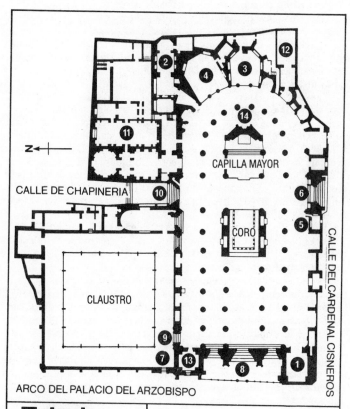

CALLE DE CHAPINERIA

CAPILLA MAYOR

CORO

CLAUSTRO

CALLE DEL CARDENAL CISNEROS

ARCO DEL PALACIO DEL ARZOBISPO

Toledo Cathedral

Points of Interest
1 Capilla Mozárabe
2 Capilla de los Reyes Nuevos
3 Capilla de San Ildefonso
4 Capilla de Santiago
5 San Cristóbalon

6 Pta de los Leones (Gate of Lions)
7 Pta Mollete-main entrance
8 Pta del Perdón
9 Pta de la Presentación
10 Pta del Reloj
11 Sacristía
12 Sala Capitular de Invierno
13 Tesoro
14 Transparente

You enter by the cloisters and the Puerta de la Presentación and you should buy the tickets you will need to see sections of the cathedral on your way in. Inside, the broad square expanse is divided into five naves, supported by 88 columns. It is probably easier to do a whole circuit on the circumference of the interior, visiting the main sights on the way, then return to the two central sections, the Capilla Mayor (Sanctuary) and the Coro (Choir), which take up the middle of the great building. While you go round, keep an eye cocked upwards to spot the myriad of statues and the magnificent stained glass. The main things to see, going clockwise from the entrance, are:

The Sacristía (Sacristy) is, in effect, the art gallery of the cathedral. It contains some quite marvelous paintings—a collection of works by El Greco, including a set of *Apostles* and the other version of *Christ Stripped of His Garments,* a *Burial of Christ* by Bellini, a marvelous portrait of *Paul III* by Titian, canvases by Bassano, Goya and Van Dyck. Other rooms contain richly embroidered vestments and illuminated manuscripts.

The Capilla de los Reyes Nuevos (Chapel of the New Kings) is often locked, but full of monuments to 14th and 15th century monarchs, including Catherine of Lancaster, the daughter of the English John of Gaunt and wife of Enrique III.

The Capilla de Santiago, a wonderful confection in flamboyant Gothic, was the creation of Count Alvaro de Luna, Master of the chivalric Order of Santiago. The beautiful altarpiece of 14 painted panels in 15th-century Flemish style surround a statue of St. James.

The Capilla de San Ildefonso, next, contains more tombs—the one in the middle being that of Cardinal Gil de Albornoz, who died in 1367 and was responsible for a fair amount of restoration work. San Ildefonso, by the way, was a bishop of Toledo in the first part of the 7th century.

The Sala Capitular de Invierno (Winter Chapter House) is entered through a fine, ornate doorway. Inside the hall is lined with 107 pictures of past Toledan bishops and cardinals—ranging from imaginary ones of the early dignitaries to highly realistic later portraits. Both the antechamber and the chapterhouse itself have magnificently carved and painted ceilings.

Back in the nave you will see the Transparente, a wildly Baroque roof opening, which seems to give a theatrical glimpse into heaven as the sunlight pours down through a mass of figures and clouds. Created in 1732, it was the work of Narciso Tomé, assisted by his two brothers, and is one of the most important Baroque conceits in Europe.

Continuing clockwise, you will pass the Gate of Lions and see the San Cristóbalon, the huge mural of St. Christopher, restored in 1638. The Capilla Mozárabe (Mozarabic Chapel) was intended for the celebration of the ancient Mozarabic liturgy.

Completing the circuit is the Tesoro (Treasury). This is a tiny room and claustrophobic when the cathedral is full of tour groups. You may have to wait in line as a guard restricts entry. Inside is a blaze of gold and color, especially from the 10-foot-high Processional Monstrance of gold and silver gilt.

Now return to the middle of the cathedral and visit the Sanctuary and Choir that you have been circling. The Sanctuary is dominated by an enormous carved altarpiece telling the story of the Life of Christ. It was carved between 1502 and 1504 by a team of artists and each small tableau is full of fascinating detail. The Sanctuary is also full of evocative tombs, especially that of Cardinal Mendoza, the strong right arm of Ferdinand and Isabella, who erected this memorial to him. The wrought and gilded iron screens of both the Sanctuary and the Choir are superb examples of Renaissance Toledo craftsmanship.

The Choir is a treasure house of carving and history. It resolves itself into three levels. The lower one, commissioned by Cardinal Mendoza, has a series of carved panels of battle scenes commemorating the final conquest of Granada and the fall of the Moors' towns and fortresses—the work of Rodrigo Alemán (1495). The next two tiers portray incidents and characters from the Old and New Testaments, plus saints, while the upper level depicts the genealogy of Christ—several figures (for example Adam and Eve) appear in both. These were the work of Philippe Vigarni and Berruguete and were done in the early 1540s. Standing just inside the screen is one of the cathedral treasures, the White Virgin, an elegant, enigmatic French 12th-century masterpiece.

Across the square from the cathedral is the Archbishop's Palace (18th century) and opposite stands the Ayuntamiento (City Hall). This is one of several buildings around Toledo in which Jorge Manuel Theotocópulos, El Greco's architect son, had a hand. Around the opposite—that is eastern—side of the cathedral is the Plaza Mayor with, sadly, nothing major about it. But just to the north of it, in Calle de las Tornerías, are the remains of a mosque which was built over Visigothic foundations.

A Treasure Hunt

Return again to the Plaza de Zocodover and refresh yourself with a drink or a cup of coffee, then prepare for the last lap, for which you will need a good street map, a compass and an acute sense of direction. You are about to plunge into the maze. Head down Calle Comercio again, taking the second street on your right, Toledo de Ohio, which leads into Calle de la Plata: follow this to the Plaza San Vicente. Diagonally opposite you, along Cardenal Lorenzana you pass on your right the former 18th-century University. Continue across Plaza Tendillas and along Esteban Illán till you arrive at the Plaza Padilla. Below you to the north west lies the Convent of Santo Domingo El Antiguo, dating from 1576 and the burial place of El Greco. To the south of the square, down the Calle San Roman, are a number of little churches, the most important of which is San Roman, now the home of the Visigoth Museum. Its tower was built in 1166 but the body of the building dates from about 1230. Its particular combination of Moorish and Christian elements makes it one of the prettiest and most interesting Mudéjar buildings in Spain.

At the eastern end of the Calle San Roman is an attractive and shady little square, the Plaza Padre Mariana. Leading out of the square is the Calle de Alfonso XII which bends and snakes its way down to the Calle de Santo Tomé, one of the city's main thoroughfares and packed with tempting souvenir shops. Beside the Hostería Aurelio bar, turn down the narrow Travesía de Santo Tomé where, in the Plaza del Conde de Fuensalida, you will find the Chapel of Santo Tomé, home of El Greco's awesome and magnificent painting, *The Burial of Count Orgaz*. The painting is displayed all by itself, cut off from the rest of the interior. To your left as you leave the chapel is the 15th-century Palace of the Counts of Fuensalida, where Isabel of Portugal, wife of Charles V, died in 1539, and just behind this stands the Taller del Moro, once the workshop of the cathedral's masons, with interesting Mudéjar plasterwork.

Leaving the square via Calle Juan de Diós and yet more souvenir shops, and turning left, you come to El Greco's House, a much restored museum containing the artist's "supposed" studio, a collection of his works or copies of his originals and several rooms furnished with 16th-century furniture. Even on a sunny day the effect is rather dreary and gives very little idea of how he must have lived and worked.

Below El Greco's House on the right, is the Sinagoga del Tránsito, rather austere but very beautiful, home of the Sephardic Museum. Built by Samuel Haleví, rich treasurer to Pedro the Cruel, in the 1360s, it became a church in 1492 after the expulsion of the Jews. Both the lovely Mudéjar decorations and the interesting items of the museum make this a worthwhile place to visit.

Now turn right along Reyes Católicos (or Santa María la Blanca as some maps call it) to the other remaining synagogue from the great days of Toledo's Jewish past, Santa María la Blanca. It has had a very chequered career as synagogue, church, barracks and store, but can still show some fine Moorish decorations. Further along the street you will come to the final stop on this tour—though there is much more to see if you have time to search—the splendid Gothic church of San Juan de los Reyes.

San Juan de los Reyes, built in 1476 by Ferdinand and Isabella to celebrate their victory over the Portuguese, is in every way a paean of triumph. It breathes the very spirit of that sumptuous age which sent Columbus across the seas and found its perfect expression in the exuberantly decorated Isabeline style, of which this monastery is one of the very finest examples. Significantly, among the first things to catch the eye are the rows of iron manacles hung on the outside walls, relics of Christian prisoners rescued from the Moors. Inside, the two-level cloister is lined with statues of saints and other religious figures, many with penetratingly carved faces. In all over 200 stone masons worked on the elaborate craftsmanship of the buildings. The church is richly embellished with great coats of arms, more saints, monograms of the two monarchs and two high-set balconies on which one can easily imagine Ferdinand and Isabella appearing in triumph. In fact the whole church is more like a great secular hall than a place of worship.

One final "must" to complete your appreciation of this lovely city, is the *panorámica*. Drive or hire a cab to take you along the Carretera de Circunvalación on the opposite side of the Tagus, crossing over the Puente San Martín and returning via the Puente de Alcántara. The view of the city standing like an impregnable island fortress encircled by the waters of the Tagus is one of the most spectacular in Spain and one immortalized by El Greco in his rare landscape *Storm Over Toledo* now in the Metropolitan Museum, New York.

PRACTICAL INFORMATION FOR TOLEDO

TOURIST OFFICE. The Toledo Tourist Office is at Puerta Nueva de Bisagra (tel. 22 08 43) on the edge of the old town on your right-hand side as you approach from Madrid.

TELEPHONE CODE. The dialing code for the city and province of Toledo is (925). This prefix need only be used when dialing from outside the province.

GETTING AROUND. Toledo is small, and its streets so narrow, that all your sightseeing will have to be done on foot. That is not to say that it is easy, for Toledo's rabbit warren of confusing streets is one of the most difficult places to find your way around in all of Spain. A couple of words of advice before you start: arm yourself with a detailed map and ignore most of the signs to major monuments as they are aimed at the car driver, not the pedestrian, and will send you all round the mulberry bush before you arrive at your destination.

The main thoroughfares of Toledo for car drivers are through the Puerta de Bisagra, up past the Puerta del Sol, along the Cuesta de las Armas and into the Plaza Zocodover continuing straight up the Cuesta del Alcázar towards the Alcázar and Alfonso VI hotel close to which there is a car park. The other reasonably uncomplicated exit and entry point is via the narrow Puerta de Cambrón, up past the San Juan de los Reyes church and along Calle Reyes Católicos (or Sta. María la Blanca) to the terrace and park just beyond the Tránsito Synagogue where there are a few parking spaces.

If you want to take a taxi to the Hospital de Tavera or the railroad station, the best cab rank is in the Plaza Zocodover although you can usually hail a cab in most parts of the city. The train station and new bus depot are too far out of town to walk to, so you will need to take a cab or else a bus from the Plaza Zocodover.

HOTELS. Toledo's hotels are often very full due to its popularity as a tourist destination and at peak times, such as during its Corpus Christi celebrations in early June, finding a room if you haven't booked in advance, can be difficult. Many of the hotels in the old part of town are hard to negotiate with a car and parking may be a problem though there is a good car park close to the Alcázar. If you are worried about parking, opt for the parador, the *Cardenal* or the *María Cristina,* or one of the smaller hotels just out of town on the far side of the Tagus, some of which offer lovely views of the city. Toledo's parador is one of Spain's most popular as much for its magnificent views of Toledo as for its high standards, and you would be well advised to book long in advance.

Parador Nacional Conde de Orgaz (E), Paseo de los Cigarrales (tel. 22 18 50). 77 rooms. The best—and by far the most expensive—hotel in Toledo. A modern parador built in typical Toledo style and beautifully located with a magnificent view of the town and the Tagus. AE, DC, MC, V.

Alfonso VI (M), General Moscardó 2 (tel. 22 26 00). 80 rooms. Excellent hotel near Alcazar with great views over parador and cathedral. AE, DC, MC, V. *Almazara* (M), Ctra. Piedrabuena 47 (tel. 22 38 66). Charming setting some three km. (two miles) out on the road to Piedrabuena, with splendid views, old-world charm and friendly service. Open mid-March to Oct. only. V. *Cardenal* (M), Paseo de Recaredo 24 (tel. 22 49 00). 27 rooms. Next best thing to a parador; ancient house built *into* the city walls; bags of character and attractive garden. Fine restaurant with open-air dining on hot summer nights. AE, DC. *Carlos V* (M), Escalerilla de la Magdalena 3 (tel. 22 21 00). 55 rooms. Modern hotel situated right in the center and offering good accommodations. *María Cristina* (M), Marqués de Mendigorría 1 (tel. 21 32 02). 43 rooms. Charming hotel, built in Castilian style and located next to bullring on road in from Madrid. Well recommended as is its restaurant *El Abside*.

Los Cigarrales (I), Ctra. Circunvalación 32 (tel. 22 00 53). 36 rooms. Pleasant country house on far side of Tagus with marvelous views over Toledo. AE, DC, MC, V. *Imperio* (I), Cadenas 7 (tel. 22 76 50). 21 rooms. Simple, central hotel offering good budget value. V. *Maravilla* (I), Barrio Rey 7 (tel. 22 33 04). 18 rooms. Old-world hotel just off Pza. Zocodover, with pleasant old-fashioned restaurant. AE, DC, MC, V. *Sol* (I), Azacanes 15 (tel. 21 36 50). 14 rooms. New good-value hotel with garage near the Puerta del Sol; no restaurant.

RESTAURANTS. Many of Toledo's restaurants are colorful typical places specializing in partridge *(perdiz)* and quail *(cordonices)* which are the regional specialties. Two exceptions to this rule are *La Tarasca* and *La Botica* which have a more French flavor to their style. There are some pleasant places to dine across the Tagus among the *cigarrales* (country homes) often with outdoor terraces and splendid views. *Note:* Most Toledo restaurants do not include IVA in their menu prices.

Asador Adolfo (M), La Granada 6 (tel. 22 73 21). Another entrance on corner of Hombre de Palo and Sinagoga. Pleasant restaurant with good service, situated near the cathedral. Roast meats are the specialty. At top end of price range. AE, DC, MC, V. *Aurelio* (M), Pza. del Ayuntamiento 8 (tel. 22 77 16). Popular restaurant with typical décor. AE, DC, MC, V. *La Botica* (M), Pza. Zocodover 13 (tel. 22 55 57). Stylish restaurant with good fare, at back of cafe on main square. AE, DC, V. *Casa Aurelio* (M), Sinagoga 6 (tel. 22 20 97) and Sinagoga 1 (tel. 22 13 92). A long-standing Toledo tradition, not far from the cathedral. The partridge and quail are especially good. Closed Wed. AE, DC, MC, V. *Cigarral Monterrey* (M), Ctra. Piedrabuena 42 (tel. 22 69 50). Popular terraced restaurant a bit out of town. AE. *Emperador* (M), Ctra. del Valle 1 (tel. 22 46 91). Atmospheric tavern just out of town where you can enjoy the view of Toledo above the Tagus. Closed Mon. *Fernando's* (M), Covarrubias 4 (tel. 21 11 26). Pleasant restaurant in new part of town, ideal for those staying at Hotel María Cristina. AE, MC, V. *Hierbabuena* (M), Bajada Cristo de la Luz. Small restaurant run by two brothers just above the Cristo de la Luz mosque. Innovative menus and a friendly welcome. MC, V. *Hostal del Cardenal* (M), Paseo de Recaredo 24 (tel. 22 08 62). Toledo's best restaurant, located in a 17th-century palace. Interesting food (gorgeous roast suckling pig) and pleasant service. At the top end of price range. AE, DC, MC, V. *La Tarasca* (M), Hombre de Palo 6 (tel. 22 43 42). Stylish restaurant on the main shopping street sporting a good menu. AE, DC, MC, V. *Venta de Aires* (M), Circo Romano 25 (tel. 22 05 45). On the edge of town, and moderately priced for its standard. Run by the same family since it was first opened in the 19th century. Cozy and rustic, indoors in winter, in a large garden in summer. Partridge specialty. AE, DC, MC, V. *Venta Cervantes* (M), Circo Romano 15 (tel. 21 28 62). With typical decor and a garden for summer dining, this restaurant offers excellent value for money. V.

Los Cuatro Tiempos (I), Sixto Ramón Parro 7 (tel. 22 37 82). Downstairs is a good tapas bar, upstairs an agreeable restaurant. MC, V.

BARS AND CAFES. The most attractive cafes for sitting outdoors and whiling away the time are to be found in the Plaza Zocodover.

Several bars line the narrow streets of the Barrio Rey just off the Plaza Zocodover. Other typical tapas bars you might like to try are:

Bar Ludeña, Pza. de la Magdalena. A colorful old bar just below the Barrio Rey, offering a wide variety of tapas and raciones, and snacks of cheese and olives at very reasonable prices. It also serves very inexpensive meals.

Los Cuatro Tiempos, Sixto Ramón Parro 5. The ground floor bar of this restaurant is well worth a visit for its splendid ceramic décor with its colorful blue and yellow tiles and wide variety of tapas. Very popular at aperitif time.

PLACES OF INTEREST. If your time is limited you should see first the cathedral, then the Chapel of Santo Tomé, followed by one of the two synagogues and the Church of San Juan de los Reyes. For a little longer tour, next include either the Hospital de Tavera or the Hospital de Santa Cruz Museum. Note that some of Toledo's monuments are closed on Sunday afternoons and all day Monday.

Alcázar (Fortress), now houses a military museum which is open mornings only 10–2. The fortress, a reconstruction, is open 10–2 and 4–7. Closed Mon.

Casa y Museo de El Greco (El Greco's House), Calle de los Alamillos. Open 10–1.45 and 4–7 (3.30–6 in winter); closed Sun. P.M. and all day Mon.

Cathedral, entrance off Pza. del Ayuntamiento. One of Spain's most outstanding cathedrals. Open daily 10.30–1 and 3.30–7 (6 in winter).

Hospital de Santa Cruz (Museum of Fine Arts, Decorative Arts and Archeology), Calle Cervantes. Open Mon. 10–2 and 4.30–6.30, Tues. to Sat. 10–6.30, Sun. 10–2.

Hospital de Tavera (Art collection), Paseo de Madrid 20. Open daily 10.30–1.30 and 3.30–6.

Monasterio de Santo Domingo El Antiguo (Cistercian Monastery), Cuesta de Santa Leocadia. Built in the 16th century by Juan de Herrera. Its church contains paintings by El Greco who was buried here, and there is a small museum with El Greco associations. Open daily 11–1.30 and 4–7 in summer; in winter Sat. 11–1.30 and 4–7, and Sun. 4–7 only.

Museo de Arte Contemporáneo (Contemporary Art Museum), Calle Bulas. Permanent Contemporary Art exhibition in a fine old 16th-century house known as the Casa de las Cadenas (House of Chains). Open Tues. to Sat. 10–2 and 4–6.30; Sun. 10–2 only; closed Mon.

Museo de los Concilios y de la Cultura Visigoda (Visigoth Museum), in the Church of San Román. A collection of Visigoth carvings, capitals and jewelry. Open Tues. to Sat. 10–2 and 4–6.30; closed Sun. P.M. and all day Mon.

San Juan de los Reyes (St. John of the Kings Monastery), Calle Reyes Católicos. Open daily 10–2 and 3.30–7 (6 in winter).

Santo Tomé, Travesía de Sto. Tomé. Chapel housing El Greco's great *Burial of Count Orgaz.* Open 10–1.45 and 3.30–6.45 (5.45 in winter).

Sinagoga de Santa María la Blanca (Jewish Synagogue), Calle Reyes Católicos. Dating from 13th century with five aisles and beautifully delicate Mudéjar tracery. Open daily 10–2 and 3.30–7 (6 in winter).

Sinagoga del Tránsito (Transito Synagogue), Calle Reyes Católicos. Houses the Sephardic Museum. Open Tues. to Sat. 10–1.45 and 4–6.45 (3.30–5.45 in winter); Sun. 10–1.45 only; closed Mon.

Taller del Moro, next to Santo Tomé. 14th and 15th century palace, a fine example of Mudéjar art. Open 10–2 and 4–6.30; closed Sun. P.M. and Mon.

SHOPPING. Toledo is a tourist's paradise when it comes to shopping for gifts and mementoes to take home. Its streets are lined with gift shops selling El Greco prints, ceramic plates and vases, embroidered cloths and endless examples of the famous Toledo **damascene** ware. When the Moors lived in Toledo, the city was famed as the best in the world for producing strong, flexible blades. The Moors perfected the technique of inlaying gold on steel which gave rise to the famous black and gold ware of today which is fashioned and shaped into numerous articles from bracelets, pendants and earrings, through plates, knives and swords to your own personalized family crest and coat of arms. Almost all the stores in Toledo stock this damascene ware but the best areas for souvenirs are around the Chapel of Santo Tomé, El Greco's House, and San Juan de los Reyes. On the edge of town off the Paseo de los Canónigos near the Roman Circus are two sword factories *Suárez* and *Antonio López,* which cater for tour groups and are interesting for their demonstrations (Mon–Fri. only) of the inlaid gold process. They stock a wide range of damascene goods and can make you personalized shields with your own family crest if you supply the design. Note, if you are purchasing large swords, wrap them in your suitcases when you fly home, or else label them with a baggage tag and be prepared to surrender them to the airplane crew for the duration of your flight. There is no problem passing U.S. customs with them but on board a plane they are classed as potentially dangerous weapons!

Ceramics from nearby Talavera are on sale all over town and are some of the best in Spain; a couple of km. out on the road to Madrid are numerous roadside stalls selling a vast range of ceramics, many of them seconds and at lower prices than in town. Embroidered cloths and napkins from the village of Lagartera in the west of Toledo province, famous for the best **embroidery** in Spain, are also on sale in the city.

A delicious delicacy of Toledo is the sweet **marzipan** *(mazapán)* sold in the candy and pastry stores throughout town. It comes in all shapes and sizes and although quite expensive and heavy to carry is well worth sampling. *Mazapanes José Barrosa,* Núñez de Arce 12, just above the Bisagra Gate, often has a good selection.

USEFUL ADDRESSES. Police Station: Plata 25. **RENFE Office:** Sillería 7 (tel. 22 12 72). **Train Station:** Paseo de la Rosa (tel. 22 30 99) across the new Azarquiel bridge. **Bus Station:** Ronda de Castilla La Mancha (tel. 21 58 50) on the new ring road between the river and the road in from Madrid.

The Knight of the Doleful Countenance

South on N401, across the National Park of Las Tablas de Daimiel, between the valleys of the Guadiana and the Jabalon, we come to Ciudad Real, a town that, sadly, has lost its former splendor. Originally a royal village founded by Alfonso X in 1225, it was elevated to the status of a city in 1420. With the expulsion of the Moors, it declined rapidly. There are two churches of interest; the Byzantine-inspired San Pedro, which dates from the 14th century, and the 16th-century Gothic cathedral of Santa María del Prado.

Southeast from Ciudad Real on C415 is the little town of Almagro, one time base of the Knights of Calatrava and today the showpiece of La Mancha. Its castle stands further south. The wooden houses on the vast Plaza Mayor provide an unusual frame for the elegant 16th-century town hall while the Corral de Comedias is Spain's only surviving 17th-century theater courtyard. It is highly reminiscent of its Elizabethan counterparts. A short way out of town is the Dominican Monastery of the Assumption, remarkable for its great church and the superb double galleries of Renaissance cloister and plateresque stairway, doors and windows.

Further east on C415, beyond Valdepeñas, Villanueva de los Infantes's lovely classical Plaza Mayor and fine houses seem unjustly neglected by tourists. To the south of Valedepeñas, a few kilometers east off N-IV, the village of Las Virtudes boasts the oldest (1641) and one of the few square bullrings in Spain.

Northeast of Ciudad Real, N420 crosses N-IV at Puerto Lápice where a signpost indicates the border of La Mancha. For *aficionados* of Cervantes, the road taken by Don Quijote on his three expeditions has been carefully reconstructed. Few will care to follow it to its conclusion on the eastern seaboard, but with a few deviations from the main road in La Mancha, some of his most amusing adventures may be re-lived. His home, and starting point, was in Argamasilla de Alba, a village of little importance, but the house of his lady love, Dulcinea, in El Toboso, northeast of Alcázar de San Juan, has produced enough romantic interest to have been declared a national monument. This modest mansion of the 16th century, Casa de la Torrecilla, was the home of Ana Martínez Zarco, whom the Spaniards have cast for the part of Dulcinea. There is an interesting Don Quijote library in the town hall.

Cuenca

N420 continues northeast from Alcázar de San Juan via Mota del Cuervo to Belmonte, a small fortified settlement that still has its original walls and city gates. Over it broods the imposing mass of its 15th-century castle, whose interior is partly in Mudéjar style. N420 crosses an arid, grayish plateau as far as Olivares, where it thrusts into the lush green valley of the Júcar. When the road rejoins the river, it is between twisting and steep rock walls jutting up from the valley. Above, the wooden balconies of Cuenca's Casas Colgadas (Hanging Houses) are suspended over the abyss that has been carved by the River Júcar's devious meanderings.

The ancient city of Cuenca was recaptured from the Moors by Alfonso VIII in 1177. The impressive part Norman, part Gothic cathedral contains magnificent *rejas* (grilles) and, in the Treasury, there are two El Grecos and a unique 14th-century Byzantine diptych. The Calle de Obispo Valero leads to the new town while another route ascends the ravine of the Júcar to the picturesque small squares of Merced and Descalzos, and back through a rocky gateway to the Plaza Mayor.

The Museum of Abstract Spanish Art was the first of its kind to open in Spain, and is housed in several of the 15th-century Casas Colgadas. Founded by the Filipino artist Fernando Zobel, it consists of representative works by Spanish artists. In April of each year Cuenca hosts an increasingly prestigious International Festival of Religious Music.

Thirty six km. (22 miles) north, mostly along the steep banks of the Júcar, is the Ciudad Encantada, the Enchanted City, where centuries of atmospheric action on the limestone has produced the fantastic illusion of houses, streets, flowers, vegetation, animals and even human beings, mysteriously frozen into stone. Less than three km. on at Rincón de Una is a fine amphitheater of natural rock.

Guadalajara

Guadalajara is a Moorish word meaning "valley of stones". The province is separated from Soria by the Guadarrama mountains, and the Tagus river flows through it. A chain of large dams and reservoirs has been constructed, a tremendous feat of engineering which may be viewed with the impressive scenery around, by taking the *Ruta de los Pantanos* (Reservoirs Route) excursion.

The city of Guadalajara is 56 km. (35 miles) northeast of Madrid on the N-II (which has been widened this far into a fast motorway) which leads to Zaragoza. Originally settled by the Moors, it was subsequently conquered by a companion of El Cid. Thereafter, it was long dominated by the powerful Mendoza family who, in the 15th century, built the Gothic-Mudéjar Infantado Palace where Philip II married his third wife, Elisabeth de Valois. Today the palace contains a Museum of Fine Arts, reached through the attractive Gothic arches of the Lion's Court.

Further evidence of the once-dominant Mendoza family can be found in the 14th-century church of Santa María de la Fuente where one of the early members of the family is buried. Another church, however, 16th-century San Ginés, contains the bulk of the Mendoza tombs. Two other churches in the town are of interest, San Nicolás, which has an especially elaborate and splendid altar, and Santiago, whose Gothic-Mudéjar magnificence has been restored to its former splendor.

Twenty-one km. (13 miles) off the N-II and 128 km. from Madrid (80 miles) is Sigüenza. Its churches, monasteries, palaces and mansions have contrived to give the town an atmosphere of rare harmony, from its alcázar (now a parador) on the hill all the way down to the banks of the Henares river.

Sigüenza's cathedral is an impressive building, more fortress than church. It was begun in 1150, though not completed until the following century. Among its works of art is the beautifully sculptured tomb of Martín Vázquez de Arce known as El Doncel, who was slain at Granada in 1486. It is an exceptionally lovely tribute from Isabella the Catholic to her page and shows him quietly reading a book.

PRACTICAL INFORMATION FOR NEW CASTILE

TOURIST OFFICES. Alcalá de Henares, Callejón de Santa María 1 (tel. 889 2694); **Alcázar de San Juan,** Avda. de Herencia 2 (tel. 54 00 59); **Almagro,** Carnicería 11 (tel. 86 07 17); **Aranjuez,** Pza. Santiago Rusiñol (tel. 891 0427); **Ciudad Real,** Avda. Alarcos 31 (tel. 21 29 25); **Cuenca,** Dalmacio García Izcara 1 (tel. 22 22 31); **Guadalajara,** Travesía de Beladiez 1 (tel. 22 06 98); **San Lorenzo de El Escorial,** Floridablanca 10 (tel. 890 1554); **Toledo,** Puerta de Bisagra (tel. 22 08 43); **Valdepeñas,** at km. 197 on the N-IV (tel. 31 18 04).

TELEPHONE CODES. The dialing codes for the provinces of New Castile are: Ciudad Real (926); Cuenca (966); Guadalajara (911); Madrid (91); Toledo (925). You need only dial these codes if you are calling from outside the province, within the same province, just dial the number. Dialing codes for all the towns we list are given under *Hotels and Restaurants* immediately after the name of the town.

GETTING AROUND NEW CASTILE. By Train. Almost all the railroad lines in this area radiate outwards from Madrid; there are very few direct connections between the other main cities. Many of the places within a 70 km. radius of the capital are well served by frequent local train services, often geared to the needs of commuters.

Train Stations and RENFE Offices. Ciudad Real Station is on the Ronda de Ciruela (tel. 22 12 13); **Cuenca** Station is on the southern edge of town at the end of Ramón y Cajal just off the N320 to Teruel and Valencia; at **San Lorenzo de El Escorial** the train station is a little out of town and you will need to take a taxi or a bus to reach the monastery; **Toledo** Station is on Paseo de la Rosa (tel. 22 30 99) about one km. east across the Puente de Azarquiel. Tickets and train information from the RENFE office in town in Sillería 7 (tel. 22 12 72) just off the Pza. Zocodover.

By Bus. There are plenty of services from Madrid to the provincial capitals and larger towns. There are also plenty of local bus services running to many of the villages in the region.

Bus Stations. Cuenca has no central bus depot; buses to Madrid leave from Teruel 2; to Teruel from Avda. República Argentina 13; to Valencia from Avda. Reyes Católicos. From **Ciudad Real,** buses to Toledo leave from Pza. Concepción 2. **Toledo** has a bus depot in the outskirts between the river and the road in from Madrid.

By Air. The only airport in the region is Madrid's Barajas Airport.

By Car. All the main roads radiate outwards from the capital. Northwest of Madrid the N-VI is a good fast road (but avoid commuter hours and traffic returning from weekend breaks). To reach El Escorial, you have two choices. Either leave N-VI at Las Rozas and follow C505 all the way to El Escorial; or stay on N-VI as far as Guadarrama and then take the exit to El Escorial and the road that passes by the Valley of the Fallen. If you are heading for Navacerrada leave N-VI along N601 which leads to both the village and pass (1,860 meters, 6,100 feet). The road to the pass is open most of the year, except immediately after heavy snow falls, though you may need chains between Dec. and early March. Though steep and twisting, the road is good and driving not too arduous so long as the visibility is good, scenery is rewarding.

The N-V southwest to Extremadura and Lisbon passes close to Talavera and Oropesa in Toledo province. The road is good by Spanish standards but its New Castile section offers some fairly unexciting scenery. The N403 from Toledo to Avila is fine, with some nice views of the mountains once it enters the Sierra de Gredos in Avila province.

The N401 from Madrid to Toledo is boring and often very crowded with long hold-ups. It passes mostly through dull, industrial landscapes though the approach to Toledo is pleasant with the road lined with ceramic stalls and a dramatic view of the Alcázar silhouetted against the city skyline. On busy days you may find it worthwhile returning to Madrid via Aranjuez and the N-IV.

The N-IV, the main Madrid–Andalusia highway is a fast road as far as Aranjuez. From Aranjuez across La Mancha by way of Puerto Lápice, Manzanares and Valdepeñas, the narrow highway is currently being widened into a two-lane *autovía,* so delays may occur at roadworks. The landscape is mostly flat with typical vistas of La Mancha; ruined windmills dotted on distant hills, vast tawny landscapes, and extensive vineyards between Manzanares and Valdepeñas where the highway is lined with huge old terracotta wine vats. It becomes more interesting scenically in the south of Ciudad Real province once it enters the foothills of the Sierra Morena just before the Despeñaperros Pass leading into Andalusia.

For Ciudad Real, branch off N-IV at Puerto Lápice and take the N420 via Daimiel, or take the more interesting N401 from Toledo direct to Ciudad Real.

For Cuenca, detour off the N-III Madrid–Valencia road onto N400 at Tarancón, or N320 at Motilla del Palancar. The road from Cuenca to the Enchanted City (Ciudad Encantada) passes through pleasant high land with mountain scenery.

A more interesting way of reaching Guadalajara than on the main N-II from Madrid, is along the N320 from Cuenca through the mountains of the Serranía de Cuenca and skirting the reservoirs of Buendía and Entrepeñas whose 100 km. (62 miles) of shoreline make up the Mar de Castilla, or inland sea of Castile. The route is scenically rewarding if not the easiest of driving. From Guadalajara the fast N-II returns to Madrid by way of Alcalá de Henares.

HOTELS AND RESTAURANTS. Toledo is the only city of any size and the major tourist attraction in the area so consequently has the best hotels. Elsewhere the choice is somewhat limited, as the region is sparsely populated, but there are plenty of functional, comfortable roadside inns along the main N roads. There are notable paradors at Alarcón, Almagro,

Chinchón, Oropesa, Sigüenza and Toledo, and a lovely converted monastery at Santa María del Paular near Rascafría.

The region's most noted eating places are undoubtedly Toledo and San Lorenzo de El Escorial which are both well endowed with a good choice of restaurants. Elsewhere there are plenty of colorful mesones which will enable you to the local fare often at very moderate prices. Partridge is the specialty of Toledo province, whilst in La Mancha you should not forget to sample the many varieties of the local cheese, *queso manchego,* or the local wines from the Valdepeñas region.

Alarcon Cuenca (966). *Parador Nacional Marqués de Villena* (E), Avda. Amigos Castillo (tel. 33 13 50). 11 rooms. In a magnificent 12th-century castle. AE, DC, MC, V. *Claridge* (I), on Madrid–Valencia road (tel. 33 11 50). 36 rooms. Pool, tennis and garden.

Alcala De Henares Madrid (91). *El Bedel* (I), Pza. San Diego 6 (tel. 889 3700). 51 rooms. Bar. V.

Restaurant. *Hostería Nacional del Estudiante* (M), Colegios 3 (tel. 888 0330). Located in the Colegio de San Jerónimo, also known as the University of the Three Languages, founded by Cardinal Cisneros in 1510. Lashings of atmosphere. AE, DC, MC, V.

Almagro Ciudad Real (926). *Parador Nacional* (E), Ronda de San Francisco (tel. 86 01 00). 55 rooms. Located in the 16th-century convent of Santa Catalina. Pool and gardens. AE, DC, MC, V.

Almuradiel Ciudad Real (926). *Los Podencos* (M), (tel. 33 90 00). 76 rooms. Pleasant, comfortable roadside inn on the main N-IV road before Despeñaperros pass. MC, V.

Aranjuez Madrid (91). *Isabel II* (M), Infants 15 (tel. 891 0945). 25 rooms. Newly opened 3-star hotel; the best bet. *Las Infantas* (I), Infantas 4 (tel. 891 1341). A simple hostel, but clean, modern and good. *Las Mercedes* (I), on the main road through town (tel. 891 0440). 37 rooms. Oldish, and a little faded but friendly and pleasant, with pool and garden where meals are served in summer.

Restaurants. Several good places on the banks of the Tagus. Be sure to taste the *fresones* (giant strawberries) and fresh asparagus when they are in season. *Casa Pablo* (M), Almíbar 20 (tel. 891 1451). Good Castilian food in a mesón setting in the heart of town. Closed Aug. *El Castillo* (M), (tel. 891 3000). In a beautiful setting in the Jardines del Príncipe. AE, DC, MC, V. *La Rana Verde* (M), Príncipe 12 (tel. 891 3238). Overlooks the Tagus. Particularly recommended for game and fish.

Chinchon Madrid (91). *Parador Nacional de Chinchón* (E), Avda. del Generalísimo 1 (tel. 894 0836). 38 rooms. 17th-century Augustinian monastery, opened as a parador in 1982. Pool.

Restaurant. *Mesón Cuevas del Vino* (M), Benito Hortelano 13 (tel. 894 0206). In a former mill and bodega. Wine served from earthenware vats.

Ciudad Real (926). *El Molino* (M), Ctra. de Carrión (tel. 22 30 50). 18 rooms. On the road to Carrión. AE, DC, V. *Castillos* (M), Avda. del Rey Santo 8 (tel. 21 36 40). 131 rooms. Parking.

Restaurant. *Miami Park* (M), Ronda Ciruela 48 (tel. 22 20 43). AE, DC, MC, V.

Cuenca (966). *Torremangana* (E–M), San Ignacio de Loyola 9 (tel. 22 33 51). 115 rooms. Modern hotel in new part of town. AE, DC, MC, V. *Alfonso VIII* (M), Parque de San Julián 3 (tel. 21 43 25). 48 rooms. Modern and comfortable in center of new town. *Cueva del Fraile* (M), Ctra. Cuenca–Buenache (tel. 21 15 71). 54 rooms. Located in a restored 16th-century building, seven kms. (four miles) northwest of town. MC, V. *Figón de Pedro* (I), Cervantes 17 (tel. 22 45 11). 28 rooms. Good modest hotel under same management as notable restaurant. MC, V. *Posada de San José* (I), Julián Romero 4 (tel. 21 13 00). 24 rooms. Charming hostel in one of the hanging houses overlooking Huécar gorge. Its rooms (not all with bath) were once convent cells. V.

Restaurants. *Mesón Casas Colgadas* (M), Canónigos (tel. 22 35 09). Now under the same management as the highly esteemed *Figón de Pedro* and well worth a visit for the magnificent views afforded from its hanging-house location. AE, DC, MC, V. *Figón de Pedro* (M), Cervantes 15 (tel. 22 68 21). Superbly atmospheric restaurant with excellent regional cuisine; a real Cuenca tradition. Closed Sun. evening. AE, DC, MC, V. *Los Claveles* (I), 18 de Julio 32 (tel. 21 38 24). Décor and dishes are typical of La Mancha—the partridge and venison are especially recommended. A little cramped. Closed Thurs. and Sept. V.

El Escorial Madrid (91). *Victoria Palace* (E–M), Juan de Toledo 4 (tel. 890 1511). 89 rooms. Charming old-world hotel near the monastery, with pool and gardens. AE, DC, MC, V. *Cristina* (I), Juan de Toledo 6 (tel. 890 1961). 16 rooms. Delightful villa with garden next to the *Victoria Palace* hotel. AE, V. *Jardín* (I), Leandro Rubio 2 (tel. 896 1007). 22 rooms. Cozy, villa-like hostel with garden. *Miranda Suizo* (I), Floridablanca 20 (tel. 890 4711). A pleasant old hotel in the center of town, with good-value restaurant. AE, DC, MC, V.

Restaurants. *Charolés* (E), Floridablanca 24 (tel. 890 5975). A good selection of meat dishes at this elegant restaurant, which boasts a pleasant terrace among its attractions. AE, DC, MC, V. *Mesón La Cueva* (E), San Antón 4 (tel. 890 1516). El Escorial's best-known restaurant, an atmospheric mesón founded back in 1768 and comprising several small rustic dining rooms. *Doblón de Oro* (E–M), Pza. de la Constitución 5 (tel. 890 4216). Outdoor dining on the plaza. AE, DC, V. *Fonda Genara* (E–M), Pza. San Lorenzo (tel. 890 4357). Elegant restaurant located in an 18th-century theater in the renovated Galeria Martin.

Alaska (M), Pza. San Lorenzo (tel. 890 4365). Castilian décor; pleasant terrace. AE, DC, MC, V. *El Candil* (M), pleasant with outdoor terrace on corner of Pza. San Lorenzo. AE, DC, MC, V. *Castilla* (M), Pza. de la Constitución 2 (tel. 890 5219). Tables outside on the plaza in season. *Madrid-Sevilla* (M), Benavente 1 (tel. 890 1519). Attractive décor and good value *menu del día*. *Mesón Serrano* (M), Floridablanca 4 (tel. 890 1704). Good Spanish food either inside or in the pleasant shady garden. V.

Guadalajara (911). *Pax* (M), on the N-II highway (tel. 21 18 00). 61 rooms. Three-star, and the best in town. Pool, tennis and gardens. AE, DC, MC, V. *España* (I), Teniente Figueroa 3 (tel. 21 13 03). 33 rooms. Simple budget hotel.
Restaurant. *El Ventorrero* (M), López de Haro 4 (tel. 21 22 51). Mesón with rustic Castilian décor run by same family since the 1880s. V.

Guadarrama Madrid (91). *Miravalle* (I), on the N-VI (tel. 850 0300). 12 rooms. Good hostel serving meals.

Manzanares Ciudad Real (926). *Parador Nacional* (M), on the main N-IV (tel. 61 04 00). 50 rooms. Modern roadside parador with pool, fine for overnighting. AE, DC, MC, V. *El Cruce* (I), at km. 173 on the N-IV (tel. 61 19 00). 37 rooms. Pleasant roadside hotel with pool. DC, V.
Restaurant. *Mesón Sancho* (M), Jesús del Perdón 22 (tel. 61 10 16). Mesón where you can taste the local wine, Manchego cheese and local crabs.

Miraflores De La Sierra Madrid (91). *Palmy* (I), Eusebio Guadalix 17 (tel. 844 3712). 21 rooms. V. *Refugio* (I), Fuente del Gazapo (tel. 844 4211). 48 rooms. Pool and garden.

La Mota Del Cuervo Cuenca (966). *Mesón de Don Quijote* (M), Francisco Costi 2 (tel. 18 02 00). 36 rooms. A good base from which to explore Don Quijote country. Excellent value, with pool, gardens and restaurant. AE, DC, MC, V.

Motilla Del Palancar Cuenca (966). *Hotel del Sol* (I), on the N-III (tel. 33 10 25). 37 rooms. Simple roadside hotel. AE, DC, MC, V.

Navacerrada Madrid (91). Winter sports area and summer resort. *La Barranca* (M), Valle de la Barranca (tel. 856 0000). 54 rooms. Recent hotel with pool; in lovely location. The best. V. *Arcipreste de Hita* (I), Praderas de San Sebastián (tel. 856 0125). 38 rooms. Simple, with pool, tennis, and great views over the lake. V. *Doña Endrina* (I), Avda. de Madrid (tel. 856 0200). 40 rooms. Castilian-style house with pool. *Las Postas* (I), Ctra. Nal. 601 (tel. 856 0250). 21 rooms. With pool and good view of the reservoir and mountains.
The following are up at the Navacerrada pass and are simple and basic. *Pasadoiro* (I), (tel. 852 1427). 36 rooms. V. *Venta Arias* (I), (tel. 852 1100). 11 rooms. AE, V.

Oropesa Toledo (925). *Parador Nacional Virrey Toledo* (E), Pza. del Palacio 1 (tel. 43 00 00). 44 rooms. A magnificent castle-cum-palace built in 1402 on a site believed to have had a castle since 1716 B.C. Commanding a beautiful view over the surrounding countryside and the mountains of the Sierra de Gredos, this is one of the original paradores (opening in 1930) and was much favored by Somerset Maugham. AE, DC, MC, V.

Puerto Lapice Ciudad Real (926). *El Aprisco* (I), (tel. 57 61 50). 17 rooms. Pool. *El Puerto* (I), (tel. 57 60 00). 37 rooms. Both are comfortable roadside inns, fine for overnighting.

Restaurant. *Venta del Quijote* (M), (tel. 57 61 10). Superbly atmospheric inn of Don Quixote fame and worth a detour from the main highway. Specializes in regional dishes from La Mancha or sample the manchegan cheese and pastries in the bar. AE, DC, V.

Rascafria Madrid (91). *Santa María del Paular* (L), El Paular (tel. 869 1011). 58 rooms. A luxury hotel located in part of a monastery dating back to 1300, and set in pine forests high in the mountains half way between Segovia and Madrid. Outdoor pool and tennis courts. AE, DC, MC, V.

Sigüenza Guadalajara (911). *Parador Nacional Castillo de Sigüenza* (E), Pza. del Castillo (tel. 39 01 00). 77 rooms, some with canopied beds. Located in a building that began life as a Visigoth castle, then became a Moorish fortress, and, finally, an episcopal palace. A truly impressive building in an interesting medieval town. AE, DC, MC, V.

Talavera De La Reina Toledo (925). *Beatriz* (M), Avda. Madrid 1 (tel. 80 76 00). Excellent, comfortable 3-star hotel with good *Anticuario* (M) restaurant. AE, MC, V. *León* (M), 3 km. out on N-V (tel. 80 29 00). 30 rooms. Good roadside hotel with garden and pool. AE, MC, V.

Toledo. See *Practical Information for Toledo* (page 153).

Valdepeñas Ciudad Real (926). *Meliá El Hidalgo* (M), out of town on the N-IV (tel. 32 32 54). 54 rooms. Motel with bungalows, pool and garden. AE, DC, MC, V. *Vista Alegre* (I), on the N-IV (tel. 32 22 04). 17 rooms. Pleasant roadside hotel fine for overnighting.

PLACES OF INTEREST. While the outstanding showpieces of New Castile are undoubtedly the Escorial monastery and the city of Toledo, another interesting way of sightseeing in this area is to follow the trail of Don Quijote's wanderings through the lands and villages of La Mancha. A useful brochure on La Mancha is available from the Spanish National Tourist Office detailing the Quijote trail and providing a helpful map.

Alcala De Henares (Madrid). **Capilla del Oidor** (Magistrate's Chapel), Pza. Cervantes. Built in the early 15th century by Pedro Díaz de Toledo, Chief Justice of Juan II, and containing a reproduction, made with the original stones, of the font in which Miguel de Cervantes was baptized on October 9, 1547. Open weekends only 11–1 and 5–7.

Capilla de San Idelfonso, Pedro Gumiel 2. 15th-century chapel containing the empty Carrara marble tomb of Cardinal Cisneros. Open weekends only, 11–1, 5–7.

Casa de Cervantes (Cervantes' House), Calle Mayor. Modern reconstruction, plus a small museum. Open daily, 10–2, 5–8; closed Mon.

Casa Consistorial (Old Courtroom), Pza. Cervantes. Houses an edition of the first Polyglot Bible, baptismal certificate of Cervantes and editions of *Don Quijote.* Open weekends only, 11–1 and 5–7.

Monasterio de las Bernardas, Pza. de las Bernardas. Baroque monastery dating from 1617 with ornate gold altar and paintings by the 17th-century artist Angelo Nardi. Open weekends only 11–1, 5–7.

Universidad Complutense (Old University), Pza. San Diego. Built in the mid-15th century by Cardinal Cisneros with a Plateresque facade by Rodrigo Gil de Hontañón. Built around three patios, the Patio Mayor, the Philosophers' Patio and the outstanding Patio of the Three Languages where classes were taught in Latin, Greek and Hebrew. Open weekends only 11–1, 5–7.

Alcazar De San Juan (Ciudad Real). A major railroad junction and growing industrial town in the heart of La Mancha.

Molinos de Viento. Six windmills, some quite well preserved, stand on the hill of San Antón.

Museo Arqueológico Fray Juan Cobo (Archeology Museum), Calle Don Quijote. Outstanding Roman mosaics, plus displays of agricultural tools. Open daily 11–1; closed Sun. To visit, apply to the City Hall (Ayuntamiento).

Santa María, Pza. Sta María. 13th-century church whose parish records include the birth certificate of Miguel de Cervantes.

Torreón de Don Juan de Austria, Calle Don Quijote. Forming part of the old city walls, this Arab tower was restored in the 17th century. Exhibition of paintings on 2nd floor. Open 11–1; closed Sun. To visit, apply to the City Hall.

Almagro (Ciudad Real). One of the outstanding showpieces of La Mancha.

Convento de la Asunción de Calatrava (Dominican Monastery of the Assumption), Campo de Calatrava. Founded in 16th century by Don Pedro de Girón, with beautiful Renaissance cloisters, Plateresque doors, and Gothic church and tombs; declared a National Monument.

Convento de San Francisco, Ronda de San Francisco. Former Franciscan Monastery. Begun in 1596, with remains of some outstanding chapels and paintings; now a parador.

Corral de Comedias (Theater Courtyard), Pza. Mayor. Classical dramas are still performed here at the end of August. Visits can be arranged through the Tourist Office between 9–2, 4–7; and on Sun. 10–2, 4.30–7.

Plaza Mayor. Fascinating 16th-century oblong main square with wooden houses with small windows and wooden balconies supported by stone pillars.

Aranjuez (Madrid). **Casa del Labrador** (Laborer's Cottage), in the Jardín del Príncipe. Built (1792 to 1803) by Charles IV and María Luisa de Parma after the Trianon at Versailles. Its lavish decoration, gilding and ornamentation are a far cry from a laborer's cottage. Open daily 10–1, 3–6; closed Tues.

Jardín del Príncipe (Prince's Garden). A large park (1763 by Boutelou) on the banks of the Tagus; ornamental fountains, sculptures and many different kinds of trees. In the park is the **Casa de Marinos** (Sailors' House) housing the vessels of six Spanish sovereigns. The park closes at 7.30 P.M.

Palacio Real (Royal Palace). Outstanding rooms are the Throne Room, the Porcelain Room and the Miniature Room. The palace houses the **Museo de Trajes** (Museum of Royal Robes). Open daily 10–1, 3–6; closed Tues.

Argamasilla De Alba (Ciudad Real). Believed to be the birthplace of the legendary Don Alonso de Quijano, otherwise known as Don Quijote.

Cueva de Medrano, Cervantes 8. Cave and cell of Cervantes in the former home of Bachiller Sansón Carrasco, where Cervantes is thought to have written the opening chapters of *Don Quijote.* To visit, apply to the Ayuntamiento (city hall).

Castillo de Peñarroya (Peñarroya Castle), 11 km. (seven miles) out on road to Ruidera. Castle with view over the lagoons of Ruidera; important in the Reconquest; and a chapel where the Virgin of Peñarroya is worshipped.

Iglesia de San Juan Bautista (Parish Church of St. John the Baptist), Pza. de España. Houses a votive painting of Rodrigo Pacheco, believed to have been the model and inspiration for Cervantes' Don Quijote.

Belmonte (Cuenca). **Castle.** Hexagonal Gothic castle-fortress. Its rooms are now empty but are still noted for their beautiful Mudéjar ceilings. Open daily 9–2 and 4–6.

Colegiata de San Bartolomé (Collegiate Church of St. Bartholomew). Superbly carved wooden choirstalls originally in Cuenca cathedral, polychrome wooden altar-pieces and the font in which the 16th-century poet Fray Luis de León was baptized.

Buitrago De Lozoya (Madrid). **Museo Picasso,** Pza. Picasso 1, in the basement of the Ayuntamiento (City Hall). Forty works by Picasso which belong to Eugenio Arias, the artist's barber. Open Tues. to Fri. 11–1 and 5–7, Sat. and Sun. 11.30–2 and 4–7; closed Mon.

Chinchon (Madrid). **Castillo de los Condes de Chinchón** (Castle of the Counts of Chinchón). 15th-century Gothic castle, privately owned but can be visited on request.

Iglesia de la Asunción (Church of the Assumption), Pza. Palacio. 16th century with good views over the rooftops of Chinchón, and housing one of the few religious paintings ever done by Goya, his Assumption of the Virgin Mary.

Ciudad Real. Catedral de Santa María del Prado. Single nave late-Gothic cathedral with 17th-century statues and a Renaissance painting by Giraldo de Merlo.

Iglesia de San Pedro. 14th and 15th century Gothic Church, now a National Monument.

Iglesia de Santiago. Ciudad Real's oldest church dating from the 13th century. Once a synagogue, it has Mudéjar carvings and a 13th-century statue of the Virgin and Child.

Puerta de Toledo. The old Toledo gateway forming part of the ancient city walls and dating from the reign of Alfonso XI; a National Monument.

Cuenca. Casa Museo Zavala (Art Gallery), Pza. de San Nicolás. In the 17th-century palace of the Cerdán family. Open Sat. 4–6, Sun. 11–1.

Cathedral, Pza. Pio XII. The only mixed Norman and Gothic cathedral in Spain; its 18th-century altar is by the architect Ventura Rodríguez. The **Cathedral Museum,** with a collection of church treasures and religious art, is open Mon. to Fri. 11–1.30, 2.30–6; Sat. 2.30–7.30, Sun. 11–2, 4.30–7.

Museo de Arte Abstracto (Museum of Abstract Art), Cañónigas, in one of the Hanging Houses. One of the first of its kind in Spain, with a collection of abstract art donated by the Juan March Foundation. Open Tues. to Fri. 11–2 and 4–6 (8 on Sat.), Sun. 11–2.30; closed Mon.

Museo de Cuenca, Obispo Valero 12. Housed in the 14th-century Casa Curato with a collection of archeological finds from the province of Cuenca. Open daily 10–2, 4–7; closed Mon.

Museo Diocesano de Arte Sacro (Diocesan Museum of Sacred Art), Obispo Valero. Open Tues. to Sat. 11–2 and 4–6, Sun. 11–2; closed Mon.

Daimiel (Ciudad Real). In the heart of the Manchegan vineyards and famous for its modern wine vaults.

Convento de las Carmelitas (Carmelite Convent), Pza. de la Paz. 17th-century; now a Historic Monument.

Santa María la Mayor and **San Pedro Apostol,** are two worthwhile 15th-century churches.

Tablas de Daimiel, 11 km. (seven miles) out of town. The marshy area formed by the Guadiana and Cigüela rivers is a paradise for all kinds of wild life and a shelter for migrating birds from all over Spain. One of Spain's five National Parks. Open 10–5 in winter, and 9–8 in summer; closed Mon. and Tues.

El Escorial (Madrid). Monastery of El Escorial. Open 10–1, 3.30–6.30 in summer; 10–1, 3.30–5.30 in winter; closed Mon. An inclusive ticket entitles you to visit all parts of the Monastery as well as the **Casita del Príncipe** (Prince's House) and the **Casita de Arriba** (Upper House) in the monastery grounds, or you can buy tickets for separate sections.

Guadalajara. Palacio del Infantado (Palace of the Duke of Infantado), Plaza Caidos. Restored after severe bombing in the Civil War. Open 9–2 and 4–9; closed Sun. P.M.

Manzanares El Real (Madrid). Attractive mountain village in the Guadarrama range very popular with Madrileños at weekends.

Castle. Built by Diego Hurtado de Mendoza on the site of a 13th-century castle in a mixture of Moorish and Renaissance styles, one of the best preserved and most beautiful castles in Spain. Magnificent views of the rugged peaks of La Pedriza and the Santillana reservoir. Open 10.30–1.30, 3–5.30; closed Mon.

Rascafria (Madrid). Monastery of El Paular, Three km. out on the Ctra. de Cotos. Founded in 1390 by Juan I, its refectory was designed by the Moorish architect Abderraman; early 15th-century church. Open 12–1, 4–4.45; closed Thurs.

Saelices (Cuenca). Ruins of Segobriga, once the capital of Celtic Spain. Ruins of thermal baths, a Roman amphitheater, theater and necropolis; near the temple of Diana. In the ruins is a **Museum,** open Tues. to Sat. 10–2 and 4–7, Sun. 10–2 only; closed Mon. with a collection of archeological finds from the site.

Sigüenza (Guadalajara). **Castillo de los Obispos** (Castle of the Bishops). 12th century, restored and converted into a parador.
Cathedral, Pza. Obispo Don Bernardo. Open daily 11.30–2.30, 4–6.

Talavera De La Reina (Toledo). Small industrial town just off the N-V noted for its ceramic tiles and pottery.
Ermita de la Virgen del Prado (Hermitage of the Virgin of the Meadow), at the approach to town on way in from Madrid. Beautifully-decorated church with *azulejos,* ceramic tiles; the oldest tiles, yellow in color, 14th to 16th centuries, are in the sacristy, the more recent tiles are predominantly blue and date from the 18th–20th centuries.

Toledo. See *Practical Information for Toledo* (page 153).

Valdepeñas (Ciudad Real). **Cooperativa Invencible,** Calle Caro Patón. Valdepeñas' largest winery processing the grapes of some 850 growers amounting to almost five million gallons of wine a year. The winery is open to visitors.
Iglesia de la Asunción (The Church of the Assumption). From the late 15th century; has been declared a National Monument.
Monumento a la Victoria (The Victory Monument), on a hill to the north of town just off the N-IV is a good look-out point and was erected by General Franco to commemorate his victory in the Civil War.
Museo los Molinos de Gregorio Prieto (Gregorio Prieto Museum), Avda. Gregorio Prieto. Over 200 works by the Valdepeñas painter. Open 12–1.30, 4–6; closed Mon.

Valle De Los Caidos (Valley of the Fallen) (Madrid). 12 km. (eight miles) from the Escorial and accessible only by car or tour bus. Open 10–7 daily (6 in winter). The basilica and cafe open at 10.30.

Villanueva De Los Infantes (Ciudad Real). **Convento de Santo Domingo,** Pza San Juan. Convent of Dominican nuns where you can visit the cell in which the great Golden Age writer, Francisco de Quevedo, died in 1645. To arrange a visit, enquire at the Ayuntamiento (town hall).
San Andrés Apostel. 16th-century church, a rare example of Italianate Gothic with a doorway believed to be by Juan de Herrera.

Viso Del Marques (Ciudad Real). **Palacio del Marqués de Santa Cruz,** six km. (four miles) off N-IV along C410 between Almuradiel and Puertollano. Sumptuous palace built by Don Alvaro de Bazán, first Marquis of Santa Cruz, between 1564 and 1585 with Italianate décor and beautiful gardens. It now houses the Museum-Archives of the Spanish Navy. Open daily 9–1, 4–6.

SHOPPING. The main items of interest in New Castile are the **damascene** ware from the city of Toledo and the numerous pottery pieces to be found all over the region, but most especially around the ceramic-making town of Talavera de la Reina. Typical Talavera **ceramics** are blue and yellow in color whereas those from nearby Puente del Arzobispo are mostly yellow and green. Ceramic stalls line the roadside on the approaches to Toledo and Talavera. Other villages with their own brand of typical ceramics are Consuegra, Mota del Cuervo and Chinchilla. Almagro is famous for its hand made **lace,** the village of Lagartera in Toledo province is well known for its embroidery, and in Cuenca you can buy drinking vessels, *porrones,* shaped like bulls. At the Escorial scented sandalwood rosaries are on sale. All over La Mancha—and elsewhere in Spain—you will find carved olivewood figures of Don Quijote and Sancho Panza.

On the gastronomic front, La Mancha produces one of Spain's most famous **cheeses,** *queso manchego.* A good place to buy these is in the picturesque *Venta del Quixote* in Puerto Lápice just off the N-IV where they are made fresh on the premises and where you can sample the cheese in the bar first. So long as you buy a whole cheese, which is preserved in a wax skin, you will have no problems taking it through customs back home. Consuegra is well known for its **saffron,** used to flavor the famous *paella,* and in Aranjuez in early spring, around March–April, the roads are lined with stalls selling fresh strawberries and asparagus.

SPORTS. Fishing. Carp is fished abundantly in La Mancha, and the Ruidera lagoons are one of the finest fishing spots. Fresh-water crabs are found around Daimiel and Argamasilla de Alba. In Madrid province there are trout in the upper reaches of the Guadarrama rivers, with good fishing around Alameda del Monte, La Pedriza and Puerto de los Cotos and magnificent trout in the Buitrago Dam. The Santillana Reservoir is famous for its carp and pike.

Hunting and shooting. Partridge, rabbit and hare are found throughout the region, with partridge being a specialty of La Mancha. The Tablas de Daimiel is one of the best places in Spain for shooting water fowl though permits must first be sought from ICONA.

Rock climbing is much practised in the Pedriza area near Manzanares el Real and there are special **jogging** tracks in Cercedilla.

Skiing. The Guadarrama mountains close to Madrid are one of Spain's main skiing areas, and villages such as the Puerto de Navacerrada, are equipped with ski lifts and ski tows. The season usually runs from late December to early April. The mountain villages are also popular with hikers, joggers and rock climbers in the summer months.

Watersports. The Mar de Castilla in Cuenca province not far from Guadalajara, comprising the reservoirs of Buendía, Entrepeñas and Bolarque, has been well landscaped and developed as a popular watersports area and is much frequented on weekends.

OLD CASTILE

The Essence of Iberia

To the north and west of the capital Madrid, lie the provinces of Old Castile: Avila, Segovia, Salamanca, Zamora, Valladolid, Palencia, Burgos, La Rioja and Soria. Salamanca and Zamora together with the province of León (which for geographical reasons we cover in another chapter) traditionally formed the old medieval kingdom of León which was united early in its history with Castile. Today, for administrative purposes, the region is known as the Autonomous Community of Castilla-León.

Castile's Epic History

Castile arose in Christian Spain in the 10th century, through a rebellion against the Kings of Asturias and León, initiated by Count Fernán González and carried on by his sons. The Kingdom of Castile was established in 957 and rights of succession granted. From a principality, Old Castile finally came to include all of central Spain until, in 1037, León and Castile were united. From then on, new territories were added, Toledo being captured in 1085, completing the region now known as New Castile.

In 1230, Castile was recognized as the representative kingdom for all Spain. Castile held its responsibilities in high regard, helping other rulers in their campaigns against the Moors, and the border castles bear witness to the region's warring abilities.

Three important contributions were made by Castile to the civilization of Spain. The first was an innovation in the legal system by which local customs as laws were adopted, in opposition to the written code. The second was the rise of a popular literature, the *Romancero,* which related past and present history in poetry and song. The most important, perhaps, concerns language. Castile started early to build its language on fixed principles, and by the 10th century, it ranked with Latin as a popular tongue. By the 15th century, Castilian had been adopted in León and Aragón and had supplanted the Mozarabic dialects of the south of Spain.

Exploring Old Castile

The provinces of Old Castile curl about the core of the capital to the west and the north. They are most often visited from Madrid, with the exception of Burgos, which is apt to be a stop on the road between Madrid and France. But the other two of the top three attractions of this region, Avila and Segovia, are usually made the object of excursions from the capital.

As it is easy to see each of the towns in this area on separate trips from Madrid, there is no particular order in which they are likely to be visited. We might as well start, therefore, with Avila, sharing a border with Toledo in New Castile, and swing round clockwise through Segovia, Salamanca, Zamora, Valladolid, Palencia, Burgos and La Rioja (capital Logroño) until we close the circle at Soria.

Mountains and Roman Roads

If you approach Avila from the north, you will travel through a hilly district, strewn with huge granite boulders and many evergreens, to make your last stage across an arid region. But if you come from Madrid, as you probably will, you run first through a countryside dotted with neat villages, then enter a valley enclosed by the foothills of the Guadarrama, and finally come to an area of bleak mountains.

Some 50 km (37 miles) from Madrid, the Guadarrama range extends along a northeast-southwest axis, and with the Gredos range, divides Spain's huge central plateau into Old and New Castile. These mountains, standing out so distinctly in the soft rays of the setting sun, were featured in many of Velázquez's paintings. The Guadarrama range, below which a toll-tunnel provides a substantial shortcut, is the center of many summer activities.

The Sierra de Gredos, separated from that of Guadarrama by the Avila plateau, might be called the sportsman's paradise. Here, within easy access of the parador at Gredos, are the game and fishing preserves, where horse riding and mountain climbing are popular pursuits. There is excellent trout fishing in the River Tormes, which runs close to the scenic road from Avila to Barco de Avila, the latter a pleasant summer resort surrounded by ramparts.

Before the Puerto del Pico pass, with its well-preserved Roman road, another branch traverses the Sierra de Gredos to the Monastery of Yuste and Plasencia. Mombeltrán possesses a lovely 15th-century Gothic church, a 16th-century hospital and a splendid 14th-century Albuquerque castle. Arenas de San Pedro is today a rather run-down small town, but it deserves a stop, not only for its Palace of the Infant Don Luis de Borbón, the Castle of the Triste Condesa, the Monastery of San Pedro de Alcántara and a 14th-century Gothic church, but also as a center for excursions to the picturesque mountain villages of Candelada and El Arena, or to the stalactite Grotto of Aguila.

Some 50 km. south of Avila, just outside the village of Guisando, lies an interesting curiosity known as Los Toros de Guisando, the Guisando Bulls. Little is known about the origins of this ancient group of granite animals, but they are thought to date back to the Celtic Age and to be not older than the 2nd century B.C. It was near here that Henry IV of Castile signed the pact depriving his daughter Juana of her rights to the throne of Castile, and proclaiming Isabella as his rightful heir.

Avila

The dramatically walled city of Avila, 1,219 meters (4,000 feet) above sea level and the highest provincial capital in Spain, is eminently worth visiting, for its historical associations and for its distinctive, unspoiled character. The winter climate is fiercely cold but the summers are not oppressively hot.

Roman Avila was converted to Christianity as early as the first century, and occupied by the Moors until reconquered by Count Raymond of Burgundy who brought it permanently under Christian control. Until the 16th century it was simply a prosperous town; then it assumed an aura of saintliness it still preserves to a remarkable degree.

This is due to Saint Teresa, the mystic whose personality lives today as vividly as it did in the 16th century, when she dedicated herself to the Way of Perfection, and trod barefoot the rocky roads of Spain. Teresa was a great administrator and founded 32 religious institutions for both men and women in different parts of Spain.

One itinerary that the traveler can follow is to the places glorified by Saint Teresa. These are the Convent of Nuestra Señora de Gracia, where she was educated; the Encarnación, where she made her profession and became Prioress; the Convent of San José or Las Madres, which was the first establishment of the Carmelite Reform; and finally, the Convent of Saint Teresa, which stands on the site of her birthplace. Her room has been converted into a chapel, with a statue of her by Gregorio Hernández; and in the adjoining museum her relics are kept—her finger, rosary, books, walking stick and the sole of her sandal.

A visit to Avila is best begun by a tour of the walls that enclose the city. There has been some restoration but this has not lessened their grandeur. They were begun in 1090 by Count Raymond on order of his father-in-law, King Alfonso VI, who decided to repopulate Avila with settlers from other provinces. Among the new citizens were master builders who undertook the work with enthusiasm, making these walls the most complete military installation in Spain in the Middle Ages. They entirely enclose the city, measuring more than two and a half km. (1½ miles), and contain 88 towers, nine gateways and several posterns. They are at their most impressive viewed from the lookout Los Cuatro Postes on the Salamanca road. In spring you will see storks nesting in the turrets of the walls. A good place to look is in the part of the walls close to the Raimundo de Borgoña parador.

There are many interesting churches, convents and fortified palaces. The cathedral resembles a castle more than a place of worship. It was begun in the 12th century and completed in the 15th. There are two important entrances, the Gate of the Apostles, with its pointed arch and statue of the Savior surrounded by reposeful figures, and the west doorway, of Baroque design. The interior is vast and dim, giving a general Gothic impression.

The church of San Pedro stands in the center of the city though just outside the walls. It is Romanesque, with a beautiful rose window. The basilica of San Vicente, Romanesque and Gothic of the 12th to the 14th centuries, is outside the walls, erected on the spot where the saint was martyred. In the center of the chapel of the convent of Santo Tomás, 15th-century Gothic, is the alabaster tomb of Prince Juan, only son of Ferdinand and Isabella. The reredos and three cloisters are exceptionally fine, providing a worthy setting for the Museum of Oriental Art.

Castles in Spain

The province of Segovia, separated from Madrid by the Guadarrama mountains, is famous for its castles, Romanesque architecture, and a Roman aqueduct. The outstanding sights, beside Segovia itself, are the towns of Pedraza and Sepúlveda, the castles of Coca and Fuentidueña, the palaces of Riofrío and La Granja.

On the road to Coca, Santa María la Real de Nieva boasts its famous relic, the *Buried Virgin*. Coca, already important in Roman times and the birthplace of Emperor Theodosius the Great, was built in the 15th century by Bishop Fonseca in flamboyant Gothic but shows strong Mudéjar influence. Today it is used as a school and only its courtyard may be visited. Cuellar castle which is open to visitors in the mornings only, dates from the 15th century and was restored, so its style is Gothic with mudéjar additions. In the 16th century a sumptuous palace was added, which once accommodated the Duke of Wellington. Twenty-nine km. (18 miles) east, mighty Fuentidueña is reached by a bridge over the Duratón. The view of Sepúlveda, 32 km. (20 miles) up the Duratón, is most impressive. The Gonzales Castle, that withstood not only many a Moorish siege but also the repeated assaults of Napoleon's armies, towers above narrow, tortuous streets, with Romanesque churches and noble palaces. Pedraza, still a walled town, is the reputed birthplace of the Emperor Trajan. Over the pretty Plaza Mayor rises a steep crag crowned by the stout walls of the 15th-century castle. Turegano was constructed in the 15th century as the fortress-castle of the bishops of Segovia. If you wish to visit the castle, enquire in the church where the sacristan has the key. But the finest of all the castles in this region lies to the south and belongs technically to New Castile. Across the Guadarrama mountains, 18 km. east of the village of Navacerrada in Madrid province, stands Manzanares el Real (15th century). Its crenelated walls and tower recall the heroic times of the Reconquest.

The quickest way to reach Segovia from Madrid is to take the N-VI and pay the toll for the Guadarrama tunnel. Then leave the freeway at San Rafael and continue along the N603 to Segovia. If there's not much traffic, you can drive the distance in just over an hour. Alternatively, stay on the highway through the village of Guadarrama, and instead of taking the tunnel, continue up over the Puerto de los Leones (1,511 meters) with superb views of both Madrid and Segovia provinces. Then drop down to San Rafael and take the N603.

A worthwhile detour off this road is to the Palace of Riofrío, built by Elizabeth Farnese, widow of Philip V, in the neo-Classical style round a central patio. It houses a small hunting museum. The palace is very cold inside so take a jacket. The vast grounds are filled with roaming deer, which come up to your car. For a small toll, drive right through the cork-oak forest, a relaxed short cut to Segovia.

An alternative, and perhaps even more rewarding route, is to leave Madrid at the Plaza de Castilla and take the C607 Colmenar El Viejo road. A short detour to the right after Guadalix takes you to the magnificent castle and lake of Manzanares el Real. C607 joins the N601 at the resort village of Navacerrada where you bear right and climb up a winding but safe road to the Puerto de Navacerrada (1,860 meters), a ski station with splendid views. You can then make the steep descent through fragrant pine forests to La Granja with its beautiful palace and gardens, and the small village nestling nearby. After that it's straight sailing right into Segovia.

La Granja

The palace of La Granja de San Ildefonso, 11 km. (7 miles) from Segovia, 85 (53 miles) from Madrid, was built by the homesick Philip V to remind him of his beloved Versailles. It has become one of the showpieces of Spain. Originally the site was occupied by a hermitage built at the order of Henry IV of Castile. Later, it was purchased by Ferdinand and Isabella and presented to the Monastery of El Parral, when a farm (granja) was started nearby. And there it is, just as the first Bourbon king of Spain had it made to his liking—statues, fountains, châteaux, retreats, trimmed hedges, formal gardens—an exquisite bit of France in a Spanish wood; Philip V and his Queen, Elizabeth Farnese, are buried in the palace's collegiate church.

Segovia

Segovia stands 998 meters (3,276 feet) above sea level, between two small streams, the Eresma and the Clamores. The first thing that will strike you about Segovia is the enormous, and still undamaged Roman aqueduct. The romantic-looking Alcázar fortress-palace rises like a huge ship on the crest of an 80-meter-high (262-foot) rock. The best view of it is from near the circular 13th-century church of the Knights Templar, just outside the town. Segovia's 16th-century cathedral rises majestically in the corner of the Plaza Mayor.

Segovia has been an important city for 2,000 years. It was the center of Celto-Iberian resistance to Roman conquest, but was occupied by the Romans and razed in the year 80 B.C. It was the capital of Alfonso El Sabio (1284), Isabella was proclaimed queen here in 1474, and here Ferdinand, her husband, swore to preserve the independent rights of Castile.

Segovia's streets are crooked and picturesque, with the cathedral built at the highest point. On entering the city, the Alcázar is not visible, but a sudden turn, and there it is poised as if ready to take off in flight. Burnt down in 1862, it was rebuilt in a fairy-castle style, decorated with huge murals, but furnished with many genuine period pieces. No less striking is the Roman aqueduct, one of the best preserved Roman remains in the world. Built of huge, uncemented boulders, it joins two somewhat distant hills. It is 823 meters (900 yards) long and its 148 arches are over 9 meters (30 feet) high. In the center, a dip in the earth made the use of two tiers of arches necessary, and at this point it towers 27 meters (90 feet) above ground level. The aqueduct served to bring water into the city from Riofrío 16 km. away. High up in a niche in one of its arches a statue of the Virgin stands demurely and somewhat incongruously—having replaced a statue of Trajan—overlooking the Plaza del Azoguejo. On the other side of the aqueduct a delightful small bronze statue of Romulus and the wolf was presented to Segovia in 1974 by the city of Rome to commemorate 2,000 years of the aqueduct's existence.

Romanesque Churches, Gothic Cathedral

Those searching for beauty instead of grandeur will seek out the churches (though sadly they are now only open for Mass), for Segovia is a Romanesque city, untouched for six centuries. Most of them were built during the 12th and the beginning of the 13th centuries and are characterized by their outer galleries, which resemble arcades and give light and air to an otherwise heavy style. The idea may have been to keep the churches cool, but it added a new beauty to following styles. The finest examples are San Martín and San Millán, the latter showing some Moorish influence in its decorations. Others include San Esteban, with a graceful tower; San Andrés with brick arches; San Lorenzo, a beautiful exterior; San Clemente, with fine porticos, apses and tower (but currently under restoration); San Miguel in whose atrium Isabella was proclaimed Queen of Castile, and San Juan de los Caballeros, today a studio for ceramics, founded by Zuloaga (closed at presstime). Deserving special mention is Vera Cruz, consecrated in 1208, one of the most notable churches of the Knights Templar in Europe.

The 16th-century cathedral was the last Gothic building to be erected in Spain, replacing the original church destroyed by the *Comuneros*. Among the works of art are a *Pietà* by Juan de Juni (1571) and a collection of valuable 17th-century Flemish tapestries in the Chapter Hall under a fine coffered ceiling. In the Capilla Mayor stands a neo-Classical marble reredos by Sabatini, in the Capilla del Sagrario a Christ by Churriguera above a ceramic altar; despite these works of art, the overall aspect of the interior is rather bare, many of its treasures having been destroyed in the Napoleonic wars, and the beauty of the cathedral is appreciated much better from the outside when viewed across the picturesque Plaza Mayor.

Segovia's main square with its cafes and ceramic stalls is a delightful place to while away a moment or two. Across the Plaza is the Tourist Office, and nearby the Calle Isabel la Católica leads into Juan Bravo with the church of San Martín and a statue of the local hero, Juan Bravo, who led the Comuneros revolt against Charles V. Continue on down the Calle Cervantes to the Plaza del Azoguejo at the foot of the aqueduct. Mentioned by Cervantes, the plaza was once a rendezvous for thieves and knaves; today it is the market place.

The Monastery of El Parral is one of the many famous convents still standing in Segovia. It was founded by Henry IV and is now a national monument. There are also the Clarisas de San Antonio el Real, a Dominican Convent established by the same king, and a Jesuit seminary.

Even new structures adhere to Segovia's architectural peculiarity (which, by the way, preserves its unity); this is the *esgrafiado*, a facade decoration that can best be seen on the entrance gates to the Alcázar, embellished with small pieces of coal!

Don't miss the view from on top of the old city ramparts near the Alcázar, or better still, from the top of the Alcázar's tower—it affords you a complete view of one of the finest old cities in the world. If you have a car, or don't mind a longer walk, leave from the aqueduct and make your way along the Ronda de Santa Lucia below the ramparts. Near the Carmelite Convent, burial place of St. John of the Cross, is a magnificent spot from which to photograph the Alcázar perched on top of a rock above the meeting place of the Eresma and Clamores streams. Then return to the city along the Carretera de los Hoyos.

Salamanca

Your first glimpse of the ancient city of Salamanca, should you be approaching from the south, is unforgettable. Beside you flows the swift River Tormes spanned by a Roman bridge with 26 arches, and beyond it rise the old houses of the city topped by the golden walls, turrets, domes and spires of the cathedral. Salamanca's history goes back to the time of Hannibal, and a Roman bridge still spans the river. Like León it suffered almost total destruction in the ebb and flow of the centuries-long struggle to eject the Moors, and its great days began only when Alfonso XI of León founded the University in 1223 (much enriched later by Alfonso the Wise who bequeathed it his own huge library of 100,000 volumes and manuscripts).

The University

Several different buildings make up the university. Starting in the Patio de las Escuelas, the facade of the main building is a veritable tapestry in stone, an outstanding example of the "Plateresque style" of decoration, so called because of its resemblance to the work of the silversmith, *platero*. You'll see a medallion of Ferdinand and Isabella on the facade, surmounted by the coat of arms of Charles V and surrounded by a profusion of heraldic emblems and floral motifs. Hiding in their midst is a frog, said to bring good luck to students in their examinations. Inside, the chapel and lecture rooms are clustered round the lower Gothic cloister, from which a majestic staircase ascends to the upper loggia and the famous library. Among the lecture rooms is the Aula de Fray Luis in which, after five years of imprisonment by the Inquisition, Luis de León opened his speech with the famous words: "As we were saying yesterday . . . " Here too in 1936 Miguel de Unamuno, the great philosopher and then Rector of the University, openly challenged the Nationalist General Millan Astray whose only retort was his sinister slogan "Viva la muerte" (Long live death).

To the right of the main entrance lies the Rectory, housed in the former Hospital del Estudio founded in 1413. The chapel is used as an assembly hall and has a strikingly beautiful polychrome coffered ceiling. Here too

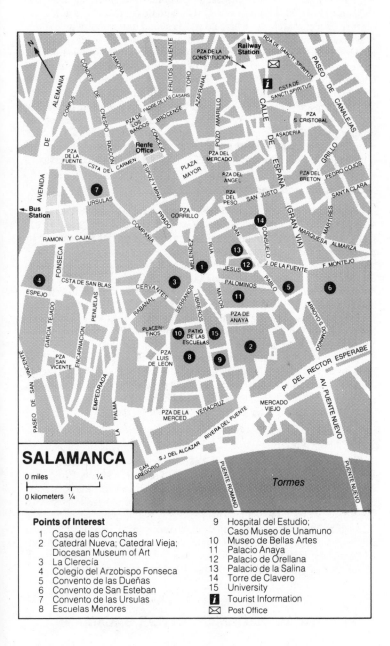

SALAMANCA

0 miles ¼

0 kilometers ¼

Tormes

Points of Interest

1. Casa de las Conchas
2. Catedral Nueva; Catedral Vieja; Diocesan Museum of Art
3. La Clerecía
4. Colegio del Arzobispo Fonseca
5. Convento de las Dueñas
6. Convento de San Esteban
7. Convento de las Ursulas
8. Escuelas Menores

9. Hospital del Estudio; Caso Museo de Unamuno
10. Museo de Bellas Artes
11. Palacio Anaya
12. Palacio de Orellana
13. Palacio de la Salina
14. Torre de Clavero
15. University

i Tourist Information

✉ Post Office

is the House and Library of Miguel de Unamuno, who lived here between 1900 and 1914. On the south side of the Patio de las Escuelas is the 17th-century Escuelas Menores which served as a kind of university preparatory school. The walls of the charming cloistered courtyard are covered with *vitores* testifying to the enthusiasm of successful candidates. Next door is one of the entrances to the Fine Arts Museum located in the house of Queen Isabella's physician, Dr. Alvarez Abarca; the other entrance is on the opposite side of the building in Plaza Fray Luis de León.

Higher up the Calle Serranos spreads the larger Pontifical University La Clerecía, the former Jesuit College whose church is typical of the order's styles. On the opposite corner is the famous Casa de las Conchas whose facade is adorned with the shell motif of St. James, symbol of the pilgrim to Santiago. Nearby is the Dominican Theological University.

Cathedrals and Convents

Not content with three universities, Salamanca also possesses two cathedrals. The three-meter-thick (10-foot) walls of the Old were built by the Cid's chaplain, Don Jerónimo de Perigueux, in the early 12th century. In the center of the 53-panel reredos stands the *Vírgen de la Vega,* patroness of Salamanca, a 13th-century copper statue adorned with Limoges enamels. The lovely cloister is surrounded by numerous chapels housing many notable works of art, among them a superb triptych by Fernando Gallego, Salamanca's greatest painter. Though outmoded by 1513, the Cathedral Chapter clung to Gothic and after some 200 years the graceful vaults and towers of the New Cathedral were at last finished. The interior is rather bare, except for the Baroque choir and some of the chapels.

Across the Plaza stands the 18th-century Anaya Palace, and a short walk away you will come across the 16th-century convent of Las Dueñas with its remarkable double cloisters. Close by is the even more extravagant stone filigree of the church of San Esteban belonging to a Dominican monastery, where the Cloister of the Kings should be seen.

The Plaza Mayor

On the way back to the center you pass the Renaissance palaces of Orellana and La Salina next to the 15th-century Torre del Clavero. From here it is only a short walk to Salamanca's greatest jewel, its Plaza Mayor. Spain's most perfect square was begun in 1729 and completed in 1755 with Churriguera's Royal Pavilion. The Town Hall is a harmonious part of the arcaded buildings round the trapezium-shaped square, used for bullfights till the last century, but now given over to open-air cafés. Sitting surrounded by such perfection you simply don't feel like moving away. It is a touch of splendor, right in the heart of this delightful university town.

PRACTICAL INFORMATION FOR SALAMANCA

TOURIST OFFICE. The Salamanca branch of the Castilla-León Tourist Office is on Gran Vía (Calle de España) 39 (tel. 24 37 30). There is also a Municipal Information kiosk in the Pza. Mayor at the top of the steps leading down into the Pza. del Mercado (tel. 21 83 42).

TELEPHONE CODE. The dialing code for the city and province of Salamanca is (923).

GETTING AROUND. Salamanca is not a large city and all the sights are within walking distance of one another within the central area bounded by the ring road. With the exception of the parador and the *Regio,* all the hotels are located in this central area with one or two out near the station. Both the train station and the bus depot are some way from the center; both are reached by short cab rides or city bus. The most central cab stand is on Pza. Poeta Iglesias just off the Pza. Mayor, though cabs can be hailed all over town.

HOTELS. Many of Salamanca's central hotels are fairly old but they have mostly been renovated and offer comfortable accommodations. The two hotels outside the city center, the parador and the *Regio,* are the only hotels with pools. During Salamanca's fiestas mayores in mid-September, hotel accommodations can be hard to come by if you haven't booked in advance.

Expensive

Gran Hotel, Pza. del Poeta Iglesias 5 (tel. 21 35 00). 100 rooms. The grand hotel of old, very central just off Pza. Mayor, but much in need of a facelift; old-world *Feudal* restaurant. AE, DC, MC, V.

Monterrey, Azafranal 21 (tel. 21 44 00). 89 rooms. Pleasant old-style hotel in center, recently renovated and with good *El Fogón* restaurant. AE, DC, MC, V.

Parador, Teso de la Feria 2 (tel. 22 87 00). 110 rooms; pool. A modern parador with spacious rooms, standing on far side of river with good views of city. AE, DC, MC, V.

Moderate

Alfonso X, Toro 44 (tel. 21 44 01). 66 rooms. An older hotel, backing onto *Monterrey* with whom it shares the same management. AE, DC, MC, V.

Castellano III, San Francisco Javier 2 (tel. 25 16 11). 73 rooms. One of Salamanca's newest hotels; comfortable and recommended. MC, V.

Regio, three km. out on road to Madrid (tel. 20 02 50). 118 rooms. Part of a large hotel, pool and restaurant complex very popular with locals at weekends. Best suited to those with car. AE, DC, MC, V.

Inexpensive

Ceylan, San Teodoro 7 (tel. 21 26 03). 32 rooms. Simple old hotel, central and renovated. V.

Condal, Santa Eulalia 2 (tel. 21 84 00). 70 rooms. Comfortable and very central, the best in this category. DC.

Emperatriz, Compañía 44 (tel. 21 92 00). 37 rooms. A charming old-world hotel in an historic building near La Clerecía and university area.

Pasaje, Espoz y Mina 23 (tel. 21 20 03). 62 rooms. Right in the center and connected to the Pza. Mayor via an arcade on the west side. AE, V.

RESTAURANTS. Two regional specialties of Salamanca are *chanfaina,* a rice dish with lamb, chicken and chorizo sausage, and *farinato,* a local sausage made in the province. Be prepared for some of Salamanca's restaurants to close for a month in summer, often for the whole of July, or the whole of August.

Expensive

Chez Victor, Espoz y Mina 26 (tel. 21 31 23). In recent years this has become the most highly thought of restaurant in town, with superb cooking and friendly, pleasant service. Closed Sun. evening, Mon. and Aug. AE, V.

Nuevo Candil, Pza. de la Reina 2 (tel. 21 50 58). The two *Candil* restaurants are a long-standing institution in Salamanca, offering consistently high standards and a pleasant setting for dining. The set menu is (M). AE, DC, MC, V.

Venecia, Pza. del Mercado 5 (tel. 21 67 44). Another leading and traditional restaurant just off Pza. Mayor. Closed Mon. AE, DC, MC, V.

Moderate

El Candil, Ruiz Aguilera 10 (tel. 21 72 39). A popular atmospheric mesón dedicated to good eating. Always crowded. AE, DC, MC, V.

El Fogón, Dean Polo Benito 3 (tel. 21 44 00). This is the restaurant of the *Monterrey* hotel, but it is open to non-residents too, and is recommended by locals. AE, DC, MC, V.

El Mesón, Pza. Poeta Iglesias 10 (tel. 21 72 22). Typical Castilian mesón. AE, V.

La Olla, Pza. del Mercado 12 (tel. 25 38 04). In the market square just off the Plaza Mayor; consistently good.

La Posada, Aire 1 (tel. 21 72 51). Excellent restaurant, popular with locals. Closed first two weeks of Aug. AE, DC, MC, V.

Rio Chico, Pza. del Ejército 4 (tel. 24 18 78). Recently opened, and managed by *Río Plata* (below), it is fast gaining a good reputation.

Río Plata, Pza. del Peso 1 (tel. 21 90 05). Small and atmospheric, serving superb food; a real find. Closed Mon. and July.

CAFES AND BARS. Cafes. It would be hard to beat Salamanca's beautiful Plaza Mayor as a setting for sidewalk cafes and you are unlikely to want to look further. Of the many enticing cafes that pack the square with their outdoor terraces, two of the best-known are **Las Torres** at #26 and **Novelty** at #1; the latter first opened in 1905. Although any of the Plaza Mayor's cafes are ideal for a coffee or drink at any time of day, they are at their best around 1 P.M. when the locals are having their pre-lunch aperitifs, and again in the evening between 7–9 P.M. when the crowds arrive for the *paseo* hour.

Bars. Being a university city Salamanca has plenty of atmospheric bars and mesones well suited to those in search of evening *tapas* and a glass of wine or beer. Some of the most colorful mesones are to be found at the back of the Plaza Mayor in the arcades of the Plaza Mercado on the east side of the square. Of the half dozen or so mesones here, where you'll be spoilt for choice when it comes to *tapas,* cheeses and hams, **La Covachuela** at Pza. Mercado 24 is one of the best. There's often someone playing the guitar in one of these bars, maybe even a group of musicians from the university *tuna.*

Another good area for atmospheric bars is along and around the Calle Meléndez. Here you have everything from traditional Spanish mesones, to new chic piano bars and pub-style drinking places. In all of them you are free to just drink, or to order snacks and light refreshments.

PLACES OF INTEREST. To see all the sights listed below at a comfortable pace and to have time for shopping and some leisurely drinks in the Plaza Mayor, will take about three full days, though if your time is limited you can absorb much of the atmosphere of Salamanca in less time. Double check the opening hours of monuments with the Tourist Office.

Casa Museo de Unamuno, next to the university on Patio de las Escuelas. Home of the renowned philosopher Miguel de Unamuno when he was Rector of Salamanca university, now a small museum. Open Mon. to Fri. 4–7; Sat., Sun. and fiestas 11–1; closed Aug.

Cathedrals—Old and New. Open 10–1 and 3.30–6 summer, 9.30–1.15 and 3.30–5.45 winter.

La Clerecía, Calle de la Compañía. Jesuit Baroque church and Pontifical University begun in the reign of Philip III with some notable paintings, especially Luis Salvador Carmona's *Christ*. Closed for restoration, but check locally.

Colegio del Arzobispo Fonseca (Los Irlandeses), San Pablo. College of Archbishop Fonseca, also known as the Irish College, boasting a beautiful Renaissance patio and church with a Berruguete retablo. Open 9–2 and 4–8.

Convento de las Dueñas, Pza. Concilio de Trento. Open 10–1 and 4–7 in summer; 10.30–1 and 4–5.30 in winter; Sun. 11–2 and 4–7.

Convento de las Ursulas, Ursulas. Early 16th-century convent and church with a small museum. Open 9.30–12.30 and 4–6.

Convento de San Esteban (Monastery of St. Stephen). A magnificent example of 16th-century Plateresque style. Ornately-carved facade and an altar by Churriguera. Open daily 9–1 and 4–7.

Museo de Bellas Artes (Fine Arts Museum), Patio de las Escuelas. Valuable art collection in 15th-century house. Open 10–2 and 4–7, Sun. 10–2 only; closed Mon.

Pontifical University—La Clerecía. Open Mon. to Fri. 9–1.30 and 4.30–8.30; Sat. 9.30–1.30 only.

Torre del Clavero. The Clavero Tower built in the 15th century houses the Municipal Museum of the History of Salamanca. Open 10–2 and 4.30–7.30. Closed 2nd and 4th Sun. of month, Sat. P.M. and every Mon. and fiesta.

University, Patio de las Escuelas. The oldest university in Spain. Open 9–1.30 and 4–6, Sat. 9.30–1.30 only, Sun. and fiestas 11–1.

SHOPPING. The best buys in Salamanca are hand-made leather **cowboy boots** and the typical silver and black **charro jewelry.** Boots can be bought either ready made or—if you have time—made to measure. Consult the Tourist Office for stockists.

The regional charro jewelry is a specialty of Salamanca, though it can also be purchased elsewhere. Charro rings are the most popular though you can also buy earrings, bracelets and brooches; they are characterized by a silver-and-black flower head with the petals picked out in silver against a black (charred silver) background. They are stocked in most of

the shops around the Plaza Mayor, or in the Calle Tostado just below the
Palacio de Anaya is a small shop and craftroom where you can order them
to your own design.

USEFUL ADDRESSES. Police Station, Rda. de Sancti Spiritus 2 (tel.
24 53 11). **Train Station,** Paseo de la Estación (tel. 22 57 42). **RENFE
Office,** Pza. Libertad 10 (tel. 21 24 54). **Bus Station,** Filiberto Villalobos
33 (tel. 23 67 17).

Travel Agents, *Viajes Meliá,* Avda. Alemania 2 (tel. 22 84 54); *Viajes
Salamanca,* Rua Antigua 3 (tel. 21 87 18); *Wagon-Lits Cooks,* Ruiz Aguilera 2–10 (tel. 21 21 62).

Alba de Tormes

In a southeasterly direction from Salamanca, you can take a pleasant
side trip to Alba de Tormes 19 km. (12 miles) on C510. Alba's historic
importance stems from its dukedom created in 1469—the illustrious
Duchess of Alba is the present title holder—and from its being the last
resting place of Santa Teresa of Avila. Perched high on a hill, dominating
the low-lying flat lands, the restored Armería Tower is all that remains
of the old ducal castle.

St. Teresa died in 1582 in the Carmelite convent on the opposite shore
of the Tormes, spanned by the 20 arches of the medieval bridge. Her mortal remains, or those that are not scattered elsewhere in Spain, are kept
in the church and devoted hands have sought to reconstruct the setting
of her last days on earth for the edification of visitors.

Ciudad Rodrigo

If you are on your way to Portugal, you should pause at the ancient
town of Ciudad Rodrigo 87 km. (54 miles) on N620 from Salamanca.
Named after its liberator from the Arabs, Count Rodrigo Gonzales Girón,
it contains some beautiful 16th-century manorial houses near the picturesque Plaza Mayor. The British Dukes of Wellington are also Lords of
Ciudad Rodrigo, as it was here that the Iron Duke inflicted a decisive defeat upon the forces of Napoleon in 1808. Wellington's troops were drunk
with blood, gunpowder and alcohol, and they proceeded to sack the city,
which burned for a week. The depredations as a whole were charged up
to the French, however. Spaniards are fond of repeating in a tone of voice
like that of Job on his pallet, "The Arabs polished, Napoleon demolished."

The city walls lining the banks of the Agueda are still standing. The
fortress is now a parador. The more recent (16th century) Casa Montarco
has retained more of its original flavor. Don't miss the cathedral, whose
construction began in the 12th century. Rodrigo de Alemán studded the
country with carved choirstalls of mystical or pagan inspiration. The ones
he designed for Ciudad Rodrigo's cathedral will astound you by the stark-
ness of their realism. The Chapel of Cerralbo houses a fine Ribera painting.

La Alberca

If you are not bound for Portugal but wish to return to Salamanca by
a different route, or alternatively to head south to Extremadura, you will

get the maximum of sightseeing by leaving Ciudad Rodrigo on the C515 and heading for the Monastery of Nuestra Señora de la Peña de Francia which sits astride a mountain some 1,830 meters (6,000 feet) high and commands a magnificent view of the surrounding countryside. Only five km. from here lies the delightful town of La Alberca which you should on no account miss.

The whole town has been classified a national monument. To visit it, go down to the calvary cross and continue on foot through the narrow passageways which are paved with steps. Practically all the houses have stables on their ground floors, and the upstairs living quarters are profusely blooming with plants. La Alberca with its cobbled streets and arcaded Plaza Mayor is famous for its folklore and its *Loa,* or Mystery Play, performed on August 15 and 16 for the Feast of the Assumption, when its inhabitants wear national costume and perform their local songs and dances.

To the south towards the Portuguese border lie the shadowy valleys of Las Batuecas, where prehistoric cave paintings and small hermitages emphasize the primeval landscape. Continue eastwards via Miranda del Castañar with its castles and mansions, San Martín del Castañar below a soaring fortress, and through the oak and chestnut forests of the sierra till you come to Bejar, a picturesque town lying beside the main N630 and distinguished by a 16th-century ducal palace and the beautifully landscaped gardens of El Bosque. From here you can turn north back towards Salamanca or else head south, via the Bejar pass and in only a few kilometers you will enter the remote and fascinating land of Extremadura.

Zamora

Zamora was an old frontier fortress and you cannot drive the 65 km. from Salamanca to Zamora through this pleasantly hilly countryside, with the dark mountains of the north Portuguese province of Braganza occasionally visible far to the west, without realizing that this is frontier country. Crumbling but still formidable medieval castles face west towards their troublesome neighbors, who broke away from Spain only in the 12th century.

The little city of Zamora is perched defensively upon a steep hill, and it was here Doña Urraca, wicked daughter of King Ferdinand I, shut herself in to resist the besieging forces of her brother Sancho in 1072. Just outside the defiant walls of Zamora she had Sancho murdered. Under his younger brother Alfonso, there began the second great wave of the Reconquest, led by the gigantic, almost legendary figure of El Cid Campeador.

Sightseers in Zamora feel almost as if they had been whisked off to the Orient. The Arabs have left their stamp here through the intermediary, so to speak, of the Mozárabes; the latter were a paradoxically united group of both Christians and Moslems who staged an uprising against the Eastern potentates in Córdoba without waiting for the Reconquest. This bit of history explains why Zamora was constantly war-torn.

The distinguishing feature of the local Palace of Justice is its shield, ornamented by the figure of a monkey, which has led to its being referred to disrespectfully as the Casa de los Momos, or House of Grimaces. The Holy Week Museum is installed in a restored palace close to the church of Santa María la Nueva. The cathedral is unfortunately disfigured by a ponderous tower that throws its proportions off kilter. In Zamora, you will derive a certain consolation from the mellow Flemish tapestries that are the pride of the museum: they hang in the charming cathedral cloister. Beforehand, pay a little visit to the choirstalls; the work of Rodrigo de Alemán, they are full of wickedly amusing, natural touches. Visit also the interior of San Claudio's church and of Santiago El Viejo, the scene of the solemn ceremony in which El Cid received his knighthood. (That, of course, didn't keep him from being expelled from the town later on.) The beautiful Renaissance parador of the Condes de Alba y Aliste should not be missed.

Not far from El Cid's 11th-century house, a 15-arch stone bridge spans the river and brings you to the Cabanales suburb. Try to find time to see Santo Domingo, Santa María de la Orta (the order of the Knights Hospitaler), Santo Tomé and Santiago del Burgo. Before leaving the subject of churches, we should also mention San Pedro de la Nave (a quarter of an hour away), founded in Visigothic times.

If you are now heading north from Zamora, towards León and Galicia, you will pass through the old town of Benavente, with a comfortable parador, and here you may choose to turn westwards on the N525 passing through the mountains of the Sierra de Cabrera before entering Galicia in the province of Orense. Just before you leave Zamora province, you will come to Puebla de Sanabria, where there is a parador, but even more important, it is only a few kilometers to the loveliest mountain lake in Spain, the Lago de Villachica, where tree-covered hills crowd down to the water's edge. With the mountains of Portugal to the south, and of Galicia and León to the north, it is a magical spot in which to enjoy some lovely country scenery.

If, after Zamora, you are staying within the confines of Old Castile, then you will branch east towards Toro and its Roman bridge, 30 km. distant, halfway between Zamora and Tordesillas in the province of Valladolid. In the impressive church of Santa María la Mayor, look out for the wooden retable, and the painting of the *Virgin and the Fly,* for which the great Queen Isabella is said to have posed.

Valladolid, Province of Kings

Valladolid is another province rich in castles and ancient architectural remains, overshadowed, as usual, by the provincial capital in the heart of the endless wheat fields of the plateau, 193 km. (120 miles) north of Madrid. At an altitude of 692 meters (2,270 feet), the climate is somewhat harsh in summer and winter, but the Pisuerga river provides enough water to enable the beautiful gardens in and around the town to thrive despite the otherwise arid nature of the country.

In September, Valladolid celebrates the *Ferias Mayores,* or Great Fair; but if you happen to be in the vicinity during Easter week, do not miss the Semana Santa processions. Even for those not particularly interested in religious festivals, it is a great artistic experience to see passing before you, along the city streets, the fabulously beautiful statues created by famous *imagineros castellanos* so long ago. It was in Castile that this distinctive type of polychrome religious sculpture originated. Valladolid saw its beginnings and today preserves the finest examples of this work.

As is the case with many Spanish cities, the early history of Valladolid is dominated by one man. He was Count Pedro Ansurez, the town's governor and benefactor in the time of Alfonso VI. He provided it with its name, Belad Walid, an Arabic phrase meaning "the town of the governor." During much of the 13th century, Valladolid was the residence of the governors of Castile. The Cortes met here some ten times, until its return for good to Madrid at the beginning of the 17th century. Napoleon, too, set up his headquarters here in 1809.

Shades of Columbus and Cervantes

Wandering around this pleasant, but in many ways somewhat dilapidated, city, your first impression may be one of decaying old houses, often in rack and ruin, interspersed with modern buildings, many of them faceless and anaemic, though some have been built in traditional Castilian style. But hidden among the arcades of its sadly neglected center you will come across a wealth of interesting old churches, museums and historic houses, all bearing witness to the greatness of Valladolid's historic past. Strolling along the city streets you will come upon the house where Columbus died in 1506. The house, now a well laid out museum chronicling the history of the New World, is actually a reconstruction, the original one having been demolished in 1965; a stone in the garden marks the actual site of Columbus' deathbed. Other historic houses include the old home of Cervantes, which is now a museum, and the Atheneum, located in the house of José Zorrilla, author of *Don Juan Tenorio.* One of Spain's most popular dramas, the latter is performed all over the country every year in November.

Los Pimenteles, the birthplace of Philip II, still stands, as does Las Aldabas, where Henry IV was born. Among many other palaces is the Casa de los Viveros, where Ferdinand and Isabella were married in 1469. Not all the events in Valladolid were happy ones, however. Just off the Plaza Mayor, used in ancient times for a bullring and for *autos da fé,* is the small square of the Ochavo, where you may see the spot upon which Don Alvaro de Luna, minister and favorite of King Juan II, was beheaded in 1453.

The cathedral, of late Renaissance style, was begun by Juan de Herrera and continued by Diego de Praves, while the upper part of the facade was added by Churriguera in his own individual Baroque, but never completed. Juan de Juni's splendid reredos stands out in the classically austere interior of 32 Corinthian columns. The Collegiate Church next door is now the Diocesan Museum with lovely reredos, jewelry and above all the silver monstrance by Juan de Arfe, which is 1.82 meters (6 feet) high and weighs 63 kilograms (140 pounds). Almost facing the magnificent entrance arch is El Salvador with a Flemish reredos; backing onto the cathedral stands Santa María Antigua, founded in the 11th century and reconstructed in the 13th, whose Romanesque tower is an architectural gem.

Nearby Las Angustias is famous for its high altar designed by Velázquez, alas only the lesser Cristóbal, and Juan de Juni's *Vírgen de los Cuchillos* (Our Lady of the Knives). Beyond the Archiepiscopal Palace, the church of La Cruz and the house of the painter Berruguete, rises the fortress-like 15th-century San Benito, whose Renaissance cloisters have become the *Auditorio Patio Herreriano* for theatrical performances. It is an impressive church if somewhat bare inside, since, as with many of Valladolid's churches, its works of art have all been removed to the Sculpture Museum.

Across the Plaza del Poniente you come first to the church of San Lorenzo and then the circular Convent of Santa Ana, founded by Philip II and rebuilt by Sabatini; three Goyas and a sculpture by Fernández adorn the church. On the far side of the Campo Grande park the Royal College of Augustinian Fathers, built in 1759, houses the recent Oriental Museum boasting a magnificent collection of Chinese and Philippino art.

For those who love books, the College of Santa Cruz, founded by Cardinal Mendoza in 1479, contains a library of rare volumes. Across the Plaza Santa Cruz the austere building of the University is enlivened by a Baroque portal.

This still leaves Valladolid's two greatest monuments, both on the prodigious Plaza San Pablo, adjoining the palace of Philip II. The facade of the 15th-century Dominican Monastery of San Pablo resembles in its Plateresque profusion a Gothic reredos; inside the lack of church furniture is more than compensated for by the ornate doors of the north and south transepts and the beautiful gold and blue roof beams studded with interesting bosses. Its Plateresque magnificence is rivaled only by the entrance and cloisters of the College of San Gregorio, now Spain's outstanding National Museum of Polychrome Sculpture, built between 1488 and 1496 for Bishop Alonso de Burgos, confessor of Ferdinand and Isabella; his coat of arms appears in the center of the facade. Inside is a patio of exquisite design, its lower, twisted columns upholding an open, lavishly carved gallery.

Here is displayed that polychrome sculpture to which Spanish artists brought a brilliant and original genius. Abandoning marble and bronze, these creators worked with wood—pine, oak and cedar—and added color. The method of execution was peculiar to Spain. Once the figure had been carved from wood, it was polished and the polychrome was applied by painters who specialized in this art. The process was highly technical and the results have never been equaled elsewhere.

The interior of San Gregorio is well adapted for these exhibits though some of the exhibits themselves are not very clearly labelled and you will benefit from purchasing a detailed guidebook. The spacious rooms are rich in statues, carvings and fragments. Alfonso de Berruguete's magnificent retablo executed between 1526–32 from the Church of San Benito, is mounted on blue velvet walls in Rooms I–III; Diego de Siloé worked on the elaborately carved pews in Room XI; Juan de Juni is represented by his touching *Encierro de Cristo* in Room XV, Pedro de Mena by his Mary Magdalene, beautiful in its simplicity; and Gregorio Fernández by his *Cristo Yacente*. In Room XXVIII note the head of St. Paul (San Pablo) by Juan Alonso Villabrille y Ron—it helps if you hold a mirror to the mouth to see the details of finely carved tongue and teeth. Many of the museum's priceless *pasos* are carried through the streets in Valladolid's Holy Week processions but remain in the museum for the rest of the year.

Excursions from Valladolid

If this formidable array of miscellaneous architecture should prove insufficient, there are castles and churches galore beyond the capital. Only 11 km. (seven miles) down the Pisuerga rise the cylindrical towers of mighty Simancas, a Moorish castle reconstructed by Alfonso III. Since the reign of Charles V it has served as the General Archive of the Kingdom and over 30 million documents are kept in its 52 rooms. Beautifully renovated, but not generally open to visitors, it's a splendid sight from the old road, but is bypassed by the new.

Medina de Ríoseco in the northern Tierra de Campos abounds in churches ranging from Gothic to Baroque, while Villalón goes in for Mudéjar and Plateresque. A rectangular keep with four turrets was added in the 15th century to guard Fuensaldaña Castle; Mota del Marqués and Torrelobatón serve as impressively stern reminders of the embattled past as Iscar and Portillo, where Don Alvaro de Luna was imprisoned.

South of the Duero, Olmedo, immortalized by Lope de Vega in his *Gentleman of Olmedo,* has preserved its ramparts and numerous churches. Nava del Rey not only possesses a Gothic-Renaissance church, but also produces excellent wines of the sherry type in the enormous vineyards which extend over this part of the province.

At Medina del Campo, the churches of San Antolín and San Martín contain reredos sculptured in part by Berruguete and Becerra. Other tokens of past glory are the Casa Blanca, the Casa Consistorial, and the Dueñas family mansion. Above all don't miss the superb castle of La Mota; though not open to visitors, it is marvelously well preserved, with a deep moat, towers, drawbridge and barbican. Here Isabella the Catholic breathed her last. It later served as a state prison, holding at various periods such choice inmates as Hernando Pizarro, Rodrigo Calderón and Cesare Borgia. There is also the pleasant Plaza de España, a picturesque square surrounded by noble old houses, the City Hall, 16th-century Collegiate church and the former slaughterhouse.

East from Valladolid along the course of the Duero, Peñafiel Castle was built in the 10th century, but the present unusual silhouette of a ship run aground dates from the 14th. At Valbuena de Duero stands the 12th-century Cistercian Monastery of St. Bernard.

The Mad Queen and the Mapmaker

Lastly, Tordesillas, where Queen Joan (Juana la Loca), mad daughter of Ferdinand and Isabella and mother of the Emperor Charles V, lived out her distraught existence long after the death of her husband, Philip I of Spain. She was so passionately in love with him that, when he died young, she refused to let his body be buried and carried the open coffin with her on her travels for three years before being confined at Tordesillas. She lived here for 49 years, a long time to stay in prison, even when the view over the Duero is unrivaled.

Prior to that, when Spain and Portugal were busily dividing up the "new world to be discovered," it was at Tordesillas, in 1494, that they reached an agreement, amending an earlier arbitral decree issued by the Borgia Pope Alexander VI. As a result, much of Latin America was settled by Spaniards, whereas Brazil became Portuguese, largely through an error in calculation, either involuntary or deliberate, committed by a certain cartographer named Amerigo Vespucci . . . yes, the very one.

The restored Convent-Palace of Santa Clara was originally the residence of King Pedro I. The Mudéjar style is particularly striking in the patio—sometimes referred to as the Alhambra of Castile—and in the gilt-adorned chapel. The tomb of the founder, Friar Fernando de la Cueva, is a further fine example of 15th-century Mudéjar art. Here also are the musical instruments of the Mad Queen, but her apartments were in an adjoining palace, of which, after a fire in 1974, only the church and tower of San Antolín remain.

The Communal Bull

In this part of the country the big fiestas are held in September. In small towns that can't afford arenas, a makeshift bullring is set up in the Plaza Mayor, where bull and fighters confront one another—for no celebration is complete without the gory encounter between man and beast. All exits from the square are barred off, it is surrounded by wood panels resembling campaign-billboards, sand is sprinkled on the ground, and then, on with the corrida! Everybody chips in to buy the bull; the people living in the square invite their friends to come and watch from windows and balconies.

This particular kind of bullfighting is governed by a set of regulations that make it something quite different from what the average visitor sees. It begins with a few ordinary passes at the bull in the improvised arena, and the banderillas are put in place. But the bull is then let loose to run through the town, perhaps even into the countryside if he can make it. The entire male population, on foot or on horseback, dashes off in pursuit, bent on killing the bull. The putting to death has to be done within established limits and rules; no firearms or poisons are allowed. The amateur matadors are usually armed with spears. Whoever strikes down the bull is borne in triumph and is awarded a prize and the bull automatically becomes the property of the community having jurisdiction over the territory in which the bull gets slaughtered. If he escapes beyond the town limits it's the neighbors who will do the feasting!

Palencia

The province of Palencia owes its wealth of old monasteries to the position it occupies across the famous pilgrimage route which led from France across northern Spain to the tomb of St. James the Apostle (in Spanish, Santiago) at Santiago de Compostela.

The lowlands of the River Pisuerga form the western boundary of Palencia; it is separated from Santander by the Cantabrian range. In general the landscape and climate of the region—called Tierra de Campos—is a blend of the dry Castilian plateau and the less severe north.

In the 12th century the city of Palencia was the seat of the Castilian kings and the Cortes. It was reduced in importance by Charles V, however, who never forgave it for its part in the revolt of the Comuneros. The cathedral was begun in the 14th century, with an unusual Plateresque altar and stone sculptures by Gil de Siloé. Next in importance is the church of San Miguel, 13th-century Gothic. The Plaza Mayor is typical and the city abounds in *alamedas* and gardens.

If you can give up a day, do not neglect a trip to the Mirador de Tierra de Campos, only 18 km. from Palencia near the village of Autillo del Pino. From this vantage point on a clear day, you can look out over a distance of some 50–60 km. upon the region known as the Tierra de Campos, stretching through the provinces of Valladolid and Palencia. Nor should you neglect *Las Rutas Románicas,* a little tour along the Pilgrim's Way which includes Fromista, with its Benedictine Monastery of San Martín, continuing to Villalcázar de Sirga, on a third-class road. Its Alcázar was a royal grant to the Knights Templar and in the Santiago Chapel, in the church of Santa María la Blanca, is the solitary tomb of a knight of the times. A fine reredos and some superb carved tombstones make the visit to this church—too important for the town's present-day population— more than worthwhile. Coming back through Carrión de los Condes, court of kings and seat of counts, you will visit the church of Santa María de la Victoria del Camino and other buildings. Only eight km. from Palencia is the Castle of Paradilla del Alcor; and nearby, in the village of Antillo del Pino, stop for one of the finest overall views in this part of Old Castile.

Burgos, the Shield of Castile

Castile of the Middle Ages, with its wealth of architecture, comes to life in the province of Burgos; a varied and rich land irrigated by the headwaters of the Ebro river. Burgos is reputed to speak the purest Castilian in Spain, which is understandable, since the language had its origin here, becoming the national tongue only later.

The city of Burgos straddles the River Arlanzón halfway between Madrid and San Sebastián. Though the Gothic character of the inner core has been preserved, many of the 156,000 inhabitants are engaged in industrial projects that have created dreary suburbs. The Holy Week processions are beautiful, especially on Good Friday. If you are in Burgos during Corpus Christi, visit the Monasterio de las Huelgas the next day for the procession called *Corpillos.*

Burgos was founded in the 9th century by a Castilian count. For a time it was the royal residence and the capital of Old Castile. It joined the Comuneros against Charles V, but appeased his wrath by erecting the triumphal Arco de Santa María, a curious gateway with towers, pinnacles, and statues. Many battles of the War of Independence were fought nearby and, during the Civil War, it was the headquarters of General Franco.

Burgos has two glories. One of the country's finest Gothic cathedrals, whose twin spires rise up to greet you long before you reach the city, stands here. In addition, it is the city of El Cid, the national hero who embodies the Spanish idea of chivalry. His equestrian statue in the city center is one of Burgos' great landmarks.

The first stone of Burgos cathedral was laid in the reign of Saint Ferdinand III by Bishop Mauricio in 1221 and the work was continued for the next 30 years. The facade and towers were finished in the 14th century; Juan de Colonia executed the Condestable Chapel and the tracery of the spires in the 15th century; the dome dates from the 16th century. The exterior, of the most exuberant flamboyant Gothic, culminates in the fine 13th-century sculpture on the Sarmental and Coronería gateways.

The interior of the cathedral is imposing in its grandeur and can be studied only superficially during a first visit. The Condestable Chapel, for example, is so large and elaborately decorated that it leaves you breathless. The Escalera Dorada, a flight of double steps with heavy gilt balustrades leading to the Puerta de la Coronería, and the door itself were designed by Diego de Siloé. The reredos in the Chapel of Santa Ana is by his son, Gil de Siloé; the whole church, in fact, is a treasure house of sculpture by famous artists. Do not miss the superb ironwork. This craft reached its highest point in the Spanish Gothic. The cloister on the southeast side of the cathedral is 13th-century Gothic, and contains many statues of interest. It's advisable to engage a guide, since the greatest treasures are locked up. Two of the cathedral's more intriguing features are the bizarre image of Christ covered in a cow hide in the Santo Cristo Chapel, and high up in the nave just inside the West Door, the famous Papamoscas (flycatcher) Clock—watch the bird open its mouth as it strikes the hour.

Other churches and important places to see in Burgos are San Esteban, San Nicolás with a stunningly beautiful altarpiece by Simón de Colonia (1505), San Gil; the celebrated Casa del Cordón of the 15th century, where Columbus was received by Ferdinand and Isabella when he returned from his second voyage to America; and the Marceliano Santa María museum in the ruined cloisters of the Monastery of San Juan.

Three splendid Gothic monuments lie on the outskirts. To the west, the convent of Las Huelgas Reales, originally a summer villa of the kings of Castile, was converted into a majestically endowed convent for noble ladies by Alfonso VIII in 1187. The Gothic church is flanked by Romanesque cloisters and Mudéjar chapels. The kneeling figures of Alfonso and his wife, Eleanor, daughter of Henry II of England, are on either side of the altar in the main chapel, while their tombs are behind the double screen that conceals the nuns from the public. Here also you will see the banner captured from the Moors in the Battle of Las Navas de Tolosa (1212). The collection of medieval fabrics may be unique, but is rather tattered.

Closer to the river is the Hospital del Rey, another foundation of Alfonso VIII, now a sadly neglected old men's home, but the Puerta de Romeros and the Casa de Romeros are Plateresque at its best.

The Cartuja de Miraflores in the eastern suburbs is approached by a drive lined with poplars and elms. It was founded in 1441 by Juan II, the poet king, and rebuilt by Simón de Colonia. The reredos of its Isabelline Gothic church is by Gil de Siloé, gilded with the first gold brought back from America. Gil, one of the greatest wandering artists of the Middle Ages, carved the tombs of Juan II, his queen, Isabel of Portugal, and Prince Alfonso in alabaster by order of Queen Isabella.

El Cid

Five km. farther on is the Monastery of San Pedro de Cardeña where El Cid took leave of his wife before going into exile. The exploits of El Cid Campeador (lord champion)—whose actual name was Rodrigo Díaz de Vivar—are immortalized in the greatest Spanish epic poem, *El Cantar del Mío Cid.* You can visit El Solar del Cid, the site of the house where he once lived and see the coffer he filled with sand instead of treasure won from the Moors. He left the coffer as security for a loan, but when it was opened, the sand was found to have turned miraculously to gold. See the church of Santa Agueda, which lives in history because it was here that the Cid made the new King Alfonso VI swear that he had had no part in the death of his brother Sancho during the siege of Palencia. Finally, in the transept of the cathedral, is his tomb, beside that of his wife, Doña Jimena.

The whole of Castile is dotted with too many noble castles, churches and monasteries to enumerate. The 58 km. (36 miles) south to the most renowned, the Benedictine Monastery of Santo Domingo de Silos with its marvelous 11th-century cloister pass through Quintanilla de las Viñas, proud of its Visigothic church; and the ancient town of Covarrubias, in whose collegiate church two outstanding works of art can be seen: a triptych of Diego de Siloé and a polychrome sculpture by Berruguete. The walls of historic Lerma enclose a ducal palace, not open to visitors, and a 17th-century collegiate church.

In the north beyond the Ebro, the Castle of Medina de Pomar looks down on an Alcázar, a convent and the old Jewish quarter, and near the summer resort of Villarcayo stands the 11th-century Romanesque Abbey of Tejada.

La Rioja, Vineyard of Spain—and Soria, the Undiscovered

Most travelers bypass the provinces of La Rioja and Soria, although neither is far from the main road from San Sebastián to Madrid, and both are logical stops on the way to Zaragoza.

Logroño, capital of the province of La Rioja, is beautifully situated on the Ebro, crossed here by two bridges, one of stone, constructed in the 13th century by Juan de Ortega. It was dominated first by the Romans, then by the Saracens. In 1076 it came under the rule of Alfonso I of Castile, and in 1521 the city defeated the invading army of the French. The finest table wines in Spain come from this beautiful province, which is equally rich in game and the sport afforded by its clear rivers, alive with trout and freshwater crayfish, called *cangrejos.*

Other places to visit in La Rioja are Calahorra, one of the oldest Iberian towns on the peninsula, once used as a refuge against the Romans; Santo Domingo de la Calzada, whose early Gothic cathedral is dominated by a Baroque tower, inside which is a lovely 13th-century reredos and—unique in Christendom—a white cock which crows lustily during the service from a cage opposite the saint's tomb; and Santa María, containing a handsome cloister and tombs of the kings of Castile.

Soria might be called the "Red City," from the color of its sunbeaten soil, from which bricks and tiles are made. Lying on a plateau on the right bank of the Duero, it came under the rule of Castile in 1136, during the reign of Alfonso VII. There are several fine Romanesque churches—San Juan de Rabanera, San Pedro, the French-inspired Santo Domingo, and Nuestra Señora de la Mayor—but the most important is San Juan del Duero, with its ancient cloister. Soria was the city adopted by the poet Antonio Machado who immortalized many of its landscapes in his much loved volume *Tierras de Castilla.*

Only seven km. north of Soria is the ancient city of Numancia, celebrated for its heroic resistance to the Romans. Destroyed by them in 134 B.C., its remains were discovered in 1854 by Eduardo Saavedra. There is, however, precious little to see. But the Numantine Museum in Soria is filled with artifacts from the excavations and is well worth a visit.

Medinaceli, 72 km. (45 miles) south of Soria, was an important stronghold of the Moors and contains tombs of the Medinaceli family, who, in the Middle Ages, were claimants to the Spanish throne. Their ancient castle still stands, and so does the Roman arch of the 2nd or 3rd century,

the only one with a triple archway surviving in Spain. The village is picturesquely perched on a hill and is well worth a visit, especially for those traveling the Madrid-Barcelona road.

PRACTICAL INFORMATION FOR OLD CASTILE

TOURIST OFFICES. Avila, Pza. Catedral 4 (tel. 21 13 87); **Burgos,**
Pza. Alonso Martínez 7 (tel. 20 31 25); **Ciudad Rodrigo,** Arco de Amay-
uelas 6 (tel. 46 05 61); **Fromista,** Paseo Central; **Logroño,** Miguel Villanueva 10 (tel. 21 54 97); **Medina de Rioseco,** Pza. Generalísimo (tel. 70
08 25); **Palencia,** Mayor 105 (tel. 72 00 68); **Salamanca,** España 39 (tel.
24 37 30) and Pza. Mayor 10 (tel. 21 83 42); **Segovia,** Pza. Mayor 10 (tel.
43 03 28); **Soria,** Pza. Ramón y Cajal (tel. 21 20 52); **Tordesillas,** Pza.
Mayor 1 (tel. 77 00 61); **Valladolid,** Pza. de Zorilla 3 (tel. 35 18 01); **Zamora,** Santa Clara 20 (tel. 51 18 45).

TELEPHONE CODES. The dialing codes for the provinces of Old Castile are: Avila (918), Burgos (947), La Rioja-Logroño (941), Palencia
(988), Salamanca (923), Segovia (911), Soria (975), Valladolid (983), Zamora (988). Only dial these codes if you are calling from outside the province. Dialing codes for all the towns we list are given under *Hotels and
Restaurants* immediately after the name of the town.

GETTING AROUND OLD CASTILE. By Train. All the provincial
capitals with the exception of Logroño, are on fast frequent routes from
Madrid. To Avila and Segovia there is a frequent *cercanías* (suburban)
service from Madrid (Atocha and Chamartín).

Old Castile has some of the best train services in Spain. Four major rail
junctions provide interconnecting points for most places—Medina del
Campo (Valladolid), Venta de Baños (Palencia), Aranda del Duero (Burgos) and Miranda de Ebro (Burgos).

Train Stations and RENFE Offices. Avila station is on the eastern edge
of town (tel. 22 65 79); **Burgos** station is at the end of Avda. Conde de
Guadalhorce (tel. 20 35 60) and the RENFE office is at La Moneda 21
(tel. 20 91 31); **Logroño** station is on the Pza. de Europa (tel. 25 49 35)
and the RENFE office is at Calvo Sotelo 13 (tel. 25 88 55); **Palencia** station
is by the Jardinillos (tel. 74 30 19); **Segovia** station is on Paseo Obispo
Quesada out along the Ctra. de Villacastín (tel. 42 15 63) and is reached
by bus 3 from the Pza. Mayor; **Soria** station is the Estación del Cañuelo
(tel. 22 28 67) and the RENFE office is on Pza. del Olivo 5 (tel. 21 21
84); **Valladolid** station is at the far end of Paseo Campo Grande (tel. 30
35 18) and the RENFE office is on Divina Pastora 6 (tel. 30 80 52); **Zamora** station is a long way out of town to the northeast reached by Avda.
de las Tres Cruces, and the RENFE office in town is on Santa Clara not
far from the Tourist Office.

By Bus. There are plenty of services from Madrid city to the provincial
capitals of the region, and plenty of services from the capitals out to the
smaller towns of each province.

Bus Stations. With the exception of Soria, all the provincial capitals have central bus depots. **Avila,** on the Avda. de Madrid; **Burgos,** Miranda 4 (tel. 20 55 75); **Palencia,** near the train station; **Segovia,** corner of Ezequiel González; **Valladolid,** Puente Colgante 2 (tel. 23 63 08); **Zamora,** near the bullring.

By Air. The only city in Old Castile to have a regular airport is Valladolid with daily flights to Barcelona Mon. to Fri. The airport is 14 km. out on N601 to León (tel. 56 01 62). Valladolid's Iberia office is on Gamazo 17 (tel. 30 06 66/30 07 77). Salamanca has an airport but it is only used for charter flights and private planes.

By Car. The main highways crossing Old Castile are the N-I running north from Madrid to Burgos and on to the French border at Irún, and the N-VI running northwest from Madrid and the main starting point for Avila, Segovia and Valladolid. All the other main N roads in the region offer easy driving, if not always good surfaces.

Much of Old Castile is flat high plateau land and the only mountain areas are in the outlying corners of the region.

HOTELS AND RESTAURANTS.

HOTELS AND RESTAURANTS. All the provincial capitals of Old Castile are well endowed with a range of hotels, and in the smaller towns and along the roads there is no shortage of moderate hotels and roadside hostels. There are historic paradors in Avila, Ciudad Rodrigo, Zamora and Santo Domingo de la Calzada, and good modern paradors in Segovia, Salamanca, Soria and Tordesillas.

Old Castile is famed for its suckling pig *(cochinillo)* and roast meats, especially roast lamb *(cordero asado),* and the gastronomic capital for such specialties is undoubtedly Segovia which boasts one of Spain's best known restaurants, the *Mesón de Cándido.* Valladolid is another fine gourmet city with an unusual number of good restaurants for a town of its size. Standing on the traditional Galicia–Madrid truck route, it specializes in fish dishes as well as meat, unusual for inland Castile.

Aguilar De Campo. Palencia (988). *Valentín* (M), Avda. del Generalísimo 21 (tel. 12 21 50). 50 rooms. Bar and garden. AE, DC, MC, V.

Alba De Tormes. Salamanca (923). *Benedictino* (I), Las Benitas 6 (tel. 30 00 25). 40 rooms. Parking and garden. DC.

La Alberca. Salamanca (923). *Las Batuecas* (I), Ctra. de Batuecas (tel. 43 70 09). 24 rooms. Two-star hotel with parking and garden. V.

Alfaro. La Rioja (941). *Palacios* (I), Ctra. de Zaragoza (tel. 18 01 00). 86 rooms. Pool, tennis, garden and bar. AE, DC, MC, V.

Aranda De Duero. Burgos (947). *Los Bronces* (M), 1 km. north on N-I (tel. 50 08 50). 29 rooms. AE, DC, MC, V. *Montehermoso* (I), 5 km. north on N-I (tel. 50 15 50). 54 rooms. Both are modern roadside hotels. AE, DC, MC, V. *Motel Tudanca* (I), 7 km. south on N-I (tel. 50 60 11). 20 rooms. Ideal spot for overnighting. AE, DC, V. *Tres Condes* (I), Avda. Castilla 66 (tel. 50 24 00). 35 rooms. In town. AE, DC, MC, V.

Restaurants. *Casa Florencio* (M), Arias de Miranda 14 (tel. 50 02 30). Good roast lamb. DC, V. *Mesón de la Villa* (M), Alejandro Rodríguez de Varcárcel 3 (tel. 50 10 25). Renowned for great Castilian roasts. Closed Mon. and most of Oct.

Arnedillo. La Rioja (941). *Del Balneario* (M), Balneario (tel. 39 40 00). 181 rooms. Pool, tennis and gardens. Spa hotel, open mid-June to mid-Oct. only.

Arnedo. La Rioja (941). *Victoria* (M), Constitución 97 (tel. 38 01 00). 48 rooms. Pool, garden and tennis.

Avila (918). *Palacio de Valderrábanos* (E), Pza. de la Catedral 9 (tel. 21 10 23). 73 rooms. Luxuriously appointed and highly recommended hotel situated in 15th-century mansion opposite the cathedral. AE, DC, MC, V. *Parador Nacional Raimundo de Borgoña* (E), Marqués de Canales y Chozas 16 (tel. 21 13 40). 62 rooms. Beautifully located in a 15th-century palace which forms part of Avila's famous city walls. AE, DC, MC, V.

Don Carmelo (M), Paseo de Don Carmelo 30 (tel. 22 80 50). 60 rooms. Good modern hotel close to rail station. V.

Cuatro Postes (M), Ctra. Salamanca 23 (tel. 21 29 44). 36 rooms. A modern hotel just outside town, with splendid view of the walled city. *Reina Isabel* (I), Avda. de José Antonio 17 (tel. 22 02 00). 44 rooms. AE, DC, MC, V. *Rey Niño* (I), Pza. de José Tomé 1 (tel. 21 14 04). 24 rooms. Good value in the heart of town. Closed Oct. to Apr. V.

Restaurants. *Parador* (E), within the hotel (see above). Castilian cuisine; try their *cocidos* or the *yemas de Santa Teresa* (a sweet dessert resembling egg yolks). *Las Cancelas* (M), Cruz Vieja 6 (tel. 21 22 49). Popular family-run mesón serving local dishes at good-value prices. Closed Wed. evening. *Piquio* (M), Estrada 4 (tel. 21 14 18). Veal, lamb and suckling pig specialties; popular with the locals. AE, V. *El Rastro* (M), Pza. del Rastro 1 (tel. 21 12 19). Ancient inn serving local specialties, including Avila's famous veal and *yemas de Santa Teresa*. AE, DC, MC, V. *El Torreón* (M), Tostado 1 (tel. 21 31 71). Situated in the old Velada Palace, near the cathedral. Food excellent. AE, V.

Bejar. Salamanca (923). *Colón* (I), Colón 42 (tel. 40 06 50). 54 rooms. Garden and bar. AE, DC, V.

Benavente. Zamora (988). *Parador Nacional Rey Fernando II de León* (E), Paseo de Ramón y Cajal (tel. 63 03 00). 30 rooms. Situated in a 15th-century castle. AE, DC, MC, V.

Burgos (947). *Landa Palace* (L), 4 km. south off the N-I (tel. 20 63 43). 39 rooms, pool, garden. One of the great hotels of Spain, in a transplanted 14th-century castle. Praised by readers for its charm—not to mention its magnificent marble bathrooms. V. *Almirante Bonifaz* (E), Vitoria 22 (tel. 20 69 43). 79 rooms. Highly recommended for comfort and excellent service. AE, DC, MC, V. *Condestable* (E), Vitoria 8 (tel. 26 71 25). 82 rooms. Comfortable, central hotel with good standards. AE, DC, MC, V. *Mesón del Cid* (E-M), Pza. de Santa María 8 (tel. 20 87 15). 30 rooms. Magnificently located opposite the cathedral. AE, DC, MC, V. *Cordón* (M),

La Puebla 6 (tel. 26 50 00). 35 rooms. Comfortable and functional opposite Casa del Cordón. AE, DC, V. *Corona de Castilla* (M), Madrid 15 (tel. 26 21 42). 52 rooms. Modern hotel situated in a dull part of town. AE, DC, V. *Fernán Gonzáles* (M), Calera 17 (tel. 20 94 41). 64 rooms. Overlooking river and city. V. *España* (I), Paseo del Espolón 32 (tel. 20 63 40). 66 rooms. Pleasant central location on the promenade. Friendly, though somewhat shabby. *Norte y Londres* (I), Pza. Alonso Martínez 10 (tel. 26 41 25). 55 rooms. Central and close to mesones. Lots of old-world charm and décor, friendly service. V.

Restaurants. *Los Chapiteles* (E), Gen. Santocildes 7 (tel. 20 59 98). Elegant décor, considered the best in town. Closed Wed. evening and Sun. AE, DC, MC, V. *Landa Palace* (E), within the hotel (see above). Delightful; unbeatable for beauty and atmosphere. AE, DC, MC, V.

Arriaga (M), Laín Calvo 4 (tel. 20 20 21). Old fashioned, a real old Burgos tradition. Closed Mon. AE, DC, MC, V. *La Becada* (M), Pza. Santo Domingo de Guzmán 18 (tel. 20 85 13). Recent restaurant fast gaining a name for good food. Closed Sun. night and late Aug. AE, DC, MC, V. *Casa Ojeda* (M), Vitoria 5 (tel. 20 90 52). Charming Castilian setting overlooking the Casa del Cordón. AE, DC, MC, V. *Gaona* (M), Paloma 41 (tel. 20 61 91). Long established and reliable, close to cathedral; fish specialties. Closed Wed. except July to Sept. AE, DC, MC, V.

Mesón del Cid (M), Pza. de Sta. María 8 (tel. 20 59 71). In a 15th-century house opposite the cathedral, home of one of Spain's first printing presses. Good food and atmosphere. Closed Sun. evening. AE, DC, MC, V. *Papamoscas* (M), Llana de Afuera (tel. 20 45 65). In a square behind the cathedral; outdoor tables have a fine view of the sculptured east facade, and indoors is a typically atmospheric mesón. AE, DC, MC, V. *Rincón de España* (M), Nuño Rasura 11 (tel. 20 59 55). An elegant dining room and large covered terrace for summer dining. AE, DC, MC, V.

Villaluenga (I), Laín Calvo 20 (tel. 20 61 54). A simple, family-run *económico,* friendly and very popular. Great value.

Calahorra. La Rioja (941). *Parador Nacional Marco Fabio Quintiliano* (M), Era Alta (tel. 13 03 58). 63 rooms. Modern, with beautiful décor and good facilities. AE, DC, MC, V.

Cervera De Pisuerga. Palencia (988). *Parador Nacional de Fuentes Carrionas* (E), Ctra. de Ruesga (tel. 87 00 75). 80 rooms. Modern parador in a mountain setting overlooking a reservoir. Good view of Picos de Europa from the balcony. AE, DC, MC, V.

Ciudad Rodrigo. Salamanca (923). *Parador Nacional Enrique II* (E), Pza. del Castillo 1 (tel. 46 01 50). 27 rooms. Located in a 15th-century castle set in a pleasant garden. AE, DC, MC, V. *Conde Rodrigo* (I), Pza. del Salvador 7 (tel. 46 14 04). 31 rooms. Charming and friendly. V.

Covarrubias. Burgos (947). *Arlanza* (M), Pza. Mayor 11 (tel. 40 30 25). 38 rooms. Situated in an historic building, a semi-parador. Saturdays (except July and Aug.) there are medieval banquets. Closed Dec. through Mar. AE, DC, MC, V.

La Granja De San Ildefonso. Segovia (911). *Roma* (I), Guardas 2 (tel. 47 07 52). 16 rooms. Hostel situated at entrance to palace. Open July to Sept. only. V.
Restaurant. *Dolar* (M), Valenciana 1 (tel. 47 02 69). Good value, simple home cooking. Closed Wed. MC, V.

Ledesma. Salamanca (923). *Balneario de Ledesma* (I) (tel. 57 02 50). 214 rooms. Spa hotel with pool and garden.

Logroño. La Rioja (941). *Los Bracos* (E), Bretón de los Herreros 29 (tel. 22 66 08). 72 rooms. Comfortable and modern, central. AE, DC, MC, V. *Carlton Rioja* (E), Gran Vía del Rey Juan Carlos I, 5 (tel. 24 21 00). 120 rooms. The best hotel in Logroño, large and modern. AE, DC, MC, V. *Gran Hotel* (M), General Vara de Rey 5 (tel. 25 21 00). 69 rooms. A pleasant old-timer with garden and garage. AE, DC, MC, V. *Murrieta* (M), Marqués de Murrieta 1 (tel. 22 41 50). 113 rooms. Modern and well situated with good restaurant.
Restaurants. *La Merced* (E), Marqués de San Nicolás 109 (tel. 22 11 66). Outstanding restaurant in a grand old house offering excellent food and service. Admirable wine list and a "wine museum." Closed Sun. and early Aug. AE, DC, MC, V. *Machado* (E–M), Portales 49, 1st floor (tel. 24 84 56). Elegant décor and excellent cuisine. Closed Sun. and Aug. AE, DC, V. *Asador González* (M), Carnicerías 3 (tel. 25 12 96). Serves the best roast goat in Spain. Known also as *La Chata.* Closed Sun. *El Cachetero (M),* Laurel 3 (tel. 22 84 63). A "must," much frequented by artists, bullfighters, and the famous. Closed Sun., Wed night and mid–July to mid–Aug.

Medinaceli. Soria (975). *Nico Hotel 70* (M), Ctra. Nal. II (tel. 32 60 11). 22 rooms. Recent; pool. AE, DC, MC, V.

Medina Del Campo. Valladolid (983). *La Mota* (I), Fernando el Católico 4 (tel. 80 04 50). 40 rooms. V.
Restaurant. *Madrid* (M), Fernando el Católico 1 (tel. 80 01 34). V.

Medina De Pomar. Burgos (947). *Las Merindades* (I), Pza. Somovilla (tel. 11 08 22). 23 rooms. A fairly recent hotel in a 16th-century house.

Medina De Rioseco. Valladolid (983). *Los Almirantes* (M), San Francisco 2 (tel. 70 01 25). 30 rooms. Good views. Pool and recommended restaurant.

Miranda De Ebro. Burgos (947). *Tudanca* (M), Ctra. Madrid–Irún 45 (tel. 31 18 43). 124 rooms. Garden and bar.

Monzon De Campos. Palencia (988). *Castillo de Monzón* (M), (tel. 80 80 75). 10 rooms. Situated in a small, comfortable castle. Good restaurant. AE, DC, MC, V.

Navarredonda De Gredos. Avila (918). *Parador Nacional de Gredos* (M), (tel. 34 80 48). 77 rooms. Beautifully located some two or three km. (a mile or two) out of town in the Gredos mountains, this was the first of the government-run paradores; Alfonso XIII chose the site in 1926. Has since been refurbished and enlarged. AE, DC, MC, V.

Las Navas Del Marques. Avila (91). *San Marcos* (I), Pza. Ciudad Ducal (tel. 897 01 01). 16 rooms. Three-star hotel with a garden, and located in a pinegrove. Closed Oct. to Mar.
Restaurant. *Magalia* (M), Paseo de las Damas (tel. 897 02 10). Agreeable restaurant overlooking pinegrove. The meat dishes are especially good. AE, DC, MC, V.

Palencia (988). *Castilla la Vieja* (M), Casado del Alisal 26 (tel. 74 90 44). 87 rooms. Central. AE, DC, V. *Rey Sancho de Castilla* (M), Avda. Ponce de León (tel. 72 53 00). 100 rooms. Pool and tennis. AE, DC, V. *Monclús* (I), Menéndez Pelayo 3 (tel. 74 43 00). 40 rooms. Central. V.
Restaurants. *Casa Damián* (M), Martínez de Azcoitia 9 (tel. 74 46 28), and *Lorenzo* (M), Avda. Casado del Alisal 10 (tel. 74 35 45), are owned by two brothers. Both offer small menus of good, simple food. *Gran San Bernardo* (M), Avda. República Argentina (tel. 72 59 49). A smarter restaurant with good standards, but not so central. AE, DC, MC, V.

Pancorvo. Burgos (947). *El Molino* (M), at km. 306 on the N-I (tel. 35 40 50). 48 rooms. Pool and gardens.

Pedraza. Segovia (911). **Restaurants.** *Hostería Pintor Zuloaga* (E), Matadero 1 (tel. 50 40 88). Atmospheric state-run restaurant. Closed Tues. except in summer. AE, DC, MC, V. *El Yantar de Pedraza* (M), Pza. Mayor (tel. 32). Very typical with tiny menu but well recommended. Closed Mon. except in summer. AE, MC, V.

Puebla De Sanabria. Zamora (988). *Parador Nacional* (M), Ctra. de Zamora (tel. 62 00 01). 44 rooms. Modern, small and quiet. AE, DC, MC, V.

Salamanca. See *Practical Information for Salamanca* (page 178).

Santa Maria De Huerta. Soria (975). *Parador Nacional* (M), at km. 180 on the N-II (tel. 32 70 11). 40 rooms. A small modern roadside parador, fine for overnighting. AE, DC, MC, V.

Santo Domingo De La Calzada. La Rioja (941). *Parador Nacional* (E), Pza. del Santo 3 (tel. 34 03 00). 27 rooms. Situated in an old pilgrim hostel of the Way of St. James dating back to the 11th century. AE, DC, MC, V.

Santo Domingo De Silos. Burgos (947). *Tres Coronas* (M), Pza. Mayor 6 (tel. 38 07 27). 16 rooms. Small family-run hotel with good restaurant. MC, V.

Segovia (911). *Parador Nacional* (E), (tel. 43 04 62). 80 rooms, pool. A little way out to the north of town, this modern parador offers magnificent views over Segovia. AE, DC, MC, V. *Los Arcos* (E–M), Ezequiel González 24 (tel. 43 74 62). 59 rooms. Modern, functional hotel in new part of town, renovated and reopened in 1987. *Los Linajes* (E–M), Dr. Velasco 9 (tel. 43 12 01). 55 rooms. Delightful modern Castilian-style hotel in the heart of the old town, close to San Esteban church; splendid views. AE, DC, MC, V. *Acueducto* (M), Padre Claret 10 (tel. 42 48 00). Comfortable older hotel with balconies overlooking the famous aqueduct. AE, DC, MC, V. *Puerta de Segovia* (M), (tel. 43 71 61). 118 rooms. Three km. (two miles) out of town on the N110 at La Lastrilla. Modern, but functional and dull. Pool and tennis. AE, DC, V. *Las Sirenas* (M–I), Juan Bravo 30 (tel. 43 40 11). 39 rooms. Pleasant, centrally-situated hostel overlooking San Martín church. AE, DC, V.

Restaurants. *Parador Nacional* (E), within the hotel (see above), has acquired a good local reputation. *Casa Duque* (E–M), Cervantes 12 (tel. 43 05 37). Several floors of beautifully decorated traditional restaurants. Lots of color and local atmosphere—and Castilian specialties on the menu. AE, DC, V. *Mesón de Cándido* (E–M), Pza. del Azoguejo 5 (tel. 42 81 02). The most famous restaurant in Segovia—if not in the whole of Spain. Seven dining rooms pulsate with atmosphere; bullfighting memorabilia and photos of all the dignitaries, from many countries, who have dined here during the restaurant's long history. Reserve a table early to get one of the windows facing the aqueduct. Specialties are suckling pig and roast lamb. AE, DC, MC, V.

El Bernardino (M), Cervantes 2 (tel. 43 32 25). Pleasant décor, friendly service—and some superb views. As well as the traditional roast meats, it does a very good paella. AE, DC, MC, V. *César* (M), Ruíz de Alda 10 (tel. 42 81 01). Close to the aqueduct and very pleasant. Specializes in fish (unusual for Segovia) and fresh vegetables. Closed Wed. and Nov. AE, DC. *El Hidalgo* (M), José Canalejas 3 (tel. 42 81 90). Attractive restaurant opened in 1988 behind the Church of San Martín in a 13th-century palace with ancient beamed ceilings, gallery, and charming enclosed patio. Closed Mon. AE, MC, V. *Mesón Don José María* (M), Cronista Lecea 11 (tel. 43 44 84). Modern but built in traditional style; popular with Segovianos for good food at reasonable prices. AE, DC, V. *La Oficina* (M), Cronista Lecea 10 (tel. 43 16 43). Just off Pza. Mayor, opposite Don José María (see above). Dating back to 1893 with two delightful dining rooms brimming with paintings and knick-knacks. AE, DC, MC, V. *La Taurina* (I), Pza. Mayor 8 (tel. 43 05 77). Typical Segovian décor, bullfighting ambience. Friendly service. AE, DC, MC, V.

Soria (975). *Parador Nacional Antonio Machado* (E), Parque del Castillo (tel. 21 34 45). 34 rooms. Small and modern, located in a park with good views over the Duero and the city. AE, DC, MC, V. *Alfonso VIII* (M), Alfonso VIII 10 (tel. 22 62 11). 103 rooms. Traditional central hotel. AE, DC, MC, V. *Caballero* (M), Eduardo Saavedra 4 (tel. 22 01 00). 84 rooms. The most recent, situated on the edge of town just off the road to Valladolid. AE, DC, V. *Mesón Leonor* (M), Paseo del Mirón (tel. 22 02 50). 32 rooms. Pleasantly located on a hill near Numancia ruins. AE, DC, MC, V.

Restaurants. *Maroto* (M), Paseo del Espolón 20 (tel. 22 40 86). One of the best. AE, DC, MC, V. *Mesón Castellano* (M), Pza. Mayor 2 (tel. 21 30 45). DC, MC, V. *Casa Garrido* (I), Manuel Vicente Tutor (tel. 22 20 68). Closed Wed. and Nov. AE, DC, MC, V.

El Tiemblo. Avila (91). *Las Jaras* (M), (tel. 862 50 36). 17 rooms. Next to the Burguillo reservoir. Open June to Sept. only. *Los Toros de Guisando* (I), Avda. de Madrid 5 (tel. 862 50 11). 36 rooms. A top hostel with pool. MC, V.

Tordesillas. Valladolid (983). *El Montico* (M), Ctra. Burgos–Salamanca (tel. 77 07 51). A good hotel, with pool, tennis and garden. AE, DC, MC, V. *Parador Nacional* (M), Ctra. Nal. 620 (tel. 77 00 51). 73 rooms. One of the modern paradors. Pool. AE, DC, MC, V.

Toro. Zamora (988). *Juan II* (I), Pza. del Espolón 1 (tel. 69 03 00). Modern and friendly, with views over the Duero plain or the massive church. Excellent food and local wine. AE, DC, V.

Valladolid (983). *Felipe IV* (E), Gamazo 16 (tel. 30 70 00). 130 rooms. Modern, somewhat impersonal. Bar, bingo and parking among the many facilities. AE, DC, MC, V. *Olid Meliá* (E), Pza. de San Miguel 10 (tel. 35 72 00). 237 rooms. The best hotel in Valladolid, located in the old part of the town. Good service, and an excellent—though pricey—restaurant. AE, DC, MC, V. *Meliá Parque* (E–M), García Morato 17 (tel. 47 01 00). 300 rooms. The biggest and most recent (1982), but in a dull part of town next to the bus depot. AE, DC, MC, V. *Imperial* (M), Peso 4 (tel. 33 03 00). 80 rooms. Older hotel just off Pza. Mayor; fine but a little faded. AE, DC, MC, V. *Mozart* (M), Menéndez Pelayo 7 (tel. 29 78 88). 30 rooms. A newly opened hotel right in the center. *Roma* (M), Héroes del Alcázar de Toledo 8 (tel. 35 46 66). 38 rooms. Central, but parking difficult.

Restaurants. *La Goya* (E), Puente Colgante 79 (tel. 35 57 24). Garden dining on the edge of town across the Pisuerga river. Closed Sun. evening and all day Mon., also Aug. *El Hueco* (E), Campañas 4 (tel. 33 76 69). Atmospheric cellar restaurant below a lively mesón; superb daily specials. AE, V. *Mesón La Fragua* (E), Paseo de Zorrilla 10 (tel. 33 71 02). Top cuisine—try the rich suckling lamb—in comfortable mesón atmosphere. Closed Sun. evening. AE, DC, MC, V.

Atrio (M), Atrio de Santiago 5 (tel. 35 18 43). Neighborhood bar/restaurant with *belle époque* décor and pleasant outdoor terrace opposite the Roma hotel. AE, DC, MC, V. *El Figón de Recoletos* (M), Recoletos 3 (tel. 39 60 43). A stylish, well-recommended restaurant with good menu and wine list. *Mesón Cervantes* (M), Rastro 6 (tel. 30 61 38). Good Castilian restaurant close to Cervantes' house; one of the best. Closed Mon. and Nov. AE, DC, MC, V. *Mesón La Viña* (M), Ferrari 5. Going since 1913 with a cozy upstairs dining room. On Marina Escobar is a whole cluster of good medium-priced restaurants. One of the best is *Mesón Pañero* (M), Marina Escobar 1 (tel. 30 16 73). AE, DC, MC, V.

Machaquito (I), Caridad 2 (tel. 35 13 51). Simple setting but the food is tops; good value. AE, DC, MC, V. *Mesón Combarro* (I), Correos 3. The most popular of the numerous cheap eating places on this street; something of an institution, so book ahead.

Zamora (988). *Parador Nacional Condes de Alba y Aliste* (E), Pza. de Cánovas 1 (tel. 51 44 97). 19 rooms. One of the most magnificent paradores in Spain, located in the old town in a converted medieval palace with many antiques. Garden and pool. AE, DC, MC, V. *Dos Infantas* (M), Cortinas de San Miguel 3 (tel. 51 28 75). 68 rooms. Modern. AE, DC, MC, V.

Cuatro Naciones (I), Avda. José Antonio 11 (tel. 53 22 75). 40 rooms. Modern, somewhat antiseptic hotel, though clean and comfortable. *Rey Don Sancho* (I), Ctra. Villacastín–Vigo (tel. 52 34 00). 76 rooms. A typical, well-run, roadside hostel. Good value, if a little downbeat. AE, DC, MC, V. *El Sayagues* (I), Pza. Puentica 2 (tel. 52 55 11). 56 rooms. Quiet, simple hostel. Reasonably priced restaurant.

Restaurants. *París* (E), Avda. de Portugal 14 (tel. 51 43 25). The best in town. AE, DC, MC, V. *Rey Don Sancho II* (M), Pza. Marina Española (tel. 52 60 54). Regional specialties and good service. AE, DC, MC, V. *Serafín* (M), Pza. de Maestro Haedo 10 (tel. 51 43 16). Especially recommended for seafood. AE, DC, MC, V. *Valderey* (I), Benavente 7. Has a bar with good tapas and, next door, a pleasant restaurant.

PLACES OF INTEREST. Old Castile has more than its fair share of interesting sights as well as some of Spain's finest museums and universities. The most notable monuments in Old Castile are the cathedral in Burgos, the Roman aqueduct in Segovia, the university of Salamanca and the National Museum of Polychrome Sculpture in Valladolid. Many of the castles for which these lands are famed are unfortunately not open to visitors and can only be viewed from the outside; those which are open to view are listed below.

Alba De Tormes (Salamanca). **Convento de las Carmelitas** (Carmelite Convent). Open 9–2 and 4–8.

Aranda De Duero (Burgos). **Santa María.** Church founded by the Catholic Kings in the 15th century with a typically Isabelline Gothic facade and magnificent Plateresque doorway.

Arenas De San Pedro (Avila). **Convento de San Pedro de Alcántara.** 17th-century Franciscan monastery, three km. from Arenas.

Cuevas del Cerro de Aguila (Caves of Aguila), 10 km. from village. Impressive stalactite grotto. Open 10–6 (7 in summer).

Arnedo (La Rioja). **Monasterio de Vico,** Ctra. de Préjano. Cistercian convent. Exhibition and sale of decorated porcelain. Open 10–12.30 and 4–6.

Avila. Basilica de San Vicente. Vast Romanesque basilica. Open 10–1 and 4–6.

Cathedral. Impressive fortress-like cathedral begun in 1107, finished in 14th century; with the alabaster tomb of Cardinal Alonso de Madrigal. Open 8–1 and 3–7 (5 in winter). Museum opens at 10 A.M. Sun. and fiestas 11–7 (5 in winter).

Convento de San José, Saveno. Santa Teresa's first foundation, with small museum housing relics of the saint, and a 17th-century church. Open 10–1 and 3.30–6.

Convento de Santa Teresa de Jesús, Pza. de la Santa. Open 9–1.30 and 3.30–9.

Monasterio de la Encarnación, Paseo de la Encarnación. Convent of the Incarnation where Santa Teresa took her vows. Open 9.30–1 and 4–6.

Monasterio de Santo Tomás, Pza. de Granada. 15th-century Gothic monastery; residence of the Catholic Monarchs and later a university. Its cloisters house the **Museum of Oriental Art.** Open 10–12.30 and 4–7.

Museo Provincial, Pza. de Nalvillos 3. Provincial Museum in 15th-century building; archeological collection and popular art including tapestries and ceramic tiles. Open Tues. to Sat. 10–1.30 and 7–9, Sun. 11–1.30; closed Mon.

Bejar (Salamanca). **Museo Mateo Hernández,** Pza. Martín Mateos. Works of art in the old church of San Gil. Open Oct. through June, Sat., Sun. and fiestas 11–2; July through Sept. 11–1 daily.

Palacio de los Duques de Bejar. Palace of the Dukes of Bejar with a double-galleried Renaissance patio decorated with the shields of ancient Bejar families; a National Monument.

Santa María. Notable 13th-century church with fine paintings.

Benavente (Zamora). **San Juan del Mercado,** Pza. Encomienda. 12th-century Romanesque church; fine Journey of the Magi carving on the south door. Open 9.30–1 and 7.30–9.

Santa María de Azogue, Calvo Sotelo. Romanesque exterior and early Gothic interior. Inside are some fine sculptures including two 12th-century Annunciations. Open 9.30–1 and 7.30–9.

Torre del Caracol (Snail Tower). 16th–17th-century tower, the only remnant of the Pimentel Palace which was burnt down by Napoleon's troops, and now incorporated in the parador. Splendid views of the surrounding countryside from the terrace.

Burgos. Arco de Santa María, overlooking the river at junction Avda. Gen. Franco and Paseo del Espolón. The present gate dates from the 14th–16th centuries and on its sculptured facade is the Virgin Mary surrounded by Charles V, Fernán González and El Cid, and below the founder and 10th century governors of the city.

Casa del Cordón (House of Ropes), Pza. Calvo Sotelo. Built at the end of the 15th century by the Constable of Castile, for his wife. Only the outside and the patio can be seen; currently under restoration.

Cathedral. Open 10–1.30 and 4–6.30.

Museo Arqueológico (Archeology Museum), Casa Miranda on Calle Miranda. Housed in a 16th-century palace. Open 10–1.30 and 5–7; closed Mon.

Museo Marceliano de Santa María, Pza. de San Juan. Charming art gallery in the remains of the San Juan Monastery, with over 150 paintings by the Burgos artist Marceliano Santa María (1866–1952). Open 10–2 in summer, and 11–2 and 5–8 in winter; closed Sun. P.M. and Mon.

San Esteban. Beautiful Gothic church badly damaged in the 1813 explosion which destroyed the Castle. Valuable collection of tapestries, paintings of the Castilian school showing Flemish influence, and several tombs. Open 10–2.

San Gil. 13th–14th century, long a prison. Notable are the Chapel of the Nativity and the Chapel of the Three Kings, the wrought iron pulpit and a statue of *La Dolorosa* by Gregorio Fernández. Open 11–1 and 3–7 (5 in winter).

San Nicolás, Pza. de Sta. María. Open Tues. to Fri. 12–2 and 6.30–8, Mon. 9–9, Sat. 10–12, Sun. 9–1.15 and 4.45–6.

Outside the city are:

Cartuja de Miraflores, three km. southeast. Open 10.15–3 and 4–7 (6 in winter); Sun. 11.30–12.30, 1–3 and 4–7. Mass at 10.15 on Sundays.

Hospital del Rey, three km. west on road to Valladolid. Founded as a hospice for pilgrims on the Camino de Santiago. Fine Renaissance patio and splendidly-carved church door. Only the outside and entrance can be seen.

Monasterio de las Huelgas, one km. southwest, reached by Bus 5 from El Cid statue. Open Tues. to Fri. 11–2 and 4–6; Sat. and Sun. 11–2 only; closed Mon.

San Pedro de Cardeña, ten km. from Burgos and reached by Bus 9 from El Cid. Trappist monastery dating from 899 but rebuilt in 11th century. Famous Cloister of the Martyrs and one-time resting place of the bodies of El Cid and Doña Jimena. Open 9.30–1 and 4–7, Sun. and fiestas 12–2 and 4–7.

Calahorra (La Rioja). Ancient city of Celtic origin and named Calagurris by the Romans. Seat of a bishopric since the 5th century.

Cathedral. 12th-century with Baroque facade. Notable choir, sacristy and Gothic chapels. Houses the **Diocesan Museum** with a valuable collection of religious art from diocesan churches. Open Sun. only 12–2.

Ciudad Rodrigo (Salamanca). **Ayuntamiento,** Pza. Mayor 21. The City Hall, in a splendid Renaissance palace with galleried facade.

Casa de los Aguilas, Dámaso Ledesma. Now the Post Office, with Gothic doorway and Plateresque grills and ornamentation.

Cathedral. Romanesque cathedral begun in 1165 with Gothic and Plateresque additions, outstanding cloisters and choirstalls. Open 8–12 and 4–8.

Palacio de los Castros, Pza. del Conde. Outstanding example of a Plateresque palace, today the residence of the Counts of Montarco.

Palacio del Príncipe, Juan Arias. Pure Plateresque palace with fine patio, stairway and ornamentation, former home of the Prince of Melito. Calvary scene by Juan de Juni in its chapel.

Covarrubias (Burgos). **Colegiata y Museo Parroquial** (Collegiate Church and Parochial Museum), Chindasvinto 3. 15th-century church containing the tombs of Fernán González and his wife Doña Sancha, and Princess Christine of Norway. The Museum has a rich collection of church art including paintings by Pedro Berruguete and Van Eyck and a 15th-century triptych of the Three Kings by Gil de Siloé. Open 10–2 and 4–7; closed Tues. in winter.

Torreón de Fernán González. 10th-century tower in which, according to legend, Doña Urraca was imprisoned by her father Fernán González in 1039.

Fromista (Palencia). Charming old village standing on the Camino de Santiago and with remains of an old Jewish quarter and synagogue.

San Martín, Pza. San Martín. An outstanding example of Romanesque church architecture. Open 10–2 and 4–8. Closed Mon.

Santa María del Castillo, Pza. del Castillo. Renaissance and Plateresque church with an altarpiece of 29 Flemish paintings depicting the Salvation of Mankind from Paradise to the Assumption of the Virgin Mary.

La Granja De San Ildefonso (Segovia). Royal Palace and Tapestry Museum

are open 10–1.30 and 3–5, Sun. 10–2; closed Mon., and the gardens close at 7 P.M. In summer, May through Oct., the fountains play on certain days only, usually Thurs., Sat., and Sun. To check, call 911–47 00 19 or ask at the Segovia Tourist Office.

Medina Del Campo (Valladolid). Castillo de la Mota.

Mudéjar castle, former residence of the Catholic Kings, and where Isabella died on November 24, 1504. Splendidly preserved but not open to the public.

Palacio de las Dueñas, Santa Teresa. Attractive brick palace showing clear Mudéjar influence.

Medina De Pomar (Burgos). Monasterio de Santa Clara, Santa Clara

1. Beautiful grilles, a statue of the dead Christ by Gregorio Fernández and a museum with many fine treasures. Open 10–1 and 5–7.

Medina De Rioseco (Valladolid).

Historic town with many fine churches and exceptionally beautiful Holy Week processions.

Santa María de la Asunción, Pza. Sta María. 16th-century Gothic church with Baroque tower, altar by Esteban Jordán, splendid Benavente chapel and several works by Juan de Juni. Open June through Oct. 11–2.30 and 4.30–7.30; Nov. through May, weekends only 11–1.30.

Najera (La Rioja). Monasterio de Santa María la Real.

Founded by King García of Navarre; church rebuilt 1422–1453. Royal Pantheon and 12th-century tomb of Doña Blanca de Navarra. The cloisters are the setting in July of each year for historical plays. Open 10–12.30 and 4–6.30.

Palencia. Cathedral,

Pza. San Antolín. Interesting crypt and a Museum containing El Greco's *San Sebastián,* the four Fonseca tapestries, and a triptych by Pedro Berruguete. Open 10.30–1 and 4–6.30, Sun. and fiestas 9–2.

Paredes De Nava (Palencia).

Birthplace of the painter Pedro Berruguete, his sculptor son Alonso Berruguete, and Jorge de Manrique.

Santa Eulalia. With a Romanesque tower and an altarpiece by Pedro Berruguete. Good **museum** containing many valuable works of art reflecting the village's great artistic heritage. Open 11–2 and 4–7.

Peñafiel (Valladolid). Peñafiel Castle.

Magnificent 14th-century castle. Open 11–2 and 4–6.

Piedrahita (Avila). Palace of the Duchess of Alba,

Calle Palacio. Today used as a school; where Goya painted *La Vendimia, La Maja Desnuda* and *La Maja Vestida.* Open Mon. to Fri. 10–1 and 3–5; closed in school holidays.

Puebla De Sanabria (Zamora). **Castle.** 15th-century castle important in Spain's long wars with Portugal; at present under restoration.

Monasterio de San Martín de Castañeda. Splendid 12th-century Cistercian monastery. Open 10–2 and 4.30–8.30; closed Mon.

Riofrio (Segovia). **Palacio de Ríofrio,** 11 km. from Segovia. Open 10–1.30 and 3–5, Sun. 10–2; closed Tues.

Salamanca. See *Practical Information for Salamanca* (page 178).

San Millan De La Cogolla (La Rioja). **Monasterio de Suso.** 11th-century monastery built in Mozarabic style containing the tombs of the seven Infantes de Lara. Open 10–2 and 3–dusk.

Monasterio de Yuso. Renaissance monastery often referred to as the Escorial of La Rioja. Its library houses some rare volumes and its treasury a collection of 11th-century Romanesque ivory plaques. Open Apr. through Oct. 10.30–12.30 and 4.30–7; Nov. through Mar. 10.30–12.30 and 4–6. Closed Mon.

Santa Maria De Huerta (Soria). **Cistercian Monastery.** Built by Alfonso VIII in 1162. Open 9–1 and 3.30–6 (7 in summer), Sun. 11–12.

Santo Domingo De La Calzada (La Rioja). **Cathedral.** 13th-century cathedral with a Renaissance altar and choir and Flemish triptychs. Santo Domingo is buried in the crypt, his tomb is in the south transept. Open 9–1 and 5–8.30 (7.30 Sun.).

Convento de las Bernardas. 17th-century convent housing the Baroque pantheon of the Manso de Zúñiga family.

Convento de San Francisco. Designed by Juan de Herrera with a magnificent retable.

Santo Domingo De Silos (Burgos). **Monasterio de Santo Domingo.** Monastery built in the 11th century, destroyed by the Moors and rebuilt by St. Dominic. Magnificent Romanesque cloisters and a museum with many valuable treasures. Open summer 10–1 and 4–7, Sun. 12–1 and 4–7; in winter 10–12.45 and 3.30–6.30, Sun. 12–12.45 and 3.30–6.30.

Segovia. Alcázar. Period furniture, paintings, murals, and weapons; good views from its terrace and top of tower. Open daily 10–7 (6 in winter).

Cathedral, Pza. Mayor. Open daily 9–7 in summer, and in winter Mon. to Fri. 9.30–1 and 3–6, Sat. and Sun. 9.30–6.

Convento de las Carmelitas (Carmelite Convent). Open daily 10–1.30 and 4–7.

Convento de San Antonio El Real. Open Mon. to Sat. 10–1 and 4–6, Sun. 11–1 and 4–6.

Iglesia de la Vera Cruz. 12th-century church with 12 sides founded by the Knights Templar; a National Monument. Open 10.30–1.30 and 3.30–7 (6 in winter); closed Mon.

Monasterio de El Parral. Open Mon. to Sat. 9–1 and 3–6.30, Sun. 9–12 only.

Museo de Bellas Artes (Fine Arts Museum). The collection includes a Rembrandt engraving; housed in a 16th-century building. Open Tues. to Sat. 10–2 and 4–6, Sun. 10–2 only; closed Mon.

Soria. Catedral de San Pedro. 16th-century Gothic cathedral with a magnificent cloister from the 12th century.

Museo Numantino, Paseo del Espolón. Archeological finds from the Iberian city of Numancia, 7 km. north of Soria. Closed at presstime for restoration, so check.

Numancia ruins, 8 km. out towards Garray. Excavations of the Iberian town of Numancia famous for its resistence to Scipio's legions in 133 B.C. Open 10–2 and 4–7 in summer, 10.30–1.30 and 3.30–6 in winter.

San Juan de Duero, Ctra. de Almajano. Small Romanesque church now a Museum of Archeology, with a magnificent adjoining cloister. A National Monument. Open 10–2 and 4–7; closed Mon. and Sun. morning.

San Juan de Rabanera, Calle Caballeros. Fine Romanesque church, a National Monument, with two notable polychrome crucifixes.

Santo Domingo, Pza. Condes de Lérida. Its facade, a copy of Notre Dame de Poitiers in France, is one of the most outstanding examples of Romanesque art in Spain; another National Monument.

Tordesillas (Valladolid). **Monasterio de las Claras.** Palace built for Alfonso XI and converted into a convent by his son Pedro the Cruel, in which he installed his mistress María de Padilla. Sumptuously decorated in Moorish style reminiscent of the Alhambra in Granada to remind the homesick María of her native Andalusia. Juana la Loca was long imprisoned in an adjoining apartment. Open 9–1 and 4–8 (3–7 in winter).

San Antolín. The Alderete Chapel contains a Plateresque tomb and retable by Juan de Juni and a worthwhile museum.

Toro (Zamora). **Casa Museo Delhy Tejero,** Pza. Delhy Tejero. Home of the artist Delhy Tejero (1910–1968) with over 100 of her paintings exhibited on the ground floor. The house still belongs to her family and the museum is open to the public when the family are at home.

Colegiata de Santa María la Mayor, Pza. la Cierva 4. 12th-century Romanesque Collegiate Church with a notable west door, the Pórtico de la Gloria. Open 10.30–1.30 and 5–7 in summer; 12–1 and 7–8 in winter.

Convento de Sancti Spiritus. 14th-century convent with the tombs of Beatrice of Portugal, Queen of Castile, and Santa Sofía.

San Lorenzo. 12th–13th century Mudéjar church with an altar by Fernando Gallego and the tombs of Don Pedro de Castilla and his wife. If closed, apply to the caretaker of the Collegiate Church.

Valladolid. Casa de Cervantes, Rastro 7. Cervantes' home furnished in 17th-century style, with a small museum and library. Open 10–6, Sun. 10–2; closed Mon.

Casa Museo de Colón (Columbus' House) Calle Colón. Delightful small museum showing Columbus' journeys and the history of Latin America from its Discovery through Independence. Open 11–2 and 4–7, Sun. 11–1.

Casa de Zorilla, Fray Luis de Granada 1. Birthplace of José Zorilla, author of *Don Juan Tenorio.* Open 10–1 and 4.30–6.30; closed Sun. P.M.

Cathedral and **Diocesan Museum.** Open 10–2 and 5–8, Sun. 9.30–2 only.

Monasterio de Santa Ana, Pza. Sta Ana. Collection of religious art and sculpture, a painting by Goya and a magnificent statue of the *Dead Christ* by Gregorio Hernández. Open 11–1.30 and 4–6; Sun. 4–6 only.

Museo Nacional de Escultura (National Museum of Polychrome Sculpture). The magnificent Colegio de San Gregorio makes a perfect setting for one of Spain's leading museums. Open 9–2, and 4.30–7, Sun. 10–2; closed Mon.

Museo Oriental, Paseo de Filipinos 7. Oriental Museum housed in the Iglesia de los Padres Agustinos. Splendid collection of Oriental art, porcelain, bronzes, coins, all attractively displayed. Open Mon. to Sat. 4–7, Sun. 10–2.

Museo de Pintura (Art Gallery) located in the Church of La Pasión. Paintings by 16th–18th century Valladolid artists. Open 10–2 and 4–7, Sun. 10–2 only; closed Mon. and fiestas, also Aug.

Zamora. Cathedral, Pza. Pio XII. Beautiful Byzantine cupola; some fine tapestries in its museum. Open 11–1 only.

Museo de la Semana Santa (Holy Week Museum), Pza. de Sta. María la Nueva. Interesting museum with 35 *pasos* from the Holy Week processions and the robes of the various brotherhoods which carry them. Open 11–2 and 4–7, Sun. 10.30–2 only.

Portillón de la Traición (Betrayal Gate), Pza. del Castillo. Gateway through which Bellido Dolfos entered the city after betraying King Sancho II. Good views of the city walls.

WINE TASTING. The Rioja vineyards produce the best wine in Spain and there are several bodegas you can visit throughout the province and numerous places where you can taste the different wines; look out for *degustación* signs.

The small town of Haro is the capital of the vineyards of the Alta Rioja and here there are two places you might enjoy. **La Catedral de los Vinos,** Santo Tomás 4 (tel. 31 02 93) is open 7 days a week and sells a vast selection of wines from all the best vineyards in the area, including *gran reservas.* **Juan González Muga,** Pza. de la Paz 5 (tel. 31 14 25) is a firm specializing in *gran reservas* and which runs a wine club for the distribution of vintage Riojas. The store sells a wide selection of the best wines and there is a large room given over to tasting the various vintages. Its collection boasts some of the rarest and most valuable of Rioja wines.

The province of Valladolid is also well known for its vineyards. Peñafiel is famous for its red wines and here there are two good bodegas where you can purchase wine, the **Bodegas del Botero** in the old Jewish quarter, and the **Bodega Ribera Duero,** Avda. Gen. Sanjurjo 64, which bottles one of the best of the region's red wines "Protos" as well as Peñafiel and Ribera Duero.

The village of Rueda on the N-VI is famous for its white wines and here there are numerous bodegas, many of them around km. 170 and 171 on the N-VI, where you can stop to sample and purchase wines.

SPORTS. There are few opportunities for participatory sports in Old Castile but the region is popular for fishing and hunting. Trout streams abound and the Sanabria Lake near Puebla de Sanabria in the extreme northwest of Zamora province is a very popular spot for fishing in mountain scenery. The Sierra de Gredos in Avila province has long been one of the country's most favored hunting grounds.

ASTURIAS, LEÓN AND GALICIA

The End of the Cockleshell Way

Finisterre—world's end—was Galicia's name until the discovery of America, for west of it lay nothing but the ocean, and if you were so foolish as to sail on, you could expect to slip over the edge and plunge down into the abyss.

Along the coast of Asturias and Galicia, the sea is often rough and cold (though the deep estuaries are sheltered and calm), and the landscape inland is as green and lush as southern Ireland. Here you find barren mountains, variable skies, and ancient, gray stone towns nestling among tall trees.

Although some visitors may find the northwest insufficiently Spanish to fit in with their previous notions, in fact it is far more Spanish than is typically Moorish Andalusia. For it was precisely to Asturias that the most doggedly independent of the Spanish people withdrew when the Moorish invasion in the 8th century swept over their country and on, almost to the gates of Paris.

Grimly barricaded behind mountains that rise from 1,525 to 2,440 meters (5,000 to 8,000 feet), they learned through hunger, cold and hardship the spiritual austerity and physical courage that are still such marked national characteristics. Pelayo, who was descended from the Goths, swore an oath with other princes to fight against the Muslim invaders. At the

208

Battle of Covadonga in 718 they won their first victory; the Reconquista had begun. It was to end nearly 800 years later with the capture of Granada.

In a cave near Covadonga, in eastern Asturias, you will find the sarcophagus of the valiant knight and the statue of the Virgin who assisted in the defeat of the Moors.

Asturias was never conquered and Galicia was early liberated from the Moors. Although neighboring León was the setting for desperate advances and retreats for a century and a half, it then became the Christian capital of Spain, remaining so until the medieval kingdoms of León and Castile were united under the crown of Castile, and Castile rose to lead the Reconquest that was to dominate the course of Spanish history throughout the Middle Ages. Thus, the northwest's claim to be more truly Spanish than any other part of Spain seems to be historically justified.

Although this northwestern corner of Spain is primarily agricultural, the coal mines of Asturias are of vital importance to the economy of the whole country, while the great Galician port of El Ferrol is Spain's chief naval and shipbuilding base. The ports of La Coruña and Vigo, also in Galicia, and the smaller Asturian port and seaside resort of Gijón are all thriving commercial towns, but once away from the sea, these are provinces with fat cattle, (Asturias is known as "the dairy of Spain"), excellent salmon and trout fishing, pine-clad hills, and occasional snow-capped mountains.

León and Pajares

León, almost exactly 320 km. (200 miles) by road from Madrid and 840 meters (2,750 feet) above sea level, is the gateway to the northern and northwestern provinces of Asturias and Galicia.

In the 11th century León was the capital of Christian Spain, but with the liberation of Toledo in 1085 the warrior court moved there, so as to be nearer to the still enslaved provinces of the south. With the unification of the kingdoms of León and Castile, the latter became dominant, and the old city slowly declined in importance. Although it is full of 10th–, 11th– and 12th–century churches, monasteries and convents, León is unique in two ways—first, the almost incredibly beautiful 13th-century stained-glass windows of the cathedral. There are 230 of them, 12 meters (40 feet) high, and once within the dark interior of the perfect Gothic building, you will find yourself walking in a patterned maze of glowing colors of an unearthly depth and intensity. The second is the 11th-century church of San Isidoro el Real, housing the body of the saint; its vault possesses the most beautiful wall-paintings of the 12th century in Spain.

León also has the former convent of San Marcos, today a five-star hotel of great charm, and the church of Nuestro Señor del Camino. The 14th-century Palace of the Counts of Luna has interesting coats of arms; San Marceló guards the saint's remains in an urn on the high altar and has some fine statues; San Marcos, once a pilgrims' hospice, 12th century, then the H.Q. of the Order of Santiago has lovely choirstalls and cloisters. The Casa de Botines, with its four fairytale towers in the Plaza Sto. Domingo, was built by Gaudí at the end of the 19th century.

Sixty km. (38 miles) north of León, N630 climbs to the famous 1,356-meter (4,450-foot) Pájares Pass (with a gradient of one in seven on the far side), which marks the border between the provinces of León and Asturias. Here there is a matchless view in spring and autumn over the mountains of Asturias.

Asturias

Oviedo, the Asturian capital, lying at the foot of Mt. Naranco, was capital of Christian Spain during the 9th century, through the reigns of three kings, Alfonso II (792–842), Ramiro I (842–850) and Alfonso III (866–910). All three of these monarchs left their mark on the town. Alfonso II built the city's most treasured monument, its famous Cámara Santa (Holy Chamber) in which the treasures of Christian Spain were hidden during the long struggle with the Infidel Moors. The chest of relics can still be seen, and in the sanctuary are the two famous crosses, the Cross of Los Angeles and the Cross of La Victoria. The Angels' Cross dates from 808 and marks the beginning of the court in Asturias. The Victory Cross, 100 years on (908), is in fact a jeweled sheath made to cover the oak cross borne by the valiant Pelayo at the Battle of Covadonga.

Oviedo's splendid flamboyant Gothic cathedral was erected in the 14th–16th centuries around the shrine of the Cámara Santa. Only one of its two projected towers was completed. Its Chapel of the Chaste King was intended as a royal pantheon and merits special attention, as does the reredos behind the main altar which was fashioned by a number of distinguished 16th-century artists and sculptors.

Several of the buildings in Oviedo are pre-Romanesque in style; this is also called *Ramiresque,* after King Ramiro I, who originated it. This pre-Romanesque style is very austere and is found nowhere else. At the beginning of the 9th century, only the capital, Oviedo, was enriched by splendid buildings, such as the Church of Santullano built by King Alfonso II in 812–842. But only a century later the countryside round about and the small town became fired with ambition to do things on a grand scale. King Ramiro was personally responsible for the building of Santa María del Naranco, originally as a palace for himself and only later converted into a church, and for the Church of San Miguel del Lillo, both on the outskirts of the city on the slopes of Mt. Naranco. Both are magnificent examples of Ramiresque style.

The fountain of Fonclada, built by Alfonso III, is another of Oviedo's most ancient relics. The facade of the university was built in 1598. Inside you can see paintings by Ribera and Zurbarán. There is also an *Apostolado* by El Greco in the ducal palace of El Parque.

The inland area between Llanes, Gijón and Oviedo is interesting. Places to visit are San Antolín de Bedón (monastery dating from the 10th and 11th centuries), Santiago de Gobiendes, Priesca (San Salvador, consecrated in the 10th century), Villaviciosa at the head of the Ría with San Juan de Amandi (12th-century) and San Salvador de Valdediós (9th-century). But of all the attractions of Asturias, the excursions most highly recommended are inland to the mountains, to the little town of Cangas de Onís with its Roman bridge spanning the lovely Sella Gorge, and the nearby 11th-century Monastery of San Juan de Corias; to Covadonga eight km. (five miles) away, with its Shrine of the Blessed Virgin—among the votive gifts in the treasury is a crown with over 1,000 diamonds—and memories of the valiant Pelayo, and nearby the beautiful mountain lakes of Enol and Ercina where the traveler can gaze from the Mirador de la Reina at one of the loveliest views in the world. From Mt. Orandi the River Deva falls in cascade after cascade to reach the bottom of the valley, and above Covadonga the mountains of the National Park tower upwards around the mighty Peña Santa.

Gijón, which is bigger than Oviedo, is an industrial town and at the same time a port (the new port is at El Musel, a few kilometers farther on), a university town and a holiday resort. The large beach of San Lorenzo has excellent bathing and an attractive esplanade. There are certainly plenty of opportunities for taking a dip and acquiring a tan on the coast of Asturias. From Llanes to Salinas, with Ribadesella and Colunga lying in between, summer visitors will find everything they need for an enjoyable holiday.

Luarca has a savage beauty which distinguishes it from its rivals, a splendid beach, and the prettiest little fishing port you can imagine. Cudillero and Navía will not disappoint you, either. The last little Asturian town, Castropol, is perched on a promontory.

Discovering Galicia

Galicia, consisting of the four provinces of Lugo, La Coruña, Pontevedra and Orense, is considerably larger than Asturias, and, consequently, unless you have a car, requires more planning in order to explore it comfortably on a short holiday.

One road from Castropol skirts the inlet to Ribadeo, then to Mondoñedo, a somber town with an imposing cathedral. It dates from the 13th century, but as usual a great number of alterations were carried out in the 16th and 18th centuries. The road then bends round to the west toward Villalba, but at Mondoñedo you can return to the Lugo road, via Ríotorto. This allows you to stop at Meira, where you will find the pure lines of Cistercian architecture at the monastery, originally under Benedictine supervision. (From the 12th century, it came under the rule of Clairvaux.) The church (13th century) is very beautiful.

Except for a Napoleonic interlude, Lugo has rested in relative peace for the last 1,000 years, and stands today, still surrounded by well over a kilometer of high medieval walls, perched on a hill overlooking the River Miño. There is quite a wide road around the walls and about 50 semicircular towers. A surprise awaits you in the cathedral—the passages between the naves are walled up, but the choir, at least, is surrounded by glass. The chapels all around are overloaded with a lavish display of Rococo bric-à-brac.

The 14th-century Santo Domingo is one more of the countless beautiful churches that are so thickly spread over the whole country. Near the bridge over the Miño are the ruins of Roman sulphur baths, where the medicinal water still gushes out at 43°C (110°F).

It is 97 km. (60 miles) from Lugo to La Coruña, and the road (N-VI) runs through pleasant, hilly country. Your trip will take you from 483 meters (1,584 feet) above sea level, the altitude of Lugo, all the way down to zero, since La Coruña is on the coast.

The tourist who is anxious to see everything will take N540 from Lugo, then C547 to Mellid, taking a look at the magnificent ruins of the ancient and imposing monastery of Sobrado de los Monjes (782), 24 km. north

of Mellid. It was immense at one time and was *the* leading religious authority in Galicia. It was, of course, Cistercian. The present church dates from
the 17th century. It is the cloisters that will hold the visitor's attention;
they are abandoned and are overgrown with a romantic covering of weeds,
filling one with nostalgia and an awareness of history. Few Galician
churches are as beautiful as the church at Sobrado. The sacristy deserves
a glance and the kitchen is just as it was in the 15th century.

Betanzos, nearer the coast, has retained much of its medieval character—part of the old walls still stand—and is a very interesting town. Fernán Pérez de Andrade, who lived in the 14th century, was undoubtedly
a man of good taste, for he has left a splendid palace for us to visit. Notable
churches here include San Francisco with the tomb of Fernán Pérez de
Andrade who rests on a bear and a wild boar, Santa María de Azogue
built by the Guild of Mariners, and Santiago built by the Guild of Taylors
with its Pórtico de la Gloria inspired by the great doorway of Santiago.

As you have to pass through Betanzos if you are going to La Coruña,
you might as well go to nearby El Ferrol del Caudillo. General Franco
was born there, and it would appear to be one of the finest natural harbors
in the world. There is not much we can say about it, except that the parador is very comfortable. It is the region itself that is charming, with its
white-washed houses; the windows are framed in dark gray stone and the
woodwork is painted green, or sometimes blue. The old houses often have
a glazed balcony or loggia with small panes of glass added on to the front.

North of El Ferrol, you may wish to explore one of the least frequented
corners of Spain, where lonely beaches, often made up of "black" sand,
stretch eastward toward Asturias. Picturesque Vivero has several hotels
and the smaller fishing villages of Cedeira and Ortigueira have simple hostels.

La Coruña

An important port, especially for oil shipments, La Coruña is a mixture
of modern and historical buildings—with the modern not always in the
best of taste. The wooden balconies of the old houses with their small
panes of glass are a distinctive feature. It can also boast a fair number of
restaurants offering the fine seafood for which Galicia is famous. And, indeed, this city (of 230,000 inhabitants) does have a history. Romans, Visigoths, Arabs, Charles V and Napoleon—as you will see later on—have
all left some trace behind them. So have the sardines and the canneries
which have made it rich. There is a fine, large harbor. A few centuries
ago, it witnessed the preparation of the most powerful fleet of that era.
Philip II was so proud of it that he christened it the Invincible Armada,
but it never returned. It was defeated by a storm and by the fire-ship plan
thought up by an ingenious Englishman, Sir Francis Drake, possibly while
bowling.

La Coruña is built on a narrow point jutting out into the Atlantic, and
is surrounded by sandy bathing beaches. The showpiece is its Hercules'
Tower, which dates from the time of Breogan and was restored by the
Emperor Trajan—himself, by the way, born in Spain—for use as a lighthouse. Breogan was a Celtic chieftain, who erected the tower in celebration
of his tribe's removal to Ireland.

The tomb of Sir John Moore, the British general who was fatally wounded in his retreat to La Coruña before Napoleon's Marshals Soult and Ney,
is in the beautiful San Carlos gardens.

The Ciudad Vieja (Old City) is an interesting quarter where stately palaces rub shoulders with humble dwellings. The oldest house in La Coruña
stands on the Calle de las Damas, the Calle del Sinagoga evokes memories
of the Jewish community and the Calle de Tavernas of the bawdy sailors'
quarter of the 18th century.

Those with a taste for sightseeing may enjoy a visit to the Convent of
San Francisco, where King Charles I of Spain called a meeting of the Cortes in 1520 in order to raise the funds necessary to ensure his election as
the Holy Roman Emperor, under his better-known title of Charles V.

Santiago de Compostela

The showpiece of Galicia is undoubtedly Santiago de Compostela, the
holy city, one of the three chief places of pilgrimage of the Middle Ages.

It is possible to follow the pilgrims' route, the Camino de Santiago,
down from France, across the north of Spain to Santiago. It is, in fact,
a fascinating exercise in medieval tourism. Unbelievable as it may seem,
the crowds that "took the cockleshell" and made the journey sometimes
numbered as many as two million in a year.

Some guidebooks generously allow the traveler three hours to explore
Santiago de Compostela. Setting aside sentiment, faith and the ever-
present possibility of falling in love with this very beautiful city, one can
acquire a really lasting impression by merely visiting the enormous rectangular Plaza del Obradoiro, magnificently framed by the cathedral, the
Hostal de los Reyes Católicos, the San Jerónimo College and the Rajoy
Palace, now the city hall. By stretching things, you could add a quarter
of an hour for a stroll through the city and another fifteen minutes for
a short walk in the park known as Paseo de Herradura, which offers a
superb view of the city.

On the other hand, one could well spend a day in and around the great
cathedral and it would be a day worth remembering. The west entrance,
known as the Fachada del Obradoiro, approached from the plaza by a qua-
druple flight of steps, is a wonderfully ornate masterpiece. The south door,
or Puerta de las Platerías, Silversmiths' Door, dating from 1104, faces the
Casa del Cabildo and is partly concealed by the Clock Tower, but you
can see that the huge corbel on the left is in the form of a cockleshell—the
sign of St. James the Apostle which all pilgrims who visited here carried.
The marble outer shafts are carved with tiers of figures in a bewildering
confusion. At the east end is the Puerta Santa (1611), open only when St.
James's Day falls on a Sunday. The north door is less notable.

When the visitor enters the cathedral (from the front, or Obradoiro,
side), he is struck by the gigantic but harmonious proportions of the three
naves. Walk under the Pórtico de la Gloria, the work of the famed Maestro
Mateo and one of the crowning achievements of 12th-century sculpture.
In the crypt beneath the Capilla Mayor, a silver urn contains the remains
of the Apostle, and his two disciples, St. Theodore and St. Athanasius.
The *botafumeiro,* normally kept in the library, is the large censer which
is lit on special occasions and, despite its great weight, hung from the roof

and sent swinging over the heads of the congregation. It takes six men to keep it in motion.

Next to the cathedral is the Archbishop's Palace, one of the most beautiful to be found even in this land of ancient palaces. The town is ringed with historic monasteries, churches and pilgrims' hostels.

The feast day of St. James, July 25, is Santiago de Compostela's big moment, but a moment that begins the night before and that continues for a week. This is the time to come (making sure you have hotel accommodation first), if you want to participate. However, it is distinctly not the time to come if you want to be able to move leisurely about the cathedral and along the arcaded streets of the ancient city.

The visit is now over for hurried travelers. But others might be interested in two monuments left from the 6th century: the Church of San Felix de Solovo, the oldest in Santiago (for it pre-dates the discovery of the Apostle's remains), which was rebuilt in the 12th century; and the San Martín Pinario Monastery (599). On Plaza Quintana facing the cathedral, there is the immense bare wall of San Pelayo de Ante-Altares. To its left stand two charming old houses, of which one, the Baroque Casa de la Parra, is famous.

Tradition has it that Saint Francis of Assisi himself founded the monastery that bears his name. After seeing this, to do a thorough job, you might stroll along Rua del Villar (to glance at the Casa del Déan) and Rua Nova; then stop for a moment in front of the portal of Los Canónigos, and, on Plaza de Platerías, in front of the imaginative delirium of the Baroque decoration displayed by the Casa del Cabildo.

If you are lucky enough to be staying overnight, be prepared for the town to change into a colorful, fascinating maelstrom as darkness falls. Like many other Spanish towns, Santiago has a character all its own, and it comes roaring out at night.

At the Gates of Portugal

To the south of Santiago, the indentations along the Atlantic coast become more and more marked. There is a succession of deep inlets, called *rías,* and estuaries that seem to go on forever. These are the lush green fjords, where the air smells of iodine and salt. It is a region of delightful houses and courteous people.

After Santiago, Pontevedra, 56 km. south, has to be an anticlimax. Though it dates back to Roman times and is rich in antiquities, with a fine 16th-century church, Santa María la Mayor, with a doorway made of glittering gray granite, most of the town is not particularly interesting. But it does have some old sections with a certain charm of their own, and its historical museum is well worth a visit. A stroll through the ancient streets surrounding the museum can be most rewarding. The Gothic church of San Francisco overlooks the Plaza Herrería which is lively in the early evening, and the parador in the 18th-century Maceda palace is worth a look. Your main memory is of the extremely odd contours of the Peregrina chapel. Pontevedra is notable chiefly for its beautiful position at the head of the Ría, a deep bay cutting far into the land.

It is from Pontevedra, by a corniche road that offers some of the most beautiful coastal scenery in Spain, that one reaches the resort paradise of the island of La Toja, with its balmy climate, fine bathing, and many mineral springs. There are a great many beaches along the way. In the villages, you come past old *pazos* or palaces and seigniorial mansions, especially in Villagarcía and Cambados. Also notice the traditional *hórreos* on each property, where farmers formerly stored their grain, looking like boxes supported on six stone pillars, with the inevitable cross on each side of the roof. On the Ría, you will see a strange type of craft—like a raft with a hut on it—moored to the bottom by means of a cage made of stakes. These are mussel beds. On the island of La Toja there are three hotels, one of them a famous deluxe resort, and a little bit of everything else besides, including gardens, cafés, beaches, minigolf, a casino and pigeon shooting—in fact, everything that man has devised for his vacation happiness. The light is magnificent and there is one scene you should not miss— the fisherman walking on the waters at low tide, pushing his boat with his hands.

There are two monasteries to see on the way—the monastery of Poyo, which is almost on the outskirts of Pontevedra on the road to La Toja, and the monastery at Armenteira, a little farther away, beyond Combarro.

Little remains of the first one, which is Benedictine. The present church dates from the 16th century and the cloister from the 18th. But the trip is particularly worth making for the wonderful view you get of the Ría and also for the sake of the choirs which can be heard there on Saturday evenings. The building occupied by the Galician novices stands beside the church. (Remember that women are forbidden to enter.)

The second monastery, at Armenteira, is Cistercian, and dates back to 1162. It is long abandoned, but its magnificent Romanesque architecture, including church, cloisters and monkish dependencies, has now been tastefully restored.

Vigo

The port of Vigo is 27 km. south of Pontevedra, and is one of the best places in Galicia to choose as a holiday center—particularly for visitors not possessing a car. From Vigo, there are excellent bus communications and you can cross the wide bay by ferry to Cangas de Morrazo, Santa Tecla and the Portuguese frontier.

You seldom see a port so miraculously endowed by nature as that of Vigo. A series of islets defends the entrance to the deep roadstead. Here again, we come across the name of Sir Francis Drake, who captured and plundered the town so prettily built in the form of an amphitheater. As a result of the Franco-Spanish differences with Britain during the war of the Spanish Succession, legend says the sea bed here is covered with a layer of gold. A British squadron attacked a convoy, heavily laden with treasure from America, sending all its ships to the bottom.

A stay in Vigo is pleasant and restful. There are no historical monuments to visit and the tourist can relax. But it is worth going up to the Castro or fortress, from where you can get a magnificent panoramic view of the city.

Orense

Orense, the most distant from La Coruña of the four provincial capitals of Galicia is, like Lugo, of Roman origin, and contains excellent thermal springs.

Orense's name comes from *oro* (gold), not the gold from the New World which was both a blessing and a curse to Spain, but the gold from the Sil, that was panned there. It is a more modest town today but you can nevertheless spend a pleasant hour or two strolling through the streets of the old town. The cathedral, unfortunately, is stifled by the walls of the houses surrounding it. There you can see a fairly successful replica of the Door of Glory in Santiago, but this one is called the Door of Paradise. Calvo Sotelo, whose murder triggered off the Civil War in 1936, represented Orense in the Spanish parliament.

South of Orense is Celanova, with its extraordinary monastery of San Salvador, which is Benedictine and goes back to the 10th century. All that remains of it is the Chapel of San Miguel, a unique example of the Mozarabic style in Spain that has survived intact.

And there is the inevitable Cistercian monastery—Santa María la Real de Osera is about 64 km. away. The original buildings were almost entirely destroyed by fire in 1552. The new buildings are in Renaissance and Baroque styles. The chapter house is the part to visit in particular.

Go and see it even if you have had a surfeit of churches and monasteries—go and see it for the sheer pleasure of driving through the delightful Galician countryside. You may have seen the grain storehouses in Asturias, perched high on pillars. Here you will see the *hórreos*. They are smaller and more elongated—curious structures, sometimes very old and worm-eaten. There they stand beside the houses, each one like a sarcophagus piously preserved by the head of the family. And yet, all they contain is maize. There are many forests of pine and eucalyptus and accompanying sawmills. And in Galicia you will see a sight that no longer exists anywhere else in Spain, not even in Andalusia, for here the women toiling in the fields are clad from head to toe in black peasant garb, with long flowing skirts and thick knitted stockings; a scene more reminiscent of the 19th than late-20th century. But, however attractive the countryside, the traveler is reluctant to leave Galicia for yet another reason—the cooking here is the best in Spain.

PRACTICAL INFORMATION FOR
ASTURIAS, LEÓN AND GALICIA

TOURIST OFFICES. Astorga, Pza. de España (tel. 61 68 38); **La Coruña,** Dársena de la Marina (tel. 22 18 22); **Gijón,** Marqués de San Esteban 1 (tel. 34 11 67); **León,** Pza. de Regla 4 (tel. 23 70 82); **Llanes,** Nemesio Sobrino 1 (tel. 40 01 64); **Luarca,** Pza. Alfonso X el Sabio (tel. 64 00 83); **Lugo,** Pza. de España 27 (tel. 23 13 61); **Orense,** Curros Enríquez 1 (tel. 23 47 17); **Oviedo,** Pza. de la Catedral 6 (tel. 21 33 85); **Ponferrada,** Avda. de la Puebla 1 (tel. 41 55 37); **Pontevedra,** Gen. Mola 3 (tel. 85 08 14); **Ribadeo,** Pza. de España (tel. 11 06 89); **Santiago de Compostela,** Rua Villar 43 (tel. 58 40 81) and Pza. del Obradoiro 1 (tel. 58 29 00 ext. 125); **Vigo,** Jardines de las Avenidas (tel. 43 05 77).

TELEPHONE CODES. The dialing codes for the provinces of Asturias, León and the four provinces of Galicia are: Asturias (985), La Coruña

(981), León (987), Lugo (982), Orense (988), Pontevedra (986). You need only dial these codes when calling from outside the province. Dialing codes for all the towns we list are given under *Hotels and Restaurants* immediately after the name of the town.

GETTING AROUND. By Train. Galicia, Asturias and León are all linked to Madrid by fast, frequent train services; the distances are considerable, and you may well want to opt for one of the overnight trains with a bed or couchette which leave Oviedo, La Coruña or Madrid in the evening and arrive at their destination around breakfast time. Trains from Madrid to the north coast leave from Chamartín, and to Galicia from the Estación del Norte; there are a few services such as Madrid–La Coruña via León which leave from either station, so always doublecheck.

RENFE links this area with the rest of Spain but some of the most useful intercity routes within the area, especially the route along the north coast from San Sebastián in the east all the way to El Ferrol in the west, is run by the independent FEVE company. *EurRail* and *Inter Rail* passes are not valid on this line, nor is the RENFE Tourist Card. Cities served by FEVE have different railroad stations for FEVE and RENFE lines. The tourist offices in the cities of the north coast can help with information about FEVE services.

Stations and RENFE Offices. La Coruna, station is on Marqués de Figueroa in the south of town and is connected to the center by frequent public buses, RENFE office is at Fontán 3 (tel. 22 19 48). **León,** RENFE station is on Avda. de Astorga (tel. 22 37 04/08/12); the FEVE station, Estación de Matallana for trains to Bilbao, is on Avda. del Padre Isla (tel. 22 59 19); and the central RENFE office is at Travesía Roa de la Vega 26 (tel. 22 26 25). **Lugo,** station is northeast of town off N640, the road to Meira, and the RENFE office is on Pza. de España 27 (tel. 22 55 03). **Orense,** station is out of town to northwest, just off Pontevedra road and is a taxi or bus ride from the center. **Oviedo,** RENFE station, the Estación del Norte, is at the far end of Calle Uria (tel. 24 33 64); the Asturias FEVE station for trains to El Ferrol is on Calle Jovellanos (tel. 21 90 26); the Basque FEVE station for trains to Santander and Bilbao is on Calle Económicos (tel. 28 01 50). **Pontevedra,** the station is a short ride out along Virgen del Camino, and the RENFE office is on Conde de Gondomar 3 (tel. 85 19 05). **Santiago de Compostela,** the station (tel. 59 60 50) is at the far end of Calle Hórreo (Gen. Franco) in the south of town. **Vigo,** station on Alfonso XIII.

By Bus. Long distance services from Madrid to the region mostly leave from the Estación del Sur. There are plenty of services from town to town within the region.

Bus Stations. La Coruña, Santiago, Pontevedra and Lugo are the only cities with central bus stations, elsewhere buses leave from various points according to their destination. **La Coruña** bus station is on Caballeros (tel. 23 96 44) and is reached from the town center on public bus. **Santiago** bus station is on Avda. de Rodríguez de Viguri, some way out of town but connected by frequent buses to the Pza.Galicia. **Pontevedra** bus station is in the south of town off the Virgen del Camino on Alfereces Provisionales. **Lugo** bus station is off Avda.Angel López Pérez.

By Air. There are four airports in the region—La Coruña, Santiago, Vigo, and Asturias. All have flights to main Spanish cities, Santiago also has flights to London.

By Car. There are some short stretches of toll freeways *(autopistas)* in this area, the A8 and A66 Gijón–Avilés–Oviedo triangle, the A8 from southern Asturias to just south of León, the A9 from La Coruña to Santiago, and its continuation from Pontevedra to Vigo. Though as the main attraction of this region is the scenery you may well choose to opt for the more scenic N roads. If you stick to the main N-roads linking the major cities, surfaces are good and driving, even where mountain passes are involved, is not difficult. Off the N roads, surfaces can be poor and in several places the C roads are very high and winding.

Much of the region is very mountainous and negotiating some of the roads in the Picos de Europa mountains in eastern Asturias and northeastern León requires a good head for heights. So too do the C roads crossing through the mountains further west in Asturias into León province. These involve some of the country's highest passes.

Much of Galicia is mountainous too, but here the hills are more rounded and less awe-inspiring than the mountains further east. Any of the coastal roads, whether along the Cantabrian shores of Asturias and Galicia, or Galicia's Atlantic coast, may well take longer to drive than you would think from the distances involved. This is due to the indented nature of the coast, with its numerous *rías* (estuaries), and to the extensive roadwork currently being undertaken.

HOTELS AND RESTAURANTS. The region's most outstanding hotels from the point of view of sheer comfort, luxury and, in some cases, historical atmosphere, are the *San Marcos* in León, the *Hostal de los Reyes Católicos* in Santiago, the *Reconquista* in Oviedo and the *Gran Hotel* on the island of La Toja; the *Gran Hotel de Sella* in Ribadesella in Asturias is another reliable old favorite. Pontevedra, Bayona and Villalba all have historic paradores though most of the paradores in this area (and there are several) are modern and have been built more for the beauty of their location or as convenient roadside inns.

Galicia is famed throughout Spain for the variety and quality of its shellfish, and its magnificent seafood restaurants are rivalled only by those of the Basque country. For lovers of fresh seafood Galicia is a gastronomic paradise. Asturias too, has its own notable cuisine. Its lush meadows are known as the dairy of Spain and its cheeses, including the famous *queso cabrales,* cream desserts and yoghurt products should all be tried. Don't forget to try Asturian cider—many of the restaurants have cider bars in their entrances—or the typical *fabada asturiana,* a bean stew.

Astorga. León (987). *Gaudí* (M), Eduardo de Castro 6 (tel. 61 56 54). 35 rooms. Comfortable, close to historic center. AE, V. *Pradorrey* (M), at km.331 on N-VI (tel. 61 57 29). 64 rooms. Good motel five km. (three miles) north of town. AE, DC, MC, V.

Bayona. Pontevedra (986). *Parador Nacional Conde de Gondomar* (E), Monterreal (tel. 35 50 00). 128 rooms. Modern parador inside old castle walls. Pleasant location. Pool and tennis. AE, DC, MC, V.

Cambados. Pontevedra (986). *Parador Nacional del Albariño* (E), Paseo Cervantes (tel. 54 22 50). 63 rooms. Modern, with regional décor. AE, DC, MC, V.

Cangas De Onis. Asturias (985). *Ventura* (M), Avda. de Covadonga (tel. 84 82 00). 22 rooms. Simple and pleasant. AE, DC, V.

Colombres. Asturias (985). *San Angel* (M), on the N634 (tel. 41 20 00). 77 rooms. Superb ocean views. Pool, gardens and bar. AE, DC, MC, V. *Mirador de La Franca* (M), Colombres (tel. 41 21 45). 52 rooms.

Corcubion. La Coruña (981). *Motel El Hórreo* (M), Santa Isabel (tel. 74 55 00). 40 rooms. On the estuary. Pool and bar.

La Coruña (981). *Atlántico* (E), Jardines de Méndez Núñez 2 (tel. 22 65 00). 200 rooms. Right in the center. AE, DC, MC, V. *Finisterre* (E), Paseo del Parrote (tel. 20 54 00). 127 rooms. The best hotel in town, beautifully situated on the bay, commanding a sweeping view. Pool, gardens, sauna, tennis and bingo. AE, DC, MC, V. *Ciudad de la Coruña-Eurotel* (M), Polígono de Adormideras (tel. 21 11 00). 131 rooms. Comfortable and well recommended, out of center near Tower of Hercules; shuttlebus service to town. AE, DC, MC, V. *Riazor* (M), Andén de Riazor (tel. 25 34 00). 168 rooms. Overlooking Riazor beach and close to the center. Comfortable, one of the best. AE, DC, MC, V. *Almirante* (I), Paseo de Ronda 54 (tel. 25 96 00). 20 rooms. V. *España* (I), Juana de Vega 7 (tel. 22 45 06). 84 rooms. Modern, in town center. AE, DC, MC, V. *Los Lagos* (I), Polígono Residencial de Elviña (tel. 28 62 99). 35 rooms. Pool, tennis and gardens. *Santa Catalina* (I), Travesía de Santa Catalina 1 (tel. 22 66 09). 32 rooms. A modern hostel, central and close to good restaurants.

Restaurants. *El Rápido* (E), Estrella 7 (tel. 22 42 21). Excellent shellfish, but pricey. AE, DC, MC, V. *Duna-2* (E–M), Estrella 2/4 (tel. 22 70 23). One of the best in town and very popular with locals. The admirable management organizes special weeks of regional cooking, when chefs are invited to prepare regional specialties. *El Coral* (M), Estrella 5 (tel. 22 10 82). Seafood and regional specialties. AE, DC, MC, V. *Mesón de la Cazuela* (M), Callejón de la Estaca (tel. 22 24 48). Just off Avda. de la Marina. Typical décor and outdoor terrace. *Naveiro* (M), San Andrés 129 (tel. 22 90 24). Good-value traditional restaurant specializing in Galician cuisine and seasonal dishes.

Covadonga. Asturias (985). *Pelayo* (M), Covadonga (tel. 84 60 00). 55 rooms. Oldish hotel in exceptional location—an ideal mountain retreat. The church bells (Covadonga is a shrine) may keep you awake.

El Ferrol Del Caudillo. La Coruña (981). *Almirante* (M), Frutos Saavedra 2 (tel. 32 53 11). 122 rooms. Modern hotel in center. AE. *Parador Nacional* (M), Almirante Vierna (tel. 35 67 20). 39 rooms. Pleasant parador with good views over the Ría and a well recommended restaurant. AE, DC, MC, V.

Gijon. Asturias (985). *Hernán Cortés* (E), Fernández Vallín 5 (tel. 34 60 00). 109 rooms. Old hotel right in the center. AE, DC, MC, V. *Parador*

Nacional Molino Viejo (E), Parque de Isabel la Católica (tel. 37 05 11). 40 rooms. A little way out of town. A modern copy of an old Asturian windmill. AE, DC, MC, V. *Príncipe de Asturias* (E), Manso 2 (tel. 36 71 11). 80 rooms. Close to the beach. AE, DC, MC, V. *León* (M), Ctra. de la Costa 45 (tel. 37 01 11). 156 rooms. V. *Pathos* (M), Contracay 5 (tel. 35 25 46). 56 rooms. Only two streets from the beach, but rather functional and unexciting. *Robledo* (M), Alfredo Truán 2 (tel. 35 59 40). 138 rooms. In the center. AE, DC, MC, V.

Restaurants. *Las Delicias* (E), Barrio Fuejo (tel. 36 02 27). Four km. (two-and-a-half miles) out, in Somió. This is the best, with good shellfish, and an outdoor terrace in summer. AE, DC, MC, V. *El Retiro* (E–M), Begoña 28 (tel. 35 00 30). Very central and lively. Generous portions. Cider and seafood served at the bar. AE, DC, MC, V. *Casa Victor* (M), Carmen 11 (tel. 35 00 93). Everything cooked to order—patience needed—but the fish is superb as well as good value. *Zagal* (M), Trinidad 6 (tel. 35 13 98). Small and popular with good food and service. AE, DC, MC, V.

León. (987). *San Marcos* (L–E), Pza. San Marcos 7 (tel. 23 73 00). 258 rooms. Elegant hotel in 16th-century hospice; magnificent plateresque façade and antique furnishings. One of the great hotels of Spain. AE, DC, MC, V. *Conde Luna* (E), Independencia 7 (tel. 20 65 12). 154 rooms; pool. Good traditional hotel in center. AE, DC, MC, V. *Quindós* (M), José Antonio 24 (tel. 23 62 00). 96 rooms. Very comfortable, excellent value. AE, DC, MC, V. *Ríosol* (M), Avda. de Palencia 3 (tel. 22 36 50). 141 rooms. Functional but comfortable. AE, DC, MC, V. *París* (I), Generalísimo 20 (tel. 23 86 00). 77 rooms. Simple, older hotel.

Restaurants. *Adonías* (M), Santa Nonia 16 (tel. 25 26 65). Agreeable rustic décor and good local products. AE, DC, MC, V. *Bodega Regia* (M), Pza. San Martín 8 (tel. 25 41 00). In a beautiful 12th-century building, specializing in traditional Leonese dishes. AE, DC, MC, V. *Casa Pozo* (M), Pza. San Marceló 15 (tel. 22 30 39). A real León tradition going strong for over a century and still in the same family; good home cooking. AE, DC, V. *El Racimo de Oro (M),* Caño Vadillo 2 (tel. 25 75 75). Family-run restaurant serving good local produce in an old 17th century *mesón.* MC, V. *El Faisán Dorado* (I), Cantareros 2 (tel. 25 66 09). A bright and novel restaurant with imaginative cuisine and good service. Closed Sun. evening and Mon. V.

Llanes. Asturias (985). *Las Brisas* (M), La Arquera (tel. 40 17 26). 33 rooms. Recently opened, very comfortable. *Don Paco* (M), Parque de Posada Herrera (tel. 40 01 50). 42 rooms. In a 17th-century palace near the sea. Open June through Sept. only. AE, MC, V. *Montemar* (M), Jenaro Riestra (tel. 40 01 00). 41 rooms. Recent and close to beach. AE, MC, V.

Luarca. Asturias (985). *Gayoso-Hotel* (M), Paseo de Gómez 4 (tel. 64 00 54). 26 rooms. At upper end of price range. MC, V. *Hostal Gayoso* (M), Pza. Alfonso X el Sabio (tel. 64 00 50). 26 rooms. Under same ownership as the hotel. A well established hostel run by same family for over 120 years. MC, V.

Restaurants. *Casa Consuelo* (M), 6 km. out in Otur (tel. 64 08 44). Long established Asturian tradition founded in 1935. Excellent wine list and local cider. AE, DC, MC, V. *Leonés* (M), Pza. Alfonso el Sabio (tel. 64 09

95). Popular family-run restaurant serving delicious pastries. Closed Thurs. in winter. AE, MC, V.

Lugo (982). *Gran Hotel Lugo* (E–M), Avda. Ramón Ferreiro (tel. 22 41 52). 169 rooms. The best in town. AE, DC, MC, V. *Méndez Núñez* (M), Reina 1 (tel. 23 07 11). 94 rooms. Central and highly recommended.

Restaurants. *Mesón de Alberto* (M), Cruz 4 (tel. 22 83 10). Good Galician specialties. AE, MC, V. *Verruga* (M), Cruz 12 (tel. 22 98 55). Long-established restaurant with a good reputation. Closed Mon. AE, DC, MC, V.

Orense (988). *San Martín* (M), Curros Enríquez 1 (tel. 23 56 11). 60 rooms. The best in town, with good amenities. AE, DC, MC, V. *Sila* (M), Avda. de la Habana 61 (tel. 23 63 11). 64 rooms. *Barcelona* (I), Avda. Pontevedra 13 (tel. 22 08 00). 47 rooms. Pleasant location overlooking a square in the old part of town. DC, MC, V. *Padre Feijoo* (I), Pza. Eugenio Montes 1 (tel. 22 31 00). 53 rooms. Centrally located close to the Old Town and with good restaurants nearby. DC, MC, V. *Paroque* (I), Parque de San Lázaro 24 (tel. 23 36 11). 57 rooms. Very central, close to cafes and shops.

Restaurants. *San Miguel* (E), San Miguel 12 (tel. 22 12 45). The best in town—excellent shellfish. Closed Tues. AE, DC, MC, V. *Carroleiro* (M), San Miguel 10 (tel. 22 05 66). Old-world décor and charm, plus good service. AE, DC, MC, V. *Martín Fierro* (M), Avda. Sáenz Diez 65 (tel. 23 48 20). Modern and elegant, with terrace overlooking the river. Specializes in Argentinian *parrilladas*. AE, DC, MC, V. *Pingallo* (M), San Miguel 6 (tel. 22 00 57). The best bet, price-wise, of the restaurants on this street. V.

Oviedo (985). *La Reconquista* (L), Gil de Jaz 16 (tel. 24 11 00). 139 rooms. Luxurious 5-star hotel; book well in advance. AE, DC, MC, V. *Gran Hotel España* (E), Jovellanos 2 (tel. 22 05 96). 89 rooms. Recently renovated, very central. AE, DC, MC, V. *La Jirafa* (E), Pelayo 6 (tel. 22 22 44). 89 rooms. Comfortable, friendly service. AE, MC, V. *Ramiro I* (E), Calvo Sotelo 13 (tel. 23 28 50). 83 rooms. A little out of center, on the N630 from León. AE, DC, MC, V. *Regente* (E), Jovellanos 31 (tel. 22 23 43). 88 rooms. Central and comfortable; under same management as *España*. AE, DC, MC, V. *La Gruta* (M), Alto de Buenavista (tel. 23 24 50). 55 rooms. Modern hotel on edge of town with good views. AE, DC, MC, V. *Principado* (M), San Francisco 6 (tel. 21 77 92). 55 rooms. Stylish hotel opposite Old University; excellent restaurant. AE, DC, MC, V. *Bardón* (M–I), Covadonga 7 (tel. 22 52 93). 40 rooms. Very central, well recommended.

Restaurants. *Casa Fermín* (E), San Francisco 8 (tel. 21 64 52). Next to *Principado* hotel and with a fine reputation for good food. AE, DC, MC, V. *Trascorrales* (E), Pza Trascorrales 19 (tel. 22 24 41). Famous Asturian restaurant in a lovely old house. AE, DC, MC, V. *La Goleta* (E–M), Covadonga 32 (tel. 21 38 47). Small restaurant specializing in fish and seafood. Closed Sun. and July. AE, DC, MC, V. Booking advisable in all three.

Ponferrada. León (987). *Hotel Del Temple* (M), Avda. de Portugal 2 (tel. 41 00 58). 114 rooms. In a medieval palace. Pool. AE, DC, MC, V. *Conde Silva* (M), Avda. de Astorga 2 (tel. 41 04 07). 60 rooms. AE, DC, MC, V.

Pontevedra (986). *Parador Nacional Casa del Barón* (E), Maceda (tel. 85 58 00). 47 rooms. Magnificent palace right in town. AE, DC, MC, V. *Rías Bajas* (M), Daniel de la Sota 7 (tel. 85 51 00). 100 rooms. Modern and central. AE, DC, MC, V. *Virgen del Camino* (M), Virgen del Camino 55 (tel. 85 59 04). 53 rooms. AE, DC, MC, V. *Comercio* (I), González Besada 3 (tel. 85 12 17). 26 rooms. Recent with pleasant, helpful service.

Restaurants. *Doña Antonia* (E), Soportales de la Herrería 9 (tel. 84 72 74). Delightful small restaurant (only 9 tables) overlooking the Pza. Herrería. Closed Sun. MC, V. *Casa Román* (M), Augusto García Sánchez 12 (tel. 84 35 60). One of the best. AE, DC, MC, V. *Casa Rua* (M), Avda. de Carbacerías 12 (tel. 85 62 61). Good moderately priced restaurant at bottom of Campo de la Torre. MC, V.

Two km. (just over a mile) out, at **San Salvador de Poyo,** is *Casa Solla* (M), Ctra. de La Toja (tel. 85 26 78). Exquisite food and beautiful surroundings make this one of Galicia's best. Closed Thurs., and Sun. evenings. V.

Puebla De Lillo. León (987). *Toneo* (M), Las Piedras (tel. 73 50 25). 130 rooms. Set in the Cantabrian mountains above the Porma reservoir near the border with Asturias.

Ribadeo. Lugo (982). *Parador Nacional* (E), Amador Fernández (tel. 11 08 25). 47 rooms. Modern parador with rooms overlooking estuary. AE, DC, MC, V. *Eo* (M), Avda. de Asturias 5 (tel. 11 07 50). 20 rooms, pool. Magnificent views over the *ría*. MC, V.

Ribadesella. Asturias (985). *Gran Hotel del Sella* (E), La Playa (tel. 86 01 50). 74 rooms. Pool, tennis, bar and garden at the beach. Open Apr. through Sept. only. DC, MC, V. *La Playa* (M), La Playa 42 (tel. 86 01 00). 12 rooms. Garden. Open Apr. to Sept. only.

Santiago De Compostela. La Coruña (981). *Araguaney* (L), Alfredo Brañas 5 (tel. 59 59 00). 57 rooms, pool. A new luxury hotel primarily for businessmen, and only 15 minutes' walk from center. AE, DC, MC, V. *Reyes Católicos* (L), Pza. de España 1 (tel. 58 22 00). 157 rooms. A former pilgrims' hostel built by Ferdinand and Isabella—end 15th century—and a legend. Lashings of atmosphere, superb location right by the cathedral. However, it is starting to show its age. Its architecture and setting make it one of the great hotels of Spain, but reports have been mixed regarding food and service. AE, DC, MC, V.

Compostela (E), Gen. Franco 1 (tel. 58 57 00). 99 rooms. Central and close to the Old Town; another famous hotel in a historic building. Rooms are old-fashioned but comfortable. MC, V. *Peregrino* (E), Avda. Rosalía de Castro (tel. 59 18 50). 148 rooms. Modern, a little way out on the road to Pontevedra. Somewhat austere. Pool, gardens, bar. AE, DC, MC, V. *Los Tilos* (E), (tel. 59 79 72). 84 rooms. Two km. (just over a mile) out, on the road to La Estrada. Comfortable, typical chain hotel. AE, DC, MC, V. All above are very low (E).

Gelmírez (M), Gen. Franco 92 (tel. 56 11 00). 138 rooms. Modern and only a short walk from the center; rather functional. MC, V. *Santiago Apóstol* (M), La Grela 6 (tel. 58 71 38). 80 rooms. Just out of town, on the Lugo road. New. AE, DC, MC, V.

Rey Fernando (I), Fernando III el Santo 30 (tel. 59 35 50). 24 rooms. A 2-star hotel not far from station. *Universal* (I), Pza. Galicia 2 (tel. 58 58 00). 56 rooms. Simple but adequate hotel close to center. AE, DC, MC, V.

Restaurants. *Don Gaiferos* (E), Rua Nova 23 (tel. 58 38 94). Elegant, modern décor. AE, DC, MC, V. *El Retablo* (E), Rua Nova 13 (tel. 56 59 50). Attractive setting in an old antiques shop. Food generally good, especially the desserts, but service could be better. Closed Sun. evening and Mon. AE, DC, MC, V. *Vilas* (E), Rosalía de Castro 88 (tel. 59 10 00). Opened in 1915, it's been serving top Galician cuisine ever since and is something of a tradition in the city, as is its annexe *Anexo Vilas* (E), Avda. de Villagarcía 21 (tel. 59 83 87). AE, DC, MC, V.

El Franco (M), Calle del Franco 28. One of the best on a street jampacked with restaurants. *Las Huertas* (M), Huertas 16 (tel. 56 19 79). Recent restaurant in an old house not far from cathedral, fast gaining popularity. MC, V. *La Tacita de Oro* (M), Gen. Franco 31 (tel. 56 32 55). A longstanding tradition among Santiago restaurants; well patronized by locals. AE, DC, MC, V.

El Asesino (I), Pza. Universidad 16 (tel. 58 15 68). Modest tavern serving basic home cooking for over 110 years; a real Santiago institution. Closed Sat. night and Sun.

Camilo (I), Raina 4 (tel. 58 15 68). Delightful, first-floor restaurant overlooking Pza. Fonseca. Local Galician cuisine, simple and charming, with Ribero wine served from white china bowls. Closed weekends.

Cafes. *Alameda* (M), on corner of Calle del Franco and Avda. Figueroa, has tables on the sidewalk and is popular in the early evening. It also has a restaurant serving meals and *platos combinados. Derby* (M), on corner of Pza. Galicia, is a charming old-world cafe notable for its good service. *Fonseca* (I), on Pza. Fonseca, has tables in the square, and serves generous tapas.

Taramundi. Asturias (985). *La Rectoral* (E–M), (tel. 63 40 60). 12 rooms. A newly-opened, delightful hotel in a lovely rural setting on borders of Asturias and Galicia. MC, V.

La Toja. Pontevedra (986). *Gran Hotel* (L), (tel. 73 00 25). 201 rooms. Between the sea and the pinewoods, this magnificent spot has just about everything—a marvelous situation, tennis courts, golf links, pool, and private beach. It also houses the island's casino. AE, DC, MC, V.

Louxo (E), (tel. 73 02 00). 96 rooms. Four-star hotel, again marvelously located, and with golf, tennis and pool. AE, DC, MC, V. *Balneario* (M), (tel. 73 01 50). 43 rooms. One-star hotel with pool, tennis, golf and gardens. Open June through Aug. only.

Tuy. Pontevedra (986). *Parador Nacional San Telmo* (E), (tel. 60 03 09). 16 rooms. One km. (just over half a mile) out of town. Characteristic local building. Pool and gardens. AE, DC, MC, V.

Verin. Orense (988). *Parador Nacional de Monterrey* (M), (tel. 41 00 75). 23 rooms. Four km. (two-and-a-half miles) out of town, a modern parador with pool and gardens. AE, DC, MC, V.

Vigo. Pontevedra (986). *Bahía de Vigo* (E), Cánovas del Castillo 5 (tel. 22 67 00). 107 rooms. Comfortable, well-equipped rooms. AE, DC, MC, V. *Ciudad de Vigo* (E), Concepción Arenal 4 (tel. 22 78 20). 101 rooms. Modern. AE, DC, MC, V. *Samil Playa* (E), Playa Samil (tel. 23 25 30). 127 rooms. About six km. (nearly four miles) out of town. Pool, tennis and disco. AE, DC, MC. V. *Ensenada* (M), Alfonso XIII 35 (tel. 22 61 00). 109 rooms. Modern. AE, DC, MC, V. *México* (M), Vía Norte 10 (tel. 43 16 66). 112 rooms. AE, DC, MC, V. *Estación* (I), Alfonso XIII 43 (tel. 43 89 11). 22 rooms. Good budget bet in an otherwise costly district. AE, DC, MC, V.

Restaurants. *El Mosquito* (E–M), Pza. Villavícencio 4 (tel. 43 35 70). A long-standing Vigo tradition; good seafood. DC, V. *Puesto Piloto Alcabre* (M), Avda. Atlántica 194 (tel. 29 79 75). Good fish and seafood. AE, DC, V. *Sibaris* (M), García Barbón 168 (tel. 22 15 26). Very popular and one of the best. Closed Sun. AE, MC, V.

Villafranca Del Bierzo. León (987). *Parador Nacional* (M), Avda. de Calvo Sotelo (tel. 54 01 75). 40 rooms. Modern. Garden. AE, DC, MC, V.

Villagarcia De Arosa. Pontevedra (986). *Pazo O Rial* (M), El Rial 1 (tel. 50 56 22). 60 rooms, pool. An old mansion set in pinewood. AE, MC, V.

Restaurants. *Chocolate* (M), Avda. Cambados 151 (tel. 50 11 99). Outstanding and famous, with moderate prices. AE, DC, MC, V. *Lolina* (M), Pza. Muelle 1 (tel. 50 12 81). Well known for superb seafood. MC, V.

Villalba. Lugo (982). *Parador Nacional Condes de Villalba* (E), Valeriano Valdesuso (tel. 51 00 11). 6 rooms. A genuinely medieval castle. AE, DC, MC, V.

Vivero. Lugo (982). *Tebar* (I), Nicolás Cora 70 (tel. 56 01 00). 27 rooms. Recent. AE, DC, MC, V. *Las Sirenas* (I), Sacido Covas Vivero (tel. 56 02 00). 29 rooms. Near beach, with good views. Garden.

PLACES OF INTEREST. The cities of Oviedo, León and Santiago have a wealth of notable buildings, and the early Romanesque churches of Asturias and Galicia, and the ancient Ramiresque-style architecture found only in Asturias, make rewarding sightseeing; but generally speaking, this is a region visited more for the beauty of its landscapes and seascapes than for its monuments.

Astorga (León). **Cathedral of Santa María.** Open 8–12 and 4.30–7 in winter, 11–2 and 3.30–6.30 in summer. Its **Museum,** with a collection of statues of the Virgin, gold plate and a 10th-century cask, is open 11–2 and 3.30–4.30 in winter, 10–2 and 4–8 in summer.

Ergástula Romana (Roman Tunnel). Dark, sinister tunnel thought to have been used as a slave prison in Roman times; a National Monument.

Palacio Episcopal (Episcopal Palace). Fantastic white granite palace begun by Antoní Gaudí in 1889 and completed in 1913 by Ricardo Guereta. It houses a **Museum of the Camino de Santiago** and a contemporary art gallery. Open 11–2 and 3.30–6.30 in winter, 10–2 and 4–8 in summer; closed Mon. in winter.

Seminario Diocesano (Diocesan Seminary). Seminary built in 18th century with cloisters by Gaudí. Note the paintings of the Evangelists in the chapel's enormous dome.

Aviles (Asturias). **Capilla de los Alas** (Alas Chapel) in San Nicolás church. 14th-century chapel built to house the tomb of Pedro Juan de los Alas in 1348. Open 9–1 and 5.30–8.15. In the main church the tomb of Don Pedro Menéndez de Avilés is also worthy of note.

Palacio de Camposagrado, Plazuela de Camposagrado. Outstanding 17th-century Asturian palace.

Bayona (Pontevedra). **Santa María.** 13th-century Romanesque basilica. Open 10–1.30 and 4–8.

Virgen de la Roca. Statue of the Virgin of the Rocks, patroness of sailors, standing 1 km. out on a headland overlooking the Ría of Vigo. Magnificent views over the Cíes Islands.

La Coruña. Jardines de San Carlos (San Carlos Gardens). Former fort now a park; tomb of Sir John Moore. Open 8 A.M. to dusk.

Museo Arqueológico, Castillo de San Antón. Interesting Archeological Museum in 16th-century fort. Open 10–2 all year, and 4–8 in summer. Closed Mon.

Museo de Bellas Artes (Fine Arts Museum), Pza. Pintor Sotomayor. Paintings from the Spanish, Flemish, Italian and Galician schools. Open 10–2 all year, in summer 4–6 also. Adjoining is the **Casa Museo de Emilia Pardo Bazán,** a small museum dedicated to this writer's life and work. Open 10–12; closed Sun.

Torre de Hércules (Hercules Tower). On the furthest point of the peninsula 2 km. from center. 242 steps to climb to the top, the only Roman lighthouse still in use. Open 10–1.30 and 4–7.30.

Covadonga. (Asturias). **Parque Nacional de la Sierra de Covadonga.** National Park and Nature Reserve with many protected species of flowers and animals, in the mountains of Covadonga and the Peña Santa.

Gijon (Asturias). **Casa Museo de Jovellanos,** Pza.de Jovellanos. Birthplace of the writer Gaspar Melchor de Jovellanos (1744–1811). Mementoes, an art gallery, and the famous polychrome sculpture *Retablo de Mar* by Sebastián Miranda. Open 10–1 and 4–8, Sun. 10–1.30; closed Mon.

Pueblo de Asturias. Model village of a typical Asturian pueblo. Houses two interesting museums, the **Museo de Cerámica Popular** with Asturian ceramics, and the **Museo de la Gaita** (Bagpipe Museum) with a bagpipe workshop and collection of bagpipes from all over the world. Open 10–7.

León. Basílica de San Isidoro. Romanesque basilica with the remains of San Isidoro and pantheon of the Kings of León. Open 9–2 and 4–6. Its **Museum** houses an important collection of Roman and medieval artefacts including valuable medieval banners. Open 9–2, 3.30–8 in summer; 10–1.30, 4–6.30 in winter.

Cathedral, Pza. de la Regla. 13th-century Gothic cathedral with magnificent stained glass windows (over 130). Closed Sun. afternoon. The **Ca-**

thedral Museum in the north transept has a rich collection of sacred art including a Mozarabic Bible. Open 9–1.30 and 4–7.30; closed Fri.

Museo Arqueológico, Pza. San Marcos, within the Hostal San Marcos. Limoges enamels, a statue of Christ by Carrizo, a Mozarabic cross, medieval tombs and portraits of the Knights of the Order of Santiago. Open 10–2, 4–6; closed Mon.

Nuestra Señora del Mercado, Pza. Sta María del Camino. 13th-century Romanesque church with attractive wrought iron grilles. Open 8.30–12 and 5.30–8.30.

Lugo. Cathedral. Neo-Classical with some Gothic and Romanesque. See the Chapel of the Virgin of the Big Eyes *(Ojos Grandes)* and the altar by Cornelis de Holanda.

Museo Provincial, Pza.de la Soledad. Collection of sundials, and pre-Roman and Celtic artefacts. Open 10–2 and 4–7. Closed Sat. P.M. and Sun.

San Pedro. Pza. de la Soledad. National Monument. Visit with the same ticket as the Provincial Museum. Open 9–1, 4–8.

Orense. Cathedral with splendid **Pórtico del Paraíso** (Gate of Paradise). **Museum,** in the 13th-century cloisters, includes some 10th-century rock-crystal chess pieces. Open 10.30–1, 3.30–7.30.

Museo Arqueológico, Pza. Mayor. Former Bishops' Palace, with wide range of archeological, Romanesque, Gothic and Baroque items. Open 10–1 and 5–8; closed Mon.

Oviedo (Asturias). **Cathedral,** Pza. Alfonso II el Casto. 14th–15th-century built around the Cámara Santa of Alfonso II (792–842). Open 10–1, 4–8 in summer; 10–1, 4–6 in winter.

Museo Arqueológico, San Vicente. Archeology Museum with collections of prehistoric Celtic, Roman and pre-Romanesque artefacts housed in the Monastery of Santa María la Real. Open 11.30–1.30 and 4–6. Closed Mon.

Museo de Bellas Artes (Fine Arts Museum), Santa Ana. In the old Velarde Palace. Open 11.30–1.30 and 5–8. Closed Mon. in winter; Sun. in summer.

San Miguel de Lillo, Ctra. de los Monumentos. 2 km. out on the slopes of Mt. Naranco. Ancient pre-Romanesque church built by King Ramiro I (842–850). Magnificent views over Oviedo. Open 10–1 and 4–7; in winter 10–1 only.

Santa María del Naranco, Ctra. de los Monumentos. Palace and church built by King Ramiro I in the 9th century. Open 10–1 and 4–7; in winter 10–1 only.

Peñalba De Santiago (León). **Monastery of Peñalba.** 10th-century, in Mozarabic style. Open 9–1 and 3–5. Closed Tues., and Sat. P.M.

Ponferrada (León). The name—iron bridge—comes from the bridge built in the 11th century, to help pilgrims on their way to Santiago.

Castillo de los Templarios, Flórez Osorio 4. Castle of the Knights Templar. Originally Roman, later reconstructed by the Knights Templar; one of the most important examples of medieval military architecture. Open 9–1 and 3–7; closed Sun. in winter, Tues. in summer.

Nuestra Señora de Vizbayo and **San Andrés,** the two most notable churches; the former with horseshoe arches, the latter built in the 17th century with a Baroque altar and a 13th-century statue of *Cristo de las Maravillas.*

Pontevedra. Museo Provincial, Sarmiento 51. Provincial Museum housed in two 18th-century mansions, with a collection of prehistoric and pre-Roman artefacts. Also visited on the same ticket are the **Santo Domingo ruins** housing a lapidary museum, and the **Casa de Fernández López** with an exhibition of paintings by contemporary Galician artists. Open 11–1.30 and 5–8; closed Sun. afternoon.

Ribadesella (Asturias). **Tito Bustillo Cave,** in Ardines, south of the bridge. Cave used as a dwelling in the paleolithic period around 20,000 B.C. Magnificent stalactites and prehistoric paintings of animals including horses, stags and does; second in importance only to the Altamira cave paintings. Open Apr. to Sept. 9–1 and 3.30–6.30. Limited to 400 visitors each day.

Sahagun (León). **Monasterio de Santa Cruz,** Avda. Dres. Bermejo y Calderón 8. Benedictine convent. Open summer only, 11–1, 5–7.

5 km. from Sahagún is the **Castle of General Campos,** a 16th-century fort; National Monument.

Santiago De Compostela. We suggest that you contact the Santiago Tourist Office for the latest details of church and other monuments' opening times.

SPORTS. Watersports. The coast of Asturias offers some good bathing beaches, the most popular spots for swimming are the beaches of Ribadesella, Colunga, Llanes, Salinas and Luarca, all in Asturias province. In Galicia the island of La Toja is a paradise for sports lovers and here you can go swimming, wind surfing or waterskiing, not to mention its opportunities for tennis, golf or shooting, or gambling in the island's luxury casino. Canoeing is popular on the River Sella in Asturias and the annual kayak race on the Sella is one of the big events of the year.

Mountain sports. The Cantabrian range between Asturias and León provinces is one of Spain's most important skiing areas. Skiing installations have been built in the Picos de Europa in eastern Asturias and around the Puerto de Pájares on the Asturias-León border. Mountain climbing and hiking are also popular and the difficult and dangerous ascent of El Naranjo de Bulnes in Asturias is a well known challenge to mountaineers. Qualified guides can be hired to escort groups on easy hikes or on more adventurous mountain climbs. Contact Mountain School, Camping Naranjo de Bulnes, Arenas de Cabrales, (Asturias), tel. (958) 84 51 78. There are mountain refuges scattered around the Picos de Europa.

Hunting and shooting. The entire region is rich in hunting grounds for both big and small game. Mountain goat, wild boar, chamois, roebuck, stag and even bears are hunted in the mountain ranges of Asturias, the Montes de León and in the provinces of Galicia, especially in the Ancares

National Reserve. The reservoirs of Sil, Orbigo and Porma in León province, and the estuaries of Galicia are good shooting grounds for waterfowl.

Fishing. Salmon and trout abound in the rivers Sella, Narcea, Eo, Deva and Cares in Asturias, and there are numerous trout reserves in the rivers of León, and throughout Galicia. Deep sea fishing, especially for shellfish, is excellent off the shores of Galicia.

THE BASQUE COUNTRY AND CANTABRIA

The Individualist North

Spain's Atlantic coast facing north across the Bay of Biscay is a much more fertile region than any we have so far explored. Its eastern half, covering the Basque Country and Cantabria, has green landscape and high peaks more reminiscent of the Swiss alps than the usual image of Spain. Though mountainous it is also one of Spain's most heavily industrialized areas, which unfortunately mars much of its natural beauty, particularly along the coastal strip of the Basque Country.

The Spanish Basque Country (the Basque lands extend over the Pyrenees into France) is made up of the three provinces of Alava (capital Vitoria), Vizcaya (capital Bilbao), and Spain's smallest province, Guipúzcoa (capital San Sebastián). The two million Basques have their own language, which bears no resemblance to Spanish, their own TV and radio stations, their own flag and police force (wearing red berets), their own regional parliament and a long history of fierce national pride and coveted self-government, if not independence from the rest of Spain. Of the 16 self-governing regions now operating in Spain, the Basque Country was the first to lead the movement towards decentralization once democracy was established, and the first to pass its Statute of Autonomy. The Basque Country's western neighbor Cantabria, with its capital Santander, is a single province, historically part of Old Castile but today a newly-created autonomous region.

The Basque Country

Although heavily populated and full of individuality, Vascongadas is a tiny region—only some 145 km. (90 miles) from east to west and 72 from north to south—and roads are amongst the best in Spain.

Let us briefly sum up what the area has to offer that cannot always be found in other parts of Spain.

Firstly, in San Sebastián, there is a city expressly created for the tourist, with every kind of comfort for a pleasant summer holiday and boasting two of the best beaches in Spain. Because it is only a few kilometers from the French frontier, it is a place that is used to the peculiar habits of foreigners and where foreigners, therefore, can feel at home. Secondly, the Basque country, with its northern sea, temperate heat, and rugged coast. Thirdly, the rough and ready Basque himself, with his passion for all forms of outdoor sport, large meals, hard liquor and hard work, is far easier for the Anglo-Saxon to understand than the proud, passionate, but austere Castilian.

No one knows for certain the origin of the Basque race and language, but it is believed that the Basques are the descendants of the original Iberians, who inhabited the peninsula even before the Celts arrived some 3,500 years ago, and were driven by successive waves of conquerors, Phoenician, Roman, Visigoth and Moorish, into the fastnesses of the Pyrenees and, by one of those inexplicable twists of history, somehow survived as a distinct entity. In any case, they are not Spaniards in appearance, origin, character or language.

In appearance they tend to be short, wide of shoulder and hip, barrel-chested, and with the typical mountaineer's short, sturdy legs. They are huge eaters and drinkers, hard working, and shrewd, superb natural singers like the Welsh, and talk a language which, to the novice, sounds as if it is composed exclusively of the letters U, G, LL, RR, TH and ZZ.

Basque cooking is one of the greatest cuisines of Spain, and is fast gaining an international reputation. The freshness and preparation of Basque seafood dishes is legendary and the Basque love and pride in the national cuisine is manifested in the preservation of the traditional eating clubs. There are some 50 of these clubs in San Sebastián alone and around 100 of them through the whole Basque Country. Once a week or so, groups of Basque men gather in these clubs and take it in turn to prepare and cook a meal for their fellow club members. This intriguing institution is still a totally male preserve.

Here we should just mention the current terrorist situation in the Basque Country. Bombings, kidnappings and assassinations carried out by ETA, the Basque separatist movement, are fairly frequent throughout the region, but they are directed at the police, banks and prominent businessmen and not normally against tourists. The danger to tourists would seem to be minimal. Avoid Rentería near the French frontier, one of the worst affected places.

Guipúzcoa

From the French frontier onward, the coastline of Guipúzcoa is an un-interrupted chain of superb beaches, of which the most famous is San Sebastián. San Sebastián, or Donostia as the Basques call it, is only 20 km. (12 miles) from the French frontier at the River Bidasoa, which is spanned by the bridge that links Spanish Irún with French Hendaye.

It is a pleasant city, designed to provide the tourist with an ideal setting in which to pass the summer months. It is never excessively hot and the streets are wide, and fresh with the breezes of Biscay. There are luxurious shops, hotels, restaurants, bars and nightclubs, and all the sightseeing is within a day's run. In July San Sebastián is the setting for a well known International Jazz Festival, in mid-August it celebrates its *Semana Grande* with huge fireworks displays and much merrymaking, while in September it hosts the prestigious San Sebastián International Film Festival.

For serious sightseeing we can recommend the collection in the San Telmo Museum, or a trip to Hernani, an attractive town where the church shelters some beautiful (and little-known) gilded wood carvings. Also of interest are two old churches—the exuberantly Baroque Santa María and the 16th-century San Vicente, both in the old town, between Mount Urgull and the Alameda. A stroll along the picturesque harbor front with its colorful old houses, fishing boats and plentiful outdoor restaurants is a delight; so too are the narrow streets, squares and market place of the old town.

But before reaching San Sebastián, shortly after Irún, it's worth a detour to Fuenterrabía to see its medieval citadel and castle of Charles V, now a parador, and interesting harbor.

Other places of interest along the coast, not far from San Sebastián, are Deva, with a fine bathing beach, and the charming little ports of Zumaya and Guetaria. Nearby Zarauz is a most pleasant and attractive bathing resort. To the west are the picturesque fishing villages of Ondárroa, Lequeitio and Bermeo, while inland, at Loyola, is the austere monastery and Baroque church built around the house where St Ignatius, founder of the Jesuit order, was born in 1491.

There are many other places worth stopping at. The modern basilica of Aránzazu fits in ideally with the wooded hills surrounding it. At Azpeitia, in the mountains, you will see some very pretty houses. There is also Elgoibar, which has a lovely gateway, the manor house of Val de l'Espina at Ermua, the church of Santa María de Galdácano, Vergara, Azcoitia, Oñate and a great many other places.

One word of warning, however: rain is frequent all the year round on this north coast!

Alava

Vitoria (198,000 inhabitants), capital of the province of Alava and seat of the Basque regional parliament, is only 65 km. (40 miles) by road from Bilbao, and 116 from San Sebastián via Tolosa. Although only some 56 km. in a direct line from the coast at its nearest point, Vitoria is 536 meters (1,760 feet) above sea level. The gray stone houses with high bay windows, combined with a tendency to Scotch mists, call to mind an English country town, more than anything Spanish.

It is an interesting little town set in beautiful country. In the town hall you can still see the special knife—the Machete Vitoriano—over which the Attorney General must place his hands while he is sworn into office, this being a reminder that he will be beheaded if he fails to give satisfaction!

There are Van Dyck and Rubens paintings side by side with a 12th-century Virgin in the cathedral of Santa María, but of greater importance to the locals is the jasper White Virgin of Vitoria in the 12th-century church of San Miguel. She is carried through the streets in procession, with much bell ringing followed by fireworks, on August 12. The high altar before which she stands is unusually beautiful.

It was Sancho VI, King of Navarre, who founded Vitoria in 1181 on the site of the ancient city of Gasteiz (to which name it has now reverted amongst Basque-speaking people). The old and the new towns are quite separate. The Provincial Museum contains canvases by Ribera and Alonso Cano, together with some interesting modern works. In the Plaza de la Virgen Blanca stands a monument commemorating the terrible defeat inflicted by Wellington on Napoleon's forces on June 21, 1813, just outside the town. The famous Machete used to be preserved inside a niche in the apse of San Miguel. The Plaza del Machete backs on to the church. In that square stands the palace of Villasuso, displaying a very fine coat of arms.

It is worth taking some short side trips into the countryside around Vitoria as much of the real charm of the Basque Country lies in its ancient mountain villages, and any road inland will take you through half a dozen that have not changed materially since Columbus borrowed the money from great Queen Isabella to discover America, and thus inaugurate the European dollar gap.

Vizcaya

Bilbao, with a population of something under half a million, is the largest city in the Basque country, and is heavily industrial. It lies some 11 km. from the sea, but ships of 4,000 tons can navigate the River Nervión to the city docks.

Iron ore is mined in the locality, and the largest blast furnaces in Spain are to be found around Bilbao. It is an industrial center and port far more than a tourist resort, but in the summer months the luxurious villas of the residential suburbs of Santurce and Portugalete fill with guests from Madrid.

Bilbao is relatively modern, being founded as late (for Spain) as the year 1300 and is less overpoweringly endowed with ancient buildings than is commonly the case in Spain. The Old Quarter, the heart of the old town, merits a walking tour—it is now a pedestrian zone. It includes, among many interesting old buildings, the Cathedral, which dates from just after the founding of the town and has early 15th century Gothic cloisters. Do not fail to visit the quite exceptional collection of Grecos, Riberas and Goyas in the Museo de Bellas Artes, in the park halfway up the Gran Vía—particularly the Goyas.

If archeology interests you, you might visit from Bilbao the prehistoric caves of Basondo. If, on the other hand, you are an enthusiastic oyster eater, then steal off by yourself to the little fishing village of Plencia, 29 km. from Bilbao where, as well as enjoying the oysters, you can see the

13th-century castle of Butrón. Then there is Pedernales Bay (with the Chacharramendi Islands) backed by Mount Urguiola, which is crowned with old palaces. Bilbao's most frequented beach is at Algorta though the pollution here is unpleasant.

Guernica, with its sacred oak tree under which sovereigns since the Middle Ages have sworn to respect the freedom and privileges of the Basque people, stands as a symbol of independence in the heart of every Basque. Ruthlessly bombed by the Luftwaffe in April 1937, with the blessing of General Franco, and immortalized by Picasso's vivid portrayal of its sufferings, it has been almost totally rebuilt, and lies about 32 km. to the northeast of Bilbao. The countryside you pass through is wooded with a sprinkling of meadows; it is like a miniature Switzerland, except around Amorebieta, which is spoilt by industrialization.

Other musts near here are Mundaca and the extraordinary panorama of the Nervión estuary, especially at low tide. Most important of all, you should go on north a few more miles till you reach Bermeo, the prettiest fishing port of Spain. You see houses set in tiers on the steep cliff, washing drying at the windows and the fleet of gaily colored fishing boats, all neatly lined up in the harbor. It is a painter's dream. But remember that it is advisable to go there before September 15th. The fishermen depart after that date for their annual season of deep-sea fishing and the three docks are then pathetically empty.

You can return to Bilbao by way of Mungula and Miranda, an area of woods and mountains and, alas, factories. From a tourist's point of view, the scenery is not striking. Most cars turn off to the right on reaching Mungula and return to the coast.

While you are northwest of Bilbao, drive past the castle of Santurce, just to sample the delicious grilled sardines, or *sardinas asadas,* in the street, before going on to Castro Urdiales. The latter is a compulsory stop and is the oldest town on the coast. The Vikings destroyed the ancient Flaviobriga, which dated from Roman times. A fortress was built, and a fort was also erected in the little cove of Urdiales, where the lighthouse dominates the castle. Whatever you do, be sure to visit Nuestra Señora de la Anunciación, a splendid ocher-colored building. When Cesare Borgia escaped in 1506 from the castle of La Mota at Medina del Campo, where he had been held captive, it was in Castro Urdiales that he found a temporary refuge.

Cantabria

If you are looking for a summer vacation with swimming, fishing, hunting, tennis, golf, yachting and all the other pastimes dear to the heart of a sportsman, you will find it in the province of Santander, now officially designated Cantabria. Situated in the north of Spain, its shoreline bordering the Bay of Biscay is dotted with bathing beaches. The terrain of the province varies from warm, fertile valleys rich in fruit trees to the snow-capped mountains of the Picos de Europa. During the season there is good skiing and other winter sports.

Mention should be made of the spas of this region, which have been little publicized and offer relief from afflictions ranging from arthritis to respiratory troubles. Many of them, such as Solares, are only a short distance from the city of Santander.

The province of Cantabria is also rich in small villages, each with its own personality, and, of course, there are the prehistoric paintings discovered in the caves of Altamira in 1875. Much of the folklore of this region has been lost, but romerías are still held locally.

The city of Santander is first mentioned historically only in 1068, when it was called the Port of San Emeterio. Later, the city was converted into a fortress, and given an arsenal and shipbuilding yards. Its commerce flourished in medieval times, especially after the discovery of America, and its ships contributed to the reconquest of Seville. In 1941 a fire caused by a freak tornado gutted the city, making necessary almost total reconstruction, so that Santander is perhaps the most modern Spanish city today, one practically devoid of ancient remains. (The only significant one is the 12th-century crypt of the former cathedral). The atmosphere of Santander is distinctly nautical, with its docks and old fishing quarter. Throughout August the city plays host to an International Festival of Music and Ballet.

Santander has three fine, sandy beaches (though the water isn't free from industrial pollution): Magdalena, nearest to town; El Sardinero, smartest, equipped with good hotels and all nautical paraphernalia for holidaymakers; and finally Mataleñas, near the beautiful camping site of Bellavista.

Prehistoric Altamira

Even for those not historically or artistically minded, a visit to the caves of Altamira is a must, just as a reminder that there were people living over 13,000 years ago who were advanced enough to make colored pigments and draw amazing pictures of the animals that existed at that time. These decorations were made when most of the northern part of Europe was still in the glacial period, with only a small strip of land visible in Spain between the mountains and the Bay of Biscay. Men dressed in skins, and retired to caves at night to protect themselves from the wild beasts. Even then, a desire for beauty burned in the breasts of these prehistoric nomads, expressing itself in the ornamentation of their homes. These artists, with only charcoal, ocher and hematites, were able to make every shade of yellow, red and gray.

The first cave was discovered in 1875, another in 1928. Perhaps the most expressive observation about them was made by a Frenchman who called them "The Sistine Chapel of the Ice Age." The caves are 29 km. west of Santander and three km. from Santillana del Mar. But before you set your heart on seeing the famous paintings for yourself, a word of caution about the current visiting situation.

The huge crowds of people that flocked to see the famous caves over the years seriously endangered the paintings. The problems of atmospheric control, dust, general wear and tear on the rock surfaces and a whole host of other factors inimical to the safety of these enormously important works, forced the authorities to close the caves completely from 1977 to early 1982. It now appears, however, that the condition of the paintings has improved as a result of this closure. The current situation is that the caves are open to limited groups of visitors only—just how many people are allowed in each day is regulated by the prevailing humidity levels. But take comfort in the fact that if your efforts are thwarted, you can still enjoy a visit to the adjacent museum and audiovisual center, and there are also other caves at Santillana del Mar, as well as the caves at Puente Viesgo 23 km. away, which may be open to the public when the Altamira Caves are closed.

Santillana del Mar

Santillana del Mar is an old village that would still be fast asleep if it were not for these prehistoric discoveries. Nothing has happened here since the 15th century, yet it still remains fresh and lovely. Some of the finer houses are adorned with heraldic coats of arms and emblems, some quite ancient and illustrious. Be sure to visit the 12th-century collegiate church, the most important Romanesque building in the region. The tomb of Santa Juliana (a corrupt form of whose name the town bears) stands in its center. In summer, concerts are given in the exquisite cloisters. The former palace of Carreda Bracho has been turned into a really delightful parador. Santillana del Mar is an adorable little village. The inhabitants add mischievously, "This is the town of the three lies. It has never been holy (*santa*) and it is not flat (*llana*) and the sea (*mar*) is six kilometers away!"

There is scarcely a village or town in the province of Santander that is not distinctive from some point of view. Laredo, with its curious 13th-century church, is where Charles V came to worship after his abdication; Comillas, a small port with two beaches and a pontifical university; Noja, with the beach of La Isla; Reinosa, near the Romanesque churches of Bolmir and Retorillo; Potes, with beautiful scenery and a medieval tower; Limpias, for its famous crucifix.

Here in the inaccessible mountains of northern Spain, the Christian Spaniards took refuge from the Moors in the 8th century and began the reconquest of Spain. This range spreads over three provinces; the highest peaks are under perpetual snow. They are a challenge to mountain climbers, who have opened many clubs in the vicinity, where guides are available. From the Refugio de Aliva high in the Picos de Europa mountains, excursion are organized all year round. One of the most popular trips, or overnight stops for visitors is to the mountain parador of Fuente De, high above Potes. The parador (book well in advance) serves as a base for mountain excursions, and from here a cable car whisks you high up into the mountains for stunning views.

PRACTICAL INFORMATION FOR
THE BASQUE COUNTRY AND CANTABRIA

TOURIST OFFICES. Bilbao, Alameda Mazarredo (tel. 424 4819); **Comillas,** Aldea 6 (tel. 72 07 68); **Irún,** Puente de Santiago (tel. 62 22 39) and in the Estación del Norte (tel. 61 15 24); **Laredo,** Alameda Miramar (tel. 60 54 92); **Potes,** Pza. Capitán Palacios; **San Sebastián,** Reina Regente (tel. 42 10 02), and on corner of Andía and Miramar; **Santander,** Pza. Velarde 1 (tel. 31 07 08), and Jardines de Pereda; **Santillana del Mar,**

Pza. Ramón Pelayo (tel. 81 82 51); **Torrelavega,** Ruíz Tagle 6 (tel. 89 29 82); **Vitoria,** Parque de la Florida (tel. 24 95 64); **Zarauz,** Navarra (tel. 83 09 90).

TELEPHONE CODES. The dialing codes for the Basque provinces and Cantabria are: Alava (945); Guipúzcoa (943); Vizcaya (94); Cantabria (942). You need only dial these codes when calling from outside the province. Dialing codes for all the towns we list are given under *Hotels and Restaurants* immediately after the name of the town.

GETTING AROUND. By Train. Trains from Madrid to the Basque Country and Cantabria all leave from Madrid Chamartín. The distances are such that the journey can easily be made in an overnight train with a couchette or sleeper.

Stations and RENFE Offices. Always double check your station of departure as RENFE and FEVE operate out of different stations, and in the case of Bilbao and San Sebastián there are several different departure points for local and suburban services. *EurRail, InterRail,* and *RENFE Tourist Card* passes are not valid on FEVE routes.

The following will serve as a brief guide to the main stations. **Bilbao** RENFE station is the Estación del Norte (also known as the Estación de Abando) on Hurtado de Mendoza. Then there are separate stations for the FEVE lines to León, Santander and San Sebastián. **San Sebastián** has three stations: the RENFE station is the Estación del Norte on Avda. de Francia (tel. 28 30 89) for the Irún–Madrid mainline service; the FEVE station for trains to Hendaye is the Estación de la Frontera (tel. 45 51 60) on Calle Easo; and the FEVE station for trains to Bilbao is the Estación de Amara (or Estación Vascongadas) (tel. 45 01 31) also on Easo but a little before the Estación de la Frontera. San Sebastián's central RENFE office is on Camino 1 (tel. 42 64 30). In **Santander** the RENFE and FEVE stations are both together on Calle Rodriguez quite close to the center of town. The RENFE office is on Paseo de Pereda 25 (tel. 21 23 87). **Vitoria** station is at the very end of Eduardo Dato (tel. 23 20 30).

By Bus. Services from Madrid direct to the north coast only run in summer; in winter or for more frequent services, make connections in Burgos. The two principal services, one to Santander, the other to San Sebastián and Vitoria via Burgos, both leave from Alenza 20 in Madrid and there is just one bus a day on each route.

Bus Stations. In **Bilbao,** buses to most places including Logroño, Vitoria, Pamplona and Zaragoza leave from Henao 29 right in the center; buses to Santander, Burgos, and Madrid leave from Autonomía 17. In **Santander,** buses to Burgos, Irún, Ontaneda and Gijón leave from F. Vial 8, and to Castro and Logroño from the Bar Machichaco on Calderón de la Barca 9. **San Sebastián's** bus station is on Pza. Pio XII. **Vitoria's** bus station is on Francia 24.

By Air. All four provincial capitals—Bilbao, Santander, San Sebastián, and Vitoria—have airports, and the region is well-connected to other parts of Spain, and France and England, by air routes.

By Car. The Basque Country is well served by fast tollways *(autopistas)* and if you are simply passing through and not planning to do a lot of sightseeing, these are well worth the cost. The A1/A8 runs from the French frontier along the coast to Bilbao with exits for San Sebastián and other intermediate stops. The A1 branches inland at Elgoibar to Burgos with exits for Vitoria. From Bilbao the A68 runs southeast via Logroño to Zaragoza.

The N1 from the French border to Madrid via San Sebastián, Vitoria and Burgos is a very busy road and should be avoided at all costs at the beginning and end of both July and August when it is jammed solid with French vacationers. You are unlikely to fare much better on the A1 *autopista* at these times. All the main N roads in the region offer reasonable driving, though the N634 from Bilbao to Santander snakes its way laboriously along the coast offering some good views of the Bay of Biscay but some slow going. The two inland N roads from Santander, the N623 to Burgos, and the N611 to Reinosa and Palencia, both pass through mountains, and skirt opposite ends of the Ebro reservoir. The scenery here is picturesque and the villages around the reservoir are popular summer resorts and weekend haunts.

In the extreme west of the region in the Picos de Europa mountains in Cantabria province, the best road up into the mountains is the N621 to Potes and Fuente De where there is a mountain parador and a cable car to take you up a further 2500 ft. The road is good right up to the parador. To continue on to León along N621 via Riaño involves some very high mountain driving over the 1609-meter Puerto de Sangloria pass. A slightly lower route is the C627 via the 1350-meter Puerto de Piedrasluengas on the Cantabria-Palencia border, continuing on via the parador at Cervera de Pisuerga to the N611 and Palencia.

HOTELS AND RESTAURANTS. All four provincial capitals are well endowed with good hotels, and San Sebastián and Santander being long established summer capitals offer a wide choice of accommodations. Many of the hotels in Santander and San Sebastián open for the summer only, and some of them only from July–Sept. Hotels in San Sebastián will be heavily booked for the Jazz Festival in July, for the city's *Semana Grande* celebrations around Aug. 15 and again in Sept. for the Film Festival; hotels in Santander are usually heavily booked in July and Aug. but especially during the city's Summer Music and Dance Festival.

There are four paradores in the region, at Argomaniz in Alava, Fuenterrabía in Guipúzcoa, and at Santillaña del Mar and Fuente De in Cantabria.

Basque cuisine, whether traditional or *nouvelle,* is renowned throughout Spain as one of the country's very finest culinary traditions. Excellent restaurants are to be found throughout the Basque provinces but San Sebastián boasts more than its fair share of the nation's top restaurants. Seafood is the specialty of the region and while in Guipúzcoa you should make sure to try some of the local cider and the local white wine called *txakoli* which comes from Guetaria.

Argomaniz. Alava (945). *Parador Nacional de Argómaniz* (M), Ctra. Nal. Madrid–Irún (tel. 28 22 00). 54 rooms. An ancient palace situated some 13 km. (eight miles) from Vitoria. Wonderful views. AE, DC, MC, V.

Bilbao. Vizcaya (94). *Ercilla* (L), Ercilla 37 (tel. 443 88 00). 350 rooms. Large, modern, four-star hotel with many amenities—but the rates are high. Excellent *Bermeo* restaurant. AE, DC, MC, V. *Villa de Bilbao* (L), Gran Vía de López de Haro 87 (tel. 441 60 00). 142 rooms. A top-class hotel with all amenities. AE, DC, MC, V. *Aránzazu* (E), Rodríguez Arias 66 (tel. 441 32 00). 171 rooms. Good hotel with many amenities. AE, DC, MC, V. *Carlton* (E), Pza. Federico Moyua 2 (tel. 416 22 00). 142 rooms. A much older four-star hotel, but still one of the best. AE, DC, MC, V. *Avenida* (E–M), Avda. Zumalacarregui 40 (tel. 412 4300). 116 rooms. *Conde Duque* (E–M), Campo Volantín 22 (tel. 445 60 00). 66 rooms. *Nervión* (E–M), Campo Volantín 11 (tel. 445 47 00). 351 rooms. AE, DC, MC, V.

Cantábrico (M), Miravilla 8 (tel. 415 28 11). 40 rooms. *Zabálburu* (M–I), Pza. Martínez Artola 8 (tel. 443 71 00). 27 rooms. *San Mamés* (I), Luis Briñas 15 (tel. 441 79 00). 36 rooms.

Restaurants. *Guria* (L), Gran Vía de Lopez de Haro 66 (tel. 441 05 43). With an atmosphere that matches the excellence of the food. AE, DC, MC, V. *Goizeko-Kabi* (E), Particular de Estraunza 4 (tel. 441 50 04). Far-and-away the best cuisine in town; outstanding. Closed Sun. AE, DC, MC, V. *Victor* (E), Pza. Nueva 2 (tel. 415 16 78). A reliable Bilbao stand-by, going strong since the 1940s. AE, DC, MC, V.

Castro Urdiales. Cantabria (942). *Las Rocas* (M), Ctra. de la Playa (tel. 86 04 04). 61 rooms. Modern, right on the beach; high rates July to Aug. *Miramar* (M), Avda. de la Playa 1 (tel. 86 02 00). 33 rooms. Near the beach. Bar. AE, DC, MC, V. *Vista Alegre* (M), Barrio Brazomar (tel. 86 01 50). 19 rooms. A good roadside hotel on the main Santander–Bilbao highway, near the beach.

Cestona. Guipúzcoa (943). *Arocena* (M), Paseo San Juan 12 (tel. 86 70 40). 109 rooms, pool. The best hotel in town, modern and comfortable. AE, MC, V. *Gran Hotel Balneario Cestona* (M), Paseo San Juan (tel. 86 71 40). 110 rooms. Traditional spa hotel with extensive grounds. Note that most Cestona hotels open July through Sept. only.

Comillas. Cantabria (942). *Paraíso* (I), Pza. (tel. 72 00 30). 36 rooms. Three-star hotel open April through Oct. *Casal del Castro* (M), San Jerónimo (tel. 72 00 36). 45 rooms. The best hotel in town. Gardens and bowling green. Open Apr. to mid-September. AE, DC, MC, V. *Joseín* (I), Santa Lucía 27 (tel. 72 02 25). 23 rooms.

Deva. Guipúzcoa (943). *Miramar* (M), José Joaquín Aztiria (tel. 60 11 44). 60 rooms. Comfortable. AE, DC, MC, V.

Fuente De. Cantabria (942). *Parador Nacional Río Deva* (M), (tel. 73 00 01). 78 rooms. 3½ km. (2 miles) from Espinama. Peaceful, with fabulous views; an ideal base for mountain excursions. Book well in advance. AE, DC, MC, V.

Fuenterrabia. Guipúzcoa (943). *Pampinot* (L), Kale Nagusia 3 (tel. 64 06 00). 8 rooms. Small and exclusive though only classed as a 3-star hotel. (E) rates Oct. to May. *Parador Nacional El Emperador* (E), Pza.

Armas del Castillo (tel. 64 21 40). 16 rooms. Superb medieval citadel, a former palace of Charles V; one of the great paradors. AE, DC, MC, V. *Guadalupe* (M), Ciudad de Peñíscola (tel. 64 16 50). 34 rooms. Pleasant location. Pool. Open June through Sept. only. *Jauregui* (M), San Pedro 31 (tel. 64 14 00). 53 rooms. The next best. DC, MC, V.

Restaurant. *Ramón Roteta* (E), Villa Ainara, (tel. 64 16 93). Exquisite setting in a private villa with garden; superb cuisine—a "must." MC, V.

Guetaria. Guipúzcoa (943). **Restaurants.** *Elcano* (E), Herrerieta 2 (tel. 83 16 14). Specializes in grills and fresh seafood. Try the local *txakoli* white wine. AE, MC, V. *Kaia y Asador Kai-Pe* (E), General Arnao 10 (tel. 83 24 14). Good for seafood. Country-style decor, good views of the sea and coast. AE, DC, MC, V.

Laredo. Cantabria (942). *El Ancla* (E), González Gallego 10 (tel. 60 55 00). 25 rooms. Garden and bar. AE, V. *Riscó* (M), Alto de Laredo (tel. 60 50 30). 25 rooms. On mountainside; good restaurant and splendid view over the bay. *Cosmopol* (M), Avda. de la Victoria (tel. 60 54 00). 60 rooms. Pool.

Pasajes De San Juan. Guipúzcoa (943). **Restaurant.** *Casa Cámara* (E), San Juan 79 (tel. 35 66 02). Top seafood for over 100 years. Magnificent view.

Reinosa. Cantabria (942). *Corza Blanca* (M), Ctra. Reinosa-Tres Mares (tel. 75 10 99). 44 rooms, pool. *Vejo* (M), Avda. Cantabria 15 (tel. 75 17 00). 71 rooms. Best in town. Modern with a good restaurant. AE, DC, MC, V.

San Sebastián. Guipúzcoa (943) *María Cristina* (L), Paseo República Argentina (tel. 42 67 70). 139 rooms. Recently reopened after extensive renovations which have retained its turn-of-the-century charm. Now with 5-star rating, San Sebastián's leading hotel. AE, DC, MC, V. *Costa Vasca* (E), Avda. Pío Baroja 9 (tel. 21 10 11). 203 rooms. A modern, if rather characterless, hotel; ten minute walk from Ondaretta beach up a steep hill. In need of renovation. AE, DC, MC, V. *Londres y de Inglaterra* (E), Zubieta 2 (tel. 42 69 89). 119 rooms. One of the grand old-timers, though recent renovations have removed much of its original charm. Magnificent views over Igueldo bay. AE, DC, MC, V. *Monte Igueldo* (E), on Mt. Igueldo (tel. 21 02 11). 121 rooms. Reached by a 20-minute drive up a winding road. Superb views, but the hotel itself lacks character. AE, DC, MC, V. *Orly* (E), Pza. de Zaragoza 4 (tel. 46 32 00). 63 rooms. Central and popular. AE, DC, MC, V. *San Sebastián* (E), Avda. de Zumalacárregui 20 (tel. 21 44 00). 94 rooms. Near Ondarreta beach. Rooms facing the highway are hot and noisy. Pool and gardens. AE, DC, MC, V.

Gudamendi (M), Barrio de Igueldo (tel. 21 41 11). 30 rooms. Pleasant situation on Mt. Igueldo. Garden. *Niza* (M), Zubieta 56 (tel. 42 66 63). 41 rooms. Off Pza. Zaragoza, near the beach. Old-world charm. AE, DC, MC, V. *Parma* (M), Gen. Jauregui 11 (tel. 42 88 93). 19 rooms. Impeccably clean, with sea views, modern decor, and deluxe bathrooms.

Restaurants. *Akelarre* (L), Barrio de Igueldo (tel. 21 20 52). Magnificent views and food. AE, DC, MC, V. *Arzak* (L), Alto de Miracruz 21 (tel. 28

55 93). Just in the outskirts, on the road to Fuenterrabía. Unusual, and excellently-prepared food in intimate cottage setting. Internationally famous; reserve long in advance. With *Akelarre,* rates among Spain's top restaurants. AE, DC, MC, V.

Juanito Kojua (E), Puerto 14 (tel. 42 01 80). Long famous throughout Spain for its succulent seafood. Simple decor, but popular so expect to wait. AE, V. *Lanziego* (E), Triunfo 3 (tel. 46 23 84). A recent addition with a growing reputation for good Basque cooking with a French flavor. AE, MC, V. *Nicolasa* (E), Aldamar 4 (tel. 42 17 62). Elegant, with superb cuisine. Another of Spain's all-time great restaurants. AE, DC, MC, V. *Txomin* (E), Avda. Infanta Beatriz (tel. 21 07 05). Near Ondarreta beach. Top food in a rustic setting. AE, DC, MC, V. *Urepel* (E), Paseo de Salamanca 3 (tel. 42 40 40). AE, DC, MC, V.

Salduba (M), Pescadería 6 (tel. 42 56 27). One of the Old Town's most venerable favorites. Outstanding fish dishes. AE, MC, V.

Santander. Cantabria (942). *Real* (L), Paseo de Pérez Galdós 28 (tel. 27 25 50). 123 rooms. Once one of the finest hotels in Europe. Luxury restaurant. AE, DC, MC, V. *Bahía* (E), Alfonso XIII 6 (tel. 22 17 00). 181 rooms. A leading hotel close to ferry terminal. AE, DC, MC, V. *Santemar* (E), Joaquín Costa 28 (tel. 27 29 00). 350 rooms. Good standards but very functional. AE, DC, MC, V. *María Isabel* (M), Avda. de García Lago (tel. 27 18 50). 63 rooms. At the end of Sardinero beach, with splendid views from the large balconied rooms. Pool and garden. *Rhin* (M), Reina Victoria 155 (tel. 27 43 00). 95 rooms. Very popular with good views over Sardinero beach. AE, V. *Sardinero* (M), Pza. de Italia 1 (tel. 27 11 00). 113 rooms. Close to the beach. AE, DC, MC, V. *Europa* (I), Avda. Reina Victoria 145/7 (tel. 27 07 49). 25 rooms. Two-star hostel across the street from Sardinero beach. Excellent value, and run by friendly, helpful owners. Open Apr. to Sept. only.

Restaurants. *Bar El Puerto* (E), Hernán Cortés 63 (tel. 21 30 01). An old-timer, famous for the best shellfish in Cantabria, excellent meat dishes too. AE, DC, MC, V. *Rhin* (E), Pza. de Italia 2 (tel. 27 30 34). Long-time favorite at Sardinero beach with wonderful views. AE, V. *Posada del Mar* (E–M), Juan de la Cosa 3 (tel. 21 30 23). Fine food served in a rustic setting. Try their fish soup and *merluza posada.* AE, MC, V. *La Sardina* (E–M), Dr. Fleming 3 (tel. 27 10 35). Atmospheric, decorated like a fishing boat and specializing, naturally enough, in fish. One of the best. AE, DC, V.

Bodega Cigaleña (M), Daoiz y Velarde 19 (tel. 21 30 62). Rustic bodega, lively with lots of atmosphere, good wines. AE, DC, V. *Cañadio* (M), Gómez Oreña 15 (tel. 31 41 49). In center of town and very popular with locals. AE, DC, MC, V. *Chiqui* (M), Avda. García Lago (tel. 27 10 08). On Sardinero beach. Elegant; wonderful sea views. AE, MC, V. *Il Giardinetto* (M), Joaquín Costa 18 (tel. 27 31 96). Italian restaurant serving pizzas, pasta and zabaglione. Very good value. AE, DC, MC, V. *Piquío* (M), Avda. de los Castros (tel. 27 55 03). Good views of sea and gardens, attractive decor, generous portions. MC, V.

Twelve km. (seven-and-a-half miles) out, at **Puente Arce,** is *El Molino* (E), (tel. 57 40 52). A legend for its location in an old windmill and once radical experimentation with nouvelle cuisine; consistently high standards. Superb decor. Well worth a visit. AE, DC, V.

Santillana Del Mar. Cantabria (942). *Parador Nacional Gil Blas* (E), Pza. Ramón Pelayo 11 (tel. 81 80 00). 24 rooms. In an 18th-century manor house. AE, DC, MC, V. *Los Infantes* (M), Avda. Le Dorat 1 (tel. 81 81 00). 30 rooms. In seigniorial style, in keeping with the village. V. *Altamira* (M–I), Cantón 1 (tel. 81 80 25). 28 rooms. A lovely old house, huge rooms and a delightful patio in back ideal for evening drinks. AE, DC, MC, V.

Restaurant. *Mesón de los Blasones* (E–M), Pza. de Gándara (tel. 81 80 70). Delicious food in a charming atmosphere. Good service. AE, MC, V.

Torrelavega. Cantabria (942). *Marqués de Santillana* (M), Marqués de Santillana 6 (tel. 89 29 34). 32 rooms. AE, MC, V. *Saja* (M), Alcalde del Río 22 (tel. 89 27 50). 45 rooms. DC, MC, V. *Regio* (I), José María de Pereda 34 (tel. 88 15 05). 24 rooms.

Vitoria. Alava (945). *El Caserón* (L), Camino de Armentía 5 (tel. 23 00 48). 5 rooms, pool. In a picturesque setting 2 km. out of town, this is principally a restaurant, but it has rooms for overnight guests. *Canciller Ayala* (E), Ramón y Cajal 5 (tel. 13 00 00). 184 rooms. Best in town. AE, DC, MC, V. *Gasteiz* (E), Avda. Gasteiz 19 (tel. 22 81 00). 150 rooms. Elegant, luxurious. AE, DC, MC, V. *General Alava* (M), Avda. de Gasteiz 53 (tel. 22 22 00). 105 rooms. A traditional hotel on the main avenue. AE, DC, MC, V. *Páramo* (I), Gen. Alava 11 (tel. 23 04 50). 40 rooms. Central.

Restaurants. *Dos Hermanas* (E), Madre Vedruña 10 (tel. 24 36 96). Established over 100 years ago, though now in new premises. Traditional Basque cooking. AE, DC, MC, V. *El Portalón* (E), Correría 151 (tel. 22 49 89). In 15th-century house, rustic-style decor; a favorite. AE, DC, MC, V.

Zarauz. Guipúzcoa (943). *La Perla* (M), Avda. de Navarra 1 (tel. 83 08 00). 72 rooms. *Zarauz* (M), Avda. de Navarra 26 (tel. 83 02 00). 82 rooms. Garden. V. *Paris* (I), Avda. de Navarra (tel. 83 05 00). 28 rooms. Popular. Pool.

Restaurant. *Karlos Arguiñano* (E), Mendilauta 13 (tel. 83 01 78). Not to be missed, some of the best cuisine in Spain. MC, V.

PLACES OF INTEREST. The Basque Country and Cantabria is a region visited more for its splendid mountain scenery, the charm of its summer seaside resorts and picturesque fishing ports than for any really great and famous monuments. But as anywhere in Spain the towns and villages have their historic churches and monasteries and one unusual feature of Cantabria, and to a lesser extent, Vizcaya, is the number of prehistoric caves, many of them with wall paintings, which are dotted around the countryside.

Bermeo (Vizcaya). **Torre de Ercilla** (Ercilla Tower), Torrontero Emparaza 1. Gothic tower, now housing the city library and a **Fishing Museum.** Open 10–2 and 5–7.30; closed Mon.

Bilbao (Vizcaya). **Museo de Bellas Artes** (Fine Arts Museum), Parque de Doña Casilda Iturriza. Excellent art gallery with sections dedicated to Dutch, Flemish and Italian painters and the Spanish collection, with works by El Greco, Ribera, Velázquez, Zurbarán and Goya. Open 10–1.30 and 4.30–7; Sun. 11–2; closed Mon.

Museo Histórico y Arqueológico, Cruz 4–6. Finds from the prehistoric caves of Santimamiñe and others in Vizcaya province, Roman finds from the Forua cavern and Neolithic pottery. Open 10.30–1.30, 4–7; closed Sun. P.M. and Mon.

Comillas (Cantabria). Palacio del Marqués de Comillas.

Comillas (Cantabria). **Palacio del Marqués de Comillas.** Attractive residence of the Marquis of Comillas with a folly by Gaudí in its park, known as El Capricho. Open 10–12, 4–6.

Fuente De (Cantabria). **Monasterio de Santo Toribio de Liebana.** Founded in the 7th century, is at the end of a road—turn left as you leave Potes.

Guernica (Vizcaya). **Casa de Juntas,** Allendesalazar. The City Council building was one of the few houses to escape damage in the Luftwaffe bombing of 1937; restored, it now serves as a meeting place for the municipal councils of Vizcaya; houses a museum, some interesting Basque archives and the sacred oak, both the new tree and the remains of the old one. The **Church of Santa María la Antigua,** where Castilian Kings swore to respect the freedom of the Basques, is within its precincts. Open 10–2, 4–7 (6 in winter); closed Sun. mornings.

Santimamiñe Caves, on the road to Elanchove. Prehistoric caves beneath the hermitage of Santimamiñe, with large chambers, numerous stalagmites and wall paintings from the Paleolithic era. Conducted visits at 10.30, 12, 4 and 5.30. Closed Mon.

Loyola (Guipúzcoa). **Monastery of San Ignacio de Loyola.** Jesuit monastery erected in the 17th century around the manorhouse of the Loyola family near Azpeitia, birthplace of St. Ignatius Loyola, 1491. Important pilgrimage center, especially on July 31, the fiesta of San Ignacio. The **Basilica** is built in Italian style with a dome by Churriguera, and the **Santa Casa** (Sacred House) to the right of the Basilica has an exhibition on the life and works of the saint.

Marquina (Vizcaya). **Colegiata de Cenarruza.** Collegiate Church founded in 968 but rebuilt in the 16th century. Outstanding altar and cloisters both in Plateresque style; a National Monument.

Two km. from the center is the old village of Bolivar and the **Casa Natal de Simón Bolivar,** birthplace of the South American freedom fighter.

Pasajes (Guipúzcoa). **Museo Victor Hugo,** San Juan 63. A recent museum with mementoes of the great French poet on the ground floor whose home this once was; and upstairs a museum of the famous ships built in Pasajes. Details of opening hours were not available at presstime.

Puente Viesgo (Cantabria). Of the several limestone caves here, visit **El Castillo** dating back to the Paleolithic Age with traces of some 750 cave paintings and 50 ocher hand prints. Check opening times in Santander Tourist Office.

San Sebastián (Guipúzcoa). **Biblioteca Municipal,** Pza. de la Constitución. Municipal Library, plus a good art gallery. Open 9–8; closed Sat. P.M. and all day Sun.

Museo de San Telmo, Pza. Ignacio Zuloaga. Outstanding museum, with frescoes by Sert, paintings by Zuloaga and a vast collection of religious art and archeology. Open 10–1.30 and 3.30–5.30; closed Sun. P.M. and Mon. A.M.

Santander (Cantabria). **Biblioteca Menéndez Pelayo,** Rubio 4. Library with 45,000 volumes bequeathed by Menéndez Pelayo to his native town; statue of the great historian by Mariano Benlliure. Open 9–1.30; closed Sun. **Museo de Bellas Artes** (Fine Arts Museum), Calle Rubio. Paintings from the Flemish, Italian and Spanish schools of the 17th and 18th centuries, and contemporary local paintings. Open 11–1, 5–9; closed Sun.

Museo Marítimo, San Martín de Abajo, near the Nautical School. Maritime Museum with one of Spain's most important aquariums. Open 11–1, 4–7; closed Mon.

Museo de Prehistoria y Arqueología, Casimiro Sainz 4. Prehistoric objects from the caves of Cantabria province, some dating back 15,000 years. Open 9–2; closed Mon.

Museo de Velarde, eight km. (five miles) out in Muriedas. Cantabrian folk museum and mementoes of Pedro Velarde, leader of the Madrid uprising of May 2, 1808, immortalized by Goya. Open 11–1 and 4–7 in summer; 10–1 and 4–6 in winter; closed Mon.

Santander Casino, in El Sardinero. Open 7 P.M.–4 A.M. daily.

Santillana Del Mar (Cantabria). **Altamira Caves,** 2 km. outside. The adjacent **Museum** with a video presentation and models of the rock formations and paintings is open to everyone, Mon. to Sat. 9–1 and 4–6, Sun. 10–1. If you want to ensure a visit to the caves, write well in advance to: Centro de Investigaciones y Museo de Altamira, Santillana del Mar (Cantabria).

Colegiata de Santillana. 12th-century Romanesque Collegiate Church, interesting cloisters and capitals. Open 9–1, 4–8.

Fundación Santillana, Torre de Don Borja in the Pza. Mayor. Interesting art exhibitions, and displays of ceramics, folklore etc. Open 11–1, 4–8; closed Tues. and Oct. till mid-Nov.

Monasterio Regina Coeli. Museum of the 16th century and collection of art typical of the mountain region, housed in 17th-century house. Open 10–1, 3–4 in winter; 9–1, 4–8 in summer. Closed Wed. in winter and Feb.

Vitoria (Alava). **Armería,** Palacio de Ajuria-Enea, Fray Francisco de Vitoria 3. Historic weapons from many ages. Open Tues. to Fri. 11–2 and 5–7, Sat. and Sun. 11–2 only; closed Mon.

Museo de Arqueología, Correría 116. Archeological excavations from the Paleolithic era to the Middle Ages. Open Tues. to Fri. 10–2 and 5–7, Sat. and Sun. 11–2 only; closed Mon.

Museo de Bellas Artes (Fine Arts Museum), Palacio de Agusti, Paseo de Fray Francisco 8. Religious art from Alava and contemporary paintings. Open Tues. to Fri. 10–2 and 5–7, Sat. and Sun. 11–2 only; closed Mon.

Museo de Heráldica, 12 km. (8 miles) out of Mendoza. Collection of heraldic shields and coats of arms from former noble mansions, installed in 13th-century Mendoza tower. Open Tues. to Fri. 11–2 and 5–7, Sat. and Sun. 11–2 only; Closed Mon.

SPORTS. Golf. There are two 18-hole golf clubs near Bilbao, the Club de Campo de la Bilbaina 14 km. northeast on the road to Bermeo, the other at Neguri 17 km. northwest. San Sebastián golf club is at Jaizkibel 14 km. out along the N-I, and Santander's Pedreña golf club is 24 km. out of town.

Watersports. San Sebastián has two of the country's most famous bathing beaches and Santander's El Sardinero beach is another famous stretch of sand though sea pollution around the city is now something of a problem. Bathing around Bilbao is not advised due to industrial pollution. Many of the small villages along the Cantabrian coast have fine beaches where the water is cleaner than close to the capital city.

Winter sports and Mountain Climbing and Hiking. The Picos de Europa in Cantabria province around Fuente De have winter sports installations, a cable car, and ideal mountain excursions and hiking trails. For guided walks into these mountains, see the Asturias chapter.

Basque sports. Pelota (*jai alai* in Basque) is the Basque national sport. Enquire at the local tourist offices or look in the local press for times of games; a pelota match is a worthwhile experience. Other traditional Basque sports and competitions are mountain climbing, wood-chopping, and rowing—many instances of these can be seen in the local fiestas.

NAVARRE AND ARAGÓN

Mountains and Miraculous Virgins

East of Castile lie Navarre, a single province, and Aragón, made up of three: Huesca, Zaragoza and Teruel. In Navarre, there is only one name that will ring a bell for most people, that of Pamplona, which attracts tourists at one time during the year and for one reason—the running of the bulls. Zaragoza is the capital of Aragón, and on the Madrid-Barcelona route, while Teruel is virtually *Terra Incognita* for foreigners, though some of them may have stopped, more or less accidentally, at its capital city on the way between Madrid and Valencia. This area might be visited from several points: from Barcelona, Madrid or San Sebastián, from across the border in France, or by anyone arriving by boat in Santander and heading for the Mediterranean coast in the Barcelona–Valencia area.

Like all the provinces bordering on the Pyrenees, Navarre and Huesca can be recommended for summer visits because of their cool mountain climate. They also offer a good choice of mountain resorts, which are even more popular for winter sports.

Navarre

The history of Navarre, one of the four Christian kingdoms into which northern Spain was divided during the period when the Moors held the south, has always been linked with that of the neighboring Basque country. Isolated castles, imposing monasteries and fortified walled towns all bear witness to Navarre's stormy past. But it is an area visited as much

for the natural beauty of its Pyrenean scenery as for its history, as exemplified in Roncesvalles, famed from the *Song of Roland* and one of the loveliest crossings into France; the Irati and Salazar valleys, leading to the
higher crossing at Puerto de Larrau; or the Baztan valley. But the landscape is not entirely mountainous for there is a great contrast betwen the
green valleys and high Pyrenean mountains in the north and the arid yellow flatlands of the south of the province where the countryside opens out
onto the great Castilian meseta.

One of the province's notable features is its great wealth of Romanesque
churches, chapels and monasteries. These grew up in such abundance between the 11th and 13th centuries when Navarre lay on the medieval pilgrimage route from France to the shrine of St. James the Apostle in Santiago de Compostela in Galicia. The Camino de Santiago passed through
Navarre in two places, one route entering through the Roncesvalles pass,
and the other crossing the southern half of the province from Aragón and
Sangüesa in the east to Logroño and Castile in the west. The famous Roncesvalles pass has witnessed three great retreats in the course of Spain's
history: here in 778 Charlemagne's army, having sacked Pamplona and
expelled the Moors, was retreating into France when its rearguard, led
by Roland, was attacked and savagely massacred by Basques who resented
the foreign invasion of their territory; here in 1813 at the end of the Peninsular War, the defeated Napoleonic forces fought their last battle before
fleeing across the mountains into France; and through here between the
years 1937–39 thousands of Spanish refugees fled over the Pyrenees to take
refuge in France as General Franco's Nationalist forces gained control of
Spain. Because it was so small a kingdom, Navarre became only one modern province and is an exception to the general rule that Spanish provinces
are named for their capital cities. Navarre has kept its ancient name instead of taking that of its chief city, Pamplona.

The Running of the Bulls

Pamplona's big moment comes at the time of the Fiesta de San Fermín,
between July 6 and 14. The cross streets along the route from the corral
to the bullring are shut off, and while tourists and other non-combatants
watch from windows and balconies, the bulls are coursed through the
main streets of the town to the bullring. Ahead of them run the youths
of Navarre, ducking and dodging the charges of the infuriated animals
in time-honored tradition. This is the place that provided background for
Ernest Hemingway's *The Sun Also Rises* (or *Fiesta,* depending on which
edition you read) and you will know, if you read the book, that Pamplona
is set in good fishing country. One of its attractions is the 15th-century
cathedral, which contains the marble tombs of Carlos II of Navarre and
his wife, and boasts one of the most beautiful Gothic cloisters in Spain.
These cloisters house the Diocesan Museum with a good collection of religious art from the Middle Ages and the Renaissance.

Close to the city walls and housed in a 16th-century building is the
Museo de Navarra, with an archeological collection, a good display of historic costumes and an art gallery.

The Ciudadela (Citadel) was built in the reign of Philip II. Concerts
and exhibitions are held in some of its rooms and the garden is laid out
with Basque sculptures and is often used for open-air concerts. Other at-

tractions of Pamplona include the 13th-century San Nicolás, 14th-century San Cernín, and the city ramparts.

Forty-three km. (27 miles) southwest by N111, Estella on the Ega river was in the late 12th century the residence of King Sancho the Wise, whose palace is an unusually fine example of Romanesque civil architecture. No less remarkable is the church of San Pedro de la Rúa with lovely cloisters, the palaces of the nobles and churches down to the 16th century. Nearly two km. south is the Benedictine abbey of Irache, eight km. (five miles) north the Cistercian abbey of Iranzu, and 20 km. (13 miles) east Puente la Reina is graced by old churches and a bridge over the Arga.

Southeast from Pamplona on N240, Sangüesa features the church of Santa María with a superb Romanesque portal, several 12th- and 13th-century churches, the royal palace of the same period, the 15th-century palace of the Duque de Granada and a bridge over the Aragón river. A few kilometers to the west rises the 13th-century castle of Javier, where St Francis Xavier, Apostle of the Indies and Japan, was born in 1506. Now a Jesuit college, the castle is well worth a visit.

Continuing on the N240 your route now takes you along the northern side of the long artificial lake of Yesa, formed by the damming of the Aragón and popular with campers. Here on the slopes of the Sierra de Leyre the 11th-century Leyre monastery, Spain's first large Romanesque building, has been restored.

Aragón

Aragón, together with Catalonia, was united to Spain when its King Ferdinand married Isabella, Queen of Castile and León, in the 15th century, but, as with other Spanish medieval kingdoms, its frontiers are still remembered by the inhabitants, who possess their own separate customs and traditions.

Today Aragón consists of the provinces of Huesca, Zaragoza and Teruel, which together form a strip little more than 160 km. (100 miles) wide, but which thrusts 400 km. (250 miles) south from the central Pyrenees almost to the Mediterranean port of Valencia.

The outstanding natural and architectural sites of Huesca, touristically the most attractive province, can be included in one roundtrip. The N240 climbs northwest from the capital via Ayerbe and then follows the Río Gállego to Santa María. Here, it meets the N330 which turns northeast, skirting the Reservoir de la Peña, famous for its trout and dominated by Spain's most important Romanesque castle, Loarre, perched on a crag. The castle commands a magnificent view over the Aragón plain and was built by King Sancho Ramirez of Navarre as a base from which to lead his resistance to the Moorish conquerors.

After leaving the Gállego, a further 11 km. (seven miles) of a branch west (left) lead to the monastery of San Juan de la Peña. Set among green meadows the *new* monastery is a fairly recent structure (1714). Almost 2 km. down the mountain the *old* monastery is distinguished by its 10th-century lower church, its upper church, which was hollowed into the rock in the 13th century, and the well preserved though roofless cloister, the pantheon where the heroes of Aragón were buried. Lastly, there is the setting itself. Right in the heart of a mountain wilderness, the enclosure stands on uneven ground, overhung dramatically by a huge mass of rock.

And there is a legend. The Holy Grail was kept here because San Juan de la Peña was used as a Christian fortress to resist the Arab invaders. In 713 Zaragoza fell into their hands, then Huesca; the inhabitants fled to the Pyrenees. Amongst them were two young men, Voto and Félix. The former, who was a keen huntsman, was pursuing a stag when the cornered animal leapt over the edge of a precipice and the huntsman, feeling that he was about to topple over too, commended his soul to John the Baptist. Miraculously, he was held there on the very edge of the precipice. When he went in search of the shattered remains of the stag, he came upon the body of a hermit who had died in the cave beneath the crag. From the inscription that the hermit had carved on the stone before he died, the young man learned that the cave was dedicated to John the Baptist. Voto and his brother promptly renounced the world and went to live in the cave which had such miraculous associations for them. History was enacted here, too. It was in this monastery that men took the oath to fight against the Muslim invader.

The N330 passes over the 1,080-meter (3,543 feet) high Puerto de Oroel on the remaining 16 km. (10 miles) to Jaca, an important crossroads and a good base for exploring the region.

Jaca and the Pyrenees

A favorite residence of medieval Aragonese kings, the ancient town of Jaca is still surrounded by the walls built in 1592 together with the imposing citadel, upon foundations dating from 194 B.C. The 10th-century Romanesque cathedral (spoiled by centuries of alterations) is flanked by the Plateresque town hall, the Museum of Romanesque Art and a Benedictine convent; two bridges, Romanesque San Miguel and Gothic San Cristóbal, span the Río Aragón.

North of Jaca on N330 the road passes by the tiny village of Villanua famous for its caves with stalactites and stalagmites, before coming to Canfranc, the customs station with France, while right on the border is Candanchú, 1,676 meters (5,500 feet) above sea level and a popular summer and winter sports resort; to the east, beyond Panticosa, some of the highest peaks in the Pyrenees tower 3,298 meters (11,000 feet) into the usually cloudless blue sky.

Owing to the mountains it is necessary to return to Jaca and then turn east on the C134 which follows the railroad to Sabiñánigo where there are some fine samples of Mudéjar architecture. From there, the northern section of the C136 climbs the lovely Valle de Terna to the thermal spa of Panticosa, recommended for bronchitis and rheumatism, but now even more important as a winter sports center. A more elegant spot, however, is El Formigal above Sallent de Gállego on the way to France. C140 branches east (right) to the beautiful National Park and game reserve of Ordesa, where a wealth of wildlife may be seen amid completely unspoilt magnificent scenery. Just before the park, Torla is a charming village with some fine old houses and a picturesque Plaza Mayor.

To complete this tour of Huesca province you can either return to Sabiñánigo, and from there take the southern section of C136 direct to Huesca over the Puerto de Monrepos, 1,262 meters (4,200 feet), or if you wish to make a much bigger loop return via Boltaña and Barbastro by taking C138 along the Ara and Cinca rivers to Barbastro which has a 16th-century cathedral, an episcopal palace and an interesting town hall on the colonnaded Plaza Mayor.

A westerly turn from Barbastro along N240 leads back to Huesca. But first you might like to make a short detour southeast on N240, the road to Lérida, as far as Monzón, situated between the Cinca and Sosa rivers. It can boast many fine old houses and a dominating brick castle which once belonged to the Knights Templar. You should also see the Collegiate Church of Nuestra Señora del Romeral, with an outstanding Mudéjar tower and a fine 16th-century town hall.

Huesca

If you are approaching Huesca from the north, the first glimpse you will get is of the cathedral, built over the mosque that took the place of the original church. The alabaster altar piece is very fine indeed. The cloister, which dates further back, is Romanesque, except for one Gothic wing. Works by Goya, Guido Reni, Gilarte and Crespi Carducci are among the masterpieces exhibited in the museum. But the finest section of all is devoted to the primitives.

The House of Culture (a community center) is situated within the old Sertoria, or university, which was restored in the 17th century. You can still see a piece of the original Roman wall. San Pedro el Viejo, which is a national monument, was erected over the remains of a pagan temple; it is one of the oldest churches in Spain, and has a Romanesque cloister and the tombs of Ramiro II and Alfonso I of Aragón. Other interesting sites in the town are the churches of San Agustín, San Miguel and San Lorenzo. The Renaissance architecture of the town hall has served as a model for much of the inner town, which thus presents an unusually harmonious character.

Today Huesca has a history going back to 400 B.C. It was liberated from the Moors in 1096. During the Civil War it was in the front line for the entire two and a half years as a Franco stronghold, and suffered considerable damage. It has been somewhat over-restored.

Between Huesca and Zaragoza, no halts are suggested, except perhaps for the ancient village of Almudévar, which has a strange and disproportionately large church and the ruins of a castle.

Zaragoza

Zaragoza (sometimes written Saragossa by English-speaking peoples and pronounced Tharagotha by the Spaniards) is the capital of Aragón, 72 km. (45 miles) by road or rail from Huesca. In that relatively short distance, however, the green of the Pyrenees foothills has given way to a desolate, tawny-colored plateau, blasted by shade temperatures of over 38°C (100°F) in summer, swept by icy winds in winter and, in years of drought, the peasants would gladly exchange a liter of wine for a liter of water to save their dying cattle.

Yet despite the desolation of its immediate surroundings, Zaragoza is, and always has been, a city of great strategic importance. Its name is a corruption of Caesar Augustus, who made it his headquarters while carrying out the campaigns that were to end the two centuries of struggle necessary for Rome to subdue Spain. The great Charlemagne arrived at its walls in the year 777, but was unable to take the city. Liberated from the Moors in 1118, it immediately became the capital of the Kingdom of Aragón. Its year-long resistance to Napoleon in 1808–9 is an example of the great courage and endurance of which the Spaniards are capable.

Being almost exactly equidistant between Madrid and Barcelona, it is an obvious stopping place for travelers by road or rail, though it should be said that, other than its Basilica of the Virgin of the Pillar, it now has little to offer the tourist. Its once picturesque old center now lies in a disgraceful state of repair, and its modern quarters are of little interest to the visitor. To its credit, it does have some interesting art museums, a university founded in 1567, and the most famous officers' training academy in Spain, where the Prince of Asturias, heir to the Spanish throne, studied in 1986. Its other claim to fame is its proximity to the birthplace of Francisco de Goya (1746–1828), and it therefore boasts several works of the man whom many consider the greatest of all Spanish artists.

Its cathedral of San Salvador, known as La Seo, is in a mixture of styles and stands on the site of a former mosque. Its 15th-century dome is best seen from the chapel of La Perroquieta. Inside are a Tapestry Museum, with 60 Flemish and French tapestries, and a Sacristy with religious and other works of art.

Of far greater interest than the cathedral—despite some Goya frescos and a Tapestry Museum—is the 18th-century Basilica de la Vírgen del Pilar, set upon the banks of Spain's largest river, the Ebro, a site traditionally chosen by St James the Apostle. With its cupolas and blue tiling, its Baroque magnificence seems at first sight to belong to Baghdad rather than Aragón. Inside, the tremendous sweep of its 129-meter-long (422-foot) and 64-meter-long (211-foot) nave makes you feel as though you are in some strange underground city. The Virgin herself is a small 15th-century carving, not over 30 cm. (one foot) high, set on a silver-inlaid jasper pillar, itself deeply worn by 250 years of kisses from the devout (including Pope John Paul II in 1984). To the right of the Chapel of the Virgin are displayed two bombs thrown at the Basilica in August 1936 and believed to have been defused by the Virgin. Goya contributed to the frescoes in the choir of the chapel; there is an incredible wealth of jewels, gold plate and priceless Flemish and Spanish tapestries to be seen in the museum, many of which accompany the little Virgin on her ceremonial procession through the city on October 12, her feast day and a national holiday throughout Spain. The Basilica also contains two paintings by Velázquez.

The modern administrative buildings that have gone up along the spacious Plaza del Pilar blend in remarkably well, and the pinkish brown of the brick provides a pleasing unifying element between the Roman ramparts on one end and the Lonja, the 16th-century Exchange, on the other. The octagonal Mudéjar tower of San Pablo rises above the old quarter, graced by Renaissance and Baroque palaces.

The other architectural highlight of Zaragoza is the restored Castle of Aljafería, situated in particularly ugly surroundings. It began life as an 11th-century Moorish palace, then became the residence of the Christian kings after the Reconquest and finally was a center of the Inquisition. The walls still serve as a reminder of an age when gold came flowing in from the New World.

The Museum of Camón Aznar and the Museum of Zaragoza are well worth a visit, and both contain rooms dedicated to Goya's *caprichos*. Goya fans should not miss his frieze illustrating the life of the Virgin, in the 16th-century Cartuja d'Aula Dei, 13 km. (8 miles) out of town, although only men will be able to see it as the monastery is inhabited by an enclosed order.

The main road from Zaragoza to Madrid passes through Calatayud, with interesting Mudéjar church towers, to Alhama de Aragón 114 km. (71 miles) further on, where almost on the borders of the province, there is a welcome release from the desolation of the scenery. By branching off for 19 km. (12 miles) to Nuévalos, you can reach the famous 12th-century Monasterio de Piedra, well worth a visit. Founded by the Cistercian order, much of it has now been turned into a delightful hotel, but you can still admire the Homenaje Tower which dates from the 12th century. The monastery is set in a delightful park where there are signposted walks which take you past lakes, grottos and waterfalls to some splendid *miradores* (viewing places).

The N330 from Zaragoza to Teruel leads southwards through some of the best Aragonese vineyards to Daroca. Lovers of Goya's paintings may wish to make a detour off this road east along C221 to the tiny village of Fuendetodos where, in 1746, Francisco Goya was born. After a somewhat chequered history the artist's birthplace, a small two-roomed cottage, was restored and opened to the public in 1985. And with the opening of a Goya museum in 1986, this dusty and rather obscure village may at last find its place on the map.

Moving on to Daroca you come to one of the oldest towns in Spain. Its medieval walls measure almost two km. in length and enclose 100 towers and churches of all styles. The Corpus Christi procession and ensuing popular fiestas here take on extraordinary proportions. The Basilica of Santa María, originally Romanesque but much restored in the 16th century, houses the revered altarcloths in which, according to legend, the consecrated host was hidden when the Moors attacked Valencia in 1238; when removed the wafers were said to have left their impression in blood upon the cloths. The holy relics were claimed by Teruel, Calatayud and Daroca, and to solve the dispute, were placed on the back of a donkey. Wherever the animal stopped, there the relics would remain. The donkey bore them from Valencia to Daroca where it dropped dead, and there they have remained, being put on public display each year on Corpus Christi.

Teruel

Teruel, on the River Turia, is 185 km. (115 miles) from Zaragoza, and is the smallest of the three provincial capitals of Aragón. It stands 915 meters (3,000 feet) above sea level, and provides an interesting halt on the way to the coast, some 105 km. (65 miles) away.

The town's chief fame is due to its medieval lovers, Diego Marcilla and Isabela de Segura, who, separated by their parents, both died of broken hearts. In death, their mummified bodies are united in the church of San Pedro. El Portal de la Andaquilla (Andaquilla Gate) situated close to the tower of San Martín is one of the most famous landmarks in the remains of the old city walls. It was through this gate that Diego entered Teruel on his return from battle to discover that the arranged wedding of his beloved Isabel was taking place. Teruel's other claim to fame is for its four Mudéjar towers, notable for the way in which they were built separately from the church to which they belonged, in a style more reminiscent of a Muslim minaret than the belfry of a Christian church. The four towers are the twin towers of San Martín and San Salvador and those of the cathedral of Santa María and San Pedro. Although the churches are usually open only during Mass, the towers can be admired at any time, and are particularly beautiful at night when floodlit. Another worthwhile sight in this ancient city is the aqueduct of Los Arcos, constructed by a French engineer, Pierre Vedel, in the 16th century.

Teruel changed hands twice during the Civil War, and was the point from which in 1938 Franco made his decisive thrust down to the sea, fatally cutting Republican territory in two.

A worthwhile excursion is a visit to Albarracín, 32 km. (20 miles) to the west. This small Moorish fortified town, perched in the mountains 1,100 meters high (3,600 feet), remains medieval though signs of tourism are now beginning to creep in. Its church has a number of fine 16th-century Flemish tapestries. A little way to the southeast is Callejón del Plou, where there are prehistoric cave paintings of red bulls; at Navazo, there are other paintings of human but snakeheaded figures against a background of black and white bulls. Although these paintings belong to the dawn of time, they still retain an extraordinary vividness of color and movement.

For most people, however, the road leads south into the province of Castellón, through Viver to Segorbe, 87 km. (54 miles) from Teruel, from which the Mediterranean is only half an hour away by car. This walled town, set between two castle-crowned peaks, is rich in reminders of its Roman past.

To the northeast of Teruel towards the border with Castellón province, lies a wild and off-the-beaten-track area known as the Maestrazgo which offers the more adventurous traveler who will not mind braving hair-raising and possibly boulder-strewn roads, some stunning and dramatic scenery full of gorges, precipices and rocky crags. Scattered throughout the Maestrazgo region are villages which have changed little in the last hundred years and in whose streets and squares it is not hard to evoke the image of El Cid Campeador who some nine centuries ago, waged war on the Moors in this rugged land. Cantavieja, with its porticoed Plaza Mayor, and L'Iglesuela del Cid, with its hermitage before whose Virgin the Champion is said to have prayed, are just two of many such places.

On the edge of the Maestrazgo in the north of Teruel province, where N420 meets N232, lies Alcañiz, but devotees of the film world might first like to stop off briefly in the small village of Calanda just south of Alcañiz where the film director Luis Buñuel was born. While here be sure to see Calanda's plaza. Alcañiz like Calanda, is set among fertile olive groves and produces some of the best olive oil in Aragón. Its castle of Calatravos dates back to the 12th century and is now a parador, though most of the buildings are somewhat more modern, dating only from the 18th century. The town is dominated by the Baroque Collegiate Church of Santa María and in the Plaza Mayor are two lovely old buildings, the Gothic Lonja, site of a medieval market, and the Renaissance Ayuntamiento or City Hall.

From Zaragoza to Pamplona

Having explored the areas to the southwest and southeast of Zaragoza and, earlier, the area to the northeast, all that remains now is the northwest, the road to Tudela and Pamplona.

Before actually reaching Tudela, it is a good idea to take the turning (it is on the left if you are coming from Zaragoza) to Magallón and Borja. Early in the 12th century it was given to Don Pedro de Atares, the founder of a family which was later destined to become famous—the Borgias. It is now just a sleepy market town that the tourist passes through on the way to the Monastery of Veruela. The monastery is located on the outskirts of the village of Vera and the road to it is not good.

Veruela dates back to 1146. It looks like a fortress from the outside. The first Borgia, Don Pedro de Atares, its founder, handed it over to the Cistercians. The Jesuits were banished from Spain in 1932, but they have been back at the monastery since 1940. The church is magnificent; the cloister has been partly rebuilt. The restoration of the Chapter House has been accomplished most successfully. Features worth noticing are the many tombs and the ambulatory.

Tarazona on the road from Zaragoza to Soria is an interesting Mudéjar town whose cathedral, begun in the 12th century, is a good example of the Mudéjar decorative use of brick, and whose dome was built to the same design as Zaragoza's cathedral. Its 15th-century cloisters are particularly outstanding and have been successfully restored. Brick is equally pleasingly used in the other Mudéjar churches, while the former Lonja, now the city hall, is decorated with Renaissance reliefs of the Labors of Hercules and a frieze depicting the entry of Charles V into Bologna for his coronation. Tarazona's ancient bullring dates back to the 18th century and is interestingly octagonal in shape and has been converted into dwellings.

The N121 branches northeast, back to Navarre, where Tudela's 12th-century cathedral is a particularly interesting example of the transition from Romanesque to Gothic; there is a superb carving on the doorway depicting the Last Judgment. Unfortunately, the effect is lost, as it is not set far enough back for you to see it in perspective. The town itself is bustling and alive. Everything about the place has a quaint charm that is most appealing. The Plaza de los Fueros is quite delightful, with its wrought-iron balconies.

When you cross the Romanesque bridge over the Ebro (17 arches and 380 meters [1,247 feet] long), you return to dreary hillocks, dotted with grayish plants and tufts of thyme. Continue north on N121 to Caparroso, where C124 branches east (right) following the River Aragón for 16 km. (10 miles) to Carcastillo and the Cistercian abbey of Nuestra Señora de la Oliva, set right in the heart of the vineyards. This region has a wealth of interesting buildings. Carlos II, the Wicked, added a Gothic nave and gate to the 12th-century fortress church of San Martin de Unx. The 12th-century church of Ujué, a few kilometers to the north of Oliva, is built over an unusual crypt and possesses a fine portal and beautiful 16th-century reredos.

Back on N121, Olite's parador is part of the erstwhile residence of the kings of Navarre. The castle hosts a music, dance and drama festival each August. Bridging the transition from the 14th to the 15th centuries, Carlos

III restored the castle in the French style, with a touch of Mudéjar poly-chromed woods, ornate pavements and *azulejos.* The royal chapel became the church of Santa María; more ancient (11th century) and more beautiful is the church of San Pedro, whose Romanesque cloisters and portal are finely worked.

Tafalla, 6.5 km. to the north, likewise possesses a Santa María and San Pedro, moreover convents of San Francisco and of the Immaculate Conception. Some 11 km. northwest, stout towers strengthen the walls enclosing Artajona's Gothic San Saturnino and San Pedro with the miraculous statue of Our Lady of Jerusalem.

An alternative route from Zaragoza back to Pamplona takes you through the northeast of Zaragoza province along C127 to Ejea de los Caballeros and through Sos del Rey Católico to Sangüesa in Navarre before joining up again with the N240 Pamplona to Huesca road. Ejea de los Caballeros lying in the heart of a cereal growing region, is one of those towns which are often dubbed "the granary of Spain." It has two notable Romanesque churches, Santa María de la Corona, consecrated in 1174, and El Salvador dating from the 13th century. Sos del Rey Católico is one of the most interesting small towns of the region and its chief claim to fame—and hence its name—stems from the fact that it was the birthplace in 1452 of the Catholic Monarch Ferdinand of Aragón. The town was built as a fort to defend Aragón from attacks from neighboring Navarre, and is surrounded by fortified walls with seven gates. Today many of its steep narrow streets are still cobbled and lined with handsome old mansions. The Church of El Salvador and San Esteban is a fortified Romanesque church with a large crypt known as the lower church. It has some splendid paintings and houses the Parochial Museum. The Hermitage of Santa Lucía is another notable church, dating from the early 13th century, and has an interesting painted roof. Three km. out of town is the Monastery of Nuestra Señora de Valentuñana, a well-preserved Carmelite convent with much of its original furnishings and an interesting collection of South American artefacts. All together, Sos del Rey Católico is a delightful example of a medieval town.

PRACTICAL INFORMATION FOR
NAVARRE AND ARAGÓN

TOURIST OFFICES. In **Navarre** province (948): *Cintruénigo,* Barón de la Torre 62 (tel. 77 33 40); *Pamplona,* Duque de Ahumada 3 (tel. 22 07 48); *Sangüesa,* Mercado 2 (tel. 87 03 29); *Tudela,* Pza. de los Fueros (tel. 82 15 39). In **Huesca** province (974): *Huesca,* Coso Alto 21 (tel. 22 57 78); *Jaca,* Pza. Calvo Sotelo (tel. 36 00 98). In **Teruel** province (974): *Teruel,* Tomás Nogués 1 (tel. 60 22 79). In **Zaragoza** province (976): *Caspe,* Pza. de España 8 (tel. 63 11 31); *Ejea de los Caballeros,* Costa 2 (tel. 66 10 08); *Tarazona,* Ayuntamiento (City Hall), (tel. 64 01 00); *Zaragoza,* Pza. del Sas 7 (tel. 22 11 17); in the Torreón de la Zuda, Glorieta Pio XII (tel. 23 00 27); and in the Pza. del Pilar opposite the Basilica.

TELEPHONE CODES. Dialing codes are: Navarre province (948); Huesca province (974); Teruel province (974); Zaragoza province (976). Dialing codes for all the towns we list are given under *Hotels and Restaurants* immediately after the name of the town. The codes need only be used when dialing from outside the province.

GETTING AROUND NAVARRE AND ARAGÓN. By Train. The

focal point of the Aragón–Navarre rail system is Zaragoza which lies right in the center of the region and at the midway point on the important Madrid–Barcelona railway line. South from Zaragoza there is a direct line to Teruel and Valencia. To the east there are two routes to Barcelona, one via Caspe, Reus and Tarragona, the other via Lérida. To the north trains run from Zaragoza to Huesca and on up to Ayerbe, Jaca and Canfranc in the Pyrenees with connections over the border to Pau in France. To the northwest trains run from Zaragoza to Pamplona, Alsasua, San Sebastián and Irún on the French frontier; and from Zaragoza to Logroño, Miranda de Ebro and Bilbao. To the west, direct to Madrid via Calatayud and Guadalajara.

From Pamplona there are twice daily trains direct to Madrid via Soria, or frequent trains to Alsasua for connections onto the Irún–Burgos–Madrid line.

Train Stations and RENFE offices: *Huesca,* Calle Zaragoza in the south of town; *Pamplona,* the station (tel. 12 69 81) is out of town off the road to San Sebastián. *Teruel,* Camino de la Estación (tel. 60 26 49); *Zaragoza,* the Estación Portillo is off Avda. Clave (tel. 21 11 66), and the RENFE office is at San Clemente 13 (tel. 23 38 02).

By Bus. Bus routes provide the most comprehensive public transport in this area and are far more numerous than train services. In **Huesca** the main bus station is at Parque 3 on the Pza. Navarra, though some buses to Pamplona leave from Costa 23; in **Pamplona** the bus station is at Conde Oliveto 2; in **Teruel** it is on Ronda 18 de Julio; **Zaragoza** as yet has no central bus station, though one is being built, and buses leave from many places, so enquire at the Tourist Office.

By Air. Pamplona and Zaragoza both have domestic airports.

By Car. The region is quite well served by *autopistas* (freeways) for which you will have to pay a toll. The A15 runs from Irurzun in Navarre to Pamplona and southwards towards Tudela where it joins the A68 from Bilbao–Logroño–Zaragoza, which links with the A2 Zaragoza–Barcelona freeway. Of the other main N-roads in the region, the most important is the east–west Barcelona–Madrid road, the N-II. In the northern parts of Navarre and Huesca provinces the roads leading through the Pyrenees are high and winding and offer some spectacular mountain scenery. If you are planning to cross into France via the Pyrenees the main routes across the mountains are the N121 from Pamplona and then the C133 to Irún which is the least mountainous road, or alternatively you can continue on N121 via Elizondo and Urdax. The other two routes are the C135 from Pamplona through the famous Roncesvalles pass, and the N330 from Jaca to Candanchú and the Puerto de Somport. The C137 through the Roncal valley to Isaba offers some of the best Pyrenean scenery.

There are customs posts in the following places: Irún-Behovia in Guipúzcoa province; Vera de Bidaso, Echalar, Lizuniaga, Errazu, Eugui, Valcarlos, Ochagavía and Isaba all in Navarre province; and at Canfranc, Sallent de Gállego and Bielsa in Huesca province.

HOTELS AND RESTAURANTS. During the San Fermín festival in Pamplona in July, hotel rooms are exceedingly difficult to come by if you have not booked long in advance. The town will be booked to bursting point and beyond, and the prices of all accommodations from luxury hotels to rented rooms will double or triple at this time. Zaragoza, too, can be difficult during the *fiestas del Pilar* around Oct. 12.

There are several spa towns in the region whose hotels, much favored by elderly ladies, often have a faded air about them. Many of these have pools and very modest prices and are often open in summer only. There are many mountain-type chalet hotels in the Pyrenean resorts in Navarre and Huesca provinces. Most of these open for the skiing season (Dec. through Apr.) when their prices are highest, and again in the summer for July through Aug. (sometimes Sept.) when their prices drop considerably.

Albarracin. Teruel (974). *Albarracín* (M), Azagra (tel. 71 00 11). 30 rooms. In a 16th-century house. AE, DC, MC, V.

Alcañiz. Teruel (974). *Parador de la Concordia* (E), Castillo de los Calatravos (tel. 83 04 00). 12 rooms. In converted Calatrava castle just outside town. AE, DC, MC, V. *Meseguer* (I), Maestrazgo 9 (tel. 83 10 02). 30 rooms. Simple comfortable hostel with modernized rooms and good restaurant. V.

Alfajarin. Zaragoza (976). *Casino Montesblancos* (E), (tel. 10 00 04). This hotel together with four restaurants is part of the hilltop casino complex 20 km. (13 miles) from Zaragoza on the N-II. Luxurious with pool, tennis and casino. AE, DC, MC, V.

Alhama De Aragon. Zaragoza (976). Spa town. *Termas* (M) July to mid-Oct. and (I) the rest of the year. Gen. Franco 20 (tel. 84 00 11). Typical old-fashioned spa hotel catering for clients who come to "take the waters." AE, MC, V. *Guajardo* (I), Gen. Franco 3 (tel. 84 00 02). 84 rooms; pool.

Alsasua. Navarra (948). *Alaska* (I), ten km. (six miles) out of town on Burgos–San Sebastián road (tel. 56 28 02). 29 rooms; garden and pool; good views. V.

Ayegui. Navarra (948). *Irache* (M), (tel. 55 11 50). Quietly situated pleasant hotel with pool, on the N-III just beyond Estella. MC, V.

Baños De Panticosa. Huesca (974). *Gran Hotel* (I), (tel. 48 71 37). 54 rooms, tennis, and garden. Recently renovated. Open mid-June to mid-Sept. only. *Mediodía* (I), (tel. 48 71 61). 52 rooms; tennis and garden. Under same management as *Gran Hotel;* open all year.

Barbastro. Huesca (974). *Rey Sancho Ramirez* (M) at km. 163 on the N-240 (tel. 31 00 50). 81 rooms. Well-maintained hotel on edge of town with pool, good restaurant and pleasant views. AE, V
Restaurant. *Flor* (M), Goya 3 (tel. 31 10 56). Good food and service. AE, DC, MC, V.

Bielsa. Huesca (974). *Parador Monte Perdido* (E), Valle de Pineta (tel. 50 10 11). 14 km. (nine miles) from the village, a modern parador with 16 rooms and superb views of the surrounding mountains. (M) rates Nov. to June. AE, DC, MC, V.

Calatayud. Zaragoza (976). *Calatayud* (M), García Olaya 17 (tel. 88 13 23). 63 rooms; garden and parking; on main Madrid–Barcelona highway. V.

Candanchu. Huesca (974). *Candanchu* (M), (tel. 37 30 25), 48 rooms. The oldest but well renovated. AE, DC, V. *Edelweiss* (M), (tel. 37 32 00), 76 rooms. AE, DC, V. *Pirineos* (M), (tel. 37 30 00). Apartment hotel. *Tobazo* (I), (tel. 37 31 25). With popular sun terrace overlooking ski slopes. These hotels are only open for the skiing season, Dec. through Apr., and in July and Aug.

Cerler. Huesca (974). *Monte Alba* (E) in skiing season, (M) in summer (tel. 55 11 36). Open Dec. through Apr. and June through Sept. Good recent hotel in delightful setting; ideal mountain base. Pool, sauna and solarium.

Daroca. Zaragoza (976). *Daroca* (I), Mayor 42 (tel. 80 00 00). 20 rooms. Simple 2-star hotel. *El Ruejo* (I), Mayor 112 (tel. 80 10 86). 14 rooms. Clean, bright, family-run pension in part of an historic building; good inexpensive meals.

Ejea De Los Caballeros. Zaragoza (976). *Cinco Villas* (M), Paseo del Muro 10 (tel. 66 03 00). 30 rooms; comfortable. DC, MC, V.

Elizondo. Navarra (948). *Baztan* (M), (tel. 58 00 50). 84 rooms; pool.

Esquedas. Huesca (974). **Restaurant.** *Venta el Sotón* (M), on N240 14 km. (nine miles) west of Huesca (tel. 27 02 41). Outstanding country restaurant, one of best in Aragon. Closed Mon. AE, DC, MC, V.

Fitero. Navarra (948). *Balneario Bécquer* (M), (tel. 77 61 00). 218 rooms; pool, tennis and garden. Old but renovated hotel. Pope Benedict XV and the poet Gustavo Adolfo Bécquer both stayed here. Open mid-June to mid-Oct. *Balneario Virrey Palafox* (M), 3 km. outside the village (tel. 77 62 75). 55 rooms. Modern, under same management and shares same facilities as *Bécquer.* Open July through Sept. only.

El Grado. Huesca (974). *El Tozal* (M), Las Planas (tel. 30 40 00). 35 rooms. Recent, with delightful decor and good views of Río Cinca. V.

Huesca (974). *Pedro I de Aragón* (M), Parque 34 (tel. 22 03 00). 52 rooms; good restaurant. DC, MC, V. *Montearagón* (M–I), on N-240 (tel. 22 23 50). 27 rooms; pool. One km. out on road to Lérida with own bull-ring. V. *Mirasol* (I), Ramón y Cajal 29 (tel. 22 37 60). 13 rooms. Small family-run hostel right in center. Spotless and good value.

Restaurants. *Navas* (M), San Lorenzo 15 (tel. 22 47 38). Outstanding restaurant with innovative cuisine. AE, DC, MC, V. *Sauras* (I), Zaragoza 2 (tel. 24 46 60) is a long-standing tradition.

Isaba. Navarra (948). *Isaba* (M), on highway (tel. 89 30 00). Pleasantly situated with parking and garden. V.

Jaca. Huesca (974). *Oroel* (M), Avda. de Francia 37 (tel. 36 24 11). 124 rooms. Modern apartment hotel but with full hotel service; restaurant and self-service cafeteria. AE, DC, V. *Gran Hotel* (M), Paseo Gen. Franco 1 (tel. 36 09 00). 98 rooms. Renovated 1950's-style and recently enlarged; pool and delightful garden. AE, DC, V. *Conde de Aznar* (M–I), Paseo Gen. Franco 3 (tel. 36 10 50). 23 rooms; some cheaper. Pleasant family-run, mountain-style hotel. MC, V. *Pradas* (I), Obispo 12 (tel. 36 11 50). 39 rooms. AE, DC, V.

Restaurants. *La Cocina Aragonesa* (E), Cervantes 5 (tel. 36 10 50). Specializes in typical Aragonese dishes; belongs to Conde Aznar hotel. Closed Tues. MC, V. *Gaston* (M), Avda. Primo de Rivera 14 (tel. 36 29 09). Pleasant atmosphere and good food. AE, MC, V.

Monzon. Huesca (974). *Vianetto* (I), Avda. de Lérida 25 (tel. 40 19 00). 84 rooms. Modest but pleasant. MC, V.

Restaurant. *Mesón del Carpintero* (M), San Antonio 15 (tel. 40 10 66). Family-run restaurant with good basic cooking. MC, V.

Nuevalos. Zaragoza (976). *Monasterio de Piedra* (M), (tel. 84 90 11). In a 12th-century Cistercian monastery overlooking lake and waterfalls. Pool and tennis. AE, DC. *Las Truchas* (I), (tel. 84 90 40). On the Cillas–Alhama road. 36 rooms; pool, mini-golf and tennis.

Olite. Navarra (948). *Parador Príncipe de Viana* (E) July to Oct., otherwise (M), Pza. de las Teobaldas 2 (tel. 74 00 00). 48 rooms; built among a 12th-century castle. AE, DC, MC, V.

Pamplona. Navarra (948). Remember that hotel prices rocket during the San Fermines in July. *Los Tres Reyes* (L), Jardines de la Taconera (tel. 22 66 00). 168 rooms; pool and garden among its many amenities. AE, DC, MC, V.

Ciudad de Pamplona (M), Iturrama 21 (tel. 26 60 11). 117 rooms; good amenities but out of center. DC, MC, V. *Maisonnave* (M), Nueva 20 (tel. 22 26 00). 160 rooms. Very central, in the old part of town. AE, DC, MC, V. *Orhi* (M), Leyre 7 (tel. 22 85 00). 55 rooms. Central, close to bullring. MC, V. *Sancho Ramírez* (M), Sancho Ramírez 11 (tel. 27 17 12). Recent hostel on edge of town; good restaurant. MC, V. *Yoldi* (M), Avda. San Ignacio 11 (tel. 22 48 00). 48 rooms. Central, recently renovated; patronized by bullfighters during San Fermines. DC, MC, V. *Eslava* (I), Pza. Vírgen de la O 7 (tel. 22 22 70). 28 rooms. Older hotel, in the old town, with good views. AE, DC, V.

Restaurants. *Hartza* (E), Juan de Lebrit 19 (tel. 22 45 68). High standards, offering a small menu based on fresh seasonal produce. Very popular; booking essential. Closed Mon. and last two weeks of July. AE, MC, V. *Josetxo* (E), Pza. Príncipe de Viana 1 (tel. 22 20 97). Famous for over 30 years and now in the new premises; the best. Closed Sun. and Aug. AE, V. *Alhambra* (M), Bergamín 7 (tel. 24 50 07). Has an excellent reputation. Closed Sun. AE, DC, MC, V. *Europa* (M), Espoz y Mina 11 (tel. 28 18 00). Just off the Pza. Castilla and very popular. Closed Sun. AE, DC, MC, V.

Ribaforada. Navarra (948). *Sancho El Fuerte* (M), on N-232 (tel. 86 40 25). 133 rooms; pool. A very reasonable 3-star hotel.

Sabiñanigo. Huesca (974). *La Pardina* (M), Sta. Orosia 36 (tel. 48 09 75). 64 rooms; pool and garden. Delightful quiet hotel on edge of town on road to Jaca.

Sallent De Gallego. Huesca (974). Leading Pyrenean skiing resort. *Eguzki-Lore* (E), in winter, (M) in summer (tel. 48 80 75). 32 rooms. Typical mountain hotel with good restaurant. Open Jan. through Apr. and July through Aug. AE, DC, MC, V. *Formigal* (E), in winter, (M) in summer (tel. 48 80 00). 119 rooms. Open Dec. through Apr. and July through Aug. AE, DC, MC, V. *Nievesol* (M), (tel. 48 80 34). 162 rooms; pool and tennis.

Sos Del Rey Catolico. Zaragoza (976). *Parador Fernando de Aragón* (M), (tel. 88 80 11). 66 rooms. Modern regional-style parador in historic town. Great views from the terrace. AE, DC, MC, V.

Teruel (974). *Parador Nacional* (M), two km. (one mile) out of town on N-234 (tel. 60 18 00). 60 rooms. Recently renovated modern parador. AE, DC, MC, V. *Reina Cristina* (M), Pasaje Ovalo 1 (tel. 60 68 60). 62 rooms. Good modern hotel in town center; with good *Figón* restaurant. AE, DC, MC, V. *Civera* (I), Avda. Sagunto 23 (tel. 60 23 00). 73 rooms; modern, simple and comfortable.

Torla. Huesca (974). *Ordesa* (I), (tel. 48 61 25). 69 rooms, pool. Eight km. (five miles) out at the entrance to Ordesa National Park. Pleasant and good base for mountain excursions. Open Apr. to mid-Oct. only. V.

Tudela. Navarra (948). *Morase* (M), Paseo de Invierno 2 (tel. 82 17 00). 26 rooms. 3-star hostel in pleasant location; good restaurant. AE, DC, MC, V. *Santamaría* (M), San Marcial 14 (tel. 82 12 00). 54 rooms. *Hostal de Tudela* (I), (tel. 82 05 58). 16 rooms. Well run hostel on edge of town on road to Zaragoza. MC, V.

Restaurant. *El Choko* (M), Pza. de los Fueros 6 (tel. 82 10 19). Good food. Closed Mon. MC, V.

Villarluengo. Teruel (974). *La Trucha* (M), Las Fabricas (tel. 8). 53 rooms. An old paper factory dating back to 1789 and converted to a hotel in the 70s. Surrounded by woods, beside a river much favored by fishermen. Pool and tennis. AE, DC, MC, V.

Villanueva De Gallego. Zaragoza (976). **Restaurant.** *Las Casa del Ventero* (M), Paseo 18 de Julio 24 (tel. 11 51 87). Outstanding French restaurant 14 km. (nine miles) from Zaragoza. Decor not special but food worth the trip. Open Tues. to Fri. dinner only, Sat. lunch and dinner, Sun. lunch only. Closed Sun. night and Aug. DC, MC.

Zaragoza (976). *Corona de Aragón* (L), Avda. César Augusto 13 (tel. 43 01 00). 251 rooms. Zaragoza's leading deluxe hotel; pool. AE, DC, MC, V. *Gran Hotel* (L), Costa 5 (tel. 22 19 01). 138 rooms. Excellent stylish older hotel recently refurbished. AE, DC, MC, V. *Palafox* (L–E), Casa Jiménez (tel. 23 77 00). 184 rooms. Very central with large underground carpark; superb accommodations; pool. DC, MC, V. *Don Yo* (E), Bruil 4 (tel. 22 67 41). 181 rooms. Close to the Post Office just off Paseo de la Independencia. A good and lively hotel renowned for its American breakfasts. AE, DC, MC, V. *Goya* (E), Cinco de Marzo 5 (tel. 22 93 31). 150 rooms. Modern, spacious hotel. MC, V. *Rey Alfonso I* (E), Coso 17 (tel. 21 82 90). 117 rooms. Modern, central and functional. AE, DC, MC, V.

Conquistador (M), Hernán Cortés 21 (tel. 21 49 88). Comfortable hotel opened in 1985; the best of the 3-stars. AE, DC, MC, V. *Europa* (M), Alfonso I 19 (tel. 22 49 01). 54 rooms. Older hotel, very central on mainstreet. AE, DC, MC, V. *Oriente* (M), Coso 11 (tel. 22 19 60). 87 rooms. Central, close to the Rey Alfonso I, with good service. V. *Paris* (M), Pedro María Ric 14 (tel. 23 65 37). 62 rooms. A little further out than most. AE, DC, MC, V.

Conde Blanco (I), Predicadores 84 (tel. 44 14 11). 83 rooms. Modest, functional hotel, geared to businessmen. *Gran Vía* (I), Gran Vía 38 (tel. 22 92 13). 41 rooms. AE, DC, V. *Los Molinos* (I), San Miguel 28 (tel. 22 49 80). Central.

Restaurants. *Los Borrachos* (E), Sagasta 64 (tel. 27 50 36). Delicious food and good service. Game and fish specialties. Reader recommended. AE, DC, MC, V. *El Cachirulo* (E), (tel. 33 16 74). Four km. (two and a half miles) out of town on N-232 to Logroño. Superb food, Aragonese atmosphere and folk music. MC, V. *Costa Vasca* (E), Valenzuela 13 (tel. 21 73 39). Top Basque dishes specializing in fish. Its *puddings* (a kind of terrine or mousse) are also recommended. One of the most highly rated restaurants in the area. Closed Sun. AE, DC, MC, V. *Villa de Zarauz* (E), Mefisto 4 (tel. 21 56 99). Excellent restaurant with atmospheric bar in entrance. Closed Sat. lunch and all day Sun. AE, DC, MC, V. *Casa Tena* (E–M), Pza. San Francisco 8 (tel. 35 80 22). Agreeable restaurant, noted especially for its roast meats. AE, DC, MC, V.

Casa Martín (M), Pza. San Francisco. Stylish green and white decor, modern and bright with good *menu del día*. DC, V. *Mesón del Carmen* (M), Hernán Cortés 4 (tel. 21 11 51). Old fashioned, long standing tradition; drab appearance but you eat well. AE, DC, MC, V.

Casa Colás (I), Mártires 10. Excellent budget restaurant, very popular with locals, and just about the only restaurant in the old town center.

Zuera. Zaragoza (976). *Las Galias* (I) at km. 26 on the Zarago-za–Huesca road (tel. 68 00 24). 25 rooms. Small 3-star hostel with pool and garden. Very pleasant; exceptionally good restaurant. AE, DC, MC, V.

PLACES OF INTEREST. Opening hours given are liable to frequent change and it is always wise, especially in the case of the many remote monasteries in this region, to double check opening times with the local tourist offices, before setting out on a special trip.

Ainsa (Huesca). **Museo del Alto Aragón,** Concepción Arenal 6. Muse-um of Upper Aragón with paintings and sculptures by contemporary art-ists. Open 7–10 P.M.; closed Sun.

Carcastillo (Navarra). **Monastery of La Oliva.** Cistercian monastery in transitional Romanesque style and a National Monument. Open daily 9–12.30 and 3–6.30.

Daroca (Zaragoza). **Basílica de Santa María de los Corporales,** Pza. de la Colegial 2. The museum is open 10–12 and 4–6, closed Sun.; and the church 9.30–1.30 and 4–8.
Santo Domingo de Silos. 13th-century church with a stone and brick tower and an interesting museum containing pictures, portraits and sculp-tures. Open daily 9.30–1 and 3–8.

Estella (Navarra). **Casa de Fray Diego de Estella.** Birthplace in 1524 of the Franciscan writer Fray Diego; fine Plateresque building. Open Mon. to Sat. 7 P.M.–9 P.M. Sun. 12–2.
San Pedro de la Rúa. Outstanding 12th-century church. To visit, obtain key from Calle Fray Diego 13.
Monasterio de Irache, 2 km. out on Logroño road. National Monu-ment; inhabited by Benedictine monks, a former pilgrims' hospice on the Camino de Santiago. Open daily 9.30–1 and 3.30–7.
Monasterio de Iranzu, 7 km. north on San Sebastián road. 12th-century Cistercian monastery. Open 9–2 and 4–8.30.

Fuendetodos (Zaragoza). **Casa de Goya,** Goya's birthplace and child-hood home. For opening hours, ask at Zaragoza Tourist Office.

Huesca. **Museo Arqueológico Provincial** (Archeological Museum), housed in the University in Pza. Universidad. Objects from the Roman city and paintings from the 15th century to the present day housed in the old university building in the 12th-century palace of the kings of Aragón. Open 10–2; closed Mon.
Museo Diocesano (Diocesan Museum), Pza. Catedral 9. 2nd-century Roman finds, 13th-century murals by Bierge and some interesting exam-ples of religious art. Open daily 11–1.

Javier (Navarra). **Javier Castle.** Medieval castle 52 km. from Pamplo-na, birthplace of San Francisco Xavier. The castle is open 9–1 and 4–7 and in summer *son-et-lumière* spectacles some weekends; for details en-quire at the Pamplona tourist office. Special celebrations are held in the basilica during the first week of March which draw pilgrims from all over the region.

Loarre (Huesca). **Castle of Loarre.** Striking 11th-century castle with two impressive towers perched high on a rocky crag overlooking the plains of Aragon. Difficult to reach if you haven't a car but well worth a visit. So is the adjoining Romanesque **church** and **crypt.** The castle is open 9–2 and 4–8 but doublecheck these times with the Huesca tourist office.

Monzon (Huesca). **Monzón Castle.** Once the residence of King Jaime I El Conquistador. Open 10–1 and 5–8 in summer; 11.30–1 and 3–5 in winter.

Olite (Navarra). **Olite Castle.** Open daily 11–1 and 5–7 (3–5 in winter).

Pamplona (Navarra). **Catedral** and **Museo Diocesano.** Cathedral open 8–1.30 and 4–8 in summer; 8–11.30 and 6–8 in winter. Diocesan Museum in the magnificent Gothic cloister open 10.30–1.30 and 4–7 in summer only.

Frontón Euskal Jai Berri (Pelota Court), 6 km. out in Huarte. Pelota is played on Thurs., Sat. and Sun.; also fiestas, at 4 P.M.

Museo de Navarra (Provincial Museum of Navarre), Santo Domingo. Has been closed for renovations; check locally.

Sabiñanigo (Huesca). **Museo Angel Orensanz,** Puente de Sardas. Interesting folk museum with a good collection of agricultural instruments, cooking utensils, looms and sculptures by the artist Angel Orensanz. Open 10–1 and 5–8 in summer, 11–1 and 4–7 in winter; closed Mon. and Tues.

Tarazona (Zaragoza). **Cathedral.** Open daily 11–1 and 4–6. Also of interest are the **Bishops Palace,** the **City Hall** and the octagonal **Bull Ring.**

Teruel. **The Cathedral.** Dating from 1176, but only became a cathedral in 1587. Its Mudéjar tower is one of the famous four towers of Teruel. Open daily 8–9.

Mausoleum of the Lovers, in a chapel adjoining San Pedro. Open daily 9–1 and 3–10; Sun. and fiestas 9–1 and 3–9.

Museo de Artes Populares (Museum of Popular Arts). This collection of household items and tools from the surrounding villages of Teruel province is housed in the basement of the Diputación Provincial.

Museo Arqueológico Provincial (Archeological Museum) is housed in the modern Casa de Cultura in Pza. Pérez Prado. Interesting section on caves and troglodite dwellings. Open daily 10.30–2 and 5–7; Sun. 10.30–2.

Tudela (Navarra). **Cathedral.** Open 8.30–1 and 4.30–8.

Villanua (Huesca). Village in picturesque mountain setting in the valley of the River Aragón and famous for its caves. The most popular is the **Guixas** or Old Cave which is almost one km. deep, and the **Rebeco** and **Esjamundos caves** are full of stalactites, stalagmites and lakes. To visit the caves, obtain the key from the guardian.

Yesa (Navarra). **Monastery of Leyre.** 11th-century monastery in dramatic situation five km. above the Yesa reservoir. The road is good but very steep towards the end. Open daily 8 A.M.–9.30 P.M. but best to double-check with the Pamplona tourist office.

Zaragoza. Aljafería (Moorish Castle). Open daily 9–1.

Audiencia (Renaissance palace), Conde de Aranda. Beautiful palace built in 1551 for the Counts of Morata. Open 10–2; closed Sun.

Basílica de la Vírgen del Pilar (Basilica of the Virgin of the Pillar), Pza. del Pilar. Baroque basilica and Zaragoza's number one sight. Its museum, the **Museo Pilarista,** is open daily 9–2 and 4–6.

Cartuja de Aula Dei (Carthusian Monastery), Barrio de Montañana on the road to Lérida. Founded by Hernando de Aragón, grandson of Ferdinand the Catholic king, in 1564. A beautiful building with some magnificent frescoes by Goya on the church ceiling. Only men may visit as it is an enclosed order.

La Seo (Cathedral of San Salvador), Pza. de La Seo. **Museo de Tapices** (Tapestry Museum) open daily 9–2, 4–6. **Museo Capitular** (Chapter Museum) same times.

Museo Camón Aznar, Epoz y Mina 23. Splendid collection of paintings including Goya's *Caprichos,* housed in the Renaissance Pardo palace and donated by the art historian Camón Aznar. Very worthwhile. Open Tues. to Sat. 10–2, Sun. 11–1.45; closed Mon. and Aug.

Museo Etnológico (Folk Museum), in Primo de Rivera Park. Has an especially good collection of Aragonese costumes. Open Tues. to Sat. 4–8, Sun. 10–2; closed Mon. and fiestas, (double check with tourist office).

Museo Pablo Gargallo, in the Palacio de Argillo, Pza. San Felipe. Delightful display of modern sculpture by Pablo Gargallo (1881–1934). Open 10–1 and 5–7, Sun. 11–2; closed Tues.

Museo de Zaragoza (Zaragoza Museum), Pza. de los Sitios 6. Important provincial museum with an Archeological Section housing finds from prehistory to the Muslim era including some fine mosaics; an excellent picture gallery (Bellas Artes section) with some good Aragonese primitives, a room dedicated to some of the best works of Goya and another to Goya's Los Caprichos etchings. Open Tues. to Sun. 10–2; closed Mon. and fiestas.

SPORTS. Hunting and Fishing are popular pastimes throughout the region, especially in northern Aragón, though for both of these you will need a permit. Salmon and trout are fished in the streams and rivers of Navarre and Huesca, and in parts of Teruel province too. Game in northern Aragon includes chamois, wild boar, rabbits, hares, quail, partridge and deer. There are eight game reserves in the Pyrenees.

Ice Skating is available at Jaca's Palacio de Hielo.

Skiing. The Pyrenean provinces of Huesca and Navarre are one of Spain's principal skiing areas. In Huesca province there are ski resorts at Panticosa, Candanchú and El Formigal-Sallent de Gállego; instruction is available at all of these. Other resorts are Cerler-Benasque, Valle de Astún-Aisa and Guarrinza. In Navarre province the main resorts are Burguete and Isaba.

NATIONAL PARKS AND NATURE RESERVES. The northern part of Huesca province is rich in nature reserves, the most outstanding being the National Park of Ordesa which covers some 2,200 hectares (5,440 acres) at the foot of the Tres Sorores massif and is dominated by the peak of Monte Perdido, 3,355 metres (11,000 feet). The nearest villages to the park are Broto and Tola. Apart from its stunning scenery, the park is a veritable paradise for flora and fauna and its wild life population includes wild boar, chamois, ermine, foxes, martens, otters, eagles, vultures and falcons.

CATALONIA

Gateway to the Mediterranean

Catalonia (in Spanish *Cataluña,* in Catalan, *Catalunya*) constitutes a bridge between France and Spain. Barcelona's Prat de Llobregat airport handles some four million passengers annually. The quickest access by road is on the A17 Perpignan–Barcelona toll-road crossing the border at La Junquera, though more attractive crossings into Catalonia, whether by road or rail, are over the Pyrenees at Puigcerdà or along the Côte Vermeille in Roussillon (French Catalonia) to Port Bou, where the railroad turns inland to Figueras, while the road meanders along the Costa Brava to Cadaqués.

Roussillon, Catalonia and the Balearic Islands had a common history in the Middle Ages, and this community of fate has been reflected in their architecture, customs, dances, music, habits and costumes. It is, of course, mirrored above all in the common language, which is different from Castilian. Catalan is related to Provençal, with an admixture of harsh intonation that robs it of the soft, musical cadences of Provençal, but at the same time adds vigor and dynamism to it. Catalan is spoken from Perpignan to Valencia and, with variations, in the Balearic Islands. It has some affinities with French.

Of the industry of the Catalans, there can be no doubt: they boast of their modern factories, especially for textiles, which rank with the finest in the world. Also, they are much more commercially minded than other Spaniards. Catalonia, with Barcelona as its cultural center, was one of the greatest seats of nautical, maritime and astronomical knowledge during the Middle Ages, and Catalans were famous for their seafaring exploits.

Wine, oil, fruit and cork have been the staples of Catalonia for hundreds of years, and, with the exception of cork which has been ousted by plastics, they still are today. Food is the least exotic here of all the Spanish provinces and the least strange to foreign palates and stomachs. The Catalans take pride in the preparation of their food; travelers often find that the cuisine in many Catalan places can stand comparison with that of France.

Spanish Catalonia, divided today into the four provinces of Gerona (called Girona by the Catalans), Barcelona, Tarragona and Lérida (known in Catalan as Lleida), has enjoyed a turbulent, rich history that has scattered its monuments throughout the province with a truly generous hand. Geography and the quirks of historical development have contributed largely to the distinct character of Catalonia, which differs in so many respects from that of the kingdoms of central Spain. The mountains stretching along the Ebro and the desert-like plains of Aragón separate Catalonia from central Spain; consequently, Catalonia looked toward the Mediterranean as its natural outlet, and so acquired maritime characteristics.

Barcelona's Hinterland

The environs of Barcelona abound in places of great interest to lovers both of landscape and of antiquity—San Cugat del Vallés, with a lovely Benedictine abbey; Tarrasa, the ancient Egara, which has charming examples of pre-Roman architecture; Llobregat's river with a Roman bridge. But the main site, easily reached from the Martorell freeway exit, is the world-famous monastery of Montserrat, where medieval legend placed the Holy Grail, a claim contested by many other places.

The countless legends that surround Montserrat, which inspired Wagner's opera *Parsifal,* are undoubtedly rooted in the fantastic and strangely unreal appearance of this mountain. It juts up abruptly some 1,135 meters (3,725 feet) above the valley of the Llobregat river and is outlined with monoliths that look like immense stone figures. The best view of the supernatural wall is to be had from some distance away on the road to Manresa.

Founded in A.D. 880, the monastery has some 300 Benedictine monks today. Each year, thousands of pilgrims go there to see its chief treasure, the Black Virgin of Montserrat, which is supposed to have been carved by St. Luke. But even the vast monastic complex is dwarfed by the grandeur of the jagged mountain peaks. From the highest, called San Jerónimo and accessible by cablecar, a large section of the coast and the entire range of the eastern Pyrenees are visible on a clear day. Except for the church and the Virgin's Sanctuary, you cannot visit the monastery, and the village itself is swamped by tourism. El Greco, Correggio and Caravaggio are represented in the monastery museum, while the music-lover will have an unforgettable experience listening to the Escolanía, the boys' choir founded 700 years ago, singing at morning mass, at the Salve and at the end of vespers.

The granite Sierra de Montseny, away to the northeast, deserves a separate excursion, to include the drive up from San Celoni, near the freeway, to the Santa Fé hermitage, from where there are sensational views. The road to Montseny itself traverses the entire sierra to Tona on N152, while the branch to Viladrau and Arbucias winds along the sierra's northern slopes.

Around Catalonia

To explore Catalonia properly, we need to move further away from Barcelona. There are three directions from which to choose—ignoring the Costa Brava, which will be treated later. Southward along the coast is for the beaches near Barcelona or the inland toll-road for Tarragona and Valencia; westward into the province of Lérida is also the way to Madrid, or, if you turn north from its capital, to Andorra. Northward takes you to the playgrounds of the Pyrenees, their spas, their resorts, in winter their ski centers, and to the ancient town of Puigcerdà. The most traveled of all these routes is the coastal road south.

Costa Dorada

A freeway leads past the Prat de Llobregat airport to the resort of Castelldeféls, but then the overcrowded coastal road narrows to Sitges, to which the people of Barcelona flock for bathing. It is an attractive town, proud of its flowers, which carpet the streets during the Corpus Christi processions. There is an excellent beach at Sitges, the fishing is good, and if you are a golfer, you can play on the local links. The town has several museums; most interesting is the Cau-Ferrat, founded by the artist Rusiñol, which contains some of his own paintings, but a greater attraction is provided by two canvases of El Greco. Connoisseurs of wrought ironwork will be delighted to find here a beautiful collection of *cruz terminal,* crosses once erected to delimit town boundaries.

Unless bound for the coastal resorts of Villanova i la Geltrú, Cubellas, Calafell or Torredembarra, motorists are advised to avoid the traffic jams on the overcrowded N340, not least because the parallel freeway offers an attractive alternative through vineyards and olive groves.

The A2 freeway, as it branches west to Lérida, passes two superb monasteries. The first is the Cistercian monastery of Santes Creus, founded in 1159. The three austere aisles and the unusual 14th-century apse combine with the newly restored cloisters and the courtyard of the royal palace to make a complex of great beauty.

Another turning off the highway leads to Montblanc, whose ancient gates are too narrow for cars. A walk through its narrow streets reveals Gothic churches with lovely stained glass windows, a 16th-century hospital and fine medieval mansions. Eight km. (five miles) further on is the second monastery: that of Santa María at Poblet. This splendid Cistercian foundation at the foot of the Prades mountains, is the most complete and representative masterpiece of Spanish medieval monastic architecture. Started in 1153, it took three centuries to complete. The monastery suffered extensive damage in the 1835 revolution, and monks of the reformed Cistercian order have successfully carrried out the difficult task of restoration. Monks and novices pray again before the splendid retable over the tombs of the Catalan rulers, sleep in the cold, austere dormitory, eat their frugal meals in the stark refectory, while a fountain plays in the rose garden. The cloister is outstanding for lightness and severity, two elements that you rarely find so deftly blended as at Poblet.

Tarragona

Tarraco, renamed Colonia Julia Tarraconensis by Julius Caesar in 45
B.C., was one of Rome's principal strongholds in Spain (it has only about
117,000 inhabitants today whereas in Roman times it had a quarter of a
million) and, even before reaching it, you pass by the triumphal arch of
Bara, unrestored and undamaged, which dates back to the 3rd century
B.C. English engineers constructed in 1707 the glacis on which the Archeological Promenade skirts the formidable 3rd-century B.C. Ibero-Roman
ramparts above the "cyclopean" walls, containing blocks of stone so huge
that is is impossible to explain how they could have been raised before
the age of machinery, even by employing thousands of slaves. Visigothic,
Moorish and Catalan towers guard the Roman gates.

From the sea Tarragona looks like an evocation of, and a scene from,
the Middle Ages; viewed from the air, it presents a picture of wonderful
clarity though the view as you approach by road is somewhat less impressive. In Roman times, it was regarded as one of the empire's finest urban
creations; its wine was already famous and its population was the first in
Spain to gain Roman citizen status. Signposts indicate Scipio's tower, the
amphitheater and the perfectly preserved three-tier aqueduct some four
km. (three miles) outside the city, while the Praetorium stands next to a
medieval masterpiece built from the stones of these Roman monuments.

A flight of steps leads up to the cathedral, which is 13th century.
Though never finished, the clustered columns of the stark interior contrast
dramatically with the idyllic cloister round the rose garden. The showpiece
of the rich treasury is a rare Gothic tapestry. From the "Mediterranean
Balcony" at the head of the main avenue, the Rambla Nova, the view extends over a series of fine beaches.

Just off the highway, 77 km. (48 miles) to the southwest is Tortosa, nestling since Roman times in a superb setting on the left bank of the Ebro.
The 14th-century cathedral and the 16th-century college of St. Aloysius
Gonzaga rise majestically above the medieval quarter. The soil around
here is very rich, producing superb fruit and vegetables. A particularly
lovely drive follows the Ebro upstream to the dam at Flix and to the last
of the impressive chain of artificial lakes formed by the Ebro, Cinca and
Segre, and finally, through idyllic olive groves and green hills, to Lérida.

Lérida (Lleida)

The road west from Barcelona leads to Zaragoza and eventually to Madrid after passing through the least known of the four provinces of Catalonia—indeed, the principal place of interest between Barcelona and Lérida
occurs before the provincial border is passed. In Igualada, you might enjoy
stopping to look at the old people's home, with its curious Gaudí-esque
facade of unhewn stone and pebbles.

In its own distinctive way, Lérida equals many another provincial capital. Though it is an industrial town, the old quarters of the city are picturesque, and certain streets are shut off to traffic to make things easier for
pedestrians and shoppers. The streets are all bursting with life, full of
bright sunshine and welcome shade. Some streets have the protective *tol-
dos* stretched across to ward off the heat of the sun's rays.

From whichever direction you approach Lérida, you see the upper part of a mighty building rising above what looks like a fortified castle atop a hill on the banks of the Segre river. This is the ancient La Séo Cathedral—deconsecrated, converted into a fort, burned, and pillaged. However its restoration has entirely recaptured the majesty of this grandiose edifice, all the more deeply impressive for having survived disaster. You may admire the cleverly conceived square cloister, and the intricate fretwork portals and columns. To top it all you have a glorious, sweeping view out over the plain. There is also a New Cathedral, neo-Classical, from the mid-18th century, which has also undergone restoration.

Side Trip to Andorra

From Lérida a scenically very rewarding route is the narrow C1313 leading north via Balaguer up the Segre valley and then along the shores of the artificial lake, the Pantano d'Oliana, into the tiny country of Andorra.

The way to Andorra lies through the little town of La Seu d'Urgell—the only way to go in winter, for snow can block the passes from France, and then Andorra may only be entered from Spain. Seu d'Urgell is unimportant now—though its cheese is very popular—but in the 13th century, the date from which its old cathedral stems, it was of sufficient note to justify being given two co-princes. The Bishop of Urgell was one, the Count of Foix, the other. And today Andorra still, nominally at least, is ruled by these two co-princes, the Bishop and the President of France to whom the Count of Foix ceded the title. The Councils of the Valleys of Andorra really govern themselves and so are independent of the powers that theoretically hold them in feudal fief.

If you slip into this patriarchal and minute country, with its deep gorges and savage mountain scenery, there are two places that are most likely to attract you—Andorra la Vella, the capital, and Les Escaldes, a spa, better equipped even than the capital to put up visitors. The visit offers a rare combination of natural beauty and strictly practical benefits, as the duty-free status of Andorra makes it a shopper's paradise—provided you hold a foreign passport you are simply waved through the customs. The only snag is parking, as the narrow valley, hemmed in by majestic mountains on all sides, literally has not enough space to accommodate the uninterrupted influx of cars.

You may escape from this traffic into the idyllic upper valleys, or pass through Andorra entering France over the highest road pass in the Pyrenees, blocked by snow half the year and thus ideal skiing terrain. Or you may keep on C1313 which turns east (right) just before the Andorran frontier, following the Segre for 50 km. (31 miles) to another border crossing at Puigcerdà, which can also be reached directly from Barcelona via Vic and Ripoll.

Puigcerdà was once the capital of the Cerdagne, a Pyrenean land straddling the present Franco-Spanish frontier. High in the mountains, it has a 18-hole golf course and is a center for the summer and winter vacation resorts of the Pyrenees—Super-Molina (Spain's top winter sports resort), Nuria, Camprodon, and Puigcerdà itself, and the spa of Ribes de Freser.

The Green Catalonia

Travelers interested in discovering for themselves the real Catalonia, the one that is seldom available to tourists in a rush, should try another itinerary that is highly recommended. Between the frontier and Barcelona, there is a roundabout route from Figueras, due west on C260 and C150 to Olot and Ripoll, then veering obliquely south on N152 via Vic to bring you to the capital of the province.

Here, you will see land that is carefully tilled and productive, a living green refutation of the proverbially arid reputation of Spanish soil. The landscape is endlessly changing, alternating between hills and wooded dales. On a sheer basalt cliff overhanging the Fluvia River, Castellfollit juts out like the prow of a ship. The road passes through the rather disappointing town; what looks from afar like a story-book village loses its charm close-up. Don't plan to stop anywhere before Sant Joan de les Abadesses, where the church possesses a handsomely carved wood calvary cross.

In recent years the general appearance of villages, particularly in Catalonia, has undergone a curious change. Capital resulting from the booming tourist industry of the 1960s and '70s has been invested in storage silos built along outlines closely resembling those of the generally square church steeples, somehow reminiscent of Tuscany. Everywhere, new camping grounds and swimming pools have mushroomed. If you're bent on finding the old-world atmosphere of Spanish rural existence, you will have to avoid the international traffic sweeping down to Barcelona and stick to back roads.

Probably the most pleasant sights in the Catalonian countryside are the farms. The multitude of buildings of austere grayish or pinkish stone, with their staggered levels of rooftops and ubiquitous square towers, give the farmhouses an immutable, centuries-old look of fortresses, exactly the way they must have looked in more heroic times.

Churches confer dignity on the villages. Church architecture is pretty much the same everywhere here: Romanesque—either real or imitation—with Baroque façades added on. The tiniest village boasts its main square, framed by arcades, and a *rambla,* or promenade (from *rable,* a species of tree), where it is fun to sit and watch the villagers stroll up and down during the sacred evening *paseo.*

Olot has managed to preserve most of its original flavor. Even its new quarters catch your eye, with their modern church that flaunts a springboard-shaped steeple and a gigantic monk's head sculptured by Iloret on its façade. This is the church of St. Peter the Martyr, whose name has been extended to the surrounding neighborhood.

The town of Ripoll was considerably disfigured by turn-of-the-century industrialization. It commands a halt, nevertheless: the 11th-century monastery of Santa María is worth a visit. The portal is one of the outstanding achievements of Romanesque art and so are the cloisters with their double colonnades.

Vic sits in the middle of the plain at the confluence of the Guri and the Heder rivers, 488 meters (1,600 feet) above sea level: it's the business and industrial center for the region. It possesses a handsome Baroque cathedral (St Peter's), whose Byzantine tower dates back to the 11th and 12th centuries, and an interesting museum. The cathedral is decorated with very powerful modern murals painted twice by José María Sert because the first series was destroyed in the Civil War.

If you wish to detour here, take N141 to Moià—notice its church tower with the odd "lobster-claw" fretwork—and then go on to Manresa, where you will catch your first glimpse of the fantastic ridge of Montserrat, looming up to your left.

Instead of passing thorough Moià and Manresa, you can keep to N152 through La Garriga, a charming medieval town set in a rich agricultural valley, and in a few more kilometers find yourself once more in Catalonia's first city, Barcelona.

PRACTICAL INFORMATION FOR CATALONIA

TOURIST OFFICES. Andorra, Dr Villanova (tel. 202 14); **Arenys de Mar,** Po Xifré 25 (tel. 792 1537); **Calafell,** Vilamar 1 (tel. 69 17 59); **Cambrils,** Pl. Creu de la Missió (tel. 36 11 59); **Cardona,** Pl. Fira 1 (tel. 869 1000); **Castelldefels,** Pl. Rosa de los Vientos (tel. 664 2301); **Lérida,** Arc del Pont (tel. 24 81 20); **Manresa,** Pza. Mayor 1; **Olot,** Mulleras 33 (tel. 26 01 41); **Puigcerdà,** Querol (tel. 88 05 42); **Ripoll,** Pl. Abat Oliva (tel. 70 23 51); **Salou,** Expl. del Muelle (tel. 38 02 33); **Sant Cugat del Valles,** Pl. Barcelona 17; **Sitges,** Po de Vilafranca (tel. 894 1230); **Tarragona,** Fortuny 4 (tel. 23 34 15); **Terrassa,** Pl. Eduardo Maristany (tel. 894 1213); **Valls,** Pl. Blat 1 (tel. 60 10 43); **Vic,** Ciutat 1 (tel. 886 2091); **Vilafranca del Penedés,** Cort 14; **Vilanova i la Geltrú,** Pl. de la Villa 8.

TELEPHONE CODES. The dialing codes for the four provinces of Catalonia are: Barcelona (93); Gerona (972); Lérida (973); Tarragona (977). Dialing codes for all the towns we list are given under *Hotels and Restaurants* immediately after the name of the town. You need only dial these codes if you are calling from outside the province.

GETTING AROUND. By Train. The main train routes across Catalonia all start from the Catalonian capital, Barcelona. The principal routes are Barcelona–Tarragona–Zaragoza and on to Madrid; Barcelona–Manresa–Lérida–Zaragoza; and the coastal route Barcelona–Sitges–Tarragona– Salou–Cambrils–Ametlla del Mar–Tortosa and on out of Catalonia to Castellón and Valencia. There is one route from Barcelona into the Pyrenees and this is the line to Andorra via Vic, Ripoll, Ribes de Freser, Puigcerdà and La Tour de Carol on the French border. In high summer only (July–Sept.) there is a connection at Ribes de Freser for Nuria.

Other train routes in Catalonia are from Lérida to Tarragona via Reus; and north from Lérida to Pobla de Segur which is as far as the line goes.

Lérida station is on the Plaça de Berenguer IV at the far end of Rambla de Ferran, and there is a RENFE booking office at Rambla de Ferran 20 (tel. 23 74 67). Tarragona station is close to the sea at the far end of Passeig de les Palmeres, and the RENFE office is at Rambla Nova 40 (tel. 23 52 94).

From Barcelona (Plaça de Espanya) there are local services to Martorell and Manresa, and from this line you can connect onto a cable car to Montserrat, a dramatic way of approaching the monastery; also to Martorell and Igualada. From Barcelona (Passeig de Gracià) there are local services to Terrassa and Sabadell.

By Bus. Bus services provide the most comprehensive way of getting about, particularly in the mountainous Pyrenean regions, and further south to some of the more remote inland villages and monasteries. As with trains the biggest network is based on Barcelona, though bus services connect almost all the places you might want to visit in Catalonia. The main termini in Barcelona are—Ronda Universitat 4 and Estación del Norte. The other two main bus centers are Lérida and Tarragona.

By Air. Barcelona is Catalonia's main airport with numerous international flights as well as services to most major Spanish cities. Gerona airport deals with thousands of charter flights from northern Europe.

By Boat. There are regular sailings from Barcelona to the Balearic islands of Majorca, Minorca and Ibiza.

By Car. Catalonia is one of the few areas in Spain well served by fast freeways *(autopistas),* and whatever your destination from Barcelona you can make good use of these, if you so choose. Remember that tolls are fairly high. For the coastal road south from Barcelona to Tarragona you have a choice of the A7 *autopista* or the N340. The A7 is both fast and scenic. Inland, westwards, from Barcelona you have the choice of the A2 *autopista* or the N-II via Igualada, both leading to Lérida and Zaragoza. The N-II passes closer to the mountain range of Montserrat but there is a good view of this strange saw-toothed range from both roads. Scenically they are both pleasing in the vicinity of Barcelona as they pass through mountains and the vine-growing region around Vilafranca del Penedès, but become less so as they cross the plains near Lérida.

The three main routes northwards into the Pyrenees towards the French border are N152 from Barcelona to Vic, Ripoll and Ribes de Freser then through the ski resorts of La Molina, Super Molina, and Alp to the border at Bourg-Madame; C1313 from Lérida to La Seu d'Urgell following the winding course of the Segre river; and C147 from Balaguer, north of Lérida, following the River Noguera right up into the Pyrenees, skirting the National Park of Aigües Torres, to the Vall d'Aran. All of these involve some high mountain driving with plenty of twists and turns, but the last route, the C147 is perhaps the most demanding.

HOTELS AND RESTAURANTS. The hotels of the Costa Brava resorts as well as those of Gerona and Figueras are dealt with in the Costa Brava chapter, and Barcelona has its own chapter too. There are six paradores in this area: at Cardona and Vic in Barcelona province; at Arties, La Seu d'Urgell and Viella in Lérida province; and at Tortosa in Tarragona province. Many of the Pyrenean hotels in the provinces of Lérida and Gerona are only open during the winter sports months and in some cases, in high summer season, in July and August.

Alfes. Lérida (973). *Lleida* (M), at km. 142 on the A2 freeway (tel. 11 60 23). A comfortable and typical freeway hotel close to the exit to Lérida.

Ametlla Del Valles. Barcelona (93). *Hotel del Valles* (M), Autovía de la Ametlla (tel. 843 0600). 54 rooms with pool, tennis and garden; a reasonable roadside hotel.

Andorra. Tiny republic perched in the Pyrenees, easily approached from La Seu d'Urgell. At **Andorra la Vella** (9738) *Andorra Palace* (E), Prat de la Creu (tel. 21 072). Tennis, pool, mountain views. AE, DC, MC, V. *Andorra Park* (E), (tel. 20 979). Good amenities and away from the noise; pool. *Eden Roc* (E), Avda. Dr Mitjavila (tel. 21 000). AE, DC, MC, V. *President* (M), Avda. Santa Coloma. (tel. 22 922). Restaurant has magnificent views. AE, DC, V. *L'Isard* (M), (tel. 20 096). 55 rooms all with bath. AE, DC, MC, V. *Florida* (I), (tel. 20 105). Small; no restaurant. *Internacional* (I), (tel. 21 422). Good value. **Restaurants.** *Chez Jacques* (E), Avda. Tarragona 163 (tel. 20 325). Outstanding and highly imaginative cuisine. *Moli dels Fanals* (M), Dr. Vilanova (tel. 21 381). In an old windmill in center of town; good set menus. AE, DC, MC, V. *Versalles* (M), Cap del Carre 1 (tel. 21 331). Tiny French bistro; good value. V.

At **Les Escaldes**, spa with many hotels: *Valira* (E), (tel. 20 565). 42 rooms all with bath. *Roc Blanc* (E), (tel. 21 486). Pool and fine restaurant. *La Pubilla* (I), (tel. 20 981). Good value. *Comtes d'Urgell* (M), at Engordany (tel. 20 621). 200 rooms. **Restaurant.** *1900* (E), Unió 11 (tel. 26 716). Best in Andorra—outstanding. AE, DC, V.

At **La Massana:** *Rutlan* (M), (tel. 35 000). 100 rooms; pool. *La Massana* (I), (tel. 35 222). 50 rooms all with bath; pool. **Restaurant.** *La Borda de l'Avi* (M), (tel. 35 154). Good local food; well recommended. AE, DC, MC, V.

Arenys De Mar. Barcelona (93). *Raymond* (M), Paseo Xifre 1 (tel. 792 1700). 33 rooms. *Carlos I* (I), Passeig de Catalunya 10 (tel. 792 0383). 100 rooms; pool. *Titus* (I), at km. 662 on N-II. (tel. 791 0300). 44 rooms; pool and garden.

Restaurants. *Portinyol* (E), Escollera de Levante (tel. 792 0009). Good views of beach and good seafood. Closed Mon. AE, DC, MC, V. *Hispania* (E), Reial 54 (tel. 791 0457). Outstanding restaurant, one of the best in Catalonia. Closed Sun. night and Tues. two km. south on the N-II. AE, MC, V.

Arties. Lérida (973). *Parador Don Gaspar de Portola* (E), (tel. 64 08 01). 40 rooms; in magnificent mountain setting between the Viella tunnel and the Bonaigua pass. AE, DC, MC, V.

Balaguer. Lérida (973). *Conde Jaime de Urgel* (M), Avda. Pedro IV (tel. 44 56 04). 60 rooms, a semi parador with pool and many amenities; on the banks of the River Segre. DC, MC, V. *Mirador del Segre* (I), Carrer la Banqueta 3 (tel. 44 57 50). 33 rooms.

Barruera. Lérida (973). *Manantial* (E), Caldas de Bohí (tel. 69 01 91). 119 rooms; pool, mini-golf, gardens and bar. Situated close to the Aigües Tortes National Park and a good base for excursions. Open late June through Sept. only. *Caldas* (I), Caldas de Bohí (tel. 69 04 49). 125 rooms. Simple but comfortable spa hotel first opened in 1883. Open late June through Sept. only.

Bruc. Barcelona (93). *Bruc* (M), at km. 574 on the N-II (tel. 771 0061). Convenient roadside hotel with pool, 50 km. (31 miles) from Barcelona. One of the closest hotels to the Monastery of Montserrat. DC, MC, V.

Calafel. Tarragona (977). *Kursaal* (M), Avda. San Juan de Diós 119 (tel. 69 23 00). 4-star hotel with 39 rooms; much higher rates July to Aug. AE, DC, MC, V. *Canadá* (M), Mosén Jaime Soler 44 (tel. 69 15 00). 106 rooms; pool, garden and tennis. V. *Miramar* (M), Rambla Costa Dorada 1 (tel. 69 07 00). 201 rooms; garden, pool.

Restaurants. *Da Giorgio* (E), Angel Guimera 4 (tel. 69 11 59). Italian restaurant, open for dinner only. *La Barca* (M), San Juan de Diós 79 (tel. 69 15 59). A good fish and seafood restaurant by the beach. Closed Wed. AE, DC, MC, V.

Caldas D'estrac. Barcelona (93). *Colón* (E–M), Paz 16 (tel. 791 0500). 82 rooms; pool, tennis, bar. *Jet* (I), Santema 25 (tel. 791 0651). A good value 3-star hotel.

Caldes De Montbui. Barcelona (93). *Balneario Broquetas* (M), Plaza Font del Lleo 1 (tel. 865 0100). Oldish but good hotel with 84 rooms; pool and pleasant garden. AE, DC, MC, V. *Balneario Termas Victoria* (I), Barcelona 12 (tel. 865 0150). 91 rooms; pool and garden. V.

Calella. Barcelona (93). Not to be confused with Calella on the Costa Brava. *Mont Rosa* (M), Paseo de las Rocas (tel. 769 0508). Modern with private beach; 120 rooms, all with balconies; pool. AE, DC, MC, V. *Las Vegas* (M), Zona Riero Faro (tel. 769 0850). 94 rooms; pool. AE, DC, MC, V. *Calella Park* (I), Jubara 257 (tel. 769 0300). 51 rooms; pool; just one of the many reasonably priced 1- and 2-star hotels in this resort.

Cambrils. Tarragona (997). *Augustus I* (M), Ctra. Salou (tel. 38 11 54). 243 rooms; pool and garden. *Centurión Playa* (M), Ctra. Salou (tel. 36 14 50). Large, modern hotel with 233 rooms; pool. *Motel La Dorada* (M), at km. 229 on the N340 (tel. 36 01 50). 37 rooms; pool, tennis; very reasonable rates. *Tropicana* (I), Ctra. Salou (tel. 36 01 12). Small hotel near beach; 28 rooms; pool.

Restaurants. Cambril is blessed with some outstanding restaurants. *Can Gatell* (E), Miramar 27 (tel. 36 01 06). Serving fish and seafood dishes with many specialties from Tarragona. Closed Mon. night and all day Tues. AE, DC, MC, V. *Casa Gatell* (E), Miramar 26 (tel. 36 00 57). Excellent fish restaurant with innovative creations as well as the traditional *rovellons*, a kind of mushroom very popular in Catalonia. Closed Sun. evening and all day Mon. AE, DC, MC, V. *Eugenia* (E), Consolat de Mar 80 (tel. 36 01 68). Possibly the best of these three, with its own garden and swimming pool. Closed Tues. night and Wed. in summer; Wed., and Thurs. lunch in winter. AE, DC, MC, V.

Camprodon. Gerona (972). *Güell* (I), Plaza de España 8 (tel. 74 00 11). 43 rooms; parking. v. *Rigat* (I), Plaza del Doctor Robert 2 (tel. 74 00 13). 28 rooms, pool; mini golf, garden and bar.

Cardona. Barcelona (93). *Parador Duques de Cardona* (M), (tel. 869 1275), 65 rooms; in ancient castle of Dukes of Cardona with a lovely Gothic patio; good food and service. AE, DC, MC, V.

Castelldefels. Barcelona (93). Seaside resort just south of Barcelona. *Rey Don Jaime* (L), in Torrebarona 2.5 km. from Castelldefels (tel. 665 1300). 88 rooms; pool, tennis and gardens. *Bel-Air* (E), Paseo Marítimo 169 (tel. 665 1600). 38 rooms; pool, tennis. *Playafels* (E), Playa Ribera de San Pedro (tel. 665 1250). 34 rooms; garden and private beach. *Rancho* (E), Paseo de la Marina 212 (tel. 665 1900). 60 rooms; pool and tennis. *Mediterráneo* (M), Paseo Marítimo 294 (tel. 665 2100). 47 rooms; good view. AE, DC, MC, V. *Neptuno* (M), Paseo Garbi 74 (tel. 665 1450). 38 rooms; pool. *Rialto* (I), Paseo Marítimo 70 (tel. 665 2058). 24 rooms; garden and parking.

Restaurants. *Nautic* (M), Paseo Marítimo 374 (tel. 665 0174). A good seafood restaurant with typical decor. AE, DC, V. *La Bonne Table* (M), Avda. de la Constitución 390 (tel. 665 3755). Away from the sea front, a small French restaurant serving fine food and wine. Closed Tues. and all Nov. AE, DC, V. *Las Botas* (M), Avda. Constitución 326 (tel. 665 2132). Good value and serving some good desserts. AE, MC, V. Both are on the C246 highway.

Comarruga. Tarragona (977). *Gran Hotel Europe* (E), Avda. Palfuriana (tel. 68 04 11). Modern, overlooking the sea with pool, tennis and mini golf. DC, MC, V. *Brisamar* (I), Pza. Hermanos Trillas (tel. 68 00 11). 102 rooms; very reasonable rates. DC, MC, V. *Casa Martí* (I), Villafranca 8 (tel. 68 01 11). 106 rooms; pool. AC, DC, MC, V.

Cubelles. Barcelona (93). *Llicorella* (E), Camino San Antonio 101 (tel. 895 0044). 11 rooms, pool. Exclusive small hotel belonging to French *Relais et Châteaux* chain. It is primarily an excellent French restaurant. Closed Mon. AE, DC, MC, V.

La Garriga. Barcelona (93). *Blancafort* (M), Baños 55 (tel. 871 4600). A spa hotel with 50 rooms, pool, tennis and mini golf. AE, DC, V.

Igualada. Barcelona (93). *América* (M), at km. 557 on the N-II (tel. 803 1000). A comfortable roadside hotel with good restaurant and pool.

La Jonquera. Gerona (972). Frontier town. *Porta Catalana* (E), at km. 149 on the A17 (tel. 54 06 40). New. AE, V. *Puerta de España* (I), at km. 22 heading south on N-II (tel. 54 01 20). 26 rooms. v. *Goya* (I), at km. 782 heading north on N-II (tel. 54 00 77). 36 rooms.

Lérida. (973). *Condes de Urgel* II (M), Avda. de Barcelona 17 (tel. 20 23 00). Quite large and popular with tour groups. On the southern outskirts of town. AE, DC, MC, V. *Sansi Park* (M), Alcalde Porqueras 4 (tel. 24 40 00). 26 rooms. Recently opened small hotel just outside the old town.

AE, MC, V. *Jamaica* (I), Ctra. de Zaragoza (tel. 26 51 00). 24 rooms. *Principal* (I), Plaza Pahería 8 (tel. 24 09 00). 53 rooms; in the center.

Restaurants. *Forn del Nastasi* (E), Salmerón 10 (tel. 23 45 10). Reliable with good Catalan cooking. Closed Sun. and Mon. AE, DC, MC, V. *El Pati* (M), Pza. Noguerola 5 (tel. 23 74 32). Stylish and in a lovely old house. Closed Sun. and Aug. AE, DC, V. *Sheyton Pub* (M), Prat de la Riba 39 (tel. 23 81 97). Decor is the Spanish version of an English pub. Excellent food. DC, MC, V. *Moli de la Nora* (E), 10 km. north on C1313 in Vilanova de la Barca (tel. 19 00 17). Picturesque location in old olive-oil and grain store; delightful garden for summer dining; excellent fish and game. Well worth the trip. Closed Sun. evening and Mon. in winter. AE, DC, V.

Llivia. Gerona (972). *Llivia* (M), Ctra. de Puigcerda (tel. 89 60 00). 63 rooms; pool, tennis, bar and pleasant garden. V.

Malgrat De Mar. Barcelona (93). *Monte Playa* (I), Paseo Marítimo (tel. 761 0508). 183 rooms; pool. Also many one-star hotels along Paseo Marítimo.

Manresa. Barcelona (93). *Pedro III* (M), Muralla Sant Francesc 49 (tel. 872 4000). A central 3-star hotel.

Mataro. Barcelona (93). *Castell de Mata* (M), on N-II (tel. 790 5807). 52 rooms in an old building; pool, garden and bar. *Colón* (M), Colón 6–8 (tel. 790 5804). A recent comfortable hostel right in the center. V.

Restaurant. *Can Dimas* (E), Passeig de Callao (tel. 790 3209). Going strong for over 100 years. AE, DC, MC, V.

La Molina. Gerona (972). Winter sports resort. *Palace* (E–M), Supermolina (tel. 89 20 16). 32 rooms; pool, tennis and garden in a beautiful position right at the bottom of the ski slopes. V. *Adsera* (M), (tel. 89 20 01). 35 rooms in center, pool and garden. *Roc Blanch* (M), on road to station (tel. 89 20 75). 22 rooms; central, pool and garden. Open Dec. to Apr. and July to Sept. only. AE, MC, V. *La Solana* (M), (tel. 89 20 00). Small modern family hotel with pool and garden.

Montseny. Barcelona (93). *San Bernat* (M), Montaña Finca el Clot (tel. 847●3011). 18 rooms in quiet location with excellent views of the mountains. AE, DC, V.

Montserrat. Barcelona (93). *Abat Cisneros* (M), Plaça del Monastir (tel. 835 0201). A basic hotel with restaurant opposite the monastery. AE, DC, MC. *El Monasterio* (I), Plaça Monastir (tel. 835 0201). A simple 2-star hostel under same management as hotel. AE, DC, MC.

Olot. Gerona (972). *Montsacopa* (I), Mulleras (tel. 26 07 62). 73 rooms. Good, simple hotel in center. AE, DC, MC, V.

Restaurant. *Purgatori* (M), Bisbe Serra 58 (tel. 26 16 06). Family-run, serving good home cooking. Closed Sun. night and Mon. AE, DC, MC, V.

Prats Y Sampsor. Lérida (973). *Moixaró* (I), Ctra. Bellver-Alp (tel. 89 02 38). 32 rooms; pool and garden; the only hotel here.

Puigcerda. Gerona (972). Some 1,200 meters (3,937 feet) above sea level, delightfully situated and cool at night. *Puigcerdà Park Hotel* (M), Ctra. Barcelona (tel. 88 07 50). 54 rooms; in town. *Chalet de Golf* (M), (tel. 88 09 63). A few km. out of town along the beautiful Segre valley. 16 rooms; golf course. *Hotel del Lago* (I), Avda. Dr Piguillén (tel. 88 10 00). 16 rooms with pool; older hotel. *María Victoria* (I), Florenza 9 (tel. 88 03 00). 50 rooms; in town. AE, MC, V. *Martínez* (I), Ctra. de Llivia (tel. 88 02 50). 15 rooms, pool.

Rialp. Lérida (973). *Condes del Pallars* (M), Ctra. Esterri de Aneu (tel. 62 03 50). 103 rooms; pool, tennis, mini golf and garden. Situated on the roadside but in a quiet position with its own cinema and pelota court. DC, MC, V.

Ripoll. Gerona (972). *Solana del Ter* (M), 2 km. out on N152 south (tel. 70 10 62). Small roadside hotel with 28 rooms, pool and tennis. *Monasterio* (I), Placa Gran 4 (tel. 70 01 50). Simple central hotel with 40 rooms.

Salardu. Lérida (973). *Montarto* (E), Baqueira-Beret (tel. 64 50 75). 166 rooms; pool, tennis and bar, at the foot of the ski slopes. Open Dec. through May, and in Aug. when rates are more moderate. AE, DC, MC, V. *Tuc Blanc* (E), Baqueira-Beret (tel. 64 51 50). Another good hotel close to the ski slopes and quite luxurious. Open Dec. to Apr. and July to Aug. AE, DC, MC, V.

Restaurant. *La Borda Lobató* (M), belonging to the Montarto hotel. Pleasant relaxed atmosphere and good food. Open Dec. through May only. Closed Tues. AE, DC, MC, V.

Salou. Tarragona (977). *Negresco* (E), at Punta Dorada on road to Faro (tel. 38 03 92). Quiet position with lovely garden. *Salou Park* (M), Calle 31 (tel. 38 02 08). Comfortable with pool and good view; the best. AE, DC, MC, V. *Las Vegas* (M), Alfonso V, (tel. 38 06 54). 275 rooms; pool. *Picnic* (I), (tel. 38 01 58). 43 rooms; pool. *Planas* (I), Plaza Bonet 3 (tel. 38 01 08). 100 rooms. *Delfín Park* (I), Calle Mayor (tel. 38 03 08). 244 rooms; pool.

Restaurant. *Casa Soler* (M), Virgen del Carmen (tel. 38 04 63). AE, DC, MC, V.

Sant Carles De La Rapita. Tarragona (977). *Miami Park* (M), Avda. del Generalísimo 33 (tel. 74 03 51). 80 rooms; simple and central. AE, DC, MC, V.

Sant Hilari De Sacalm. Gerona (972). *Suizo* (M), Plaza Verdaguer 8 (tel. 86 80 00). 39 rooms; central.

Sant Pol De Mar. Barcelona (93). *Gran Sol* (M), (tel. 760 0051). 45 rooms; pool and tennis. *La Costa* (I), Carrer Nou 32 (tel. 760 0151). 17 rooms.

Sant Vicent De Mont-Alt. Barcelona (93). *Clipper* (M), Marítimo 21 (tel. 791 0800). 103 rooms; pool and garden.

Sardanyola. Barcelona (93). *Bellaterra* (E), on the A7 at Area de Bellaterra (tel. 692 6054). Modern roadside hotel with pool and golf.

Seu D'urgell. Lérida (973). *El Castell* (E), at km. 129 on Lérida road (tel. 35 07 04). 39 rooms, pool. Great views and beautiful setting. AE, DC, MC, V. *Parador Nacional* (M), Santo Domingo (tel. 35 20 00). Modern, comfortable parador on the edge of the old town; 85 rooms, pool. AE, DC, MC, V. *Nice* (I), Avda. Pau Claris 4 (tel. 35 21 00). Simple with 48 rooms.

Sitges. Barcelona (93). Crowded, popular seaside resort—especially with the young. *Calipolis* (E), Avda. Sofía (tel. 894 1500). Pleasant modern hotel. AE, DC, MC, V. *Terramar* (E), Passeig Maritim (tel. 894 0050). Right on the beach, old world charm, spacious garden, pool, golf and tennis. AE, DC, MC, V. *Antemare* (E), Avda. Virgen de Montserrat 48 (tel. 894 1908). 72 rooms with pool. *Los Pinos* (M), Passeig Maritim (tel. 894 1550). 42 rooms; pool and garden. DC, MC, V. *Romantic* (I), San Isidro 23 (tel. 894 0643). Stylish old hotel with delightful garden where you can dine; short walk to beach. MC. *Sitges Park* (I), Jesus 12 (tel. 894 0250). 79 rooms in historic building; pool and garden.

Restaurants. *El Greco* (E), Passeig de la Ribera 72 (tel. 894 2906). On quay; cozy with rustic English decor. DC, MC, V. *Fragata* (M), Passeig de la Ribera 1 (tel. 894 1086). Also on quay. AE, DC, MC, V. *Vivero* (M), Paseo Balmins (tel. 894 21 49). On the beach; tops for seafood. DC, V.

Tarragona (977). *Imperial Tarraco* (E), Rambla Vella 2 (tel. 23 30 40). In the heart of the city with good views; pool, tennis and garden. AE, DC, MC, V. *Lauria* (M), Rambla Nova 20 (tel. 23 67 12). Simple, central hotel with pool, not far from beach. AE, DC, MC, V. *París* (I), Maragall 4 (tel. 23 60 12). Central with 45 rooms on the Pza Verdaguer. AE, DC, MC, V. *Marina* (I), Vía Augusta 151 (tel. 23 30 27). 26 rooms; 2 km. from center. Open Apr. through Sept. only. AE, DC, MC, V. *Nuria* (I), Vía Augusta 217 (tel. 23 50 11). 61 rooms and close to Marina.

Restaurants. *Sol Ric* (E), Vía Augusta 227 (tel. 23 20 32). Very pleasant terrace garden, well known to locals. Regional cuisine; highly recommended. AE, DC, MC, V. *La Galería* (M), Rambla Nova 16 (tel. 23 61 43). Small welcoming restaurant in center of town, specializes in fish; pleasantly decorated with paintings by owner. Closed Wed. evening and Sun; also Sat. lunch in summer. AE, MC, V.

Torredembarra. Tarragona (977). *Costa Fina* (I), Avda. de Montserrat (tel. 64 00 75). 48 rooms; simple resort hotel. Open May to Sept. only. *Morros* (I), Pérez Galdós 8 (tel. 64 02 25). 81 rooms; simple hotel. Open March to Sept. only. AE, DC, MC, V.

Restaurant. *Morros* (M), Paseo del Mar (tel. 64 00 61). Very good food. AE, DC, MC, V.

Tortosa. Tarragona (977). *Parador Castillo de la Zuda* (M), (tel. 44 44 50). 82 rooms; located in ancient castle. Magnificent views over the town, the Ebro and mountains; pleasant garden and pool. AE, DC, MC, V.

Vallfogona De Riucorp. Tarragona (977). *Balneario* (M), on outskirts (tel. 88 00 25). Pool and tennis, in quiet setting.

Vic. Barcelona (93). *Parador Nacional* (E), 14 km. outside. (tel. 888 7211). Modern parador with 36 rooms, pool. On a hill overlooking Sau reservoir. AE, DC, V.

Restaurant. *L'Anec Blau* (M), Verdaguer 21 (tel. 885 3151). Smart with good service and a good choice of menu. Closed Mon. AE, DC, MC, V.

Viella. Lérida (973). *Tuca* (E), Ctra. Salardú (tel. 64 07 00). 4-star hotel with 118 rooms a few km. out of Viella in Betrén. AE, DC, MC, V. *Arán* (M), Avda. Castiero 5 (tel. 64 00 50). 44 rooms. AE, DC, MC, V. *Parador Valle de Arán* (M), 2 km. out of town (tel. 64 01 00). Modern parador with 135 rooms; pool. Located in the Lérida Pyrenees with beautiful views over mountains.

Restaurants. *Can Turnay* (M), Pza. Mayor (tel. 64 02 92). Simple home cooking and rustic decor. Reasonable prices. Closed May and Nov. AE. *Era Mola* (M), Curva 8 (tel. 64 08 68). French-inspired menu with duck and game specialties. Open Dec. to Apr. and July and Aug. MC, V.

Vilafranca Del Penedes. Barcelona (93). *Pedro III El Grande* (M), Pl. Penedés 2 (tel. 890 3100). 52 rooms. Comfortable modern hotel. AE, DC, MC, V.

Vilanova I La Geltru. Barcelona (93). *Cesar* (E–M), Isaac Peral 4 (tel. 815 11 25). 30 rooms; pool and pleasant terrace. Good *La Fitorra* restaurant.

Restaurants. *Chez Bernard et Marguérite* (E), Ramón Llull 4 (tel. 815 56 04). Excellent French restaurant. AE, DC, MC, V. *Peixerot* (M), Passeig Maritim 56 (tel. 815 06 25). Good fish and seafood and Penedés wine. AE, DC, V.

PLACES OF INTEREST. Opening hours given are liable to frequent change and it is always wise to doublecheck with the local tourist offices before setting out on a special trip. Most museums close on Mondays.

Arneys De Mar (Barcelona). **Museo Marés de les Puntes** (Lace Museum), Esglesia 41. One of Europe's best lace museums with a collection donated by the sculptor Federico Marés. Open Apr. through Sept. Tues. to Fri. 6–8, Sat. 11–1 and 6–9, Sun. 11–2; Oct. through Mar. open same hours but Tues., Thurs., Sat. and Sun. only.

Barruera (Lérida). Village close to the **National Park of Aigües Torres**—in this district of magnificent mountain scenery are the fine Romanesque churches of San Juan de Boi, San Clemente and Santa María de Taüll, Erill-la-Vall, Coll and Cardet, usually open 8–8.

Caldes De Montbui (Barcelona). A spa town since Roman times. **Museo de Historia,** Santa Susana 4. Archeological finds from local Iberian and Roman excavations. Open Sat. 5–8; Sun. and fiestas 11–2 and 5–8.

Museo Romántico Can Delger, Joaquín Delger 8. Library, furniture and mementoes of the Delger family and paintings and sculpture by Manolo Hugue. Open Sat. 5–8; Sun. and fiestas 11–2; 5–8.

Roman Thermal Springs, Pza. Fonto del Lleo. Thermal baths construct-ed in the time of the Emperor Hadrian. Open Mon.–Fri. 10.30–1, Sat. and Sun. 10.30–1.30 and 5–8.

Cardona (Barcelona). **Castle of the Dukes of Cardona.** Fortified castle dating back to 9th century; now contains a parador. Castle is open 9–1.
Museo de Sal (Salt Museum), Pompeu Fabra 4. Displays of salt in its original state and ornamental objects made of salt. Open Sat. and Sun. 10–2.

Igualada (Barcelona). An important leather town, 70% of all Spain's leather goods are cured and made here. **Museo de Igualada,** Ctra. de Man-resa. The City Museum's collection concentrates mainly on fabrics and costumes, both civic and religious. Open Sat. and Sun. 9–12 and 4–6.
Museo de la Piel (Leather Museum), next to the City Museum. Leather working, with fine examples of embossed work. Open Sat. and Sun. 12–2.

Lérida. Hospital of Santa María, Pza. Catedral. This 15th-century hos-pice houses several museums including the **Institute of Lérida Studies** and the **Archeological Museum,** open daily 12–2 and 6–9.
Palacio de la Pahería, Pza. de la Pahería, is 13th-century Romanesque and is now the Ayuntamiento (City Hall). It has a splendid facade and inner patio and contains the **Museo de la Pahería** with Iberian and Roman finds discovered during excavations in this building. Open Mon. to Sat. 11–2 and 6–8.

Montserrat (Barcelona). **Monastery of Montserrat.** Only the basilica of the monastery is open to visitors but it contains the shrine of the famous "Moreneta," the Black Virgin. The basilica is open throughout the day but sightseers are not allowed in during services, though they are welcome to attend Mass and to hear the singing of the famous Escolanía, the Boys' Choir, in the midday service, usually held sometime between 11.30 and 1.
Museo del Monasterio. The Monastery Museum is divided into two sec-tions. In summer the old section *(Sección Antigua)* opens 10.30–2 and 3–6, and the new *(Sección Moderna)* 10.30–2 and 3.30–6; in winter the Sección Antigua opens 10.30–2 only, and the Sección Moderna 3–6 only. Impor-tant collection of 16th–18th century Italian art, and Flemish, French and Spanish art from the 15th to 18th centuries.

Poblet (Tarragona). **Monastery of Poblet,** near L'Espluga de Francoli and Vimbodi. Open daily 10–12.30 and 3–6 (5.30 in winter).

Ripoll (Gerona). **Monastery of Santa María,** Plaza Abad Oliva. 12th-century monastery containing the tomb of Wifredo el Velloso (Wilfred the Hairy, 857–902), founder of the Catalan dynasty.
Museo Folklórico, in the Church of San Pedro beside the Monastery. Interesting Museum of Folklore detailing mountain customs, and a collec-tion of shotguns. Open daily 9–1 and 3–7, Mon. 9–1 only.

Sant Cugat Del Valles (Barcelona). **Monastery of San Cugat.** Gothic Benedictine monastery surrounded by medieval wall and with notable Romanesque cloisters. Open daily 9–1 and 3–6; closed Mon.

Sant Sadurni D'Anoia (Barcelona). **Cavas Codorniu** (Codorniu Wine Cellars). Sant Sadurni is the center of Catalonia's booming champagne (or *cava,* as it is now called) industry. The Cavas Codorniu are open Mon. to Thurs. 8–12 and 3–6, Fri. 8–12 only, but are closed in Aug. They have been declared a National Monument and have a fascinating **Wine Museum** designed by the *modernista* architect Puig i Cadafalch.

La Seu D'Urgell (Lérida). **Cathedral of San Odon.** 11th- and 12th-century Romanesque. Open daily 9–2 and 4–8; closed Sun. afternoon.
Museo Diocesano, Casa del Obispado. Religious art, sculpture and ornaments from the 10th to 18th centuries. Open Apr. to June and Oct. on Sun. only 10–1; Holy Week and July to Sept. 10–1 and 4–7; closed Nov. to Mar.

Sitges (Barcelona). **Museo Cau Ferrat,** Fonollar. Excellent museum with Spanish and Catalan paintings, two El Greco's, furniture, glass, ceramics, and photographs. Open Tues. to Sat. 10–1 and 5–7 (4–6 in winter), Sun. 10–3; closed Mon.
Museo Maricel del Mar, Fonollar. Collection of religious objects, sculpture and Romanesque and Gothic works of art. Open Tues. to Sat. 10–1 and 5–7 (4–6 in winter), Sun. 9–3; closed Mon.
Museo Romantic Can Llopis, San Gaudencio 1. Collection of clocks, musical instruments, porcelain, furniture and books from the 19th century, and 17th–19th century doll collection. Open Tues. to Sat. 10–1.30 and 5–7 (4–6 in winter), Sun. 10–2; closed Mon.

Tarragona. The **Roman Amphitheater** is next to the Parque del Milagro; the **Roman Aqueduct,** dating from the 2nd century A.D., and the second most important in Spain after the one in Segovia, is 4 km. out of town on the approach to the A7 freeway; **Scipio's Tower** is 5 km. out on the road to Barcelona.
Cathedral, Plaça de la Seu. Largest cathedral in Catalonia. Open daily 10–1 and 4–7.
Museo Arqueológico, Pza. del Rey. Archeological Museum with a good coin collection. Open Tues. to Sat. 10–1.30 and 4.30–8 (4–7 in winter), Sun. 10–2; closed Mon.
Museo de Arte Moderno, Santa Ana 8. Works by local artists. Open Tues. to Sat. 10–1 and 5–8, Sun. 11–2; closed Mon.
Museo de Historia de Tarragona, Pretorio Romano. History and development of Tarragona from Roman times to the Middle Ages. Open Tues. to Sat. 10–1 and 4.30–8 (10–1.30 and 4–7 in winter), Sun. 10–2; closed Mon.
Museo Paleocristiano, Pza. Independencia. Sarcophagus, mosaics, ceramics, glass and excavations revealing early burial chambers. Open Tues. to Sat. 10–1 and 4.30–8 (10–1.30 and 4–7 in winter), Sun. 10–2; closed Mon.
Roman Forum, Calle Lérida. Open daily 9–7.

Roman Walls and Archeological Promenade, Paseo Torroja and Avda. del Imperio. Open daily 10–8 in summer; 10–1.30 and 4.30–6.30 in winter.

Terrassa (Barcelona). **Castillo Cartuja Vallparadis,** Salmerón. Paintings, sculpture and ceramics from the 12th to 19th centuries in an old Carthusian Castle. Open Tues. to Sat. 10–1.30 and 3–7, Sun. 10–2; closed Mon.

Casa Museo Alegre de Sagrera, Font Vella 29. House with three 18th-century rooms furnished in the period; ceramics, bronzes, marble and Chinese paintings. Open Sun. 11–2 and by arrangement.

Museo Textil, Salmerón 19–21. Comprehensive collection of garments, robes and costumes connected with Terrassa's important textile industry. Open Tues. to Sat. 10–1 and 5–8, Sun. 10–2; closed Mon.

Tortosa (Tarragona). **Cathedral** 13th-century, packed with treasures including medieval Flemish tapestries. Open 8–1, 5–9.

Convent of Santo Domingo. Houses the **Archeology Museum,** a valuable collection of medieval documents and a **Folk Museum.** Open Mon. to Sat. 9–3; closed Sun.

Palacio Episcopal (Bishop's Palace), Muelle. 14th-century Gothic building. Open daily 10–2; closed Sun.

El Vendrell (Tarragona). **Casa Museu Pau Casals,** Palfuriana 14. Birthplace of the great cellist Pablo Casals with many of his mementoes. Open Mon. to Sun. 11–2 and 5–8 in summer; Mon. to Fri. 11–2, Sat. and Sun. 11–2 and 5–8 in winter.

Vic (Barcelona). **Cathedral.** Dating from 11th century but restored in neo-Classical style in the 19th century. Murals by **José María Sert.** Open daily 10–1 and 4–7.

Museo Episcopal, Plaça del Bisbe Oliva. Interesting Episcopal Museum; Romanesque art, polychrome sculptures, medieval garments, manuscripts and a painting by Lluis Borrassa from 1445. Open daily 10–1 and 4–6; Sun. and fiestas 10–1 only. Nov.–Apr. 10–1 only.

Vilafranca Del Penedes (Barcelona). The center of the Catalan vineyards and famous for its wines, especially whites. **Palacio Real,** Pza. Jaime I. Gothic palace, residence of the kings of Aragón and where King Pedro III died. Today it houses the **City Museum** (ceramics, archeology, art) and the **Wine Museum.** Palace is open daily 10–2 and 4–6; closed Mon.

Museo del Vino (Wine Museum), Pza. Jaime I. History and process of wine making, ancient utensils and presses. Open Tues. to Fri. 10–2 and 4–7, Sat. and Sun. 10–2 and 4.30–7.30; closed Mon.

Vilanova I La Geltru (Barcelona). **Castillo de la Geltrú,** Calle de la Torre. Much restored 12th-century castle housing **Museum of Contemporary Art.** Open Tues. to Sat. 10–2 and 4–7, Sun. 10–2; closed Mon.

Museo Balaguer, Avda. Victor Balaguer. 16th–20th century paintings and oriental art from China and Japan. Also Spanish furniture from 17th–19th centuries, Romanesque art and personal mementoes of Victor Balaguer. Open Tues. to Sat. 10–2 and 4–7, Sun. 10–2 only; closed Mon.

Museo del Ferrocarril (Train Museum) at the RENFE station. Steam engines, old rail cars and train memorabilia. Check visiting hours with the Tourist Office.

Museo Romántico Can Papiol, Calle Mayor 32. 19th-century house with period decor and furnishings, clocks, carriages and bicycles. Open Tues. to Sat. 10–1.30 and 5–7, Sun. 10–2; closed Mon.

NATURE RESERVES. There are several nature reserves in the Catalan Pyrenees and at Albiñana in Tarragona province. In the Vall d'Aran in northern Lérida is the magnificent National Park of Aigües Torres and Lake San Mauricio covering an area of 10,500 hectares (25,950 acres), and whose highest peak, the Comoloformo is 3,030 meters (9,940 feet). The nearest villages with accommodations to the park are Boí, Caldes de Boí, Barruera, Espot, Rialp, Sort and Esterri d'Aneu.

SPORTS. Skiing. There are ski resorts in the Catalan Pyrenees at Vallter, Nuria, La Molina and La Masella in Gerona province; and at Port del Compte, Lés, Llesuy, Super Espot, Baqueira-Beret and La Tuca de Viella in Lérida province.

Golf. Golf courses at Sitges and Sant Cugat in Barcelona province.

Tennis. Tennis clubs are numerous all along the coast of Barcelona and Tarragona provinces and many hotels both on the coast and inland have their own tennis courts.

Watersports. The coastal resorts of the Costa Dorada are ideally suited to swimming, sailing, water skiing and wind surfing; good yachting harbors at Sitges and Tarragona.

Colonia Güell —Gaudí

BARCELONA

The Catalan Capital

With a population of around two million, Barcelona, second largest city in the country, has always had an international flair and sophistication all of its own. Its high cultural level, industrial muscle and thriving maritime commerce—cemented by a language of its own—have long made Barcelona a formidable rival to Madrid, often surpassing the capital in industrial production and intellectual achievement. This has given the citizens of Barcelona a local pride—they feel that they are essentially different from the rest of Spain. With the world's richest soccer club and a fashion industry fast rivalling those of Milan and Paris, Barcelona's latest cause for rejoicing is its nomination as the host of the 1992 Olympics. A huge modernization program is underway in readiness, and the excitement and confidence of its citizens is summed up in a slogan splashed all over the city, *Barcelona, mes que mai*—"Barcelona, more than ever."

Through the centuries Catalans, and especially the citizens of Barcelona, have forged a reputation for themselves in industriousness while remaining appreciative of the pleasures of life. Like the Basques, they take great pride in their own culture. The Catalan language (they will argue fiercely that it is *not* a dialect of Spanish Castilian or French) is commonly spoken in most households, more now than in the thirty-five years when it was outlawed by the Franco regime. You will hear people speaking Catalan in the streets and shops, schooling is in Catalan, plays are put on in Catalan, a newspaper is printed in that language, and there is a Catalan radio and television station.

Though no-one would begrudge the Catalans the increasing use of their language after almost four decades of repression, the tremendous zeal with which this fiercely nationalistic people have embraced the legalization of their own tongue has led to some confusion for the foreign tourist and indeed for many non-Catalan speaking Spaniards (some 40% of Barcelona's population are not native Catalan speakers and the language barrier has proved a big obstacle for the large migrant workforce from Andalusia). Barcelona's streets are now known by both their Catalan and Castilian names and the visitor with no knowledge of Spanish may encounter some difficulty in relating the street name plaques to his street map. It is also not uncommon for theater and concert programs, and museum exhibitions to be labeled solely in Catalan so great is the determination of the City Hall to promote the use of Catalan.

The ordered cosmopolitanism of Barcelona will immediately be evident to the tourist as he explores the city. Many streets are cobbled and lined with trees as in France, and there are French-type cafés with glass-enclosed terraces in the winter which invite you to while away an hour. Drivers tend to be more careful than in Madrid, zebra crossings for pedestrians are usually respected and red lights not jumped. The food, too, is essentially different from Madrid's. You'll often be served more imaginative dishes and desserts than in the rest of the Peninsula. Tea rooms and pastry shops reminiscent of France and Germany lure afternoon idlers in the elegant section of town. This polish, however, goes hand in hand with a taste for local specialties in the portside taverns; the *paella* here rivals any made in Valencia.

The city lies between two mountains, Tibidabo and Montjuïc, but sprawls a good deal, so you will find yourself resorting to taxis, buses or the Metro (subway). The Ramblas, the traditional main street, continues to be a hive of activity at all hours of the day and night, but no really centralized section can be pinpointed; cinemas, clubs and restaurants are scattered all around the city. The Passeig de Gràcia perhaps comes closest to being an entertainment and shopping nexus.

As a large port city, there are the seamier sides as well, which makes for greater diversity and contrasts than in cities of the interior. You can opt for the luxury shops and restaurants on and off the Passeig de Gràcia or plunge into the backstreet turmoil of the ancient quarter known as the Barrio Gótico (Gothic Quarter).

The climate of Barcelona is extremely mild—witness the palm trees in some streets and squares. In summer, weather can be uncomfortably hot and muggy, and air-pollution is a mounting problem. Beaches near Barcelona are not recommended for bathers who value their health, but north on the Costa Brava and south at Castelldefels and Sitges, well-equipped but overcrowded resorts provide escape-valves.

A Little History

Barcelona's history dates back to its founding by the Phoenicians. This Greek colony was subsequently occupied by the Carthaginians in 237 B.C., who called it Barcino (after the ruling House of Barca). Later the Romans changed its name to Julia Faventia Augusta Pia Barcino and made it the capital of the Roman province of Layetania. After a spell as capital of the Goths, it was conquered in 713 by the Moors, who in turn were ousted by the Franks. Under the Counts of Barcelona, starting in 874, the city attained its independence.

In the 11th century, Ramón Berenguer I compiled a sort of constitution, the *Usatges,* which proclaimed the region's autonomy and sovereignty, but in 1137 Catalonia became part of Aragón. During the 14th and 15th centuries the city prospered immensely thanks to its maritime trade, for Aragón then ruled over such Mediterranean colonies as the Balearics, Sardinia, and the Kingdom of Naples and Sicily. Finally, in 1474 when Isabella of Castile married Ferdinand of Aragón, Barcelona became part of united Spain, and ceased to be a capital.

However, the tradition of independence has always remained uppermost in the life of Catalans and on numerous occasions over the past centuries the region has revolted against the central authority of Madrid. Catalans have jealously guarded their language and culture and still only reluctantly think of themselves as Spaniards.

During the Civil War, Barcelona was a stronghold of the Republic, and base for many anarchists and communists. It resisted the approach of Franco's troops till very nearly the end of the conflict. Franco rigorously suppressed Catalan separatism and the Catalan language. But since the establishment of regional autonomy in 1979, the Catalans have been making headway in reinstating their customs and language. In 1980 Catalans voted for their first home-rule parliament since the Civil War and both then, and at the 1984 and 1988 elections, the Catalan Nationalist Party, led by Jordi Pujol, won a majority.

Exploring Barcelona

Barcelona offers the tourist a great variety of sights ranging from some excellent museums to the weird architectural vagaries of Antonio Gaudí, the leading figure in Barcelona's *art nouveau* movement which gripped the city from 1880 till the outbreak of World War I, and was known locally as *"Modernismo."* A good spot to start your wanderings is the Plaça de Catalunya, the large, somewhat amorphous square which is the intersection of several important streets.

The Ramblas

If you leave the Plaça de Catalunya by way of the Ramblas, you reach a section of the city which is a fascinating amalgam of earthy taverns and atmospheric squares and alleys. The Ramblas, which changes its name every block or so, is a lively, thronged promenade flanked by trees, running through the center of this area. It is lined with bookshops, flower stalls, and stands crammed with bird cages and fish tanks and is one of the most colorful streets in the whole country. The traffic roars down either side of it, while the middle section is happily still devoted to the needs of pedestrians. The Ramblas is always bustling with an endless stream of browsers, tourists, sailors and businessmen. The activity is such that you don't know where to look first, whether at the stalls, the crowd, the bootblacks and lottery-ticket sellers, the cafes, or at the venerable old buildings lining the street.

All the way along, cross streets beckon you to plunge deeper into the maze-like area. In contrast to the elegance of the section north of the Plaça de Catalunya, the Ramblas is lined mostly with inexpensive hotels, hooker clubs, snack bars and old cafes. Intermingled with these are historic monuments such as the church of Nuestra Señora de Belén on the right, on the corner of Carrer Carme, and opposite it the ocher-colored Baroque Palacio de Moya built in 1702. The colored paving stones of the Rambla de las Flores (or Sant Josep) were designed by the Catalan artist Joan Miró. Again on your right, notice the Casa Antigua Figueras, with its lovely mosaic façade and exquisite old fittings, and the Palacio de la Virreina, built by a viceroy of Peru in 1778. If you branch off to the right here for a couple of blocks you come to the ancient Hospital de la Cruz surrounded by a cluster of other 15th-century buildings which are today cultural and educational institutes, including the Central Library and a school for Catalan studies. You can wander through the courtyard of the Casa de Convalecencia which is particularly impressive with its Renaissance columns and its scenes portrayed in *azulejos,* and which in summer is sometimes used for outdoor concerts or theater performances. Return to the Ramblas and a little further down on the right, you reach a famous Barcelona landmark, the Liceo Opera House, one of the oldest and largest in Europe and long the pride of the city. It was built in 1845–7 and holds an audience of 5,000.

The Plaça Reial

One of the narrow side streets on the left leads to the Plaça Reial, a porticoed square in the Mediterranean style, where several tall palm trees in the center of the square add a touch of tropical voluptuousness. Take care here as the Plaça has sadly become a meeting place for drop-outs and drug addicts. The best and safest time to visit this lovely square is on Sunday mornings when the crowds gather to listen to the orators and peruse the popular stamp and coin stalls. Just behind the Plaça, on the Carrer Escudellers, is a cluster of bars and restaurants teeming with visitors and Spaniards of every description. Some of Barcelona's oldest and most atmospheric restaurants are located here, including Los Caracoles, famous since the turn of the century for its seafood, paellas and, of course, snails.

From the Carrer Escudellers down to the port you can plunge into the area of narrow streets known as the Barrio Chino, though the Chinese have long since departed. It swarms with somewhat shady nightclubs and single men usually get inviting nods from the ladies who frequent the little bars in the humid lanes. A word of warning at this stage: purse snatching is a big problem in Barcelona, especially in the narrow streets of the Gothic Quarter. The worst affected area is the lower regions of the Gothic Quarter between the Plaça Arc del Teatre and the port; you should take extra care at all times in this area. Best leave your purse and your camera behind if you are venturing below the Plaça Reial or Nou de la Rambla, and avoid the siesta hours when the streets are often deserted.

The Port

At the bottom of the Ramblas lies the Plaça del Portal de la Pau with its bronze statue of Columbus perched on a high column; ride the elevator to the top for a fine view of the port and the city. Anchored in the water nearby is a replica of the *Santa María,* Columbus's flagship, and on the right of the Ramblas is the excellent Maritime Museum chronicling the

BARCELONA

0 Miles ½

0 Kilometers ½

(NOT ALL STREETS SHOWN)

Points of Interest

1 Arc del Triomf
2 Barri Gòtic: Catedral;
  Museu Frederic Marés;
  Plaça del Rei
3 Basilica de la Mercè
4 Castell de Montjuïc;
  Museu del Exèrcit (Army Museum)
5 Fundació Joan Miró
6 Generalitat; Ajuntament;

Palau Centelles
7 Gran Teatre del Liceu
8 Hospital de la Santa Creu
9 La Llotja
10 Museu Arqueològic
11 Museu d'Art de Catalunya
12 Museu d'Art Modern
13 Museu Etnològic
14 Museu Marítim
15 Museu Picasso

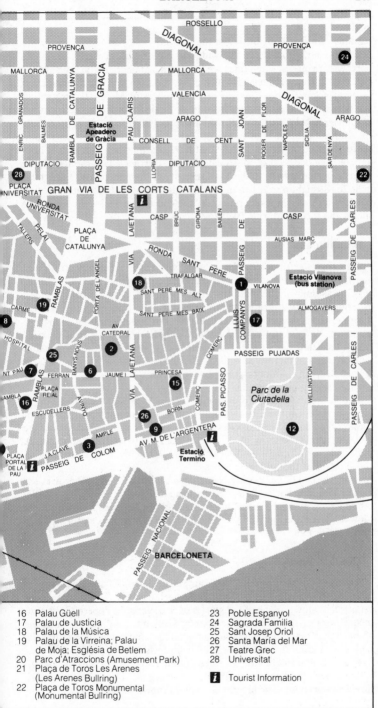

16 Palau Güell
17 Palau de Justicia
18 Palau de la Música
19 Palau de la Virreina; Palau
   de Moja; Església de Betlem
20 Parc d'Atraccions (Amusement Park)
21 Plaça de Toros Les Arenes
   (Les Arenes Bullring)
22 Plaça de Toros Monumental
   (Monumental Bullring)

23 Poble Espanyol
24 Sagrada Familia
25 Sant Josep Oriol
26 Santa María del Mar
27 Teatre Grec
28 Universitat

i Tourist Information

importance of Barcelona as a world port. The museum is housed in the medieval Reales Ataranzanas, one of Europe's oldest shipyards with the remains of a fort built by Jaime the Conqueror.

On the left, going down the wide Passeig de Colom which flanks the port where you can sometimes see battleships anchored, you come to the Plaça del Duc de Medinaceli, with a pretty fountain, and the Comandancia General, formerly the Convent of the Mothers of Mercy (1846), with a pretty patio. The facade dates from 1929. Behind it is the Baroque church of La Merced (1775), with a Renaissance portico from a previous church. La Merced contains the image of Barcelona's patron saint, the 16th-century Virgin of Mercy, whose feast day on September 24 is a local holiday and the occasion of much celebration. Further along the Passeig de Colom, on the corner of the Vía Laietana, is the main Post Office, built in 1926. Straight ahead lies the Avinguida Marquès de l'Argentera with the Lonja (Stock Market) rebuilt at the end of the 18th century on the site of the former Marine Exchange.

Barceloneta

Crossing over the busy Plaça Palau, you come eventually to the old quarter of Barceloneta, clustered onto the quay below Término station, which was built in 1755 and was traditionally the home of workers and fishermen. Today it is rather scruffy and run-down and many of its streets have a deserted, somewhat threatening air. But at lunchtime its main thoroughfare, the Passeig Nacional, or Moll de la Barceloneta, comes strikingly to life when the citizens of Barcelona flock here to feast on the delicious seafood of its numerous no-frills restaurants. As you walk past you will see people sitting outdoors, their plates piled high with shrimps, while others are digging into a paella.

The restaurants range from humble diners to traditional old favorites like Can Sole. On the Carrer Maquinista is a cluster of popular ones including the Pañol and Ramonet taverns. The latter is a lively haunt where the Catalans delight in ali-oli sandwiches (with tomato and garlic), smoked ham and *butifarra*. The rafters are so thickly hung with sausages and hams that the ceiling vanishes.

From the end of the Passeig Nacional, a cablecar *(teleférico)* crosses the port to Montjuïc Park offering some splendid views of the city. This cablecar can also be boarded at its halfway stage, the Torre de Jaume I on the Moll de Barcelona, only a short walk from the Columbus statue in Plaça Portal de la Pau.

The Cathedral

Another sightseeing route from our starting point of the Plaça de Catalunya is to walk down the Porta de l'Angel, past the Galerías Preciados department store, to one of the glories of Barcelona, its superb Gothic cathedral, one of the finest in the country. Just off the Plaça Nova, scene of an interesting antiques market on Thursday mornings, is a mural designed by Picasso for the College of Architects.

The cathedral is set in the so-called "Gothic" quarter of the city, a fascinating labyrinth of medieval streets and mansions, ideally suited for leisurely explorations. The present cathedral (known to the locals as La Seu) stands on the site of an earlier church, the Basilica of Santa Eulalia, which dated from A.D. 878. Work on the present structure was begun in 1298 under the kings of Aragón, and was completed around 1450. Such master builders as Jaime Fabré of Majorca and Master Roque are credited among its architects.

The two octagonal towers at either side of the transepts date from the 14th century, whereas the neo-Gothic facade on the Plaça Cristo Rei is modern (1892), as is the recent spire. The three rather somber naves measure 76 by 34 meters (249 by 111 feet), rising to a height of 23 meters (76 feet). The choirstalls by Matías Bonafe (the lower sections) and Lochner and Friedrich, two Germans of the late 15th century (for the upper sections) are astounding examples of the glories that wood-carving attained in the Middle Ages. See also the main altar, the crypt of Santa Eulalia, twenty-nine chapels and especially the magnificent cloister built in the Italian Renaissance style, finished by Roque in 1448, with capitals depicting scenes from the Bible.

Leaving the cathedral by the main door you come out into the Plaça Cristo Rei. On Sunday mornings in summer the citizens of Barcelona gather in the plaza to dance the traditional sardana, a living symbol of the tenacious regionalism of Catalonia. On Palm Sunday the mid-morning ceremony of the blessing of the palms on the steps in front of the cathedral is another spectacle well worth seeing.

The Gothic Quarter

Next, stroll through the Gothic Quarter, a warren of narrow streets with old churches and palaces dating from the 14th century. If you turn to your left on leaving the cathedral, you will pass the 15th-century Casa del Arcediano, home of the city's archives, before turning left again down the narrow Carrer Bisbe (Obispo) Irurita at the side of the cathedral towards the Plaça Sant Jaume (San Jaime). An alleyway off to the left leads to four Roman columns, remains of a temple dedicated to Augustus. On the west side of the plaza is the 15th-century Palau de la Generalitat, now the home of the Autonomous Government of Catalonia. Inside is an impressive courtyard with a beautifully balustraded staircase leading up to an arcaded gallery and the Patio de los Naranjos. Opening off this upper gallery is the Chapel and Salón de San Jorge—St. George being the patron saint of Catalonia—and the ornate Council Chambers. Facing it across the square is the Ajuntament, whose main facade dates from the 1840s, but just around the corner on Carrer Ciutat you can see one of its original facades dating back to 1400. Inside are the famous Salón de Ciento and the impressive mural of José María Sert in the Salón de Crónicas. Behind the Ajuntament, on the Baixada de Sant Miquel, you will come across the 15th-century Centelles Palace with a fine patio.

If on leaving the cathedral you turn instead to your right, you come face to face with the ancient Pía Almoina mansion, home of the Diocesan Museum and currently under restoration. Turn up the narrow street of the Comtes de Barcelona for a visit to the fascinating Federico Mares Museum. Across the museum's courtyard are the remains of the city's ancient Roman fortifications which can be visited on a ticket to the City of Barcelona Museum. Round the corner you will come upon the historic Plaça del Rei flanked by the Palacio Real; the Salón del Tinell, now an exhibition

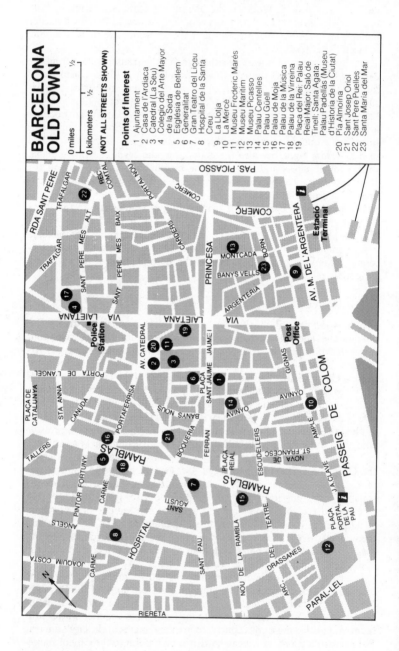

BARCELONA OLD TOWN

0 miles ½

0 kilometers ½

(NOT ALL STREETS SHOWN)

Points of Interest

1 Ajuntament
2 Casa de l'Ardiaca
3 Catedral (La Seu)
4 Colegio del Arte Mayor de la Seda
5 Església de Betlem
6 Generalitat
7 Gran Teatro del Liceu
8 Hospital de la Santa Creu
9 La Llotja
10 La Mercé
11 Museu Frederic Marés
12 Museu Marítim
13 Museu Picasso
14 Palau Centelles
15 Palau Güell
16 Palau de Moja
17 Palau de la Musica
18 Palau de la Virreina
19 Plaça de Rei: Palau Reial Major: Saló de Tinell; Santa Agata: Palau Padellàs (Museu d'Historia de la Ciutat) Pia Almoina
20 Sant Josep Oriol
21 Sant Pere Puelles
22 Santa Maria del Mar
23

hall but originally a 14th-century banqueting hall where Columbus was received by the Catholic Monarchs upon his return from America; the 14th-century Chapel of Santa Agüeda built into the old Roman walls; and the Casa Padellás which houses the Museum of the City of Barcelona.

The Picasso Museum

Next make your way to the Plaça de l'Angel between Jaume I and Vía Laietana. Cross over the broad Vía Laietana, go down the Carrer de la Princesa and turn right at the Carrer Montcada, which takes you to the Picasso Museum. The collection has been added to over the years and is now one of the world's foremost museums on the artist who spent many of his formative years in Barcelona. In 1970, the artist donated some 2,500 works to the museum, despite pressures from the French government to keep the works in that country and in the early 80s the museum expanded into a neighboring palace. The collection includes paintings, engravings and drawings ranging over his entire creative life, some dating back as far as 1895 when Picasso was only nine years old. Of special interest are his variations on Velázquez's *Las Meninas* and his sketches of Barcelona.

On leaving the Picasso Museum, walk down the Carrer Montcada whose many splendid palaces, once the homes of rich and noble Barcelona families, now house museums (the Costume Museum in particular is well worth a visit), art galleries, poster stores, and trendy bars and cafés. Montcada opens out onto the Passeig del Born, a lively nighttime area, and adjoining it lies the church of Santa María del Mar, one of the loveliest churches in Barcelona. It was built between 1329 and 1383 though some of its portals and towers are of a later date, and was designed by Jaime Fabré, one of the architects of the cathedral.

The Museum of Modern Art and the Ciudadela Park

From the Passeig del Born it is only a short walk to the Ciudadela Park, containing a cluster of museums and an excellent zoo, home of Snowflake, the world's only albino gorilla. Within the park are the Geology, Natural History and Modern Art Museums as well as the seat of the Catalan parliament and an ornate fountain by José Fontseré on which the famous Gaudí worked as an assistant.

The Museum of Modern Art—something of a misnomer since most of its paintings are 19th- or even late 18th-century—has recently made more of a concession to modern art with the opening of rooms dedicated to contemporary artists. Most of the paintings are of local fame, but it is revealing to study the late 19th-century and early 20th-century works produced in Barcelona, which proved a transition period between the Impressionists and modern nonfigurative trends. Works by Fortuny, Rusiñol, Casas, Nonell, Zuloaga, and Sunyer evoke a golden period of painting and bohemianism in Barcelona, an age which saw Picasso living here, famous artistic *tertulias* in Els Quatre Gats, and the rise of the *modernista* movement. The whole museum in fact deserves far wider recognition and is well worth a visit.

From the Arch of Triumph to the Palau de la Música

Leaving the Ciudadela Park by way of the Passeig Lluis Companys, you will see on your right the Palacio de la Justicia, the law courts, and at the end a brick triumphal arch built for the exhibition of 1888. If here you turn left and plunge into the narrow streets of the old town along Rec Comtal, you will come to a small square joining the streets of Upper and Lower St. Peter's, on which stands the church of Sant Pere Puelles, one of the oldest medieval churches in Barcelona. Then continue along Sant Pere mes alt until you come to the city's main concert hall, the Palau de la Música, a fantastic and flamboyant building erected in 1908 by Luis Domenech y Muntaner in true Gaudiesque *modernismo* style. Try to attend a concert here if only to see the magnificent interior. Finally, as you come out once more onto the Vía Laietana, note the Colegio del Arte Mayor de la Seda, a fine plastered house built between 1759 and 1763 for the Guild of Silk Weavers. From here you can wander back into the maze of streets in the Gothic Quarter heading either for the Plaça Sant Jaume and the shops along Carrer Ferran, or alternatively wind your way back up past the cathedral to our starting point of the Plaça de Catalunya.

Montjuïc Park and Its Museums

Commanding a strategic position in Montjuïc Park, laid out in 1929–30 by Forestier for the International Exhibition, is the spectacularly positioned castle. The citadel was built in 1640 by those in revolt against Philip IV. It was stormed several times, the most famous assault being in 1705 by Lord Peterborough for the Archduke Charles of Austria. In 1808, the castle was seized by the French under General Dufresne during the Peninsular War. Later, in 1842, Barcelona was bombarded from its heights. Today the castle is home to the Military Museum and weapon collection of Federico Mares. Outside is a pleasant terrace commanding magnificent views of the city and its surroundings.

The Jardines de Miramar just beneath the castle can be reached by cablecar from the Passeig Nacional in Barceloneta. There is also a cog railroad up to Montjuïc from the end of Carrer Nou de la Rambla but as it runs only when the Montjuïc funfair is open and leaves from a very depressed part of the city, it's well worth taking a cab.

The most important of the cluster of museums in the Park of Montjuïc, which includes the Museo Arqueológico (Archeology Museum) and the Joan Miró Foundation, is the Museo de Arte de Cataluña (Museum of Catalan Art and Ceramics) in the Palacio Nacional. It contains an extraordinary collection of Catalan Romanesque and Gothic art treasures, such as can be seen nowhere else in the world. The murals—a superb collection—reredos and medieval sculptures represent the zenith of this genre in Spain. More conventional Baroque and Renaissance paintings, virtually all of a religious nature, are well represented too, but it is the Romanesque works which make a visit obligatory. Among the highlights is the concave fresco Pantocrator from the church of San Clemente de Tahull.

The exhibits in the Archeological Museum date from prehistoric times to the 8th century and include many artifacts found in the Balearics as well as some from the diggings at Ampurias, the large Greek and, later,

Roman colony on the Costa Brava. The Roman items are mostly frescos and mosaics. Classical plays are performed in the nearby Greek Theater in summer.

The Joan Miró Foundation designed by Josep Lluís Sert and opened in 1975 is one of Barcelona's most exciting contemporary art galleries. Its new extension by Jaume Freixa, a pupil of Sert, was opened by Queen Sofia in 1988, but it blends in so well with Sert's original that you're unlikely to notice it's there. The foundation puts on frequent temporary exhibitions as well as housing a comprehensive collection of sketches, paintings and sculptures by Joan Miró, the Catalan artist who was born in Barcelona in 1893 and who now lies buried in the cemetery of Montjuïc. Under the Franco regime which he strongly opposed, Miró had lived quietly for several years in a self-imposed semi-exile on the island of Mallorca. When he died on Christmas Day 1983 the Catalans gave him a send-off which amounted almost to a state funeral.

The Montjuïc stadium was built in 1929 for the Exhibition and with the intention of Barcelona's hosting the 1936 Olympics—later staged by Berlin. After twice this century failing to secure the Olympic nomination, Barcelona is now celebrating the capture of its long-cherished prize by renovating the semi-derelict stadium in time for 1992, when it will seat some 80,000 people.

Also on Montjuïc is the Pueblo Español, a miniature village, with each Spanish province represented. The Pueblo, created for the 1929 Exhibition, is a kind of Spain-in-a-bottle, with the local architectural styles of each province faithfully reproduced, enabling you to wander from the walls of Avila to the wine cellars of Jérez. Though, at present, it's little more than a tourist trap selling some grossly overpriced souvenirs, it's interesting up to a point. Plans are afoot, however, to inject a shot of new life into the village before 1992, and construction work is underway to build a theater, cinema, handicrafts center, convention hall, jazz and music bars, and a children's playground. An audiovisual *Barcelona Experience* center is also planned.

Just before the park's main exit you come to a huge fountain, one of the great prides of the city, which on festive occasions and weekends in summer is made to play colored fantasies while floodlights illuminate the large Palacio Nacional behind it. A wide esplanade leads past the fair buildings used for the many exhibitions and trade fairs which Barcelona hosts. The somewhat hideous fairground complex was created originally in the 1920s and '30s, but despite its monstrous architecture, it's not unimpressive. Coming out on the rather ugly Plaça de Espanya, you are face to face with Las Arenas bullring, built in Moorish style, though it is rarely used for bullfights now. From here you can take the subway or a bus back to the Plaça de Catalunya.

The Incomparable Gaudí

One of the major attractions of Barcelona is the work of the Catalan architect, sculptor and metalsmith, Antonio Gaudí, the leading exponent of the *Modernismo* movement, a Spanish and principally Barcelonan offshoot of Art Nouveau.

Born in Reus in 1852, Gaudí met his death in Barcelona in 1926 when he was run over by a tram, dying unrecognized in a hospital two days later.

He had become a virtual recluse, dedicating his life to work on his most famous building, the Templo de la Sagrada Familia (Church of the Holy Family), in whose crypt he is buried. Aided by public subscription, Gaudí began work on the Sagrada Familia in 1882. It was far from complete on his death but had already become something of a symbol to the people of Barcelona, and during the frenzy of church burning that took place after the outbreak of the Civil War in 1936, it was the only church, other than the cathedral, that was left untouched. Today work has once again begun on the church which at present resembles a building site rather than a place of worship. Amid much controversy, the work is being carried out following Gaudí's last-known plans; it is estimated it will take a further 50 years, but could take much longer if progress continues at the present pace.

If you have never seen any of his work you should make a visit to at least one of his buildings a must. The Catalan worked more as a sculptor than an architect, changing his ideas frequently as the work progressed; molding huge masses of material with a fluidity and freedom that turned towers into candles shrouded in molten wax, staircases into swooping parabolas, doorways into troglodytes' caves.

Other specimens of Gaudí's exciting architecture are the crypt of the Güell Colony in San Baudillo, two apartment buildings, the Casa Milá and the Casa Batlló on the Passeig de Gràcia, the street lamp and bench units that line the Passeig de Gràcia, the Casa Calvet on Caspe, the Casa Vicens on Carolines, and the Palacio Güell, off the Ramblas on the Carrer Nou de la Rambla, which is now a museum dedicated to the history of Barcelona's artistic past. Perhaps most fascinating, because you can inspect it at close range is the Parque Güell on a mountain in the northwest of the city, an art nouveau extravaganza where the strange shapes have been put at the service of a park-playground, with a mosaic pagoda, undulating benches and fantastic-shaped architectural effects.

Tibidabo Mountain

Finally you may like to make the trip to the top of Tibidabo Mountain behind the city, the spot for superb views. The summit is reached by car or cab in a 20-minute drive; alternatively, you can take Bus 58 from the Plaça Catalunya to the Avda. Tibidabo is where you catch the old *tramvía blau* (1901), which connects with the funicular (rack railroad). The view over Barcelona to the Mediterranean is indeed splendid, though a similar view can be had from the much prettier Parque Güell, and on clear days— and these can be few and far between in Barcelona—you can supposedly see inland to the jagged peaks of Montserrat and even as far as the Pyrenees. The entire site might easily be idyllic were it not spoilt by an over-commercialized church, a vast radio mast, and a rather brash fairground, a classic example of the misguided exploitation of a natural beauty spot.

PRACTICAL INFORMATION FOR BARCELONA

GETTING TO TOWN FROM THE AIRPORT. The least expensive way to travel from the airport into the city center is to take the airport train to Sants Central Station. From there taxis, city buses or the metro (subway) will take you quickly to your hotel. Trains leave the airport every 30 minutes between 6 A.M. and 11 P.M. The journey takes approximately 15 minutes, and there is only one intermediate stop. From the arrivals hall, follow the signs for RENFE. During the night, when trains are not running, RENFE provides a bus service into town. There is also a daytime bus service where you can take bus EA to the Plaça de Espanya; it runs from 7.15 A.M. to 9.15 P.M. At night bus EN runs to the Plaça de Espanya.

Alternatively, you take a taxi to your destination. The cab fare into town will cost you what is on the meter (approximately 1,400–1,800 ptas.) plus an airport supplement (about 150 ptas.) and extra for luggage. Make sure the driver starts his meter when you leave the airport.

TOURIST INFORMATION. Tourist Offices are located at **Sants-Central station** (tel. 250 2594), open daily 7.30 A.M.–10.30 P.M.; **Término station** (tel. 319 2791), open Mon. to Sat. 8 A.M.–8 P.M.; **Gran Vía Corts Catalanes 658** (tel. 301 7443), open Mon. to Fri. 9–7, Sat. 9–2; **Plaça Sant Jaume** in the Ayuntamiento (tel. 318 2525), open Mon. to Fri. 9–9, Sat. 9–2; in the **Columbus monument** in Plaça Portal de la Pau, open daily except Mon. 9.30–1.30 and 4.30–8.30; and at the **airport,** open Mon. to Sat. 8–8, Sun. 8–3.

TELEPHONE CODE. The area code for the city of Barcelona and the entire Barcelona province is (93). You need only dial the (93) if you are calling from outside Barcelona province, from anywhere within the province, just dial the number. When calling Barcelona from abroad, the area code is (3).

HOW TO GET AROUND. Modern Barcelona, north of the Plaça de Catalunya, is largely built on a grid system, though there is no helpful numbering system as in the U.S. However, the old part of town—from the Plaça de Catalunya to the port and ringed by the Rondas and Ciudadela Park—is quite different altogether. Here the narrow streets wind and twist in all directions. It is an area which can only be explored on foot, so before you plunge into this fascinating labyrinth, best arm yourself with a good street map.

There is a transport information kiosk in the Plaça de Catalunya (opposite Carrer Bergara and the Banco Bilbao), open 8–7 Mon. to Fri., 8–1 on Sat., which deals mainly with city bus transport. Here you can obtain maps of the bus and metro system.

By Metro. The subway system is already fairly extensive and is currently being further enlarged. This is the cheapest form of public transport and probably the easiest to use. You pay a flat fare of 55 ptas. no matter how far you travel; on Sundays and fiestas fares are 5 ptas. higher. Savings can be made by buying a *tarjeta multiviaje* from metro station ticket offices, branches of the Caixa de Pensions de Barcelona, or from the Plaça de Catalunya transport kiosk. Blue *tarjetas* cost 300 ptas. (1988 price) and are valid for 10 rides on the metro, tramvía blau, Montjuïc funicular, and Ferrocarrils de la Generalitat suburban trains. Pocket maps of the system are sometimes available from ticket offices.

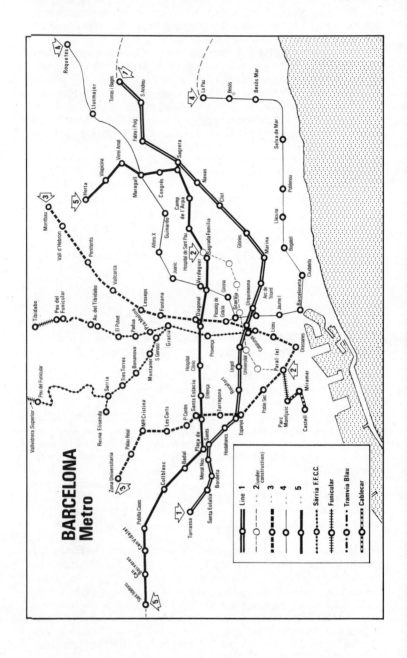

By Bus. Most of the bus routes pass through the Plaça de Catalunya; again there is a flat fare system and again it's a little higher on Sundays (about 55 ptas. and 60 ptas.). A red *tarjeta multiviaje,* good for ten rides on buses as well as the metro, tramvía blau, Montjuïc funicular, and Ferrocarrils de la Generalitat trains, costs 345 ptas. (1988 price) from the Plaça de Catalunya kiosk and is the best all-inclusive ticket. Maps of the bus network are available from the kiosk or tourist offices. To go to the beach at Castelldefels, take the UC from outside the University.

By Taxi. Taxis in Barcelona have a much higher initial charge than in other Spanish cities, making short rides expensive whereas longer rides work out much the same as elsewhere. Taxis available for hire show a *Libre* sign in daytime and a small green lamp at night. When you begin your ride a standard charge of 200 ptas. will be shown on the meter. Supplements are 40 ptas. for suitcases, 55 ptas. for leaving a train station, and 150 ptas. to or from the airport. In Zone A fares are 50 ptas. a km. between 6 A.M. and 10 P.M., and 70 ptas. a km. from 10 P.M.–6 A.M. and on weekends. Zone B costs 70 ptas. a km. during the day and 80 ptas. at night and weekends (1988 rates). Make sure your driver turns down the flag when you start your journey.

RAILROAD STATIONS. Barcelona has three mainline railroad stations, the most important being **Barcelona Central** (or **Sants**) at the end of Avda de Roma, Europe's most modern station. Next comes the ancient **Estación de Francia** (or **Término**) on Avda. Marquès del' Argentera near the port. Trains to France leave from here. There is also an underground station, **Passeig de Gracià,** at the intersection of the Passeig de Gracià and Aragó. Many trains cross Barcelona stopping at all three stations but be sure to check which station you should board your train at.

For destinations outside the Barcelona area, buy your tickets well in advance from any of the three stations. Go to the windows marked *Venta Anticipada Largo Recorrido,* open approximately 8 A.M.–9 P.M. Trains to the airport leave from Sants Station. For destinations in Catalonia, local Ferrocarrils de la Generalitat trains leave from the underground stations in the Plaça de Catalunya and the Plaça de Espanya to Martorell, Igualada, Manresa and Berga. To the Costa Brava, from the Rodalies (Cercanías) Station at Término. Trains to Montserrat leave from the Plaça d'Espanya and connect with a teleférico (cable car) for the Monastery.

BUS STATIONS. There is no central bus depot in Barcelona though buses to most Spanish destinations leave from the old **Estación del Norte** on the Avda. Vilanova. For Montserrat, a *Juliá* bus runs daily at 9 A.M. from Plaça Universitat 12. The tourist office can help with bus schedules and we would advise you always to check your departure points well in advance of your journey. *Alsina Gräells,* Ronda Universitat 4, runs buses to Lérida, Soria and Andorra; *Juliá,* Ronda Universitat 5, to Zaragoza, Huesca and Montserrat (buses leave from Plaça Universitat 12); *Montesol,* Numància 63, to Bilbao, Jaen and Seville; and to Sitges from the Estación del Norte and the Plaça Universitat.

For buses abroad, *Iberbus,* Vergara 2, have services to Italy, France, Belgium, Holland and London. *Juliá,* Ronda Universitat 5 to France, Switzerland, Germany, Scandinavia and London. *Via Tourisme,* Pau

Claris 117 to Scandinavia, Holland, Belgium, France, Germany and London.

HOTELS. For a city of its size and importance, Barcelona has long been underendowed with hotels, but, with the coming of the Olympics in 1992, the city's hotel industry is having to think afresh. New hotels are going up fast, international chains are vying for business, and of the existing hotels, many have either undergone, or will soon undergo, extensive renovation programs. At present most hotels in the downtown area around the Ramblas and the Plaça de Catalunya are older style hotels whereas the newer more modern hotels tend to be situated further out either along the Diagonal or in the residential suburbs in the hills on the far side of it. When an address is given as Gran Vía, this refers to Gran Vía de les Corts Catalanes.

Deluxe

Avenida Palace, Gran Vía 605 (tel. 301 9600). 211 rooms. Centrally located between the Passeig de Gracià and Rambla Catalunya. An elegant, old-style hotel which has been restored; rooms can be a little plain but there are several interesting features. AE, DC, MC, V.

Duques de Bergara, Bergara 11 (tel. 301 5151). 56 rooms. A recently opened hotel in a beautiful Modernista house (1898) just off Plaça de Catalunya; top marks for distinction and quiet elegance.

Princesa Sofía, Plaça Pius XII (tel. 330 7111). 505 rooms. Huge modern hotel with pool and all amenities. Located quite a long way out on the Diagonal close to the University City. Panoramic dining room on 19th floor. AE, DC, MC, V.

Ramada Renaissance, Ramblas 111 (tel. 318 6200). 210 rooms. Formerly the *Manila,* this 4-star hotel has recently been renovated to high standards of elegance and comfort.

Ritz, Gran Vía 668 (tel. 318 5200). 161 rooms. One of the original hotels founded by Cesar Ritz and still the grand old lady of Barcelona hotels. Extensive refurbishment has restored its former splendor, luxury and comfort. AE, DC, MC, V.

Sarriá Gran Hotel, Avda. Sarriá 50 (tel. 410 6060). 314 rooms. Near the Plaça Francesc Macià, and remodelled to cater for the businessman's needs. AE, DC, V.

Expensive

Arenas, Capitán Arenas 20 (tel. 204 0300). 59 rooms. Modern, in pleasant residential suburb. AE, DC, MC, V.

Balmoral, Vía Augusta 5 (tel. 217 8700). 94 rooms. Comfortable, functional hotel just off Diagonal. AE, DC, MC, V.

Barcelona, Caspe 1 (tel. 302 5858). 64 rooms. Good modern hotel very centrally located just off Rambla de Catalunya and only a short distance from Plaça de Catalunya.

Castellnou, Castellnou 61 (tel. 203 0554). 29 rooms. A new hotel out in the residential Sarrià district.

Colón, Avda. Catedral 7 (tel. 301 1404). 161 rooms. In the Gothic Quarter overlooking cathedral square. An older, cozy hotel with a charm and intimacy of its own, though the cathedral bells can be disturbing. AE, DC, MC, V.

Condes de Barcelona, Passeig de Gracià 75 (tel. 215 0616). 100 rooms. Recently opened in a superb *modernista* house; stunning decor and currently one of the most fashionable hotels in town. Top rates. AE, DC, MC, V.

Condor, Vía Augusta 127 (tel. 209 4511). 78 rooms. Parking and good amenities. In smart residential area just beyond Diagonal. AE, DC, MC, V.

Cristal, Diputació 257 (tel. 301 6600). 148 rooms. Good location close to center on corner of Rambla Catalunya. AE, DC, MC, V.

Derby, Loreto 21 (tel. 322 3215). 116 rooms. Smart modern hotel not far from Plaça Francesc Macià; a sister hotel to the more expensive Gran Derby. AE, DC, MC, V.

Gala Placidia, Vía Augusta 112 (tel. 217 8200). 31 rooms. A luxurious apartment hotel, though officially classed as 3-star. AE, DC, MC, V.

Gran Derby, Loreto 28 (tel. 322 3215). 39 rooms. A plush suites-only hotel with novel decor and high standards close to the *Sarria Gran* and *Derby* hotels. AE, DC, MC, V.

Gran Hotel Calderón, Rambla Catalunya 26 (tel. 301 0000). 244 rooms. Long a leading contender, a recent refit has given it a bright new image. Pool, sun terrace; one of the best. AE, DC, MC, V.

Hespería, Los Vergós 20 (tel. 204 5551). 144 rooms. In the residential district of Sarriá. AE, DC, MC, V.

Majestic, Passeig de Gracià 70 (tel. 215 4512). 344 rooms. Well-renovated traditional hotel with pool. AE, DC, MC, V.

Presidente, Diagonal 570 (tel. 200 2111). 161 rooms, pool. Elegant 5-star hotel on corner of Muntaner in Plaça Francesc Macià area. AE, DC, MC, V.

Putxet, Putxet 68 (tel. 212 5158). 125 rooms. Recently opened apartment hotel in the Lesseps area beyond the Diagonal; high rates. AE, DC, MC, V.

Regente, Rambla Catalunya 76 (tel. 215 2570). 78 rooms. An older-style hotel with pool on the corner of Valéncia. AE, DC, MC, V.

Royal, Ramblas 117 (tel. 301 9400). 108 rooms. Conveniently located near the top of Ramblas, the Royal has recently undergone a thorough facelift.

Moderate

Astoria, París 203 (tel. 209 8311). 109 rooms. Functional '50s-style hotel near Diagonal between Aribau and Enric Granados. AE, DC, MC, V.

Bonanova Park, Capitan Arenas 51 (tel. 204 0900). 60 rooms. In fashionable residential area in the hills beyond the Diagonal. AE, DC, MC, V.

Castellnou, Castellnou 61 (tel. 203 0554). 29 rooms. A new hotel out in the residential Sarrià district.

Covadonga, Diagonal 596 (tel. 209 5511). 76 rooms. Stylish older hotel close to Plaça Francesc Macià. AE, DC, MC, V.

Gran Vía, Gran Vía 642 (tel. 318 1900). 48 rooms. Elegant old hotel between Passeig de Gracià and Pau Claris.

Habana, Gran Vía 647 (tel. 301 0750). 65 rooms. Genteel and old-fashioned establishment on a smart central street. AE, DC, V.

Mitre, Bertrán 15 (tel. 212 1104). Small hotel quite a way from center in residential suburb. AE, DC, MC, V.

Montecarlo, Rambla dels Estudis 124 (tel. 317 5800). Some of the public rooms have retained their charming turn-of-the-century decor, but bedrooms are only functional; good location on Ramblas.

Oriente, Ramblas 45 (tel. 302 2558). 142 rooms. Barcelona's oldest hotel, opened in 1843. Its public rooms are a delight; the ballroom and dining room have lost none of their 19th-century magnificence, though the bedrooms have undergone featureless renovation and the hotel tends to cater to budget tour groups. AE, DC, MC, V.

Regencia Colón, Sagristans 13 (tel. 318 9858). 55 rooms. A somber but comfortable annexe to the Colón, close to cathedral. AE, DC, MC, V.

Rialto, Ferrán 40 (tel. 318 5212). 112 rooms. Stylish old-world hotel in heart of Gothic Quarter just off Plaça Sant Jaume. AE, DC, MC, V.

Suizo, Plaça de l'Angel 12 (tel. 315 4111). 50 rooms. A cozy old favorite on the edge of the Gothic Quarter just off Vía Laietana and overlooking Jaume I metro. AE, DC, MC, V.

Terminal, Provença 1 (tel. 321 5350). 75 rooms. Recent hotel on 7th floor of a modern block opposite Sants Station. Pleasant service and comfortable, functional rooms. AE, DC, MC, V.

Tres Torres, Calatrava 32 (tel. 417 7300). 56 rooms. Small hotel in the residential area of Tres Torres on the hill beyond the Diagonal. AE, DC, MC, V.

Wilson, Diagonal 568 (tel. 209 2511). 52 rooms. An older and traditional hotel on the Diagonal on corner of Bon Pastor and Muntaner. AE, DC, MC, V.

Inexpensive

Cataluña, Santa Anna 22 (tel. 301 9150). 40 rooms. Small hotel in the old town between Ramblas and the Porta de l'Angel just below the Plaça Catalunya.

Continental, Rambla Canaletas 136 (tel. 301 2508). 30 rooms. A deluxe hostel in a stylish old house with elegant canopies, at the top of the Ramblas near the Plaça Catalunya. Friendly reception and a long-standing favorite.

Cortes, Santa Anna 25 (tel. 317 9212). 46 rooms. Under the same management and a sister hotel to the *Cataluña*. AE, MC, V.

Internacional, Ramblas 78 (tel. 302 2566). 62 rooms. Friendly old-fashioned hotel right opposite Liceo Opera House. AE, DC, V.

Moderno, Hospital 11 (tel. 301 4154). 57 rooms. Pleasant hotel on corner of the Ramblas near Boqueria market; very popular with Spaniards.

Nouvel, Santa Anna 18 (tel. 301 8274). 76 rooms. Simple but in a charming old-fashioned house close to the *Cataluña* and *Cortés*.

Urbis, Passeig de Gracià 23 (tel. 317 2766). 61 rooms. Excellent deluxe hostel, very popular with Spaniards.

Villa de Madrid, Pza. Villa de Madrid (tel. 317 4916). 28 rooms. Modestly priced 3-star hotel in small square in Gothic Quarter just off Ramblas.

Youth Hostels. Barcelona has four Youth Hostels: the **Albergue Verge de Montserrat,** Mare de Déu del Coll 41–51 (tel. 213 8633), nearest metro: Lesseps, or buses 25 or 28; the **Albergue Pere Tarres,** Numància 149 (tel. 230 1606) not far from Sants Station; the main one is the **Albergue de Ju-**

ventud on Passeig Pujades 29 (tel. 300 3104) near the Ciudadela Park; **BCN-Xatrac** Youth Hostel, Pelai 62, overlooking the Plaça de Catalunya.

RESTAURANTS. Barcelona is well endowed with fine restaurants. Catalan cooking is wholesome with hearty portions. You'll find good paellas here and snails are also a specialty. Pasta, too, is more popular here than elsewhere in Spain. The seafood is also excellent. Other local specialties are *butifarra,* a typically Catalan sausage, and *rovellons,* an earthy-tasting mushroom. *Espinacas a la catalana* (spinach with garlic, pine nuts, and raisins) makes a tasty appetizer, and *music* is a typically Catalan dessert of dried fruits with a glass of moscatel wine. Barcelona has long been a notorious port; should you come across street walkers near any of our recommended restaurants, rest assured, they—the restaurants!—are quite respectable inside.

Many Barcelona restaurants are closed on Saturday night and Sunday, so do check in advance. Many also close for a month in summer, usually in August.

Deluxe

El Dorado Petit, Dolors Monserdá 51 (tel. 204 5153). Considered one of Barcelona's very best restaurants; exquisite cuisine and beautiful setting in a private villa. Closed Sun. and two weeks in Aug. AE, MC, V.

Finisterre, Diagonal 469 (tel. 239 5576). International dishes served in great style. Especially recommended are the *steak tartare* and the sweet *soufflés* for dessert. Closed in Aug. AE, DC, MC, V.

Orotava, Consell de Cent 335 (tel. 302 3128). This fashionable spot has a high reputation for its elegant setting and *haute cuisine.* Its seafood and game specialties are outstanding. Closed Sun. AE, DC, MC, V.

Reno, Tuset 27 (tel. 200 9129). An elegant restaurant on the corner of Travessera de Gracià much famed for its *haute cuisine* and especially well recommended for business entertainment. The *Menu Reno* is a wise choice allowing you to sample several of the best dishes. AE, DC, MC, V.

Vía Veneto, Ganduxer 10 (tel. 200 7024). Highly recommended for the best in food and professional service. Splendid decor. AE, DC, MC, V.

Expensive

Agut d'Avignon, Trinidad 3 (tel. 302 6034). Hidden at the end of the first alley on the right off Avinyó leading out of Ferran in the Gothic Quarter. Rustic atmosphere; a favorite with politicians. Catalan cuisine and game specialties in season. Reservation essential. Closed Sun., Easter Week. AE, DC, MC, V.

Ara-Cata, Dr. Ferran 33 (tel. 204 1053). Located in the residential suburb of Pedralbes, its strange name is an abbreviation of Aragón-Catalonia, the owner being Aragonés and his wife Catalan. Outstanding food. Closed Sat. and in the evenings of fiestas, Easter Week and Aug. AE, DC, MC, V.

Azulete, Vía Augusta 281 (tel. 203 5943). One of the most beautiful restaurants in Barcelona, the dining room in an old conservatory, filled with flowers and plants. Highly imaginative cooking, a mixture of Catalan, French and Italian with an interesting blend of traditional and new dishes. Closed Sat. lunch, Sun. and fiestas, and first two weeks of Aug. AE, DC, MC, V.

La Balsa, Infanta Isabel 4 (tel. 211 5048). Up in the hills just above Plaça Bonanova, this fabulous chic restaurant won an award for its architecture; original cuisine, and great outdoor terrace. Closed Sun., and Mon. lunch. AE, DC, V.

Botafumeiro, Major de Gracià 81 (tel. 218 4230). One of Barcelona's best seafood restaurants. Closed Sun. P.M., Mon., and Aug. AE, DC, MC, V.

La Cuineta, Paradis 4 (tel. 315 0111). Intimate small restaurant in 17th-century house just off Plaça Sant Jaume; specializes in Catalan cooking. Good service. Closed Mon. AE, DC, MC, V.

La Dorada, Travessera de Gracià 44 (tel. 200 6322). Under same owner-ship as the Madrid and Seville *La Doradas,* this one too serves top fish and seafood flown in daily from Andalusia. Closed Sun. and Aug. AE, DC, V.

Florián, Bertrand i Serra 20 (tel. 212 4627). A prestigious restaurant famed for unusual cuisine. The menu changes daily depending on fresh market produce, and includes international delicacies such as caviar and more humble local produce like sardines. Closed Sun. and two weeks in Aug. DC, MC, V.

La Font del Gat, Passeig Santa Madrona (tel. 224 0224). Magnificently set on Montjuïc in a large villa with patio—dining among fountains and flowers. Expensive but worth it. Catalan specialties. AE, DC.

Gorria, Diputació 421 (tel. 232 7857). Highly rated for its excellent Navarre-style cooking, good wine list, and professional service; four blocks south of Sagrada Familia. Closed Sun. and Aug. AE, DC, MC, V.

El Gran Café, Avinyó 9 (tel. 318 7986). Stylish turn-of-the-century decor in heart of Gothic Quarter; dining to piano music. Closed Sun., Easter week, and Aug. AE, DC, MC, V.

Guria, Casanova 97 (tel. 253 6325). Luxurious Basque restaurant with outstanding cuisine and service; currently one of the highest rated restaurants in town. Closed two weeks in Aug. AE, DC, MC, V.

Jaume de Provença, Provença 88 (tel. 230 0029). One of Barcelona's highest rated restaurants. Ideal for business lunches. *Haute cuisine* specialties often include baby eels rolled in smoked salmon. Closed Sun. evening, Mon., Easter Week and Aug. AE, DC, MC, V.

Neichel, Avda. de Pedralbes 16 bis (tel. 203 8408). Luxurious and elegant decor; one of Barcelona's most highly-thought-of restaurants. Closed Sun. and fiestas, Easter Week and Aug. AE, DC, MC, V.

La Odisea, Copons 7 (tel. 302 3692). Inventive restaurant near cathedral. After your meal there is a pleasant coffee lounge with piano music. Closed Sun., Easter Week and Aug. AE, DC, MC, V.

Quo Vadis, Carme 7 (tel. 317 7447). One of Barcelona's "musts". Highly original dishes; much praised. Closed Sun. and Aug. AE, DC, MC, V.

El Tunel de Muntaner, Sant Màrius 22 (tel. 212 6074). A popular restaurant on the hills behind the city not far from the Avda. Tibidabo. Its menu combines *haute cuisine* with popular home-cooking. There is a good bar at the entrance and a well stocked "boutique" for wine buffs. Closed Sat. lunch, Sun., fiestas and in Aug. AE, DC, MC, V.

Tinell, Frenería 8 (tel. 315 4604). In the heart of the Gothic Quarter just behind the cathedral. Friendly service and a delicious *sopa de ajo.*

La Venta, Plaça Dr. Andreu (tel. 212 6455). Delightful turn-of-the-century spot with tiled floors, marble-topped tables and pot-bellied stove. In a splendid setting with outdoor terrace, right beside the Tibidabo funicular. Closed Sun. DC, MC, V.

Vinya Rosa Magi, Avda. de Sarrià 17 (tel. 230 0003). Pleasant small restaurant convenient to the *Sarrià* and *Derby* hotels, specializing in Catalan and French dishes. Closed Sun. AE, DC, MC, V.

Moderate

Brasserie Flo, Jonqueres 10 (tel. 317 8037). Excellent French restaurant just off the top of Via Laietana; well decorated and good value. AE, DC, MC, V.

Can Culleretes, Quintana 5 (tel. 317 6485). This picturesque old restaurant began life as a *pastelería* in 1786 and is located on a narrow street between Boquería and Ferran just off Ramblas. Three dining rooms, walls hung with photos of visiting celebrities, it's a find and serves real Catalan cooking. Do not be put off by the hookers outside, this is a popular family restaurant. Closed Sun. evening, Mon., and two weeks in June or July.

Can Isidre, Les Flors 12 (tel. 241 1139). Long-standing tradition just off the Paral-lel and popular with artists, writers and actors. Traditional and imaginative cuisine making use of fresh produce bought daily in the Boquería market. Very highly rated but go by cab as the area's not the best. Closed Sun., Easter Week and mid-July to mid-Aug. AE, V.

Can Leopoldo, Sant Rafael 24 (tel. 241 3014). Famous for its seafood for over half-a-century; in the heart of the old town and best reached by taxi. Closed Sun. night, Mon., Easter Week and Aug. AE, MC, V.

Can Solé, Sant Carlos 4 (tel. 319 5012). Plenty of old-world charm with a nice tavern atmosphere in Barceloneta. Specializes in seafood. Closed Sat. night and Sun. Closed first two weeks of Feb. and first two weeks of Sept.

Los Caracoles, Escudellers 14 (tel. 301 2041). Famous Barcelona restaurant with wonderful decor and atmosphere. Specialty is snails. AE, DC, MC, V.

Casa Quirze, Laureà Miró 202 (tel. 371 1084). Justly famous restaurant serving mainly French-style dishes quite a long way out in Esplugues de Llobregat off the far end of the Diagonal. Closed Sun. night, Mon. and Easter Week. AE, MC, V.

La Dida, Roger de Flor 230 (tel. 207 2004). A well-recommended restaurant with atmospheric decor in the vicinity of the Plaça Joan Carlos and not too far from the Sagrada Familia church. Closed in the evening on Sun. and fiestas, and on Sat. from mid-June thru Sept, and Easter Week. AE, DC, MC, V.

Hostal Sant Jordi, Travessera de Dalt 123 (tel. 213 1037). Serving Catalan and French food of a consistently high standard; the house menu is a good choice. Closed on Sun. evenings and in Aug. AE, DC, V.

A la Menta, Passeig Manuel Girona 50 (tel. 204 1549). Atmospheric tavern serving good grilled meat. Best to reserve a table. Closed Sun. evenings and all day Sun. during Aug. AE, DC, V.

Network, Diagonal 616 (tel. 201 7238). This ultramodern cafe won a design award, and concentrates on everyday favorites—American, Mexican, and Italian—at value-for-money prices. Open till 2.30 A.M. AE, V.

Senyor Parellada, Argentería 37 (tel. 315 4010). In vogue Catalan restaurant just off Vía Laietana. Closed Sun. AE, DC, MC, V.

Sete Portes, Passeig Isabel II 14 (tel. 319 3033). Delightful restaurant going strong since 1836 and with lots of old-world charm; on the edge of the port. Open from 1 P.M. through 1 A.M. continuously. Very popular and crowded on Sundays and fiestas. AE, DC, MC, V.

Sopeta Una, Verdaguer i Callis 6 (tel. 319 6131). Delightful small restaurant with old-fashioned decor and intimate atmosphere, near Palau de la Música. Specializes in Catalan cuisine. Closed Sun. and Mon. lunch. V.

Tramonti 1980, Diagonal 501 (tel. 250 1535). Excellent Italian restaurant just beyond Plaça Francesc Macià. Its range of pastas and Italian cheeses is superb. AE, DC, MC, V.

El Tunel, Ample 33 (tel. 315 2759). An old stand-by with good old-fashioned service and reliable cooking, in the lower reaches of the Barrio Chino just off the Passeig Colom. Closed Sun. night, Mon. and mid-July thru mid-Aug.

Inexpensive

Agut, Gignàs 16 (tel. 315 1709). Good value Catalan cooking in the heart of the Barrio Chino. This simple restaurant, founded in 1914, serves only food and wine, no coffee or liquor. Closed Sun. P.M., Mon., and in July.

El Caballito Blanco, Mallorca 196 (tel. 253 1033). Long-standing popular restaurant offering a good choice of simple cooking and good selection of cheeses. Closed Sun. night, Mon., and Aug.

Del Teatre, Montseny 47 (tel. 218 6738). Located in the Teatre Lliure, this restaurant serves some original and imaginative dishes and is very good value. Closed Sun., Mon. and in Aug. AE.

Egipte, Jerusalem 3 (tel. 317 7480). Small, friendly restaurant hidden behind the Boquería market; well known to locals for its incredible value, good home cooking, and huge desserts.

Flash Flash, La Granada 25 (tel. 237 0990). Serving every imaginable kind of omelet—over 101 choices—with arty black-and-white decor. Open till 1.30 A.M. AE, DC, MC, V.

Mesón de las Ramblas, Ramblas 92 (tel. 302 1180). Pleasant bistro popular with tourists and which starts serving dinner early.

La Morera, Plaça Sant Agusti 1 (tel. 318 7555). Just off Ramblas between the market and Liceo. Smart decor and very good value.

La Ponsa, Enric Granados 89 (tel. 253 1037). A family-run restaurant serving Catalan food at very moderate prices; something of a budget institution in Barcelona. Closed Sat. night, Sun., and mid-July to mid-Aug.

Racó d'en Jaume, Provença 98 (tel. 239 7861). This is the old Jaume de Provença now reopened and serving down-to-earth good Catalan home cooking. Well worth a visit for insight into the way Catalan families eat at home. Closed Sun. night, Mon., and Aug.

Rey de la Gamba 1, 2 and 3, all on the Passeig Nacional in Barceloneta. Nothing pretentious but very popular with the locals. Great seafood and *pan tomate* at low prices.

Self Naturista, Sta. Anna 13. Popular self-service vegetarian wholefood restaurant; very cheap with long lines forming at lunchtime.

FAST FOOD. Burger King, at top of the Ramblas. The **Chicago Pizza Pie Factory,** Provença 300. A little bit of Chicago in Barcelona serving American-style pizzas, carrot cake, cheeses and garlic bread, good selection of cocktails, with American music, video and decor. **Compañía Gener-**

al de Sandwiches, Santaló 153 and Moyá 14. Great selection of sandwiches—over 100 varieties—and canapés to take away. Closed Sun. **El Drugstore,** Passeig de Gracià 71, open from early morning till very late at night for snacks and self-service meals. **Drugstore David,** Tuset 19 off the Diagonal. Every kind of hamburger, pizzas and Spanish meat dishes. Popular with the young set. **Fontanella 5,** on the corner of Fontanella and Plaça Catalunya. Pizzas and sandwiches. **Kentucky Fried Chicken,** Aribau 16, Rambla de Catalunya 113, Sants 136, and Fontanella near Plaça Catalunya. **McDonalds,** Pelai 62 on the corner of Ramblas and on Ramblas corner of Ferran. **New Kansas,** Passeig de Gracià 65 bis. Pizzas and good selection of sandwiches. **Niridia,** Diagonal 616. Pizzeria and fast food. **La Oca,** Plaça Francesc Macià 10. Smart trendy cafe serving *platos combinados,* club sandwiches and pastries; also take-away snacks. **Pizzería Samoa,** Passeig de Gracià 101. **Tropeziens,** Passeig de Gracià 83. Pizzeria and cafeteria. **Pokins** take-away hamburger chain, at Porta de l'Angel 1 and 27, Pelai 52, and Pza Francesc Macià 3.

BARS AND CAFES. Barcelona abounds in colorful old tapas bars, smart, trendy cafes where you can go for coffee and a pastry or for *platos combinados* and snack meals, jazz cafes, piano bars, and a whole range of stylish in vogue bars glorifying in the titles of *coctelerías, whiskerías* or *champanerías.* Below we list just a few of these places but, on the whole, it is best simply to wander at will and sample any which take your fancy; of one thing you can be sure—there are hundreds to choose from.

Tapas Bars. The most colorful are found in the old narrow streets on either side of the Ramblas, around the Plaça Reial, and in the area around the Picasso Museum along Carrer Princesa and surrounding the Carrer Montcada. In the port area of Barceloneta, in Carrer Maquinista the **Ramonet** and **Pañol** taverns with their garlic- and ham-strung ceilings are well worth a visit. Two well known bars very popular for their tapas are:

Alt Heidelberg, Ronda Universitat 5. Colorful bar with German beer on tap and a great variety of German sausages and tapas.

Cervecería, at the top of Ramblas opposite the Hostal Continental. Popular beerhall with a vast variety of tapas and especially good seafood.

Bars. Boadas, Tallers 1 on the corner of Ramblas. Going strong for over 50 years, this popular meeting place is famed for its cocktails.

Dry Martini, París 102. *The* place to go if your tipple is Martini. The barman has over 80 different gins with which he concocts his special martinis, and there is a *Martini del Día* on offer every day. Also a selection of whisky. Even the paintings on display are related to the Martini theme. Closed Sun. and last two weeks in Aug.

Ideal Cocktail Bar, Aribau 89 on the corner of Mallorca. A well-known cocktail bar first opened in 1931 and with some remnants of its original *Art Deco* style still there. It serves a good selection of whisky, including malts, amongst other liquors and fruit based *aguardientes,* and there are tapas and canapés to accompany your drinking. Closed Sun. and last two weeks in Aug.

Merbeye, Plaça Dr. Andreu. Next to the Tibidabo funicular, its pleasant terrace with palm trees is ideal for a coffee or early evening drink. The inside bar is very fashionable with the young and stays open till 3 A.M. Closed Sun.

Nick Havanna, Rosselló 208. Lively cocktail bar claiming to be "the ultimate bar."

Otto Zutz, Lincoln 15. One of the latest "in" places where people go to be seen. Loud, lively and open till the wee small hours.

El Paraigua, Pas. de l'Ensenyança 2, on Plaça Sant Miquel in heart of Gothic Quarter. Stylish turn-of-century style cocktail bar with classical music.

Els Quatre Gats, Montsió 5. A picturesque *tertulia* bar in the heart of the Barrio Gótico, a reconstruction of the famous original *Els Quatre Gats* which opened in 1897 and was the cafe associated with the *Belle Epoque Modernista* movement, where Picasso had one of his first shows, Albeniz and Granados played their piano compositions, Maragall read his poetry and for which Ramon Casas painted two famous murals.

Jazz Cafes. Abraxas Jazz Auditorium, Gelabert 26. Large venue with live and recorded music, mostly jazz. Well known Spanish and foreign bands. Closed Mon. and in Aug.

La Cova del Drac, Tuset 30, off the Diagonal. Bar famous for its live music, usually Catalan singing or jazz. Closed Sun.

Passeig del Born. This is one of the best streets for exciting bars and cafes and definitely one of the "in" places for the young. **Berimbau** at no. 17 has Brazilian music; **El Born** at no. 26 is a pleasant cocktail bar with a buffet; **El Copetín** at no. 19 has exciting decor and some good cocktails; **Miramelindo** at no. 15 offers a large selection of herbal liquors, fruit cocktails, pâtés and cheeses with music, usually jazz.

Champanerías. Brut, Trompetas 3 in the Picasso Museum area. A popular after-the-theater-or-cinema bar serving cocktails and champagne specialties.

La Cava del Palau, Verdaguer i Callis 10, close to the Palau de la Música. Good selection of wines and champagne cocktails served with homemade canapés and sandwiches. Wide choice of Catalan *cavas.*

La Folie, Bailén 169. One of the city's best known wine and champagne bars with good atmosphere and pleasant decor.

La Xampanyeria, Provença 236 on the corner of Enric Granados. This was the first, and is still one of the best, champanerías to open in Barcelona. Open from 7 P.M. until 2.30 A.M. and serving over 50 different Catalan wines.

Cafés and Tea Salons. Café de l'Opera, Ramblas 74. This traditional gathering place right opposite the Liceo is one of the great cafes of old; an ideal place at any time of day for a coffee or a drink.

Café Zurich, corner of Pelai and Plaça Catalunya. Barcelona's best-known meeting place, and a good place to relax and watch the world go by.

Oriente, Ramblas 45. The outdoor terrace of the Oriente hotel right on the Ramblas itself is the perfect place for a coffee or cocktail and to watch the ever-lively promenade.

Salón de Te Llibre i Serra, Ronda Sant Pere (San Pedro) 3. Exquisite tea room in a pastry shop which dates from 1907. Some 25 kinds of tea are served accompanied by sweet and savory delicacies. Closed Sunday afternoons.

Salón de Te Mauri, corner of Rambla de Catalunya and Provença. Typical tea room atmosphere and a good selection of pastries.

CITY TOURS. Tours of the city are run by *Juliá Tours,* Ronda Universitat 5 (tel. 317 6454) and *Pullmantur,* Gran Vía de les Corts Catalans 635 (tel. 318 0241). You can book these tours direct with the head offices above, or through any travel agency, or, in most cases, through your hotel.

City Tour. A half-day tour in the morning visiting the Plaça de Catalunya, the cathedral and Gothic Quarter, the City Hall (Ayuntamiento), the Passeig Colom, Montjuïc for a view over the city, and the Pueblo Español (Spanish Village).

City Tour and Picasso Museum. A half-day tour in the afternoon visiting Gaudi's Sagrada Familia and the Picasso Museum.

Panorámica y Toros. On days when there are bullfights only (usually Sundays). A drive through the city along the Diagonal, past the Church of the Holy Family, to the Monumental bullring. Seats for the bullfight and an explanation of bullfighting by the guide are included.

Night Tours. These come in various combinations including *Panorámica y Flamenco,* a panoramic drive through the city to see the illuminations followed by a flamenco show with drink included; *Gala en Scala,* cabaret show at La Scala with either dinner or just a drink; *Noche Flamenca,* dinner in a restaurant followed by visit to a flamenco show.

EXCURSIONS. These are run by *Juliá Tours* and *Pullmantur* and are booked as above.

Montserrat. Half-day excursion (morning or afternoon) to the famous Benedictine monastery of Montserrat 50 km. from Barcelona. Excursion includes a guided visit of the monastery, time to see the shrine of the Black Virgin and listen to the famous La Escolanía choir (mornings only), or a funicular ride to the top of one of the peaks of the strange saw-edged mountains (afternoons only).

Costa Brava. A full-day trip leaving Barcelona at 9 A.M. to the Costa Brava resorts including a boat cruise to Lloret de Mar. May to Oct. only, daily except Sun.

Andorra. A full-day trip, on Mon., Wed. and Fri., leaving Barcelona at 6.30 A.M. to the independent Principality of Andorra situated high in the Pyrenees between Spain and France. Lunch is included and Andorra is a mecca for tax-free shopping. Weekend trips with Sat. night in an hotel are available year round.

NIGHTLIFE. Barcelona has long had a reputation as a center of wild and wooly nightspots and there is no shortage of places putting on gay, transvestite or just plain pornographic shows. What are hard to find, however, and surprising for a city of its size, are many high-class nightclubs along the lines of, say, Paris' *Lido* or *Crazy Horse.* The places listed below should not, we hope, offend in any way, but beware the seedier night spots of the Barrio Chino and Paral-lel. *Belle Epoque* and *La Scala* are probably the best bets.

Nightclubs. Belle Epoque, Muntaner 246 (tel. 209 7385). Beautifully decorated music hall putting on good shows. Closed Sun. AE, DC, MC, V.

Gran Casino de Barcelona, 42 km. south in Sant Pere de Ribes near Sitges (tel. 893 3866). 19th-century casino with Black Jack, Boule, Roulette etc., restaurant, dancing and shows on some nights.

El Mediévolo, Gran Vía 459, between Rocafort and Calabria (tel. 325 3480). Medieval feasts and entertainment; much geared to tourists but fun.

Regine's, Av. Joan XXIII, in the Princesa Sofia hotel. Barcelona's top in-vogue club combines fashionable disco, bar, and restaurant; definitely one of the places in which to be seen, but call the hotel first to check on membership rules.

Scala Barcelona, Passeig Sant Joan 47 (tel. 232 6363). Barcelona's leading nightclub with two shows nightly, the first with dinner and cabaret, the second, around midnight, with drinks, dancing, and cabaret. Closed Mon. AE, DC, MC, V.

Flamenco. Catalans often consider this Andalusian spectacle anti-Catalan so Barcelona is not richly endowed with flamenco spots and those that there are, are aimed right at the tourist market. However, Barcelona's large Andalusian community from which many of the performers come, should offer a touch of authenticity.

Andalucía, Ramblas 27 (tel. 302 2009). Dinner from 8.30–10 followed by flamenco and Spanish dancing.

El Cordobés, Ramblas 35 (tel. 317 6653). This is the one visited by most tour groups, but it is fun and colorful.

Las Sevillanas del Patio, Aribau 242 (tel. 209 3524). Sevillanas rather than flamenco are performed here, often with audience participation.

Los Tarantos, Plaça Reial 17 (tel. 317 8098). Good flamenco show twice nightly at 10 and midnight, popular with tourists and locals.

Discos. Barcelona is very much a disco city with new and sophisticated places springing up each year. As in most Spanish cities, there are usually two sessions, *tarde* from around 7 P.M.–10 P.M., which is geared very much to the young and is usually cheaper, and *noche* beginning at 11 or 11.30 P.M. and continuing until 2 or 3 A.M. The "in" place to go changes frequently, but the following have proved reliable bets. Entrances vary from 1,000–2,000 ptas. and one drink is usually included in the price.

Duetto, Consell de Cent 294. A very popular disco appealing to a wide range of tastes with bars on three floors, videos and live shows.

Studio 54, Paral-lel 54. One of the biggest and with some "spectacular" shows which draw the crowds; lots of action. Open Fri., Sat. and Sun. only.

Trauma, Consell de Cent 228. A pleasant spot with a wide range of music and modest prices.

Up and Down, Numància 179. Very smart and fashionable (men must wear jacket and tie). Definitely one of the "in" places with loud music on the downstairs dance floor and upstairs a quieter, more sophisticated, even "snob" atmosphere. There is also a restaurant. Call 204 8809 to check membership rules.

MUSEUMS. Barcelona is well endowed with museums, the most outstanding being the Museum of Catalan Art and the Picasso Museum. Many of the best museums are now free, others have a free day on either

Sundays or Wednesdays, and holders of ISI cards, and in some cases, senior citizens, are often entitled to free entrance. Most museums close on Mondays.

Fundación Joan Miró, in Montjuïc Park. Center for the Study of Contemporary Arts founded by the artist Joan Miró and designed by Josep Lluis Sert. Collection of paintings and sculptures by Miró. Open Tues. to Sat. 11–7 (11–9.30 on Thurs.); Sun. and fiestas 10.30–2.30. Closed Mon.

Museo Arqueológico, in Montjuïc Park. Roman mosaics and displays of finds from Ampurias. Open Tues. to Sat. 9.30–1 and 4–7, Sun. 10–2 only; closed Mon.

Museo de Arte de Cataluña, in the Palacio Nacional on Montjuïc. Houses the world's greatest collection of Catalan Romanesque art. In the same building is a delightful **Ceramics Museum** which can be visited on the same ticket. Open 9–2. Closed Mon. Partially closed at presstime for renovation; check with tourist office.

Museo de Arte Moderno, in Ciudadela Park. Worthwhile collection of paintings from the late 18th century to early 20th including works by the Catalan artists Casas, Fortuny, Miró, Tàpies and Russinyol. Several rooms are now dedicated to the works of contemporary Catalan artists. Open Tues. to Sat. 9–7.30, Sun. 9–2, Mon. 3–7.30.

Museo de Autómatas del Tibidabo, in the Amusement Park on Tibidabo. Fairground automatons, mechanical dolls, electric trains, magical wizards, etc. Open Mon. to Fri. 12–2 and 3–5.45, Sat. to Sun. 12–3 and 4–7.45.

Museo de Calzado Antiguo, Plaça Sant Felip Neri in the Gothic Quarter. Museum of the history of shoes and shoe-making. Includes shoes donated by Pablo Casals. Open Sat., Sun. and fiestas only, from 11–2.

Museo de Carruajes, in the Pedralbes Palace on the Diagonal. Coach and carriage museum with a small collection of weapons and uniforms. Open Tues. to Fri. 10–1 and 4–6, Sat. and Sun. 10–2 only.

Museo de Carrozas Funebres, Sancho de Avila 2. Collection of funeral carriages dating from the middle of the 19th century onwards, and related funeral paraphernalia. Open 9–2. Closed Sun.

Museo de Cera, Pasaje de la Banca 7, at the port end of Ramblas. Wax Museum with over 300 historic and contemporary figures. Open daily 11–1.30 and 4.30–7.30.

Museo de la Ciencia, Teodoro Roviralta 55. Science Museum, including a Planetarium. Open 10–8. Closed Mon.

Museo Etnológico, Passeig Santa Madrona in Montjuïc Park. Exhibits from early civilizations worldwide. Open Tues. to Sat. 9–8.30, Sun. 9–2, Mon. 2–8.30.

Museo Federico Marés, Comtes de Barcelona 10. In the Palacio Real in the heart of the Gothic Quarter, this museum houses an important collection of religious sculpture including several wooden crucifixes, and upstairs, the personal collection of the sculptor Federico Marés, a wonderful array of *bric-à-brac* of all sorts; a fascinating museum. Open Tues. to Sat. 9–2 and 4–7, Sun. 9–2. Closed Mon.

Museo de Geología, in Ciudadela Park. Municipal Geology Museum (Martorell Museum). Open Tues. to Sun. 9–2. Closed Mon.

Museo de Historia de la Ciudad, in the Casa Padellás in the Plaça del Rei. The history of Barcelona throughout the ages with traces of the Roman city in the basement. Open Mon. 3–8, Tues. to Sat. 9–8, Sun. 9–1.30.

Museo de la Indumentaria Manuel Rocamora, Montcada 12. Interesting Costume Museum with costumes from the 16th to 20th centuries installed in one of the old palaces near the Picasso Museum. Open daily 9–2.

Museo Marítimo, Reales Atarazanas at the bottom of Ramblas. Outstanding Maritime Museum containing replicas of the galley used by Don John of Austria at the Battle of Lepanto, the first submarine, and a nautical map by Amerigo Vespucci. Open Tues. to Sat. 10–2 and 4–7, Sun. 10–2. Closed Mon.

Museo Militar, in Montjuïc Castle. Well arranged collection of arms and military uniforms from various countries and a collection of miniature soldiers. Open Tues. to Sat. 10–2 and 4–7, Sun. 10–7. Closed Mon.

Museo de la Música, Bruch 110. Musical instruments, manuscripts, scores and mementoes of great musicians. Open 9–2. Closed Mon.

Museo Picasso, Montcada 15. Important collection of sketches and paintings, donated originally by the great man himself. Open Tues. to Sun. 10–7. Closed Mon.

Museo Taurino, Plaza de Toros Monumental, Gran Vía 749. Bullfighting paraphernalia, bulls' heads, suits of light, etc., situated in the Monumental Bullring on the corner of Gran Vía and Passeig Carles I. Open 10–1 and 3.30–7; on days when there are bullfights 10–1 only.

Museo Zoología, Passeig dels Tillers in Ciudadela Park. Natural History museum in a building known as the Castle of the Three Dragons designed by Domènech i Montaner for the 1888 Exhibition. Open 9–2. Closed Mon.

HISTORIC BUILDINGS AND SITES. Antiguo Hospital de la Santa Cruz, Hospital 56. One of the principal complexes of Gothic buildings in the city with a splendid patio. Amongst the many cultural institutes housed here is the **Sala Miguel Soldevila,** with a collection of the artist's enamels. Open 10–1 and 4–8. Closed Sat. and fiestas.

Basílica de la Vírgen de la Merced, Placa de la Merced off the Passeig Colom. Baroque church containing the image of Barcelona's patron saint. Open 7 A.M.–8 P.M.

Casa Batlló, Passeig de Gràcia 43. Built for the textile manufacturer Josep Batllo in 1875–77, Gaudi gave it a splendid facelift in 1904–06 so it could outshine its neighbor, the Casa Amatller at no. 41 by Puig i Cadafalch. Now used as offices but open to visitors 8–10 A.M.

Casa Milá or **La Pedrera,** Passeig de Gràcia 92. Gaudi's splendid "stone quarry" was built in 1906–10 for Pedro Milá, Batllo's business partner. Now owned by an insurance company, which extensively cleaned and renovated it in 1988, its patio is open to visitors. You can visit the roof at 10 A.M., 11 A.M., and 12 noon, or have a drink in the **Amarcord** bar inside the building.

Gran Teatro Liceo, Ramblas 61. Begun in 1845, this is one of the grandest Opera Houses in Europe. Tours of the Opera House are conducted at 11.30 and 12.15 on Mon., Wed. and Fri. in winter, and daily Mon. to Fri. in summer.

Iglesia de Santa María del Mar, Plaça de Santa María. Beautiful early Gothic church with huge single vault and unusual columns. Open 8–1 and 4–7.30.

Iglesia del Pí, Plaça del Pí. 14th-century Gothic church of San José Oriol in delightful small square just off Ramblas. Open 8–1 and 6–9.

Lonja, Passeig de Isabel II. Neo-Classic Palace of the Exchange housing the 14th-century Gothic *Salón de Contrataciones,* The Stock Exchange, the Chamber of Commerce and Navigation and the Royal Academy of Fine Arts.

Monasterio de Pedralbes at the end of Passeig de Reina Elisenda de Montcada. Convent founded by Queen Elisenda, wife of Jaime II, in 1326. Beautiful chapel with 14th-century stained glass, rose windows and the tomb of Queen Elisenda. Important paintings and murals by the Sienese school with outstanding murals by Ferrer Bassa (1436). A rich collection of works of art. Open 10–1; closed Mon.

Palacio del Ayuntamiento, Plaça Sant Jaume. Gothic City Hall with a neo-Classical facade. Inside is the splendid *Salón de Ciento* and the *Salón de las Crónicas* with murals by José María Sert. Open during business hours.

Palacio de la Generalidad (Palau Generalitat), Plaça Sant Jaume. Gothic patio and stairway, the famous *Patio de los Naranjos,* and the Chapel and *Salón de San Jorge* with murals by Torres García. Open on Sundays only from 10–1.

Palacio Güell, Nou de la Rambla. This is one of the few of Gaudí's buildings it is possible to go inside as it houses the **Museu de les Arts de l'Espectacle,** a museum of the history of Barcelona's theater, cinema and dance. Open Mon. to Sat. 11–2 and 5–8.

Palacio (Palau) de la Música, Amadeo Vives 1, just off Vía Laietana. Magnificent concert hall by Lluis Doménech i Montaner built in *Modernista* style. Can be visited on Mondays and Fridays at 11.30.

Palacio de Pedralbes, out along the Diagonal. Temporary art exhibitions. Open Mon. to Fri. 10–1 and 4–7, Sat. and Sun. 10–2, but call 203 7501 to check.

Palau de la Virreina, Ramblas 99 on corner of Carme. Built by a viceroy of Peru in 1778 for the wife he left behind, it now serves as a major exhibition center; check to see what's showing. Open 9.30–1.30 and 4.30–9; closed Mon.

Parque Güell in which there is a house which has been turned into a **Gaudí Museum.** The museum is open on Sundays only from 10–2 and 4–6.

Pueblo Español in Montjuïc Park. The Spanish Village built in 1929 by Miguel Utrillo and Xavier Nogués for the International Exhibition. Houses, streets and plazas showing the different architectural styles of each region of Spain. Of the many small industries and crafts that used to be demonstrated here, today only a glass blowers and a printing press remain. Incorporates two museums, the **Museum of Graphic Arts** and the **Museum of Popular Arts and Crafts,** both open Tues. to Sun. 9–2; closed Mon. The village is open daily 9–7.

Reales Atarazanas, in the Porta de la Pau off Passeig Colom. 14th-century Royal shipyards built by Pedro el Grande and Pedro el Ceremonioso; the only remaining one of its kind in Europe. The **Maritime Museum** is housed here.

Sagrada Familia, between Mallorca-Provença, and Marina-Sardenya. Gaudí was first recommended as the architect of the Sagrada Familia in 1883, and after 1911 when he stopped work on the Parque Güell, he dedicated the rest of his life to this great building in whose crypt he now lies buried. Construction is still going on but you can visit part of Gaudí's original building. The site is open daily 9–8.

PARKS AND GARDENS. Parque de la Ciudadela is the closest to the city center. Its name means "Citadel Park" and the citadel, built in 1716 by Philip V, was pulled down in 1868 and replaced by public gardens laid out by Josep Fontseré. In the park are the Geology and Natural History Museums, the Museum of Modern Art, a zoo, aquarium and the Catalan Regional Parliament. The gardens, with their statues and fountains, make a pleasant place to stroll or relax.

Parque Güell, in the northwest of the city is a delightful place to visit. It was begun by Gaudí whose idea was to build a kind of garden city development to demonstrate his ideas on town planning. The project was never finished and only a few early constructions can be seen, but these constitute a superb Art Nouveau extravaganza. Not only does the park have Gaudí's incredible mosaics but also magnificent views over the city to the Mediterranean. The park is open daily, but the Gaudí Museum in one of its houses is open only on Sundays. The park has recently been undergoing restoration and although open to the public may not be seen to its best advantage; so check with the Tourist Office before you set out. To reach the park, take Metro Line 3 to Lesseps or Vallcarca and then walk—it is quite a steep climb; or alternatively take buses 24 or 28 from the Plaça de Catalunya, which go right by the park.

Parque de Montjuïc. Its name, meaning "hill of the Jews," comes from the time when Barcelona's Jewish community lived on its slopes. The gardens surrounding the hill were laid out for the International Exhibition of 1929. The Jardines de Miramar offer a splendid view over the city and the park is the home of six museums—Catalan Art, Ceramics, Archeology, Military, Ethnological and the Joan Miró Foundation—as well as the Pueblo Español, the model Spanish village, the Teatre Grec where open-air performances are held in summer, a huge amusement park and a magnificent fountain whose colored illuminations are a memorable sight on summer weekends or fiestas. There are several ways of reaching Montjuïc. Probably the most spectacular is to take the aerial cable car which runs from Barceloneta to the Jardines de Miramar. There is also the funicular from the end of Nou de la Rambla but this is more often than not out-of-order. Bus no. 61 from the Plaça de Espanya runs through the park passing the Pueblo Español, the Joan Miró Foundation and the Amusement Park every half hour on the hour and half past until 8 P.M. Bus 13 from the San Antonio Market on Borrell runs to the Plaça Espanya and on to the Pueblo Español. But public transport here is often misleading, and it's best just to walk from Plaça d'Espanya or else hail a cab.

Tibidabo. This mountain lying behind Barcelona is 1,745 ft. high and can be reached either by funicular (rack railroad) or by a winding road affording spectacular views of the city and Mediterranean. Atop the mountain is a basilica and a brash fun fair, but the view is breathtaking. To take the funicular up to the top, first take bus no. 58 or the subway (F.C. Sarrià line) to the Avda. de Tibidabo, then take the *tramvía blau,* the only remaining one of the blue trams of old, which runs to the funicular station. The funicular runs every half hour from 7.15 A.M. to 9.45 P.M.

MUSIC, MOVIES AND THEATER. To find out what is on in Barcelona, look in the daily press *(La Vanguardia, Correo Catalan, Diario de Barcelona),* or better still in the weekly *Guía del Ocio* available from newsstands all over town.

Music. Barcelona has one of the world's finest opera houses, the **Gran Teatro del Liceo** seating some 5,000 people, and which many consider to be second only to Milan's *La Scala.* The Liceo stands on the Ramblas on the corner of Sant Pau (San Pablo). The box office for advance bookings is down the side of the building in Sant Pau 1 (tel. 318 9277), open Mon. to Fri. 8–3, Sat. 9–1. Tickets for performances on the day are on sale in the Ramblas entrance (tel. 301 6787) from 11–1.30 and from 4 onwards. The main opera season runs throughout the winter from November till March, but performances may often be seen much later into the spring. The ballet season is usually April thru' May. Famous opera singers perform here frequently and the Liceo is especially well known for its Wagnerian performances. Tickets are not expensive by international standards and, if you are content with the cheaper seats, can usually be obtained right up to the day of performance itself.

The main concert hall is the **Palau de la Música,** Amadeo Vives 1, just off the Vía Laietana. Its ticket office opens Mon. to Fri. 11–1 and 5–8, Sat. 5–8 only. Tickets for performances on the day are only available from 5 P.M. onwards. Its Sunday morning concerts are a very popular Barcelona tradition. Best known amongst Barcelona's musical groups and orchestras is the *Orquesta Ciudad de Barcelona* (Barcelona City Orchestra) and the *Orfeó Català* (Catalan Choral Society). In summer concerts are sometimes held in the patio of the Antiguo Hospital de la Santa Cruz on Carrer Hospital. An *International Music Festival* is held in Barcelona in September during the city's celebrations for the feast of the Merced (around Sept. 23).

Movies. Barcelona has plenty of movie theaters but the majority of foreign films are dubbed into Spanish. Some theaters also show films in Catalan. However, if you have the patience to go through the *Guía del Ocio* looking for films marked *V.O. Subtitulada* this means that the films are being shown in their original language (often English) with Spanish subtitles. The official **Filmoteca** is on Travessera de Gracià 63 on the corner of Tusset, and shows three films a day in their original language.

Theater. Catalonia is well known for its mime theater and two well known mime troupes are *Els Joglars* and *La Claca.* An *International Mime Festival* is held most years as is a *Festival de Títeres* (Puppet Festival).

One of the best known theaters is the **Teatre Lliure** which specializes in experimental theater and satirical reviews, but as with many other Barcelona theaters, many of its performances are in Catalan. There is an open-air summer *Theater Festival* in July and August when plays, music, song and dance performances are held at the **Teatre Grec** in Montjuïc Park.

SPORTS. Bullfights. These are normally held from the end of March thru' October, usually on Sundays and for fiestas. The main ring is the **Monumental** on Gran Vía and Carles I. **Las Arenas** ring in the Plaça de Espanya is used only rarely. Tickets can be bought at the rings themselves or from the advance ticket office at Muntaner 24.

Soccer (fútbol). Barcelona's famous team, known as Barça, is one of the world's richest and grandest soccer teams. Matches are played, usually on Sundays, at the Camp Nou Stadium off Avda. Arístides Maillol which is being enlarged to hold 125,000 for the 1992 Olympics. Matches are also played at the **Sarrià Stadium,** Avda. Sarria 120.

Golf. There are five golf clubs in the area around Barcelona. The **Sant Cugat Club** about 14 km from the center; the **Prat de Llobregat Club,** the **Sant Andreu de Llanvaneres Club;** the **Vallromanes Club** and the **Terramar Club** in Sitges.

Tennis. For tennis there are the following clubs: **Barcino,** Passatge Forester 2; **Pompeia,** Travessera de Gracià 13; **La Salut,** Verge de la Salut 75; **Real Club,** Bosch i Gimpera; and the **Club Deportivo Laietano,** Sant Ramón Nonato. Rental courts at Andrés Gimeno off the highway in Castelldefels, and at Can Melich at Sant Just Desvern (take bus SJ from the Plaça Universitat for the latter).

Bowling. At the **Boliche Bolera,** Diagonal 508 and the **Bolera Novedades,** Casp 1.

Ice skating. At the **Skating Club,** Roger de Flor 168 and another at the **Palau Blau-Grana,** at the Barcelona Fútbol Club stadium, Avda. Arístides Maillol.

Swimming. Several of the 4- and 5-star hotels have pools and there are public pools on Avda. Sarrià 84, the **Piscina Montjuïc** on Avda. Miramar and the **Piscina Bernardo Picornell** in Montjuïc Park.

SHOPPING. The best shopping streets are the Passeig de Gracià (the Fifth Avenue of Barcelona); the Rambla de Catalunya; the Gran Vía between Balmes and Pau Claris; and on and around the Diagonal in the area between Ganduxer and Passeig de Gracià where there are several small boutiques in the Carrer Tusset area. For more old-fashioned, typically Spanish-style shops, explore the area between Ramblas and the Vía Laietana, especially along Carrer Ferran (Fernando). There are also lots of young fashionable stores and trendy gift shops in this area bounded by the Ramblas, Ferran, Porta de l'Angel and the Plaça Catalunya—try especially the narrow streets around the Placeta del Pi from Boquería to Portaferrisa and Canuda.

If you're feeling adventurous, you might wander over to the Major de Gracià area just above the Passeig de Gracià. This is really a small, almost independent pueblo within a large city, a warren of small, narrow streets, changing name at every corner, and filled with tiny shops where you'll find everything from old-fashioned tin lanterns to real feather dusters.

For **antiques** your best bet is to wander around the cathedral in the Barrio Gótico. Carrer de la Palla and Banys Nous have one antique shop after another. There you'll find old maps, books, paintings and furniture. And don't forget the antiques fair held on Thursday mornings in the Plaça Nova in front of the cathedral. You might also just come across some bargains at the Els Encants flea market. On the Passeig de Gracià at no. 57, the Centre d'Antiquaris, has some 75 antique stores.

Department stores. The main department stores are *El Corte Inglés* on the Plaça de Catalunya, with a newer and much bigger one on the Diagonal near the metro stop María Cristina; and the *Galerías Preciados* on Porta de l'Angel just off Plaça Catalunya, in the Plaça Françesc Macià on the Diagonal, and at Meridiana 352. All are open 10–8. Enquire about tourist discount plans.

Markets. Antiques Market. Held in the square in front of the cathedral on Thursday mornings. Antiques are often of high quality, especially the silver.

For a typical and very colorful food market, you should go to the **Boquería Market** just off the Ramblas between Carme and Hospital on any day of the week except Sunday.

Els Encants. Barcelona's flea market held on Mon., Wed., Fri. and Sat. at the end of Dos de Maig on the Plaça Glories Catalanes. Junk of all kinds; fascinating and picturesque.

San Antonio Market, held on Sunday mornings in the old market building with beautiful tiled stalls on the corner of Urgell and Tamarit at the end of Ronda Sant Antoní. Fascinating collection of second-hand books, old magazines, postcards, press cuttings, lithographs, prints, etc.

Stamp and Coin Market, held on Sunday mornings in the Plaça Reial.

Artists' Market. Paintings are on sale on Saturday mornings in the Placeta del Pi alongside the church of San José Oriol in the Gothic Quarter.

USEFUL ADDRESSES. Airlines. The *Iberia* air terminal is in the Plaça de Espanya, and the main *Iberia* office at Passeig de Gracià 30 (tel. 301 3993) on the corner of Diputació 258; open Mon. to Fri. 9–1.30 and 4–7, Sat. 9–1. For national reservations, call 301 6800; for international reservations, call 302 7656; for flight arrival and departure information, call *Inforiberia* on 301 3993. The airport number is 370 1011.

British Airways are at Passeig de Gracià 85, 4th floor (tel. 215 2112), open Mon. to Fri. 9–5. *Pan Am* are handled by *Transtur,* Avda. Drassanes 6 (tel. 301 7249). *TWA* are at Gran Vía de les Corts Catalans 634 (tel. 318 0031).

Consulates. U.S. Consulate, Vía Laietana 33 (tel. 319 9550). British Consulate, Diagonal 477 (tel. 322 2151).

Police. The main Police Station is on Vía Laietana 49 (tel. 301 6666). In an emergency, dial 091.

Car Hire. *Atesa,* Balmes 141 (tel. 237 8140); *Avis,* Casanova 209 (tel. 209 9533) and Aragó 235 (tel. 215 8430); *Hertz,* Tuset 10 (tel. 237 3737); *Ital,* Travessera de Gracià 71 (tel. 321 5141), and all are represented at the airport.

Travel Agents. *American Express,* Rosselló 257 on corner of Passeig de Gracià (tel. 217 0070), open Mon. to Fri. 9.30–6, Sat. 10–12. *Wagon Lits Cooks,* Passeig de Gracià 8 (tel. 317 5500).

Main Post Office. Plaça Antoní López at the bottom of Vía Laietana.

Telephone Exchange. Carrer Fontanella on the corner of Plaça Catalunya, open Mon. to Sat. 8.30 A.M.–9 P.M., closed Sun.

Hospital Evangélico (or of the Foreign Colonies), Alegre de Dalt 87 (tel. 219 7100).

American Visitors' Bureau, Gran Vía 591, 3rd floor (between Rambla de Catalunya and Balmes) (tel. 301 0150/0032). Services include packing and shipping of personal effects or purchases. Open 9–1.30 and 4–7, Sat. 9–1 only.

THE COSTA BRAVA

Sun, Sand and Sweet-Smelling Pines

The Costa Brava, or "rugged coast", is an extraordinarily beautiful stretch of jagged shoreline that begins at Blanes, northeast of Barcelona, and runs from there past 145 km. (90 miles) of coves and beaches blessed by the Mediterranean sun to the Franco-Spanish frontier town of Port Bou. Every step of it is a delight.

Little by little it has been discovered, and the growth of its popularity during the last 20 years has been nothing short of phenomenal. Where once there were only ten hotels along the coast, there are today thousands, all with modern facilities and most with sea-view terraces; apartment blocks have sprung up like mushrooms.

This unprecedented expansion of facilities for millions of visitors every year has inevitably encroached upon the natural beauty of the coast, yet the fantastically brilliant blue of the sea by day still contrasts with red-brown headlands and cliffs, and so do the distant lights of the sardine fishing fleet that reflect across the wine-colored waters at dusk. Neat umbrella pines still march briskly to the fringes of white sandy beaches. At least they do when they can find their way through the concrete and cars.

Around the Costa Brava

Gerona (or as the Catalans now call it, Girona), the Costa Brava's airport, handling over a million passengers annually, lies on the toll-road from France, and is connected with all the coastal resorts by regular bus services. Yet Barcelona is still the most popular starting point because so many visitors combine some sightseeing with a seaside holiday. Blanes, only 65 km. (40 miles) northeast of the Catalan capital, is the first stop on this itinerary and can be reached by train or bus as well as by car.

Blanes is the largest and least recommendable town on the Costa Brava, with a resident population of over 20,000. Its accessibility makes it popular with Spanish vacationers though industry is given precedence over tourism.

Blanes is built around the gentle curve of a bay. The open walk facing the sea and known as the Maestranza provides a pleasant locale for the typically Spanish institution of the paseo, a leisurely promenade in the cool of the evening. The bay itself is more for mooring the gaily painted boats of the fishing fleet than for bathing, but there are delightful, coarse-grained sand beaches for swimming at the head of the neighboring *calas*—deep-sea inlets—of La Forcanera and Sant Franceso.

The town itself is dominated by the medieval castle of Sant Joan, which is perched on the summit of a decoratively pointed hill a little way inland. The outbreak of the Civil War was the signal for an orgy of church burning by the Republicans both here and elsewhere in Catalonia, and the thousand-year-old church of Santa María la Antigua was one of the few survivors.

Besides an attractive botanical garden and an aquarium, you may also wish to visit the picturesque fishermen's quarters of S'Auguev and La Mossanada. Fiestas are celebrated from July 24 to July 28 in honor of St. James, patron saint of Spain, and St. Anne, and again on August 21.

From Blanes, the coastal road leads north again for five km. (three miles) to the popular resort of Lloret de Mar. Shortly after leaving Blanes, there is a side road to the right over a hill thick with vines and umbrella pines leading to the wide sweep of the Playa de Fanals.

On July 24–25 fishermen in gaily decked boats of every size and shape pay their respects to their patron saint in the hermitage of Santa Cristina. This is the famous procession known as *S'Amorra*. The religious part of the festival over, the fishermen stay on to sing, drink, and dance the sardana all night long under the vast branches of Europe's largest umbrella pine, which is festooned with colored lights. They also have a dance of their own, of Moorish origin, the *morrotxas* (the *x* in Catalan is pronounced like *ch* in Spanish). For the rest of the year, visitors content themselves with an excellent golf course.

Lloret de Mar has jumped into the front rank and is now the largest hotel and residential center of the Costa Brava. Sadly, it displays all the worst excesses of tourism, but it does have a superb sandy beach as well as a Roman ruin. This is packaged fun at its worst—or best, depending on your point of view—with the added irony that it is presided over by the image in the local hermitage of the Virgen de Alegría—Our Lady of Happiness. Though the huge masses of people who have invaded her once quiet territory would no doubt make her wonder just how the modern world goes about looking for its happiness!

Tossa de Mar

It is 13 km. (eight miles) from Lloret to Tossa de Mar, the road running parallel to the sea through small woods of oak, pine and cork trees, with clearings for vines that produce the extremely strong, slightly sweet, white wine of the district. This drive is worth doing for itself alone. The views, though often crowded, are just as often very beautiful.

Tossa was probably the first place on the Costa Brava to attract foreigners, even in the days before the Civil War; and it is also the town that has suffered most from commercialization.

Again, the center of the beach at Tossa is occupied by the fishing fleet, but its northern end just opposite the tawny-colored rock island of Illa, is clean. However, it is better to go just round the corner to the Mar Menuda beach. At the other end of Tossa beach is a headland upon which are the fairytale 12th-century fortifications of the Vila Vella or Old Town, and it is these that give Tossa its special beauty. Playa Llorell and Cala Morisca beaches are further south, and usually less crowded, because of their distance from Tossa. Remember to climb up to the 14th-century Gothic church to enjoy the narrow, 17th-century streets of the Vila Vella. The view back to the beach, seen through an arch of one of the three great towers of the still older fortifications—the Tower of the Hours, the Tower of Homage and the Jonas Tower—is surely among the loveliest.

San Felíu de Guixols to Palamós

It is only 23 km. (14 miles) from Tossa to San Felíu de Guixols but, if you take the incredibly beautiful coast road (there is an easier but longer one inland), prepare yourself for one sharp corner after another as the narrow road winds round the heads of innumerable deep-cut inlets in a way that makes driving real work. Translucent blue fingers of water thrust deep into the red rocky cliffs to which all-too-many hotels cling precariously.

San Felíu de Guixols has numerous *simpático* little bars and restaurants, a bullring and many hotels, but there is no beach worthy of the name. This is no problem, however, because a bus service runs to and from S'Agaró, the cream of Costa Brava resorts, only three km. away; people who cannot afford S'Agaró hotel prices stay in San Felíu and commute to the S'Agaró beach.

Now that it has lost its lucrative cork industry (owing to the advent of plastics), San Felíu lives from its port, its fishing, and its tourist trade. According to an old tradition, it was founded by Charlemagne, but there was a community there long before then. It was called Jecsalis, from which the present name of Guixols is derived.

S'Agaró is one of the showpieces of the Costa Brava, and you must not fail to walk along the kilometer or so of sea wall, beginning below the Hostal de la Gavina and ending at the magnificent Concha beach. This lovely little walk is invisible from either the popular bathing beach or the Hostal. S'Agaró is the creation of one man, José Ensesa, who bought the land and built upon it his idea of a perfect seaside resort; all the buildings are built in the same style. From S'Agaró you can visit some intriguing villages which lie inland; for instance, Llagostera and Caldas de Malavella with ruins of Roman thermal baths and where the famous Vichy Catalan mineral water is bottled.

Beyond S'Agaró there comes the long sweep of the Bay of Palamós, where there is a break in the coastal cliffs so typical of the Costa Brava, and here, the resort of Playa de Aro has sprawled considerably. Its many hotels are full of visitors who come to enjoy the bathing from the perfect, sandy beach which is over a kilometer long. Calonge, nearby, also has good hotels.

San Antonio de Calonge, three km. from Palamós, was once a small hamlet. It is now a lively resort well endowed with hotels. However, you may want to travel on to the attractively placed little town that rises steeply from the end of the low-lying bay.

In actual fact, Palamós is more attractive in outward appearance than it proves upon closer inspection, partly, at least, because it has been so repeatedly knocked about by war. Barbarossa and a Turkish fleet blew it to bits in 1543, the French did the same in 1694 and 1814, and the British had a go at it in 1772. Just for good measure, it was both bombed and shelled from the sea by the forces of General Franco in the 1936–9 Civil War. It is a fairly important commercial center, and has a fishing fleet that will make you reach for your camera—especially when the light is right. The neighboring beach of La Fosca is smaller, and has lovely, shallow water for swimming.

From the rather ugly little inland town of Palafrugell a number of roads radiate, leading to some of the most delightful of all the Costa Brava resorts—Calella, Llafranch, Cape San Sebastián, Tamariu and Aiguablava. None is more than six km. (four miles) away, and each has its own beach and distinct personality. Tamariu, where the umbrella pines fringe the silver-white strand, is probably the most beautiful.

Llafranch, sheltered from the northeast by 150-meter-high (500-foot) Cape San Sebastián, and continuously inhabited for some 3,000 years, was an Iberian settlement in pre-Greek and Roman times. From the 18th-century hermitage, with its Baroque sanctuary, set near the lighthouse that crowns the cape, you can see far along two of the loveliest stretches of the entire coast, both of them well worth the climb. The Botanical Gardens at Cape Roig can also only be reached from Palafrugell, via Calella. A bit difficult to find, these gardens are worth a visit by those who are interested in the flora of the Mediterranean.

The coast between Cape San Sebastián and Aiguablava is imposing in its rugged magnificence, but can be appreciated only from the sea. Here are several delightful little beaches, a number of deep calas, and the fantastic Gisbert Cave, which pierces the rock for 244 meters (800 feet) even more dramatically than the famous Blue Grotto of Capri.

Aiguablava—Catalan for blue water—is scenically the loveliest of resorts, and has the added advantage of a parador; its beach of Fornells epitomizes what Mediterranean bathing should be—deep, clear, blue water, sheltered by two headlands to form a natural yacht basin.

The neighboring town of Bagur, with its ruined medieval castle, contains a number of fine porched houses, built during the last century by those who went to Cuba to make their fortunes and returned rich to end their days in comfort in the place of their birth. The beaches of Sa Tuna, Sa Riera and Aiguafreda, however, are well over a kilometer away, which accounts for the fact that, touristically, Bagur has not advanced as much as might be expected. Nevertheless, there are a few hotels including the beautifully positioned and luxurious Aiguablava.

Anyone interested in earthenware will go inland for about 14 km. (nine miles) as far as La Bisbal, built round the 14th-century episcopal palace-fortress above the River Daró. It supplies all the markets in the country with pottery. This excursion can easily be extended to the 11th-century

Lombard-Romanesque monastery church of San Miguel at Cruilles just over a kilometer further on, returning via the 14th-century Sarriera castle at Vulpellach, the Iberic town and 11th-century church at Ullestret, the triple walls pierced by twelve gates of Peratallada, and the square towers of Pals below a well-preserved 14th-century castle. Pals, moreover, possesses the second of the Costa Brava's excellent golf courses.

North to Ampurias and Cadaqués

The southern half of the Costa Brava ends here. Northward the coastal character changes considerably until you reach Rosas. Suddenly, the road emerges from the cork and pine woods and runs between long, straight avenues of plane trees across a flat and well-watered plain with irrigation streams and ditches that intersect the rice paddies and almond groves.

This is the plain of the Lower Ampurdan. Until medieval times, an arm of the sea enabled even large ships to reach such fascinating old towns as Torroella de Montgri and Castelló de Ampurias, but gradually the silt brought down by the Rivers Ter, Fluvia and Muga cut them off from their profitable maritime trade.

Torroella de Montgri was a Royal Borough as early as 1272, and was originally surrounded by medieval walls. The Castle of Montgri on its hill-top was built between 1294 and 1301 by Jaime II of Aragón and Catalonia, but was never finished as the outer walls and four round corner towers attest.

Estartit is important as a holiday resort, with a marina berthing over 1,000 craft and extensive accommodations for tourists. Estartit's beach is of fine white sand, one of the best on the coast. It extends for more than five km.

The mass of the Medas Islands, off the coast, offer scuba divers some of the best diving in these parts. La Escala is given over mainly to fishing and the construction of boats, including the rather portly craft known as *vacas,* cows. It lies at the southern extremity of the huge sandy Bay of Rosas, next door to the really magnificent Greco-Roman ruins of the city of Ampurias, which is unquestionably the Costa Brava's number one sightseeing feature, and right by the beach.

The original trading settlement was built on the site now occupied by the attractive medieval village of San Martín de Ampurias, then an island, by Greeks from Marseille, who named it Paleopolis. During the wars against the Phoenicians in the 5th century B.C., it was decided to build a fortified settlement a couple of kilometers away on the mainland, which was called Neapolis, and it was this site that was rediscovered in 1908, and which has now been fully excavated.

More recently, a large Roman city, about ten times the size of Neapolis, and belonging to the 2nd and 3rd centuries A.D., was unearthed on its out-skirts; it is filled with many matchless mosaic pavements and household ornaments. Excavation work may go on for years to come. Visit the muse-um on the site and allow plenty of time to explore the lower (Greek) town and upper (Roman) town, from which there is a magnificent view over the Bay of Rosas. Tape machines sited near the museum enable you to hear the history of Ampurias in one of several languages for a fee. We should point out that, if you don't have time to visit Ampurias, a great deal of the best material uncovered there has been taken to the museums in Barcelona and Gerona.

At Castelló de Ampurias visit the crumbling, but still quite startlingly beautiful, 13th-century church of Santa María. Although stripped by the Republicans in 1936 of all but the superb 15th-century alabaster retable of Vicente Borrás and a few finely carved tombs of the medieval Counts of Ampurias, it is still quite remarkable. This once rich and powerful walled city has shrunk today, but the citizens are proud of their 16th-century plaza, their 13th-century palace of the Counts of Ampurias, the seven-arched, 14th-century bridge, and the two huge 15th-century convents, which however, do not equal the 11th-century convent of San Miguel de Fluvía further south.

Rosas is ten km. (six miles) from Castelló de Ampurias, at the northern end of its great bay and at the foot of the Rodes mountains, an outlying spur of the mighty Pyrenees. It is the only Costa Brava resort that faces due west, and so is justly famous for the way each summer sunset sets aflame every windowpane in the town. The old town and port cluster round the ruins of an 11th-century fortress for protection against the swift and deadly Barbary slave raids that continued all along Spain's Mediterranean coast right into the last century. For centuries fishing was the port's life-blood, but its current popularity as a tourist center has taken over. At Rosas, the fish are auctioned in the traditional manner. Once, at least, you should make a point of going down in the early evening to see the boats returning and watch the catches being unloaded and auctioned.

The Canyelles Petits beach, as a matter of fact, is better for bathing and if you wish to explore on foot round the corner of Punta Falconera, you will find a whole series of moderately unspoiled little calas, where bathing is still delightfully adventurous, such as Llado, Rustella, and the mile-deep Cala Morisca.

Cadaqués

To reach Cadaqués, 18 km. (11 miles) away by road, you have to drive over a 458-meter (1,500-foot) pass through the Sierra Alseda, but for some of the way, you will be running through almond and olive groves, and the road is good. As a town, Cadaqués is one of the most attractive of all the Costa Brava resorts, with its whitewashed houses. Its tiny beach is of a special kind of reddish blue slate, used most decoratively in houses, walls and streets, but uncomfortable to sit on, and agonizing to walk over in bare feet. Fortunately, there are a few small sandy beaches along the sides of Cabo Créus, the legend-filled headland of Cape Cross, but reached mostly only on foot, over the headland. Cadaqués has a 16th-century parish church strikingly situated, and many steep, immensely picturesque streets.

The town became an artists' haunt in the 50s, with Salvador Dalí building a house there, ornamented with huge, egg-shaped garden decorations, opposite the Port Lligat Hotel. Though it retains a good deal of its slightly bohemian atmosphere, and its moderate inaccessibility makes it attractive for those wanting to get away from things, it is now rather fashionable and is more up-market and expensive than many places on the Costa Brava.

Further on, you can reach one of the Club Méditerranée's vacation camps, famous for its skin-diving school; it is tucked away in a corner of Cabo Créus.

There remain only Puerto de la Selva, Puerto de Llansá and the frontier village of Port Bou, and, although pleasant enough, they are all unremarkable. However, if you feel like a full hour's climbing, you might ascend the nearly 610-meter (2,000-foot) summit of Cape Cross, from Puerto de la Selva, where you will find the ruins of the 10th-century monastery of Sant Pere de Roda, complete with prehistoric dolmens, anchorites' caves and haunted grottos. The marvelous view all the way from Ampurias in the south to the French Gulf of Lions in the north makes the effort well worthwhile. Alternatively, and far easier, you can drive all the way up to the monastery along the sightseeing road leading out of Villajuiga.

Inland to Figueras and Gerona

Before turning inland from our tour of coastal resorts to take a brief look at Figueras and Gerona, it is perhaps worth suggesting here that the water-level route into Spain from France can be blistering hot in summer, whether you come by train or car. Much more pleasant is the road and rail route from Toulouse in France, through such charming old towns as Foix and Ax-les-Thermes, to the frontier at Puigcerdà, some 1,067 meters (3,500 feet) up in the Pyrenees. After passing through the lovely Segre valley, this route climbs still further before gradually descending the foothills and turning south at Ribas de Freser for Barcelona.

Tourists bound for Cadaqués or Rosas frequently enter Spain by way of Cerbère and Port Bou (C252). When you reach Llansá, *don't* take the fork road to Cadaqués, unless you want a horrific (though scenically stunning) drive through Puerto de la Selva on a very narrow road; continue inland on C252 to the Rosas signpost. The main road continues to Figueras, where it links with the toll-road to Gerona.

Figueras itself is of no great moment despite the imposing bulk of the 18th-century fortress castle of San Fernando, capable, so they say, of containing an army of 10,000 men with 500 horses. This castle was the last stronghold of the Republicans at the end of the Civil War when they made Figueras their base after the fall of Barcelona. But what makes Figueras well worth a visit is its remarkable Dalí Museum given to the town of his birth by the artist himself. An original, highly amusing and eccentric museum, a visit here is a must even if you are not really a lover of Dalí's paintings.

While Figueras is unexciting, Gerona is a city of really exceptional interest. Its most famous view is of the houses that line the River Oñar, their windows always draped with an unimaginably colorful array of drying laundry!

Gerona is a town full of fine, historic buildings, the most imposing of which is the cathedral, reached up a noble flight of 90 steps. Its 18th-century Baroque facade conceals the 11th-, 12th- and 14th-century building. Inside, its architecture is unusual in that it possesses only a single 60-meter-long, 23 meter-wide, and 34 meter-high nave (200-foot-long, 75-foot-wide and 110-foot-high). It contains many priceless tapestries and a 14th-century silver altar.

Gerona was a town long before the Romans named it Gerunda, but its greatest historical glory was when it suffered no less than three sieges by 15,000 of Napoleon's best troops. In 1809, it held out for six months, the citizens forming themselves into regular battalions, one of them composed exclusively of women.

The church of San Pedro de Galligans which houses the Archeological Museum is a fine example of 12th-century Romanesque but was built on a site founded by Charlemagne in the 9th century. Along the Paseo Arqueológico are the church of San Lucas, the Capuchin convent, the Arab baths, the gates of San Cristóbal and San Daniel. Sections of cyclopean walls contain stones three meters square, which defy all explanation of how they were placed there before the invention of mechanical devices. But probably the most impressive of all Gerona's many sights are the Easter week processions, when barefoot penitents walk the narrow, ancient streets, carrying candles and wearing black hoods that conceal all but their eyes, which, illuminated by the tapers, gleam with an uncanny light.

PRACTICAL INFORMATION FOR
THE COSTA BRAVA

TOURIST OFFICES. Cadaqués, Cotche 2A (tel. 25 83 15); **La Escala,** Plaça de les Escoles 1 (tel. 77 06 03); **Estartit,** Roca Maura 29 (tel. 75 89 10); **Figueras,** Plaza del Sol (tel. 50 31 55); **Gerona,** Ciutadans (Ciudadanos) 12 (tel. 20 16 94), and Plaça de Vi 1 (tel. 20 26 79); **Llansa,** Avda. de Europa (tel. 38 01 81); **Lloret de Mar,** Plaça de la Vila 1 (tel. 36 47 35); **Palafrugell,** Carrilet 2 (tel. 30 02 28); **Palamós,** Passeig del Mar 8 (tel. 31 43 90); **Playa de Aro,** Jacinto Verdaguer 11 (tel. 81 72 84); **Rosas,** Avda. de Rhode (tel. 25 73 31); **San Antonio de Calonge,,** Avda. Catalunya (tel. 31 55 56); **San Felíu de Guixols,** Plaza de España 1 (tel. 32 03 80); **Tossa de Mar,** Iglesia 4 (tel. 34 01 00).

TELEPHONE CODE. The dialing code for the whole of Gerona province, covering the entire Costa Brava area, is (972). You need only dial this code if you are calling from outside Gerona province; within Gerona province simply dial the main number.

GETTING AROUND. By Train. Gerona lies on the main railroad line between Barcelona and the French border, and is a scheduled stop on the following international services: Barcelona–Paris, Barcelona–Marseilles–Rome, and on the Catalan Talgo service from Barcelona–Lyon–Geneva.

Local services to the region leave from Barcelona's Término (or Francia) station and go to Port Bou on the French border via Granollers, Massaret, Gerona and Figueras. An alternative branch of this service calls at Blanes, Tordera, Massaret, Gerona and Figueras. The only coastal resorts that can be reached direct by train are Blanes in the south, and Llançà, Colera and Port Bou in the north. For traveling around the region from resort to resort you would be better advised to go by bus.

By Bus. This is the best means of public transport in the region as all the coastal resorts and small inland towns are connected by local bus services, and there are regular daily services from both Barcelona and Gerona to all the main resorts. From Barcelona (Estación del Norte) there are approximately seven services a day to Gerona, and four of these continue on to Figueras. Buses from Barcelona to the Costa Brava resorts of Lloret de Mar, Tossa, San Felíu de Guixols, S'Agaró, Playa de Aro, Palamós, Palafrugell, Torroella and Bagur are run by *Empresa Sarfa* and usually leave from the Plaça Duc de Medinaceli.

Gerona's main bus station is next to the train station just off the Plaça d' Espanya, but as not all buses leave from here, it is best to check with the Tourist Office.

By Boat. Blanes, San Felíu, Palamós and Rosas are all commercial ports and some Mediterranean cruise ships call at them. The most practical means of boat transport are the *cruceros,* small local boats, which operate services all day long between most of the towns on the coast. The two main lines are *Crucero Costa Brava* running boats from Blanes to Tamariu and all intermediate resorts; and *Pasajes Costa Brava* who sail between Blanes and Playa de Aro also with intermediate stops.

By Air. Gerona airport is the Costa Brava's main airport. Its main function is as a charter airport catering for the thousands of package-tour charter flights that flood in all summer long. Many visitors to the Costa Brava also make use of Barcelona's Prat de Llobregat airport. There is no public transport between Gerona airport and the city center.

By Car. The main thoroughfares for the region are the two inland north-south routes from the French border at Le Perthus to Barcelona by way of Figueras and Gerona. These are the autopista A17 on which high tolls are levied, and the often crowded and in parts, slow N-II. On the coast the C253 winds its way from Blanes to Palamós offering some spectacular sea views, before turning inland at Palamós to Palafrugell and Gerona. In the north the C252 twists its way along the coast from Port Bou to Llançà; otherwise most of the roads connecting the coastal resorts are unclassified and though offering some stunning views may also provide for some hair-raising driving.

HOTELS AND RESTAURANTS. The vast majority of hotels on the Costa Brava have sprung up with amazing rapidity during the last fifteen years or so; they tend to be the concrete highrise type which, sadly, one has to come to expect in the over-developed coastal regions of Spain. In their favor, however, they are mostly well provided with modern amenities, all rooms have private bathrooms, and many are close to the beach. The Costa Brava, together with the Costa Blanca and Costa del Sol, is one of Spain's biggest package-deal holiday regions; so don't be surprised if the 3-star hotel of your choice is totally booked up for the whole season, or if the hotel set-up is more geared to dealing with groups than with individuals. The main season is from mid-June to mid-September, so the best times to come to find accommodations and avoid the crowds, are May and late September.

The majority of hotels on the Costa Brava are only open from March/April through Sept./Oct., so if you are planning a stay in winter, check first. For modest accommodations, most of the resorts also have many simple hostels and pensions, for the most part not included in our recommendations.

For those travelers seeking something a little out of the ordinary, there is the *parador* at Aiguablava or the deluxe *Hostal de la Gavina* at S'Agaró. For golf enthusiasts there is the *Golf Costa Brava* at Santa Cristina de Aro; and for those who enjoy older hotels, the *Trías* at Palamós.

Aiguablava. *Parador Costa Brava* (E), (tel. 62 21 62). Beautifully located modern parador; 80 rooms. Large terrace, shaded by pine trees. AE, DC, MC, V.

Bagur. *Aiguablava* (M), on Fornells beach (tel. 62 20 58). Superb management and delightful situation; pool, tennis courts; a short walk from the sea. V. *Bonaigua* (M), on Fornells beach (tel. 62 20 50). 47 rooms; good view. *Bagur* (I), Comas y Ros 8 (tel. 62 22 07). 34 rooms; in town. *Plaja* (I), Pza. Pella i Forgas (tel. 62 21 97). Friendly family hotel in center of town. V.

Restaurant. *Sa Punta* (E), Urb. Sa Punta near Pals beach (tel. 63 64 10). North of town on Pals beach. One of the top Costa Brava restaurants serving superb seafood and a great selection of *cavas.* In a lovely setting. AE, MC, V.

Blanes. *Park Blanes* (E), S'Abanell (tel 33 02 50). Close to beach with pool, mini golf and tennis. *Patacano* (I), Passeig del Mar 12 (tel. 33 00 02). A simple but cozy hostel with just six rooms and an excellent restaurant (see below). Open all year round.

Restaurant. *Casa Patacano* (M), Paseo del Mar 12 (tel. 33 00 02). Dating back to 1901. Especially good for fish and seafood. AE, DC, MC, V.

Cadaques. *Playa Sol* (E), Playa Pianch 5 (tel. 25 81 00). 49 rooms with pool, overlooking beach. *Rocamar* (E), Dr. Bartomeus (tel. 25 81 50). 70 rooms; on a cliff one km. from town; pool and tennis. *Llane Petit* (M), on Llane Petit beach (tel. 25 80 50). 35 rooms. Modern, comfortable hotel with pool and garden. *S'Aguarda* (M–I), one km. out on road to Port Lligat (tel. 25 80 82). 27 rooms. AE, MC, V. *Port Lligat* (I), Port Lligat (tel. 25 81 62). 30 rooms and pool, opposite Dalí's house.

Restaurants. *Don Quijote* (M), Avda. Caridad Seriñana (tel. 25 81 41). Pleasant bistro with terrace and vine-covered garden. Closed Tues. AE, DC, MC, V. *Es Baluard* (M), Riba Nemesio Llorens 2 (tel. 25 81 83). *La Galiota* (M), Narciso Monturiol 9 (tel. 25 81 87). Decorated with Dalí paintings; a very popular and trendy restaurant so you need to book. Fish dishes usually good. Open June through Oct. daily, and on weekends only in winter.

Caldas De Malavella. *Balneario Vichy Catalán* (M), Dr. Furest 8 (tel. 47 00 00). Pool, tennis and pleasant gardens. *Balneario Prats* (I), San Esteve 7 (tel. 47 00 51). 76 rooms; pool. Both are pleasant old spa hotels.

Calella. *Alga* (E), Avda. Costa Blanca 43 (tel. 30 00 58). 54 rooms; pool, tennis and pleasant gardens, short walk from beach. Good restaurant *El Cantir,* MC, V. *Garbi* (M), Calle del Mirto (tel. 30 01 00). 30 rooms, some cheaper; pool and garden. MC, V. *Port Bo* (I), Gelphi 4 (tel. 30 02 50). 46 rooms; tennis. Low rates for a three-star hotel. AE, MC, V.

Calonge. *Cap Roig* (E), Ctra. de Palamós (tel. 65 20 00). Large hotel; pool and tennis. *Condado de San Jorge* (E), Ctra. de Palamós (tel. 81 71 16). 36 rooms; pool. *Park Hotel San Jorge* (E), Ctra. de Palamós (tel. 65 23 11). One of the best on the Costa Brava, with many amenities.

La Escala. *Nieves Mar* (M), Paseo del Mar (tel. 77 03 00). 80 rooms; pool, garden, tennis and a good restaurant. DC, MC, V. *Voramar* (M), Paseo Luis Albert 2 (tel. 77 01 08). 40 rooms; pool and bar. AE, V.

Estartit. *Bell Aire* (M), Iglesia 39 (tel. 75 81 62). 78 rooms. Central and one of the best. V. *Club de Campo Torre Grau* (M), Descampado (tel. 75 81 60). 10 rooms; pleasant setting with pool, mini-golf and tennis. *Miramar* (M), Avda. de Roma 7 (tel. 75 86 28). 64 rooms; pool, tennis and garden. *Coral* (I), Pza. de la Iglesia 8 (tel. 75 82 00). 59 rooms; pool and garden.
Restaurant. *Les Salines* (M), Cap de la Barra 5 (tel. 75 86 11). Specializes in fresh fish—try the *crema catalana* for dessert. Open April to Sept. only. AE, DC, MC, V.

Figueras. *Presidente* (E), Ronda Ferial 33 (tel. 50 17 00). 75 rooms. Rates are (M) in winter. AE, DC, MC, V. *Ampurdán* (M), 1.5 km. out on the N-II to France (tel. 50 05 62). An adequate, comfortable, motel-type hotel with an outstanding restaurant (see below). AE, DC, MC, V. *Durán* (M), Lasauca 5 (tel. 50 12 50). In center of town, dating back to 1895. Comfortable, excellent cuisine (see below). AE, DC, MC, V. *Pirineos* (I), Ronda Barcelona 1 (tel. 50 03 12). 53 rooms. AE, DC, V. *Travé* (I), on road to Olot (tel. 50 05 91). 73 rooms; pool, garden, easy parking. AE, DC, MC, V.
Restaurants. *Ampurdán Hotel* (E), (tel. 50 05 62). Highly recommended for huge portions of delicious food and recognized by gourmets as one of Catalonia's best restaurants. Prices, bearing in mind the quality, are very reasonable. AE, DC, MC, V. *Durán Hotel* (M), (tel. 50 12 50). One of the best in Catalonia and run by the same family since 1920s. AE, DC, MC, V. *Can Jeroni* (I), Castello 36 (tel. 50 09 83). Modest eating place in market square. Open 8.30 A.M.–4 P.M. only; good basic fare and incredible value. Something of an institution though some Spanish—or Catalan—may help here. *Mas Pau* (E), five km. out on road to Olot (tel. 54 61 54), in a beautifully decorated old farmhouse with charming garden; food good as well. AE, DC, MC, V.

Gerona. *Novotel-Gerona* (E), (tel. 47 71 00). Twelve km. out just off the *autopista* A17 at exit 8. Comfortable, modern and close to airport. AE, DC, MC, V. *Costabella* (M), Avda. Francia 61 (tel. 20 25 24). Two km. north on N-II. 23 rooms; easy parking. AE, DC, MC, V. *Fornells Park* (M), (tel. 47 61 25), five km. south on N-II at Fornells de la Selva. 36 rooms; garden and pool. AE, DC, MC, V. *Ultonia* (M), Gran Vía Jaume I 22 (tel.

20 38 50); 45 rooms; is the best. AE, DC, MC, V. *Europa* (I), Julio Garreta 23 (tel. 20 27 50). In south of town just a block off the N-II. 26 rooms; AE, DC, MC, V. *Inmortal Gerona* (M), Ctra. de Barcelona 31 (tel. 20 79 00). 76 rooms; parking; low rates. *Peninsula* (I), Nou 3 (tel. 20 38 00). Quite close to river; 68 rooms.

Restaurants. *Cipresaia* (M), Carreras Peralta 5 (tel. 20 30 38). Excellent food and a good wine list from the owner's own cellars. Closed Sun. AE, MC, V. *Rosaleda* (M), Passeig Devesa (tel. 21 36 68). Pleasantly located in La Devesa Park. *Casa Marieta* (I), Pza. Independencia 5 (tel. 20 10 16). Good value.

Llafranch. *Levante* (M), Passeig Francesc Blanes 5 (tel. 30 03 66). 20 rooms; a 2-star hotel. *Paraíso* (M), Paraje Font D'en Xeco (tel. 30 04 50). 55 rooms; pool and garden. AE, DC, MC, V. *Terramar* (M), Cipsele 1 (tel. 30 02 00). An old hotel with good views. AE, DC, MC, V. *Casamar* (I), Carrer d'El Nero 3–11 (tel. 30 01 04). 24 rooms; pleasant and with the lowest rates.

Llagostera. Restaurant. *Els Tinars* (E), (tel. 83 06 26). In lovely setting with outdoor terrace five km. out, off the road to San Feliu de Guixols. Well worth the trip for its excellent Catalan cooking. Closed Mon. night. AE, DC, MC, V.

Llansa. Good beach resort with modest hotels only. *Grimar* (M), Ctra. de Port Bou (tel. 38 01 67). 38 rooms; tennis, garden. *Mendisol* (M), (tel. 38 01 00). On Grifeu beach. 32 rooms; parking and garden. *Berna* (I), Paseo Marítimo 13 (tel. 38 01 50). Central with 38 rooms.

Restaurant. *Ca'n Manuel* (M), Plaça del Port 9 (tel. 38 01 12). Large fish restaurant overlooking the port; good service. Closed Thurs. in winter. V.

Lloret De Mar. A heavily-developed resort with hundreds of 2- and 3-star resort hotels of which it is only possible to mention a few here. Its 4-star hotels are all good and *Santa Marta* and *Rigat Park* are outstanding. *Santa Marta* (L), Playa de Santa Cristina (tel. 36 49 04). 78 rooms; 3 km. out of town, isolated in its own beautiful leafy cove; swimming pool, tennis courts, spacious rooms with balconies overlooking the sea or mountains; fine cuisine. AE, DC, MC, V. *Monterrey* (L), Ctra. de Tossa (tel. 36 40 50). 229 rooms. Good standards; pool and tennis. AE, V. *Cluamarsol* (E), Jacinto Verdaguer 7 (tel. 36 57 50). 87 rooms; on the front. AE, DC, MC, V. *Rigat Park* (E), Avda. de América (tel. 36 52 00). 99 rooms. Spanish-style hotel, pleasantly situated 2 km. out at Fanals beach; private beach, pool and gardens. DC, MC. *Roger de Flor* (E), Turo de l'Estelat (tel. 36 48 00). Close to both the sea and the center of town; pleasant garden and rooms with either sea or mountain views. AE, DC, MC, V. *Excelsior* (M), Jacinto Verdaguer 16 (tel. 36 41 37). 45 rooms. Also on main promenade overlooking sea. AE, DC, MC, V. *Tropic* (M), Paseo Marítimo (tel. 36 51 54), 40 rooms. Centrally located with pool; by far the smallest and cheapest of the 4-star hotels. *Montecarlo* (I), San Jorge 11 (tel. 36 49 08). 94 rooms; pool, garden. Pleasantly situated in a pine wood. *Mundial* (I), Vicenc Bou 15 (tel. 36 43 50). 98 rooms; pool, garden and parking. *Perelló* (I), Areny 7 (tel. 36 46 62). 40 rooms; five mins. from beach.

Restaurants. *Santa Marta* (L), Playa de Santa Cristina (tel. 36 49 04). The panoramic diningroom of the Santa Marta hotel is in a beautiful setting and serves some superb cuisine; impeccable service. AE, DC, MC, V. *El Trull* (E), Playa Canyelles (tel. 36 49 28). Atmospherically decorated restaurant three km. off the road to Tossa. Noted for its fine cuisine; seafood especially recommended. AE, DC, MC, V. *La Bodega Vella* (M), Na Marina 14 (tel. 36 74 78) with typical decor. AE, DC, MC, V. *Taverna del Mar* (M), Pescadors 5 (tel. 36 40 90). Just off the front and with some good fish dishes. AE, MC, V.

Palamos. *Trías* (E), Paseo del Mar (tel. 31 41 00). Also (M) outside high season. One of the few Costa Brava old timers, established in 1900 and well maintained. Overlooking the bay with a fine restaurant. This hotel only accepts individual travelers, no tour groups. Open Easter to Oct. only. MC, V. *San Luís* (M), Avda. 11 de Septiembre 61 (tel. 31 40 50). 29 rooms; in center. *Marina* (I), Avda. 11 de Septiembre 48 (tel. 31 42 50). 62 rooms; garden. AE, DC, MC, V.

Restaurants. *María de Cadaques* (E), Notarias 39 (tel. 31 40 09). Fine restaurant popular now for 50 years; mostly seafood including the local specialty of *pollo con langosta* (chicken with lobster). Always crowded, so book. AE, DC, MC, V. *Trías* (E), Paseo del Mar (tel. 31 41 00). The restaurant of the Trías hotel is a long-standing tradition on the Costa Brava and serves some notable cuisine; impeccable service. Top end of price category. MC, V.

Playa De Aro. *Big Rock* (E), Barri de Fanals 5 (tel. 81 80 12). 5 rooms. Beautifully furnished comfortable rooms in a 17th-century house next to the renowned restaurant (see below). Superb sea views, an outstanding place to stay. AE, DC, MC, V. *Columbus* (E), Paseo del Mar (tel. 81 71 66). 110 rooms. An older hotel in a park overlooking the beach, the best in this rather brash resort. *Aromar* (M), Paseo Marítimo (tel. 81 70 54). 167 rooms. Good functional packaged-tour hotel overlooking sea. AE, DC, MC, V. *Costa Brava* (M), Punta d'en Ramis (tel. 81 73 08). 59 rooms. In a lovely position on a headland surrounded by beaches. AE, DC, MC, V.

Restaurants. *Carles Camós-Big Rock* (E), Barri de Fanals 5 (tel. 81 80 12) in the Urbanización Mas Nou. This famous restaurant moved from Palamos to this wonderful setting. Cuisine, service, and atmosphere—it's in an old Catalan farmhouse—are notable. Closed Mon. AE, DC, MC, V. *Mas Nou* (E), (tel. 81 78 53). 4 km. out on the road to Santa Cristina. Bright, yet stylish decor, excellent food and wines and very good service. AE, DC, MC, V. *La Grillade* (M), Pinar del Mar 14 (tel. 81 73 33). Good French food and outdoor dining. AE, DC, MC, V.

Puerto De La Selva. A pretty little fishing village. *Amberes* (M), Selva de Mar (tel. 38 70 30). 18 rooms; a simple, pleasant hostel close to the harbor. V. *Porto Cristo* (M), Mayor 48 (tel. 38 70 62). The only hotel. 54 rooms; central and pleasant. Both inexpensive.

Restaurant. *Ca l'Herminda* (I), Isla 7 (tel. 38 70 75). Typical decor and good fresh fish. DC, V.

Rosas. *Almadraba Park* (E), Playa Almadraba (tel. 25 65 50). Five km. out of town on a headland overlooking the sea. Good service and a fine restaurant serving many Catalan specialties. AE, DC, MC, V. *La Terraza* (E), Paseo Marítimo 19 (tel. 25 61 54). 111 rooms; by the beach with pool, tennis and garden. MC, V. *Canyelles Platja* (M), at Canyelles Petites beach (tel. 25 65 00). Beach hotel with 99 rooms. *Coral Playa* (M), Playa del Rastrillo (tel. 25 62 50). 128 rooms; garden. *Goya Park* (M), Santa Margarita (tel. 25 75 50). 224 rooms; pool. *Marián* (M), Platja Salata (tel. 25 61 08). 145 rooms; pool and tennis. Some cheaper rooms. *Moderno* (M), Paseo Marítimo 15 (tel. 25 65 58). 57 rooms overlooking the sea. One of the most expensive. *Monterrey* (M), Santa Margarita (tel. 25 66 76). 138 rooms; pool. *Casa del Mar* (I), Ctra. de Figueras (tel. 25 64 50). 28 rooms; garden.

Restaurants. *Hacienda El Bulli* (L), (tel. 25 76 51). In Cala Montjoi, this restaurant is well worth the trip. The diningroom has beautiful views and there is an outdoor patio. The food is superb with the emphasis on French *nouvelle cuisine.* Closed Mon. and for lunch on Tues. AE, DC, MC, V. *La Llar* (E), (tel. 25 53 68). Four km. (three miles) out on the road to Figueras. An excellent restaurant with its own imaginative style of cooking. Closed Thurs. except in high season. AE, DC, MC, V. *L'Antull* (M), Plaça Sant Pere 7 (tel. 25 75 73). AE, DC, MC, V. *Can Ramón* (M), Sant Elm 8 (tel. 25 69 18). Closed Mon.

S'Agaro. *Hostal de la Gavina* (L), Pza. de la Rosaleda (tel. 32 11 00). Super-deluxe hotel with rates to match. 73 rooms. Palatial setting amid tree-shaded lawns; has a Louis XV suite with genuine period furniture. Its restaurant is equally famous. Belongs to *Relais and Châteaux* and is a link in the *Leading Hotels of the World* chain. Open April through Oct. AE, DC, MC, V.

San Antonio De Calonge. *Rosa dels Vents* (E), Paseo del Mar (tel. 65 13 11). 58 rooms; garden and tennis, overlooking the sea. DC, V. *Reymar* (M), Torre Valentina (tel. 65 22 11). 49 rooms, some (I); garden, tennis. *Príncipe Ben-Hur* (M), Josep Mercader (tel. 65 11 38). Good hostel with 20 rooms; open June through Sept. only. *Rosamar* (M), Paseo del Mar 33 (tel. 65 06 61). Many rooms are (I). 63 rooms; garden and overlooking sea.

Restaurant. *Refugi de Pescadors* (M), José Mundet 44 (tel. 65 10 88). Fish and seafood restaurant. Decor resembles a boat's cabin. AE, DC, MC, V.

San Feliu De Guixols. A lovely old village behind the tourist facade. *Curhotel Hipócrates* (M), Ctra. de Sant Pol 229 (tel. 32 06 62). 85 rooms; on a headland north of town. Pool, gardens, tennis. Also a hotel for therapeutic cures. *Murla Park* (M), Passeig de Guixols 22 (tel. 32 04 50). 89 rooms; modest but comfortable hotel, close to the sea and center; good service. MC, V. *Les Noies* (I), Rambla Portalet 10 (tel. 32 04 00). 45 rooms; central, not far from the sea. AE, DC, MC. *Caleta Park* (E), at Sant Pol beach (tel. 32 00 12). 105 rooms; good beach hotel. Pool and tennis. DC, MC, V. *Montjoi* (M), at Sant Elm (tel. 32 03 00). 64 rooms; pool and garden. In pleasant location overlooking sea. AE, MC, V.

Restaurants. *Eldorado Petit* (L), Rambla Vidal 11 (tel. 32 18 18). In the very center of town. The food is exquisite, the service superb and friendly and the prices very fair for what is offered. Under the same ownership as its famous namesake in Barcelona. AE, DC, MC, V. *S'Adolitx* (M), Mayor 13 (tel. 32 18 53). AE, DC, MC, V. *Bahía* (M), Passeig del Mar 18 (tel. 32 02 19). AE, DC, MC, V. *Can Toni* (M), Sant Martiriá 29 (tel. 32 10 26). An excellent and reasonably priced restaurant offering some superb Catalan specialties and fish dishes. AE, DC, MC, V.

Santa Cristina De Aro. *Golf Costa Brava* (E), by the Costa Brava golf club (tel. 83 70 52). Pool, eight tennis courts, golf, all in a peaceful location. AE, DC, MC, V. *Cristina* (I) (tel. 83 73 52), on the Gerona road; a simple 2-star hotel with pool and garden.

Restaurant. *Les Panolles* (M) at km. 27 on the C250 (tel. 83 70 11). In a 17th-century farmhouse on the side of the road. Good Catalan cooking. Try to eat in the picturesque old part. AE, DC, MC, V.

Tamariu. *Hostalillo* (E), Bellavista 22 (tel. 30 01 58). 70 rooms; pleasant traditional hotel on the edge of the bay with good views and good service. *Jano* (M), Paseo del Mar 5 (tel. 30 04 62). 50 rooms; close to the sea. *Tamariu* (I), Paseo del Mar 3 (tel. 30 01 08). 24 rooms; close to the sea. All open May to Sept. only.

Tossa Del Mar. *Gran Hotel Reymar* (E), Playa Mar Menuda (tel. 34 03 12). 131 rooms; 4-star hotel with pool, tennis and gardens close to the La Palma beach. *Ancora* (M), Avda. de la Palma 4 (tel. 34 02 99). 58 rooms; pleasant terrace. *Mar Menuda* (M), Playa Mar Menuda (tel. 34 10 00). 40 rooms; pool, tennis and garden, close to the sea. DC, V. *Vora Mar* (M), Avda. de la Palma 19 (tel. 34 03 54). 63 rooms; garden. *Avenida* (I), Avda. de la Palma 5 (tel. 34 07 56). 50 rooms; opposite the Vora Mar. *Cap d'Or* (I), Passeig Vila Vella 1 (tel. 34 00 81). 12 rooms. Simple and pleasant at far end of Passeig del Mar.

Restaurants. *Bahía* (M), Socorro 4 (tel. 34 03 22). Good seafood; opposite the beach at the end of Paseo del Mar. AE, DC, MC, V. *Es Moli* (M), Tarull 3 (tel. 34 14 14). Outdoor dining on a leafy patio. AE, DC, MC, V.

PLACES OF INTEREST. Opening hours given are liable to frequent change and it is always wise to doublecheck with the local tourist offices before setting out on a special trip. Most museums close on Mondays, so be prepared.

Ampurias. The **Greek and Roman settlements** on this site about two km. north of La Escala are some of the most important excavations in Spain; ruins of temples and Roman villas, cisterns, mosaics and sculptures will provide a fascinating day's exploration. Open Tues. to Sun. 9–7 in summer, 10–1 and 3–5 in winter; closed Mon. Above the site is a small **museum** with diagrams and explanations of the ruins.

La Bisbal. Interesting small historic town which is famous for its pottery and is dominated by its 13th-century **Romanesque Castle.** Open Mon. to Fri. 6–9, Sat. and Sun. 11–2 and 5–9. Part of the old medieval city walls are still intact as is the **Puente Viejo,** the medieval bridge over the River Daró.

Blanes. Aquarium, Explanada del Puerto 12. Collection of Mediterranean marine life, octopus and turtles. Feeding takes place on Tues. and Fri. mornings. Open Easter to Oct. 10–8.

Jardín Botánico Mar-i-Murtra, Paseo Carlos Faust. One of the most important botanical gardens in Europe with over 4,000 plants including species from southern Africa, Mexico and Australia. Open 9–6.

Cadaques. Museo Municipal de Arte Contemporáneo, Monturiol 15. Modern art museum containing, among others, works by Dalí and Picasso. Open Mar. through Oct., 11–1 and 4–8; closed Sun. P.M.

Museo Perrot Moore (Perrot Moore Museum), Pza. Federico Rahola. Important collection of European graphic arts from the 15th to 20th centuries. Open daily 5–8 in summer; weekends only in winter.

Figueras (Gerona). **Museo del Ampurdán** (Ampurdán Museum), Rambla 1. Valuable collection of religious painting, archeology, art and history from the Ampurdán region. Art galleries with paintings from the 17th to 20th century including works by Ribera, Sorolla, and Tapiès. Open 11–1 (2 on weekends) and 4.30–8; closed Tues.

Museo Dalí (Dalí Museum), Plaza Gala-Dalí. Open daily 11.30–5.30; closed Mon. in winter.

Museo de Juguetes (Toy Museum), Rambla 10. Collection of toys from Catalonia and Valencia from 1900–1940. Open 10–12.30 and 4–7.30; closed Tues. in winter.

Gerona. Museo de la Catedral (Cathedral Museum), Pza. de la Catedral. Interesting collection of medieval Islamic art and 12th- and 13th-century tapestries including the famous Tapestry of the Creation. Open daily 9.30–1.15 and 3.30–7; in July through Sept. 9.30–8.

Museo de Arte (Museum of Art), Palacio Episcopal. Romanesque paintings and sculptures and Catalan Gothic paintings. Also modern art. Open Tues. to Sat. 10–1 and 4.30–7; closed Mon. and Sun. P.M. Entrance ticket also includes visits to the **Archeological Museum** and the **Arab Baths.**

Museo Arqueológico de Sant Pere de Galligans, Sta. Lucía 1. Local archeological finds and Romanesque art housed in 12th-century Benedictine monastery of Sant Pere—beautiful cloisters. Open Tues. to Sun. 10–1 and 4.30–7; closed Mon. and Sun. P.M.

Museo Histórico (Museum of the History of Gerona), Força 27. Concentrates especially on the 19th century; plus history of the sardana dance. Open Tues. to Sat. 10–2 and 5–7; Sun. 9.30–2.30; closed Mon. and Sun. P.M.

Baños Arabes (Arab Baths) in the Barrio Viejo. Open Tues. to Sun. 10–2 and 4–7 in summer; Oct. to Apr. 10–1 only; closed Mon. and Sun. P.M.

Llagostera. Musei Emilí Vila (Emilí Vila Museum), San Pedro 25–7. Birthplace of Emilí Vila with his paintings and works by Corot, Degas, Modigliani and Picasso. Open Mon. to Sat. 11–1 and 4–8; closed Sun.

Llivia. Museo Municipal, Forns 4. Local archeology and history and a visit to Europe's oldest pharmacy founded in 1415. Open 10–1 and 3–7 (6 in winter).

Lloret De Mar. Museo Municipal (Municipal Museum), Sant Carles. Sections on archeology, sea-faring and folklore. Recently reopened after restoration; check hours with tourist office.

Palafrugell. Museo Archivo Municipal, Cervantes 10. Archeology, ceramics and tools from the history of the cork industry. Open Mon. and Thurs. to Sat. 5–8.

Castell de Cap Roig, Cap Roig. A castle built in this century in Renaissance style, by the Russian Colonel Woevodsky. Open daily 10–6.

Cap Roig Botanical Gardens, close by, down an unsurfaced road. These are right above the sea with Mediterranean plants and rare shrubs. Open daily 8–8 in summer and 9–6 in winter.

Palamos. Museo Cau de la Costa Brava, Plaça del Forn. Ceramics and pottery, modern painting and a good coin collection. Open daily 10–1 and 4–6.30; closed Sun. P.M.

Perelada. Palace of the Counts of Perelada. Built between the 14th and 16th centuries and restored in the 19th. Part of it is now used as a luxury **casino** and it also houses a **Biblioteca**, a library with over 70,000 old books; the **Museo del Vidrio** (Glass Museum) with glass-blowing displays, and the **Museo del Vino** with displays of wine making. Library and museums open Tues. to Sat. 10–12 and 4.30–5.30; Sun. 10–12 only; closed Mon. Perelada lies in the center of the Ampurdán wine growing region and it is possible to visit some of its **wine cellars** on the edge of town.

Puerto De La Selva. Monastery of Sant Pere de Roda, on the edge of the village. Impressive medieval monastery built between the 9th and 12th centuries with a fine Romanesque 11th-century church. Open daily 9–1 and 4–7.

San Feliu De Guixols. Ruins of a **Benedictine monastery** begun in the 11th century with famous Porta Ferrada, a Romanesque doorway. The Museo Municipal (Municipal Museum), adjoining the monastery, houses Iberian, Greek and Roman remains, and paintings and carvings from the ancient monastery. Open 11–1 and 4–7 in summer; in winter on Sun. only 11–1.

Sils. Museo Claret at km. 706 on the N-II. Good collection of vintage cars and carriages, all in working order. Open 10–1 and 3–7. Closed Sun. P.M. and afternoons in winter.

Tossa De Mar. The Vila Vella, the Old Town, a Historic and Artistic Monument, boasts some fine old walls and 12th-century circular towers among its many historic buildings.

Museo Municipal Vila Vella has some well documented records, finds and paintings from this old historic center. Open Mon. to Sat. 10–1 and 4–8 (3–5 in winter); Sun. 11–1 only.

SPORTS. Golf. The Costa Brava has two 18-hole golf courses; the Club de Golf de Pals at Pals beach, and the Club de Golf Costa Brava at Santa Cristina de Aro.

Tennis. There are numerous tennis courts all along the coast and many of the resort hotels have their own tennis courts.

Watersports. Swimming, scuba diving, wind surfing and water skiing are popular all along the coast.

Sailing. Suitable yacht marinas at the following towns: Blanes, San Felíu de Guixols, Palamós, El Estartit, Rosas and Puerto de la Selva.

SOUTHEAST SPAIN

Costa del Azahar and Costa Blanca

Following the successful practice that every bit of coast must be labeled with an attractive trade name, the shores of the provinces of Castellón de la Plana and Valencia have been officially baptized Costa del Azahar—not a bad choice, as the fragrant perfume of the orange blossom *(azahar)* pervades the whole countryside. The Costa Blanca, less originally named after the dazzling white light which after all is not restricted to that particular stretch of coast, lumps together the seaside of Alicante, Murcia and parts of Almería as far south as Cape Gata, two wide arcs divided by Cape Palos.

The northern 320 km. (200 miles) used to be known as the Levante—a rather vague term simply meaning "east." In ancient times the Levante was a favored place for Phoenician trading ships, and it is interesting to note that the inhabitants today still have a strongly Semitic cast of countenance, not found elsewhere in Spain. The Phoenicians never attempted the conquest of Spain, merely contenting themselves with trading posts, to which the Ibero-Celts themselves brought the minerals the Phoenicians sought, but it was as they sailed along this stretch of coast, and gazed uneasily at the menacing mountains, that they gave to the country its present name—Spagna, meaning "the hidden land."

South and west of the Levante lie the two modern provinces that represent the medieval kingdom of Murcia—Murcia and Albacete. The latter is of little interest to tourists beyond laying claim to a few of Don Quijote's exploits and the fact that the shortest road from Madrid to the Costa Blanca runs through it, as well as the less frequented and thus much quicker inland route from Valencia via Jaén to Granada. The main road linking the Levante with Andalusia runs through Murcia.

Exploring the Southeast

The Levante is most easily approached by the Barcelona–Valencia–Alicante toll-road, though the N340, the narrower coastal road, is scenically superior, entering Castellón, the first of the two great orange-growing provinces, at Vinaroz, a little town that once belonged to the Knights Templar, and is still famous for its wine. Just beyond it, outside Benicarló, and within sight of the parador, is the promontory upon which is built the strangely romantic fortress town of Peñíscola. Roadways lead to this town of highrise apartments, modern hotels, shops and restaurants. Seen from afar, Peñíscola is dramatically picturesque, but nothing can equal this first view and wandering about this 3,000-year-old city is disappointing.

The highway and railway leave the sea after Peñíscola to pass the ruined castle of Chisvert, but to return at the fine bathing beaches of Oropesa with its Torre del Rey, a model of 16th-century military architecture, and Benicasim (a Moorish name), six km. (four miles) from the idyllic Carmelite monastery at the Desierto de las Palmas, Desert of Palms being merely an original way to indicate the scarcity of that tree among the pines and cypresses.

Castellón de la Plana is small for a provincial capital, but bustling with movement in the wide avenues. The 14th-century Gothic church of Santa María contains paintings by Zurbarán, while San Augustín is decorated with colorful tiles; the town is overlooked by the 40-meter-high (130-foot) belfry.

Next comes Villareal at the mouth of the River Mijares, with its disproportionately large church and on the Seco, closer to the sea, Burriana, with a fine Gothic church.

The first place of interest after entering the province of Valencia is Sagunto, the ramparts of whose medieval castle extend for over a kilometer across the hilltop of the ancient acropolis. These enormous fortifications which can be seen from a distance give the best view over the ruins of the Roman town which includes a theater capable of holding 7,000 spectators. Sadly, this splendid site is ruined by gigantic steel mills and cement factories.

Valencia

Sagunto is only 23 km. (14 miles) from Valencia, the third city of Spain. Valencia is the obvious capital of the Levante, being roughly equidistant from its two bigger sisters, Barcelona and Madrid. Though of surprisingly little maritime importance, Valencia has mushroomed into a huge town of characterless highrises which swamp the lovely old nucleus on the right bank of the Río Turia. It does have an Acropolis, a fortified hill, site of the ancient city with ruins going back through centuries of occupation by many races; a Roman theater dating from the 3rd century A.D., one of Spain's best-preserved Roman buildings, with magnificent acoustics still; and a ruined Temple of Diana.

Valencia was liberated from the Moors by that legendary figure El Cid at the end of the first wave of the Reconquest in 1094 but, at his death,

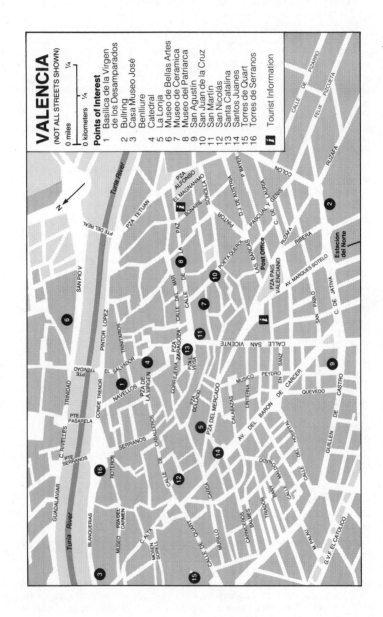

VALENCIA
(NOT ALL STREETS SHOWN)

0 miles ¼

0 kilometers ¼

Points of Interest

1 Basilica de la Virgen de los Desamparados
2 Bullring
3 Casa Museo José Benlliure
4 Catedral
5 La Lonja
6 Museo de Bellas Artes
7 Museo de Ceramica
8 Museo del Patriarca
9 San Agustín
10 San Juan de la Cruz
11 San Martín
12 San Nicolas
13 Santa Catalina
14 Santos Juanes
15 Torres de Quart
16 Torres de Serranos

i Tourist Information

it again became an Emirate, and was not permanently in Christian hands until 1238. Don Jaime I, the Conquistador King of Aragón, retook the city for Catholic Spain following a four months' siege, won with the help of troops commanded by the Archbishop of Narbonne (France). It was a true holy war—the Moors, who had been subjugated definitively by the Spaniards at the end of the 15th century were now forced to choose between exile or conversion to Christianity. Some pretended to submit and were henceforth known as Moriscos, others resisted. Accused of nefarious relationships with the Berbers, not to mention conspiracy, they were expelled from Spain in 1609.

The city picked the wrong side in the War of the Spanish Succession at the beginning of the 18th century. Later it rebelled against Napoleon, and was considerably damaged by Marshal Suchet before it surrendered in January 1812.

Today Valencia is noted for holding one of the most colorful and sensational of all Spanish fiestas, the *fallas de San José,* held for a week in March. March 19 is *San José,* St. Joseph's Day, when families throughout Spain celebrate Father's Day. (*San José* is a public holiday in the provinces of Castellón, Valencia and Alicante.) The fact that St. Joseph is not only the patron saint of fathers but also of carpenters is what gave rise to this bizarre and time-honored fiesta. Back in medieval days the guilds of carpenters burned their wood shavings in huge bonfires on St. Joseph's day. Today, after a week-long celebration of fireworks, flower-strewn floats, carnival processions, top bullfights and uncontrolled merry-making to which tourists and natives flock from all over Spain, the *fallas* reach their climax on March 19 with the burning of huge and monstrous effigies of popular and not-so-popular figures on massive bonfires.

Valencia lies on the River Turia, which enters the sea at the large port of El Grao, some three km. east. To the north are the drab and polluted beaches of Levante and Malvarrosa; south lie Nazaret and Pinedo, followed by the less crowded El Saler backed by the La Dehesa pine wood, Recati, El Perello and the string of the Las Palmeras beaches.

Valencia's historical buildings cluster round the 14th-century cathedral, which is entered by three portals, respectively Romanesque, Gothic and Rococo; but this mixture of styles has been done away with in the interior, where Renaissance and Baroque marbles have been removed, as is now the trend in Spanish churches, in a successful restoration of the original pure Gothic. There is a large treasury; one side chapel features a Goya picture of St. Francis Borgia surrounded by devils waiting eagerly for the saint's demise. Before a superb Florentine Gothic retable stands a small dark vessel, supposedly the Holy Grail, used at the Last Supper. It is amazing just how often the Holy Grail pops up in Spain. There must have been quite a Grail industry at one time.

The basilica of the Virgen de los Desamparados (Virgin of the Unsheltered) joins the cathedral near the porch which has accommodated a meeting of the water tribunal every Thursday since 1350, and where all decisions regarding the irrigation of the local crops are still made. The Plaza de la Virgen by the entrance to the cathedral and the basilica is a lovely place for a drink in the late afternoon, its many sidewalk cafes attracting the population of Valencia.

The unfinished octagonal 15th-century belfry, affectionately known as Miguelete, faces the much finer hexagonal 17th-century tower of Santa

Catalina across the Plaza de Zaragoza. San Martín, at the corner of the plaza and the main shopping street, Calle San Vicente, contains another Goya and a fine late-Gothic sculpture of the patron saint.

Down a small street on your right as you walk down Calle San Vicente, you will come across the delightful Plaza Redonda, with a market and hordes of stray cats. It is a charming old corner of the city. Return to the Calle San Vicente and this time head down one of the streets on the opposite side which will bring you to the Palace of the Marqués de Dos Aguas which today houses the National Ceramics Museum. The palace's fantastic Rococo facade centers on the figures of the *Two Waters* by Hipólito Rovira, who died demented in 1740—not really surprising after you have seen the sculptures. The museum inside the palace has a wonderful collection of ceramics and is well worth a visit. Close by is the neo-Classical University and the rather more severe facade of the Colegio del Patriarca. The college was founded by San Juan de Ribera and was begun in 1603. Inside is a small art gallery with some worthwhile paintings including works by El Greco and Morales.

Of Valencia's many historic buildings the 15th-century Lonja del Mercado on the Plaza Mercado opposite the market, is probably the most rewarding architecturally; the market itself, housed in a fine old building, is also worth a glance. The splendid 14th-century arch of the Torres de Serranos spanned a gate in the walls—which surrounded the old town till 1865—leading to one of the three bridges across the Turia. The Museum of Fine Arts in the San Pio V buildings on the north bank is considered one of the finest in Spain.

Finally, before you leave—or when you arrive, for that matter—take a look at the facade of Valencia's main railroad station near the bullring. Prettily painted with oranges and roses, it shelters some stylish old ticket counters in its lobby.

PRACTICAL INFORMATION FOR VALENCIA

TOURIST OFFICES. The main Tourist Office is at Calle de la Paz 46 (tel. 332 4096) near the Plaza Alfonso el Magnánimo. There is also a Municipal Tourist Office at Plaza del País Valenciano 1 (tel. 351 0417), at the Estación del Norte (tel. 352 2882), at Avda. Cataluña 1 (tel. 369 7932) and at the airport at Manises (tel. 153 0325).

TELEPHONE CODE. The dialing code for the city of Valencia and the entire Valencia province is (94). You need only dial this code when calling from outside Valencia province.

GETTING AROUND. Buses provide the main method of public transport and most central services start from the Plaza País Valenciano area, or to the outlying suburbs and beach areas, from the Plaza Porta del Mar. The Tourist Office can give you details of bus routes or you can ask at the transport headquarters, EMT, Gobernador Viejo 16. From the main bus depot on Avda. Menéndez Pidal (tel. 349 7222), bus 28 takes you into the center of town near the Plaza País Valenciano. Buses to Pinedo and Saler beaches leave from the Glorieta Porta de la Mar.

The train station, Estación del Norte, on Calle Játiva is very central and only involves a short walk or cab ride to most of the hotels we list.

HOTELS. With the exception of the *Rey Don Jaime,* all the hotels listed here are very much in the center of town and within easy walking distance of the main sights. Valencia has several older hotels which are well maintained and full of old-world charm and style; if you prefer more recent hotels, there is no shortage of these either. All the hotels listed below, with the exception of the airport hotel, the *Azafata Sol,* are in the city itself; but in the vicinity of Valencia, within only 15 minutes' drive or so, are some excellent luxury hotels which we have listed under Puzol and El Saler.

If you are planning to come to Valencia for its *falla* celebrations between March 12 and 19, make sure you have booked your accommodations long ahead; be prepared also for prices to rise during this time.

Deluxe

Rey Don Jaime, Avda. Baleares 2 (tel. 360 7300). 314 rooms; pool. Situated in the outskirts towards El Grao. The most expensive 4-star hotel in the city. Readers praise its excellence and delicious food. AE, DC, MC, V.

Expensive

Astoria Palace, Pza. Rodrigo Botet 5 (tel. 352 6737). 208 rooms. Modern hotel with good amenities in a pleasant central square. This is the most expensive in this category. AE, DC, MC, V.

Dimar, Gran Vía Marqués de Turia 80 (tel. 334 1807). 95 rooms. On the edge of city center, not far from river, a functional businessman's hotel. AE, DC, MC, V.

Reina Victoria, Barcas 4 (tel. 352 0487). 92 rooms. Central, elegant, old-style hotel close to the main Pza. País Valenciano. AE, DC, MC, V.

Moderate

Bristol, Abadía San Martín 3 (tel. 352 1176). 40 rooms. Well maintained old-world hotel with charm. Central but hidden away in narrow street by church of San Martín. AE, DC, MC, V.

Continental, Correos 8 (tel. 351 0926). 43 rooms. Just behind Post Office off main square. V.

Excelsior, Barcelonina 5 (tel. 351 4612). 65 rooms. Old but good, just off Pza. Rodrigo Botet, with pleasant cafeteria. AE, DC, MC, V.

Inglés, Marqués de Dos Aguas (tel. 351 6426). 62 rooms. Old-world charm, overlooking Ceramics Museum. AE, DC, MC, V.

Llar, Colón 46 (tel. 352 8460). 51 rooms. Functional, recent hotel opposite Galerías Preciados store. AE, DC, MC, V.

Metropol, Játiva 23 (tel. 351 2612). 109 rooms. Another good old-world-style hotel close to train station.

Oltra, Pza. País Valenciano 4 (tel. 352 0612). 93 rooms. Older hotel overlooking top end of main square. Rooms on front could be noisy. AE, DC, MC, V.

Sorolla, Convento Santa Clara (tel. 352 3392). 50 rooms. Functional but reasonable modern hotel on a fairly quiet street exactly half way between bullring and main square. AE, MC, V.

Inexpensive

Europa, Ribera 4 (tel. 352 0000). 81 rooms. In a central, almost traffic-free street, just off main square.

Internacional, Bailén (tel. 351 9462). 55 rooms. Good, clean, reasonably-priced hotel alongside station.

Out at **Manises,** right by the airport, is **Azafata Sol** (E), (tel. 154 6100). 130 rooms; pool. Modern, functional, airport hotel. AE, DC, MC, V.

RESTAURANTS. Valencia has some excellent restaurants and perhaps more than its fair share of expensive places to dine. Many of the better restaurants are a little way out of the center but in most cases this only involves a short drive or cab ride. Remember that Valencia is the home of Spain's national dish *paella valenciana,* and you should therefore encounter a good selection of paellas in many of its restaurants.

Expensive

Los Azahares, Avda. Navarro Reverter 16 (tel. 334 8602). Smart restaurant with select atmosphere and good service. Closed Sat. lunch and all day Sun. AE, DC, MC, V.

El Cachirulo, Cronista Almela y Vives 3 (tel. 361 1315). Typically Aragonese restaurant with rustic decor; specializes in meat dishes, though *paellas* and fish are also on the menu. Top standards. Closed Sun. evening. AE, DC, V.

Comodoro, Transits 3 (tel. 351 3815). Smart restaurant with high standards, in a narrow street in the center. Closed Sun., Holy Week, and Aug. AE, DC, V.

El Condestable, Artes Gráficas 15 (tel. 369 9250). The decor is almost medieval, with tapestries on the walls. There are just 18 tables and the food and service are of the highest standards as is the wine list; good regional wines from Valencia. Closed Sun. AE, DC, MC, V.

Eladio, Chiva 40 (tel. 326 2244). Galician restaurant some way out of center run by a husband-and-wife team from Galicia and Switzerland. Superb Galician fish dishes and mouth-watering Swiss pastries. Closed Sun. and Aug. AE, DC, MC, V.

La Hacienda, Navarro Reverter 12 (tel. 373 1859). Stylish decor with some antique furniture, old books and glass; recommended for fine cuisine. Closed Sat. lunch and all day Sun. AE, DC, MC, V.

Ma Cuina, Gran Vía Germanías 49 (tel. 341 7799). Fine Basque cooking well known to local gourmets; high prices. Adjoining is **La Taberna Vasca,** an old-world-style bar serving good wines and beer and a magnificent selection of Basque *tapas* and *raciones.* Closed Sun. AE, DC, MC, V.

Moderate

El Gourmet, Taquígrafo Martí 3 (tel. 374 5071). A very popular restaurant serving traditional Spanish dishes and nouvelle cuisine at reasonable prices. Always busy so advisable to book. Closed Sun. and mid-Aug. to mid-Sept. AE, DC, MC, V.

Lionel, Pizarro 9 (tel. 351 6566). Attractively decorated and with a good menu; a house specialty is duck served with a variety of sauces. Closed Sat. lunch and Sun. AE, DC, MC, V.

El Plat, Conde de Altea 41 (tel. 334 9638). Simple restaurant specializing in Valencian cuisine and especially noted for its rice dishes—a different paella daily is the house specialty. Closed Sun. evening, Mon., Holy Week, and Aug. AE, MC, V.

Inexpensive

Casa Cesáreo, Guillén de Castro 15 (tel. 351 4214). Both floors are prettily decorated with ceramic pots and tiles; good-value menu. Livelier at lunchtime than in the evening. Closed Sun. evening and all day Mon. AE, V.

Venta del Toboso, Mar 22 (tel. 332 3028). Charming rustic 60-year-old restaurant. Specializes in local regional dishes; impressive wine list. AE, DC, V.

For other reasonably priced restaurants, stroll along the Calle Moisén Femades which is packed with atmospheric bars and restaurants. Some you might try are **Alcázar, Río Sil** and **Palacio de la Bellota.** In summer, this street is sealed off to traffic and the restaurants take over the whole road.

BARS AND CAFES. Barrachina, Pza. País Valenciano 2. An old Valencia institution famous throughout Spain. There is a bar, cafe and restaurant here, and in the popular ground floor bar you can sample *pepitos rellenos,* bread-like rolls almost like doughnuts filled with tuna, pimienta and a variety of other fillings, *empanadas,* a kind of fish or tomato pie, and several different sausages and hams. The magnificent counter display is made up almost entirely of regional specialties.

Cervecería Madrid, Abadía San Martín, opposite Hotel Bristol. Atmospheric tavern with its walls hung with pictures and photographs. Very popular, especially at aperitif time around 8 P.M.

Cervecería Valenciana, on corner of Játiva and Bailén beside the train station. Another atmospheric *mesón* with a ham-strung ceiling.

Calle Moisén Femades is packed with atmospheric bars serving *tapas, raciones,* hams, *chorizo,* shrimp, etc. and draught beer or local wines. Just one of the many to try here is **Cervecería Pema** with lots of atmosphere and a variety of hams hanging from the ceiling.

Horchatería del Siglo, Santa Catalina. An old-world-style *horchata* cafe and ice-cream parlor, just off the Pza. Zaragoza.

PLACES OF INTEREST. The opening hours given below are only a guide as they may well change frequently; best check on the spot or with the tourist office. On no account miss seeing the **Ceramics Museum** or the **Bellas Artes** (Fine Arts) Museum.

Casa Museo José Benlliure, Blanquerías 23. The house of the painter José Benlliure containing many of the artist's works and those of his son Benlliure Ortíz. Open Mon. to Fri. 10–2.

Basílica de Nuestra Señora de los Desamparados (Our Lady of the Forsaken), Pza. de la Virgen. Open usually for services only but occasionally at other times too.

Cathedral. Entrance in Pza. de la Virgen. Open daily 10–1 and 4–6; Nov. through Feb. mornings only. Its tower, the popular **Miguelete** (or **Micalet,** in *Valenciano*) is 50 meters (164 feet) high, splendid views over city.

Jardines del Real. Behind the Bellas Artes Museum across river. Pleasant park with fountains, rose gardens, tree-lined avenues and ancient remains; also a small zoo. Open 9 to dusk.

Lonja de la Seda (Old Silk Exchange), Pza. del Mercado. Beautiful late 15th-century Gothic building with picturesque Patio de los Naranjos (Orange Tree Courtyard). Open Tues. to Fri. 11–2 and 4–6, Sat. and Sun. 10–2.

Museo de Bellas Artes (Fine Arts Museum), Colegio de San Pío V, San Pío V 9. One of the best art galleries in Spain with works by Ribalta, El Greco, Velázquez, Benlliure and Sorolla. Splendid medieval, Renaissance, Romantic and modern galleries. Open Tues. to Sat. 10–2 and 4–6; closed Sun. P.M. and all day Mon. In July and Aug, open mornings only.

Museo Fallero, Pza. Monte Olivete 4. Fallas Museum displaying the one effigy (*ninot*) from each year's Fallas celebrations which is spared the bonfire and preserved for posterity. Open Tues. to Sun. 10–2 and 4–7. Closed Mon.

Museo Nacional de Cerámica (National Ceramics Museum), Palacio de Dos Aguas, Poeta Querol 2. Magnificent display of ceramics from all over Spain, Italy and China, housed in fascinating Baroque mansion. Also a collection of antique carriages. Open Tues. to Sat. 10–2 and 4–6, Sun. 10–2 only; closed Sun. P.M. and all day Mon.

Museo del Patriarca (Museum of the Patriarch), Colegio del Patriarca, Calle de la Nave. 16th-century college founded by San Juan de Ribera with Renaissance patio and ornate church. Museum contains works by Joan de Joanes, Ribalta and El Greco. Open Sat. and Sun. only, 11–1.

Museo Taurino (Bullfighting Museum), Pasaje Dr. Serra, beside bullring. One of Spain's oldest and best bullfighting museums packed with memorabilia. Open 10–2 and 5–8.

Palacio de la Generalidad, at the end of Caballeros backing onto Pza. Manises. Seat of the home government of Valencia with two beautiful salons, the *Salón de Cortes* with worthwhile murals, and the *Sala Dorada* with intricate wood carvings.

Torres de Serranos (Serranos Towers), Pza. de Serranos. Gothic gateway in the old city walls, housing a small **Maritime Museum** with naval history from Roman times to present day. Open Tues. to Sun. 10–2; closed Mon.

Torres de Quart (Quart Towers). Mid-15th-century gateway in the old city wall. Open daily 10–1; closed Mon.

SHOPPING. There are two branches of the *Corte Inglés* department store, one in the center on Pintor Sorolla overlooking the Pza. Alfonso el Magnánimo, the other in the Nuevo Centro shopping center out near the bus station on Avda. Menéndez Pidal. Both are open 10–8 (no siesta closing). *Galerías Preciados* is on Colón opposite Llar hotel.

Valencia is an excellent place to buy the famous Lladró porcelain, or the slightly cheaper version, Nao porcelain, as both of these are made nearby. The Lladró factory is at Cardenal Benlloch 13 in Tabernes Blanques, five km. (three miles) north of Valencia, and it is sometimes possible to arrange visits to the factory; best check with the Valencia Tourist Office. In town, you might try *Cerámicas Lladró,* Poeta Querol 9 for purchases. Nao porcelain comes from the Cape Nao region south of Valencia.

Ceramics are generally a good buy in Valencia not least because so many of them are made in Manises, nine km. (six miles) west of Valencia, near the airport. There are several specialist ceramic shops in Manises, and a Municipal Museum of Ceramics in Calle Sagrario in Manises.

USEFUL ADDRESSES. Car Hire. *Avis,* Isabel la Católica 17 (tel. 351 0734), and at the airport (tel. 154 7002): *Europcar,* Antiguo Reino de Valencia 7 (tel. 374 1512) and at the airport (tel. 153 1369): *Hertz,* Segorbe 7 (tel. 341 5036), and at the airport (tel. 154 7229).

U.S. Consul. Ribera 3 (tel. 351 6973).

Police Headquarters. Gran Vía Ramón y Cajal 40 (tel. 321 4573); emergency phone (091).

RENFE Office. Pza. Alfonso el Magnánimo 2 (tel. 351 4874). Open 9–1 and 4–7.

Airlines. *Iberia,* Paz 14 (tel. 351 9737); information on Iberia flights (tel. 351 3739); airport (tel. 154 0211); *British Airways,* Moratín 14, 3rd floor (tel. 351 2284).

Post Office and **Telephones.** Both in Pza. del Pais Valenciano 24 and 27.

The Golden Apples of the Hesperides

The coastal road to the southern and more pleasant beaches runs on the thin strip of land (La Dehesa) which barely separates the sea from the Albufera lagoon, rimmed with rice-fields and pleasant pinewoods. There are large-scale duck shoots in the fall. A short distance farther on, the road here rejoins N332, near the Cullera rock.

Before continuing on this attractive road farther south toward Alicante, it is necessary to mention oranges—those golden apples that Hercules was sent to capture from nearby Majorca in legendary times.

Following years of experiment, it was found possible to spread the orange harvest over five months—from late November until the end of April—so that in spring, you will see both flower and fruit growing simultaneously on the same tree. As you drive along this road at night, the waves of perfume from the blossoms are almost overpowering.

Some 48 km. (30 miles) from Valencia, the toll road to Alicante passes a turning off to Játiva, an inland town which is well worth seeing. This is the home town of the Borjas, better known outside Spain by the Italian form of their name, Borgia. Their castle, set on the slopes of Mount Bernisa, is exactly what one has always pictured whenever one hears the phrase "castles in Spain."

By the coast road (N332) via Gandía and Villajoyosa, it is 190 km. (118 miles) from Valencia to Alicante. After leaving behind the righthand fork to Játiva, you will find yourself driving through muddy rice-fields, except where the green of the rice itself shows above the surface of the water. The abundance of rice in this area gave rise to Valencia's regional gastronomic specialty, and now the national dish of Spain, the *paella valenciana.* Ahead tawny hills mark the beginning of the Levante's loveliest province, Alicante, and the Costa Blanca.

Let yourself revel one last time amid the charms of the orange-country, for which the town of Gandía is the flourishing business center. In the palace of the Dukes of Gandía, St. Francis Borgia was born. You can visit the 17th–century state rooms and the cell in which he scourged himself. Other worthwhile buildings are the convent of Santa Clara, the monastery of San Jerónimo, the collegiate church, the town hall and the former university.

Once past Ondara with an interesting stone bullring, a short detour to the Cueva de las Calaveras (Skull Cave) on the road between Pedreguer and Benidoleig is worthwhile. At Gata de Gorgos evidence of the local craft of basketwork is all around you. Here a road branches off to Jávea and the coast. The old town of Jávea lies a few kilometers inland but its two moderately developed beaches, one with a beautifully located parador, are quite pleasant resorts.

If you look at a map of Spain you will notice the great spur of Cape Nao that drives out into the Mediterranean toward the island of Ibiza, only about 100 km. away. Turning that corner is to turn from a coast that looks toward Italy and find yourself on one that mirrors Africa. In the course of a few kilometers, the scenery changes from one of oranges and rice to one of olives and palms, from a variable, if benign, climate, to tawny aridity.

The Costa Blanca

The popular name for the stretch of coast between Cape Nao and Cape Gata is the Costa Blanca, or "white coast," including the towns of Alicante and Cartagena as well as numerous beach resorts which have, unfortunately, expanded at an uncontrolled rate, creating a kind of sub-Miami growth of endless concrete hotels and apartment houses. These catered to a surge of interest in cheap holidays in the late '60s and early '70s, which when it declined some years later, left in its wake a chain of tasteless architecture and over-developed towns.

One can get away from the worst of the property developer's excesses, however, and enjoy what is still a sun-worshippers' paradise. Here you are in the land of the carnation, a flower so prevalent that it even faintly perfumes the local wine, and here, too, you come to one of those strange but lovely places with which the entire Costa Blanca is strewn—the Peñón of Ifach (or Ifach Rock). It is located 5 km. away to the left of the main road, beyond the town of Calpe, which was utterly deserted for nearly one hundred years after Barbary pirates killed or carried off as slaves the entire population in the 17th century. The 305–meter (1,000–foot) monolith of the Peñón rises sheer from the sea into the sky, the summit conveniently accessible through a tunnel. Legend tells of the goatlike spirits that pluck to their deaths those unwise enough to scale these heights at the full of the moon. At the foot of the Peñón are two perfect sandy bathing beaches.

Back on the coastal road, which plunges periodically through tunnels in the rock, the next town we come to is Altea, an old and picturesque fishing village with white walls and blue tiled domes. Although now a developing resort, it has retained much of its charm, especially in the old quarter around the church, and is a favorite haunt of artists. An interesting short side trip here is to branch inland along the road that leads to the C3318, a beautiful mountain road on which lies the village of Polop. In its center is a fascinating collection of water taps, each donated by a different town or province, which serve to bring water from the mountains to the villagers. The people of Polop still fill up their bottles with drinking water from these taps. Returning to the N332 the next town is Benidorm, a hugely overdeveloped resort though some praise must be given to its two splendid beaches (even though the sand was specially imported from Morocco!), and hidden somewhere among the concrete blocks the original pretty village still survives. Then come Villajoyosa and San Juan, Alicante's summer resort; both of little interest but with fine beaches.

Alicante

Alicante, terminal of the toll-road, is dominated by the vast Moorish castle of Santa Bárbara, set on a rocky peak. From the palm-lined harbor, ships sail regularly to the Balearic Islands and North Africa. A glory of the city is its date-palm avenue, the Explanada, with some of the only date-palms in Europe on which the fruit ripens. The town itself has little to interest the foreign visitor other than a fine, but very crowded, sandy beach and one good art gallery, but it is very popular with Spanish holiday-makers. It makes a reasonable place to stop overnight and you can spend quite a pleasant evening strolling around the streets of its old quarter. Look out for the local specialty *turrón,* a delicious nougat sold in many varieties in the shops of the Calle Mayor, the main shopping street.

Although definitely torrid in the summer, escape from ninety in the shade is unusually easy as, only 23 km. from Alicante, there are pine woods at a height of over 1,220 meters (4,000 feet), with views across terraced vineyards to the sea.

Twenty-three km. along the inland N340 leads to Elche, with a palm forest, first planted by the Moors for the dates; it is from here that the whole of Spain is provided with the yellow palm fronds used for Palm Sunday processions, and which, once blessed, are hung on balconies to ward off evil during the coming year.

The origins of this town are ancient, even for Spain, and the remarkable stone bust known as the Dama de Elche (in Madrid's Archeological Museum) is one of the earliest examples of Iberian sculpture. The Mystery Play performed in Elche church on the Feast of the Assumption draws many visitors. Its 14th-century music is unique and the roles are all played by local townsfolk. The performances on August 14 and 15 are spectacular, involving the winching of a platform bearing the Virgin Mary and a band of guitar-playing angels 150 feet up into the dome of the church.

Palm and orange groves are scattered through market gardens up to Orihuela, on the banks of the Segura, halfway to Murcia. Enjoy strolling through Orihuela's winding little streets, and don't miss the Gothic cathedral (whose handsomest portal, however, happens to be Renaissance), the church of Santiago, and above all, the striking architectural cluster formed by the Santo Domingo monastery with its two magnificent double-storied Renaissance cloisters, and the old university buildings.

The Coastal Route

If instead of taking the inland N340, you follow the coastal N332 to Cartagena you will pass by many of Alicante's excellent beaches, all with fine clean sand and in many cases surprisingly deserted. Just south of Alicante you will be struck by the beautiful and luminous quality of the light as you drive across vast salt flats.

Along this coast is a string of small, and not highly developed resorts though they are really of very little interest. The first is Santa Pola from which you may be able to take a short excursion to the primitive Island of Tabarca, 11 km. out to sea, where old fortifications and reputed offshore treasure lure the curious.

South of Santa Pola on the way to Guardamar are long stretches of magnificent and empty sandy beaches surrounded by dunes and pine trees, a far cry from the concrete blocks to the north of Alicante. Torrevieja further south is a more developed resort mostly patronized by Spaniards. Continuing southward into Murcia province, past some uninteresting coastal towns, you will reach the Mar Menor (Smaller Sea), a huge lagoon enclosed by a strange geographical phenomenon, known as La Manga del Mar Menor, meaning "a finger" or "sleeve" of land. Although this narrow strip offers some stunning views across the Mar Menor, it has been ruined by a quite tasteless development of sprawling hotels and holiday apartments. In striking contrast to this awful development is the eery, rather bleak and primitive countryside which lies to the south of the lagoon between Cape Palos and Cartagena, though tucked away here is the La Manga Club, a vast modern sportsman's paradise with innumerable facilities for tennis, golf and even cricket.

Cartagena

Cartagena was founded by the Carthaginians in the 3rd century B.C. and, as Spain's principal Mediterranean naval base, has been the scene of numerous battles, the more recent of them being raids by Sir Francis Drake in 1588, naval engagements during the Napoleonic Wars, and a rebellion in 1873. It is a fairly uninteresting town but a suitable place for an overnight stop if you are planning the long drive south into Almería province or on to Granada. Apart from its value as a port, Cartagena has survived through 22 centuries for the same reason that attracted the Phoenicians, namely its silver, lead, iron, zinc and copper mines. Rocks rich in these ores dominate the entire 180 km. (112 miles) of Murcian shoreline from the resort of La Manga to the town of Aguilas just above the provincial border with Almería.

Near the Plaza Caudillo is a model of the first-ever submarine, invented by a Cartagena native, Isaac Peral. The Torre Ciega, a Roman tower and sepulcher dating from the 1st century A.D. has been declared a National Monument. Two of the town's most interesting churches are Santa Mariá la Vieja, built on Roman foundations, and Santa Mariá de Gracia.

Murcia

Returning now to the inland route, soon after Orihuela, the N340 enters the province of Murcia and follows the course of the Segura, though the foothills of the Sierra de Carrascoy often intervene between road and river. This is the driest region of Spain and possibly of Europe, with less than 20 days of rain annually, but near the life-giving rivers whose waters irrigate three crops a year.

The capital, Murcia, lies in the rich Segura valley. Roman statues and coins were found near the present site, and it was with Roman bricks that the Moors built the 8th-century Murcia, which was only liberated and annexed to the crown of Castile in 1243. The Murcian dialect contains many Arabic words and, in appearance, many of its inhabitants clearly reveal their Moorish ancestry.

Though begun in the 14th century, the cathedral received its magnificent Plateresque facade as late as 1737. But the Gothic Door of the Apostles dates from the 15th century, as also the splendid Isabelline chapel of the Marqués de los Vélez, with carvings by Francisco de Salcillo. The Tower, built between 1521 and 1792, is 95 meters (312 feet) high and gives fantastic views over the city and surrounding countryside. Other works by de Salcillo, pieces of an astonishing intensity, are in the Jesus Hermitage (Ermita de Jesús), now a museum, whence they are taken for Holy Week processions.

The 19th-century Casino building on the main street is well worth a peep for its style and aura of a British gentleman's club. Little is left of the old town except some dilapidated houses rising straight from the river, which you might follow to the *malecón,* the old dike built by the Romans to hold back the Segura's waters. It stretches out through palm trees and market gardens, the fertile *huertas,* so perfectly irrigated ever since the days of the Moors. You can also see out over Murcia and the huertas from the Cresta del Gallo, or Cockscomb.

Murcia is visited chiefly by tourists on their way from Alicante southwest to Granada, but equally it can be reached from Madrid by way of Albacete.

Albacete

From Madrid to Albacete, via Ocaña and Mota del Cuervo, is 250 km. (155 miles). Albacete is an agricultural town specializing in wines and saffron. Just over 900 meters (3,000 feet) above sea level, it has a picturesque 15th- and 16th-century quarter on the crest of a hill, known as Alto de la Villa, and the Hermitage of San Antonio is a good example of 17th-century architecture.

Taking N430, the southerly of the two routes from this important road junction to Valencia, you soon see the imposing 15th-century fortress-prison-castle of Chinchilla de Monte Aragón away on your left and, if the day is clear, the distant Sierra de Alcaraz rising to nearly 1,830 meters (6,000 feet), to the south. Chinchilla is an old pottery town producing attractive ware.

But most of the 146 km. (91 miles) of N301 from Albacete to Murcia run adjacent to the bleak uplands of La Mancha, where Don Quijote went adventuring, and the scenery is impressive rather than attractive. However, once across the provincial border and into Murcia, and through the Roman fortress town of Cieza, dominated by its feudal castle, the road drops some 823 meters (2,700 feet) to green farmland before reaching the provincial capital.

South from Murcia and Cartagena

From Murcia southwards, the quickest route, and the one that makes for easier driving, is the N340. Although not unpleasant and bordered by some rich agricultural land with interesting crops—in the fall you will see field after field of red peppers drying in the sun—there is little else that can be said about this road. It is fairly fast but not particularly scenic. Lorca with its small churches and convents, a 13th-century castle, a Baroque collegiate church and the Guevara palace, must once have been a romantic-looking small town. Today away from the old nucleus, it is a dismal drab place. Further on Puerto Lumbreras, an important road junction where the N342 branches west to Granada, and the N340 carries on southwards into Almería province, is little more than a glorified truck stop, though there is a comfortable, modern parador.

By far the more rewarding route scenically, though slower, twisting, and in parts abominably surfaced and cambered, is the N332 from Cartagena to Mazarrón, Aguilas and Vera in Almería province where it joins up with the N340. A few kilometers south of Cartagena the N332 traverses first almond groves and then some vivid and dramatic mountains via the Cuesta Blanca pass with frequent glimpses of the sea. Approaching the resort of Puerto de Mazarrón you will drive through field after field of tomato plants, and maybe see women in straw hats working in the fields and the large marquee-like structures where vegetables are hung to dry on trellises. Here too you may catch your first glimpse of the *plástico* form of agriculture, a seemingly primitive method of growing fruit and vegetables under oceans of ugly plastic sheeting, but which, since it caught on a decade or so ago, has completely revolutionized the fortunes of this previously impoverished corner of Spain.

Mazarrón is an unlovely town but once you have passed through it, the minerals in the rocks along the roadside provide a fascinating medley of color. The landscape here is desolate, rocky and barren but dramatic. Here, too, is the worst stretch of road from a driver's point of view as you could encounter the odd loose boulder or two and some particularly tricky cambers, but it is not impassable and can be negotiated even by more reluctant drivers. Once the road has been joined by C3211 from your right, and begins to drop down to the coast at Aguilas, driving becomes easy again. Aguilas, a coastal town of little attraction, is the last town in Murcia province, and from here you head south through the little inhabited regions of northeastern Almería.

PRACTICAL INFORMATION FOR
THE SOUTHEAST

TOURIST OFFICES. Albacete, Virrey Morcillo 1; **Alicante,** Expl. de España 2 (tel. 21 22 85); **Benicarló,** Pza. San Andrés 21B (tel. 47 31 80); **Benicasim,** Médico Segurra 4 (tel. 30 02 81); **Benidorm,** Avda. Martínez Alejos 16 (tel. 85 13 11); **Calpe,** Avda. Ejércitos Españoles 66 (tel. 83 12 50); **Cartagena,** Pza. Castellini 5 (tel. 50 75 49); **Castellón,** Pza. María Agustina 5 (tel. 22 77 03); **Cullera,** Calle del Riu 56 (tel. 152 0974); **Denia,** Patricio Ferrandiz (tel. 78 09 57); **Elche,** Parque Municipal (tel. 45 27 47); **Gandía,** Parque de la Estación (tel. 287 1600); **Játiva,** Moncada (tel. 288 2561); **Jávea,** Pza. Almirante Basterreche (tel. 79 05 00); **Lorca,** López

Gisbert (tel. 46 61 57); **Murcia,** Alejandro Seiquer 4 (tel. 21 37 16); **Ori-huela,** Francisco Díez 25 (tel. 30 12 85); **Oropesa,** Avda. de la Plana 4 (tel. 31 00 20); **Peñíscola,** Paseo Marítimo (tel. 48 02 08); **Sagunto,** La Autonomía 2 (tel. 246 1230); **Santa Pola,** Pza. Diputación (tel. 41 49 84); **Torrevieja,** Plaza de la Libertad 11 (tel. 71 07 22); **Valencia,** Paz 46 (tel. 352 2497).

Alicante, Castellón and Valencia provinces all have tourist information phone lines: **Alicante:** 965–20 00 00; **Castellón:** 964–22 10 00; **Valencia:** 96–352 4000.

TELEPHONE CODES. The dialing codes for the five provinces of the South East are: Albacete (967); Alicante (96); Castellón (964); Murcia (968); Valencia (96). Dialing codes for all the towns we list are given under *Hotels and Restaurants* immediately after the name of the town.

GETTING AROUND. By Train. Local services in the area are: Valencia–Puzol–Sagunto–Castellón; Valencia–Liria; Valencia–Gandía via Cullera and Tabernes; Valencia–Játiva–La Encina; Valencia–Játiva–Alcoy. Alicante to Murcia via Elche and Orihuela, with connections at Murcia for Granada and Cartagena. From Alicante there is the independent FEVE line north to Denia via Villajoyosa, Benidorm, Altea and Calpe.

There is no direct coastal service between Valencia and Alicante. To go from one to the other you have to travel inland via Játiva.

Rail Stations. *Albacete,* some distance from center on the far side of Paseo de la Cuba (tel. 21 20 96).

Alicante. The main RENFE station (Estación Término) is on Avda. Salamanca at the end of Avda. General Mola (tel. 22 68 40). There are two other stations for local lines: the FEVE station, for trains to Benidorm and Denia, is on Avda.Villajoyosa at the far end of Postiguet beach (tel. 26 27 31) reached by Bus C-1 from downtown, and the station for certain trains to Elche and to Santa Pola is at the end of Oscar Espla near the docks. The RENFE office is at Expl. de España 1 (tel. 21 98 67).

Castellón. The station is just behind the Parque de Ribalta (tel. 21 45 32).

Murcia. Station is out of center in south of town on Calle Industria (tel. 25 21 54). The RENFE office in town is in Calle Barrionuevo (tel. 21 28 42).

Valencia. The main RENFE station, the *Estación del Norte,* is on Calle Játiva (tel. 351 3612). The FEVE station for local services to Lliria, Buñol, Villanueva de Castellón, etc, is on Cronista Rivelles (tel. 347 3750) across the river not far from the Museo de Bellas Artes. The RENFE office is in Plaza Alfonso el Magnánimo 2 (tel. 351 4874).

By Bus. There are plenty of local and long distance bus services covering the area. **Bus Stations:** with the exception of Castellón, all the provincial capitals have bus depots. In **Castellón,** buses to Valencia and most other destinations leave from Trinidad 166. **Albacete** bus station is next to the train station. **Alicante** bus depot is on Avda. Portugal (tel. 22 07 00); **Murcia** bus depot is west of town on Pza. Casanova (tel. 29 22 11); **Valencia** bus depot is across the river on Avda. Menéndez Pidal 3 (tel. 349 7222) and is reached by bus 28 from the center.

By Boat. From Valencia and Alicante there are sailings of the *Transmediterránea* Company to the Balearic islands; these are more frequent and serve all three islands, Majorca, Minorca and Ibiza, in summer. Transmediterránea are at Expl. de España 2 (tel. 20 60 11) in Alicante; and on Avda. Manuel Soto 15 (tel. 367 0704) in Valencia. From Denia, *Isnasa* run ferries to Ibiza, and there is also a sailing to Palma. In summer there are sailings across to the island of Tabarca from both Alicante and Santa Pola. For information, call Santa Pola 541 1113 or Alicante 521 6396, or check with the local Tourist Office.

By Air. There are two international airports in the region, at Valencia and Alicante. Both have good scheduled connections with other Spanish cities and several European capitals and Alicante is also a busy charter airport serving the resorts of the Costa Blanca. Alicante airport (tel. 28 50 11) is reached by bus from outside the Calle de Portugal bus station. *Iberia,* Paseo de Soto 9 (tel. 21 86 13) in Alicante.

By Road. Coastal roads. The choice is between the toll road, the *autopista* A7 and the main N-roads which run almost parallel to the A7 the whole length of the coast from Castellón to Alicante. Tolls on the *autopista* are quite high (from Port Bou on the French border to Alicante cost in the region of 5,500 ptas in 1985). In the north of the region the A7 and the N340 run almost parallel the whole length of the Costa del Azahar from Castellón to Valencia, and scenically there is little to choose between them.

On the next stretch from Valencia to Alicante N340 branches inland via Játiva and Alcoy through some mountainous scenery with lovely views. There are two passes on this road, the Puerto de Albaída (600 meters/1,968 feet) and the Puerto de la Carrasqueta (1024 meters/3,359 feet). The stretch around Jijona is very twisty. Most tourists however, follow one of the coastal roads, either the A7 or the N332; the latter passes through many small towns and modern developments, many of them architecturally quite interesting. Both roads leave the coast for a while at Cape Nao.

At Alicante the A7 toll road ends (though on some maps you may see it continuing on to Murcia, Cartagena and Almería, this stage has not as yet been built). From Alicante southwards, you have a choice of the inland N340, or the coastal, and slower, N332. Both roads are described in some detail in the text.

Inland roads. Of the main radial routes, the most important is the N-III from Valencia to Madrid. North of Valencia, at Sagunto, the N234 branches inland to Teruel and Zaragoza; and further north at Vinaroz, the N232 turns inland via Morella and Alcañiz to Zaragoza, via the Puerto de Torre Miró pass (1,259 meters/4,131 feet) just before you leave Castellón province. From Valencia the main N430 drops southwest to Albacete, and from Alicante to Albacete the N330 joins the N430 just before Almansa. From Cartagena to Murcia the N301 passes through some low mountains (Puerto de la Cadena, 340 meters/1,115 feet) before reaching Murcia, and continues on to Albacete.

Many of the C-classified roads, especially between Valencia and Alicante, and again south of Cartagena, pass through mountains and are therefore twisty, and not always with the best surfaces, though they are all passable. The unclassified roads through the mountains are probably best avoided unless you are an adventurous driver with a good head for heights.

HOTELS AND RESTAURANTS. Many of the coastal towns in this area, such as Benidorm, are long established resorts, well supplied with modern hotels; other more recent resorts are only now being developed and will—it's to be hoped—probably never reach the size and scale of the concrete giants. These newer resorts are mostly in Alicante province south of the capital and along the coast line of Murcia, and tend to appeal to Spanish vacationers rather than visitors from abroad. Rates in 3-star hotels along the coast are mostly very reasonable. This is principally due to the large number of package-deal holiday operators using them. In high season, July and August, you may well find hotels on the coast hard to come by if they have been block-booked by travel agents, but at other times you should have no trouble finding a room. Many of the resort hotels are closed in the winter months.

If you are planning to see Valencia's *fallas* in March or the Elche Mystery Play in August, you would be wise to book accommodations well in advance, as they draw crowds from all over Spain.

Albacete (967). *Los Llanos* (high M), Avda. España 9 (tel. 22 37 50). 102 rooms. Opposite Abelardo Sanchez park. AE, DC, MC, V. *Gran Hotel* (M), Marqués de Molins 1 (tel. 21 37 87). 69 rooms. Very central. AE, DC, MC, V. *Parador de la Mancha* (M), 5 km. out on the N301 (tel. 22 94 50). 70 rooms; pool, tennis, gardens. Modern, in regional style. AE, DC, MC, V. *Albar* (M–I), Isaac Peral 3 (tel. 21 68 61). 51 rooms. Right in center. V.

Restaurants. *Las Rejas* (M), Dionisio Guardiola 7 (tel. 22 72 42). Good typical méson. Closed Sun. *Nuestro Bar* (I), Alcade Conangla 100 (tel. 22 72 15). Friendly with good regional cooking. Closed July. AE, DC, V.

Alcoy. Alicante (96). *Reconquista* (M), Puente San Jorge 1 (tel. 533 09 00). 77 rooms. DC, MC, V.

Restaurant. *La Venta del Pilar* (M), 2.5 km. out on road to Valencia (tel. 559 23 25). Atmospheric 18th-century inn serving superb food. Closed Sun., Holy Week, and Aug. AE, DC, MC, V.

Alicante. (96). *Gran Sol* (E), Avda. Mendez Núñez 3 (tel. 520 30 00). 150 rooms. Modern skyscraper right on the main street with panoramic view from bar on 32nd floor. AE, DC, MC, V. *Meliá Alicante* (E), Playa del Postiguet (tel. 520 50 00). 547 rooms. A vast apartment complex overlooking the beach.

Colegio Oficial Farmacéuticos (M), Gravina 9 (tel. 521 07 00). 46 rooms. Charming old hotel between Expl. de España and the Pza. Ayuntamiento. *Maya* (M), Manuel Peñalva y Don Violante 5 (tel. 526 12 11). 200 rooms; pool, some suites. Out of center, just off road leading north to Valencia. AE, DC, MC, V. *Palas* (M), Cervantes 5 (tel. 520 93 10). 48 rooms. Pleasant hotel with charm on the corner of Expl. de España. Nearby in the old town is another charming old hotel, the *Residencia Palas* (M), Pza. Ayuntamiento 6 (tel. 520 66 90). 53 rooms. AE, DC, MC, V.

La Balseta (I), Manero Molla 9 (tel. 520 66 33). 84 rooms. Functional hotel just off Portal de Elche. *Covadonga* (I), Pza. de los Luceros 17 (tel.

520 28 44). Good modern hotel in pleasant square in elegant part of town. Reasonable rates. AE, DC, MC, V. *La Reforma* (I), Reyes Católicos 7 (tel. 522 21 47). 52 rooms. Modern hotel, a couple of blocks from bus station. MC, V.

Restaurants. *Dársena* (E), Muelle del Puerto (tel. 520 73 99). At the port beside the Regatta Club; well known for its outstanding paellas — 25 different kinds. Closed Sun. evening and Mon. AE, MC, V. *Delfín* (E), Explanada de España 14 (tel. 521 49 11). Modern restaurant, one of the best in town. AE, DC, MC, V. *Quo Vadis* (E), Pza. Santísima Faz 3 (tel. 521 66 60). Atmospheric decor in a delightful square in the old town. AE, DC, MC, V.

La Roda (M), next to Quo Vadis, is a colorful mesón. Both have tables on the sidewalk. *Nou Manolin* (M), Villegas 4 (tel. 520 03 68). Good tapas bar on ground floor and upstairs an atmospheric restaurant serving superb paellas and good fish. Interesting display of wines with especially good champagne *(cava)* and white wines. AE, DC, MC, V.

Rincón Castellano (I), Manero Molla 12, opposite Balseta hotel (tel. 521 90 02). Charming mesón with check tablecloths and friendly service. Castilian specialties include roast pork and lamb. Excellent *menu del día.* Closed Thurs.

Altea. Alicante (96). *Cap Negret* (E), (tel. 584 12 00). At km. 32 on Valencia–Alicante highway; pool. *Altaya* (I), Generalísimo 113 (tel. 584 08 00). DC, MC, V.

Restaurants. *La Costera* (E), Costera del Mestre de Música 8 (tel. 584 02 30). Amazing restaurant as much for its bizarre decor as the "surprises" that come as part of the show each night. Good cooking with Swiss specialties. Extremely popular and often booked long ahead. Closed Wed. and Aug. DC.

Gullerías (M), San Pedro 1 (tel. 584 22 81). Pleasant location by the beach with old-world decor. Specializes in Basque cooking and the *menu estrecho y largo* allows you to sample a little of everything. AE, DC, V. *Chez Pierre* (I), Conde de Altea 22 (tel. 584 20 37). Featuring Spanish, French and Moroccan cuisine at very reasonable prices. Friendly service and very popular; best to book.

Benicarlo. Castellón (964). *Parador de la Costa del Azahar* (E–M), Avda. Papa Luna 2 (tel. 47 01 00). Modern parador with 108 rooms, pool, garden, excellent sea views and a recommended restaurant. AE, DC, MC, V.

Benicasim. Castellón (964). *Azor* (M), Paseo Marítimo (tel. 30 03 50). 88 rooms overlooking sea, pool, mini golf, tennis and garden. DC, MC, V. *Orange* (M), Gran Avenida (tel. 30 06 00). 415 rooms, pool, mini golf, tennis, garden and many other amenities. AE, DC, MC, V. *Bonaire* (M–I), Paseo Marítimo (tel. 30 08 00). 79 rooms, pool, mini golf, tennis. DC, MC, V. *Miami* (I), Gran Avenida (tel. 30 00 50). 44 rooms, pool, tennis. *Tramontaña* (I), Paseo Marítimo (tel. 30 03 00). 65 rooms, overlooking sea, garden. AE, DC, MC, V.

Restaurant. *Villa del Mar* (M), Paseo Colonia 24 (tel. 30 28 52). Lovely old house with terrace for outdoor dining. AE, DC, MC, V.

Benidorm. Alicante (96). *Gran Hotel Delfín* (L), Playa de Poniente (tel. 585 34 00). Luxury hotel away from the crowds. 87 rooms, pool, tennis, tropical gardens. AE, DC, MC, V. *Cimbel* (E), Avda. Europa (tel. 585 21 00). 144 rooms. Good views over Levante beach. AE, DC, MC, V. *Los Dalmatas* (E), Estocolmo 4 (tel. 585 19 00). 270 rooms, pool, garden. Modern and close to beach. AE, DC, MC, V. *Don Pancho* (E), Avda. Mediterráneo (tel. 585 29 50). 251 rooms, pool, garden. Well-furnished with good service; Spanish colonial and Aztec motifs in its decor. AE, DC, MC, V.

Avenida (M), Martínez Alejos 5 (tel. 585 41 08). 4-star hotel with 93 rooms. *Belroy Palace* (M), Europa 5 (tel. 585 02 03). Also 4-star, 102 rooms. *Costa Blanca* (M), Playa de Levante (tel. 585 54 50). 190 rooms, pool, gardens; 4-star. AE, DC, MC, V. *Las Garzas* (M), Avda. Marina Española (tel. 585 48 50). 306 rooms, pool, 3-star hotel on Poniente beach in quiet location. AE, DC, MC, V. *Las Ocas* (M), Gerona (tel. 585 56 58). 329 rooms, pool, tennis; 3-star hotel. AE, DC, MC, V. *Los Pelicanos* (M), Gerona (tel. 585 23 50). 476 rooms, pool, tennis, large garden. 3-star hotel. AE, DC, MC, V.

Agir (M–I), Avda. Mediterráneo 11 (tel. 585 51 62). 69 rooms. AE, DC, V. *Royal* (M–I), Vía Emilio Ortuño (tel. 585 35 00). 88 rooms and pool. V. *Bilbaíno* (I), Virgen del Sufragio 1 (tel. 585 08 05). 38 rooms.

Restaurants. *Don Luis* (E), Edif. Zeus, Dr. Orts Llorca (tel. 585 46 73). Elegant restaurant specializing in Italian and regional Spanish cuisine. Best to book. AE, DC, V. *I Fratelli* (E), Dr. Orts Llorca (tel. 585 39 79). Excellent Italian restaurant with stylish turn-of-century decor. AE, DC, MC, V. *Tiffany's* (E), Avda. Mediterráneo, Edificio Coblanca 3 (tel. 585 44 68). A top restaurant. Modern with musical entertainment while you dine. Open for dinner only. AE, DC, MC, V. *La Caserola* (M), Rincón de Loix, Avda. Bruselas 7 (tel. 585 17 19). Good French food; dining on terrace with flowers. AE, DC, MC, V.

Calpe. Alicante (96). *Venta la Chata* (M), Ptda. de la Cometa (tel. 583 03 08). 17 rooms; a charming roadhouse. AE, DC, MC, V. *Paradero Ifrach* (M), Explanada del Puerto 50 (tel. 583 03 00). On the beach a little out of town. 29 rooms, tennis.

Restaurants. *Casita Suiza* (M), Edificio Apolo in Calle Jardín (tel. 583 06 06). Swiss chalet decor and Swiss food. Closed Sun. and Mon. AE, MC, V. *Paradero de Ifrach* (M), a charming restaurant-hotel with wonderful view and good food.

Cartagena. Murcia (968). *Cartagonova* (M), Marcos Redondo 3 (tel. 50 42 00). 127 rooms, parking. AE, DC, MC, V. *Alfonso XIII* (I), Paseo Alfonso XIII 30 (tel. 52 00 00). 239 rooms. Recent, on one of main avenues on edge of town. AE, DC, MC, V.

Restaurants. *Barlovento* (M), Cuatro Santos 33 (tel. 50 66 41). Excellent seafood—the smoked fish is a good choice. AE, MC, V. *Chamonix* (M), Puerta de Murcia 11 (tel. 50 74 00). Good fish dishes. AE, DC, V. *Tino's* (M), Escorial 13 (tel. 10 10 65). Italian restaurant, pleasantly decorated with friendly service and good food. AE, DC, MC, V.

Castellon De La Plana (964). *Mindoro* (E), Moyano 4 (tel. 22 23 00). 114 rooms in town. AE, DC, MC, V. *Hotel del Golf* (M), Playa del Pinar (tel. 22 19 50). Just out of town on beach at El Grao; modern; 127 rooms, pool, tennis, golf. *Turcosa* (M), Avda. de Buenavista 1 (tel. 22 21 50). 70 rooms; five km. out in El Grau. *Doña Lola* (I), Lucena 3 (tel. 21 40 11). Pleasant small hotel across from station. Ask for a room at the back. *Myriam* (I), Obispo Salinas 1 (tel. 22 21 00). 24 rooms with TV, radio, parking. DC, V.

Restaurants. *Casino Antiguo* (M), Puerta del Sol 1 (tel. 22 28 64). Long-standing popular restaurant serving good paellas, fish, and specialties from La Mancha. At El Grao are *Club Náutico* (M), Escollera Poniente (tel. 22 24 90). Good views of port. AE, DC, MC, V. *Rafael* (M), Churruca 26 (tel. 22 20 88). Opposite fishing port with attractive decor and good seafood. Closed Sun. and early Sept. AE, DC, MC, V.

Chiva. Valencia (96). *Motel la Carreta* (M), at km. 330 on N-III (tel. 251 1100). Convenient roadside motel with pool.

Cofrentes. Valencia (96). *Balneario Hervideros Cofrentes* (I), (tel. 219 6025). Spa hotel in small inland town beside the Jucar reservoir.

Cullera. Valencia (96). *Sicania* (M), Playa del Raco (tel. 152 0143). 117 rooms, private beach, functional. AE, DC, MC, V. *Don Carlos II* (I), Avda. Cabañal 17 (tel. 152 0089). 39 rooms. AE, DC, V. *Safi* (I), Faro de Cullera (tel. 152 0577). 31 rooms, parking, garden. AE, DC, MC, V.

Restaurant. *Les Mouettes* (E), (tel. 152 00 10). On the road up to the castle. Tiny restaurant with only a dozen tables; magnificent sea views. French owner and some of the best cooking in the region. Open for dinner only. AE, DC, MC, V.

Denia. Alicante (96). *Denia* (M), Ptda. Suertes del Mar (tel. 578 12 12). 280 rooms, pool and gardens. *Los Angeles* (I), Playa de las Marinas (tel. 578 04 58). 60 rooms, tennis, garden. DC, V. *Las Rotas* (I), Ptda. Les Rotes 47 (tel. 578 03 23). 23 rooms, tennis, garden.

Restaurant. *Mesón La Troya* (M), Ctra. Les Rotes (tel. 578 14 31). Decorated with nautical motifs, clean and friendly. Try the *arroz a banda,* it's superb. Closed Mon. and Nov.

Elche. Alicante (96). *Huerto del Cura* (E), Federico García Sanchiz 14 (tel. 545 80 40). A semi-parador, with 59 rooms, delightfully set in palm grove. Good restaurant, pool, mini golf, tennis and other amenities. AE, DC, MC, V. *Cartagena* (I), Gabriel Miró 12 (tel. 546 15 50). 34 rooms, central. DC, V. *Don Jaime* (I), Avda. Primo de Rivera 5 (tel. 545 38 40). 64 rooms, central. MC, V.

Restaurants. *Els Capellans* (M), Federico Sanchiz 14 (tel. 545 80 40). At the Huerto del Cura hotel in the famous palm grove. Good paellas and fish; outdoor dining beside the pool. AE, DC, MC, V. *Parque Municipal* (M), Paseo Alfonso XIII (tel. 545 34 15). Set in park with outdoor terrace and dining under the palms; a favorite with locals. V.

Gandia. Valencia (96). Many of the hotels here are closed in winter. *Bayren I* (E), Paseo Neptuno (tel. 284 0300). 164 rooms; by lovely beach and orange groves. DC, MC, V. *Bayren II* (M), Mallorca 19 (tel. 284 0700). 125 rooms, tennis, one block from sea; low rates. AE, DC. *Riviera* (M), Paseo Neptuno 29 (tel. 284 0066). 72 rooms. Recent, bright hotel close to center and beach. V. *Safari* (M), Legazpi 3 (tel. 284 0400). 113 rooms, pool. One of the original Gandía hotels. DC. *San Luis* (M), Paseo Neptuno 6 (tel. 284 0800). 72 rooms, with seafront terrace. V. *Los Robles* (M), Formentera (tel. 284 2100). 240 rooms, pool, garden.

Restaurants. *La Gamba* (E), Ctra. Nazaret-Oliva (tel. 284 1310). In a smart house at far end of Gandía beach just into the country; superb seafood. AE, DC, MC, V. *Celler del Duc* (M), Pza. Castell (tel. 284 2082). Argentinian-range style; specializing in roast meats. MC, V. *Mesón de los Reyes* (M), Mallorca 47 (tel. 284 0078). Outdoor dining on a large terrace. AE, DC, MC, V.

Javea. Alicante (96). *Parador Costa Blanca* (E), (tel. 579 02 00). Modern parador with 60 rooms. Fine location overlooking beach; pool, garden. AE, V.

Restaurants. *La Estrella* (M), Avda. del Arenal (tel. 579 08 02). Excellent small restaurant with outdoor terrace. Bouillabaisse is recommended. V. *Villa Selina* (M), Partida Puchol 96, Ctra. del Puerto (tel. 579 06 98). Well-known in Jávea area. Open for dinner only. AE, DC, MC, V.

Lorca. Murcia (968). *Alameda* (I), Museo Valiente 8 (tel. 46 75 00). Reasonable 3-star hotel in side street off main through-road.

La Manga Del Mar Menor. Murcia (968). An ugly and architecturally disgraceful resort on what was potentially a beautiful site. *Entremares* (M), Gran Vía de la Manga (tel. 56 31 00). 245 rooms, pool, tennis; with the lowest rates. AE, DC, V. *Galua-Sol* (M), (tel. 56 32 00). 170 rooms; overlooks sandy beach, pool, tennis. AE, DC, MC, V.

Los Belones (968). *La Manga Club-Hotel* (L), (tel. 56 45 11). 47 rooms. Opened in 1983 as part of the La Manga Country Club complex. A sportsman's mecca with 13 tennis courts, two pools, golf and cricket. AE, DC, MC, V.

Restaurants. *Dos Mares* (M), Pza. Bohemia (tel. 56 30 93). Good views of sea. AE, DC, MC, V. *El Mosqui* (I), (tel. 56 30 06). Five km. (three miles) out at Cabo de Palos. Boat-shaped restaurant serving excellent *paella* and *caldero;* pleasant seafront terrace. MC, V.

Moraira. Alicante (96). *Swiss Hotel Moraira* (L), Club Moraira (tel. 574 44 54). 13 rooms. New luxury hotel on southern tip of Cape Nao. AE, DC, MC, V.

Restaurant. *El Girasol* (E), 1.5 km. out on road to Calpe (tel. 574 43 73). Owned by German Heinth Orth, who is also the chef; one of the very best restaurants in the area, with outstanding, imaginative cuisine. AE, DC, V.

Murcia (968). *Hispano II* (E), Radio Murcia 3 (tel. 21 61 52). A 3-star hotel with 35 rooms. Smart, modern, very central. AE, DC, MC, V. *Rincón de Pepe* (E), Apóstoles 34 (tel. 21 22 39). 117 rooms. Central and tastefully decorated hotel beside the famous (and excellent) restaurant of the same name. AE, DC, MC, V. *Siete Coronas Meliá* (E), Ronda de Garay 3 (tel. 21 77 71). A 4-star hotel with 108 rooms, good amenities, overlooking river. AE, DC, MC, V.

Conde de Floridablanca (E–M), Corbalán 7 (tel. 21 46 26). In narrow street just off Princesa on far side of river. AE, DC, MC, V. *Majesti* (M), San Pedro 5 (tel. 21 47 42). Central right by the Mercado de Verónica. MC, V.

Restaurants. *Rincón de Pepe* (E), Apostoles 34 (tel. 21 22 39). Famous in Murcia for its outstanding food and quaint setting. If the superb and lengthy wine list defeats you, just ask for a good wine of the region. Delicious selection of sorbets. AE, DC, MC, V. *Hispano* (M), Lucas 7 (tel. 21 61 52). Traditional Spanish dishes and nouvelle cuisine. Pleasant terrace and bar. AE, DC, MC, V.

Orihuela. Alicante (96). *Montepiedra* (M), Dehesa de Campoamor (tel. 532 03 00). 64 rooms, some cheaper; pool. *La Zenia* (M), (tel. 532 02 00). 200 rooms, pool.

Oropesa. Castellón (964). *Neptuno Stop* (I), on road to Barcelona (tel. 31 03 75). Motel with 21 rooms; pool. *El Cid* (I), Las Playetas (tel. 30 07 00). 58 rooms; by beach, pool, tennis. *Oropesa Sol* (I), Ctra. del Faro 97 (tel. 31 01 50). 50 rooms, by the beach. *Zapata* (I), Ctra. del Faro 92 (tel. 31 04 25). 65 rooms. Simple, friendly hotel near to beach. All beach hotels open Apr./May through Sept. only.

Peñiscola. Castellón (964). *Hostería del Mar* (E), (tel. 48 06 00). A semi-parador across road from beach, slightly out of town. 85 rooms; pleasant local decor, garden, and pool. Medieval banquets on Sat. AE, DC, MC, V. *Benedicto XIII* (M), (tel. 48 08 01). On hill above town; garden, pool, tennis. Tasteful decor; friendly service. MC, V. *Cartago* (M), (tel. 47 33 11). At km. 2 on road to Benicarló. 26 rooms, garden, tennis, pool. Open mid-June to mid-Sept. only. *Papa Luna* (M), (tel. 48 07 60). At km. 6.6 on road to Benicarló. Modern with 230 rooms and pool. Open mid-Mar. to mid-Oct. only.

Restaurants. *Hostería del Mar* (high M), Avda. Papa Luna 18 (tel. 48 06 00). Delightful setting in old part of town. Serves good dinners in its Banqueting Hall. *Casa Severino* (M), Príncipe 1 (tel. 48 07 03). Splendid terrace with ocean view; popular with tourists. DC, V.

Playa San Juan. Alicante (96). *Sidi San Juan Palace* (E), Pda. Cabo la Huerta (tel. 561 13 00). Luxury hotel with two pools, tennis, good views of sea. AE, DC, MC. *Almirante* (M), Avda. Niza 38 (tel. 565 01 12). Central with pool.

Puerto De Mazarron. Murcia (968). *Bahía* (M) high season, otherwise (I), Playa de la Reya (tel. 59 40 00). An older hotel with 54 rooms. DC, V. *Durán* (I), Playa de la Isla (tel. 59 40 50). Open Apr. through Sept. only. AE, MC, V.

Puerto Lumbreras. Murcia (968). *Parador Nacional* (M), on N340 (tel. 40 20 25). Functional roadside parador with 60 rooms, pleasant garden, good food. AE, DC, MC, V. *Riscal* (I), Juan Carlos I 4 (tel. 40 20 50). 48 rooms. V.

Puzol. Valencia (96). *Monte Picayo* (L), (tel. 142 0010). Luxury hotel just 15 mins. drive from Valencia. Pool, mini golf, tennis, horse riding and chance to try your hand at bull-fighting. Excellent views, peaceful surroundings; tops with the famous. Disco and one of Spain's best casinos. AE, DC, MC, V.

El Saler. Valencia (96). On the coast ten km. (six miles) south of Valencia. *Sidi Saler Palace* (L), on beach (tel. 161 0411). 272 rooms; luxury hotel with tennis, golf, pool. Its *Grill Bendinat* (E) restaurant offers outstanding cuisine, its paella and desserts are especially good. AE, DC, MC, V. *Parador Luis Vives* (E), on Alicante road (tel. 161 1186). Modern parador by beach; 58 rooms, pool, garden and right by golf course. AE, DC, MC, V.

Santa Pola. Alicante (96). *Pola Mar* (M), Playa de Levante 6 (tel. 541 32 00). 76 rooms, by beach. *Rocas Blancas* (M), at km. 17 on N332 (tel. 541 13 12). Adequate hotel with pool. On promontory overlooking bay. DC, MC, V.

Santiago De La Ribera. Murcia (968). *Lido* (M), Conde Campillo 1 (tel. 57 07 00). 32 rooms, on beach. *Ribera* (I), Explanada de Barnuevo 10 (tel. 57 02 00). 38 rooms; simple, on beach. V.

Torrevieja. Alicante (96). *Fontana* (M), Cap de Pon four km. north on Alicante road (tel. 571 41 11). 156 rooms, pool. AE, DC, MC, V. *Masa Internacional* (E), Alfredo Nobel 8 (tel. 571 1537). 27 rooms, pool, mini golf, garden, pleasant terrace. AE, DC, MC, V. *Mar Bella* (I), Avda. Alfredo Nobel 8 (tel. 71 08 28). 30 rooms. By beach two km. north on Alicante road. V.

Valencia. See *Practical Information for Valencia* (page 340).

Villajoyosa. Alicante (96). *El Montiboli* (L), (tel. 589 02 50). Epitome of luxury, overlooking sea; 52 vast rooms with sun terraces; beach surrounded by palm trees; two pools, 18 tennis courts, beauty salons and health cures. AE, DC, MC, V.

Vinaroz. Castellón (964). *Miramar* (I), Paseo Blasco Ibáñez 12 (tel. 45 14 00). Family-run hotel with 14 rooms. DC, V. *Roca* (I), Pda. San Roque, at km. 143 on main highway (tel. 45 03 50). 36 rooms, pool and tennis.
Restaurants. *Casa Pocho* (M), San Gregorio 49 (tel. 45 10 95). Small restaurant famous for its excellent seafood. Closed Sun. night and Aug. *El Langostino de Oro* (M), San Francisco 31 (tel. 45 12 04). A fish and seafood restaurant specializing in the local dish of *langostinos.* Closed Mon. AE, MC, V.

PLACES OF INTEREST. Albacete. Museo Arqueológico Provincial (Archeological Museum), Parque Abelardo Sánchez. Roman mosaics, collections from the Paleolithic era to the Middle Ages; paintings and drawings by Benjamín Palencia. Open 10–2 and 4–7; closed Sun. P.M. and Mon.

Alcoy (Alicante). **Museo de Fiestas del Casal de Sant Jordi** (Moors and Christians Festival Museum), San Miguel 60. Costumes worn in the annual celebration of St. George's Day, April 23, when mock battles between Moors and Christians take place in the streets. Open daily 10–1.30 and 5.30–8; closed Sat. and Sun. P.M.

Alicante. **Museo Arqueológico,** Gen. Mola 6. Good archeological collection on exhibition in the provincial government. Open Tues. to Sat. 9–2; closed Sun. and Mon. **Museo de la Asegurada** (Modern Art Museum), Casa de la Asegurada, Villavieja. Excellent modern art gallery with large collection of works by 20th century Spanish and foreign painters, many famous. Open daily 10–1 and 5–8; Closed Sun. P.M. and all day Mon.
Museo Bañuls, Aureliano 8. Sculpture by Daniel and Vicente Bañuls.
Castillo de Santa Bárbara (Castle of Santa Barbara) on the rock dominating the city. Inside is the **Museo de las Hogueras de San Juan** (Museum of the St. John's Day Bonfires). Objects associated with Alicante's main festival, which is celebrated around St. John's Day from June 21–24. Display of *ninots indultados*—the one effigy spared the flames in each year's celebrations. Open daily 10–1 and 4–6; closed Mon.

Benidoleig (Alicante). **La Cueva de las Calaveras** (Cave of the Skulls). Cave inhabited by prehistoric man some 40,000 years ago; arrowheads, animal bones, stalactites and stalagmites. A circle of 150 skulls was found when the caves were discovered. Legend claims they were the skulls of a Moorish king and his harem, who hid here as El Cid's army approached. Open 9 A.M.–10 P.M.

Benicasim (Castellón). **Monasterio del Desierto de las Palmas.** Ten km. from town. The monastery and museum are open daily 9–1 and 3–7.
Fábrica de Licor Carmelitano, Avda. Castellón. The place where the Carmelite friars make their popular liqueur known as Licor Carmelitano. Open daily 8.30–7 for short visits, tastings and sales.

Castellon. **Museo de Bellas Artes** (Fine Arts Museum), Caballeros 25. Gothic paintings, including some by Ribera, from the Carthusian monastery of Valldecrist. Other sections on prehistory, ceramics and sculpture. Open 10–2; closed Sun.
Convento de las Capuchinas (Capuchine Convent), Núñez de Arce. Built in 1693 containing several paintings by Zurbarán.

Denia (Alicante). **Torre del Geno,** Ptda. Les Rotes. 16th-century defense tower against Barbary pirates. Usually only visited on group tours.

Elche (Alicante). **Museo de la Alcudia,** on the road to Dolores. Archeological excavations open during daylight hours; closed Mon.
Museo de Arte Contemporáneo (Museum of Contemporary Art), Pza. del Raval. In 17th-century university buildings. Interesting collection of contemporary Spanish art including works by Juan Gris, Tapiès, Picasso, Braque and Miró. Open daily 10–1 and 5–8; closed Mon.
Huerto del Cura. "Priest's Orchard"—a flower garden planted beneath magnificent palm trees. Open mid-June to mid-Sept. from 9–8; and from 9–6 the rest of the year.

Gandia (Valencia). **Collegiate Church,** Pza. Constitución 1. 14th and 15th-century Gothic church, a National Monument. Open daily 8–12 and 6.30–8.

Palacio del Santo Duque (Ducal Palace). Ancient palace of the Dukes of Gandía (Borgias) with a splendid patio and staircase, richly decorated rooms, and a small art gallery. Open 10–12 and 5–7 in summer, 11–12 and 4.30–5.30 in winter. Closed Sun. afternoon.

Murcia. Casino, on Trapería, the main shopping street. Beautiful, stylish 19th-century building with impressive library and salons, Moorish patios, Louis XV-style ballroom and an ornate turn-of-the-century facade.

Cathedral Museum, Pza. de Belluga. In the Chapter House and cloisters of the cathedral are valuable religious paintings and the 3rd-century Roman Sarcophagus of the Muses. Open daily 10–1 and 4–7; 5–8 in summer. **Cathedral Tower.** Open daily 9–1 and 4–7; 5–8 in summer.

Museo de Bellas Artes (Fine Arts Museum), Obispo Frutos 12. Paintings and sculpture from the 16th century onwards. Open Tues. to Sun. 9–2, also 5–9 on Wed; closed Mon.

Museo de Salzillo, Pza. San Andrés 1. Museum of the Murcian sculptor Francisco de Salzillo installed in the Iglesia de Jesús church. Exhibits include a Nativity Crib and Holy Week floats. Open daily 9.30–1 and 3–6 (4–7 in summer); Sun. 10–1.

Orihuela (Alicante). **Museo Diocesano** (Diocesan Museum), Ramón y Cajal. Exhibits of religious objects, the missal of Pope Calixto II and a painting by Velázquez. Open daily 10.30–12.30; closed Sun.

Museo de la Reconquista (Museum of the Reconquest against the Moors). Moorish and Christian costumes and pieces relating to the history of the Reconquest. Open daily 11–1 and 4–7.

Peñiscola (Castellón). **Castle.** Open 10–1 and 4.30–8 in summer, 9–1.30, 3.30–6 in winter.

Sagunto (Valencia). **Museo Arqueológico** (Archeology Museum), at the entrance to the Roman Theater. Mosaics, coins and archeological finds. Open daily 10–2, 4–6 (8 in summer).

Valencia. See *Practical Information for Valencia* (page 304).

Villena (Alicante). **Museo Arqueológico Municipal** (Archeological Museum), Pza. Santiago 2. Contains the "Treasure of Villena" discovered in 1963, a magnificent collection of gold jewelry from the Bronze Age. To see the golden treasure, phone 580 0429 a couple of days ahead.

Yecla (Murcia). **Casa de los Ortega,** Calle España. Houses an **Archeology Museum,** a **Museum of Folklore** in an 18th-century wine cellar, and a **Museum of El Greco Reproductions,** 73 copies done by the artist Juan Albert. Open Mon. to Fri. 5–9.

SPORTS. Cricket. The only pitch in southern Spain is at the La Manga Club.

Golf. There are some excellent golf courses in this area: in Castellón province, the 18-hole Club del Mediterráneo just north of Castellón, and the 9-hole Costa del Azahar course at El Grao de Castellón; in Valencia province, the 9-hole course at Manises near the airport, the 18-hole Club Escorpión 19 km. (12 miles) from Valencia on the road to Liria, and at El Saler the 18-hole course right by the parador; in Alicante province, Jávea, Calpe and Altea all have a 9-hole course; and in Murcia province, the La Manga Club between Los Belones and Cape Palos is one of Spain's most luxurious sporting centers with two championship golf courses where the Spanish Open Championships have been held for the past several years.

Tennis. Most of the coastal hotels have their own tennis courts and there are several clubs along the whole stretch of the Costa del Azahar and Costa Blanca. The La Manga Club has 13 courts.

Watersports. Swimming, water skiing, windsurfing are popular all along the coast and there is the Dos Mares watersports center at La Manga del Mar Menor. Alicante province has the best beaches with fine, clean sand. Swimming around Valencia is not recommended because of water pollution, though the beaches from El Saler southwards are clean and popular. Murcia province is reckoned to have the least polluted water but the sand is generally rather drab.

SEVILLE

Prelude to Andalusia

Lying on the banks of the Guadalquivir, Seville, Spain's fourth largest city and capital of Andalusia, is one of the most beautiful and romantic cities in Europe. With its whitewashed houses brilliant with bougainvillea, ocher-colored palaces, Baroque facades, flower-filled patios and iron grilles, and a magnificent skyline, Seville is a must for any traveler to Spain.

It is a city steeped in history, and boasting literary, artistic and musical associations. The painters Velázquez and Murillo were natives of Seville, as were the poets Gustavo Adolfo Bécquer, Antonio Machado and the Nobel Prize winner, Vicente Aleixandre. Cervantes twice languished in a Sevillian jail and it was in a prison in Seville that the gallant hero Don Quijote was born. In the mansions of Seville Don Juan carried on his amorous pursuits, and in the old tobacco factory Don José first met Carmen. Seville has served as an inspiration to no fewer than four operas, *Don Giovanni, The Marriage of Figaro, The Barber of Seville,* and, of course, *Carmen.* Among its royal associations, the Saint King Ferdinand, conqueror of the Moors and liberator of Seville and Córdoba, lies buried in Seville cathedral, as does the later, and somewhat less saintly, Pedro the Cruel. Ferdinand and Isabella's son Don Juan was born here and Charles V was married here. Seville's role in the discovery of America and its subsequent wealth and embellishment as the New World trade developed, are an integral part of the city's heritage. Amerigo Vespucci and Ferdinand Magellan set sail from here, and in Seville's cathedral rest the remains of Christopher Columbus.

Start your visit here with an hour spent on a cafe terrace, with a pitcher of sangría and a plate of shrimps, watching the crowds pass by. The Sevillians around you, smoking their cigars and sipping their glasses of sherry, will be watching the crowds too. It is a local pastime, *the* local pastime, for every Andalusian has learned the great Arab maxim, "Life is much shorter than death," and he intends to relish every last bit of life before death takes a hand.

The Cathedral and Giralda Tower

Seville's cathedral can only be described in superlatives. It is the largest and the tallest in Spain, and the largest Gothic building in the world. It is the world's third largest Christian church, coming after St. Peter's in Rome and St. Paul's in London. A century and a half after Saint Ferdinand delivered Seville from the Moors, the city set about replacing its 12th-century mosque with a grandiose monument, befitting its proud and opulent station. At the time a member of the chapter is said to have proclaimed, "Let us build a church so big that we shall be held to be insane." In order to hasten the building begun in 1402, the canons renounced their incomes and lived in ascetic privation. Nothing was too fine for the church: sculptured portals, Flemish altar screens, stained-glass windows, wrought-iron grilles, marble floors, bronze candelabra. The centuries have brought further treasures in the form of votive offerings, the finest canvases of Zurbarán and Morales, and two beautiful Murillos, the *Immaculate Conception* and *Saint Anthony.*

Inside the cathedral in a silver tomb in the Capilla Real lie the precious relics of Seville's liberator, Saint Ferdinand. Another glorious mausoleum beneath the high vaults is that of Christopher Columbus. The great explorer knew triumph and disgrace, and found no repose even in death. He died at Valladolid, bitterly disillusioned. His body was first buried at Santo Domingo, then at Havana, and brought to Seville only when Spain had lost the last vestige of the New World he had discovered. (Though there is a school of thought that claims Columbus's body still lies in Santo Domingo.) The details of Columbus' long and tragic life are better understood after a study of the General Archives of the Indies, beside the cathedral. Since Seville adorned her immense shrine with gold and precious woods brought from Peru and the West Indies, it is only just that Columbus should share a place among them. And fitting too is the fact that Seville has been chosen as the site of the 1992 fair to be held in celebration of the 500th anniversary of Columbus's discovery of the New World, for which preparations are now taking place throughout the city and much of Andalusia.

Every day the bell of this colossal monument that summons the faithful to prayer rings out from a Moorish minaret. For when they had razed the old mosque, the Sevillians could not bring themselves to destroy the admirable tower of Abou Yakoub, a splendid example of Arabic art and one of the marvels of Seville. It has been topped by a five-story bell tower capped by a mammoth statue of Faith, so ingeniously mounted that its great bulk turns with the slightest breeze. This is the *giraldillo* ("something that turns") whence the magnificent tower gets its name, La Giralda. The platform at 70 meters (230 feet) is reached by a gently sloping ramp wide enough for two horsemen to pass abreast. From this splendid site you can see the irridescent panorama of Seville, the roofs of its old quarter stretching before you in ridge after ridge of harmonious pinkish-grey tiles, the pattern of its fragrant gardens, and the loop of the Guadalquivir.

The Alcázar

Close by the cathedral, past the Archives of the Indies (designed as a *lonja,* or exchange, by Juan de Herrera, architect of the Escorial) lies the Plaza de Triunfo where you will find the entrance to the Alcázar, the Mudéjar palace built by Pedro the Cruel in the 14th century on the site of the former Moorish alcázar or fortress. The high fortified walls served to defend exquisitely decorated interiors. Pass through the gate and cross the courtyard and you come to the facade of this elaborate palace whose stunningly beautiful patios are surrounded by ornate *azulejos* and delicate lace-like stucco. Second in beauty only to Granada's Alhambra, the Alcázar cannot fail to enchant you.

The Catholic Kings added their own halls and embellishments to the delicate columns of the Patio de las Doncellas, the Court of Maidens, named no doubt for the sultans' annual tribute of one hundred virgins. In the Salón de Embajadores, one of the Alcázar's most beautiful rooms, Charles V married Isabel of Portugal. He it was who built the small adjoining palace—reached through a second patio with stunning views of the Giralda—and the hall where the splendid Flemish tapestries depicting his triumphal expedition to Tunis are exhibited. The apartments in which the Spanish monarchs frequently resided in the 19th century and where Queen Isabella II was born, were restored in 1977. Finally, do not neglect to stroll in the gardens of the Alcázar, a cool haven of green and tranquility with their ornamental fountains and pool well stocked with water lilies and gold fish of every shape and size.

The Barrio Santa Cruz

On leaving the Alcázar take the picturesque alleyway to your right and you will come directly into the old Jewish area, known, somewhat ironically, as the Barrio de Santa Cruz, which, with its twisting, little byways, is a perfectly conceived set for an operetta. Old houses mingle with bars and antique shops. The streets have quaint names like Agua (water), Vida (life) and Pimienta (sweet pepper). Every whitewashed garden wall has its wrought-iron lantern and its profusion of vines or Bougainvillea. Every window hides behind a pot-bellied grille bristling with spikes, but through open doors you catch glimpses of inviting patios that remind you that Murillo once lived in one of these charming dwellings. He was buried in the Plaza Santa Cruz, and nearby his house has now been opened as a small museum. He must have loved his flagstone patio, brightened with masses of potted plants and copper vessels, and enlivened by a fountain.

Just off the Plaza Santa Cruz, the Murillo Gardens, adjacent to those of the Alcázar but hidden from them by a high wall, offer a delightful spot to rest awhile. Then you can stroll back through the other charming squares of the barrio beginning with the Plaza de los Venerables surrounded by some of the loveliest old Sevillian houses, and the location of one of the city's most picturesque bars.

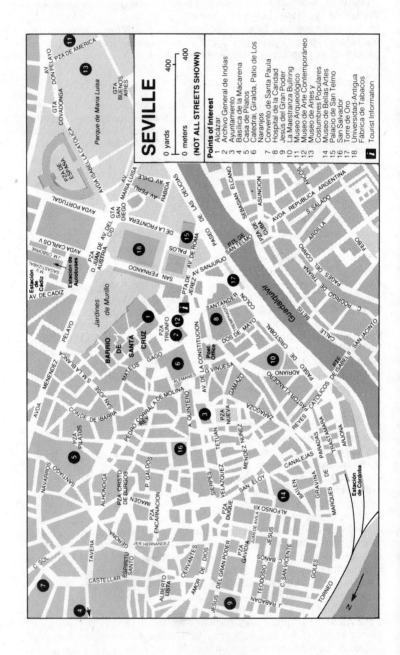

SEVILLE

0 yards　　　400

0 meters　　　400

(NOT ALL STREETS SHOWN)

Points of Interest

1　Alcázar
2　Archivo General de Indias
3　Ayuntamiento
4　Basílica de la Macarena
5　Casa de Pilatos
6　Catedral, Giralda, Patio de Los Naranjos
7　Convento de Santa Paula
8　Hospital de la Caridad
9　Jesús del Gran Poder
10　La Maestranza Bullring
11　Museo Arqueológico
12　Museo de Arte Contemporáneo
13　Museo de Artes y Costumbres Populares
14　Museo de Bellas Artes
15　Palacio de San Telmo
16　San Salvador
17　Torre de Oro
18　Universidad-Antigua Fábrica de Tabacos
i　Tourist Information

Move on (past some of Seville's best ceramic shops) to the peaceful Plaza de Doña Elvira, with its fountain and *azulejos* benches, often a popular gathering place for guitarists and onlookers, to the Plaza Alianza and pause for a moment to admire the stark simplicity of the crucifix on the wall in front of you and the delightful blue and white tiles bearing the name of the square. From here you can turn left and make your way back to the cathedral, or by turning right, plunge deeper into the heart of old Seville.

The Old Town and Pilate's House

Unlike the Barrio Santa Cruz where most of the old houses have been bought up and restored by the well-off (and which now fetch considerable prices on the property market), much of the fascinating labyrinth of narrow streets that make up this part of the old town has fallen into a sad state of decay. Its occupants moved out into the suburbs during the boom years of the Franco era, and those that remained found themselves unable to afford the maintenance costs. At present some 6,000 houses in Seville's old town lie empty or in ruins. Only 60,000 people inhabit the old quarter, where just 25 years ago there were double that number. But with the approach of the 1992 Exhibition to commemorate Columbus's discovery of America, the City Council has stepped in and the future for this once-lovely area is looking rosier. As part of the plan to help revitalize the old heart of the city, 1,000 new dwellings are to be built, easy credit terms are to be made available to owners wishing to restore their properties, and new and practical uses are being sought for those buildings which now lie empty.

Make your way to the Calle de Aguilas and the Plaza de Pilato where, on your left, stands the entrance to the Casa de Pilatos, residence of the Marquis of Medinaceli. No visit to Seville would be complete without an hour or so spent in this lovely mansion. The Duke of Tarifa, a 16th-century ancestor of the present inhabitant, returned from a pilgrimage to the Holy Land and built this palace in the style of Pontius Pilate's residence there, or so he believed. The vast patio, the fine stucco work, and the *azulejos* are much more Mudéjar in style than Roman, even to the untrained eye. On the upper floor, the furnished apartments of the Medinaceli family contain some lesser known works of Goya, Murillo and Velázquez.

La Caridad

Love is an all-important question in Seville, the city of Don Juan. He was actually called Miguel de Mañara. He was rich, licentious, careless of his life and his wealth. Leaving the scene of a drunken orgy he encountered a funeral procession and saw, with horror, that the partly decomposed corpse was his own. He accepted the apparition as a sign from God. Andalusians, with all their love of life, have a morbid preoccupation with death, and a taste for the tragic and sanguinary. It is evidenced in their passion for bullfights and in their gruesome statues of Christ and the martyrs. Miguel de Mañara renounced his worldly goods and joined the brotherhood of the Caridad, whose unsavory task it was to collect the bodies of executed men and give them burial. He died in this fine Baroque almshouse, the Caridad, where his portrait can still be seen. But the chief at-

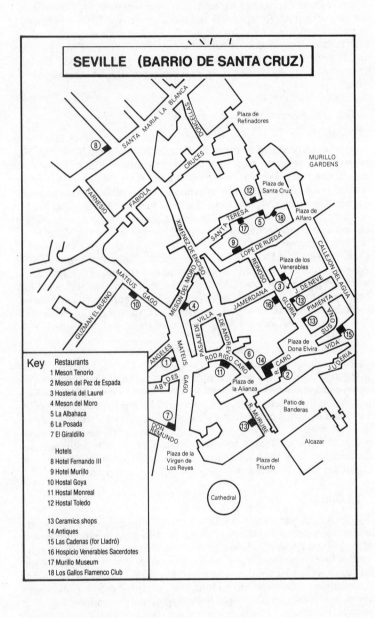

SEVILLE (BARRIO DE SANTA CRUZ)

Key

Restaurants
1 Meson Tenorio
2 Meson del Pez de Espada
3 Hosteria del Laurel
4 Meson del Moro
5 La Albahaca
6 La Posada
7 El Giraldillo

Hotels
8 Hotel Fernando III
9 Hotel Murillo
10 Hostal Goya
11 Hostal Monreal
12 Hostal Toledo

13 Ceramics shops
14 Antiques
15 Las Cadenas (for Lladró)
16 Hospicio Venerables Sacerdotes
17 Murillo Museum
18 Los Gallos Flamenco Club

traction—and a sinister one—are two paintings by Valdes Leal, commissioned by Miguel de Mañara. They realistically represent the Triumph of Death: a skeleton in knightly armor and a bishop in his coffin devoured by worms.

Murillo said that one had to hold one's nose when looking at this canvas. His own paintings cover the Caridad walls with Virgins and cherubs. He is the painter of Seville, as El Greco is that of Toledo and Goya that of Madrid. He has painted the burning tenderness of Seville in the eyes of his Virgins as he has captured the piquancy of Santa Cruz's street urchins.

Along the Banks of the Guadalquivir

The Guadalquivir banks no longer shelter graceful sailing vessels of the past, but freighters loaded with wood, lead or minerals. The port has long since lost the regal position it held when the Tribunal of the Indies met in Seville, and when the Portuguese, Magellan, came here to embark on his first trip around the world. For many years the port was paralysed by encroaching sand, but when the Tablada Canal was dug in 1926, ocean-going vessels were brought once again to Seville's shores, though today they are mostly to be seen on the widened part of the river beyond the suburbs of Triana, leaving the central part of the Guadalquivir free from commerce and industry.

There is no lovelier place for a stroll as the sun is setting than along the Calle Betis on the far side of the Guadalquivir between the San Telmo and Isabel II bridges. From here the vista of the sparkling water, the palm-lined banks and the silhouette of the Golden Tower, the Giralda and the roof of the cathedral, is simply stunning. From here too, you can glimpse Seville's bullring, the Maestranza, built in 1760–3 and the oldest bullring in Spain. The Torre de Oro, or Golden Tower, was built in 1220 as the last tower on the city's ramparts and was used to close off the harbor by means of a chain stretched across the river to another tower, long since disappeared, on the opposite bank. Its name, some believe, comes from the fact that it may once have been covered in golden tiles. The tower is 12-sided and its lantern is an 18th-century addition. Inside is a small, but pleasantly laid out Maritime Museum.

The María Luisa Park

On the fringes of the María Luisa park lie two notable buildings, one the old Tobacco Factory built in 1750–66, and today the university of Seville. At its height in the 19th century the factory employed 10,000 girls, numbering among them the legendary Carmen. The other is the Palace of San Telmo, today a seminary, and whose gardens have become the María Luisa Park. They were redesigned in 1929 for the Ibero-American exhibition, and today the sunken gardens with pools, fountains and ceramic tiles provide welcome relief from Seville's summer heat. Many of the pavilions from the 1929 exhibition still remain and are used as consulates or private schools. Be sure to see the Plaza de España, the vast semi-circular brick building which was Spain's pavilion. The ceramic-tile pictures in each of its arches represent Spain's 50 provinces and the four bridges over the ornamental lake represent the four medieval kingdoms of the Iberian peninsula. As you wander through the park, you will come across the statue to the Romantic 19th-century poet, Gustavo Adolfo Bécquer, and at the far end, is one of the loveliest spots in all Seville, the Plaza de América. A blaze of color with its deep orange sand, its flowers and shrubs, fountains in yellow, blue and ocher tiles, which attract hundreds of white doves, it is an ideal place to pass away the siesta hours.

Seville's Churches

All of Seville's churches are interesting in their own way, some are obviously reconstructed mosques, others are Spanish Baroque. The chapels are naively cluttered with artificial flowers. Golden lamps illuminate figures by Roldán and Montanés. There are Christs and Virgins with names of touching lyricism: *Our Lady of Solitude* and *Jesus Omnipotent,* the *Virgin of Sorrow* and *Christ Expiring.* The neighborhood parishes render to each saint a particular homage, but none is more revered than the Virgin of Hope. She is familiarly known as the Macarena, because her church adjoins the Macarena Gate, a remnant of the old Roman wall. As familiar to the Sevillian as the features of his sweetheart are those of the Macarena. She has been granted the City's Medal of Honor along with the somewhat dubious distinction in 1937 of having been made Captain General of the Nationalist Forces by General Queipo de Llano. She is the matador's protector and few bullfighters would dream of entering the ring without addressing a prayer to her. So great are her charms, that the famous Sevillian bullfighter Joselito spent half his personal fortune buying her four emeralds. When, in 1920, he was killed in the ring at the tender age of 25, the Macarena was dressed in widow's weeds for a full month.

Holy Week and Its Processions

The citizen of Seville is a habitual night-owl, and, during Holy Week he seldom sleeps at all. By Palm Sunday every balcony is hung with palm branches brought from the palm groves of Elche and blessed in church—a house so adorned is thought to enjoy good fortune and good health throughout the coming year. The faithful are busily acquiring merit by freshening up the statues, brushing Caiaphas' velvet robe, combing Saint John's sheepskin, and ironing the linen for the communion rail. Seville's streets and alleys become crowded with parades that continue until Good Friday. Out of their niches come all the carved stations of the cross: Jesus before Pilate or in the Garden, groups of as many as 20 sumptuous figures, richly clothed and armed, surrounded by handsome trees, rugs and draperies. These *pasos* are mounted on platforms and carried through the city by five or six dozen bearers.

Each parish offers at least one paso and one figure of Christ or Mary to the parade. These are carried under an embroidered canopy, among flaming tapers and silver lamps. The sumptuousness of the statues is unbelievable, Madonnas are dressed in capes of satin or damask, encrusted with pearls and strands of gold; diadems glitter with precious stones. Great Spanish ladies have emptied their jewel caskets to shower the Virgin with gifts. Among this splendor move hooded barefooted penitents, each wearing a robe around his waist and carrying a lighted candle. According to their *cofradía,* or brotherhood, these pilgrims wear cowls of linen or heavy pleated satin of scarlet or blue, purple or gray.

The first procession begins on Palm Sunday afternoon, the last ends with the last streaks of sunset on the evening of Good Friday. In spite of its elaborateness, the spectacle is monotonous, and so an incongruous assortment of extra mummers is introduced. In Seville these are Roman centurions, at Lorca, Biblical characters and even Mahomet and Cleopatra.

Added to the general excitement are the songs of gypsies and the constant popping of firecrackers. Make no mistake, this Holy Week is a boisterous affair. Visitors who have rented comfortable seats in the stands in the Plaza San Francisco or Plaza del Duque can watch indefinitely one tableau after another; the Andalusians are ecstatic, comfortable or not. They munch their nuts and candy, wrap their exhausted infants in shawls, and give themselves up to this supreme moment. They have waited a year to lend their joy and agonized tears to this Passion Play. In the last hours of the procession you hear their tortured songs, the *saetas*, inspired by the sufferings of Jesus.

Much the best part of the processions are the *salidas* or *entradas* when the images are first borne out of their respective churches, and when, usually sometime around 4 A.M., they are carried back into their churches. Especially spectacular are those of the image of Jesús del Gran Poder and of the Vírgen de la Macarena whose procession takes place on Holy Thursday. Following the *entradas*, it is customary to go for an early breakfast of chocolate and churros at one of the many churro stands specially set up for the Holy Week spectacle.

The Feria

This week-long fair usually takes place a couple of weeks after Easter, towards the end of April, and occasionally spilling over into May. It originated as an agricultural fair with farm implements and machinery on show, and horse, donkey and mule breeders coming from all over Andalusia to sell their animals, much of the dealing being done by gypsies. Today little of its original purpose survives, and the whole affair has turned into a huge flamenco spectacle accompanied by some of the best bullfights in the Spanish year, and luring visitors from far and wide.

On the Real de la Feria across the river, row after row of *casetas* are set up. These are tents, or small wood and canvas pavilions with striped awnings, erected by wealthy Sevillian families, by firms, by clubs, by trade unions or political parties, and maybe just by groups of friends who have clubbed together for the purpose. In these *casetas* from early evening through the small hours of the morning, the most amazing display of flamenco dancing, singing, guitar music, castanet-snapping and hand-clapping, takes place. The women of Seville, whether participants or onlookers, from the tiniest two-year-old to the plumpest grey-haired matron, proudly sport their flamenco attire, much of it made new for each year's Feria and at no mean cost. Many of the men too are attired in traditional Andalusian riding dress with broad-rimmed leather hats, short jackets and leather trousers and boots. From noon till about 3 P.M. each afternoon riders and horses parade round and round the fair ground, with frilled and flounced señoritas mounted side-saddle behind their respective beaus. Around 5 P.M. the bullfights begin in the Maestranza ring, attracting enormous crowds and top bullfighters who have come from all over the country to participate. In the evening an enormous firework display sets off the night's festivities, and if you can stand the pace and late hours, you will soon find yourself absorbed in the whole spectacle.

PRACTICAL INFORMATION FOR SEVILLE

WARNING. With the highest unemployment figures in western Europe (35% against the national average of 20%, and 41% of its youth without work) and its proximity to the drug trafficking ports on Spain's southern coast, Seville has become notorious for purse snatching and thefts from parked or even moving cars. Tourists have recently been attacked and robbed while driving their cars, and the American consul has resorted to issuing a list of warnings to American visitors to Seville. Drive with your car doors locked, take extra care with your belongings at all times, never leave anything in a parked car and keep a wary eye on scooter riders who are prone to windshield smashing and bag snatching. Take only a small amount of cash and just one credit card out with you; leave your passport, traveler's checks and other credit cards in the hotel safe; and avoid carrying purses and expensive cameras, or wearing valuable jewelry, at all times. Do not think you're safe from attack when in a crowded street. Spanish onlookers, and even the police, are notorious for not coming to your rescue. Take no risks.

GETTING TO TOWN FROM THE AIRPORT. The airport is 12 km. (seven miles) out on the road to Carmona and Córdoba. Buses meet some incoming *Iberia* flights and run to the Iberia office on Almirante Lobo 3. But the best way of getting into the city center is to take a cab directly to your hotel.

TOURIST INFORMATION. The Seville Tourist Office is at Avda. de la Constitución 21, between the Archives of the Indies and the Puerta de Jerez. Its summer opening hours are Mon. to Sat. 9.30–7.30, and 9.30–1.30 on Sun. and fiestas. In winter it may well close Sat. afternoons and all day Sun.

TELEPHONE CODES. The area code for Seville province and the city itself is (954). You need only dial this code when calling from outside Seville province.

GETTING AROUND. Seville, with its labyrinth of narrow streets, can be a difficult city to find your way about in and is best negotiated on foot. Fortunately all the main sites, except possibly for the park, are fairly close together. Arm yourself with a city map and mark your hotel on it, it may not be so easy to find at the end of a day's sightseeing!

By Taxi. If you do get lost, or are feeling weary, then take a taxi. They are plentiful and not too expensive. Make sure the driver puts his meter on at the start of the ride. As of mid-1988, fares were as follows: meter starts at 74 ptas., and goes up a few ptas. each 15 seconds. Supplements are: suitcases 25 ptas., Sundays and holidays 45 ptas., night fares 10–6 A.M.

45 ptas., to or from the airport 200 ptas. There is a 25% surcharge on rides during the April Fair. These prices will most likely rise by 1989. Taxis take up to four people.

By Bus. Local buses are orange and charge a flat fare of 60 ptas. A *bonobus* good for 10 rides can be bought at reduced cost (approximately 350 ptas.) from the main *taquilla* of TUSSAM (the Seville Transport Authority) in Plaza Nueva. Taking a bus can be confusing, however. Due to Seville's complicated one-way system, many buses return along a different route from their outward journey, so ask if you're uncertain.

By Carriage. *Coche caballos* (horse-drawn carriages) add a touch of local color to Seville's streets. A good place to hire one is in Plaza Virgen de los Reyes, outside the cathedral entrance. Four or five people can ride together. If you don't like the price quoted, be sure to bargain, but always agree your price before your ride begins. A recommended route for a buggy ride is through the María Luisa Park visiting the Plaza de España and the Plaza de América. As a guide, an hour's ride should cost around 2000 ptas.

By Metro. A metro system has been under construction for some years but little progress is being made at present.

RAILROAD STATIONS. Seville has two train stations, the *Estación de Córdoba* in Plaza de Armas for Madrid, Córdoba and Málaga and all other directions; and the *Estación de Cádiz* in Calle San Bernardo for trains to Cádiz, Huelva and Jerez. Some trains serve both stations. Be sure to check which station your train leaves from. Tickets can be bought at either station or in the RENFE office in Calle Zaragoza 29. For train information call (41 41 11), and for reservations (21 79 98). Alternatively you can buy your tickets from any travel agent displaying the blue and yellow RENFE sign.

BUS STATIONS. The principal bus depot is the *Estación de Autobuses* between José María Osborne and Manuel Vázquez Sagastizabal. For bus information, call (41 71 11). For buses to Huelva and Ayamonte, go to the *Empresa Damas* on Segura 18 (tel. 22 22 72). For buses to Badajoz and Cáceres, go to *La Estellesa* on Arenal 7 (tel. 22 58 20). Both the latter are near the bottom of Reyes Católicos.

AIRPORT. The San Pablo airport is 12 km. out. Buses run from the Iberia office (Almirante Lobo 3, tel. 22 89 01) to connect with particular flights. Iberia is the agent in Seville for all foreign airlines.

HOTELS. During Easter week and the Seville fair at the end of April hotel rooms are virtually impossible to find, many having been booked for as much as a year in advance. Rates are about double at this time and you will probably be obliged to take half or even full board terms.

Many of Seville's hotels are located in narrow streets and may be extremely hard to find if you are arriving for the first time in your own car. In which case we advise that one of you take a taxi which you can follow in your own car to the hotel. In Easter week many of the streets in the center of town may be closed to traffic altogether; most hotels will then have porters with trolleys who will collect your luggage from your car or taxi.

Deluxe

Alfonso XIII, San Fernando 2 (tel. 22 28 50). 149 rooms. Built in ornate Mudéjar style for Alfonso XIII's visit to the 1929 exhibition. Although renovated a decade ago, it is now more interesting as a survival than as a comfortable up-to-date hotel. Worth a visit for the atmosphere, though. The bar and *Itálica* restaurant are popular social venues. AE, DC, MC, V.

Colón, Canalejas 1. A traditional hotel, also built in 1929 but in a less flamboyant style than the *Alfonso XIII,* the Colón was reopened in 1988 after three years of extensive renovations. Its well known *Burladero* restaurant is also open again. The hotel is very central, just off Reyes Católicos, and has been granted a 5-star rating. AE, DC, MC, V.

Expensive

Dona María, Don Remondo 19 (tel. 22 49 90). 61 rooms. In a side street close to the cathedral, this is probably Seville's most charming hotel after the Alfonso XIII. Its rooms are small and tastefully furnished with antiques. The hotel does not have a restaurant but there is a roof-top pool with a good view of the Giralda. AE, DC, V.

Gran Hotel Lar, Pza. de Carmen Benítez 3 (tel. 41 03 61). 137 rooms. A functional hotel for businesspeople and tour groups. Standards and service are good. DC, MC, V.

Inglaterra, Pza. Nueva 7 (tel. 22 49 70). 120 rooms. A modern comfortable hotel right in the central square. Its restaurant is known for good food and excellent service. AE, DC, MC, V.

Los Lebreros, Luis Morales 2 (tel. 57 94 00). 439 rooms all of which have balconies equipped with rotating canopies to provide a choice of *sol* or *sombra.* A popular hotel for conventions, some way from center, with pool and elegant *La Dehesa* restaurant. AE, DC, MC, V.

La Macarena, San Juan Ribera 2 (tel. 37 57 00). 305 rooms. An enormous, stylish hotel, not central but near the old Moorish walls and the basilica of the famous Virgin. An elegant and comfortable place to stay with an impressive lobby, cocktail bar, inner patio and fountains. AE, DC, MC, V.

Pasarela, Avda. de la Borbolla 11 (tel. 41 55 11). 82 rooms. A fairly recent hotel located just behind the Plaza de España. AE, DC, MC, V.

Porta Coeli, Eduardo Dato 49 (tel. 57 00 40). 247 rooms. Large, modern hotel with agreeable atmosphere and service; a little out of the center. AE, DC, MC, V.

Sevilla Sol, Avda. de la Borbolla (tel. 42 26 11). This hotel behind the Pza. de España opened in 1988. Rooms are very comfortable with wide beds, spacious bathrooms, and great views over the city; every effort has been made to provide for the traveler's needs. AE, DC, MC, V.

Moderate

Alcázar, Menéndez Pelayo 10 (tel. 41 20 11). 96 rooms. Modern hotel on busy road, overlooking Murillo and Alcázar gardens. AE, DC, MC, V.

América, Jesús del Gran Poder 2 (tel. 22 09 51). 100 rooms. Modern hotel centrally located close to shops on Plaza del Duque. DC, MC, V.

Bécquer, Reyes Católicos 4 (tel. 22 89 00). 126 rooms. A pleasant, modern hotel with bar and lounge. Good service. AE, DC, MC, V.

Corregidor, Morgado 17 (tel. 38 51 11). 69 rooms. Pleasant and reasonably central. Rooms rather bare but comfortable. AE, V.

Fernando III, San José 21 (tel. 21 73 07). 156 rooms. Rooms are rather somber, but its location on the edge of the Barrio Santa Cruz, and its rooftop pool and patio, make it one of the best choices.AE, DC, V.

Giralda, Sierra Nevada 3 (tel. 41 66 61). Located just off the Avda. Recaredo, the former *Fleming* underwent extensive renovations and modernization in the mid-1980s, and now offers some of the best standards in this category. AE, DC, MC, V.

Monte Carmelo, Turia 9 (tel. 27 90 00). 68 rooms. Small, comfortable hotel in the Barrio de Los Remedios across the river. AE, MC, V.

Venecia, Trajano 31 (tel. 38 11 61). 24 rooms. A reasonably good hotel in a narrow street about half way between the Alameda de Hercules and the central Plaza del Duque. V.

Inexpensive

Ducal, Pza. de la Encarnación 19 (tel. 21 51 07). 51 rooms. An old-timer, simple and central, with large old-fashioned comfortable rooms. AE, DC, MC, V.

Internacional, Aguilas 17 (tel. 21 32 07). 26 rooms. A well-maintained and charming old-world hotel in the narrow streets near the Casa Pilatos.

Montecarlo, Gravina 51 (tel. 21 75 03). 26 rooms. Old-fashioned hotel in a picturesque house with an attractive inner courtyard decorated with ceramic tiles. AE, DC, MC, V.

Murillo, Lope de Rueda 7 (tel. 21 60 95). 61 rooms. Picturesque setting in the heart of Barrio Santa Cruz. Cannot be reached by car but a porter with a trolley will collect your luggage from your taxi. AE, DC, MC, V.

La Rábida, Castelar 24 (tel. 22 09 60). 87 rooms. A charming old-fashioned budget hotel in a central part of town. Lots of old-world atmosphere and a restaurant.

Sevilla, Daioz 5, (tel. 38 41 61). 30 rooms. Typical and quaint in an old Sevillian house overlooking a small square in the heart of town.

Simón, García de Vinuesa 19 (tel. 22 66 60). 48 rooms. In an 18th-century house with beautiful iron grilles and a delightful patio; in a narrow street in the old town just off Avda. Constitución. It may not have every comfort, but if you like charm this is the place to stay. The rooms are clean, half of them have full bathrooms, and the management is friendly. Lowest rates.

Youth Hostels. The Youth Hostel is *Residencia Juvenil Sevilla,* Isaac Peral 2 (tel. 61 31 50), and is out beyond the María Luisa Park just off the road to Jerez, the Avda. de la Palmera.

RESTAURANTS. Should you find Seville's restaurants, particularly the cheaper ones, rather empty, it is probably due to the abundance of *mesones* and *bodegas* all over town which serve a vast range of tapas at the bar but do not provide tables or waiter service. Many of the locals eat this way, particularly in the evenings. Remember too that lunch is the main meal and tends to be a rather lengthy affair. Few Sevillians begin lunch before 2.30 and many are still at the table as late as 4.30. If you are pressed for time, however, most restaurants begin serving around 1 P.M. when they will be less crowded and therefore speedier.

Expensive

La Albahaca, Pza. Santa Cruz 12 (tel. 22 07 14). Attractive old house in the heart of the Barrio Santa Cruz. Lots of atmosphere and a small menu offering creative dishes. Closed Sun. AE, DC, MC, V.

La Dorada, Vírgen de Aguas Santas 6 (tel. 45 51 00). A seafood restaurant with an outstanding variety of shellfish. With the same owner as the ones in Madrid and Barcelona, this is the original *La Dorada*. Closed Sun. evenings and Aug. AE, DC, V.

Enrique Becerra, Gamazo 2 (tel. 21 30 49). Small, intimate restaurant in old Andalusian house just off the Plaza Nueva. High standard of Andalusian cooking. Closed Sun. AE, V.

Figón del Cabildo, Pza. del Cabildo (tel. 22 01 17). A welcome innovation on the Seville restaurant scene. In a pedestrian precinct just off Avda. Constitución. Closed Sun. AE, DC, MC, V.

Maitres, Avda. República Argentina 54 (tel. 45 68 80). Los Remedios restaurant with fine cooking. Closed Sun. AE, V.

Mesón Don Raimundo, Argote de Molina 26 (tel. 22 33 55). In an old convent not far from the cathedral. Decor and atmosphere are truly Sevillian. You can also sample a *fino* and some of its splendid *tapas* in its entrance bar without dining. Closed Sun. evenings. AE, DC, MC, V.

Or-Iza, San Fernando 41 (tel. 22 72 54). Popular and highly thought-of Basque restaurant opposite the old tobacco factory. Its lively entrance bar is an attractive place to sample excellent seafood. AE, DC, MC, V.

Ox's, Betis 61 (tel. 27 95 85). This is the old *Or-Iza* and still under same management. Smart Basque restaurant on far bank of Guadalquivir, serving nouvelle cuisine; small but delicious portions. Closed Sun. and Aug. AE, DC, MC, V.

Rincón de Casana, Santo Domingo de la Calzada 13 (tel. 57 02 15). Behind Los Lebreros hotel, this smart restaurant specializes in high-quality fish, and Argentinian meat dishes. Stylish decor resembles a stately old Andalusian home. Closed Sun. and either July or Aug. AE, DC, MC, V.

Rincón de Curro, Vírgen de Luján 45 (tel. 45 02 38). In the Barrio de Los Remedios across the river, one of Seville's best restaurants; with superb fish and meat dishes. Closed Sun. night and Aug. AE, DC, MC, V.

San Marco, Cuna 6 (tel. 21 24 40). In the center of town close to the main shopping area, with French, Italian and Andalusian dishes on the menu. Closed Sun. and Aug. AE, DC, MC, V.

Taberna del Alabardero, Genaro Parladé 7 (tel. 62 75 51). Under the same ownership as its namesakes in Madrid and Marbella, this restaurant specializes in Basque cuisine. Some way out of the center off Avda. Manuel Siurot beyond María Luisa park. Closed weekends. AE, DC, MC, V.

Moderate

El Bacalao, Pza. Ponce de León 15 (tel. 21 66 70). Near the Don Paco hotel and Santa Catalina church, El Bacalao specializes, as its name suggests, in different ways of serving cod. Try the *bacalao con arroz* or *bacalao al pil-pil.* Other fish dishes are good, too. Closed Sun. and Aug. AE, DC, V.

Bodegón Torre del Oro, Santander 15 (tel. 21 42 11). A large rustic restaurant with good food; long popular with Americans. Close to the Golden Tower. AE, MC, V.

Bodegón El Riojano, Vírgen de las Montañas 12 (tel. 45 06 82). Popular Remedios restaurant with typically Andalusian dishes—good tapas and seafood in its bar. AE, DC, MC, V.

La Isla, Arfe 25 (tel. 21 26 31). Long famous for it superb seafood and paellas; in the center between the cathedral and La Caridad and well worth a visit. Closed Aug. AE, DC, MC, V.

Jamaica, Jamaica 16 (tel. 61 12 44). An old restaurant out in the Barrio de Heliópolis. Famed for having the best wine cellar in Seville and some very creative dishes. Closed Sun. evenings. AE, DC, V.

La Judería, Cano y Cueto 13 (tel. 41 20 52). Bright, modern restaurant near Hotel Fernando III that is fast gaining fame for its fish dishes from the north of Spain and its meat from Avila; very good value. Closed Tues. AE, DC, MC, V.

El Mero, Bétis 1 (tel. 33 42 52). A well thought-of and moderately priced fish restaurant close to the Isabel II bridge. Closed Tues. in summer. AE, DC, MC, V.

La Rayuela, Don Remondo 1 (tel. 21 79 52). Small restaurant in the old streets close to the old cathedral. The imaginative menu makes full use of the freshest produce, and its daily *menu de la casa* features typical Spanish dishes. Closed Sat. lunch and Sun. night. AE, DC, MC, V.

Rio Grande, Bétis 70 (tel. 27 39 56). Fine location on the banks of the Guadalquivir with a pleasant outdoor terrace and splendid views over the Golden Tower and Giralda. Good Rioja wines. AE, DC, MC, V.

San Francisco, Pza. San Francisco 10 (tel. 22 20 56). Former convent, central and close to the Ayuntamiento. Its menu is a pleasing mixture of French and Spanish inventiveness; a little pricey. Closed Sun. nights, Mon., and Aug. MC, V.

Inexpensive

La Cueva del Pez de Espada, Rodrigo Caro 18. Colorful tavern in the Barrio Santa Cruz with tables outside in Pza. Doña Elvira in summer. Consistent standards, friendly and helpful service, and sometimes live guitar music.

El Giraldillo, Plaza Vírgen de los Reyes 2 (tel. 21 45 25). Typical, colorful mesón opposite entrance to cathedral. Popular with both locals and tourists.

El Mesón, Dos de Mayo 26 (tel. 21 30 75). A typical Sevillian bodega of James Michener fame, not far from La Caridad. Great atmosphere, with bullfight decor in the first room, and photos of famous diners, including many Americans, in the inner room. Closed Mon.

Mesón Castellano, Jovellanos 6 (tel. 21 41 28). Opposite the Church of San José, this old Sevillian house is an ideal place for lunch after a morning's shopping on Calle Sierpes. Specialties are Castilian meat dishes; amazingly good value. Open for lunch only. Closed Sun. AE, DC, V.

Mesón Tenorio, Mateus Gago 9. One of many inexpensive restaurants on this street just up from the cathedral. More a bar than a restaurant but there are a few tables and a fresh and pleasant atmosphere.

Modesto, Cano y Cueto 5 (tel. 41 68 11). This typical Andalusian house with colorful tiles is popular with locals who come here for tapas. Cooking is Andalusian with Sevillian specialties, and there's a good-value *menu del día.* Closed Wed. AE, DC, MC, V.

BARS AND CAFES. Seville is loaded with bars, mesones and tavernas but, for a city of its size, surprisingly few cafes. One of the smartest places to go for a pre-dinner drink is the bar of the Alfonso XIII hotel. For more typical bars try the streets of the old town, in the Sierpes-Velázquez area, between the cathedral and Plaza del Salvador along Alvarez Quintero or Conteros, the area between Avda. Constitución and the Bullring round the Calles Dos de Mayo and García Vinuesa, and Calle Mateos Gago leading away from the cathedral and bordering on the edge of the Barrio de Santa Cruz. If you want to sit out on the sidewalk, there are plenty of bars with outdoor terraces in Calle Alemanes down the side of the cathedral overlooking the wall of the Patio de los Naranjos. The following is a small selection of the more colorful bars.

Bar Alhucema, Carlos Canal 20A. Charming small bar in a converted grocery shop near the Hotel Inglaterra.

La Alicantina, Pza. del Salvador 2. An ancient beer hall beside El Salvador church with wonderful *tapas,* especially seafood.

La Campana, corner of Sierpes and Campana. Delightful old-world cafe and pastry shop, the nearest Seville has to a traditional cafe-cum-tearoom.

Casa Morales, García de Vinuesa 11. A lively bodega just off Avda. Constitución where people go for *vino tinto* and fried fish. Closed Sundays and fiestas.

Casa Román, Plaza de los Venerables. A picturesque bar with atmospheric paintings and the ceiling strung with hams. In one of the prettiest squares in the Barrio Santa Cruz. Closed Sundays.

Cervecería Giralda, Mateus Gago 1. Traditional old beerhall near cathedral with several sidewalk tables.

El Rinconcillo, Gerona 42. 1670 inn and long a Bohemian haunt. Wide range of *tapas* and *raciones* which you can well make a meal of. Closed Wednesdays.

NIGHTLIFE. There is no cabaret of international standing in Seville and the few nightclubs there are, such as *La Trocha* and *La Koutoubia,* really require a knowledge of Spanish and the Spanish scene, to enjoy their shows. However, for a night's entertainment, your best bet is to try one of the flamenco shows while you are in this capital of flamenco. Though patronized more by tourists than locals, they make for a good night out and provide the chance to see some excellent performances interspersed with numbers of more mass appeal. Tickets are normally on sale in hotels; otherwise make your reservations directly with the club, by calling during the evening—there is rarely anyone there during the day. Reservations are essential for larger groups.

Flamenco. El Arenal, Rodo 7 (tel. 21 64 92). The well known *Tablao de Curro Vélez* puts on a reasonably authentic flamenco show, probably not best suited to flamenco newcomers. El Arenal is closed in January and February when the group travels abroad, often performing in the U.S.

Los Gallos, Plaza de Santa Cruz 11 (tel. 21 69 81). Small and intimate deep in the Barrio Santa Cruz. Good, fairly pure flamenco.

El Patio Sevillano, Paseo de Colón (tel. 21 41 20). This one caters mainly to tour groups; the show is very colorful and the costumes superb. Mixture of regional Spanish dances (often performed to taped music) and pure flamenco numbers by some outstanding guitarists, singers and dancers. If you haven't seen flamenco before, this is probably the best choice. Two or three shows nightly.

TOURS AND EXCURSIONS. As most of the sights of Seville have to be visited on foot, day coach tours for individual tourists are not as common as they are in other cities. However, if you are interested in a guided tour, enquire at your hotel or the Tourist Office. If you would like to hire a guide to show you the sights, contact **Guidetur de Sevilla,** Cuna 41–2°-A (tel. 22 23 74/5); their office is open 9–1.30 and 5–8. You will see many guided parties in Seville, but these are usually part of an all-inclusive package tour visiting Seville as one of several stops on its itinerary. The following are side trips you might like to make if you have a day to spare; contact the Tourist Office for details and helpful information.

Boat rides on the Guadalquivir. River trips on the Guadalquivir with guided commentary leave from the Muelle Torre del Oro near the Golden Tower and last one hour. Details are posted in the Tourist Office and in many hotels, or you can call *Cruceros Guadalquivir* (tel. 77 08 10) or *Cruceros Sevilla* (tel. 12 19 34).

Itálica. The Roman excavations of Itálica lie nine km. (six miles) from Seville just beyond the village of Santiponce on the road to Huelva. One of the earliest Roman settlements in Spain, its huge amphitheater and some interesting mosaics have survived. There are traces in other excavations of a forum and a theater. Most of the small artefacts found on the site have been moved to the Museum of Archeology in Seville. Buses to Italica leave from Marqués de Paradas near the Córdoba railroad station. The excavations are open Tues. to Sat. 9–5.30, Sun. and fiestas 9–3; closed Mon. Do not neglect to visit the nearby **Monastery of San Isidro del Campo** just outside the village of Santiponce, founded by Guzmán el Bueno; it contains his tomb and a magnificent reredos by Martínez Montañés.

Visit to a bull farm and ranch. It is sometimes possible to visit the **Cortijo de Juan Gómez,** at Los Palacios (tel. 86 50 00), 32 km. (20 miles) from Seville on the road to Jerez. There is a bullfighting museum, a small bullring where you will have the chance to "fight" a young bull, see the magnificent thoroughbred Andalusian horses and have lunch or an aperitif in the farm's restaurant. The ranch usually only accepts groups of 30 people or more, but enquire at the Tourist Office or contact *Promociones Turísticas Reunidas,* Avda. República Argentina 9 (tel. 27 75 51).

The *Cortijo Pino Montano,* out along Avda. Pino Montano about five km. (three miles) from central Seville, is a fun place to go for lunch or dinner in summer or fiesta time. You can visit the stables or try your hand at fighting baby bulls. Its interesting small museum has portraits of a previous owner, the bullfighter Ignacio Sánchez Mejías, whose death in the ring in 1935 was immortalized by the poet García Lorca. Its phone no. is 43 42 11 and it is wise to book.

MUSEUMS AND GALLERIES. Most are free to holders of I.S.I. cards, and to Spaniards with I.D., but not to foreign visitors, except on Saturdays. Although we give opening times below, it is always wise to double check as they change frequently.

Museo Arqueológico (Archeological Museum), Pza. de America in the María Luisa Park. Collection of finds from the province of Seville including several from the Roman Itálica excavations. Open Tues. to Sun. 10–2; closed Mon.

Museo de Arte Contemporáneo (Contemporary Art Museum), Santo Tomás 5, beside the Archives of the Indies. Small permanent collection and interesting temporary exhibitions in an old house. Open Tues. to Fri. 9–2, Sat. and Sun. 11–2; closed Mon.

Museo de Artes y Costumbres Populares (Museum of Folk Art and Customs), in the Plaza de América in María Luisa Park. Open Tues. to Sun. 10–2; closed Mon. and fiestas.

Museo de Bellas Artes (Fine Arts Museum), Pza. del Museo 9. Good collection of Murillo, Valdés, Leal and Zurbarán housed in a delightful old convent. Currently closed for restoration.

Museo Marítimo (Maritime Museum), in the Golden Tower near San Telmo bridge. Open Tues. to Sat. 10–2, Sun. 10–1; closed Mon.

Museo Murillo (Murillo's House), Santa Teresa 8. In the Barrio Santa Cruz. Open Tues. to Fri. 10–2 and 4–7, Sat. and Sun. 10–2 only; closed Mon.

PLACES OF INTEREST. Alcázar (Reales Alcázares), entrance in Plaza del Triunfo. Open daily 9–12.45 and 3–5.45. Entrance free on Saturdays.

Archivo General de Indias (Lonja), Avda. de la Constitución. Interesting collection of documents of the discovery, conquest and colonization of America. Open Mon. to Fri. 10–1.

Ayuntamiento (City Hall), in the Pza. San Francisco at the end of Avda. Constitución. Early 16th-century building, a fine example of Spanish Plateresque. Ask permission to visit the inside.

Basílica de la Macarena, near the Macarena Gate. Open 9–1 and 5–9. To the side of the church is the **Museo Devocional y Artístico.** Open 9–12.30 and 5.30–7.30.

Casa de Pilatos (Pilate's House), Pza. de Pilatos. Open daily 9–6.30.

Catedral y Giralda, Pza. Vírgen de los Reyes. Open 10.30–1.30 and 4.30–6.30 in summer, 10.30–1 and 4–6 in winter; Sun. 10.30–1.

Convento de Santa Paula, Calle Santa Paula. 15th-century Gothic convent with a superb ceramic facade. Inside the church are some beautiful *azulejos,* notable paintings and furnishings, and sculptures by Martínez Montañés. Open daily 9–1 and 4–6.30.

Hospicio de Venerables Sacerdotes, in the square of the same name in the Barrio Santa Cruz. Baroque chapel and collection of *pasos* (floats) from the Cruz de Mayo processions. Closed at presstime, but check locally.

Hospital de la Caridad, Calle Temprado. Open 9.30–1.30 and 4–7.

Iglesia del Salvador, Pza. del Salvador. 17th-century Baroque church built on the site of an old Arab mosque and containing the processional images of Jesús de Pasión and San Cristóbal, both by Martínez Montañés, and *El Cristo del Amor* by Juan de Mesa. Open 8–11 and 6.30–9.

La Maestranza, Paseo de Colón. Oldest and most beautiful bullring in Spain, with an interesting art gallery in an adjoining annexe.

Templo del Gran Poder, Calle Jesús del Gran Poder. Famous processional statue of Jesús del Gran Poder (Christ Omnipotent) by Juan de Mesa. Open daily 8–1.30 and 6–9.

PARKS AND GARDENS. María Luisa Park. This is probably the prettiest park in Spain, with a fascinating mixture of formal designs and wild vegetation. Also fountains, cafes, small sequestered nooks, where one may sit and read or dream. Its beautiful villas were built for the Hispanic-American exhibition of 1929, each pavilion representing a different Latin American country.

Also beautiful are the **Murillo Gardens** on the edge of the Barrio Santa Cruz and the delightful **Alcázar Gardens** with their patios, flowering shrubs and ornamental pools and fountains. The latter can be visited on a ticket to the palace.

MUSIC, MOVIES AND THEATERS. To find out what is on look in the local press, in either the *ABC,* the *Correo de Andalucía,* the *Sudoeste* or *Nueva Andalucía.* Alternatively, pick up a copy of the monthly leaflet *Giraldillo,* available free from the Tourist Office and several other places around town. This lists classical music and jazz events, movies and theater preformances, art exhibitions and dance events.

Music. There is no concert hall as such but classical concerts are held in the *cathedral* and in the *Iglesia del Salvador,* also sometimes in the *Escuela de Estudios Hispanoamericanos.* Opera and ballet performances are staged at the *Teatro Lope de Vega.*

Jazz. The two jazz venues are *Acuarela Jazz,* Alameda de Hércules 86 with daily events, and *Be Bop Jazz,* Sol 40.

Movies. For films in English, look in the press or *Giraldillo* for films marked *V.O. Subtitulada* (V.O. = Original Version).

Theater. Seville has two theaters, the *Teatro Lope de Vega,* Avda. de María Luisa (tel. 23 21 03) whose season runs Sept. through July; and the *Teatro Alvarez Quintero,* Laraña 4 (tel. 22 02 39) whose season runs Sept. 15 through May 31.

SPORTS. Bullfights. Bullfights take place at the Maestranza bullring on the Paseo de Colón, usually on Sundays between Easter and October. The best season is during the April Fair when fights take place each day. Tickets can be bought in advance from the ticket windows at the ring or from the kiosks in Calle Sierpes (these charge a commission).

Soccer (Fútbol). Seville has two stadiums, the **Estadio Benito Villamarín,** which is out along the Paseo de la Palmera on the road to Jerez; and the **Estadio Sánchez Pizjuán,** which is on Eduardo Dato just off the road to Granada and Málaga.

Swimming. There are pools at the hotels Alfonso XIII, Doña María, Los Lebreros, Macarena, Don Paco and Fernando III. Municipal pools are the *Piscina Sevilla* (summer only) on Avda. Ciudad Jardín 81, and at the sports complex on Avda. Cristo de la Expiración. There is another pool at the camp site, *Camping Sevilla,* six km. (four miles) out on the road to Córdoba.

SHOPPING. Seville's main shopping streets are in the area bounded by the Calles Sierpes, Tetuan, and Velázquez, the Plaza de la Magdalena and the Plaza del Duque. The *Corte Inglés* **department store** in Plaza del Duque stays open during siesta hours and has a cafeteria on the top floor. There is a new and much bigger *Corte Inglés* opposite the Los Lebreros hotel on Luis Montoto. *Galerías Preciados* is in Plaza de la Magdalena.

Antiques and **ceramics** are best in the Barrio Santa Cruz. Try the antique shops in Rodrigo Caro between the Plazas Alianza and Doña Elvira. Other good antique shops are at Mateus Gago 4 and 5, Placentines 8, both near the cathedral, Avda. de la Constitución 5 and in the Plaza del Cabildo precinct just off Constitución. Good ceramic shops are in Romero Murube, on the corner of Vida and Callejón del Agua, and in Calle Gloria where *Cerámicas Sevilla* at no. 5 specializes in hand-painted plates by local artists. Another smart ceramics shop is *Martian Ceramics,* Sierpes 76 near the Plaza Nueva. There are also two old **ceramics factories** out in the Barrio de Triana, the *Cerámica Santa Ana,* San Jorge 31, and the *Cerámica Montalván,* Alfarería 23.

For **fans,** try *Casa Rubio,* Sierpes 56. For **folk costumes,** try *Establecimiento Lina,* Plaza Santa Cruz 12; and for **flamenco** dresses, *Pardales* at Cuna 23. Children's flamenco dresses are usually cheapest in souvenir shops around the cathedral. **Lace** mantillas and tablecloths as well as woven and embroidered cloths are good at *Feliciano Foronda,* Alvarez Quintero 52. A good **souvenir** shop with a wide selection of Lladró porcelain is *Las Cadenas,* Calle Vida in the Barrio Santa Cruz. Good bookshops are *Pascual Lázaro,* Sierpes 2–4, and *Libros Vértice,* Mateus Gago 24, which also has guidebooks and novels in English.

Street Markets. If you enjoy rummaging through market stalls, the following may be of interest. Alameda de Hércules, craft market on Sunday mornings; Plaza de la Alfalfa, pet market on Sunday mornings; El Jueves Antiques Market, in Calle Feria on Thursday mornings; Plaza del Cabildo, coin and stamp market on Sunday mornings; Plaza del Duque, daily craft and jewelry stalls.

USEFUL ADDRESSES. Consulates. *U.S. Consulate,* Paseo de las Delicias 7 (tel. 23 18 85). *British Consulate,* Pza. Nueva 8 (tel. 22 88 75).

Police Headquarters (lost passports, stolen purses), Pza. de la Gavidia (tel. 22 88 40). Emergency phone no. 091.

Post Office, Avda. Constitución 32.

Telephone Exchange, Pza. Nueva 3. Open 10–2 and 5.30–10; closed Sun.

Car Hire. *Avis,* Avda. Constitución 15 (tel. 21 53 70); *Budget,* Reyes Católicos 4 (tel. 22 46 78); *Europcar,* Recaredo 32 (tel. 41 95 06); *Hertz,* Avda. República Argentina 3 (tel. 27 88 87); *Ital,* Avda. República Argentina 9 (tel. 27 75 51). *Atesa, Avis, Europcar* and *Hertz* are all at the airport too.

Travel Agents. *American Express* is represented by *Viajes Alhambra,* Teniente Coronel Segui 6 (tel. 21 29 23). *Juliá Tours,* Bilbao 12 (tel. 22 49 10). *Wagon Lits Cooks,* Avda. de la Constitución 4 (tel. 21 89 05).

Airlines. *Iberia,* Almirante Lobo 3 (tel. 22 89 01). For reservations, call (21 88 00). Iberia is the agent for all foreign airlines in Seville.

ANDALUSIA

Costa del Sol and Costa de la Luz

Andalusia is the fabulous land that armchair tourists mistake for Spain. If you believe the travel posters, every girl is called Carmen, wears a carnation in her hair, spends her days swooning over a matador bloodying up a bull and her nights swooning over guitar serenades wafted to her window through the heavy perfume of orange blossoms. Somewhere in the background a fountain plays seductively and the Alhambra looms against the sky. The more sophisticated may add the specter of a hooded penitent or one of Murillo's little beggars.

The odd thing is that Andalusia really *is* rather like that. In spite of a century of blatant advertising, comic opera settings and terrible tourist souvenirs that turn up all over the world, Andalusia remains mysterious, original, incredibly romantic and reeking with atmosphere. In fact, supremely worth visiting, for the first—or the fifty-first—time.

If you're happy to do no more than visit Seville's cathedral, Córdoba's mosque and Granada's Alhambra, you'll get along without too much trouble or difficulty. The roads are adequate, there'll be sherry and serenades; you can buy a black lace mantilla. All the beautiful Spanish postcards you've ever seen will come to life for you. And in a week you can tour the entire region and enjoy it very much. But that is not the only way, or even the best way.

For there is so much to see in Andalusia—too much for a mere week's stay. To know and understand Andalusia fully would take not a week, but a lifetime. For Andalusia has everything. There is the glamor of candlelight reflected upon gold brocade, the hooded, barefoot figures of marching penitents, and the sudden wailing lament of impromptu flamenco saetas sung as the Holy Week processions pass through the darkened streets of Seville, Granada or Málaga. There is the comfort and sophistication of great seaside hotels on the Costa del Sol and Costa de la Luz, respectively Andalusia's Mediterranean and Atlantic shores, backed by fortress towns half as old as time, and vast tawny sierras where eagles wheel toward the unclouded sun. Andalusia is fierce, virile, beautiful, and pagan—it is *never* dull!

Huelva and the Discovery of the New World

West of Seville, the Odiel and Tinto rivers flow through the dreary plains, dyed red by copper deposits. Huelva, between the two busy rivers, is still an active port. A huge monument to Columbus by the American sculptress, Mrs Whitney, stands in the estuary, but it is from Palos, now a fishing village higher up the Tinto, that Columbus' three caravels departed for America.

The coastal road continues east for 45 km. (28 miles) to Mazagón, an up-and-coming resort, with a parador, at the beginning of the endless sands of the Playa de Castilla. It then follows the beach to Torre de la Higuera, now more often known as Matalascañas, an uninteresting cluster of concrete hotels popular mainly with Spaniards. The coastal road ends here. Behind Matalascañas lie the 1,300 square km. (500 square miles) of the Coto Doñana National Park extending east to Las Marismas, a paradise for ornithologists, and which can only be visited on organized pre-booked excursions. If at Torre de Higuera you branch inland along the C445 you pass through El Rocío, the sanctuary of the famous virgin whose Whitsuntide *romería* is one of the most beautiful of all Spain's fiestas, before driving through extensive vineyards and the small town of Almonte to rejoin the main Seville-Huelva road.

So Huelva is necessarily approached from Seville. The N431 passes through several nice little towns, such as Sanlúcar la Mayor, La Palma del Condado, and Niebla, an ancient settlement on the Tinto, all of them with interesting churches in a blend of Mudéjar and Gothic styles. Niebla still has its original walls, with their four Moorish gateways also revealing Roman and Visigothic traces. Equally deserving of a visit, Santa María la Granada is a curious 10th-century Mozarabic church, once converted into a mosque and subsequently enhanced by Gothic and Mudéjar adjuncts.

Huelva was founded by the Phoenicians; the bulk of its humming industry comes from the exportation of copper ore and from canneries. But a visit to the old monastery at La Rábida, at the confluence of the Odiel and the Tinto, will repay the more historically minded. In 1484, Christopher Columbus, down on his luck and practically at the end of his rope, found refuge and assistance here. The monks who had taken him in grew to realize the significance of his scientific investigations, and interceded on his behalf with the king and queen. Those heroic times have left vivid traces in the church, the room in which Columbus conferred with the monks, the cloister and the patio. The return to the main roads leads through Palos and extensive vineyards to Moguer with its splendid 14th-century Santa Clara monastery.

Beyond Huelva N431 continues to Ayamonte, a small fishing hamlet next door to Portugal. The way to the frontier is paved with endless, shining beaches, including La Antilla and Isla Cristina.

A trip to Aracena in the Sierra Morena mountains, in the north of Huelva province, is worthwhile to see the Gruta de Maravillas, an impressive stalactite cave with underground lagoon. While there, be sure to sample some of the local *serrano* ham from nearby Jabugo, famous for its acorn-fed gray pigs. A little to the south at the spectacular mines of Minas de Riotinto, copper has been mined for 3,500 years. Closeby a Roman necropolis is under excavation.

En Route from Seville to Córdoba

The Guadalquivir, which the Arabs called the Great River, was once navigable as far as Córdoba. Galleys moored at the splendid ports along the river banks. Today, you can see the imposing ruins at Itálica, founded by Scipio, and the birthplace of three emperors, Hadrian among them. Vestiges of castles, sanctuaries and thermal baths remain at Arva. But the most moving Roman ruin is the necropolis at Carmona, with 900 family tombs chiseled out of the rock. Its walls are decorated with leaves and birds, and pierced with niches for urns. An adjoining museum with archeological finds, completes the picture.

Carmona itself is a small and typically Moorish town that has managed to preserve its naturalness. As you wander through its narrow, twisting streets, bordered by unpretentious little houses punctuated here and there by an occasional palace, with the bright sunlight playing in and out among the intricacies of wrought-iron balconies, suddenly you come upon the extraordinary San Pedro church, begun in 1466; its interior is an unbroken mass of sculptures and gilded surfaces. Nearby stands the Gothic church of Santa María, designed by the architect of Seville's cathedral, and embellished by primitive paintings, a triptych, and a calvary cross. For a great view out over the plains, climb up to the Alcázar, the once proud Moorish citadel with its scattered ruins, now the site of Carmona's parador.

Not so long ago, there was nothing but an expanse of wasteland as far as you could see along this route. Vast agricultural projects, however, have already changed the desolate aspect of the plain that was fertile enough when the Romans and Arabs cultivated it with dogged labor. One of Spain's most urgent problems, the rehabilitation of this sterile ground, has been tackled energetically.

Ecija, a dazzling white cluster, passed successively through Greek, Roman, Visigothic and Moorish hands. You will find plenty of Renaissance and Baroque palaces to see here. Gothic art is also represented in the Santa María and Santiago churches. In Santa Cruz, dominated by its high-standing Moorish tower, there is a Greco-Byzantine icon, presented in the 6th century by St. Gregory the Great to the local bishop, while several china monuments and fountains add a far-eastern flavor to the reputedly hottest town in Europe, dubbed by most Spaniards *El Sartén de Andalucía* (The Frying Pan of Andalusia).

Córdoba

If you visit the ancient city of the caliphs in midsummer, you will find it blanched, torrid and still, under an unrelenting sun with the stores and many of the monuments shutting up shop for the day at lunchtime. You may seek a breath of fresh air on the river banks, but you won't find it. So try to visit Córdoba earlier or later in the year; early May during the *Fiesta de los Patios* when the citizens of some of the lovely old houses in the old town fill their patios with flowers and open them to the public, is a wonderful time to visit. But if you have no choice, it is still a worthwhile trip to see the old Arab mills and the arches of a splendid Roman bridge, later rebuilt by the Moors, which testify together to the city's rich history.

Originally, Córdoba was only an olive oil center, but a strange destiny was in store for this curve of the Guadalquivir. Its lush fields saw the ferocious encounter of Caesar and his rival Pompey the Younger, in which 22,000 soldiers perished. Later, under Arab domination, there were intrigues and struggles among the emirs, often settled by means of poison, dagger or silken strangler's cord. Retaken by Saint King Ferdinand in 1236, the city suffered additional misfortunes as a Christian frontier town. Again, during the Napoleonic invasion, the name of Córdoba had tragic implications.

There is, of course, a modern Córdoba, arising from the activity of the Sierra copper mines and electric equipment factories, to which the many factories and ugly apartment blocks on the outer edges of the city, testify only too well.

But the great drawing card of Córdoba is the 8th-century mosque (Mezquita). Despite continuing restoration, and a program of revitalization now underway for the old section of the city, the outside of the mosque still presents a dilapidated aspect. Grass grows between its paving stones, the mosaics are chipped, the walls cracked by a scorching sun. It began as a Roman temple erected in honor of Janus and is now dedicated to the Virgin. Abdu'r Rahman intended it to surpass all other Arab mosques in grandeur.

Crossing the threshold, you are immediately confronted with evidence of the magnificent Moorish civilization. Some 850 columns rise in a forest of onyx, jasper, marble and granite, reflecting all the colors of the rainbow in oblique rays of light. The ceiling is of carved and delicately tinted cedar. Topping the pillars are capitals remaining from the Visigoth church that was razed to make a place for the mosque. Many of the bronze and copper lamps that illuminate the building were made from church bells carried from Santiago de Compostela by Christian slaves.

The pilgrims' knees have worn away the stone floor in many places. The *maksoureh,* a kind of anteroom (which now precedes the "new," 11th-century, mihrab), was reserved for the caliphs and their guests. Its central part, with its delicate mosaic and plasterwork, is a masterpiece of oriental art.

The Legacy of the Moors

To the eternal glory of the caliphs, it may be said that they made Córdoba not merely rich and powerful, but one of the greatest centers of art and philosophy of their epoch. In this city, where Seneca studied, there developed a stream of illustrious thinkers, among them Averroes, the great Arabian scholar, and the Jewish philosopher, Maimónides. One emir was as proud of his mastery of algebra as he was of the beauty of his favorites.

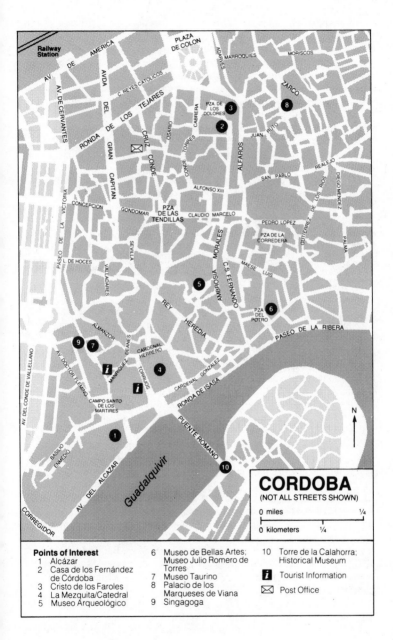

CORDOBA
(NOT ALL STREETS SHOWN)

0 miles ¼
0 kilometers ¼

N

Points of Interest
1 Alcázar
2 Casa de los Fernández de Córdoba
3 Cristo de los Faroles
4 La Mezquita/Catedral
5 Museo Arqueológico

6 Museo de Bellas Artes; Museo Julio Romero de Torres
7 Museo Taurino
8 Palacio de los Marqueses de Viana
9 Singagoga

10 Torre de la Calahorra; Historical Museum

i Tourist Information

✉ Post Office

Dazzling and erudite, this was the Córdoba that brought marble from Tarragona and Carthage for its mosque, and perfumed wood from Lebanon for its chamber of odalisques. This was the Córdoba whose citizens refused to disturb a stone of their wonderful mosque after Saint Ferdinand had driven out the Moors, but blessed the building and consecrated it to the Virgin. Alas, three centuries later, a clergy more zealous than esthetic decided to erect a church in the midst of the Moorish columns. The citizens fought bitterly against this outrage, and even threatened the lives of workers who undertook the demolition. But Charles V had given his consent to the construction, and so, at great expense, the *crucero* was built. It is a splendid Baroque affair, and would be stunning were it not a heavy, awkward mass in this airy forest of columns. The Emperor later lamented his decision accusing the clergy of building something commonplace in the midst of much beauty.

The mosque is best seen during a summer sunset, when its tawny walls are gilded by the dying rays of light. If you climb to the top of the mosque's tower you will be rewarded by a magnificent view over the rooftops of the old city to the Guadalquivir. In her niche on the nearby street of Cardenal Herrero, the Virgin of Lanterns stands demurely behind a lantern-hung grille, rather like a lovely lady awaiting a serenade. A little further on, in a narrow alleyway off to your left, the Callejón de las Flores, with its houses decked with hanging flower baskets, is straight off a picture postcard, and the patios here boast some of the best foliage, ceramics and wrought-iron grilles of the whole city.

Now retrace your steps along Cardenal Herrero and move westwards through the labyrinth of narrow streets lined with old (and in some cases, sadly crumbling) white houses, filigree silver and embossed leather shops, to the Judería, the old Jewish quarter. Here on the Plaza de las Bulas is the recently restored Museum of Bullfighting housed in two adjoining Córdoban mansions built around a patio. With a magnificent collection of memorabilia, paintings, posters, and rooms dedicated to the great Cordoban toreros Lagartijo, Guerrita and the immortal Manolete, killed in the ring in 1947, this charming museum is well worth a visit even if you are not a dedicated *aficionado* of the bullfight.

Right next to the museum in the Plaza de Tiberiades is a modern statue of the Jewish philosopher Maimónides, and just a few paces up Judíos, you come to the only remaining old synagogue in Andalusia. Standing in the heart of the Judería, it proudly bears its stucco ornamentation and its 14th-century Hebrew inscriptions. Just across the way through an archway, you enter an inner courtyard, called the Zoco, a former Arab souk, which in summer has some pleasant shops and stalls and sometimes a bar open. Only a short walk away you come to the Plaza Campo Santo de los Mártires where you can see the excavations of the Baños Arabes (Arab Baths), and on the far side of the square the entrance to the Moorish palace of the Alcázar, rebuilt in Mudéjar-style by Alfonso XI in the early 14th century.

The modern city of Córdoba centers around the busy Plaza de las Tendillas. From here you can explore the old, winding streets that lead out of the square to the north and east. One of the places where you can sense most deeply the city's somnolent pace is on the Plaza de los Dolores (Square of Sufferings), surrounded by the Convento de Capuchinos. Here, in the center of the square, eight lanterns hanging from twisted wrought-iron brackets shed their light on a Calvary scene. Anyone intrigued by the legend of the bullfighter Manolete may like to visit the monument to this most famous of Córdoban sons, near the church of Santa Marina de las Aguas Santas.

Moving south towards the river, seek out the Plaza de la Corredera (or Constitución), an intriguing if somewhat dilapidated square dating from around 1690, where a market is held every morning. There was once a prison beneath the square, the city garotte was sited here, and bullfights were also staged. From here make your way to the Plaza del Potro, where the inn is reputed to have extended hospitality to Cervantes' hero Don Quijote. Today, restored, it houses displays of local arts and crafts. To the side of the square is the Museum of Fine Arts, housed in a former Charity Hospital founded by the Catholic Monarchs, who, incidentally, twice received Columbus here and finally agreed to support the voyage which led to his discovery of the New World. Across the courtyard from the Fine Arts Museum is the house, now a museum too, of the early 20th-century Córdoban artist, Julio Romero de Torres who died in 1930. It is full of his paintings depicting, often ironically, life in turn-of-the-century Córdoba, and is one of the many small treasure houses of this ancient city.

PRACTICAL INFORMATION FOR CÓRDOBA

TOURIST OFFICES. The main Tourist Office is at Torrijos 10 in the Palacio de Congresos y Exposiciones beside the mosque (tel. 47 12 35). Open Mon. to Fri. 9.30–2.30 and 5–7, Sat. 9.30–1.30; closed Sun., fiestas, and afternoons from June to Sept. The Municipal Tourist Office is in Pza. de Judás Levi (tel. 29 07 40) in the Judería, halfway between the mosque and the synagogue. Open 9–2. In the afternoons tourist information is available in the Alcázar.

TELEPHONE CODE. The dialing code for the city and province of Córdoba is (957). This prefix need only be used when dialing from outside the province.

GETTING AROUND. Córdoba is a compact city and all the main sights are within walking distance of each other. Many of the places you will want to visit are in the old city where most of the streets are *only* navigable on foot. Public transport is by city bus but you are unlikely to need them. Taxi stands are plentiful with the main ones in the Plaza Tendillas, on the Avda. Gran Capitán, outside the Meliá hotel and on Cardinal Herrero close to the mosque.

A more original and picturesque way of getting around the city is to hire a horse buggy *(coche caballo)*. These seat four or possibly five people and you should agree the price (about 2000 ptas.) with the driver *before* you set off, also your route. The main places for hiring these are in Torrijos, the street alongside the mosque, outside the Meliá hotel, and in the Camposanto de los Mártires.

HOTELS. For a city visited by so many tourists Córdoba has surprisingly few hotels at present; however, plans for three new hotels are underway.

Our *Moderate* (3-star) recommendations are high with rates very close to (E) category. At presstime there are no really moderately priced hotels. Most hotels are central and within walking distance of the sights and shopping center. *Los Gallos* is a little further out than most and the parador is 3.5 km. north of the center.

Expensive

Adarve, Magistral González Francés 15 (tel. 48 11 02). 103 rooms. Delightful new hotel on eastern side of mosque in heart of old city. Built in Andalusian Moorish-style with a charming patio and ceramic decor. The best bet. AE, DC, MC, V.

El Gran Capitán, Avda. de América 5 (tel. 47 02 50). 100 rooms. Modern with good standards not far from Pza. Colón. AE, DC, MC, V.

Meliá Córdoba, Jardines de la Victoria (tel. 29 80 66). 106 rooms; pool. An older hotel with large rooms and pleasant garden, but beginning to show its age. AE, DC, MC, V.

Parador La Arruzafa, Avda. de la Arruzafa 33 (tel. 27 59 00). 83 rooms; pool. North of town on the road to El Brillante. Modern parador in pleasant location built on site of an Arab palace; good mountain and city views, but not one of the great paradores. AE, DC, MC, V.

Moderate

El Califa, Lope de Hoces 14 (tel. 29 94 00). 50 rooms. Small hotel, modern, in reasonably quiet central location. Does not accept tour groups.

Los Gallos, Avda. Medina Azahara 7 (tel. 23 55 00). 105 rooms; pool. Good accommodations, a little out of center near bullring. Built originally by the famous bullfighter El Cordobés, now part of a chain—caters largely for tour groups. AE, DC, MC, V.

Maimónides, Torrijos 4 (tel. 47 15 00). 61 rooms. Lovely location in heart of historic area right next to mosque. Impressive lobby but some rooms upstairs are beginning to show their age. AE, DC, MC, V.

Inexpensive

Colón, Alhaken II 4 (tel. 47 00 17). 40 rooms. Functional hotel hidden just off Avda. Gran Capitán; excellent value.

Marisa, Cardenal Herrero 6 (tel. 47 31 42). 28 rooms. Charming old Andalusian house in picturesque street right by mosque. AE, DC, V.

Selu, Eduardo Dato 7 (tel. 47 65 00). 118 rooms. Recent right in center. Takes a lot of budget tour groups, but accommodations are comfortable. AE, DC, V.

El Triunfo, Cardenal González 79 (tel. 47 55 00). 26 rooms. Clean, bright 2-star hostel on south side of mosque. A good budget find. MC, V.

RESTAURANTS. Córdoba offers a good choice of restaurants which are recommended both for high gastronomic standards and atmospheric decor. There are also several elegant modern restaurants which are becoming very popular with the locals. Córdoba's pride and joy on the gastronomic front is the *Caballo Rojo*.

Expensive

El Caballo Rojo, Cardenal Herrero 28 (tel. 47 53 75). Atmospheric Andalusian decor and superb food. Known throughout Andalusia and winner of national gastronomy prize. Beside mosque. AE, DC, MC, V.

Oscar, Pza. Chirinos 6 (tel. 47 75 17). Pleasantly modern with an increasing reputation for fine seafood. Closed Sun. a DC, MC, V.

Moderate

La Almudaina, Campo Santo de los Mártires 1 (tel. 47 43 42). Attractive location in an old school overlooking the walls of the Alcázar, at the entrance to the Judería. Andalusian patio, Córdoban decor and cooking. Closed Sun. evening. AE, DC, MC, V.

El Blason, José Zorrilla 11 (tel. 48 06 25). Under the same management as the famous *Caballo Rojo,* this charming restaurant with its atmospheric Cordoban decor, is fast gaining an excellent name for fine food and unbeatable ambience. Specialties include *salmón con naranjas* (salmon with oranges) and *ternera con salsa de alcaparrones* (roast beef in caper sauce). Closed Sun. evenings in summer. AE, DC, MC, V.

El Cardenal, Cardenal Herrero 14 (tel. 48 03 46). Near the mosque and Marisa hotel, this new restaurant offers a stylish setting. A marble staircase with oriental carpets leads up to the first-floor dining room, which is attractively decorated with works of art. Good food and professional service complement the cool, agreeable atmosphere. Closed Sun. evening and Mon. AE, DC, V.

El Churrasco, Romero 16 (tel. 29 08 19). Atmospheric restaurant with colorful mesón and Andalusian patio, in the heart of the Judería. Its grilled meat dishes are outstanding, especially the *buey cebón* and the *churrasco;* good selection of fish dishes too. One of the best. Closed Thurs. and Aug. AE, DC, MC, V.

Ciros, Paseo de la Victoria 19, corner of Concepción (tel. 29 04 64). Modern restaurant and cafetería serving seafood and *nouvelle cuisine.* AE, DC, MC, V.

Mesón Bandolero, Torrijos 8 (tel. 47 64 91). This beautifully decorated mesón is in an old Córdoban mansion on the site of Averröes' birthplace. Popular with tourists. AE, DC, MC, V.

Inexpensive

Café Juda Levi, Plaza Juda Levi 1. Inexpensive café in the heart of the Juderia offering several set menus in a picturesque Cordoban atmosphere. Tourist oriented but ideal for a light lunch or quick snack. V.

Los Patios, Cardenal Herrero 16 (tel. 22 83 40). Tourist oriented self-service cafeteria in delightful outdoor patio. Fixed price, help-yourself buffet, and menu in English.

El Triunfo, Cardenal González 79 (tel. 47 55 00). Typical Andalusian-style tavern with small outdoor patio, close to mosque. Good for quick meals and snacks.

BARS AND CAFES. There are several pleasant outdoor cafes in the central square, the Plaza de Tendillas. The streets around Victorio Rivera to the north, and Jesús y María to the south, are also lined with bars and cafes offering inexpensive snacks and tapas. The old Andalusian mesones, packed with atmosphere and color are mostly in the narrow streets of the old town, in the Judería, and to the east of the mosque between it and the Plaza del Potro. Some of them are quite difficult to find as this old quarter is inadequately mapped. It may be easier just to stroll around and

sample those that you come across on your wanderings—there is no shortage of colorful taverns in Córdoba.

Casa Pepe, Romero 1. Popular old tavern with good tapas and excellent
fish.

Casa Rubio, Puerto de Almodóvar 5. One of Córdoba's oldest taverns,
serving delicious tapas.

Mesón de la Luna, Calleja de la Luna. Colorful mesón in a garden.

Los Pilares, Angel Saavedra 2. Another typical Córdoban tavern serving good tapas and hams.

Sociedad de Plateros, Pza. de Séneca 4. A good selection of tapas and
wines from the Montilla-Morilés region in the south of Córdoba province.

PLACES OF INTEREST. Although Córdoba is chiefly known for its
mosque, it has some other outstanding monuments too. It is always worth
double checking the opening hours given below to avoid disappointment;
in July and Aug. many places close down at lunchtime and do not reopen
in the afternoon due to the extreme heat. Summer opening hours begin
on May 1.

Alcázar de los Reyes Cristianos (Alcazar of the Catholic Monarchs),
off the Pza. Campo Santo de los Mártires. Lovely gardens and interesting
Roman mosaics. Open 9.30–1.30 and 4–7 (5–8 May to Sept.); closed Mon.
Gardens open and illuminated in summer 10 P.M.–12 P.M.

Mezquita (Mosque and Cathedral). Open daily 10.30–1.30 and
3.30–5.30 in winter; 10.30–1.30 and 4–7 in summer.

Museo Arqueológico Provincial (Archeological Museum), just off Pza.
Jerónimo Páez. Interesting collection from Córdoba's past civilizations,
including a Roman pavement. Open 10–2 and 6–8 (5–7 in winter), Sun.
10–1.30; closed Mon.

Museo Provincial de Bellas Artes (Fine Arts Museum), Pza. del Potro.
In the ancient Hospital of Charity. Collection of Spanish art from several
centuries and a room dedicated to the sculptor Mateo Inurria. Open Tues.
to Sat. 10–2 and 6–8 (5–7 in winter), Sun. 10–1.30; closed Mon.

Museo de Julio Romero de Torres, opposite the Bellas Artes Museum.
Good collection of the artist's work with many paintings inspired by *belle
époque* and 1920s women. Open Tues. to Sat. 10–1.45 and 5–7 (4–6 in winter), Sun. 10–1.45; closed Mon.

Museo Taurino (Bullfighting Museum), Pza. Maimónides (or Bulas).
Bullfighting memorabilia. Open Tues. to Sat. 9.30–1.30 and 4–7 (5–8 May
to Sept.), Sun. and fiestas 9.30–1.30 only; closed Mon.

Palacio de los Marqueses de Viana (Palace of the Marquis of Viana),
Pza. de Don Gome. Magnificent; 14 beautiful patios, a library and works
of art. Open June to Sept. 9–2; closed Wed. Oct.–May 10–1 and 4–6, Sun.
10–2; closed Wed. Patios are open at night in summer.

Ruinas de Medina Azahara. Open 10–2 and 6–8 in summer, but double
check Sun. and winter hours with tourist office. A taxi there and back with
1 hour's waiting time costs around 1,800 ptas.

Sinagoga, Calle Judío. Andalusia's only remaining synagogue, dating
from 14th century with Hebrew and Mudéjar stucco tracery. Open Tues.
to Sat. 10–2 and 5–7, Sun. 10–2 only; closed Mon.

Torre de la Calahorra (Calahorra Tower). On far side of Guadalquivir
across the Roman bridge. Built in 1369 to guard the entrance to Córdoba,
today it houses the city's **Historical Museum.** Open Mon. to Sat. 10.30–6,

Sun. 10–2.30 and 4–7; in summer (from Apr. 1) it's open 10–2 and 5.30–8.30.

SHOPPING. Typical Córdoban crafts are filigree silver and embossed leather and you will find plenty of shops stocking them. The best area to try is around the mosque in the Calles Torrijo, Cardenal Herrero and Deanes. Another good place to hunt for souvenirs is in the Zoco, the old Arab souk near the Synagogue and Bullfighting Museum in Calle Judíos, though the shops and stalls here may only be open in the summer months.

The main department stores, *Galerías Preciados* and the *Corte Inglés* are on Ronda de los Tejares and Avda.Gran Capitán.

USEFUL ADDRESSES. Police Station, Avda. Dr. Fleming 2 (tel. 47 75 00). **Iberia,** Ronda de los Tejares 3 (tel. 47 12 27). **Train Station,** Avda. de América (tel. 47 93 02). **RENFE Office,** Ronda de los Tejares 10 (tel. 47 58 84). **Post Office,** Cruz Conde 21. **Telephones,** Pza Tendillas.

Bus Depots. There is no central depot. Buses to Madrid via N-IV, and to Valencia, leave from Paseo de la Victoria 29; to Madrid via Ciudad Real, from Paseo de la Victoria 5; to Jaén and Seville, from Avda. Cervantes 22; to Granada, Málaga and Badajoz, from Avda. Medina Azahara 29.

Travel Agents, *Viajes Marsans,* Manuel de Sandoval 2 (tel. 47 46 19). *Vincit,* Alonso Burgos 1 (tel. 47 23 16) run city sightseeing tours. *Wagons-Lits Viajes,* Cruz Conde 28 (tel. 47 25 36).

Car Hire, *Avis,* Pza. de Colón 28 (tel. 47 68 62).

Las Ermitas and Medina Azahara

There is a nice, typically Spanish contrast in two wholly dissimilar sidetrips that you can make in the surrounding area. One is to Las Ermitas, a few kilometers to the northwest on the Sierra slopes, where several hermits continue to perpetuate the early traditions of the original church, identical to those observed by the members of the faithful who established themselves here in the 4th century! Today, their membership is scattered, but they bide their time, saying prayers and tilling the soil, like the true peasant-monks that they are.

The second sidetrip, in a completely opposite mood, takes you to the site where once stood a splendid oriental monument built for a beloved woman: about 11 km. (seven miles) west of Córdoba are the ruins of Medina Azahara, a palace erected by a 10th-century caliph for his favorite. The Hall of the Ambassadors has been rebuilt and in a small museum, a few relics of the vanished marble have been collected. According to the storytellers of the time, there were no fewer than 4,300 columns of gleaming white, green and pink marble supporting an inlaid wood ceiling. (See page 392.)

Roads to Granada

The quickest route from Córdoba to Granada, N432 allows for a sidetrip from Alcalá la Real to Montefrío with its Gothic-Renaissance church and castle built into the Moorish fortress, the early 18th-century pure Plateresque San Antonio and the late 18th-century neo-Classical circular church of the Encarnación. Five km. away, at Peñas de los Gitanos, is one of the rare remains of the late paleolithic Iberian period, the settlement of Hipo-Nova.

N331 passes across the Cordoban campiña (fertile region) through the vineyards of the Montilla-Morilés region, becoming increasingly well known for their fortified, sherry-type wine, before reaching Lucena, then to Antequera where it links up with the Seville–Granada road.

The third, and in some ways the most rewarding route from Córdoba to Granada is by way of Andújar and Bailén on the main N-IV Madrid-Seville highway, and thence via Jaén to Granada. Turn off at Andújar up a beautiful winding road for 32 km. (20 miles) to the fantastic mountain-top shrine of Nuestra Señora de la Cabeza. The church is set above the stark ridges of the Sierra Morena, wildly remote, in forests famous for wild boar shooting, so completely out of the 20th century as to be mildly alarming. During the Spanish Civil War, the Falangists and members of the Guardia Civil settled in for a last stand in this sanctuary, which they thought would be relatively easy to defend. Completely shut off, the garrison withstood an eight months' siege, towards the end of which the provisions parachuted in by the Nationalist forces failed to cope with the increasing problem of famine. It was finally forced to surrender to the Republicans, who set the sanctuary on fire. (The present shrine is a reconstruction.)

The land surrounding this stretch of the N-IV is one of the most fertile regions of Andalusia and you will see evidence of this in the orchards of Córdoba province, and once into Jaén, in the vast sea of olive groves. Bailén is the road junction at which one turns south to Jaén and Granada. Napoleon's troops were defeated here in 1808, on July 16, while on another July 16—in the year 1212—the decisive Battle of the Reconquest was fought on the plain of Las Navas de Tolosa, to the north of Bailén. A crusade instigated by Pope Innocent II brought together troops from Castile, Aragón and Navarre fighting side by side with Germans, Frenchmen and Italians. The Muslim forces, commanded by Emir Mohammed Abou Abd Allah, stood ready for the fray. When the clash between cross and crescent got under way, the outcome seemed dubious for some time, until the Moors abandoned the fight and this part of Andalusia was restored to Christendom. Just to the north of Bailén on the side of the N-IV there is a large and rather imposing monument to this most significant of Reconquista battles.

If you entered Andalusia on the N322 from Albacete, you will have passed through the silvery sea of vast olive groves which stretches from the superbly rugged outlines of the Sierra de Alcaraz and the Sierra de Segura to Ubeda and Baeza. If not, continue east of Bailén to Ubeda to rejoin the Granada road at Jaén, a sidetrip of some 97 km. (60 miles), but actually only 51 km. (32 miles) more than the direct route.

Ubeda is worth the detour. Its winding streets spill out abruptly into the resplendent Santa María Square with the superb El Salvador church. The parador, a former palace with period-style furnishings, is the ideal place to stay for absorbing the feeling of the town. The cloister of Santa María, the Convent of La Trinidad and the Casa de las Cadenas (House of the Chains . . . it was once a prison) are all very interesting, and at every turn you encounter stately residences and churches. St. John of the Cross died here, at the end of the 16th century, though he is buried in Segovia.

An attractive sidetrip from Ubeda is to the small, mountain village of Cazorla located at the end of a bumpy road high up in the mountains of the Sierra de Cazorla. There is a parador here, popular with hunters and by those who love peace and quiet. Cazorla, though easily reached by bus from Jaén, really is off the beaten track and its narrow streets of low white houses winding their way up the mountain slopes, and its squares with their brilliant dashes of color from bougainvillea or, at Easter time, Judas trees, cannot fail to delight you.

From Ubeda you will come to Baeza, once the seat of a small university and still a treasure house of early Renaissance and Plateresque architecture. Be sure to see the fabulous Benavente Palace which shelters a seminary behind its Gothic facade and curious gallery.

Jaén, unlike most Andalusian cities, has more dignity than charm. Just as its austere pines and chestnut trees replace the palm and olive groves of the south, so are its citizens more taciturn than their neighbors. The people of Jaén tell the story of two brothers unjustly condemned to death by King Ferdinand IV. Before the victims were hurled to their deaths from the sinister precipice of Peña de los Carvajales, they called upon heaven to avenge them. Their properly vindictive Spanish God almost immediately summoned the king to his own Last Judgement. The road winding down to Granada through increasingly green country provides a promising introduction to the serene languor of the Granada plateau.

From Seville to Granada

The 258 km. (about 170 miles) of N334 and N342 take you from Seville's sweltering plains to Granada's more temperate hills at the foot of the Sierra Nevada, by the shortest route.

Like so many of its sister cities in Spain, Osuna (now bypassed by the main road) is rich in both Moorish and Roman history, particularly the latter. However, the city bears the distinctive stamp of the 16th century, as exemplified by its collegiate church on the hilltop. There you will find an exquisite two-story patio, plus the tombs of the Dukes of Osuna, descendants of the Borgia Pope Alexander VI, set in a crypt constituting a remarkable Renaissance pantheon. Osuna is a good example of the legacy of the Moors in this part of Spain. In the main street note the great number of *celosías,* the wooden shutter-like grilles that cover the windows overlooking the street. These are a Moorish legacy. *Celosía* is the Spanish word for "jealousy" and these grilles were designed to allow Moorish women to look out onto the street but at the same time to preserve their modesty and prevent passers-by looking in on them.

After Aguadulce the road passes through Estepa and La Roda with views over the Fuente de Piedra lake, home to Europe's largest colony of flamingoes, to reach Antequera, the crossroads of Andalusia.

Several roads meet outside and bypass Antequera, but it is well worth the small detour if you remember what particular stage this town represented in the Reconquest. Following the great Christian victories over the Moors in the 13th century, the latter maintained themselves for another 200 years in Granada. The spirit of Reconquest entered into a state of hibernation. One of its chief awakenings occurred in 1410 with the capture of Antequera from the Arabs, who left a mighty fortress on the town heights, in whose midst there is now a parador.

Near Antequera are the Menga Galleries, a prehistoric site where huge dolmens form arches. The mystery of their origin is as unfathomable as that of all other similar monuments of the dim past. The architect, Le Corbusier, inscribed the visitors' book: "To my predecessors."

Towering in front of you as you continue on the road to Granada is the dramatic silhouette of the Peña de los Enamorados, the "Lovers' Leap" of a medieval legend which recounts how a Moorish princess once eloped with her lover, a Christian shepherd boy, for the night, and next day the ill-fated lovers cast themselves to their deaths off this famous peak. Some say the impressive silhouette of the mountain resembles the profile of an American Indian, Andalusians often claim it as the profile of the bullfighter Manolete.

N342 continues through picturesque countryside with many rocks and canyons. The Genil river divides Loja's narrow, winding lanes of white houses dominated by a 9th-century Moorish fortress, 16th-century San Gabriel has exquisite Mudéjar ceilings attributed to Diego de Siloé; Santa María, the Santa Clara monastery and the Hospital de la Misericordia are also interesting. The Genil flows through a wild gorge where waterfalls hurtle down between the rocks.

Descending onto Granada's richly irrigated plain, the road bypasses Santa Fé, founded in 1491 during the siege of Granada as a campsite for the Christian troops. Here the last bastion of the Muslim world was surrendered to Ferdinand and Isabella, and here the Catholic Monarchs granted Columbus the ships to discover the New World.

Granada

When Boabdil, the last Moorish king of Granada, surrendered the city to Ferdinand and Isabella, he left his palace by the Puerta de Los Siete Suelos (Gate of the Seven Sighs) and asked that this gate be sealed forever. His heart-broken sobs found a lasting echo in Arab hearts, for of all Spain, the Moors deplored most the loss of Granada, and mourn it still in their evening prayers. Of all their treasured cities Granada was their chief delight.

As their standard was raised on the tower of the Alhambra, the Catholic Monarchs knelt among their soldiers and monks to thank God for victory. That January day in 1492 was for them a day of pure, transcendent joy. They wished to be buried in Granada, and built the flamboyant Gothic Royal Chapel where they have lain side by side since 1521, later joined by their daughter Juana la Loca. Though the Catholic Monarchs are remembered throughout the sanctuary—their statues on bas reliefs and pillars, their escutcheons on walls, their banners among vaults, and their crown and scepter in the sacristy—their grandson, Charles V, decided it was too small a chapel for so much glory. He commissioned Diego de Siloé to design a huge cathedral which was not finished until 1667. But even this Renaissance masterpiece, in spite of stained-glass windows, paintings by El Greco and Ribera, carvings by Alonso Cano, and an admirable portal in the Great Chapel, like all the rest of Granada's monuments, is overshadowed by the glorious silhouette of the Alhambra which dominates the entire city, Moorish and Christian alike.

The Alhambra, Seat of Caliphs and Kings

Signs indicate the narrow Cuesta de Gomerez that mounts a stiff grade to the cool vale where Wellington had elm trees planted to add a bit of English greenery to the Andalusian scene. Soon you reach the first door of the first wall, and cross the threshold straight into the Arabian Nights. You find your eyes roving from lacy walls, painted ceilings, and scintillating domes to multicolored tiles and gold mosaics. Sometimes a breath of air strays in from a garden or the dripping of a fountain carries a touch of welcome coolness. You are in a realm of little columns, festooned arches and mysterious inscriptions.

Each of the towers of the Alhambra has its secret, each stone the trace of a name or a drop of blood. It was this fascinating riddle that held Washington Irving so long in Granada, attempting to capture every secret nuance. An Arab proverb says that God gives to those he loves a means of living in Granada.

The most antique vestige in the Alhambra is the 9th-century Moorish fortress of the Alcazaba. The great hulk of its watchtower still stands out impressively. The very first Cross of the Reconquest was proudly erected on its terrace, from which you can enjoy a sweeping panorama of the city. The two towers overlooking the Square of the Cisterns date from more recent times. The sorting of these souvenirs is simple: first come the defense structures, the outer walls with their huge square towers and fortified doors. Next, around the Court of Myrtles, the official residence. This contains the Hall of Benediction, under a cedar cupola. The walls are covered with the inscription "Allah alone is Conqueror". Next is the Ambassadors' Hall, the scene of many lavish receptions given by the Moorish kings under its polychrome cedarwood cupola. Then comes the Council Room, or Mexuar, which Charles V used as a chapel.

Finally, radiating from the Lions' Court, the private apartments: the Sala de las Dos Hermanas, which was the harem, decorated with two marble slabs so alike that they have given the room its name, the Hall of the Two Sisters; the Room of Secrets, with its whispering alcoves; the marble baths, perforated like incense burners for escaping steam and perfumes; and the Sala de los Abencerrajes, where a sultan, jealous either of his throne or of his favorite, had 36 princes beheaded and watched their blood flow into the Fountain of Lions.

The Hand and the Key

The history of the Alhambra is woven through seven centuries. It begins with the Arab epoch, full of intrigues of the seraglio, the pomp, conspiracy and voluptuousness of the court. Its leading figures are poets, emirs, assassins, alchemists, eunuchs and spies. On the first door of the ramparts, called the Puerta de la Justicia, the Arabs wisely carved the hand of Fatima, whose five fingers evoke the five laws of the Koran. On the second door, a key was engraved. And the legend was that the Alhambra would remain inviolable until the day when the hand of the first door took the key that opened the second. The prophecy was fulfilled. Dissolute and cruel, the kings of Granada were so engrossed in their quarrels and viciousness that they forgot the great rules imposed by Allah. Through destructive internal warfare, they themselves opened the door to the invader.

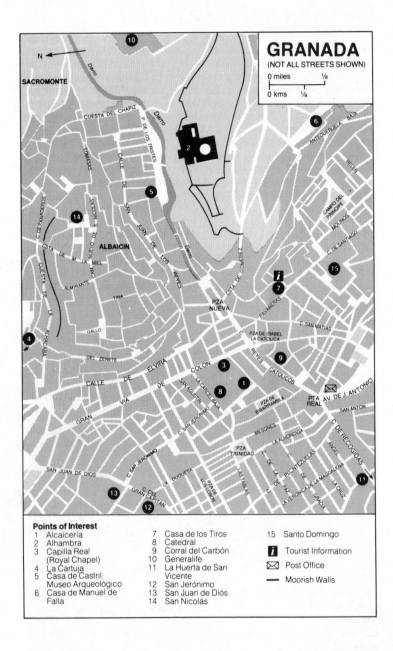

GRANADA
(NOT ALL STREETS SHOWN)

0 miles   ⅛
0 kms   ⅛

Points of Interest

1 Alcaicería
2 Alhambra
3 Capilla Real
 (Royal Chapel)
4 La Cartuja
5 Casa de Castril;
 Museo Arqueológico
6 Casa de Manuel de
 Falla

7 Casa de los Tiros
8 Catedral
9 Corral del Carbón
10 Generalife
11 La Huerta de San
 Vicente
12 San Jerónimo
13 San Juan de Diós
14 San Nicolás

15 Santo Domingo

ℹ️ Tourist Information

✉️ Post Office

— Moorish Walls

The Catholic Monarchs were at once enraptured and scandalized by the subtle splendors of the Moorish palace, built in the most fragile of materials—clay. They attempted to live there, but Christian habits did not conform easily to the exotic setting. Charles V upset the order of the gardens and chambers by superimposing a huge, square Renaissance palace on the Cerro del Sol. Though less incongruous than his church within the mosque of Córdoba, the palace was never finished and the Alhambra was abandoned for centuries. Water grew stale in the pools, the fragile stucco garlands crumbled, and the ancient royal palace became a refuge for every stray dog, beggar, gypsy and tramp, who made themselves comfortable among the mosaics and marbles. When Wellington entered Spain on his Napoleonic hunt, he was delighted with Granada, sent all the indigents flying, and himself appropriated the apartments of Charles V.

The circular court of Charles' palace with its near-perfect acoustics provides a magnificent setting for the annual Granada International Festival of Music and Dance, held in late June and early July, drawing dancers, musicians and orchestras of high repute from all over the world. The upper floor houses the Fine Arts Museum.

Earlier this century the Alhambra was expertly restored to a convincing semblance of its past glory but wear and tear, caused by natural decay and millions of visitors, has now necessitated further restoration. Renovations are underway and some rooms and the baths are temporarily closed.

The Generalife

The Alhambra, as its Arabic name indicates, is ocher-red. The *Gennat-al-Arif* ("Garden of the Builder") is white. Standing on the hill nearest their palace, it was the summer residence of the caliphs. Every detail was conceived with an eye to cool, relaxed repose. Its perfect proportions rely on understatement and intimacy—a design for sweet privacy. The battlements are not all decorated, serving merely as white frames for the landscape spread below them. The deep blue sky and a land studded with delightful bouquets of gardens stretch away into the distance. The gardens of the Generalife, fragrant with roses and jasmine, are hedged in by yew trees. Open to the sky, the great reception hall is animated by a constant shower of crystal drops from slender fountains that play above a mirror of sparkling water and water even flows down the handrails of the upper garden's staircase. The open-air theater is backed by stately cypresses.

From the Alhambra to the Campo del Príncipe

If you still have the energy to walk back into town, so much the better, as there is a different route down from the one you came up, which affords some spectacular views. If you are driving you will have to descend part of the way along this route due to the vagaries of the one-way system of access to the Alhambra. Head off down the street named Antequeruela Baja where soon on your left, another rather deserted and dilapidated road, Antequeruela Alta, leads up past some lovely old Granada houses, some of them now sadly neglected, to the house where the Cádiz-born composer, Manuel de Falla, lived and composed for many years. The house is now a small museum and is furnished with many of his possessions. In a delightful position, with a small terraced garden, it is a gem of a small Andalusian house of the 1920s and 30s and well worth a visit, though the caretaker only speaks Spanish and the only literature available is also in Spanish. Above the house at the end of Antequeruela Alta is the Manuel de Falla Concert Hall and Auditorium, a recent and important musical venue in Granada. Falla was a great friend and colleague of the poet and dramatist Federico García Lorca, who was born in the village of Fuentevaqueros just outside Granada in 1898, and who was killed by the Fascists just one month after the outbreak of the Civil War. Throughout the Franco era, the exact circumstances of Lorca's death and his burial place, were kept shrouded in secrecy. Today his genius is openly acknowledged in his homeland as well as abroad, and in 1986 his native city commemorated the 50th anniversary of his death by opening his birthplace and summer home as museums.

Return to the Antequeruela Baja and wind your way down, preferably armed with a good map, to the Campo del Príncipe. In the center of this delightful square is a much venerated statue of La Cruz del Cristo de los Faroles (Christ of the Lanterns) where women come to offer flowers and pray in front of Christ Crucified. The square is also surrounded by some excellent tapa bars and is quite lively at lunchtime and in the early evening, though you should take extra care here if there are gangs of youths around. From here it is not a long walk to the Casa de los Tiros on Calle Pavaneras, a 16th-century mansion built around a patio, which today houses the Granada Tourist Office, and if reopened after a period of restoration, a small museum of Granada artesanry, ceramics, gypsy customs and souvenirs of the Empress Eugenie, wife of Napoleon III. A little further on you will come out on to the Plaza de Isabel la Católica with its statue of Columbus presenting Queen Isabella with his maps of the New World.

Ahead of you lies one of the principal thoroughfares of the city, the Gran Vía de Colón with, to the left, the Cathedral and Royal Chapel and the narrow streets of the Alcaicería, the old Moorish silk exchange, and now a paradise for souvenir hunters, with its shops packed full of brass and silver; to the right of the Gran Vía between Colón and Elvira are old streets lined with bars and inexpensive restaurants, and beyond, you plunge into the tangle of narrow streets climbing steeply, and with no logical pattern whatsoever, up the hill of the Albaicín.

The Albaicín, The Sacromonte, and La Cartuja

At dusk the ravine of the Darro is already bathed in shadows; you can hear the shallow torrent roar under tiny bridges, and the crowds are settling in the cafes of the Plaza Nueva for their evening aperitifs. Narrow streets part dilapidated, part hiding beautiful *cármenes* (Granada's private villas with fragrant gardens) wind up the slopes of the Albaicín, which retains its original Moorish atmosphere, though the numerous mosques have long been converted into Baroque churches. The plaza in front of the church of San Nicolás affords the loveliest view of the sunset on the Alhambra's ocher walls and on the snowcapped peaks of the Sierra Nevada.

Suddenly the night is a profound blue, and one by one, the lamps on the Sacromonte begin to twinkle. The hour has come for a visit to the gypsy caves. Granada's symbol is an open pomegranate (*grenada* in Spanish), because the city opens on a triple hill with all the beauty of this exotic fruit, which the caliphs imported from the Orient. But the name Granada derives from the word *garnathah,* mountain cave, for the Sacromonte is riddled with caverns. They might have sheltered early Christians, for when searchers were looking there for the emirs' buried treasures they found, instead, a vast collection of bones. Some of these they assumed belonged to San Cecilio, the city's patron saint, and so the hill was sanctified and a monastery built on its summit.

You begin the ascent of the Sacromonte near the picturesque and mildly dangerous gypsy quarter. The *cuevas* (or caves) that penetrate the chalky cliff are like the grottos of Arab legends, spread with thick, richly-colored rugs and gleaming with copper utensils. The women never vary their traditional dance dress, a tight gown split to the waist, with a long flounced train. They wear their black hair plastered to their heads. Each family is a tribe in itself, and the minute you venture into the Sacromonte, filthy, handsome children drag you off to the family lair, whether you like it or not. You will sit through a performance given by mama, sisters, aunts and cousins, all intent on playing guitars and dancing—sometimes not too well. It may be costly, for the children are extremely tenacious, and you must cross their grimy paws with a good bit of silver in order to gain your freedom. Meanwhile, the interior of the cave is worth studying. You will see grandfather's photograph hanging on the wall beside the Virgin Mary and an assortment of banderillas retrieved from bullfights. But don't be so carried away by the scene that you forget your purse. Many of these gypsies are thieves and scarcely bother to hide the fact. So never carry more money to the Sacromonte than you can well lose, avoid the too-private party, and go, preferably, with a Spaniard you can trust to show you about the place. Your visit will be more interesting, and will be less likely to end badly. In summer there are agencies running organized evening excursions to these shows, sometimes including a drink in the Albaicín first; the quality of these so-called shows often leaves much to be desired, but they do offer a safe means of visiting the Sacromonte, if you are unable to find a friendly local to escort you there.

Finally, before leaving Granada, you should see some of the city's other monuments, notably its splendid Carthusian monastery, known as La Cartuja, whose Baroque sacristy has been called the Christian Alhambra because of its delicate stucco work. Though possibly over-ornate for some tastes, the Cartuja is important enough to rank alongside the Cathedral and Royal Chapel. Of Granada's many churches the most outstanding are the Gothic Santo Domingo, on the square of the same name and not many minutes' walk from the Tourist Office, and right across town, the Renaissance San Jerónimo, where the Gran Capitán, Gonzalo de Córdoba, is buried. Close to the latter is San Juan de Diós, burial place of the saint, its namesake, and a good example of Granada Baroque.

The Sierra Nevada Route

If you have a day to spare in Granada, one of the most popular of side trips is into the mountains of the Sierra Nevada. The Sierra is one of the prime beauties of Granada. This mountain range rises behind the city like the background of a mural. 55 km. (34 miles) of one of Europe's most magnificent mountain roads lead to lakes, meadows, wild torrents, and to the snow-capped Mulhacén (3,500 meters, 11,477 feet), Spain's highest peak, while the road itself reaches an altitude of 3,050 meters (10,000 feet) at the Pico de Veleta, in the heart of the mountains. Ski-lifts and cablecars facilitate skiing from a choice of hotels and refuges for many months of the year and this is one of Spain's most popular ski resorts. It must be said, however, that to visit it in high summer is something of a disappointment as the resort itself is of little beauty, though the breathtaking panorama southwards from the Pico de Veleta above, more than compensates for the drabness of a closed-up out-of-season resort.

PRACTICAL INFORMATION FOR GRANADA

TOURIST OFFICE. The Granada Tourist Office is in the Casa de los Tiros on Calle Pavaneras 19 (tel. 22 10 22). Open 9.30–2 and 5–7.30. Closed Sat. afternoon and Sun.

TELEPHONE CODE. The dialing code for the city and province of Granada is (958). This prefix need only be used when dialing from outside the province.

GETTING AROUND. Transport around the city is by public bus although you can mostly visit the sights and shops on foot. If you don't want to walk up to the Alhambra, take a cab or else a bus from the Plaza Nueva. To reach the train station on Avda. de Andaluces or the departure point of Empresa Bacoma buses to Murcia, Alicante, Valencia and Barcelona, board a bus along Recogidas and on the Gran Vía de Colón. A bus departs to the airport 75 mins. before each flight from the Plaza Isabel la Católica at the intersection of Gran Vía de Colón and Reyes Católicos. From the main bus station on the Camino de Ronda there are several buses into town. Circular bus no. 11 is the most useful, passing the Puerta Real, Gran Vía, the train station, bus station on Camino de Ronda, and back via Recogidas to Puerta Real. City buses operate on a flat fare system but you do not need to have exact change.

Cab fares to the Alhambra or the Cartuja (Carthusian Monastery) will not cost very much. There are cab stands all over the city but the best place to get one is in the Puerta Real-José Antonio area. At night if you hire a cab to take you into the Albaicín, or up into the Sacromonte, make sure the driver puts his meter on. If you ask the driver to wait around and bring you back again, there is, in theory, a legal waiting charge (*hora parada* on the fare list inside the cab) but the driver is more likely to want to agree a price with you, so ask beforehand, especially in the case of the Sacromonte. There will be an evening supplement to pay on top of the fare shown on the meter.

HOTELS. Granada is plentifully endowed with hotels, both old and new, though some of the more expensive ones do not come up to the standards expected in this category. Hotels divide roughly into two locations: those up on the Alhambra hill and those down in the town. Those up near the Alhambra are in the more picturesque location but need a cab or bus to reach town. Granada's parador is one of Spain's most popular hotels, so book at least six months in advance; the same applies to the picturesque America hostel. You should also make early reservations if you are planning a visit during Granada's International Music and Dance Festival, held in late June to early July.

Expensive

Alhambra Palace, Peña Partida 2 (tel. 22 14 68). 127 rooms. In Moorish style, red-ocher palace on hill near the Alhambra with magnificent views and stylish decor. Ask for a room with a view over the city. AE, DC, MC, V.

Carmen, José Antonio 62 (tel. 25 83 00). 205 rooms. Central hotel in town with generally good standards. AE, DC, MC, V.

Luz Granada, Avda. Constitución 18 (tel. 20 40 61). 174 rooms, many amenities but impersonal and geared to tour groups. AE, DC, MC, V.

Meliá Granada, Angel Ganivet 7 (tel. 22 74 00). 221 rooms. Central; its bar is a smart meeting place for locals but rooms can be both shabby and noisy. AE, DC, MC, V.

Parador San Francisco, Alhambra (tel. 22 14 40). 39 rooms. Magnificently located in an old convent within the precincts of the Alhambra. Rates approaching (L). Book long ahead. AE, DC, MC, V.

Moderate

Los Alixares, Alixares del Generalife (tel. 22 55 06). 148 rooms. Modern hotel high up on Alhambra hill. Rooms are rather bare and it caters largely to tour groups. Pleasant bar and lounge and one of the few hotels in Granada with a pool. AE, DC, MC, V.

América, Real de la Alhambra 53 (tel. 22 74 71). 14 rooms. A simple but charming hostel in magnificent location close to Alhambra. Very popular; open Mar. through Oct. only. Book ahead.

Los Angeles, Cuesta Escoriaza 17 (tel. 22 14 24). 100 rooms. Hotel has a complicated layout and some rooms are showing their age; it is also very geared to tour groups. Advantages are its pleasant leafy surroundings and its outdoor pool. AE, DC, MC, V.

Condor, Avda. Constitución 6 (tel. 28 37 11). 101 rooms. Modern functional hotel near the *Luz Granada* on the road in from Málaga and Seville. Good in its category but unexciting. AE, DC, MC, V.

Dauro, Acera del Darro 19 (tel. 22 21 56). 36 rooms. Good new hotel, reasonably central; serves breakfast only, no restaurant. AE, DC, MC, V.

Guadalupe, Avda. de los Alixares (tel. 22 34 23). 44 rooms. Modern, functional but quite pleasant hotel on Alhambra hill. AE, DC, MC, V.

Juan Miguel, Acera del Darro 24 (tel. 25 89 12). 66 rooms. Comfortable, modern hotel in the center; the most expensive.

Kenia, Molinos 65 (tel. 22 75 06). 16 rooms. Quiet hotel in residential section, with attentive service. Large, leafy garden.

Presidente, Recogidas 11 (tel. 25 36 12). 30 rooms. Recent and central with good standards. AE, DC, MC, V.

Victoria, Puerta Real (tel. 25 77 00). Old-world charm right in heart of town. Rooms on front could be noisy. AE, DC, MC, V.

Inexpensive

Inglaterra, Cetti Meriem 6 (tel. 22 15 59). 40 rooms. Old Andalusian house with period style; right in center.

Macia, Pza. Nueva 4 (tel. 22 75 36). 40 rooms. Modern, functional, in agreeable central square. AE, DC, MC, V.

Manuel de Falla, Antequeruela Baja 4 (tel. 22 75 45). 22 rooms. Simple, one-star hotel, open Apr. to Oct. only, in a charming old Andalusian house well located just down hill from *Alhambra Palace.* Ideal for those who prefer atmosphere to creature comforts.

Montecarlo, José Antonio 44 (tel. 25 79 00). 74 rooms. Old-world hotel in center of town.

RESTAURANTS. Though Granada has plenty of quite good restaurants, it lacks any guaranteed to be a gastronomic delight. However, several of our selections provide colorful atmospheric decor, and generally good food. Be prepared for some restaurants to be closed at the height of the season.

Expensive

Baroca, Pedro Antonio de Alarcón 34 (tel. 26 50 61). One block above the Camino de Ronda, now considered one of Granada's best; its desserts are especially good. Closed Sun. and Aug. AE, DC, MC, V.

Cunini (E), Pescadería 9 (tel. 26 37 01). Located in the cathedral area, and long praised for the high quality of its seafood. It has another entrance on Capuchina 14. Closed Sun. evening. AE, DC, MC, V.

Moderate

Carmen de San Miguel, Pza.Torres Bermejas 3 (tel. 22 67 23). Superb setting on hill near *Alhambra Palace,* with magnificent views over Granada, and an outdoor terrace. Now owned by Baroca. Closed Sun. V.

Colombia, Antequeruela Baja 1 (tel. 22 74 33). In a beautiful location on the back of the Alhambra hill. Terrace offers magnificent views of the city and sometimes live guitar music. Touristy but fun. Closed Sun. AE, DC, MC, V.

Los Leones, José Antonio 10 (tel. 25 50 07). One of Granada's classics, going strong since 1920; good service. Closed Mon. evening and Tues. AE, DC, MC, V.

Mesón Antonio, Ecce Homo 6 (tel. 22 95 99). Simple, homely restaurant in typical Andalusian house just off the Campo del Príncipe. Roasts cooked in charcoal oven and a strong Basque influence in many dishes. Closed Sun., July through Aug.

Sevilla, Oficios 14 (tel. 22 12 23). Beside the cathedral in the Alcaicería with typical Granadino decor, picturesque and small. Superb tapas bar at the entrance. Closed Sun. evening. AE, DC, MC, V.

Inexpensive

Altamura, Avda. Andaluces 2 (tel. 27 29 08). Italian spot on first floor of new building near station. Home-made pasta and pizzas and good Italian meat dishes. Closed Mon. evening and Tues., also mid-July to mid-Sept.

Mesón Andaluz, Cetti Meriem 10. Near the Inglaterra hotel; pleasant service and large menu. Closed Tues.

Los Manueles, Zaragoza 2 (tel. 22 34 15). An old Granada tradition, ceramic tiles, and smoked hams hanging from the ceiling. Reasonable prices and good old-fashioned service.

Outside Granada are two restaurants worth visiting: **El Molino (E)**, Camino de las Fuentes (tel. 78 02 47) is in **Durcal** on the road to Lanjarón, set in an old mill and famous for its revival of traditional Granada dishes. Closed Sun. and Mon.; be sure to book. AE, V. In **Cenes de la Vega** on the road to the Sierra Nevada, **Ruta del Veleta (M)**, (tel. 48 61 34), is famous for its succulent meat, and high-quality fish dishes from Cantábrica. Closed Sun. night. AE, DC, MC, V.

BARS AND CAFES. Bars. The main areas for good colorful tapas bars are: around the Campo del Príncipe; in the narrow streets on either side of Reyes Católicos, especially to the right, around Calle Zaragoza; in the narrow streets between Colón and Elvira, off and around Almireceros; along Calle de Mesones leading from Puerta Real to the Plaza de Trinidad; and in the Albaicín.

Cafes. The main cafe areas are: in the Pza. Mariana and Pza. del Campillo just off José Antonio and Carrera del Genil; in the Pza. Nueva, and in the Pza. de Bib-Rambla which is very popular in the late afternoon and unspoilt by traffic.

EXCURSIONS. Fuente Vaqueros. Village 11 km. from Granada where Federico García Lorca was born June 5, 1898. His birthplace was opened as a museum in 1986 and is open 10–1 and 6–8 with tours every hour; closed Mon. The nearby village of **Valderrubio** inspired his *Libro de Poemas* and *La Casa de Bernarda Alba*. Buses from Alsina Graëlls, Camino de Ronda. **Viznar,** where Lorca was assassinated and where he is believed to be buried, is just off the N342 to Guadix, or buses from Arco de Elvira.

Sierra Nevada. The main—and very worthwhile—sidetrip from Granada is into the mountains of the Sierra Nevada to the Pico de Veleta, Spain's second highest mountain. However hot the weather is in Granada, be sure to take a warm wrap, sunglasses and a headscarf. Buses leave at 9 A.M. daily, including Sundays, from outside the Hotel Zaida between the Acera de Darro and the Carrera del Genil, and arrive back in Granada at 6 P.M. The journey to the Sierra Nevada village takes around one hour and the fare is very low.

Lanjarón, Another possible daytrip from Granada is to the spa town of Lanjarón in the mountains of the Sierra Nevada. You can drive there and back in a day or else go by bus. There is little to see in the way of monuments in Lanjarón but the setting and old-world atmosphere are lovely.

Alpujarras. High in the mountains beyond Lanjarón and Orgiva, Pampaneira, Bubión and Capileira are the most visited of the remote and picturesque villages of the Alpujarras. Enquire at the tourist office for details of the once-weekly Alpujarras excursion.

Santa Fe. Just eight km. (five miles) west of Granada, this village was founded in 1491, and is often referred to as the "Cradle of America" due to Columbus signing here the agreements which led to the discovery of the New World. There are some interesting old buildings and an excellent leather store. The gateways to the town, built by Ferdinand and Isabella in 1491, have been declared National Monuments.

PLACES OF INTEREST. Granada's Alhambra is Spain's most beautiful monument and along with the Prado in Madrid, the most visited. Next, in order of priority come the Royal Chapel, the Cathedral and the Cartuja. Visiting hours often vary from summer to winter and should be double checked. The walls of the Granada tourist office are a mine of information with details of every aspect of Granada displayed on innumerable maps of the city.

Alhambra and Generalife. Open Apr. to Sept., Mon. to Sat. 9.30–8.30, Sun. 9.30–6. Also at night when floodlit, Wed. to Sat., 10–12 midnight. The ticket office closes 45 minutes before closing time; earlier in winter, around 6 P.M. Admission free on Sun. after 3 P.M. Visitors with little children or backpacks should be warned that the rules on what can be taken into the grounds are very strict—rucksacks, babies' slings, any largish bag are all prohibited.

Baños Arabes (Arab Baths) on the Carrera del Darro. Dating from the 11th century and known as El Bañuelo. Open daily 9–6.

Capilla Real (Royal Chapel). Containing the tombs of Ferdinand and Isabella, the Catholic Monarchs, their daughter Juana la Loja, and Felipe el Hermoso. Open daily 11–1 and 3–6 (possibly 4–7 in summer).

Casa Museo Angel Barrios (Angel Barrios Museum), within Alhambra precincts. Home of the guitarist Angel Barrios, a friend of García Lorca; documents and memorabilia from the musician's life. Open 3–6; closed Sun. and fiestas.

Casa Museo Manuel de Falla (Manuel de Falla Museum), Antequeruela Alta. The home of the composer. Open daily 10–2 and 4–6 (7 June through Sept.); closed Mon.

Casa de los Pisas (House of the Pisas), just off Pza. Nueva. 16th-century house with an interesting combination of architectural styles. Open daily 9.30–1 and 3.30–6; closed Sun.

Cartuja (Carthusian Monastery). Dates from 1516; richly ornamental. Open daily 11–1 and 3–6 (possibly 4–7 in summer).

Catedral (Cathedral). Dating from 1529. Open daily 11–1 and 3–6 (possibly 4–7 in summer).

Corral del Carbón (Arab Inn). The only one in Spain, adapted by the Christians for use as a theater and today used to display Spanish craftwork and expensive furniture. Closed at presstime for restoration.

La Huerta de San Vicente (García Lorca's summer home), Calle Arabial and Vírgen Blanca. Delightful Andalusian house and garden with family portraits and memorabilia, the bedroom and desk of the great poet. Open 10–1 and 4–7 (but doublecheck with Tourist Office).

Museo Arqueológico de la Casa de Castril (Archeological Museum), Carrera del Darro 41. 16th-century house with a collection of Greek and Roman sculpture and coins. Open 10–2; closed Mon.

Museo Bellas Artes (Fine Arts Museum) on the upper floor of Charles V's Palace in the Alhambra. Open Tues. to Sun. 10–2; closed Mon.

Museo Hispano Musulmán (Museum of Hispanic Islamic Art), within the Alhambra. Open daily 10–2; closed Sun. and fiestas.

San Jerónimo (St. Jerome's), Rector López Argueta 9. Magnificent Renaissance Monastery, containing the tomb of the Gran Capitán, Gonzalo Fernández de Córdoba. Open daily 10–1.30 and 4–7.

San Juan de Diós (St. John of God). Baroque church, containing the mortal remains of San Juan de Diós. Open daily 10–1 and 4–6.

Santo Domingo. Adjoining the convent of the same name; one of Granada's largest churches, begun in 1512. Open daily 11–1 and 5–8.

FLAMENCO. Although there are several "impromptu"—and often terrible—flamenco displays in the caves of the Sacromonte, there are also two regular flamenco clubs in Granada. Both cater to tourists and tour groups, but their shows are reliable, costing around 1,800 ptas, and can usually be booked through hotels.

Jardines Neptuno, Recogidas (tel. 25 11 12). At the very bottom of Recogidas across the Camino de Ronda. A club set in a pleasant garden with outdoor pool; the show is a mixture of classic Spanish dance, ballet and flamenco.

Reina Mora, Mirador de San Cristóbal (tel. 27 82 28). To reach this club, drive up the road that leads to Murcia, the Ctra. de Murcia. To make reservations during the day when the club is closed, call 20 20 06 or 20 12 11. Mixture of flamenco and regional dances; probably the better of the two.

SHOPPING. Granada's main shopping streets are the Reyes Católicos, Zacatín and Angel Ganivet. The *Galerías Preciados* department store is on the Carrera del Genil, and *Corte Inglés* on Recogidas. The narrow streets of the Alcaicería are a paradise for souvenir hunters; so is the Cuesta de Gomérez leading up to the Alhambra.

The main things to look out for in Granada are: brass and copperware, a legacy of the Moors; ceramics, especially the typical green-and-blue Fajalauza pottery; marquetry—boxes, tables, chess sets, music boxes made in ornate wooden patterns and inlaid with mother of pearl; and woven goods from the villages of the Alpujarras—shoulder bags, rugs, wall hangings in which the colors red, green and black predominate.

USEFUL ADDRESSES. Police Station, Pza. de los Campos (tel. 22 49 84). **Train Station,** Avda. de Andaluces (tel. 23 34 08). **RENFE Office,** Reyes Católicos 63 (tel. 22 31 19). **Iberia,** Pza. de Isabel la Católica 2 (tel. 22 14 52).

Bus Station, The main—*Alsina Graëlls*—bus station is on the Camino de Ronda (tel. 25 13 58). Buses to Murcia, Alicante, Valencia and Barcelona are run by *Empresa Bacoma* and leave from Avda. Andaluces 12 (tel. 23 18 83) near the train station.

Roads from Granada

Most of eastern N342—linking at Puerta Lumbreras with N340 to the Costa Blanca, Murcia and the terminus of the motorway at Alicante—lies within the borders of Andalusia. The only town of note along the way is Guadix.

As the road leaves Granada it offers some spectacular views over the city before winding through forests and low mountains. Ceramics stalls in their dozens line the approach route to Purullena. Before bursting into indignant denunciation of the cave dwellings here, go and look inside one or two. They are warm in winter, cool in summer, and have electricity laid on. Perhaps they are not so healthy or romantic as a caravan—but they are a great deal more comfortable. Recently there has been a boom in this troglodyte real estate. Many of the cave homes, which only a few years ago cost as little as 25,000 pesetas, are now selling at over half a million pesetas. There is even a troglodyte disco for the young of Purullena; once a country inn serving food and drink to the mule trains on their way to Granada, this cave is now equipped with the latest disco equipment and film projectors and can hold up to 500 people.

After Purullena, the approach to Guadix is lined by some weird rock formations of the kind almost unknown in Europe, and more reminiscent of a Utah canyon than anything European.

Guadix is really a rather unexciting town though there are a few old mansions with spectacular facades nestling beneath a Baroque church of sandstone, and the remains of an old fortress alcazaba. From here on, the road is lined with uninviting truck-stop hostels and eating places, and some more cave dwellings with white-painted facades and chimneys sticking straight up out of the rock.

Forty-five km. (28 miles) further on, Baza lies at the center of a vast basin surrounded by distant mountains. The road continues through desolate mountain scenery, with crumbling fortresses set upon vast ocher-colored crags, to the provincial border at Las Vertientes.

From Mojácar to Almeria

From Huércal-Overa it is a short drive to the village of Mojácar, the only place of note on this eastern coast of Almería province. Mojácar nestles a couple of miles inland on a mountainside overlooking the sea and far-stretching plain to the north. The views from this village of neatly restored white houses is truly magnificent, and the village itself, although touristy, has been tastefully developed. Down on the coast are an unexciting parador and some reasonable sandy beaches, often deserted, though the sand here is the gray gritty kind of the Costa del Sol, rather than the fine white sand of the Costa Blanca.

The drive from Mojácar to Almería along N340 offers some vivid scenery around the little village of Sorbas perched on a cliff, before straightening out on the way to Tabernas. Tabernas is quite a sizeable town and though it experienced something of a boom in the days of Spanish spaghetti westerns, has little of real interest other than its old-fashioned, unspoilt air. After Tabernas the road drops down past two film sets, the one still in use but open to visitors when filming is not taking place, and the second, which has now been turned into a mini-Hollywood playground, rather incongruous in the midst of so much desolate desert scenery.

The N340 is soon joined by the N324 from Guadix which travels through the rugged ranges of the Sierra de Baza and the Sierra Nevada.

South from Granada

An attractive choice of roads leads south from Granada to the Costa del Sol. N321 branches after Loja to Málaga to descend steeply to the unattractive outskirts of Spain's fifth largest city. The old Granada–Málaga road, the C340 passes the 4th-century Roman hypogeum and a Moorish tower at Gabia la Grande just outside Granada, as well as the Moorish baths of Alhama, a spa for rheumatic diseases, before hitting the coast at Vélez-Málaga. But the shortest, and most spectacular route is due south on the N323 from Granada to Motril. Not far south of Granada the road reaches the spot known as Puerto del Suspiro del Moro—the Pass of the Moor's Sigh—and it was from here, reputedly, that Boabdil, last ruler of the Moorish kingdom of Granada, stopped and looked back on the city he had surrendered to the Catholic Monarchs. As he wept over his loss, his mother is supposed to have scorned "You weep like a boy for the city you could not hold as a man."

Lanjarón and the Alpujarras

A worthwhile detour from this road is east to the old spa town of Lanjarón lying high in the mountains at the beginning of the Alpujarra range. With its faded, old-world air, this is a delightful town retaining all its authentic Spanish qualities. As you enter Lanjarón you will pass the bottling factory which dispatches so many thousands of bottles of Lanjarón mineral water to far-flung corners of Spain. Although busy in July and August, Lanjarón is otherwise somewhat off the beaten track for most travelers. It is worth visiting for itself or as a starting point for an adventure into the Alpujarras. This should only be attempted by those who do not suffer from vertigo at high altitudes or from altitude-related respiratory problems. The road to Trevélez, once famous for the best hams in Spain, is the highest road in Europe and should only be attempted by the bravest of mountain drivers. The C332 from Orjiva to Yegen is full of curves but adequately surfaced and quite passable if you take it carefully. It affords spectacular views of the mountains dotted with tiny white villages and over the river bed fed by hundreds of twisting gulleys. The villages of the Alpujarras were the last stronghold of the defeated Moors after 1492, and it was from these remote heights that they launched their last revolt against Christian Spain in 1568. The villages were later repopulated by Galicians and Asturians from the north of Spain who perfected Moorish weaving techniques and produced the famous Alpujarra textiles goods in which red, green and white predominate.

Returning via Lanjarón to the N323, the road descends through a series of mountain bends with spectacular views to the coast at Motril.

The Costa del Sol—Motril to Almería

When you reach sea level at Motril, you are in the center of the sugar cane country. Motril was another of the Moorish strongholds, and possesses a fine, early 16th-century collegiate church.

Situated halfway between Almería and Málaga, east and west respectively, Motril has developed into a beach resort of the Costa del Sol, which stretches from Cape Gata in the east to Tarifa in the west.

The road to Almería passes the small and unimportant resorts of Torrenueva, Castell de Ferro (the pleasantest), Adra on an elevation between two beaches, bypasses Roquetas and rejoins the coast at Aguadulce. Once into Almería province, the road is drab and the ugly resorts are all best avoided.

Almería is the capital of the grape industry. As late as November you will see the peasant women delicately packing the huge green clusters destined for the Christmas tables of Paris, London or Stockholm. Almería is dominated by the Alcazaba fortress built by the Caliph Abdu'r Rahman, entered by the Gothic gate of the Reyes Católicos and provided with a bell tower by Carlos III. The fortifications command a sweeping view over the port and city, whose core still consists of distinctly oriental flat-roofed houses in a maze of narrow, winding alleys, though now framed by modern blocks of flats.

Buttressed towers give the 16th-century Gothic cathedral the look of a castle, despite the Renaissance facade. Other landmarks are the 18th-century Renaissance churches of Santo Domingo and Santiago. One small mosque has survived by being consecrated as San Pedro. Almería is fine for one night's stop, but it is one of Andalusia's least interesting capitals.

Motril to Málaga

If you turn westward at Motril toward Málaga, along the mostly widened but still cluttered coastal road, you'll see some delightful scenery—giant cliffs, tropical sugar-cane plantations and date palm trees outlined against the sea. The main road bypasses Salobreña, a delightfully typical, and as yet upspoilt, white village built on a steep hill, and brings you next past wonderful seascapes and avocado groves to Almuñécar, a fishing village since Phoenician times, 3,000 years ago. Here too, is a ruined Moorish castle where once the kings of Granada kept their treasure. It is now a pleasant enough small-time resort though its beach is shingle rather than sand.

Thirty-four km. (21 miles) further on comes Nerja, a rapidly developing resort despite its poor shingle beaches, but still very pleasant out of high season. It boasts a fantastic lookout place, known as the Balcony of Europe, set high above the sea, and a huge stalactite cave, discovered in 1959 by a shepherd boy looking for his ball, which has been converted into an auditorium for concerts, ballet performances and similar entertainments. The cave, a kind of underground cathedral, contains the world's longest-known stalactite (200 feet, 61 meters), and is well worth a visit. Nearby are the "village" developments of El Capistrano, one of the Costa del Sol's architectural showpieces, whose villas and Andalusian-style homes have been a big hit with the British and American colonies. From Nerja to Málaga the road affords some pleasant seaviews but the towns of Torrox, Torre del Mar and Rincón de la Victoria are unenchanting and do not merit a stop.

Málaga

Málaga, after vast expansion in the 1970s, is today a city attractive in its center and eastern approaches, yet hideous in the urban sprawl of its western outskirts where the huge high-rises marching determinedly towards Torremolinos now encroach on its traditional sugar cane fields. A city whose wine, fruit and sugar commerce once rivaled that of the Levantine and Catalan coasts, Málaga now suffers one of the highest unemployment and crime rates in Spain. Its old center, largely unspoilt, combines both prosperity and dilapidation; away from the main street much of it is run-down and mildly dangerous. But it has its attractive side too, with many lovely villas set in exotic foliage, and you can dine in the 14th-century Moorish fortress of Gibralfaro or at one of the rough and ready fishermen's restaurants on Pedregalejos beach.

This sprawling city, protected by mountains from the inclemencies of the north, was formerly, with San Sebastián, Palma de Mallorca and Alicante, one of the great seaside capitals of Spain, though today most tourists head for Torremolinos and Marbella further down the coast rather than the city itself. Statistics show that its winter climate is equaled in hours of sunshine by only one other European town—in southern Sicily.

Málaga cathedral was begun in the 16th century, but it has never been finished, and lacks a second tower to balance the single existing one, with its fifteen bells. Almost miraculously the lovely wood carvings of the enclosed central choir, the work of the 17th-century artist, Pedro de Mena, survived the Civil War unharmed. The wood is occasionally carved wafer-thin to express the fold of a robe or the shape of a finger, and must surely be among the greatest masterpieces of its kind. Besides the choir stalls, there are canvases by Alonso Cano, who was also the architect of the cathedral, by Morales, Van Dyck and Andrea del Sarto.

If you have shopping to do, the best shops are in Calle Larios, not far from the Renaissance cathedral. Or you can walk through the park (or more exactly, the parks, for they are divided into a series of gardens of different types) to the old Moorish Alcazaba, with its own lovely flower gardens set among the grim 11th-century walls of the fortress which now houses the Archeological Museum. Over 3,000 years of history are perpetuated in the walls of this fortress. From the heights on which the Gibralfaro Castle stands, you can look down over Málaga and the port. The view is magnificent but you would be well advised, if you drive up here, to make sure there are plenty of other people about before getting out to enjoy it as there have been reports of muggings. The parador located here is a delightful place to dine, or indeed to stay, as its views are unbeatable.

West from Málaga

Leaving Málaga and traveling westward along the coastal road, past fields of sugar cane, we come to Torremolinos (the main highway now bypasses it, so turn off at the indicated place), not all that long ago merely a small village, with the asset of an eight-km.-long beach (five-mile). Overdeveloped and a prey to the packaged tour operators, Torremolinos is also the leading foreign colony in Spain. Swarms of English, French and American residents, as well as the hordes of tourists, crowd its streets in season. Shops and restaurants, nightclubs and bars, at every price from luxury to budget, make this one of the most incredible examples of 20th-century tourism run riot.

Benalmádena Costa, with a good Casino and amusement park, and Fuengirola are somewhat simpler; each has several kilometers of rather grubby sandy beach. An interesting detour of only a few kilometers is to drive inland from either Torremolinos or Fuengirola to the hillside village of Mijas. This picturesque mountain village with its narrow streets of whitewashed houses affords pleasing views over the Mediterranean. The town has become something of an artists' colony, retirement haven and tourist paradise; it offers numerous souvenir shopping for, in particular, leather, woven rugs, Lladró and ceramics.

Marbella has grand hotels, scattered over no less than four beaches. Its cafes and shops reflect a much more up-market tourism than elsewhere on the coast and prices here are among the highest in Spain. If you can see it through the thronging crowds, the old center around the picturesque Plaza de los Naranjos still has much that is beautiful and typically Andalusian. All around are luxurious residential estates in well-elected beauty spots, comprising hotels, bungalows, golf-courses and other vast sporting facilities. The ritzy marina at Puerto Banus, just west of Marbella, is a sight in itself. The picturesque waterfront, the huge flashy yachts, the parade of beautiful people that goes on late into the night in its 100 or so restaurants, rivals even St. Tropez in trendy glamor. The nearby mosque and residence of King Fahd of Saudi Arabia on Marbella's Golden Mile are signs of the growing importance of Arab property holders and speculators in the neighborhood.

A road climbs from Marbella to picturesque Ojen where you should try to see the cemetery with its rows of chambers for burial urns, and a further nine km. (six miles) to a delightful small hotel, a former state-owned *refugio,* set among the peaks of the Sierra Blanca. Another branch, C339, affording some splendid views and safe driving, winds from San Pedro de Alcántara up through wild, eagle-haunted scenery to Ronda. Yet the most spectacular if longer approach to that fascinating town is from further south, shortly after San Roque, take the C3331 to Jimena, then C341 up the Guadarranque valley past the church of Nuestra Señora de los Angeles till you enjoy near Gaucín a truly breathtaking view over the coast to the mighty rock of Gibraltar and distant Africa.

Continuing west along the coast, we pass through Estepona, once a simple fishing port and now just about the last of the development sprawl westward. It has a pleasant seafront promenade and behind the busy, unlovely highway the old town retains much of its original charm. The four-lane highway ends when the road turns inland to San Roque. This little town was built within sight of Gibraltar by the Spaniards, who chose to evacuate the fortress when it was captured by the British in 1704. From here it is 13 km. (over eight miles) along an avenue of eucalyptus, to the port of Algeciras, but only eight km. (five miles) to La Línea and Gibraltar where since February 1985 the border has been opened to visitors after 16 years of closure.

Algeciras and Cádiz

Algeciras is the southern rail terminus, and a grim port from which three ferries sail daily in just over two hours across to Tangier in North Africa, even more frequently to Ceuta, with smaller Melilla Spain's last foothold in North Africa. Though endowed with a 15th-century cathedral and fortress, Ceuta's 170,000 inhabitants and the crowds of visitors, mostly daytrippers, are only interested in the town's free port status, which makes it a shoppers' paradise a mere hour's sailing from Algeciras. The customs inspection there is very thorough, not for tax-free purchases of tourists, but for Moroccan hashish. The crossing is shorter than that through Tangier (only an hour) and is, of course, less expensive. A boat train connects with Madrid, an overnight run, and, in season, there is also a car-ferry train service from Madrid. Across the bay towers Gibraltar.

Through hills dotted with motel colonies and camping sites, we reach Tarifa, Spain's southernmost point, and may, on a clear day, see, across the narrow Straits of Gibraltar, the coast of Africa, with the foothills of the Rif low on the horizon. Tarifa, a charming white town, is well worth a short stop, just to stroll through the spotless streets, flowered gardens, and explore the Alcázar. Though the castle is now a military base, it can be visited at specified hours.

The Costa de la Luz

After Tarifa, the sea is no longer the warm, gentle Mediterranean, but the Atlantic, and we lose sight of it for a while, for N340 runs through vast wheat fields. Along that coastline which we cannot see is Cape Trafalgar, where Nelson found victory and death in 1805. At certain times of the year, the tuna swarm along the coastal waters here. They are fished for with nets; the small boats close in with their nets, tightening the circle while the men lash out at the fish. The tuna are massacred in a furious mêlée; their blood dyes the ocean purple.

The road next passes the foot of the steep hill upon the crown of which clusters the romantic-looking town of Vejer (well worth the three-km. detour), and after passing the white village of Chiclana and several branches to bathing beaches reaches San Fernando, the huge industrial zone that surrounds and pollutes the entire inlet.

Cádiz

The historic port of Cádiz is built upon a long narrow peninsula; it claims to be the oldest continuously inhabited settlement in western Europe. Drake bombarded the city in 1587, and the Duke of Essex sacked it in 1596, probably in revenge for its contribution to the "Invincible Armada" that was to have conquered England; little of the ancient town survives, therefore. The historic castle of Medina Sidonia, the Armada's commander, is not far inland.

Once you cross the narrow isthmus into the city, you immediately see why Cádiz is called "the cup of silver," for the atmosphere sparkles with a radiant sort of dust, brilliant as mica. The city is African in appearance, with palm trees, white houses, cupolas, and street stalls piled with oranges. But its most striking features are the churches in their green gardens and the silvery harbor.

This admirable, landlocked haven has made Cádiz a typical, busy, brawling southern port. The picturesque rabbit warren of its narrow back streets and delightful squares is noisy each night with singing and hands clapping out the unmistakable beat of flamenco.

The city possesses a small but worthwhile art collection (works by Murillo and Zurbarán) in its Museo de Bellas Artes on Plaza de Mina. The small oratory of Santa Cueva contains several lesser-known works by Goya, and in Santa Catalina Chapel, sadly no longer open to visitors, there is a deeply moving tribute to Murillo's memory; with various others of his works, here hangs Murillo's last painting, entitled *The Mystic Marriage of St. Catherine*. While working on it in 1682, the artist fell from his scaffolding and died of his injuries. Also of interest is the church of San Felipe Neri, where the Cortes of Cádiz were held and where the 1812 Constitution was proclaimed.

The composer Manuel de Falla, one of Cádiz's native sons, lies buried in the crypt of the neo-Classical cathedral.

From Cádiz, you turn north again, on the last segment of our Andalusian circle, north to Jerez and Seville, our starting point. The toll-road crosses the bay on a bridge to Puerto Real and bypasses the points of interest. So back to N-IV, down the isthmus through San Fernando with its formidable grille windows, past the attractive little town of Puerto de Santa María, famous for its fish restaurants and succulent giant shrimp, a local delicacy, from which sherry used to be shipped before the railway linked Jerez with Cádiz, and past the gleaming salt marshes of the flat river delta of the Guadalquivir.

You now encounter a chalky desert region, where the Moors and the Visigoths fought the famous battle of Guadalete in 711, settling the rulership of all but the remote northern provinces of Spain for the next 500 years. This land and the river are as charged with history as the Guadalquivir was charged with the blood of men who fought on its banks to defend the peninsula from Islam. There is little to break the monotony of brambles and scrub grass—only an occasional isolated castle or a flight of wheeling eagles. And then we reach the orderly vineyards that announce Jerez de la Frontera.

Jerez de la Frontera

The home of sherry is surrounded by immense vineyards whose grapes have funded a host of beautiful churches and palaces. Jerez is justly proud of its famous heady wine, flamenco dancers and *cante jondo* singers, improvisers who give vent to restrained, tragic passion in subtle modulations. Its Spanish Riding School breeds and trains the magnificent Andalusian horses that are the pride and joy of its May Horse Fair.

A visit to the bodegas of González Byass is an exciting experience even if you do not care for sherry, for there you will see casks signed by visiting notables—royalty, writers, bullfighters, musicians—and perhaps taste a few drops from the 1850 cask. If you do, you will not like it. It is almost like vinegar. But a drop or two in your ordinary 14-year-old wine will make it taste like nectar.

At the Harvest Festival in the second week in September, the grapes are blessed in a colorful pageant in an exquisite setting, the triple staircase and portal of the 17th-century collegiate church whose five naves are crowned by an octagonal cupola flanked by a Moorish tower. Amongst other outstanding religious buildings are the Convent of Santo Domingo, Isabelline San Miguel with its splendid lateral chapels, reredos and Plateresque gate, Mudéjar San Dionisio and Gothic Santiago. They are all flanked by the Renaissance and Baroque palaces of the Marqueses de Montana, de Bertemati, Requelme and de Campo Real.

However, despite these notable buildings and the ever-present lure of its bodegas, Jerez is not somewhere the visitor is likely to want to linger. The crime rate is high, with both unemployment and drug addiction being major problems. It is on the latter that the numerous purse-snatchings and muggings that occur in its streets can be blamed. Despite this rather gloomy picture, the City Council has recently launched a scheme to breathe new life into the town and improve its run-down image. Measures have been taken to make the historic bodegas more accessible to the public by replacing their enclosing fences with railings so their gardens and patios are on view; extensive renovations have been carried out in the town center; a flamenco museum has recently been opened; and Jerez's motorcycle circuit is once again drawing the crowds for Spain's Grand Prix races. A much-needed tourist office opened its doors in 1987 and two new hotels followed soon afterwards; hopefully things are now taking a turn for the better.

Six km. (four miles) east of Jerez lies the famous 15th-century Carthusian monastery of La Cartuja. Its elaborate Renaissance facade contrasts dramatically with its austere Gothic interior and vast cloisters. It was once a stud farm, and its strain of horses is still the pride of the Feria de Mayo, the spectacular Horse Fair held each year in May.

Twenty-four km. (15 miles) west through seemingly endless expanses of the renowned manzanilla vineyards you reach Sanlúcar de Barrameda, at the mouth of the Guadalquivir. In 1498 Columbus sailed from here on his third voyage to the Americas; 20 years later Magellan steered his ships out of the same harbor on the start of his world-circling exploit. The Church of Nuestra Señora de la O, with its splendid panelling, Mudéjar gate and 18th-century reredos and which antedates both these intrepid explorers, has now been declared a national monument. The main palaces in the town, all of which are worth seeing, are those of the Orléans-Bourbons and the Condes de Niebla. The Castle of Santiago guards the river mouth.

Fine beaches extend along the town's southern promontory to Chipiona, where the Roman general Scipio the "African" built a beacon tower. Further south past many fine sandy beaches lies Rota, a white village below a medieval castle, and now a U.S. naval base and popular summer resort.

One final trip that is well worth making leads in a different direction. East from Jerez and towards Málaga the road passes through the picturesque mountain town of Ronda.

Roads to Ronda

N342 leads first of all to Arcos de la Frontera, perched dramatically on a wild crag and crowned by a castle above the gorge of the Gaudalete river. Santa María in the Plaza España in the old town is a fascinating blend of architectural styles and here also is the parador and a balcony with splendid views. Further on towards Ronda you will see silhouetted against the sky to your right the virtually impregnable Arab fortress of Zahara de la Sierra, which held out until 1483 against the Christian forces. Zahara is perhaps the most typical and worthwhile of the so-called "White Towns" of this route; another is Grazalema (warning: do not attempt the tortuous winding 531 route over the Puerto de las Palomas between Zahara and Grazalema, stick to the more conventional approaches).

A final rewarding detour before reaching Ronda, would be to the little known Pileta Caves beyond Montejaque and Benaojón, reached through some magnificent mountain scenery. A guardian from the farm down in the valley will show you round the caves but the system for contacting him is primitive and typically Spanish. Your patience, however, will be well rewarded by the prehistoric wall paintings and the caves' weird stalactite and stalagmite formations.

Ronda was the last stronghold of the legendary Andalusian bandits and scene of the last great rising of the Moors against Ferdinand and Isabella. Its setting is unforgettable, perched above a rocky cleft over 90 meters (300 feet) deep, spanned by three bridges.

Ronda, one of the oldest towns in Spain, has always attracted artists and writers: two famous admirers were Goya and Hemingway. If the

Rondians have often sheltered bandits and snapped their fingers at customs officers, it is because they had only one road to guard, and that a narrow mule path. Well protected in the midst of eroded cliffs, it has always been difficult to reach.

Ronda's outstanding feature is the spectacular bridge, the Puente Nuevo (1761), from whose lantern-lit parapet you can have a paralyzingly firsthand view of El Tajo, the gorge dividing the town. Deep down in the chasm are the two other bridges, Puente Viejo and Puente San Miguel, the former on Roman foundations.

The older section of town, called Ciudad, lies south of the gorge. Its Collegiate Church, once a mosque, was later rededicated to the Virgen de la Encarnación and successive restorations added the three late Gothic naves and Baroque altar. Look also for the Casa del Rey Moro, an 11th-century residence of the Moorish ruler of the area, and the Casa de Mondragón, home of several early Spanish monarchs. The residence of the Marqués de Salvatierra, also in Ciudad, is occasionally open to visitors. Alongside the river are the excavated remains of some old Arab baths (though gangs of youths threaten tourists for money round here; so it's as well to be careful). In the new (15th- and 16th-century) part of town, called Mercadillo, are the town hall, the Paseo de la Merced gardens, a spectacular cliffside walk, the splendid turn-of-the-century Reina Victoria hotel, and the 200-year-old bullring, the second oldest in Spain, which has changed little since it was built in 1784. The ring is open to visitors and bullfights are held here just once a year during the September fiesta. Ronda is considered the cradle of modern bullfighting and mementoes of its famous 18th-century son, Pedro Romero, father of the art, loom large all over town.

PRACTICAL INFORMATION FOR ANDALUSIA

TOURIST OFFICES. Algeciras, Avda. de la Marina (tel. 60 09 11); **Almería,** Hermanos Machado 4, 5th floor (tel. 23 08 58); **Almuñécar,** Puerta del Mar (tel. 63 11 25); **Antequera,** Palacio de Nájera, Coso Viejo (tel. 84 14 27); **Baeza,** Plaza del Pópulo (tel. 74 04 44); **Benalmádena,** Avda. de Alay (tel. 44 34 49); **Cádiz,** Calderón de la Barca 1 (tel. 21 13 13); **Carboneras,** Pza. del Castillo (tel. 45 40 59); **Carmona,** El Salvador 2 (tel. 14 00 11); **Ecija,** Avda. Andalucía (tel. 83 30 62); **Estepona,** Paseo Marítimo Pedro Manrique (tel. 80 09 13); **Fuengirola,** Pza. del Ayuntamiento (tel. 47 95 00); **Huelva,** Vázquez López 5 (tel. 25 74 03); **Jaen,** Avda. de Madrid 10A (tel. 22 27 37); **Jerez de la Frontera,** Alameda Cristina 7 (tel. 33 11 50); **Málaga,** Marqués de Larios 5 (tel. 21 34 45), at the airport in the International Terminal (tel. 31 60 00 ext. 5433), and the National Terminal (tel. 31 20 44); **Marbella,** Miguel Cano 1 (tel. 77 14 42); **Osuna,** in the Museo Arqueológico, San Antón (tel. 81 12 07), and in the Colegiata, Extramuros (tel. 81 04 44); **Puerto de Santa María,** Guadalete (tel. 85 75 45); **Ronda,** Pza. de España 1 (tel. 87 12 72); **Torre-**

molinos, La Nogalera 517 (tel. 38 15 78); **Ubeda,** Pza. de los Caidos (tel. 75 08 97).

TELEPHONE CODES. The dialing codes for the eight provinces of Andalusia are: Almería (951); Cádiz (956); Córdoba (957); Granada (958); Huelva (955); Jaén (953); Málaga (952); Seville (954). These codes apply to all towns within the same province and need only be dialed if you are calling from outside that province. They are given under *Hotels and Restaurants* immediately after the name of the town.

GETTING AROUND. By Train. Traveling between the major Andalusian cities by train is not always as straightforward as one might expect. This is mainly due to the mountainous nature of much of Andalusia. Unless you are traveling on a Eurail pass and determined to stick to it, it is usually easier and more direct to go from city to city within Andalusia by bus. Trains often take very roundabout routes, involve several changes and spend a lot of time in tunnels. There is a good local train service between Málaga and Fuengirola, calling at Málaga airport, Torremolinos, Benalmádena, Carvajal, and Los Boliches. Trains run every half hour between 6 A.M. and approximately 11 P.M.

Train Stations and RENFE Offices. Almería, off Ctra. de Ronda in southeast of city (tel. 22 11 35); RENFE Office, Alcalde Muñóz 1 (tel. 23 12 07). **Cádiz,** station is near port between isthmus and old town (tel. 26 43 02). **Huelva,** station is off Avda. de Italia (tel. 24 66 66). **Jaén,** station is at end of Paseo de la Estación (tel. 21 17 56). **Málaga,** station is on Calle Cuarteles, west of center across river (tel. 31 25 00); RENFE Office, Strachan 2 (off Calle Larios) (tel. 21 31 22). The station for the local service to Torremolinos and Fuengirola is Málaga Guadalmedina, across the river opposite the *Corte Inglés* store.

By Bus. For journeys within Andalusia this is the most practical and direct means of transport. There are also plenty of bus connections into the area from Barcelona, Madrid, Valencia and other large cities.

Bus Stations. Almería, Pza. de Barcelona (tel. 22 10 11) in west of town; **Cádiz,** *Los Amarillos,* Ramón de Carranza 31 for Rota and Sanlucar de Barrameda, *Comes,* Pza. de España for Tarifa and Algeciras; **Huelva,** Avda. de Italia (tel. 24 66 66) near station for Seville and Granada, Avda. de Portugal 9 for coastal resorts; **Jaén,** Pza. Coca de la Pinera; **Málaga,** main Alsina Graëlls station for all destinations except Costa del Sol, is at Pza. de Toros Vieja 2 (tel. 31 04 00), for all destinations west of Málaga on Costa del Sol, the Portillo bus station is at Córdoba 7 (tel. 22 73 00); **Torremolinos,** Portillo bus station with services to Algeciras, La Linea, Gibraltar, Ronda, Coin and Mijas and all Costa del Sol destinations, is on Calle Hoyo opposite the *Hostal Victoria.*

By Air. The main airports in the region are, first Málaga, with many scheduled and charter international flights as well as good domestic connections, then Seville with a few international flights and several domestic flights. There are also airports at Almería, Córdoba, Granada, Jerez de la Frontera and Gibraltar.

By Car. The main highway in Andalusia is the N-IV from Madrid to Cádiz via Córdoba and Seville. It is currently undergoing extensive road-works as it is widened into an *autovía* (expressway), so expect some delays. The only toll road in the area is the *autopista* A4 from Seville to Cádiz via Jerez, and a tiny stretch of the A49 westwards from Seville to Huelva.

The other major road in Andalusia is the coastal N340. From Almería to Adra, this is fairly flat and easy driving; from Adra to Málaga the twisty coastal road has been widened and resurfaced. The long stretch of the main part of the Costa del Sol from Málaga to Algeciras is flat, with only a few curves. It is, however, the most notorious road in Spain for serious accidents, so drive with extra care at all times. Here it is useful to know that in most places, if you want to turn left, you do so by exiting right and turning on a loop road usually controlled by traffic lights. A huge reconstruction program including the building of a Marbella bypass is scheduled for this section, and work was begun in 1987.

Think twice before attempting any of the unclassified roads either in the mountain ranges behind the Costa del Sol, or in the Sierra Morena in the north; though some may be passable, others are high and twisty with no barriers and sheer drops. This also applies to some C roads, so it is always best to make enquiries first if you are planning such a route.

EXCURSIONS. Organized excursions from the Costa del Sol are run mostly by **Juliatour** and **Pullmantour** and can be booked through any travel agency and most hotels. Nearly all hotels display prices and details.

Excursions. *Granada:* one day; *Córdoba:* one day; *Seville and Córdoba:* two days; *Seville:* one day; *Ronda:* one day; *Tangiers:* one day; *Ceuta-Tetuan:* one day; *Ceuta-Tetuan-Tangiers:* two days; *Gibraltar:* one day; *Alpujarras:* one day (Sun. only).

Local tours. Half-day tour of *Málaga:* mornings; half-day to *Nerja caves:* afternoon; half-day to *Mijas:* afternoon; *Marbella-Puerto Banus:* half-day, morning; *Burro safari in Coin:* one day; *Countryside tour:* Alhaurín, Coin, Ojén, Monda: one day (Tues., Thurs., Sat. only); *Night Tours* include a barbecue evening, a bullfighting evening, and a night at the Torrequebrada Casino.

Tours run by local agencies, and usually only available in high season, include: *Cazorla; Chorro Gorge; Casares: Antequera and Torcal; Coto Do-naña National Park.*

HOTELS AND RESTAURANTS. The most highly developed region of the Costa del Sol is between Málaga and Marbella where concrete blocks shot up with alarming rapidity 10–20 years ago, completely transforming what were once sleepy Andalusian fishing villages. East from Málaga, Nerja too has tripled its original size and been more or less spoilt. The popularity of this area for package holidays never wanes, and a large proportion of the Costa del Sol hotels are block-booked in high season by foreign package tour operators. Though the stampede of British sunseekers continues relentlessly, the sheer number of hotels means that rooms are usually available even in July and August.

From Marbella to Estepona there has been some interesting resort development in recent years, including the magnificent marina at Puerto Banús, happily much more in keeping with traditional Andalusian architecture.

Of late there have been quite a few developments around Almería, until recently a more neglected part of the Costa del Sol. Roquetas de Mar, Aguadulce and Dalía are just a few of these ugly "urbanizations" in what is mostly an unlovely part of the coast, and for this reason we include few listings for these places. Resorts are also being developed along the Costa de la Luz in Cádiz and Huelva provinces. The mushrooming concrete blocks of Matalascañas, close to the Coto Doñana Nature Reserve, have already caused an outcry from ecologists. The regional government has intervened to preserve the character of the area, and it is to be hoped that this coast will not take on the alarming proportions of the Torremolinos sprawl.

The range of *paradores* in Andalusia is excellent, there being no fewer than 16 in the whole region.

Algeciras. Cádiz (956). *Reina Cristina* (E), Paseo de la Conferencia (tel. 60 26 22). Once famous hotel with tropical garden and terrace with view of Gibraltar and the mountains of Africa beyond, but it now caters largely to tour groups; tennis, pool and nightclubs. AE, DC, MC, V. *Octavio* (E–M), San Bernardo 1 (tel. 65 24 61). 80 rooms. Recent, functional hotel in uninteresting part of town. AE, DC, MC, V.

Alarde (M), Alfonso XI 4 (tel. 66 01 08). 68 rooms, modern and central. AE, DC, MC, V. *Al-Mar* (M), Avda. de la Marina 2 (tel. 65 46 61). 192 rooms. Recent hotel opposite port entrance. AE, DC, MC, V. *Anglo Hispano* (I), Avda. Villanueva (tel. 60 01 00). 30 rooms. Bright and modest, in center. MC, V.

Restaurants. *Iris* (M), San Bernardo 1 (tel. 65 58 06). Close to bus and train station. AE, DC, V. *Marea Baja* (M), Trafalgar 2 (tel. 66 36 54). Superb seafood. Closed Sun. AE, DC, MC, V. *Pazo de Edelmiro* (I), Pza. Miguel Martín 1 (tel. 66 63 55). Very central. AE.

Almería (951). *Gran Hotel Almería* (E), Avda. Reina Regente 4 (tel. 23 80 11). 124 rooms; pool. Right on the bottom of the main street overlooking the port. AE, DC, MC, V. *Costasol* (M), Avda. de Almería 58 (tel. 23 40 11). 55 rooms. Typical 3-star hotel with smart lobby on the main street. AE, DC, MC, V. *Torreluz II* (M), Pza. Flores 1 (tel. 23 47 99). 67 rooms. Functional, pleasant hotel, in central square. It has two sister hotels, one (I) and one (E) 4-star hotel in same square. AE, DC, MC, V. *Guerry* (I), Avda. de Almería 47 (tel. 23 11 77). 40 rooms. A simple, clean, 2-star hostel on main street.

Outside town on the road to Málaga, and fine if you have a car, are: *Playaluz* (E), Bahía el Palmer (tel. 34 05 04). 156 rooms; pool, tennis and golf. A good resort-type hotel on sea side of highway six km. (four miles) out. AE, DC, MC, V. *Solymar* (E), 2.5 km. out on Málaga road (tel. 23 46 22). 15 rooms. Functional, with view of sea and fishing port.

Restaurants. *Anfora* (M), González Garbín 25 (tel. 23 13 74). Its reputation for fresh food and especially fine fish dishes make it one of the best restaurants in town. Closed Sun. and end of July. AE, V. *Rincón de Juan Pedro* (M), Pza. del Carmen 6 (tel. 23 51 84). Atmospheric mesón with bar and restaurant on ground floor and pretty cellar restaurant. Very good food and pleasant service. Try the *lenguado a la naranja* (sole in orange sauce). Closed Sun. AE, DC, MC, V. *Imperial* (I), Puerta Purchena 5 (tel.

23 17 40). Plain decor but excellent value and very popular with Spanish families at lunchtime; good old-fashioned service. Closed Wed. in winter.

Almuñecar. Granada (958). *Goya* (I), Avda. Gen. Galindo (tel. 63 05 50). 24 rooms. Simple, clean hotel, a short walk from beach. AE. *Playa de San Cristobal* (I), Pza. San Cristobal 5 (tel. 63 11 12). Simple hotel overlooking a rock that separates two beaches.
Restaurants. *Vecchia Firenze* (M), in La Fabriquilla off Alta del Mar (tel. 63 19 04). Italian restaurant with elegant *belle époque* decor. Original menu, Italian and Spanish specialties. Also (I) pizzas and pastas. Closed Tues. AE, DC, MC, V. *Los Geranios* (M), Placeta de la Rosa 4 (tel. 63 07 24). Popular Belgian-owned restaurant with picturesque decor. Friendly but the food can disappoint. Closed Wed. AE, DC, MC, V.

Andujar. Jaén (953). *Hotel Del Val* (I), just outside on Madrid road (tel. 50 09 50). 79 rooms; pool, gardens, bar, good food in modern restaurant. AE, V.

Antequera. Málaga (952). *Parador Nacional* (M), García del Olmo (tel. 84 00 61). 55 rooms; pool. Parador with splendid views and good food. AE, DC, MC, V.

Arcos de la Frontera. Cádiz (956). *Parador Casa del Corregidor* (E), Pza. de España (tel. 70 05 00). 21 rooms; attractively sited in old town; recently renovated. AE, DC, MC, V. *El Convento* (M), Maldonado 2 (tel. 70 23 33). 4 rooms. Tiny, welcoming hotel in part of an old convent perched on the cliff edge. The friendly owners take pride in offering good accommodations and food; charming.

Ayamonte. Huelva (955). *Parador Costa de la Luz* (E), El Castillito (tel. 32 07 00). Great position overlooking mouth of the Guadalquivir and Portugal. 20 rooms, pool. AE, DC, MC, V. *Don Diego* (M), Ramón y Cajal (tel. 32 02 50). 45 rooms. V.

Bailen. Jaén (953). *Parador Nacional* (M), (tel. 67 01 00). 86 rooms; modern with pool. AE, DC, MC, V. *Motel Don Lope de Sosa* (I), (tel. 67 00 58). 27 rooms, garden and good restaurant. AE, DC, MC, V. *Zodiaco* (I), (tel. 67 10 58). 52 rooms; modern with good restaurant. DC, V. All three are on main highway, NIV.

Los Barrios. Cádiz (956), near Algeciras. *Guadacorte* (E), (tel. 66 45 00). 118 rooms. Facilities include pool, tennis, garden. AE, DC, V. *La Posada del Terol* (M), Barriada de Palmones Playa (tel. 66 15 50). 24 rooms, pool.

Benalmadena Costa. Málaga (952). *Triton* (L), Avda. Antonio Machado 29 (tel. 44 32 40). 190 rooms, pool, tennis, sauna, private beach. AE, DC, MC, V. *Riviera* (E), Avda. Antonio Machado 49 (tel. 44 12 40). Overlooking beach, with pool. AE, DC, MC, V. *Villasol* (I), Avda. Antonio Machado (tel. 44 19 96). 76 rooms, pool. AE, DC, V. All three are close together on sea-side of main highway at Torremolinos end.

Restaurants. *Casa Juan* (M), Avda. del Mar (tel. 44 38 39). Good food and outstanding service, just 5 minutes walk from the main hotel area. Open for dinner only in summer; closed Tues. AE, DC, MC, V. *La Rueda* (M), San Miguel 2 (tel. 44 82 21). One of the best. Closed Tues. and Aug. DC, MC, V. *Ventorrillo de la Perra* (M), Julio Romero (tel. 44 19 66). Atmospheric inn, at Arroyo de la Miel, more original than most coastal tourist restaurants. Closed Mon. AE, DC, MC, V.

Bubion. Granada (958). *Villa Turística del Poqueira* (M), Barrio Alto (tel. 76 31 11). 43 rooms. Attractive bungalow complex opened in 1986 in wonderful setting; the only good accommodations at present in the Alpujarras.

Cadiz (956). In the old town: *Atlántico* (E), Parque Genovés 9 (tel. 21 23 01). 153 rooms. In a magnificent position on headland. AE, DC, MC, V. *Francia y París* (M), Pza. San Francisco (tel. 22 23 48). 69 rooms. Pleasant old-world hotel. AE, DC, MC, V. *Isecotel* (E–M), Amílcar Barca 35 (tel. 25 54 01). Modern hotel on the isthmus; large elegant apartments overlooking beach. *San Remo* (M), Paseo Marítimo 3 (tel. 25 22 02). Also overlooks beach.

Restaurants. *El Anteojo* (E), Alameda de Apodaca 22 (tel. 21 36 39). Elegant and modern; upstairs panoramic dining room with view over bay, downstairs a pleasant terrace. AE, DC, MC, V. *El Faro* (E–M), San Felix 15 (tel. 21 10 68). Recommended by locals; especially good seafood. *Curro El Cojo* (M), Paseo Marítimo 2 (tel. 25 31 86). Elegant and near Isecotel. Superb meat dishes, mainly pork. DC, V. *La Montera* (M), Veedor 3 (tel. 21 14 73). Opened in 1987 in a beautifully restored 18th-century palace. The decor and setting are magnificent and the cuisine, mostly Basque, shows great promise. Closed Sun. AE, V.

La Carolina. Jaén (953). *La Perdiz* (M), (tel. 66 03 00). 89 rooms. Pleasant hotel with pool; at top of Despeñaperros pass on main N-IV highway. AE, MC, V.

Carmona. Seville (954). *Parador Alcázar del Rey Don Pedro* (E), (tel. 14 10 10). 55 rooms; pool. In the ruins of a Moorish fortress; magnificently overlooks vast plain. AE, DC, MC, V.

Cazorla. Jaén (953). *Parador El Adelantado* (E), 27 km. (17 miles) from village high up in the sierra (tel. 72 10 75). 33 rooms. Superb site in mountian game reserve; good shooting. AE, DC, MC, V. In the village are: *Andalucía* (I), Martínez Ferlero 41 (tel. 72 12 68). 11 rooms. Recently-opened small hotel. MC, V. *Cazorla* (I), Pza. La Corredera 4 (tel. 72 02 03). 22 rooms. Modest village hotel with good-value meals.

Córdoba. See *Practical Information for Córdoba* (page 389).

Estepona. Málaga (952). The following are all closer to San Pedro de Alcántara than Estepona itself: *Atalaya Park* (E), (tel. 78 13 00). 239 rooms. 18-hole golf course, private beach, pool, all sports facilities, nightclubs and all delights of an excellent resort hotel. AE, DC, MC, V. *Stakis Paraíso* (E), (tel. 78 30 00). 201 rooms. Revolving restaurant, disco, beach, tennis and golf. AE, DC, MC, V. *Santa Marta* (M), (tel. 78 07 16). 37 rooms; pool. Chalet bungalows, some a little shabby but pleasant garden location. Good lunches served by pool. AE, DC, V. In Estepona itself, and both very basic, are: *Caracas* (M), Avda. San Lorenzo 50 (tel. 80 08 00). 27 rooms. DC, MC, V. *Dobar* (I), Avda. España 178 (tel. 80 06 00). 39 rooms. On main, busy highway, overlooking sea.

Restaurants. *El Libro Amarillo* (The Yellow Book) (E), (tel. 80 04 84). Five km. out on road to Málaga. One of the Costa's most famous restaurants, American owned; excellent food and outstanding service. Book well in advance. Open for dinner only; closed Sun. and Jan. AE, MC, V. *El Molino* (E), 12 km. (eight miles) out on Málaga road (tel. 78 23 37). In an old windmill, good French cuisine. Open for dinner only. Closed Tues., Sun., and Jan. AE, MC, V. In Estepona are: *La Pulga que Tose* (E–M), Pozo de la Pila 25 (tel. 80 27 49). Charming old house in heart of old town; excellent food and atmosphere. Open for dinner only; closed Sun. MC, V. *Costa del Sol* (M), San Roque 23 (tel. 80 11 01). Good French cuisine, in side street near bus station. AE, MC, V. *La Fuente* (M), San Antonio 48. Chargrilled steaks, spare ribs and U.S.A. specials. *Mesón Arni* (M), Mondéjar 16. Mexican specialties; open for dinner only. MC, V.

Out at the **Puerto Deportivo** (yacht marina) to the west of town (entrance opposite building) are several restaurants where you can take your pick. Some of the best are *Antonio* (E), *El Puerto* (E–M) and *Rafael* (E).

Fuengirola. Málaga (952). *Las Palmeras* (E), Rey de España (tel. 47 27 00). 432 rooms. Vast hotel and apartment complex overlooking harbor, on corner of Jacinto Benavente. AE, DC, MC, V. *Florida* (M), Paseo Marítimo (tel. 47 61 00). 116 rooms. Smaller hotel of character, set in pleasant garden with palm trees, pool and pool-side bar. DC, V. *Mare Nostrum* (M), on highway (tel. 47 11 00). Attractive curved layout enables every room to get the sun. Pool, private beach, mini golf, tennis. *El Puerto* (M), (tel. 47 01 00). 320 rooms. On Paseo Marítimo. Good. Most expensive in this category. AE, DC, V. *Las Rampas* (I), Jacinto Benavente (tel. 47 09 00). Above shopping center, right in center, short walk to beach; good value.

Restaurants. *La Cazuela* (M), Miguel Márques 8 (tel. 47 46 34). In house of local character just of Pza. Picasso; small and popular. *Don Pedro* (M), Pza. Picasso 1 (tel. 47 30 43). Good restaurant in heart of town, specializing in Basque and fish dishes. Closed Mon. and Aug. and Sept. AE, MC, V. *Mateo* (M), Marina Nacional 36 (tel. 47 26 06). Swiss restaurant behind Edif. Perla 4; specialties are cheese or beef fondue. *Monopol* (M), Palangreros 7 (tel. 47 44 48). International cuisine in pleasant central surroundings. Closed Thurs. and July. AE, V.

In **Los Boliches** are: *La Langosta* (E), Francisco Cano 1 (tel. 47 50 49). Quality restaurant with long-standing reputation. Specialties are lobster, sole and steak. Open for dinner only. Closed Sun. AE, DC, MC, V. *Don Bigote* (M), Francisco Cano 39 (tel. 47 50 94). Relaxed atmosphere with a typical Andalusian patio. Open for dinner only. AE, MC, V. *La Sirena* (M), Francisco Cano 18 (tel. 47 50 46). Atmospheric Thai restaurant. Closed Tues. and Wed. lunch. AE, MC, V.

Granada. See *Practical Information for Granada* (page 402).

Guadix. Granada (958). *Comercio* (I), Mira de Amezcua 3 (tel. 66 05 00). 21 rooms. In a well-maintained stylish old house; central; clean and simple with a good-value restaurant. v.

Huelva (955). *Luz Huelva* (E), Alameda Sumdheim 26 (tel. 25 00 11). 105 rooms; pool. Functional, geared to businessmen. *Tartessos* (M), Avda. Martín Alonso Pinzón 13 (tel. 24 56 11). 112 rooms, some suites, with good *Doñana* (M) restaurant (tel. 24 27 73). DC, v. *Costa de la Luz* (I), Jose María Amo 8 (tel. 25 64 22). 35 rooms; central.

Restaurants. *Los Gordos* (M), Carmen 14 (tel. 24 62 66). An old Huelva institution noted for its fine fresh fish. Closed Sat. evening, Sun. and in Aug. AE, DC, v. *Las Meigas* (M), Pza. América (tel. 23 00 98). In the Inverluz complex. Fine Basque and Galician dishes. Closed Sun. in July and Aug. DC, MC, v. *La Muralla* (M), San Salvador 17 (tel. 25 50 77). One of the best, close to the Esperanza Gardens; prices a little high. Closed Sun. and end of Aug. AE, DC, MC, v. *La Cazuela* (I), Garcí Gernández 5 (tel. 25 80 96). Pleasantly decorated and good value, near the Pza. Niña. Closed Sun. P.M. v.

Jaén (953). *Parador Castillo de Santa Catalina* (E), Castillo de Santa Catalina (tel. 26 44 11). 43 rooms. Beautifully situated, converted castle with monastic-style balconied rooms. AE, DC, MC, v. *Condestable Iranzo* (M), Paseo de la Estacíon 32 (tel. 22 28 00). 147 rooms. Modern and central; rooms on front can be noisy. *Xauen* (M), Pza. de Dean Mazas 3 (tel. 26 40 11). 35 rooms. Central, older hotel, well run and friendly. v. *Europa* (I), Pza. de Belén 1 (tel. 22 27 00). 36 rooms, no breakfast. AE, DC, MC, v. *Rey Fernando* (I), Pza. de Coca de la Piñera 7 (tel. 25 18 40). 36 rooms, with garage; old-fashioned. AE, DC, MC, v.

Restaurants. Best and most spectacular meals in the parador, perched on top of a mountain commanding a magnificent view of city. *Jockey Club* (M), Paseo de la Estación 20 (tel. 21 10 18). The most luxurious. Closed on Sun. and Aug. AE, DC, MC, v. *Nelson* (M), Paseo de la Estación 33 (tel. 22 92 01). Small menu making good use of fresh market produce. Closed Sun. AE, v.

Jerez de la Frontera. Cádiz (956). *Jerez* (L), Avda. Alvaro Domecq 35 (tel. 33 06 00). 120 rooms; pool. Luxurious hotel set in beautiful gardens. AE, DC, MC, v. *Royal Sherry Park* (E), Avda. Alvaro Domecq 11 bis (tel. 30 30 11). 173 rooms. Brand-new, superior hotel with pool and restaurant. AE, MC, v. *Avenida Jerez* (E–M), Avda. Alvaro Domecq 10 (tel. 34 74 11). 95 rooms. Another new hotel with many amenities. *Capele* (E–M), Gen. Franco 58 (tel. 34 64 00). Good functional 3-star hotel in center. AE, DC, MC, v. *Motel Aloha* (M), on N-IV (tel. 33 25 00). 27 rooms, pleasant location, pool. A few km. out on Seville road. *El Coloso* (I), Pedro Alonso 13 (tel. 34 90 08). Friendly oldish hotel, simple and adequate if a bit shabby.

Restaurants. *El Bosque* (E), Alcade Alvaro Domecq 26 (tel. 33 33 33). Lovely setting in park. Closed Sun. AE, DC, MC, v. *Tendido* 6 (E-M), Circo 10 (tel. 34 48 35). Opposite bullring; specilizes in seafood. Popular at lunchtime, so book. Colorful, atmospheric decor and good service. Closed Sun. AE, DC, MC, v. *La Posada* (M), Arboledilla 2 (tel. 33 34 20). Tiny restaurant with even smaller menu but the daily specials are lovingly chosen. *Venta Antonio* (M), five km. out on road to Sanlucar (tel. 33 05 35). Excellent food with fresh fish bought daily in Sanlucar. Very reasonable prices for the quality. AE, DC, MC, V.

Lanjarón. Granada (958). Aged spa town where most of the hotels are open in summer only. *Paraíso* (I), Gen. Franco 18 (tel. 77 00 12). 49 rooms. Modern, friendly and good. AE, V. The rest of Lanjarón's hotels are simple and elderly. If you like old-world spa charm, you could try *Andalucía* (I), Gen. Franco 15 (tel. 77 01 36). 57 rooms; pool. Ancient with lovely rambling garden. Open mid-June to Sept. only. *España* (I), Gen. Franco 44 (tel. 77 01 87). 36 rooms. Old yellow and white mansion. Closed Jan. and Feb.

Loja. Granada (958). *Manzanil* (I), on main road (tel. 32 17 11). 49 rooms. Good hotel for overnighting; very reasonable. AE, DC, V.

Twenty-one km. from Loja towards Las Salinas is *La Bobadilla* (L), Finca la Bobadilla (tel. 32 18 61). 35 suites. Luxury hotel complex in the heart of the Andalusian countryside; with its own church, 4-channel satellite TV, Jacuzzi, Turkish saunas and facilities for sports, swimming, fishing and shooting. Its *La Finca* restaurant (L) is outstanding.

Málaga (952). *Guadalmar* (E), ten km. (six miles) out off road to airport (tel. 31 90 00). 195 rooms. Good resort hotel by beach with tennis, pool, gardens, disco; but you need a car, it's a long way from anywhere. AE, DC, MC, V. *Málaga Palacio* (E), Cortina del Muelle 1 (tel. 21 51 85). 228 rooms; pool. Central, overlooking port, but needs renovation. AE, DC, MC, V. *Parador de Gibralfaro* (E), on mountain top three km. from center (tel. 22 19 02). 12 rooms. Beside Moorish castle, beautiful view over bay; recently renovated, and a good place to dine. AE, DC, MC, V. *Los Naranjos* (E–M), Paseo Sancha 35 (tel. 22 43 17). 41 rooms. Short distance from center on pleasant avenue; rooms on front can be noisy. AE, DC, MC, V.

Bahía (M), Somera 8 (tel. 22 43 05). 44 rooms. Central but in dull location; functional. *Don Curro* (M), Sancha de Lara 7 (tel. 22 72 00). 105 rooms. Centrally located between Calle Larios and cathedral, but not very inviting. AE, DC, MC, V. *Las Vegas* (M), Paseo de Sancha 22 (tel. 21 77 12). 73 rooms; pool. On busy avenue with dining room overlooking Paseo Marítimo and sea. One of the best. AE, DC, V. *Victoria* (I), Sancha de Lara. A good budget bet in an old house in the center of town.

Restaurants. *La Alegría* (E), Marin García 10 (tel. 22 41 43). Famous fish and seafood restaurant, in center close to Calle Larios. Closed Sat. AE, DC, V. *Café de Paris* (E), Vélez-Málaga (tel. 22 50 43). Smart restaurant in Paseo Marítimo area; its owner is a former chef of *Maxim's* in Paris, *Horcher* in Madrid and *La Hacienda,* Marbella. AE, DC, MC, V. *Antonio Martín* (M), Paseo Marítimo (tel. 22 21 13). Very popular, dining on terrace, in harbor area. DC, V. *Casa Pedro* (M), Quitapenas 121 (tel. 29 00 13). On El Palo Beach. Famous for seafood and fish. Huge dining room overlooking ocean. Popular—extremely so on Sun. Closed Mon. and Nov. AE, DC, V. *El Estribo* (M), Trinidad Grund 28 (tel. 22 13 14). Atmospheric Andalusian mesón with great tapas bar. Colorful and serving local dishes and Arab cous-cous. Closed Sun. MC, V. *Guerola* (M), Esparteros 8 (tel. 22 31 21). Central, tables outdoors in summer; original menu. *Refectorio IV* (M), Cervantes 10 (tel. 22 33 97). Good restaurant behind bullring in Paseo Marítimo area. Closed Sun. AE, MC, V. *La Taberna del Pintor* (M), Maestranza 6 (tel. 21 53 15). Steaks and Argentinian-style grilled meats. Closed Sun. AE, MC, V. *La Cancela* (I), Denis Belgrano 3 (tel. 22 31 25). Pleasant, typical and popular with locals. Good food, dining on sidewalk in summer.

On **Pedregalojos and El Palo beaches** (Málaga–Nerja road) there is a cluster of excellent seafood beach restaurants in summer. Especially good are *El Cabra,* Copo 21 and *El Lirio,* Copo 15.

Marbella. Málaga (952). *Don Carlos* (L), 13 km. (eight miles) east of Marbella on road to Malaga (tel. 83 11 40). 232 rooms. 16 acres of land-scaped grounds between beach and hotel. Two dining rooms, coffee shop, cocktail lounge. AE, DC, MC, V. *Hotel del Golf Plaza* (L), (tel. 81 17 50). 22 rooms. Luxurious and small in an isolated position, surrounded by golf course. AE, DC, MC, V. *Marbella Club* (L), out of town on road to Cádiz (tel. 77 13 00). 76 rooms, beautiful gardens, pool and bungalow accommo-dations; a 4-star hotel officially but its rooms are deluxe. AE, DC, MC, V. *Meliá Don Pepe* (L), Finca Las Marinas (tel. 77 03 00). 218 rooms. Super deluxe hotel with every amenity. Ask for room facing sea; larger rooms face onto parking lot, road and bleak mountains. AE, DC, MC, V. *Los Mon-teros* (L), on road to Málaga (tel. 77 17 00). 171 rooms; 18-hole golf course, tennis, pools, horseback riding. Marbella's most expensive hotel. AE, DC, MC, V. *Puente Romano* (L), on road to Cádiz (tel. 77 01 00). 198 rooms. Spectacular hotel and apartment complex. The "village" located between the Marbella Club and Puerto Banús has a genuine Roman bridge in its beautifully landscaped grounds which run from the roadside down to the beach. Two pools, all amenities, enormous disco. AE, DC, MC, V. These last three are classed *super deluxe.*

Andalucía Plaza (E), six km. (four miles) out on Cádiz road in front of Puerto Banús (tel. 78 20 00). 424 rooms, three golf courses, five pools and popular with conventions—not always good for the individual travel-er. AE, DC, MC, V. *El Fuerte* (E), Llano de San Luís (tel. 77 05 00). 146 rooms, pool. In center of Marbella overlooking Paseo Marítimo. AE, DC, V. *Marbella-Dinamar Club* (E), on Cádiz road near Puerto Banús (tel. 78 15 00). 117 rooms, private beach, pool, sauna, tennis. Formerly the Mar-bella Holiday Inn, this hotel has seen better days. AE, DC, MC, V.

Las Chapas (M), some way out on Málaga road (tel. 83 13 75). 117 rooms, pool, tennis and features a ring for teaching bull-fighting with hornless calves. AE, DC, MC, V. *Don Miguel* (M), Camino del Trapiche (tel. 77 28 00). 501 rooms; pool. Pleasantly set in own grounds at foot of mountains behind central Marbella. *Estrella del Mar* (M), on Málaga road (tel. 83 12 75). 98 rooms, by beach, pool, sauna, bowling. *Guadalpín* (M), about 1.5 km. out on road to Cádiz (tel. 77 11 00). 110 rooms, bar, gardens, restaurant; good value.

All the following are only (I) by Marbella standards. *Alfil* (I), Ricardo Soriano 19 (tel. 77 23 50). 40 rooms. Recently renovated hotel on main street. Bright, cheerful, and cheap for Marbella. *Club Pinomar* (I), on road to Málaga (tel. 83 13 45). 431 rooms. Many amenities including pool, mini golf, tennis and bowling. *Lima* (I), Avda. Antonio Belón 2 (tel. 77 05 00). 64 rooms. In town between main street and beach. *El Rodeo* (I), Victor de la Serna 2 (tel. 77 51 00). 100 rooms; pool. One block behind main street.

Restaurants. *La Hacienda* (L), Urb. Las Chapas (tel. 83 12 67). 12 km. (eight miles) out towards Málaga, in Las Chapas on north side of highway. Owned by Belgian Paul Schiff and rated one of the best in Spain. Closed Mon., for lunch in Aug., and mid-Nov. to mid-Dec. AE, DC, MC, V. *La Meridiana* (L), Camino de la Cruz, Las Lomas (tel. 77 61 90). One km. above the mosque on Puerto Banús side of Marbella. Famous for freshness of ingredients and original Bauhaus-type architecture. Closed Thurs., for lunch July to mid-Sept., and Jan. and Feb. AE, DC, MC, V. *Le Restaurant* (L), Rodeo Beach Club in Urb. Nueva Andalusia (tel. 81 06 26). Owned by famous French chef Roger Vergé; superb French cuisine in delightful surroundings with terrace overlooking sea. Open for dinner only. Closed Sun. and from Nov. to Easter. AE, DC, MC, V.

Cenicienta (E), Cánovas del Castillo (tel. 77 43 18). Friendly professional service, and high standards of cuisine await you in this pleasant restaurant with garden and pine grove on the ring road. *El Corzo Grill* (E), in Los Monteros hotel (tel. 77 17 00). Elegant gourmet dining. AE, DC, MC, V. *La Fonda* (E), Pza. Santo Cristo 10 (tel. 77 25 12). Another great Marbella restaurant. Owned by Horcher of Madrid; located in an old Andalusian house; hard to beat for sheer beauty and excellence. Be sure to book; dinner only. Closed Sun. AE, DC, V. *Gran Marisquería Santiago* (E), Paseo Marítimo (tel. 77 00 78). One of the best displays of fresh shellfish in Marbella. AE, DC, MC, V. *El Refugio* (E), (tel. 77 18 48). Andalusian house with terrace on hill three km. north of Marbella on Ojén road. Perfect service and unbeatable food. Closed Sun., Mon., and Feb. Open for dinner only. AE, MC, V.

La Belle Epoque (E–M), Vírgen de los Dolores 14 (tel. 77 84 45). Stylish decor and fine cuisine, in heart of town. *Mena* (M), Pza. de los Naranjos 10 (tel. 77 15 97). Great decor, or dine in the lovely square. Nearby on Vírgen de los Dolores and Los Remedios is a cluster of picturesque (M) and (I) restaurants such as *Casa Eladio* (M), *Marbella Patio* (M), and *El Balcón de la Vírgen* (I).

At **Puerto Banús** you'll be hard pressed to choose from the array of restaurants that grace the waterfront. The following are recommended: *Cipriano* (E), (tel. 81 10 77). Great fish. AE, DC, MC, V. *Don Leone* (E), (tel. 81 17 16). Open daily. No credit cards. *Taberna del Alabadero* (M), (tel. 81 27 94). AE, DC, MC, V. *Taberna del Puerto Pepito* (M), (tel. 81 53 44). Closed Wed. AE, DC, V.

Puerto Banús also has two excellent Indian restaurants: *Mumtaz* (E), (tel. 78 20 90). Northern Indian and Tandoori specialties. AE, MC, V. *Khans* (E), at far end of Muelle Ribera (tel. 78 43 71). Lovely decor with rainbow silk canopy and Indian classical music. AE, DC, MC, V.

Mazagón. Huelva (955). *Parador Cristóbal Colón* (E), Ctra. Mazagón–Moguer (tel. 37 60 00). 20 rooms; pool, tennis, garden. Quiet position, surrounded by pinegroves, with wonderful views over beach. AE, DC, MC, V.

Mijas. Málaga (952). *Byblos Andaluz* (L), Urb. Mijas-Golf (tel. 47 30 50). 135 rooms. Luxurious hotel situated between 2 golf courses, with provisions for every kind of sport and therapeutic treatment. AE, DC, MC, V. *Mijas* (E), Urb. Tamisa (tel. 48 58 00). 106 rooms; pool. Beautifully located hotel with rose garden, terrace, outdoor lunchtime buffets and stylish English teas; peaceful and delightful. AE, DC, MC, V.

Restaurants. *Valparaiso* (E), (tel. 48 59 96). Pleasant villa on road leading up to Mijas from Fuengirola. Dining to piano music. Dinner only. Closed Sun. AE, MC, V. *El Padrastro* (M), Paseo del Compás (tel. 48 50 00). Stunning view and good food; reached by elevator from main square. Closed Thurs. AE, DC, V. *Mirlo Blanco* (M), Pza. Constitución (tel. 48 57 00). Small, typical restaurant specializing in Basque cooking, in heart of old Mijas. AE, MC, V. *La Reja* (M), Caños 9 (tel. 48 50 68). Charming restaurant with two dining rooms overlooking main square, pleasant bar and an (I) pizzeria. AE, DC, V.

Mojacar. Almería (951). Only two hotels in the village itself and though they both have magnificent views, they cater mainly for tour groups; mediocre standards and service, but their location is a virtue. *Mojácar* (M), (tel. 47 81 50). 98 rooms, pool. Insist on a room with a view: *El Moresco* (E–M), tel 47 80 25). 147 rooms; pool. Much the better of the two. AE, DC, MC, V.

Down on the coast are: *Parador Reyes Católicos* (E), (tel. 47 82 50). 98 rooms; pool. Modern parador overlooking beach. AE, DC, MC, V. *Indalo* (E–M), (tel. 47 80 01). 308 rooms; pool. Vast hotel at far end of coastal development on road to Carboneras. AE, DC, V. *Continental* (M), (tel. 47 82 25). 23 rooms. Simple, motel type hostel on beach.

Restaurants. Both in the village are: *Mamabel's* (E), (tel. 47 80 44). Down steps near entrance to Hotel Mojácar. Lovely turn-of-century decor; food is good but not outstanding and prices are rather high. Closed Wed. in winter and Nov. AE, V. *El Palacio de Mojácar* (M), Pza. del Cano (tel. 47 82 79). In a lovely old Mojácar house with exposed beams and fireplaces. Friendly owner. Menu is small with some original dishes. Closed Thurs. and Nov.–Feb. AE, MC, V.

Nerja. Málaga (952). *Mónica* (E) (tel. 52 11 00). Luxurious new hotel with pool, tennis and disco; recommended. AE, DC, MC, V. *Parador de Nerja* (E), El Tablazo (tel. 52 00 50). 60 rooms, pool, pleasant gardens with view of sea. AE, DC, MC, V. *Balcón de Europa* (M), Paseo Balcón de Europa 5 (tel. 52 08 00). 105 rooms; a little faded but in lovely location with own private beach. AE, DC, MC, V. *Portofino* (I), Puerta del Mar 2 (tel. 52 01 50). 12 rooms; charming small hotel just off Balcón de Europa, with good restaurant with sea views. MC, V.

Restaurants. *Rey Alfonso* (high M), beneath the Balcón de Europa (tel. 52 01 95). Circular dining room with magnificent views over sea. Closed Wed. *Casa Luque* (M), Pza. Cavana 2 (tel. 52 10 04). In an old Andalusian house behind the Balcón de Europa church. Good small menu. Closed Wed. AE, MC, V. *Paco y Eva* (M), Barrio 50 (tel. 52 15 24). Friendly service, good Spanish cooking. *Cortijo* (I), Barrio 26. Family-run restaurant in a lovely old house. DC, MC, V.

Ojen. Málaga (952). *Hostelería de Juanar* (M), (tel. 88 10 00). Ten km. (six miles) beyond Ojen up in the sierra. Mountain refuge and hunting lodge converted into a charming small hotel. King Juan Carlos and Charles de Gaulle have stayed. AE, DC, MC, V.

428 SPAIN

Puerto de Santa Maria. Cádiz (956). *Melía Caballo Blanco* (E), on road to Cádiz (tel. 86 37 45). 94 rooms; pool. Nicely furnished, bungalows in garden, beach nearby. AE, DC, MC, V. *Puertobahía* (M), Playa de Valdegrana (tel. 86 27 21). 330 rooms; pool. Good amenities, close to beach. V.

Restaurants. Puerto is famous throughout Spain for its seafood restaurants. *Alboronia* (M), Santo Domingo 24 (tel. 85 16 09). In a beautiful 18th-century house with attractive garden patio and outstanding cuisine. Closed Sat. lunch, Sun., and Feb. AE, DC, MC, V. *El Patio* (M), Pza. Herrería (tel. 86 45 06) is one of the best. AE, DC, MC, V. In **Valdelagrana** are *Don Peppone* (E), Cáceres 1 (tel. 86 10 99), AE, DC, V. and *El Fogón* (M), Avda. Paz. 20 (tel. 86 39 02), DC, V. Both are famous.

Punta Umbria. Huelva (955). *Pato Amarillo* (M), Urb. Everluz (tel. 31 12 50). 120 rooms, some suites, pool and disco. Open June through Oct. AE, MC, V. *Pato Rojo* (M), Avda. Oceano (tel. 31 16 00). 60 rooms, magnificent view; with good value *Don Diego* restaurant (I). Open June through Oct. only. MC, V.

Restaurants. *Al Ayamontino* (M), Avda. Andulucía 13 (tel. 31 03 16). Going strong for over 50 years; good fish and regional dishes. DC, MC, V. *La Esperanza* (I), Pza. Pérez Pastor 7 (tel. 31 10 45). Run by same family since its founding in 1915; good home cooking.

Ronda. Málaga (952). *Reina Victoria* (E), Jerez 25 (tel. 87 12 40). 89 rooms; pool. Spectacularly placed in gardens on the very lip of a gorge, with impressive view; old-world atmosphere and rather faded. Popular with package tours. DC, V. *Polo* (M), Mariano Xouviron 9 (tel. 87 24 47). 33 rooms. Good old-style hotel. AE, DC, V. *Royal* (I), Vírgen de la Paz 42 (tel. 87 11 41). 25 rooms. Comfortable and good value.

Restaurants. *Don Miguel* (M), Villanueva 4 (tel. 87 10 90). Dining on terrace overlooking gorge. Atmospheric mesón decor. Closed Tues. night, Wed. in winter, Sun. in summer. AE, DC, MC, V. *Pedro Romero* (M), Virgen de la Paz (tel. 87 10 61). Opposite bullring with—yes, bullfight decor. AE, DC, MC, V. *Mesón Santiago* (I), Marina 3 (tel. 87 15 59). Typical Andalusian decor and pretty patio for summer dining. Open for lunch only. MC, V.

Rota. Cádiz (956). *Caribe* (M), Avda. de la Marina 62 (tel. 81 07 00). 42 rooms, some suites, pool. *Playa de la Luz* (M), Arroyo Hondo (tel. 81 05 00). 285 rooms, many amenities including pool. By the sea. surrounded by pinegroves. AE, MC, V.

Salobreña. Granada (958). Unspoilt Andalusian village on steep hill. Hotels and restaurants are all outside village. *Solobreña* (M), (tel. 61 02 61). Four km. out on road to Málaga. 80 rooms, pool and gardens. In a bend in mountains overlooking sea. AE, DC, V. *Salambina* (I), one km. out on Málaga road (tel. 61 00 37). 37 rooms, simple. AE, DC, MC, V.

Restaurant. *Mesón Durán* (I), 3.5 km. out on road to Málaga (tel. 61 01 14). Typical decor. Closed Wed. AE, DC, MC, V.

San Pedro de Alcantara. Málaga (952). *Golf Hotel Guadalmina* (E), Hacienda Guadalmina (tel. 78 14 00). A bungalow-hotel near beach; pool, tennis, golf, many other amenities. AE, DC, MC, V. *Alcotán* (I), on main highway (tel. 78 05 38). 84 rooms, pleasant location, pool and gardens. *El Pueblo Andaluz* (M), (tel. 78 05 97). 179 rooms, pool. On highway on Marbella side of San Pedro. *See also* **Estepona.**

San Roque. Cádiz (956). **Restaurants.** *Los Remos* (E), Playa de Guadarranque (tel. 76 08 12). Famous for its seafood, among the best on the coast. AE, DC, MC, V. *Don Benito* (M), Pza. de Armas 10 (tel. 78 07 78). In a pleasant old house with good French cooking. Closed Tues. V.

Sanlucar de Barrameda. Cádiz (956). *Guadalquivir* (M), Calzada del Ejército (tel. 36 07 42). 85 rooms, central.

Seville. See separate chapter on *Seville.*

Sierra Nevada. Granada (958). Most hotels open Dec. through May only. The Parador is open all year. *Meliá Sierra Nevada* (E), (tel. 48 04 00). 35 km. (22 miles) from Granada, at an altitude of 2,500 meters (8,200 feet). 32 rooms; pool, bar and restaurant. Very high rates. Open Dec. through Apr. AE, DC, MC, V. *Nevasur* (M), (tel. 48 03 50). 50 rooms, Open Dec. through May. Family-type accommodations. V. *Parador Sierra Nevada* (M), (tel. 48 02 00). 32 rooms. Small modern parador built in mountain style; the most pleasant.
Restaurant. *Cuniní Sierra Nevada* (M), San José 1 (tel. 48 01 70). Fish and seafood specialties. Open Dec. through Apr. AE, DC, V.

Sotogrande. Cádiz (956). *Tenis Hotel Sotogrande* (L), off main highway near Guardiaro (tel. 79 21 00). The Sotogrande estate lies between the beach and the foothills of the Sierra Almenara. It offers magnificent sports facilities, 3 golf courses, riding, polo, tennis, pelota and shooting. There is a long, wide, sandy beach and large yachting center. Highly recommended for sporty types. AE, DC, MC, V.

Tarifa. Cádiz (956). *Balcón de España* (M), on main road (tel. 68 43 26). 40 rooms, pool. AE. *Mesón de Sancho* (M), on road to Algeciras (tel. 68 49 00). A bungalow-hotel with pool. AE, DC, MC, V.

Torremolinos. Málaga (952). All hotels except *El Pozo* have pool. *Cervantes* (E), Las Mercedes (tel. 38 40 33). 393 rooms. Busy, cosmopolitan hotel in heart of town with an excellent panoramic restaurant on the top floor. AE, DC, MC, V. *Meliá Costa del Sol* (E), Huerta Nueva (tel. 38 66 77). 540 rooms. Apartment complex at Bajondillo Beach at end of Paseo Marítimo. AE, DC, MC, V. *Parador del Golf* (E), (tel. 38 12 55). 40 rooms. Modern parador at Málaga golf course halfway between Málaga and Torremolinos. AE, DC, MC, V. *Príncipe Sol* (E), at the end of Paseo Marítimo (tel. 38 41 00). 577 rooms. A little out of the ordinary with eastern style and marvelous buffets. AE, DC, V. *Tropicana* (E), Tropico 6 (tel. 38 66 00). 86 rooms. By the beach, beyond Carihuela. AE, DC, MC, V. *Al Andalus* (E July-Sept.) otherwise (M), Avda. de Montemar (tel. 38 12 00). 164 rooms; pool, tennis. AE, DC, V. *Amaragua* (M), (tel. 38 47 00). 198 rooms. Pleasant leafy location beyond Carihuela. AE, DC, MC, V. *Carihuela Palace* (M), Avda. Carlota Alessandri 27 (tel. 38 02 00). 156 rooms. Set back from the main highway, agreable resort hotel. *Eden* (M), Las Mercedes (tel. 38 46 00). 94 rooms. On a cliff in town center, all rooms have a sea view. *Lago Rojo* (M), Miami 1 (tel. 38 76 66). 144 rooms. Well maintained apartments all with balconies at back of main street of Carihuela. AE, DC, MC, V. *Miami* (I), Aladino 14 (tel. 38 52 55). 26 rooms. Charming Andalusian villa in a shady garden; helpful and friendly staff. *El Pozo* (I), Casablanca (tel. 38 06 22). 31 rooms. A pleasant Andalusian house in center. *Prammelinos* (I), Carlota Alessandri 180 (tel. 38 19 55). In garden full of palm trees, on highway leading out to Benalmádena. 35 rooms. AE, MC, V.

Restaurants. *Caballo Vasco* (E), Casablanca (tel. 38 23 36). Smart restaurant in center specializing in Basque cuisine. Closed Mon. and Nov. AE, DC, MC, V. *La Pampa* (M), Casablanca (tel. 38 10 41). Hamburgers, steaks, mixed grills, barbecue at reasonable prices. AE, DC, V. *Florida* (M), Casablanca 15 (tel. 38 73 66). Hot and cold buffet at fixed price and small à la carte menu. Dancing to live music. *León de Castilla* (M), in Pueblo Blanco off Casablanca (tel. 38 69 59). Large, elegant Spanish cooking, good wines; rustic decor. *La Primavera* (M), Guetaria (tel. 38 09 09). In attractive villa with outdoor patio with lots of flowers and foliage. Setting is a definite plus, service is professional, food average but well presented; a good place to dine outdoors. AE, DC, MC, V. *La Rioja* (M), in Pueblo Blanco off Casablanca. Atmospheric dining with good wines; meat dishes only, no fish. *Viking* (M), Casablanca 1 (tel. 38 10 41). Cozy and intimate spot with good Danish food. *El Atrio* (M), a delightful small French restaurant in Pza. de los Tientos in Pueblo Blanco. Dinner only. Closed Sun.

La Luna (I), San Miguel. Two flights up with terrace and rustic decor. Very popular. *La Pergola* (I), in Casablanca. Large pizzeria also serving (M) dishes.

On **Bajondillo** Beach are several good fish restaurants popular in summer.

The real gourmet area of Torremolinos is the **Carihuela.** To reach the Carihuela, turn left off the highway at Las Palomas hotel and make your way down to the beach and the Calles de Bulto and Carmen. It is fun to stroll along the promenade and choose your own restaurant from the many that line the beach, but here are a few suggestions:

Antonio (M), Bulto 79 (tel. 38 52 10). Attractive restaurant right at far end of Carihuela. Closed Mon. AE, DC, V. *El Cangrejo* (M), Bulto 25 (tel. 38 04 79). Even if you are not intent on full scale dining, you should visit its bar to sample some of the magnificent shellfish *hors d'oeuvres. Casa Prudencio* (M), Carmen 43 (tel. 38 14 52). Also well-known for its seafood. *Casa Guaquín* (M–I), Carmen 37 (tel. 38 45 30). and *La Concha* (M–I) at Bulto 35 are both pleasant bistros with a wide choice of menu. *El Roqueo* (M), Carmen 35 (tel. 38 49 46). Currently one of the most popular of the Carihuela restaurants, serving superb fish dishes. Closed Tues. and Nov. V.

A short walk from the Carihuela is *Europa* (M), Vía Imperial 322 (tel. 38 09 87). Pleasant restaurant with large garden and outdoor dining; much patronized by locals, especially for Sun. lunch. AE, V.

Ubeda. Jaén (953). *Parador Condestable Dávalos* (E), Pza. Vázquez Molina (tel. 75 03 45). 25 rooms. In a 16th-century palace, one of the oldest and loveliest of Spain's paradores. AE, DC, MC, V. *Consuelo* (I), Avda.

Ramón y Cajal 12 (tel. 75 08 40). 39 rooms. Simple, modern hotel not far from bus station.

PLACES OF INTEREST. Life everywhere else in Spain, it is always a good idea to check opening hours before making a special trip, particularly to more out-of-the-way places. Local tourist information offices should be able to help you with this.

Almería. Alcazaba (Arab fortress). With magnificent views over city and Mediterranean. Open 10–2 and 4–8 in summer, 9–1 and 3–7 in winter.

Antequera (Málaga). **Colegiata de Santa María la Mayor** (Collegiate Church of Sta. María), Pza. Sta. María. Fine Renaissance building with Plateresque facade, a National Monument.

Cueva de Menga (Menga Caves). Entrance one km. out of town at the Los Dólmenes gas station. Funeral chamber with 15 giant monoliths of ancient origin; a National Monument. Open daily 10–1, 4–6 (8 in summer). Close by is the smaller **Viera Cave,** open 10–1 and 3–5 (5–7 in summer).

Museo Municipal (Municipal Museum), in the Palacio de Najera. Mainly archeological collection, with 1st-century bronze Efebo de Antequera, one of Spain's most beautiful Roman statues. Open Tues. to Sat. 10–1.30, Sun. 11–1; closed Mon.

Aracena (Huelva). **Gruta de las Maravillas** (The Marvelous Caves), Pozo de Nieve. Caves with beautiful natural colors, lakes, stalactites and stalagmites. Open 11–7 in summer; in winter the caves are officially open 10–6 but usually only for group visits.

Aroche (Huelva). **Museo del Santo Rosario** (Rosary Museum). More than 1,000 rosaries donated by Pope John XXIII, King Juan Carlos and President Kennedy, etc. Open daily 10–1.

Cádiz. Cathedral, Pza. Pio XII. Open Mon. to Fri. 5.30 to 7.30, Sat. 9.30–10.30 and 5.30–8, Sun. 11–1.

Church of San Felipe Neri (St. Philip Neri), Santa Inés. Famous *Immaculate Conception* by Murillo. Open daily 12–2, 5–7; closed Sun. and July.

Museo de Bellas Artes (Fine Arts Museum), Pza. Mina. Worthwhile small art gallery with works by Murillo, Alonso Cano, and fine collection of Zurbarán canvases. Open Mon. to Fri. 10–2 and 5.30–8, Sat. 10–2 only.

Carmona (Seville). **Roman Necropolis,** Jorge Bonsor. Roman burial chambers with room for over 900 urns. Open Tues. to Sat., 10–2, 4–6; closed Sun. and Mon.

Cazorla (Jaén). **Museo de Arte y Costumbres Populares Alto Guadalquivir,** in the Castillo de la Yedra. Display of popular art. Open daily 9–1.

Córdoba. See *Practical Information for Córdoba* (page 389).

Granada. See *Practical Information for Granada* (page 402).

Huelva. Monumento a Cristobal Colón (Monument to Christopher Columbus), Punta del Sebo. Given by the United States and dedicated to the memory of Columbus and the discoverers of America.

Museo de Bellas Artes (Fine Arts Museum), Alameda Sundheim 13. Archeological finds from Huelva province and paintings by Vázquez Díaz. Open 10–2 and 4–7; closed Mon. and Aug.

Jaén. Cathedral. Open daily 8.30–1.30 and 4.30–7. Its **museum** is worth seeing.

Museo Provincial, Paseo de la Estación. Interesting Greek, Roman and Iberian ceramics. Open Tues. to Sat. 10–2, 4–7; closed Sun. and Mon.

Jerez de la Frontera (Cádiz). See also under *Sherry Tasting* below.

Church of San Marcos (St. Mark's Church), Pza. San Marcos. One of Jerez's most beautiful churches. Open daily 12.30–2, Sun. 11–12.30. Also 6.30–8 in summer.

Escuela de Arte Ecuestre (tel. 31 11 11). Call to arrange a visit to this famous Spanish Riding School. Performances are often open to public.

Museo Flamenco, Pza. de las Angustias (tel. 34 89 93). Opened in 1988. Call or check times with tourist office.

Málaga. Alcazaba (Moorish Fortress), Alcazabilla. Lovely views of Mediterranean. Open daily 10–1, 2–7 (5–8 in summer); Sun. 10–2.

Museo de Artes y Tradiciones Populares (Folk Museum), Pasillo de Santa Isabel 10. Houses costumes, cooking utensils, etc. Open daily 10–1, 4–7; closed Mon. and mid-Aug through mid-Sept.

Museo de Bellas Artes (Fine Arts Museum), San Agustín 6. Collection includes works by Murillo, Zurbanán, Ribera, Alonso Cano. Open Tues. to Sat. 10–1.30, 4–7 (5–8 in summer); closed Sun. P.M. and all day Mon.

Medina Azahara (Córdoba). Ruins of **Moorish Palace** on road to Almodovar. Open 10–2 and 4–6, Sun. 10–1.30; closed Mon.

Moguer (Huelva). **Casa Museo de Juan Ramón Jiménez,** J.R. Jiménez 10. Childhood home of writer, evoked in *Platero y yo.* Memorial collection. Open 10–2 and 4–8.

Convento de Santa Clara (St. Clara Convent), Pza. Santa Clara. National Monument with fine tombs and **Museum of Sacred Art.** Open daily 11–1, 4–6; closed Sun., and Mon. P.M.

Nerja (Málaga). **Nerja Caves,** 4 km. out off the road to Almuñécar. Paleolithic caves 12,000–20,000 years old with magnificent stalactites and stalagmites. Open May through Sept. 9.30–9; Oct. through Apr. 10–1.30 and 4–7.

Osuna (Seville). **Museo Arqueológico** (Archeological Museum), Pza. de la Duquesa. Iberian and Roman remains. Open 10–1 and 4–6.30; closed Mon.

Museo de la Colegiata (Collegiate Museum). 16th-century paintings with five works by Ribera. Open 10.30–1 and 4–6.30; closed Mon.

Monasterio de la Encarnación (Monastery of the Incarnation). Religious art collection and lovely patio decorated with 16th-century Sevillian tiles. Open 10–1.30 and 4–6.30; closed Mon.

Palos de la Frontera (Huelva). Columbus sailed from here for the New World. **Monasterio de la Rábida.** Where Columbus met Friar Juan Pérez who interceded on his behalf with Queen Isabella. Visits every half hour from 10–1.30 and 4–8; closed Mon.

Pizarra (Málaga). **Museo Hollander.** Exceptional collection of paintings and objets d'art collected by the Hollander family from the U.S. and on display in their own home, a converted 18th-century farmhouse. To visit, call 48 31 63.

Rincon de la Victoria (Málaga). **Cueva del Tesoro** (Treasure Cave), El Cantal. Prehistoric cave with artificial lake and *son et lumière* spectacles. Open daily 10–2, 4–7; closed Mon. in winter.

Salobreña (Granada). Unspoilt Andalusian village perched on a rock. **Arab Castle,** Andrés Segovia. Fantastic views. Open daily 9–2, 5–8.

Seville. See separate chapter on *Seville.*

Tarifa (Cádiz). **Baelo Roman Ruins.** On N340 ten km. (six miles) towards Cádiz. Important Roman excavations including aqueduct, town walls, theater, necropolis and several early tombs. Open 9–2 and 4–6; closed Sun. P.M. and Mon.
Castillo de los Guzmanes, Sancho IV el Bravo. 10th-century castle of Guzmán el Bueno fame. Open Sun. to Wed. 9.30–1.30.

SHERRY TASTING. *Bodegas* (wineries) can be visited in Jerez de la Frontera (the famous home of sherry), in Puerto de Santa María which also produces many fine *finos* and *amontillados,* in Sanlucár de Barrameda, well known for its tangy *manzanillas* (these three are close together in Cádiz province) and Chiclana de la Frontera. They all close in August for a month's holiday, and do not accept visitors in September when they are busy with the grape harvest.
Jerez. Some of the best-known bodegas are those of González Byass, and Humbert and Williams. González Byass have conducted tours every day except Sat., Sun., and public holidays. They are free, but *must* be booked 24 hours in advance. Humbert and Williams charge for their tours. Pedro Domecq have no tours at all.
Puerto de Santa María. Bodega Osborne, Calle Comedia (tel. 86 16 00). Open Mon. to Fri. 9.45–1.30; Sat. 9.45–12.15; Bodega Terry, Santísima Trinidad 2 (tel. 86 14 00). Open 8–1, but call to check.

AMUSEMENT PARKS. Tivoli World at Arroyo de la Miel, near Benalmadena Costa. A good amusement park near Benalmadena Costa with live shows including cancan dancing. Good restaurants offering a variety of food from Chinese, Danish, Tex-Mex to Moroccan. Especially good is a Provençal restaurant with mainly French food and a terrace from which you can watch Spanish ballet and dance. Tivoli World features a very good amusement park at Western Sq., including a Wild West show, Big Wheel, Octopus, 30 or so attractions, among them Mouseland and model trains. An open-air auditorium seats 4,000 with two good shows on Sat. and Sun. (usually 8 and 10 P.M.) Tivoli World is open Mar. to Oct.; opening time varies from 4–6 P.M., and is midday on certain Sundays. Show times posted at entrance, or call 44 28 48 for details.

Aqua Park, (tel. 38 88 88), just off the Torremolinos bypass near the Palacio de Congresos Conference Center. Water chutes, slides, artificial waves, water mountains and swimming pools. Open Apr. to Oct. 10 A.M–10 P.M.

PARKS AND RESERVES. Coto Doñana in Huelva province is a magnificent National Park, Europe's largest game reserve, covering 77,000 hectares (250,000 acres) of swampland known as *marismas.* It is a paradise for ornithologists with over 125 species of birds including Europe's last pink flamingoes. National Park authorities run day trips lasting four hours in Land Rovers through the reserve. The Park's information center is two km. out of Matalascañas. Tours (maximum of 56 people) leave daily except Monday and must be booked well in advance. They are conducted in Spanish only, but complementary English information packs are available from the information center.

Best time for bird watching is May through June and Sept. through Oct. July through August is too hot and the marshes become cracked mud. Binoculars essential. To book trip, write or call: Parque Nacional Doñana, Cooperativa Marisma del Rocio, Centro de Recepción, Matalascañas, Almonte (Huelva), tel. (955) 43 04 32. Treks start from the information center and sometimes collect passengers from resort hotels of Matalascañas.

SPORTS. Golf. The Costa del Sol is a paradise for golfers with five famous 18-hole championship courses, all in the vicinity of Estepona and San Pedro de Alcántara: *Aloha* (tel. 78 23 88); *Atalaya Park* (tel. 78 18 94); *Las Brisas* (tel. 78 03 00) in Nueva Andalucía; *Guadalmina* (tel. 78 13 17); and *Nueva Andalucía* (tel. 81 82 00). Many of the Costa's hotels have their own golf courses.

Tennis is also well catered for. Most hotels have their own courts and there is Lew Hoade's famous tennis club in Fuengirola.

Yachting can be enjoyed all along the Costa del Sol with notable marinas at Estepona, and the outstanding and trendy Puerto Banús, just west of Marbella.

Watersports. Swimming in the sea isn't always pleasant due to gray, gritty sand, pebbles and poor pollution control. Measures are now being taken by several of the Costa's towns to remedy this latter situation and pump their sewage much further out to sea, but all hotels of 3-stars and above must, by law, have their own pools and many 1- and 2-star hotels do too.

Waterskiing is available in many resorts.

EXTREMADURA

Land of the Conquistadores

The region of Extremadura, lying between Castile and Andalusia, partakes of the characteristics of both Kingdoms. Its landscapes are big and broad, with limitless horizons even when vast plains are broken by hills and valleys. Two of Spain's great rivers, the Tagus and the Guadiana, water these lands and then flow on through Portugal to meet the Atlantic Ocean. The Sierra de Gata and the Sierra de Gredos form natural mountain barriers to the north as do the slopes (gentle at this point) of the Sierra Morena to the south. The poet José María Gabriel y Galán has immortalized this scenery in simple and effective verse.

Asters and peonies grow wild, with rock roses on the hillsides where eagles nest. Fruit trees thrive, sheep roam the slopes, and in some sections acorns furnish food for pigs. Delicious jams are made from the fruits, and ham and sausage from the pork. Extremadura is famous for these products.

Time stood still in these harsh lands, whose population was drained to the Americas. Only recently has Spain's second wave of prosperity produced even in the remote west the large blocks of flats, whose deadening concrete sameness encroaches on the walled towns, fine churches and stately manor houses from which the Conquistadores sailed forth. After briefly touching down in Cuba, Hernán Cortés conquered Mexico with a handful of troops, lost it during the *Noche Triste,* and recaptured it, only to lose it again. Francisco Pizarro, the illiterate hog-raiser from Trujillo, conquered the Incas in Peru, while Pedro de Valdivia from Villanueva de la Serena added Chile to the Spanish possessions. Vasco Núñez de Balboa, to whom Queen Isabella was so attached that she didn't want him to sail, crossed the unexplored continent and 'claimed' the Pacific Ocean for his sovereigns. Another native of Jerez de los Caballeros, Hernando de Soto, thrust northward following the Mississippi upstream and became one of the first white men to set foot in what is now the United States. By the time violent death had overtaken them, they had brought Spain great wealth and vast territories.

If you are lucky you will run into a local fiesta that, in its naive charm, will be unlike anything that you have ever seen before. In Extremadura, celebrations that take place on the Feast of the Holy Cross on May 3 and at carnival time are among the best known, and weddings and baptisms retain traditional aspects long forgotten in other parts of the country. The local dances show the influence of Andalusia; the *seguidilla* is the most popular. Some Extremaduran dances are reminiscent of the Scottish sword dance and people say that they were learned from Wellington's Scottish troopers.

Whether you enter Extremadura from the north, continuing on N630 from Salamanca, or come in from Madrid, via Talavera de la Reina and Oropesa, on N-V, you enter the province of Cáceres; but coming from Madrid, your first good-sized town is Trujillo, while on the route we are following, it will be Plasencia.

Plasencia, Yuste, Coria and Alcántara

The location of Plasencia is somewhat similar to that of Toledo. It lies on a fertile, craggy promontory with the River Jerte flowing below and surrounding it on three sides. An important city in Roman times, it was reconquered from the Moors by Alfonso III of Castile in 1180. He built its double line of walls with their 60 towers, which are, however, almost entirely hidden by encroaching houses. The entire town has been declared of outstanding artistic and historic interest. The weekly market held on Tuesdays in the Plaza Mayor is well worth seeing and dates from the 13th century.

The cathedral, begun in 1498 in flamboyant Gothic, was finished in unmistakable Renaissance. The interior is of noble proportions and contains some rare works of art. The choirstalls, carved by Rodrigo Alemán, have been declared "the most Rabelaisian in Christendom."

Other churches worth seeing are the 15th-century Gothic San Nicolás and San Ildefonso, both containing beautiful tombs; San Pedro, a blend of Romanesque and Mudéjar; and the convent of San Vicente, whose sacristy is decorated with rare antique tiles. Still showing signs of former grandeur are the medieval manors, notably the Casa de Dos Torres, with its 13th-century door, and the Casa de las Bóvedas, which has a lovely garden.

The monastery of Yuste was founded in 1414, ravaged by the French in 1809, partly restored by the Marqués de Mirabel and is today guarded by Jerónimos monks. Forty-eight km. (30 miles) east of Plasencia in the wooded foothills of the Sierra de Gredos, Yuste possesses no scenic or architectural features which might explain its choice by the ruler of the largest part of Christendom. Yet Charles V declared this part of the country to be "perpetual spring." In 1555, when only 55 years old, tired of kingly responsibilities, he renounced his empire and retired to this bleak heart of Spain. The Emperor seems to have been torn between a desire for monastic simplicity and his gluttony, as well as between renunciation of the world and the anxiety over the Dutch policy of his son and heir, Philip II, to which he gave famous vent during a visit by the latter. Charles V died here in 1558 and his body rested in Yuste until 1574, when it was removed to the Escorial.

In nearby Cuacos, in the Plaza Don Juan de Austria, you can visit the Casa Jeromín where Don Juan of Austria lived while his father, Charles V, was at Yuste.

On the highway from Ciudad Rodrigo to Cáceres, there's an interesting stop at Coria which has kept its original walls, the best preserved in all of Roman Europe—483 meters (1,585 feet) long and 8 meters (25 feet) wide, with watch-towers 4 meters (13 feet) high. The castle and the cathedral are well worth the trip: the cathedral's single nave is Spain's largest.

Alcántara, derived from El Kantara, the Arabic word for bridge, is perched on a rocky point 48 km. northwest of Cáceres. In the early 13th century, it was rescued from the Moorish clutch by the Knights of Calatrava, who lived in the San Benito monastery. There are also elegant mansions, Santa María de Almocover (a 13th-century Romanesque church with paintings by Luis de Morales), and the bridge built under Trajan's reign during the second century; its strikingly pure arches are made of granite blocks assembled without any cement.

Cáceres and Trujillo

If you wish to visit a living example of a feudal town, stop off at Cáceres, with its steep, narrow, twisted streets, its medieval palaces, towers and temples. It was rebuilt by the Moors who called it Qazrix and whose ramparts still encircle the old city, topped by a dozen of the original 30 towers. Joined to the Kingdom of León by Alfonso IX in 1227, the whole of the walled city has remained intact with its fortified palaces, of which those of the Golfines, Pereros, Sánchez-Paredes and Solís, as well as the Cigüeñas Tower, are outstanding.

The visit is best begun from the vast Plaza Mayor beneath the Bujaco Tower; ascend the stairway to the Arco de la Estrella. Below the patio of the Baroque Veletas Mansion, which houses the Provincial Museum, is a large Moorish cistern. Opposite, on the highest point, stands the church of San Mateo, originally a mosque.

The 16th-century tower of Santa María—which has an outstanding Baroque altarpiece—looks over the modern statue of San Pedro de Alcántara on the delightful Plaza de Santa María, flanked by the Episcopal Palace, the Casa de Ovando and the Mayoralgo Palace with its Mudéjar patio. Some further architectural gems lie outside the walls, the Renaissance Santa Clara Convent on the one end, the Godoy Palace, facing the church of Santiago on the other. The whole town, old and new, spreads below the sanctuary of the Virgen de la Montaña, from which the view extends to the distant peaks of the sierras.

Pizarro, conqueror of Peru, was born in Trujillo, 48 km. east of Cáceres, and the palace of the Marqueses de la Conquista built with treasure brought back from the New World, still stands in the Plaza Mayor, one of the loveliest, with its 16th-century palaces—their corner balconies typical of the region, and swathed in aristocratic coats of arms—and the equestrian statue of Pizarro, executed like its duplicate in Lima by the American sculptor Charles Carey Rumsey. Pizarro's tomb is in the church of Santa María, which is also noted for its 15th-century reredos on whose 25 panels Fernando Gallego painted the *Life of the Virgin*.

Steep narrow lanes climb to the well-preserved Moorish castle. The convent of San Miguel and Santa Isabel was founded by Queen Isabella; triumphal arches recall victorious battles.

Guadalupe

The monastery of Guadalupe lies in an alpine setting 77 km. (48 miles) east of Trujillo and is well worth a visit. Let the monks be your hosts for the night or stay in the parador, a converted convent. Before getting down to exploring the vast monastery, spend a few minutes wandering through the little village with its quaint and archaic pillared houses. The monastery is the home of men who pay eternal homage to a physical representation of the Virgin which sits on a throne, with jewel-crowned head, protected by fortress-like walls. All the great of Spain have passed before her shrine.

The discovery of Our Lady of Guadalupe was a miracle of the year 1300. The Virgin appeared to a cowherd, blinding him by her brilliance, telling him to look for a statue of her that had been buried in the vicinity under a bramble bush. This statue, said to have been carved by Saint Luke, was unearthed and a chapel built on the spot, which gave way to a bigger church founded by Alfonso XI, endowed later, with benefices added. The facade of the church faces the village and its interior has Baroque decorations added in the 18th century. The magnificent 16th-century grilles were made by Giraldo de Merlo and Jorge Manuel Theotocópulos, the son of El Greco. The vestry is built like a church, with a chapel to St. Jerome decorated with superb paintings by Zurbarán. The vestry behind the altar contains sculpture by La Roldana and nine paintings by Luca Giordano. It is impossible to describe the jeweled robes, chalices, gold-and-silver-embroidered vestments, and other treasures that exist here in such profusion. A unique feature of the monastery is its Mudéjar cloister with its open pavilion decorated in brickwork and colored tiles.

Mérida and Badajoz

But this has taken us far east of our north–south route, to which we must now return. Pursuing it from either Trujillo or Cáceres brings us, in 84 km. (52 miles) from the former or 71 from the latter, to the city of Mérida in the province of Badajoz, where more important traces of the Roman epoch remain than in any other place in Spain, including a magnificent theater where classic dramas are still performed at night against a uniquely well-preserved backdrop of Corinthian columns.

Until quite recently, this Roman theater was buried under tilled land. It is 22 meters (71 feet) high and seats 4,000 on the partially restored marble tiers. The Archeological Museum is already Spain's most important, but further excavations are in progress.

In addition to this main Roman site, there is a very worn Arch of Trajan, and on the outskirts the high arches of the aqueduct, known locally as Los Milagros (the Miracles), a smaller bridge over the Albarrega and a truly monumental one over the Guadiana.

Forty-three km. (27 miles) east at Medellín, Hernán Cortés, the most dashing of the Conquistadores, was born in 1485. Unlike Pizarro, Cortés came from a prominent family and had studied at Salamanca. The pedestal of his equestrian statue bears the names of his heroic exploits: Mexico, Tabasco, Otumba, Tlaxcala. Across the Guadiana, spanned by a 17th-century bridge, rises a mighty castle protected by the square Homage Tower.

Another 14 km. takes us through well-irrigated farmland to Villanueva de la Serena, birthplace of Chile's conqueror, Pedro de Valdivia, commemorated by a bronze statue. Other attractions are the Baroque Asunción church, the convents of the Concepción and of the Franciscans, a number of hermitages and the 16th-century Town Hall.

Further east the Guadiana and its tributaries have been dammed up in a series of artificial lakes, which provide excellent fishing, especially at Lake Cijara in the 25,000-hectare National Reserve.

The last station on the trail of the Conquistadores is the birthplace of Núñez de Balboa and Hernando de Soto. The mansions and dazzling white houses of Jerez de los Caballeros, topped by the slender towers of numerous churches and ringed by ancient walls, lie in a broad plain framed by gentle hills planted with olive and cork trees, on the southern confines of Extremadura.

The charming small town of Zafra with its arcaded squares and white washed houses is one of the oldest in Extremadura and is well worth a short visit or even an overnight stay. Its 15th-century castle was built by Lorenzo de Figueroa and has a notable patio attributed to Juan de Herrera, architect of the Escorial. This splendid building which once gave hospitality to Hernán Cortés, is now a remarkable parador. Take a stroll through the nearby streets to see the Plaza Grande and Plaza Chica which have been expertly restored and boast several picturesque houses and noble facades.

Way over to the west, close to the border with Portugal, Olivenza is a graceful town showing a strong Portuguese influence in the Manueline style Gothic architecture of its two churches, Santa María Magdalena and Santa María del Castillo, and its early 14th-century castle. The facade of the Charity Hospice, founded 1501 by Manuel I of Portugal, is decorated with the arms of both Spain and Portugal.

Finally we come to Badajoz, capital of Spain's largest province. Though traces of its important role in Roman and Moorish times are still in evidence, today Badajoz is a rather run-down town which offers little to lure the tourist miles from his route; though should you be passing through on your way to Portugal, it perhaps justifies a visit of an hour or so. It must be said at this stage that its inhabitants are amongst the friendliest and most welcoming in Spain. On the left bank of the Guadiana, it is credited with a continuous, clear summer sky and a short winter. Founded by Romans as Pax Augusta, it reached its greatest importance in Moorish times as capital of the taifa, or kingdom; and the Alcazaba, residence of the Moorish kings, still dominates the walled section from the La Muela hill. The castle's battlements enclose the octagonal Espantaperros (Dog scarer, dog being a Moorish term of abuse for Christians) Tower, and the Archeological Museum within the fortifications.

Just below the fortifications lies the sadly dilapidated Plaza Alta which, until it was allowed to fall into its present state of decay, must have ranked high amongst those picturesque squares for which Spain is famous. It is worth spending a few minutes here if only to reflect on the motive that drives thousands of Spaniards to abandon their traditional homes in favor of the monstrous, faceless apartment blocks which now desecrate the outer limits of so many of their beautiful cities.

Other places to see in the lower town are: the cathedral, in some ways more akin to a fortress than a church, the intimate Plaza de Cervantes, with the writer's statue, the former gateway to the walled city (the Puerta de las Palmas), the Museum of Fine Arts, the bridge across the Guadiana and the lovely gardens that afford sweeping views over Vauban's fortifications.

PRACTICAL INFORMATION FOR EXTREMADURA

TOURIST OFFICES. Alcántara, Avda. de Mérida 21 (tel. 39 00 02). **Badajoz,** Pasaje de San Juan (tel. 22 27 63) just off Pza. de España; **Cáceres,** in Pza. Mayor (tel. 24 63 47); **Mérida,** Calle del Puente 9 (tel. 31 53 53); **Plasencia,** Trujillo 17 (tel. 41 27 66); **Trujillo,** Pza. Mayor 18 (tel. 32 06 53); **Zafra,** Pza. de España (tel. 55 10 36).

TELEPHONE CODES. The dialing code for the province of Badajoz is (924), and for the province of Cáceres (927). You need only dial these codes when calling from outside the province; within the same province, dial only the number. Dialing codes for all the towns we list are given under *Hotels and Restaurants* immediately after the name of the town.

GETTING AROUND. By Train. There are trains to Cáceres and Badajoz from Madrid and Seville, stopping at a few of the smaller towns on the way. Both Cáceres and Badajoz can also be reached from Lisbon. There is also a line from Cáceres to Badajos.

Train Stations. Badajoz Station (tel. 23 71 70) is across the river over the Puente de Palmas and the RENFE office is on Avda. de Celada 3 (tel. 22 45 62). **Cáceres** Station is on the N630 at km. 213 (tel. 22 50 61) and is connected to the center by Bus no. 1; the RENFE office is in Pza. Concepción 27 (tel. 21 36 06). **Mérida** Station (tel. 31 81 09)—and the Bus Depot—are at the end of Calle Cardero.

By Bus. There are plenty of buses running from Madrid or Seville to Mérida, Badajoz and Cáceres. There is a bus connection between Cáceres, Trujillo and Guadalupe, between Plasencia, Cuacos (for Yuste), and between Plasencia, Jarandilla, and Salamanca. Buses also run between Badajoz and Córdoba, Lisbon, Mérida, Jerez de los Caballeros, and Zafra.

Cáceres and Mérida both have bus depots. **Cáceres** Bus Station is on Gil Cordero (tel. 22 06 00) and **Mérida** Bus Station is near the train station at the end of Cardero. **Badajoz** main bus depot is on Avda. Pardaleras for Madrid, Andalusia, and most places south; for Cáceres and most places north buses leave from Joaquim Sama; for Portugal, check with the Tourist Office.

By Air. Badajoz has a small air base located 14 km. (nine miles) east of town at Talavera la Real (tel. 25 11 11). There are no *Iberia* flights to Badajoz, only *Aviaco. Iberia* in Badajoz is in the Hotel Zurbarán (tel. 22 06 15); *Aviaco* at the airport (tel. 25 35 98).

By Car. The main east-west route is the N-V from Madrid to Lisbon passing through Trujillo, Mérida and Badajoz. To reach Cáceres from Madrid, take the N-V as far as Trujillo, then N521 to Cáceres. Both of these are well surfaced roads with good views.

The main north-south axis is the N630 Salamanca–Plasencia–Cáceres–Mérida–Seville road. In the north this is a good road with easy driving, passing through the mountains of the Sierra de Gredos between Salamanca and Plasencia, then leveling out and offering some good views over the reservoirs of the Tagus, before skirting the outer edges of Cáceres. South of Cáceres, once into Badajoz province, the surface becomes very bumpy and is badly maintained as far as Mérida. South of Mérida N630 crosses the vineyards around Almendralejos and finally enters the mountains just before leaving Extremadura and continuing through Huelva province on its way to Seville. Although passing through mountains in both the north and the south of the region, N630 does not involve any very high or very twisty mountain driving.

The N523 from Badajoz to Cáceres is poorly maintained, particularly in Badajoz province, with a dreadful surface and camber, but does not involve any otherwise arduous driving. The N432 from the N630 via Zafra to Badajoz is a fairly good road with easy driving and some quite pleasant views.

The road to Guadalupe, the C401 Mérida–Toledo road, is now well surfaced and easy to drive along. The C501 Plasencia–Avila road skirts the Sierra de Gredos range, passing close to the Monastery of Yuste, the parador at Jarandilla, and close to the Sierra de Gredos parador.

HOTELS AND RESTAURANTS. Extremadura is a remote region, and apart from the two provincial capitals Badajoz and Cáceres, the only towns of any size are Mérida and Plasencia. Consequently there are fewer hotels here than in most parts of Spain, though accommodations are adequate and rates are usually very reasonable. Extremadura has four notable paradors, all located in historic buildings and convenient for some of the major sights: the *Parador Zurbarán* in Guadalupe; the *Parador Carlos V* in Jarandilla; the *Parador Vía de la Plata* in Mérida; and the *Parador Hernán Cortés* in Zafra.

Extremeño cooking is usually wholesome and comes in generous portions. Extremadura is famous for its meat dishes such as *cocido extremeño* (boiled meat and vegetables) and *caldereta* (lamb stew), and for its hams (especially those from Montánchez), its sausages and *chorizos.* Several wines are produced in Badajoz province and some of the best are Almendralejo white, Salvatierra red and Medellín rosé.

Badajoz (924). *Gran Hotel Zurbarán* (M), Paseo de Castelar 6 (tel. 22 37 41). 215 rooms. The only 4-star hotel in town but it needs renovating; close to the river. Pool. AE, DC, MC, V. *Lisboa* (M), Avda. de Elvas 13 (tel. 23 82 00). 176 rooms. On far side of the river with a good view over the town. V. *Río* (M), Avda. de Elvas (tel. 23 76 00). 90 rooms. Also across the river. Pool. AE, DC, MC, V. *Cervantes* (I), Tercio 2 (tel. 22 51 10). 25 rooms. Good budget hostel centrally located on the corner of Pza. Cervantes; low rates. *Conde Duque* (I), Muñoz Torrero 27 (tel. 22 46 41). 35 rooms. Modern and central. AE, DC, MC, V.

Restaurants. *Caballo Blanco* (M), Avda. de Europa 7A (tel. 23 42 21). Situated in the outskirts of town; modern and elegant. AE, DC, V. *Los Gabrieles* (M), Vicente Barrantes 21 (tel. 22 00 01). Close to central Pza. de España. Recommended by locals. AE, DC, MC, V. *Manila* (M), corner of Pza. San Francisco (Gen. Franco). A good restaurant upstairs, downstairs a popular, wellstocked tapas bar (latter (I)). *Mesón El Tronco* (M), Muñoz Torero 16 (tel. 22 20 76). Atmospheric mesón serving local specialties. Closed Sun. DC, V. *El Sótano* (M), Virgen de la Soledad 6 (tel. 22 31 61). Near Pza. de España, popular.

Cáceres (927). *Alcántara* (M), Avda. Virgen de Guadalupe 14 (tel. 22 89 00). 67 rooms. AE, DC, MC, V. *Extremadura* (M), Avda. Virgen de Guadalupe 5 (tel. 22 16 04). 68 rooms; pool. Readers report it a bit nondescript. AE, DC, MC, V. *Alvarez* (I), Parras 20 (tel. 24 64 00). 37 rooms. Friendly old-world hotel, central and comfortable. AE, DC, V. *Ara,* (I), Juan XXIII 3 (tel. 22 39 58). 62 rooms. Good facilities for a one-star hotel, though not right in the center. Noise from an adjacent discotheque can be disturbing. V.

Restaurant. *Figón Eustaquio* (M), Pza. San Juan 12 (tel. 24 81 94). Rustic decor. Plenty of local color. DC, MC, V.

Guadalupe. Cáceres (927). *Parador Nacional Zurbarán* (M), Marqués de la Romana 10 (tel. 36 70 75). 45 rooms. In an old convent. Pool and garden; lovely location. AE, DC, MC, V. *Hospedería del Real Monasterio* (I), Pza. Juan Carlos 1 (tel. 36 70 00). 46 rooms. Accommodations in the monastery annexe; a good alternative to the parador.

Restaurant. *Mesón El Cordero* (I), Convento 11 (tel. 36 71 31). Typical, with good home cooking. Closed Mon. and Feb.

Jarandilla de la Vera. Cáceres (927). *Parador Nacional Carlos V* (E), Ctra. Plasencia (tel. 56 01 17). 53 rooms. Late 14th-century castle associated with Charles V. AE, DC, MC, V.

Mérida. Badajoz (924). *Las Lomas* (E), on N-V highway (tel. 31 10 11). 139 rooms; pool. Good modern motel on edge of town. *Parador Nacional Vía de la Plata* (E), Pza. de la Constitución 3 (tel. 31 38 00). 45 rooms. One of the best paradores, situated in a magnificent old convent in the town center. Excellent restaurant. AE, DC, MC, V. *Emperatriz* (M), Pza. de España 19 (tel. 31 31 11). 41 rooms. In a medieval palace on the main square. *Nova Roma* (M), Suárez Somonte 42 (tel. 31 12 01). 28 rooms. Modern and comfortable. MC, V. *Zeus* (I), on the N-V (tel. 31 81 11). 44 rooms.

Restaurants. The *Parador* (E), see above, has an excellent restaurant. AE, DC, MC, V. *Nicolás* (M), Félix Valverde Lillo 13 (tel. 31 96 10). In a lovely old house in the center but the food and service do not always match up to the setting. AE, DC, MC, V.

Plasencia. Cáceres (927). *Alfonso VIII* (M), Alfonso VIII 32 (tel. 41 02 50). 56 rooms. Excellent value and a good restaurant. DC, V.

Trujillo. Cáceres (927). *Parador Nacional de Trujillo* (E), (tel. 32 13 50). 46 rooms. Recently opened parador in 16th-century Santa Catalina convent. AE, DC, MC, V. *Las Cigüeñas* (M), Ctra. Madrid–Lisboa (tel. 32 12 50). Pleasant, functional roadside hotel with garden.
Restaurant. *Hostal Pizarro* (I), Pza. Mayor (tel. 32 02 55). Good simple home cooking. V.

Zafra Badajoz (924). *Huerta Honda* (E), Avda. López Asme (tel. 55 08 00). 48 rooms. Modern, Andalusian-style hotel, centrally located near the parador. Atmospheric mesón-type restaurant, pool. DC, V. *Parador Nacional Hernán Cortés* (M), Pza. Corazón de María (tel. 55 02 00). 28 rooms. Remarkable parador, located in a majestic fortified palace, built between 1437 and 1443. Hernán Cortés, conqueror of Mexico, lived here before leaving for the New World. In the center of town. Pool and gardens. AE, DC, MC, V.

PLACES OF INTEREST. As so many of the villages and towns in Extremadura are so very remote, it is well worth calling in at the Tourist Offices in Badajoz and Cáceres and double checking opening hours. Many of the places mentioned below are kept locked and you will need to obtain the key from the local caretaker. If in doubt, check in Badajoz and Cáceres, or ask locally.

Badajoz. Museo Arqueológico, La Galera. Archeological museum in a former mosque. Open 10–2 and 5–7 (4–6 in winter); closed Sun. P.M. and Mon. A.M. **Museo de Bellas Artes** (Fine Arts Museum), Menéndez Valdés 32. In former Convent of Sta. Catalina now the Diputacion Provincial. With works by Zurbarán and several contemporary Extremeño artists. Open 10–2 and 4–6 in winter; 9.30–2 and 5–7 in summer; closed Sun.

Cáceres. Casa de los Caballos (Museum of Contemporary Art). On the edge of the old city behind the Casa de las Veletas.
Casa del Mono, in the walled city, houses the Museo de Bellas Artes (Fine Arts Museum).
Casa de las Veletas. Fortified, 15th-century with Baroque facade. Contains the Museo Provincial—artefacts from early eras plus important numismatic collection. Open 10.30–3.30 and 4–7; closed Sun.

Guadalupe (Cáceres). The **Monastery;** Mudéjar and Gothic cloisters, and beautiful sacristy hung with works of the 17th-century Extremeño artist Zurbarán. Open daily 9–1 and 3.30–6.30.

Mérida (Badajoz). **Alcazaba** (Moorish Castle). Built on a Roman site. Inside is a cistern with Visigoth pilasters and an archeological workshop. Open daily 8–1 and 4–7.
Museo Nacional de Arte Romano (National Museum of Roman Art). A striking new museum opened in 1986 and destined to house the best collection of Roman artefacts in Spain. Incorporates part of a Roman road

discovered during its construction. Open Tues. to Sat. 10–2 and 5–7 (4–6 in winter), Sun. 10–2 only; closed Mon.

Teatro Romano (Roman Theater). Mérida's finest monument was built by Agrippa in 24 B.C. and presented to the citizens of Mérida. In the same garden is the **Roman Amphitheater** built in 8 B.C. with room for 14,000 spectators. Both are open 8–8 (7 in winter) and can be visited on the same ticket.

Plasencia (Cáceres). **Catedral Nueva.** Gothic cathedral built in 15th–17th centuries by Diego de Siloé (and others) with choir stalls by Rodrigo Alemán. Open 9–1 and 4–6. **Catedral Vieja,** the old Romanesque cathedral from the 13th century is open the same hours.

Trujillo (Cáceres). **Castillo** (Castle). Moorish fortress which can be visited all day. **Iglesia de Santa Mariá la Mayor.** Beautiful, ravaged church, with famous alterpiece. If closed, the key is with a lady nearby.

Palacio Orellana, Pza. Juan de Tena 2. Outstanding patio and gallery, inhabited by a religious order. Open daily, 9–1, 4–8.

Plaza Mayor, Among the many interesting houses here—Palacio Duques de San Carlos, now inhabited by an enclosed order of nuns; balcony with doubleheaded eagle; open daily 9–1, 3–6.

Yuste (Cáceres). **Monastery.** The Monastery of Yuste where Charles V spent the last years of his life is two km. from the village of Cuacos. Open daily 9–1, 4–6.

TOURS. In the tourist season the Cáceres Tourist Office provides a guide hire service for the following tours, and one of their guides speaks English; Visit of Cáceres Old Town; Panoramic Visit of Cáceres; Nighttime Visit of Cáceres; Trujillo; Guadalupe; Plasencia; Cáceres Province Tour.

SPORTS. There are few opportunities for participatory sports in Extremadura but fishing, hunting and shooting are all popular.

Fishing. The cold, fast-flowing rivers of northern Extremadura abound in trout. The River Jerte is especially well stocked and the most popular fishing spot is the Garganta del Infierno (Hell's Throat). Other species of fish are found in the Guadiana River, the lakes of Cijara, Montijo-Lobón, Orellana, Piedra Aguda and Valuengo and in the lagoons of Cornalvo and Prosperina.

Hunting and Shooting. Rabbits, hare, partridge, quail, wild turkey, pigeons, duck, stags and wild boar can be hunted throughout Extremadura. The **Cijara Nature Reserve,** near Herrera de Duque, in the eastern corner of Badajoz province in the foothills of the mountains of Toledo, is a paradise for hunters. Permits must be obtained from ICONA, the national game and wild life board; details from Spanish National Tourist Offices.

THE ROCK OF GIBRALTAR

Tariq's Mountain

The future of the tiny British Crown Colony fondly nicknamed Gib, which dominates the Straits that divide Africa from Europe at the point where the Atlantic Ocean becomes the Mediterranean Sea, remains unclear. When Spain, which lays claim to Gibraltar on both geographical and historical grounds, applied for membership of both the E.E.C. and N.A.T.O., the contentious issue of Gibraltar proved a major stumbling block. After much negotiation between Spain and Britain, the border between Gibraltar and La Linea was finally reopened completely in February 1985 after nearly 16 years of closure (it was ordered shut by Franco in June 1969). The British, while happy to see the border reopened—indeed their side of the border has always remained symbolically open—are unwilling and to some extent unable to cede the rock to the Spanish, not least because the vast majority of Gibraltarians are determined to retain their colonial status and British institutions, despite years of friction and uncertainty. Gibraltar is also a vital N.A.T.O. port. The Spanish joined N.A.T.O. in 1982, voted in favor of staying in the Alliance in March 1986, and now clearly find it acutely embarrassing to use the port while Gibraltar itself remains in British hands. Fundamentally, however, they consider it an absurd anachronism that a part of Spain, as they see it, should remain in the hands of a foreign government, even if it is a friendly one, though, if anything, this final fact makes the problem all the more difficult.

Though 1986 saw Spain become a full member of the E.E.C. and confirm its intention to stay in N.A.T.O., the thorny question of Gibraltar is still seeking a solution. Nevertheless, some three million tourists a year are now flocking into the tiny British colony from across the Spanish border, and huge and expensive plans are afoot to develop the Rock's tourist potential, including building a modern tourist complex with a deluxe hotel, marina, casino, and shopping center. £1.5 million has been invested in a facelift for the four major hotels now that the long lean years of isolation from its Spanish neighbors on the Costa del Sol are finally over.

Home of the Barbary Apes

In ancient times, Gibraltar was one of the two Pillars of Hercules that marked the western limit of the known world; its position dominating the narrow entrance to the Mediterranean led to its seizure by the Moors in 711 as a preliminary to the conquest of Spain. They held it for longer than either the Spaniards or the British have ever done, a fact to which tribute is paid unconsciously whenever anyone pronounces its name, for Gibraltar is a corruption of Jebel Tariq, or Tariq's Mountain—Tariq was the Moorish commander who built the first fort of Gibraltar.

For nearly 750 years, Tariq's Rock was held by the Moors, until the Spaniards captured it in 1462 on the Feast Day of St. Bernard, now co-patron saint of the colony jointly with Our Lady of Europe, whose shrine has stood at the southernmost tip of Gibraltar for more than 500 years. The English, heading an Anglo-Dutch fleet in the War of the Spanish Succession, captured the Rock in 1704, after three days of fighting. After several years of skirmishing in the vicinity, Gibraltar was ceded to England by the Treaty of Utrecht in 1713. With the exception of the Great Siege, when a Franco-Spanish force battled at its ramparts for three years (1779–82), Gibraltar has lived a relatively peaceful existence ever since. During the two world wars, it served the Allies well as an important naval and air base.

The city of Gibraltar is always crowded, which is hardly surprising bearing in mind the geography of the Rock, which is just under five kilometers long and just over one kilometer wide on average. The upper reaches, which rise to a height of 522 meters (1,385 feet), are remarkably peaceful and a haven for the Rock's varied flora and fauna. A large proportion of the almost 30,000 inhabitants live within the medieval city walls. Pedestrians vie for space in its narrow almost sidewalkless streets. Though this is British territory, driving is on the right. Those wishing to drive into Gibraltar from Spain will require the following documentation: evidence of insurance, certificate of registration, nationality plate, and a valid driving license. Parking is a problem. After the reopening of the border in 1985, six of the Rock's tennis courts had to go to make way for a much-needed coach park. Some 8,000 visitors a day flock into this tiny enclave, attracted by its history, flowers and birds, VAT-free shopping, or just to visit the apes, and there can be few other places in the world where one is forced to enter by walking or driving across an airport runway.

Why should tourists fight their way into this crowded area, to sweat under the muggy prevailing wind, the energy-stealing Levante? Sights are not many, but the whole place is a spectacle in itself, with its remnants of a Moorish castle, its red-tiled roofs and pink houses, influenced by Spain, its police wearing the old-fashioned helmets of the London policemen, and its colorful, noisy, teeming, polyglot, permanent and temporary population. The main reasons are curiosity, the free port status, and—for the 100,000 expatriate Britons living on the Costa del Sol—the lure of British groceries and, not least, Marks and Spencers.

You must go to the upper Rock to visit the famous Barbary apes, the only wild apes in Europe, who are believed to know a passage under the sea from the caves of Gibraltar to the caves near Tetuán, in Morocco, on the other side of the 16 kilometers of water that constitute the Straits of Gibraltar. Legend also says that while the apes remain, Britain will continue to hold the Rock. Nobody puts any stock in that, of course, yet during the war, when the number of apes and Britain's fortunes were dwindling simultaneously, no less a person than Winston Churchill issued orders for maintenance of the ape contingent. Their numbers were built up, Britain's fortunes turned, coincidentally or not, as you may choose to believe, and today there are more than 60 apes split into two packs—the Queen's Gate and Middle Hill packs.

The famous Galleries of the Rock were carved out during the Great Siege, and although the only attack on Gibraltar since then was by aircraft in 1940, over 32 kilometers of tunnel were excavated during World War II, in preparation for a possible invasion.

Not far away from the stolid apes, you can explore the famous caves, especially the latest to be discovered, Lower St. Michael's Cave, revealed during fortification work in 1942, with its stalactites, underground lake, and mysterious subterranean breeze (perhaps coming from Africa?) Upper St. Michael's Cave was known to the Romans, and comprises a series of linked caverns. The most beautiful is the Cathedral Cave behind the auditorium, which seats 1,000 inside the Rock and hosts concerts during the annual Arts Festival.

A skull of Neanderthal man was found in Forbes Quarry some eight years *before* the great discovery in Germany. A replica is kept in the Gibraltar Museum, which is built above a complete 14th-century Moorish bath. You can discover the history of Gibraltar here and admire a large-scale model of the Rock as it was in 1865.

A memorable excursion will take you to see the wild dolphins in the Bay of Gibraltar. Or you can take a walk down the Mediterranean Steps, zig-zagging down the side of the Rock from the highest point; or a ramble in the Almeda Gardens. You can visit the little fishing village of Catalan Bay, populated by the descendants of Italian fishermen, who came here in the 18th century, or Trafalgar Cemetery, where some of the dead of that battle are buried. In addition, you can enjoy the laser experience in the World War II tunnels or take a stroll in the Marina. Or you can use the Rock as a base from which to visit Morocco—just 20 minutes away by plane, or one hour by sea—and Spain's Costa del Sol and Costa de la Luz.

PRACTICAL INFORMATION FOR GIBRALTAR

GETTING TO GIBRALTAR. By Plane. Currently *British Airways* and *Air Europe,* in conjunction with *GB Airways* operate daily flights from London Gatwick, and also flights from Manchester. Both operate the latest Boeing 737 jets on the route, taking about 2½ to 2¾ hours for the non-stop flight. In addition there are some charter flights from the U.K. in conjunction with package holidays, details of which are available from all good travel agents or from the Gibraltar Government Tourist Office, 179 Strand, London, WC2R 1EH.

Negotiations are well underway for *Iberia* to have landing rights in Gibraltar, which means that by 1989, flights between Gibraltar and other Spanish airports may well have been inaugurated.

By Road. Tourists and British and American residents of the Costa del Sol flock across the border daily in search of cheap purchases, causing a big parking problem on the Rock and long delays at customs. If you are driving a British car and have a British driving license, you need only your passport, driving license and insurance certificate to enter Gibraltar. If you are driving a Spanish car and hold a foreign license, you will need the above, plus vehicle registration documentation and a nationality plate.

Tours from Spain. *Juliá Tours, Pullmantour* and numerous cheaper small agencies operate one-day tours to Gibraltar from Costa del Sol resorts, daily except Sundays. A much cheaper way to visit the Rock is to take the regular *Portillo* bus as far as La Linea, then walk over the border, or alternatively *Portillo* buses run a daily Gibraltar trip in summer from Torremolinos, at a much lower cost than the commercial tours. Details from Portillo bus stations.

North Africa Trips. *GB Airways* runs two 20-minute flights a day to Tangier in Morocco, daily in summer, four days a week in winter. There are also day trips by air to Tetuan in the summer. A sea service by fast catamaran to Tangier runs daily in summer, a little less often in winter. Day trips to Tangier, including an optional tour of the city and its environs, can be arranged either by air or sea or a combination of both.

GETTING AROUND GIBRALTAR. Taxis carry a pink tariff card which you can ask to see. Fares are around £1 a mile, or longer trips by arrangement. There is a bus service, but as Gibraltar is so small, it is easy to walk almost everywhere. The cablecar to the restaurant on top of the Rock runs Mon. to Sat. but not on Sun.

HOTELS AND RESTAURANTS. The Rock is not over-blessed with hotels, and accommodation is tight in summer. However, winter visitors will find things easier. Out hotel grading system is divided into three categories. Expensive (E) £60 and up, Moderate (M) £30–45, Inexpensive (I) £16–25. All prices are for 2 people in a double room.

There is good selection of restaurants—this is by no means an exhaustive list—varying from small, select ones through the hotel restaurants, down to fast food. Chinese, Indian, Spanish, Italian, French and even the English tearoom can be found. Prices are fairly high after Spain and service and/or cover charge is often added to the bill.

Our restaurant grading system is as follows—Expensive (E) £15 and up; Moderate (M) £7.50–£12. Prices are per person for a 3-course meal without drinks.

Hotels

Holiday Inn (E), 87 Governor's Parade (tel. 70500). 123 rooms with bath, TV. Rooftop pool, sauna, nightclub. A very comfortable hotel recently renovated; in town center. AE, DC, MC, V.

The Rock (E), 3 Europa Rd. (tel. 73000). A £250,000 refurbishing is underway aimed at restoring its reputation as one of the luxury hotels of Europe; comfortable old-fashioned English atmosphere. Overlooks the harbor; pool. AE, DC.

Bristol (M), 10 Cathedral Sq. (tel. 76800). 60 rooms with bath or shower. In town, with a small garden with pool and bar. AE, DC, MC, V.

Caleta Palace (M) Catalan Bay Rd. (tel. 76501). 200 rooms with bath or shower, most with balcony, telephone. Restaurant, bars, disco, pool, boutique. On the cliff overhanging the picturesque village of Catalan Bay; the main package tour hotel. AE, DC, MC, V.

Continental (M), 1–3 Engineer Lane (tel. 76900). 18 rooms. Small hotel, geared to businessmen, on corner of Main St.

Gibraltar Beach (M), Sandy Bay (tel. 76191). 18 rooms and 103 apartments. Pleasant modern hotel on the beach on east side of Rock.

Montarik (I), Main St. (tel. 77065). 64 rooms with bath or shower. Bar, sun terrace with superb view of the sea and sunsets.

Queen's (I), Boyd St. (tel. 74000). 62 rooms, some with bath. Just outside the city walls with good views of the Rock and bay.

Self-catering apartments are also available at **Aparthotel Ocean Heights**, Montagu Place (tel. 75548), and **Gibraltar Beach Apartments**, Sandy Bay (tel. 76191).

Restaurants

La Bayuca (E), 21 Turnbull's Lane (tel. 75119). A long-standing restaurant, famed for its onion soup and Mediterranean dishes. Closed Tues., and Sun lunch. AE, DC, MC, V.

Casino (E), Europa Rd. (tel. 76666). Barbecues in the Japanese garden in summer; the dining room has great panoramic views. Open daily 10 A.M. to 4 P.M. AE, DC, MC, V.

Country Cottage (E), 13 Giro's Passage (tel. 70084). English cooking, specialties include steak and kidney pie, Angus steak and roasts. Bar and garden, opposite Roman Catholic cathedral. Closed Sun. AE, MC, V.

Spinning Wheel (E), 9 Horse Barrack Lane (tel. 76091). International cuisine, bar and terrace. Reservations advisable. Closed Sun. AE, DC, MC, V.

Strings (E), 44 Cornwall's Lane (tel. 78800). Bistro serving British, Spanish and Moroccan dishes; game and seasonal dishes on the blackboard specials. Closed Mon. and for lunch at weekends.

Bacchus Bistro (M), 28 John Mackintosh Sq. (tel. 71168). Informal bistro with pleasant outdoor terrace on the central Piazza.

El Patio (M), 54 Irish Town (tel. 70822). Ideal for anyone missing Spanish food. Basque-owned with delicious seafood. Closed Sat. lunch and Sun. June. V.

Woods (M), Marina Bay (tel. 79241). Excellent fish dishes. Closed Sat. and Sun lunch. AE, DC, MC, V.

TOURS. A city walking tour leaflet is available from the Tourist Office, as is information on dolphin safaris, fishing and boat cruises. **Church Tours.** A guided walking tour of places of worship, including the two cathedrals, leaves the Piazza Tourist Office on Wednesday at 10 A.M. **City Walls Tour.** Guided walking tour of sea walls and defenses leaves from the Koehler Gun in Casemates Sq. on Fridays at 10.30 A.M. **Bus Tours.** Numerous tour operators ply for business near the frontier. Guided minibus tours are a good way of seeing all the Rock. **Calypso Tours,** 21 Horse Back Lane (tel. 76520) run excellent 2-hour tours.

MUSEUMS. Gibraltar Museum, Bomb House Lane (tel. 74289). Tells the Rock's story from prehistoric times through the Great Siege of 1779–1783 and the battle of Trafalgar up to the present day. Open Mon. to Sat. 10–6.

Moorish Castle, built by the Moorish conquerors and restored in 1333. Only a ruined tower remains with marks in its walls made by cannonballs during the Great Siege. Open 10–7 (10–5.30 in winter).

St. Michael's Cave, halfway to the Rock summit (tel. 76400). A natural cave 1000 ft. above sea-level with a fantastic display of stalactites and stalagmites. Open 10–7 (5.30 in winter).

Upper Galleries. Tunnels cut out of the sheer rock over 1000 meters deep with gun embrasures from a previous era are now displayed with tableaux so lifelike that the tourist moves stealthily. During World War II army engineers excavated some 40 km. of tunneling even deeper into the rock. Obey directions and do not get lost! Open 10–7 (5.30 in winter).

SHOPPING. Shopping has always been a big attraction in Gibraltar, not least because of the many duty-free, or rather duty-reduced, goods. Alcohol and tobacco prices are somewhat lower than in Spain, but the real bargains are in electrical and hi-fi goods, cameras, watches and certain fashion accessories.

USEFUL ADDRESSES. *Gibraltar Tourist Office,* Cathedral Sq. and The Piazza, John Mackintosh Sq. (tel. 76400). Open 8.45–5.30. *GB Airways,* Blands Office, Cloister Bldg., Market Ln. (tel. 79200, ext. 225).

Emergency numbers: police 190; fire brigade and ambulance 199; St. Bernard's Hospital 79700.

THE BALEARIC ISLANDS

Mallorca, Menorca, Ibiza and Formentera

Until comparatively recent times, this group of 16 islands was officially divided into two groups, one consisting of Mallorca (usually known to English people as Majorca) and Menorca, to which the name "Balearic" refers (originated by the Greeks who found there the *balearii,* or stone-slingers), along with Cabrera and seven uninhabited islands, and the other, the more western group, of Ibiza, Formentera and four other islets, which were known as the Pityuses or Pine Islands. Today, however, this whole area, a geological continuation of the Andalusian mountain range which runs under the sea from Cape Nao on the mainland, is included under the Spanish name Baleares, and is a separate, semi-autonomous province of Spain, with Palma de Mallorca as its capital.

Although each island has its own local Mallorquín patois with a strong French influence, the language, basic customs and race are akin to Catalan, rather than Spanish. The islanders, despite their stormy history as the pawns in the struggle between overwhelmingly more powerful peoples, have preserved a distinct character and personality different not only from those outside, but also from each other. They have also managed to preserve some remarkably unspoiled countryside and ancient small towns in contrast to the ugly modernity forced on many coastal areas by the pressures of mass tourism.

A Little History

The Balearics provided Hannibal (reputedly born on the small island of Conejera, northwest of Ibiza) with his only regiment of stoneslingers, which won fame in many battles with Rome. Even earlier, in the semi-mythical times of the Greek Argonauts, it was in Mallorca that Hercules found the Golden Apples (oranges), and here that the last High Priestesses of the Mother Cult held court in the mysterious depths of the Caves of Drach, one of the five official gateways to the underworld of the Ancients.

The Vandals seized the islands from the Romans in A.D. 455 and, except for a brief Byzantine reconquest under Belisarius, held them until the Moors took over in 798. For four centuries, Palma was the home port of particularly skillful and bloodthirsty pirates, who ravaged the coast as far as Italy and menaced communications. It was not until 1229 that Jaime of Aragón broke the Moorish hold upon the islands and proclaimed himself King of Mallorca. Many of the islands' finest old buildings date from this period of independent Mallorquín kings. Under its fourth king Mallorca was conquered by Pedro IV of Aragón in 1343, and became part of Spain. In the War of the Spanish Succession, Mallorca escaped the wrath of Marlborough and the British fleet by siding with the Austrian Pretender against Louis XIV's grandson Philip V, but Menorca was occupied continuously by the British, except for an interval of 17 years, from 1708 until 1802.

Mallorca lies roughly 210 km. (130 miles) south of Barcelona, and 225 east of Valencia. Mahón, Menorca's largest city, is 161 km. (100 miles) northeast, and Ibiza 113 km. (70 miles) southwest of Palma. Ibiza, the southernmost of the islands, is only 105 km. (65 miles) from the mainland, its nearest ports of contact being Valencia and Alicante.

Weather Matters

All year round, Mallorca has an especially fine climate, though winters can be cold and damp. Generally speaking, Ibiza is hotter and Menorca colder than Mallorca in all seasons, but these are relative differences. The swimming season runs from April to November.

In Mallorca, the best seasons are May-June and September (though the entire island is a mass of pale pink almond blossoms in February). Rain is more likely in February–April and October–November. Palma itself can be almost uncomfortably hot in July–August, but the countryside is cooler, especially by the sea. Along the southern coast of Mallorca, the season is from April until October, inclusive. The northern coast, being more exposed, is for the summer only, with the notable exception of Formentor, which lies in a huge, sheltered bay at the northeast tip of the island. Here you can swim in March and November. The huge open beaches of Pollensa, Alcudia and Cala Ratjada in the northeast are also summer-only centers.

Menorca's climate is totally different from that of its big sister, with changeable skies, cooler temperatures, and greener vistas. It is at its best from May to September.

Ibiza, the hottest of the three (it can be blistering in midsummer), allows swimming at any time of the year. As the locals say, "Mallorca looks to Spain, Menorca looks to France, and Ibiza looks to Africa."

Mallorca

The Balearics are among the most touristically developed islands in the Mediterranean, with plenty of modern accommodations and easy accessibility, giving many northern Europeans their first experience of Mediterranean sun. Mallorca is the big sister, being some 97 km. long by 80 wide—with a total area of 3,641 square km.—and having a population of about 590,000, almost half of which lives in the capital city, Palma. The floating population increases year by year. In fact, Mallorca arguably welcomes more visitors than any other place in Spain: more than five million in 1988. The population of Ibiza is 71,000; Menorca, 62,000.

Visitors to Palma who come by sea are likely to be impressed by their first view of some outstanding landmarks including the magnificent 13th-century Gothic cathedral, the nearby almost contemporary Lonja (the former exchange) and the Convent Church of San Francisco, with its exquisite cloisters, and the 14th-century Castle of Bellver, stronghold of the kings of Mallorca in medieval times. In the center of the bay, a low cliff rises immediately above the port, and from here to the Bellver, or western end of the bay, known as El Terreno, are the countless hotels, brilliantly illuminated at night, in witness of the island's popularity. When arriving by air the approach from airport to city is rather less impressive, along a modern dual highway until one reaches the waterfront, dominated by the cathedral, and city center.

In Palma itself, there remain areas of picturesque, narrow, winding 17th-century streets. You will find a stroll through the old town quite as rewarding as the obligatory visits to the cathedral and Bellver Castle.

The cathedral looks at its best from the sea because only from a distance is it possible to appreciate its majestic proportions. The central of the three great naves, forested by 14 graceful 22-meter- (66-foot) high pillars, is 74 meters (244 feet) long and 46 (150 feet) wide, and although it is rather dark and austere in appearance, it contains many treasures. Here are the tombs of two of Mallorca's four kings, and also of the anti-Pope Clement VII, who died in 1447, all illuminated by one vast and beautiful rose window, the world's largest. It was built between 1230 and 1601, the cloisters being 18th-century Baroque. Expressive sculptures adorn the fine Gothic doorway which faces out toward the sea, while the interior of the cathedral and its museum contain many pictures, carved stalls, altar pieces and gold plate.

Of special interest to Americans is the 14th-century monastery of San Francisco, from which Junipero Serra, a native of Mallorca, departed for California, where he founded the city he named for his alma mater. Important features of the monastery are its superb cloister and church.

Almost next door to the cathedral is the huge Almudaina Palace which served in turn as residence of the Moorish governors, the Walis, and the independent Mallorquín kings. It contains superb Gothic and Romanesque palace rooms and chapels which are unfortunately not open to the public, as this is now the military Governor General's headquarters. However, there is a museum within the palace with a general collection of antiques, which is open.

At the other end of the city, it is a long and hot climb to Bellver—as no doubt an attacking enemy was intended to discover—so take a taxi.

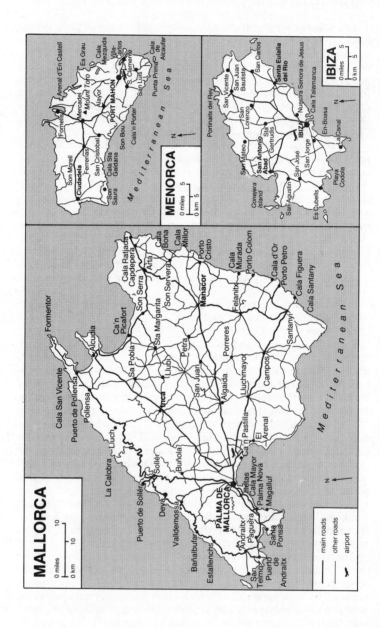

Even then, you still have to climb up a circular stone stairway to reach the top of the tower. The view along the coast and inland across pine forests and almond groves makes the effort well worth while. The castle was built by King Jaime II at the beginning of the 14th century and contains a most attractive circular courtyard and historical museum.

Also worth seeing in Palma is the Lonja, the former exchange, now used for exhibitions. Started in 1426, it is one of the most interesting examples of the Spanish Gothic style, remarkable for the clearcut elegance of its lines. Until early this century the sea came up to its walls.

But Palma is not just a place for sightseeing. It is a wonderful place simply to wander in, sit and enjoy a drink or a good seafood lunch or, especially, shop. The leatherwork of Mallorca is excellent, as are the ceramics, glasswares, artificial pearls, woodcarvings and wrought ironwork. These are of the best quality and very reasonable. This is also a good hunting ground for antiques, real and reproduction.

There are numerous good bathing beaches strung along the 19 km. (nearly 12 miles) of the Bay of Palma, but due to poor planning during the early boom days of tourism development a number of high-rise resorts of garish character and lack of any charm were allowed to grow. Other parts of the island provide a refreshing contrast to these awful commercial centers.

Excursions Around Mallorca

For visitors with an urge to explore, Mallorca lends itself to a number of half-day and full-day excursions, all of which can be made from Palma. Attractions close to the city include the extensive Marineland, with dolphin shows, and the gambling casino, but for those who would like to experience the full scenic and sightseeing diversity of the island, we recommend taking a self-drive hire car to explore a number of routes. The first of these takes you westward to Cala Mayor, Palma Nova, the beach at Paguera, Andraitx, Camp de Mar and Puerto de Andraitx. This excursion can be combined, in a single day, with the second one, below.

The second itinerary takes a full day, northwest to Bañalbufar and Estallenchs for the best coastal scenery, then back to Valldemosa and on north through Deya to Sóller and Puerto de Sóller. You can return by a different route over a mountain pass to visit Alfabia, the Moorish gardens near Buñola. Total distance 121 km. (75 miles).

The third, also all day, heads northeast through Inca to Alcudia, then on to Formentor in the extreme northeast before returning via Pollensa, the monastery at Lluch and the spectacular coastal scenery around La Calobra. Total distance, 170 km. (100 miles).

The fourth turns east from Palma for Manacor, Porto Cristo and the fabulous Caves of Drach, Son Servera and the Caves of Artá, and back, at the end of the day, via Inca. Total distance, 193 km. (120 miles). This distance can be reduced by returning from Artá to Palma via Manacor.

A fifth excursion turns south through Lluchmayor (with a short detour to the mountain monastery of Randa), to Campos, Cala Figuera, Santañy, Cala d'Or and Cala Marsal. Total distance, 158 km. (98 miles).

These trips, of course, include only the highlights of Mallorca. The island has any number of half-hidden little bays and romantic mountain villages that can be discovered only by settling down outside of Palma and

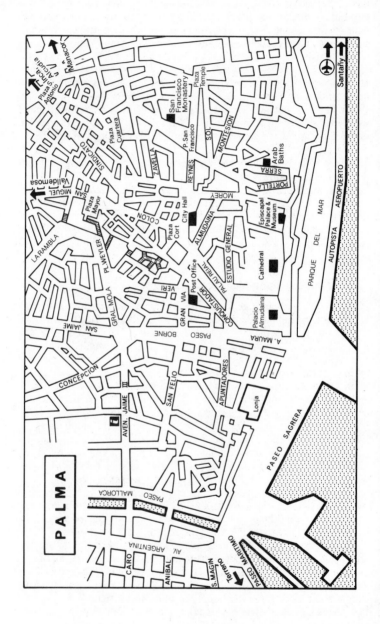

PALMA

exploring a particular region in detail. Despite its great and growing popularity, Mallorca, fortunately, is just large enough for this kind of discovery still to be possible. One still undeveloped spot is Petra, 40 km. (25 miles) from Palma, with its Fray Junipero Serra, a museum-library honoring the founder of California's chain of Spanish missions. Next door is the house where Father Serra was born in 1713.

Although Mallorca has few railway lines, these (with the exception of the one to Sóller) are not to be taken seriously by anyone except an antiquarian. Do your exploring by road, either on one of the excursion buses that visit most places of interest or, ideally, by hired car. If hiring a car, note that most gas stations are closed on Sundays and holidays and that use of seat belts is obligatory outside towns (there is a heavy fine).

Palma West to Puerto de Andraitx

This excursion takes you through all the new holiday resorts from the fashionable Terreno at the west end of Palma Bay, to Bendinat, Cala Mayor, C'as Catalá, Illetas and Palma Nova, from where there are various boat services direct to Palma. This region, rich in pine forests, is full of historical associations, but much of it has been spoiled by touristic and property development.

Palma Nova and Magalluf are huge developments of hotels and apartment blocks, conjured out of thin air. There was absolutely nothing there three decades ago except the hills sweeping down to the sand and the sea. It is the symbol of what modern Mallorca is all about.

The road crosses a broad headland to return to the sea at the great Paguera beach, Cala Fornells, and, branching off to the left, Camp de Mar. This last has a particularly fine sandy beach, and from it, a wooden bridge heads to a tiny, rocky island. On the island is a cafe-bar-restaurant justly famous for its deliciously fresh lobsters and prawns. Back on the main road you will be four km. (two-and-a-half miles) from the little agricultural town of Andraitx, and another four from Puerto de Andraitx, a picturesque little fishing town and, now, marina with a growing number of good hotels and restaurants. From here, once you are clear of the deep rocky bay, the coast is magnificent. From Puerto de Andraitx you can make a delightful six-km. (three-and-three-quarter-mile) walk to the fishing village of San Telmo, from where boat excursions serve the totally unspoilt island of Dragonera.

There is an alternative inland route home from Andraitx through Capdella and Calvia, through hilly country green with almond groves.

Palma North to Puerto de Sóller

Crossing the island at its narrowest point, the road from Palma winds north and slightly west for some 27 km. (17 miles), twisting through orange groves and around mountains in such a way that you will need an hour to reach the sea and Bañalbufar. En route, you pass the fine old manor house of Son Forteza, near Esporlas, where there are some fine 17th-century mansions that once belonged to Spanish nobles. Esporlas itself, set picturesquely above the bed of a dry river, is famous for its especially lightweight woolen skirts, banded with bright color. Nearby, La Granja is an 18th-century farm with lovely gardens and restaurant which also presents folkdance shows and handicraft displays.

Bañalbufar is also attractive, though its wealth is not from tourists. The land is steeply terraced for the cultivation of a winter crop of potatoes and a summer crop of the strongest flavored tomatoes in all Spain, much in demand for use in ketchup.

Just beyond Bañalbufar you come to a ruined stone lookout tower, reached by a narrow stone bridge. This is known as the Tower of the Owls, and from it you can see the finest stretch of majestic coastal scenery anywhere in the Mediterranean. If you want to save yourself a twisting 28-km. (17½-mile) ride south of Bañalbufar to Andraitx, you can get a fair idea from here of what the remaining stretch is like by driving eight km. (five miles) to Estallenchs, and then turn north for 18 km. (11 miles) to Valldemossa. However, if all the narrow twists and turns do not put you off, go on the exciting trip to the south as far as the Belvedere of Ricardo Roca; the spectacular view is worth it.

Valldemossa

A great deal of sentimental nonsense has been written about Valldemossa (principally by German and French authors), because Chopin and George Sand spent a miserable winter here in 1838. This whole cult is false, chilly, and quite unmoving. True, the boom of the church clock can be recognized in Chopin's Prelude, Opus 28, No. 2, but the cells where the famous lovers stayed seem phoney today. The two pianos used by the great composer, together with the fresh white rose that is laid each morning on the keyboard, may be authentic, but George Sand's "silk" stockings are surely 20th-century nylon. Those who get a thrill from contemplating the scene of an illicit affair, even after more than a century, might recall that while the lovers stayed here, Chopin's consumption got worse, and the locals stoned George Sand until she gave up wearing trousers in public. At least the lovely little flower-filled garden outside Chopin's cell is genuine and charming, and so is the view down into the wooded valley. Valldemossa also boasts several aristocratic residences, and a Chopin Festival, in July to August. Points of interest in the monastery include the small Chopin–George Sand Museum, a recreation of an ancient apothecary's shop and an old library.

The scenery beyond Valldemossa grows more enchanting with every kilometer until you reach Deya, whose inhabitants still gather on the beach at the sound of a conch shell, the signal of the fishing fleet's return. Deya was the home of the British poet and novelist Robert Graves until he died in December 1985.

The coast beyond Deya is haunted by the late Luis Salvator of Toscana, Archduke of Austria, who wrote an extremely influential six-volume work on the Balearics, and built himself two large houses here, high above the sea, together with a special carriage road leading to his private anchorage. The house, "Son Marroig," is now open to the public. Concerts of Baroque music are held year-round every Sunday at 5.30 P.M. in winter, 6.30 P.M. summer.

Sóller, a major orange-growing center, contains little of tourist interest, but it is only five kilometers to Puerto de Sóller, one of the few safe ports along the whole 97-km. (60-mile) length of the island's cliff-bound northern coast. It is more than safe; it is almost closed off, so that you cannot see the open sea from the port, only the neat, circular bay itself, surrounded by the ubiquitous hotels. A delightful way to reach Sóller is by the little antique train which runs five times daily from Palma. In Sóller this connects with an equally antique tram to the Puerto.

By car you can return south, direct to Palma over a 610-meter (2,000-foot) pass, from which there is a fine view. As you descend, you will see the gnarled and twisted shapes of thousand-year-old olive trees, seeming to writhe as if in agony. A pleasant stop is in the lovely old mansion and Moorish gardens of Alfabia, or, just off the main road, the old town of Bunyola with its impressive Baroque church.

Alternatively, you can take the road that leads up the valley from Sóller to Fornalutx, a peaceful mountain village, and beyond to the Puig Mayor, at 1,440 meters (2,317 feet) the highest mountain on the island. This used to be a trip that could be done only on foot or donkey, but now the road curls right up to the top, giving breathtaking views back to the sea. Once over the top you can return to Palma via Inca.

Palma Northeast to Formentor

The journey from Palma through Inca to the north coast provides an excellent opportunity of getting to know the varied character of the landscape of Mallorca. At the first town clear of Palma, Santa María, you can sample a glass of delightful anisette in a bodega full of local color and run by a Franciscan convent called Minimos.

Inca is an easy drive of 27 km. (17 miles) from Palma along the road to Alcudia, and can also be reached by daily train or bus from Palma. It is famous for its market on Thursday morning, its old shops, its folk dances, particularly those to be seen at Corpus Christi and on August 2, and for its 13th-century church of Santa María la Mayor—worth visiting, despite the defacing 18th-century additions. Most visitors stop off at the Celler Ca'n Ripoll, where 12 vast and ancient olive-wood casks each once held 4,000 liters of the modest local wine. The wine varies from the sweet muscatel to a dry red that tastes like a medium sherry. Try the roast suckling pig, or any other of the numerous delightful tasty tapas they have to offer. This region owes a good deal of its prosperity to the large shoe factories and to the leather industry in general. In Lloseta, approximately three km. northwest of Inca, you'll find the Palacio Ayamans, a noble family's old mansion with authentic furniture and antiques; open daily in summer, except Sundays.

Around Inca, the soil is so good and the water so plentiful that farmers can raise three crops a year from the same field. Everywhere the landscape is dotted with the typical Mallorquín windmills, used to draw up this precious water, although motor pumps have now mostly taken over the job. On the main road, after Inca and just before the turnoff to Campanet, a large tower on the left marks the location of an interesting hand-blown glass factory.

Alcudia is some 53 km. (33 miles) from Palma, situated on the southern of the two large sand-beached bays in the extreme northeast. It is an ancient town, site of the main Roman settlement on the island, then called Pollentia. It has a small, rustic, Roman theater, modest museum and restored medieval walls and gates. Alcudia was the last stronghold of the Moors when Jaime the Conqueror landed in the west of the island. Its name means 'the hill' in Arabic. Its streets are picturesque, but few stop to look at the old town, although its markets, held on Tuesday and Sunday mornings, attract many tourists in summer.

Puerto de Alcudia lies in the northern corner of the huge sweep of the Bay of Alcudia—32 km. (20 miles) of unbroken beach of almost-white sand, though the road swings inland at Ca'n Picafort less than halfway along. Inland, it is flat and swampy (there is an important migratory bird sanctuary here called S'Albufera), but the number of apartment blocks and summer villas here has boomed. Smaller and less commercially developed is the Bay of Pollensa, north of Alcudia. Both bays are famous for sailing and windsurfing. Each has good marina facilities, hotels, restaurants, nightclubs and holiday apartments. Near Ca'n Picafort there is a good, but commercial, camping site.

Pollensa, Formentor and Lluch

Puerto de Pollensa has been a favorite vacation spot on the island for many years. The water here sparkles because there is nearly always a breeze, and thus it is seldom uncomfortably hot.

The ten-km. (six-mile) drive to Formentor, over a tawny-colored headland, is one of the most beautiful on the island, with glimpses of a romantic island set in a sea so blue as to seem impossible. Alternatively, motor-boats take passengers from Puerto de Pollensa to Formentor's superbly sheltered, pine-girt bathing beach. If you go to Formentor by road, and can spare the time, continue for 13 km. (eight miles) to Cala Figuera and the lighthouse at Cabo Formentor, which is the island's wildly beautiful northeastern tip.

After returning to Puerto de Pollensa, take the road for Pollensa, but do not fail to turn off to the right (just before reaching the town) for five km. (three miles) to Cala San Vicente with its delightful views and pleasant restaurants. Pollensa itself is an ancient little town. Its fine old Baroque church, by the tree-lined square where a charming market is held on Sunday mornings, its narrow streets and fine old buildings, are all worth a visit. During July and August, the art and music festival is held, with musicians of international repute. There are splendid views from the Calvario (365 steps) and Puig Maria, the hill and monastery facing Pollensa. A stiff climb, but a good view, with refreshments available at the top. After Pollensa, the road runs for 18 km. (11 miles) through mountainous country to the attractive and ancient monastery of Lluch.

Lluch has both a strong personality all its own and a wonderful sense of timeless peace. The small image of the Virgin of Lluch, Mallorca's patron saint, was found miraculously in 1208, and is the object of pilgrimages from all over the island. There is a small, but interesting, folk culture museum. The surrounding countryside, with several strange triple crosses, or Calvarios, crowning the hills, is unforgettable.

If you have some extra time, drive the 20 km. (12½ miles) each way up the incredible corniche road to La Calobra. The country is so wild here, on the lower slopes of 1,440-meter-high (4,756-foot) Puig Mayor, that you might be in the remotest Atlas Mountains, but if it is scenery you want (and your nerve and engine are to be relied upon) then you will not be disappointed. (This point can also be reached from Sóller.)

From Lluch, the road runs south past the Sanctuary of Cristo Rey to Inca and thence back to Palma.

To the Caves of Drach

The straight run of 48 km. (30 miles) from Palma eastward to Manacor provides a good general impression of the rich agricultural central part of the island. Before Manacor, in Algaida, is an old handblown glass factory, Gordiola. Manacor is Mallorca's second largest town and manufactures furniture and ceramics. Once there, you should not miss the great cultured pearl and gold filigree shop, Perlas Majorica, in the main square, the rectangular 15th-century parish church, or the 13th-century Torre del Palau, once part of a palace of the kings of Mallorca.

The sea is only about 12 km. (seven-and-a-half miles) further on at the delightful little resort of Porto Cristo, where there is an excellent bathing beach at the edge of the sheltered waters of the cala. Another eight km. (five miles) brings you to the huge and famous Cuevas del Drach (Dragon Caves).

To describe adequately the nightmare splendors of this freak of nature would be impossible. The weird stalactites and stalagmites are really extraordinary. After walking for a kilometer or so through tunnels, caves and grottoes, you reach a large underground lake, named after its discoverer, Matel, and said to be the largest in all Europe, beside which seats are arranged for 2,000 people in a natural auditorium.

The lights go out, and after a breathless pause, a faintly illuminated boat, propelled by muffled oars and containing a small orchestra of stringed instruments playing terribly sugary classics, glides across the deep, totally still water. You can leave by boat across the lake (high in the roof you can see the roots of a tree straggling through from the surface) and then climb a long flight of stone steps, having spent nearly two hours underground. Although interesting, the caves are usually overcrowded with tourists, which can spoil the magic.

Ten km. (six miles) north of Porto Cristo, the road forks to reach Cala Millor and the lovely beaches of Son Severa. The amenities at Cala Millor and Cala Bona are catching up with the areas nearer to Palma. One of the main attractions has been the great sandy sweep of Artá Bay. Then, after an inland sweep to avoid an impassable headland, you reach the sea again, high above the exquisite beach of Cala Cañyamel, to enter the Caves of Artá. While those of Drach were only rediscovered some 60 years ago (they were well known in ancient times), the Caves of Artá have been visited since the 18th century. They are more somber, as the rock is almost black, less fanciful, but "architecturally" even more impressive, giving you the impression of being inside a vast Baroque cathedral. The Hall of the Flags, or Sala de las Banderas, is, for example, about 40 meters (130 feet) high. They also have the attraction of being less crowded than those of Drach.

Retracing your route five km. (three miles) back, the road forks north to Capdepera, with its 14th-century castle, and Cala Ratjada, the island's easternmost point, where the sleepy little port has been turned into a top-notch resort. Indeed, so has a lot of this part of the coast.

The way back to Inca, through olive, almond and fruit orchards, is as varied and beautiful as any of the inland roads. The road passes through the small agricultural market towns of Son Serra, Sta. Margarita and Muro, each with its main square and surprisingly well-endowed church.

In Muro you will find an interesting small folk and craft museum, the Museo Etnológico.

Palma to the Southeast

This excursion runs along the little-known south coast of the island: Palma–Lluchmayor–Monastery of Randa–Campos–Santañy–Cala Figuera–Santañy–Alquero Blanco–Calonge–Cala D'Or–Calonge–Porto Colon–Felanitx–Porreras–Lluchmayor–Palma; nearly 160 km. (100 miles) of alternately peaceful and majestic scenery, with some fine beaches and picturesque small fishing harbors.

At Lluchmayor, King Jaime III of Mallorca was killed by Pedro IV of Aragón, the kingdom of Mallorca then being permanently joined to the kingdom of Aragón (14th century). Randa, to the north of Lluchmayor, was where the celebrated theologian, philosopher and alchemist, Ramón Llull, lived and worked in the 13th century.

Felanitx is a charming old town, well restored and picturesque. From the 500-meter-high (164-foot) Puig San Salvador one has breathtaking views across the island. Other spots worth a mention are the superb bathing beaches and surroundings of Cala D'Or, Cala Santañy, Cala Marsal and a dozen others that pierce a stretch of not more than 13 km. (eight miles) of coast, with Cala D'Or at the center.

A detour of six km. (near four miles) each way from Lluchmayor to the monastery of Puig Randa is in order merely to obtain a view over the whole southwestern part of Mallorca, and 48 km. (30 miles) away to the little island of Cabrera, a view you will not readily forget.

Menorca

Menorca, with a population of 62,000, is second in size among the Balearic Islands—roughly 50 km. (30 miles) long by 20 km. (12½ miles) wide, and a total area of 710 square km., with a shoreline of over 285 km. (177 miles)—it possesses a much more temperate climate than any other of the islands, and so is greener than Ibiza or most of Mallorca. Besides regular car and passenger ships from Barcelona and Palma, there are daily scheduled air services, complemented by direct charter flights from England. The excellent main road runs like a backbone for 45 km. (28 miles) from the capital, Port Mahón in the southeast, to the former capital of Ciudadela in the northwest.

There is another good road about halfway across the island, which runs north from this main lateral road, from Mercadal, for eight km. (five miles) to the port of Fornells. For the rest, if you wish to explore the extremely lovely coastline, with its many splendid beaches, there are roads which run off the main highway, and lead down to the sea. They are not the best in the world, but adequate. By and large, exploration is more fun by boat than by car.

The Menorcans tend to have a more relaxed attitude to life than the Mallorcans. Local industries are leathercraft and the making of world-famous costume jewellery, in addition to agriculture, which covers a greater proportion of the island than in Mallorca. A faint echo of the British period can be caught in the two gin distilleries and a small-scale industry in the making of reproduction furniture. The British flavor of the 18th-

century architecture has by now been almost completely mellowed by the
local influence. The island has charm and a distinctly different flavor to
the other Balearic islands. It offers, increasingly, new hotels, good restaurants and varied nightlife encouraged by tourism, but still operates at a
gentler pace.

Some History

All over the island, you will come across prehistoric dolmens, taulas
and talayots, megalithic rock structures, believed to have been erected between 2,000–4,000 years ago, that at Talati resembling a miniature Stone-
henge. Phoenicians, Greeks, Carthaginians (these last led by Hannibal's
brother Magon) preceded the Romans, who conquered the island in 122
B.C. and named the capital Portus Magonis, and all left something of their
cultural heritage. The Fine Arts Museum has a collection of coins, ceramics, glass and statuary. It is located in the cloisters of the church of San
Francisco.

The Vandals, Byzantines (under Belisarius), Moors and, briefly, Catalans, obtained possession, until it was unified under the independent Kingdom of Mallorca in the 13th century. It was not until Ferdinand and Isabella that Menorca became part of Spain, late in the 15th century.

Barbarossa, the Turkish pirate (or admiral, according to whether you
are reading Christian or Turkish history), sacked both Mahón and Ciudadela in 1558, and the island was seized by the British fleet in 1708. This
was confirmed by the Treaty of Utrecht in 1713. The French ousted the
British in 1756 for seven years and a Franco-Spanish force did so again
in 1782, this time for 16 years. Nelson occupied it for four years until Britain finally left after the Treaty of Amiens in 1802.

The British influence is noticeable in their fortress city of Georgetown,
now called Villa-Carlos, at the entrance to the great harbor, where the
windows are of the horizontal sash type unknown elsewhere in Spain.

Fishing is wonderful round Menorca, and the inhabitants are proud of
having invented mayonnaise sauce (*mahones*) to go with it.

Menorca's Different Colors

Menorca as a whole is most strangely unlike Mallorca, lacking much
of the latter's golden-beige of the old, and blue-and-white of the new,
buildings. Here the predominant colors are white, green and terracotta.
You cannot fail to be struck by the sense of unassailable calm, combined
with a faint trace of 18th-century English dignity. It is more severe, both
in appearance and climate, as it lacks a mountain range to protect it from
fierce north winds in winter. The south and west are more fruitful and
have a denser population.

The superb natural harbor leading to Mahón is hardly equaled in size
by any other Mediterranean port, and it is completely sheltered. The city,
famous for its cheese, has several fine churches, including the María la
Mayor with its beautiful organ, and a lovely city hall.

During their long occupation the British spent a million pounds on forti-
fying the entrance to the harbor, and even constructed a secret underground passage between San Felipe and Fort Marlborough. The Golden
Farm on the north side of the harbor was the home of Nelson during his
brief stay on the island.

There is more of historic interest to see in the former capital of Ciudadela than in Port Mahón, including several very fine 17th-century palaces (notably those of the Conde de Torre Saura y Moya and the Marques d'Escella), and a 14th-century cathedral, while the fine old town hall and the churches of San Agustín, San Francisco and Nuestra Señora del Rosario all add an enchantingly medieval atmosphere to the little town. Down by the port, a number of picturesque harborside restaurants cater to the yachtsmen and summer tourists.

If you turn off the Mahón-Ciudadela road at Ferrerías and drive eight km. (five miles) south you come to the small resort of Santa Galdana where several hotels now cater to tourists. Once a delightful cove with calm waters and a good sandy beach surrounded by a pinewood, this is one of the few places in Menorca to have suffered at the hands of the developers.

Santo Tomás a few kilometers down the coast offers much better bathing with a fine sandy beach. But probably the best bathing beach on Menorca is that of Son Bou reached by a good stretch of road from Alayor. The water here is clean and excellent for swimming or wind-surfing and acres of fine sand stretch away into the distance. Although popular, it is never too crowded.

Other readily accessible beaches include Cala Mezquida, five km. (three miles) from Port Mahón, and Cala de Alcaufar, Es Grau, Arenal d'En Castell, Punta Prima and Cala'n Porter, all within 24 km. (15 miles) of Mahón.

Menorca's highest hill is 360-meter (1,180-foot) Mount Toro, from which, on a clear day, you can see almost the entire outline of the island. At the top, which can be reached by car, is a charming old monastery and a huge, open-air statue of Christ. In Menorca there is less opportunity than in Mallorca for those who are in search of excitement, but the island does offer more than adequate comfort, a gentle beauty and a deep sense of peace.

Ibiza

The smallest and most southern of the Balearic Big Three is about 35 km. (22 miles) long by 26 km. (16 miles) wide, with a total area of 541 square km. It still preserves some of the pine forests for which the Greeks called it *Pitiousa,* the Pine Island, but now blended with almond, olive and fig groves, even occasional palms; the sun seems to burn more fiercely from an almost-always cloudless sky.

The hordes of antiquity had more than a nodding acquaintance with the island of Ibiza; Phoenicians, Carthaginians, Romans, Vandals, Moors and, finally, the soldiers of Aragón and Spain, all were on the premises at one time or another. Each succeeding occupant bequeathed a new name to the island, and yet we are not at all surprised to discover how these different names resemble one another: Aivis, Ebysos, Ebusus, Yebisah, Eivissa, Ibiza . . . the island derives its own distinctive personality from the subtle blending of these sundry civilizations. Over a long span of centuries, up until quite recent times, visitors to Ibiza were few and far between, and hence the island preserved its customs and traditions intact. The busy airport has put an end to this isolation, Ibiza being less than half an hour's flying time from Valencia, barely an hour from Barcelona, and only 20 minutes from Palma.

The island has 71,000 inhabitants of whom approximately 31,000 live in the capital, locally known as La Ciudad—the city. The island's highest point is 472-meter (1,550-foot) Atalaya de San José, and it is generally far more hilly than placid Menorca.

The City

La Ciudad (The City) rises steeply from the water's edge, blindingly white, fascinatingly uneven as to roof levels, its walls splashed everywhere with the violent scarlet of geranium, carnation or purple bougainvillaea. This, you will feel at once, is what people who have never been there mean when they talk longingly of the perfect Mediterranean, escapist island.

A dazzling genuine medieval fortress crowns the city's heights—this is the Dalt Vila, or upper town, built up and added to by Charles V and Philip II. The lower town, nestling snugly below, is a spread of antique buildings shining forth in all their whitewashed intensity. Only two entrancegates give access to the upper town, which is enclosed by ramparts. Of these gateways, the Portal de las Tablas, which you can reach from the Plaza del Mercado, features two Roman statues, which were excavated during the building of the walls and placed in niches to guard the passage.

The Dalt Vila abounds in natural observation points, the largest of which is Cathedral Square, where you will also find the castle and the Bishops' Palace. Many budding young artists have studios in the fine old residences, some of which have been restored while others are now derelict. The Dalt Vila is also where some of the city's best restaurants are located. Many have tables placed outdoors on the quaint, cobblestone streets and squares, or on terraces overlooking the harbor. Visit the old fishing quarter, the picturesque Barrio Sa Penya, with its typical bars, cellars, and restaurants. All better hotels are out of town at the beaches. Try to visit the Museo Puig des Molins which contains a unique collection of Punic artifacts recovered from various excavations throughout the island. On the same hill, Puig des Moulins; there is a large necropolis, or ancient burial ground, known as Ereso. It can only be visited with special permission. After browsing through the tourist shops here (which are especially noted for fashions) you will likely head back to the Dalt Vila or to nearby Figueretas.

For a slice of the island's more trendy, cosmopolitan life, and extraordinary characters, try people-watching at the Mar y Sol cafe, on the corner of the harbor, or in the Zoo bar in the evening.

The Rest of the Island

The only towns beside La Ciudad are Santa Eulalia del Río and San Antonio Abad. The latter is now the island's most important tourist center, due to its burgeoning hotels, pleasant esplanade and yacht harbor, and numerous bars, restaurants and discos. Santa Eulalia is smaller and by far the pleasanter of the two, with its quieter beach, tree-lined square, old streets and peaceful atmosphere. San Juan Bautista lies five km. (three miles) inland from the simple little resort of Portinatx del Rey in the extreme north. Buses (there is no railroad) link them together and all distances are short, so there is little need to hire a car for traveling between the towns. However, it is worthwhile for exploring the more remote spots in the northeast and southwest of the island. These can also be reached by sea, which can be arranged inexpensively by local travel agencies.

Ibiza's coast is cliff-like for the most part, but deeply penetrated by calas, or inlets, where the water is marvelously calm, and at the head of which there is usually a sandy beach circled by pine trees. Some of these calas do have small hotels, but other facilities are usually very limited. Among the best of the calas are those just north of Santa Eulalia, notably Playa dés Caná, Cala Nova, Cala Llena and Cala Mestilla. All are perfect for diving and underwater fishing. Just north of San Antonio is Cala Grassio and, west of it, is the delicious Cala Bassa, from which you can see the sizeable, but now uninhabited, island of Conejera.

Santa Eulalia del Río was founded in about 700 B.C. by the Carthaginians, and its triple fortifications were familiar to the earliest voyagers. Its principal sight is the extraordinary African kraal-shaped church.

The road to the salt marshes (Las Salinas), on the southern part of the island, passes through San Jorge: the church here and the one in the picturesque village of San José are Ibiza's two most delightfully typical churches, definitely among the sights to be seen. After following the beaches of En-Bossa, you reach the marshes, which were worked by the early Carthaginians, who also exploited salt mines on Formentera. It's quite a show to see the salt being extracted and loaded onto the narrow-gauge industrial railway.

Codolar beach, to the west of southernmost La Canal, and not far from the airport, provides ample stretches of unrationed sand.

Cave paintings and ceramic objects believed to date from 1800 B.C. indicate that the island itself has been inhabited since the dawn of civilized time. But for most visitors, Ibiza is less an exercise in sightseeing than an adventure in sea, sun and underwater mysteries.

Formentera

Every day, large motor-boats chug out of Ibiza harbor and make the 18-km. (11-mile) crossing to Formentera in an hour or so. The route lies through a straggle of uninhabited islands, and you may even be convoyed all the way by a school of porpoises and flying fish.

Looking westward, you will glimpse the spectacular island of Vedrá, rising for 366 meters (1,200 feet) sheer from the water. Its only inhabitants are blue lizards.

Once among the salt pans of Formentera's only port, Cala Sabina, an old bus makes it up the five sloping kilometers (three miles) to the "capital" of San Francisco Javier. There is not much trace of 20th-century technology in all Formentera's 16 km. (ten miles) of length by two-and-a-half km. (one-and-a-half miles) width, but there are several good hotels and some spotlessly clean pensions where you need spend only a reasonable amount of pesetas a day, and that will include plenty of the excellent local wine.

The island is really two highish peaks linked by an eight-km.-long (five miles), narrow, low-lying waist, on both sides of which are unbroken and untouched sweeps of beach. The smaller, higher, eastern knob, known as La Mola (192 meters, 630 feet), has plentiful water and, as a result, grazing for the cows that produce the exquisite Formentera cheeses. Here also grow the grapes famous since Roman times. The hilltops are sprinkled with busy windmills, grinding the rich corn that covers the whole island in the spring.

PRACTICAL INFORMATION FOR
THE BALEARIC ISLANDS

GETTING THERE. Most European capitals are connected by air to Palma, capital of Mallorca, either by regular, scheduled, airline services, or by charter operators. There are also varied air services to Ibiza and Menorca. *Iberia* has daily flights between London (Heathrow) and Palma, and several flights weekly from London to Mahón, on Menorca, and to Ibiza. All British tour operators offer budget charter flights, and *Iberia* and *Air Europe* have special excursion fares. Financial savings are especially worthwhile with charter flights from Gatwick or Luton during the off season. London to Palma flight time is two hours.

Iberia flies from New York, Miami and Los Angeles to Madrid and offers special discount APEX fares; you can then connect for Palma in less than an hour. It also maintains regular services between Spanish mainland cities and the Balearics. From Barcelona or Valencia it takes about 35 minutes to reach Palma.

Iberia has direct services from Marseille and from Nice to Palma, as well as from Paris, Brussels, Rome, Zurich, Frankfurt and Geneva, and operates flights between the islands. All air services are crowded during the Christmas, Easter and summer (July to August) seasons and reservations should be made well in advance.

From the airport into Palma you can take either a taxi (about 1,000 ptas.) or the public bus service which operates half-hourly to the city center. A taxi to the main nearby resort of Arenal will cost around 1,500 ptas., to a northern resort, such as Pollensa, about 6,000 ptas. Baggage is charged extra.

To reach the islands by boat, *Compañía Trasmediterránea* has the following passenger and car ferry services to Palma: daily by night and thrice weekly by day from Barcelona (eight hrs.); from Valencia daily except Sun. (nine hrs.). It also links Palma and Ibiza twice weekly during summer (four-and-a-half hrs.), and Palma–Port Mahón (Menorca) every Sun. (six-and-a-half hrs.). Ferries from Valencia operate two times a week during the summer to Ibiza and once to Mahón via Palma. There is also a car-ferry link between Sète, in southern France, and Mallorca and Ibiza, twice a week from mid-June to mid-Sept. If traveling with a car, note that embarcation and booking conditions in Barcelona port can be chaotic, so reserve well ahead and arrive early to claim your place. Ferries are often full during summer season. A passenger hydrojet service between Palma and Ibiza operates daily from May 1 until Oct. 30.

GETTING AROUND MALLORCA. There are several daily bus services between the various resorts throughout the island and the capital, Palma, which make a whole day excursion cheap and easy. Most leave from the Plaza España, or Cafe Alcalá, Avda. A. Rossello. The Tourist Office provides timetables.

There is a delightfully old-fashioned train that goes through the mountains to Sóller, with five trips daily. Another line takes a circuitous route from Palma to Inca.

Car hire is from: *Atesa,* Antonio Ribas 33 (tel. 27 04 04), *Avis* (tel. 23 07 20) and *Hertz* (tel. 23 23 74), both on Paseo Marítimo, at nos. 16 and 13 respectively, and *Ital,* Avda. Conde de Sallent 13 (tel. 71 55 56), all in Palma. Or from any of the dozens of small firms all over the island. *Avis, Hertz* and *Europcar* have booths at the airport, and it is usually not necessary to book in advance except for high season. You can pay by credit card. It is also possible to hire motor scooters and bicycles. Remember that some of the mountain roads in Mallorca are narrow and serpentine, and that driving is on the left. Note also that most filling stations close on Sundays, and that the wearing of seat belts is compulsory. Speed limits: expressways 120 km.p.h., country roads 100 km.p.h., in towns 50 km.p.h., or according to signs.

Sightseeing coaches, run by reliable travel agencies such as *Iberia, Marsans, Melía* etc., pick you up at your hotel and take you to Valldemossa Monastery, Formentor and Pollensa, the caves of Artá and Drach, Sóller, etc. There are also a number of boat tours out of such places as Palma or Alcudia.

The other islands. Transportation here offers a choice between hire car, bus, taxi, bicycle, donkey or your own two feet. All the important roads are good; but away from the few highroads, the road surfaces can be very bad.

You can rent cars in all the main towns. In Ciudadela, Menorca, *Avis* are at Conquistador 81 (tel. 38 11 74), and *Atesa* at Poligono Industrial (tel. 38 47 36). In Mahón, Menorca, *Avis* are at the airport. *Hertz* at Vassallo 14. In Ibiza, *Avis* and *Hertz* are both at the airport, *Atesa* at Ramón Muntaner 17 (tel. 30 59 17) and *Autos Ibiza,* Calle Mallor 3 (tel. 30 25 66).

Note that standards of driving are generally poor, many of the locals having only graduated to cars from mule carts; and, in addition, many tourist drivers either come from the U.K. and so are used to driving on the left, or else are concentrating more on the scenery than on their driving.

HOTELS. Many of the Balearic hotels, especially on the smaller islands and in the less developed resorts, are only open from April through October and tend to be *very* full during the high summer season, July and August. Be sure to check first if you are planning a winter break, and do book in advance during high summer. Many of the larger modern hotels deal mainly with package-tour groups; they often have their own discos and provide entertainments and sporting facilities. Most of the hotels have their own dining rooms and many holiday-makers eat in their hotels rather than in restaurants, which is a pity as there are excellent restaurants of varied styles and price levels on the island. We have recommended specific restaurants where we know them to be worthwhile, but exploring on your own can result in some excellent alternatives. Try the characterful local cuisine: grilled meats, pork, lamb and rabbit, also seafood. And remember that tapas, or bar snacks, are both good and cheap.

Hotel prices in the Balearics tend to be cheaper than mainland cities. To telephone any of our hotels from outside the Balearics, the area dialing code is (971). From outside Spain omit the 9. Within the islands, just dial the number. Ibiza appears as Eivissa in telephone directories and many tourist brochures.

FORMENTERA

A tiny, rather plain island with good beaches, but there is not much to see or do. In recent years the island has become a haven for topless—and bottomless—sun worshippers.

San Fernando. *Rocabella* (M), on Es Pujols beach (tel. 32 01 85). 40 rooms. Good in its category.

San Francisco Javier. *Iberotel Club La Mola* (E), on Mitjorn beach (tel. 32 00 75). 328 rooms in very peaceful surroundings, with sea view, tennis, pool. *Formentera Playa* (M). 211 rooms. Also on Mitjorn beach (tel. 32 00 00). *Sa Volta* (M), near Es Pujols beach (tel. 32 01 20). 18 rooms. *Italia* (I), Playa Mitjorn. 18 rooms.

IBIZA

A pleasant, small island well-suited to beach holidays. Ibiza town is colorful and worth a visit, but otherwise there is not a lot to see. If you want a quiet, restful vacation, avoid the overdeveloped resort of San Antonio Abad. Santa Eulalia offers most resort facilities, and is less noisy and generally more pleasant than San Antonio. However, the best places for peace and quiet are probably San Vincente and Portinatx in the north.

Ibiza. *El Corsario* (M), Poniente 5 (tel. 30 12 48). 14 rooms. In an interesting old building perched atop the Dalt Vila; pleasant accommodations and superb views.

At **Figueretas Beach:** *Los Molinos* (E), Ramón Muntaner 60 (tel. 30 22 50). 147 rooms. Pool. AE, DC, MC, V. *Cenit* (M), Archiduque Luis Salvador (tel. 30 14 04). 62 rooms. Good views from a quiet situation. *Ibiza Playa* (M), Playa de Figueretas, by the beach (tel. 30 28 04). 155 rooms. Pool, gardens, and a good view of the sea. MC, V.

At **Playa D'En Bossa:** *Torre del Mar* (E), (tel. 30 30 50). 217 rooms. One of the best; with nightclub and other amenities. *Algarb* (M), (tel. 30 17 16). 408 rooms. Pool. *Goleta* (M), (tel. 30 21 58). 252 rooms. Pool, gardens and nightclub. *Tres Carabelas* (M), (tel. 30 24 16). 245 rooms. Pool, gardens and nightclub.

At **Talamanca beach:** *Iberotel Playa Real* (E–M), Apartado 425 (tel. 31 21 12). 237 rooms. Pool and mini golf. *Argos* (M), (tel. 31 21 62). 106 rooms. Pool, gardens—and good views. *El Corso* (M), Playa Talamanca (tel. 31 23 12). Pool, tennis. MC, V.

Restaurants. *Dalt Vila* (E), Playa Luis Tor (tel. 30 00 52). In the old city and excellent. *Ca'n Riquet* (M), Avda. Bartolomé de Roselló 13 (tel. 31 42 26). Specializes in fish soups. *Celler Balear* (M), Avda. Ignacio Wallis (tel. 31 19 65). Opposite the San Antonio bus stop. Good for fish and seafood—try the *zarzuela de mariscos* or the *rape marinera*. *El Vesubio*

(M), Navarra 19 (tel. 31 00 26). A good Galician restaurant on Figuertas beach. *El Olivo* (M), Pza. Dalt Vila (tel. 30 06 80). Another good one in the old city.

Casino. *Casino de Ibiza,* Paseo Marítimo (tel. 30 48 50).

Portinatx. Excellent, though small and crowded, beach on the northern coast, near San Juan Bautista, set among pinewoods. *El Greco* (M), Apartado 361 (tel. 33 30 48). 242 rooms. A package hotel; pool. *Presidente Playa* (M), (tel. 33 30 14). 270 rooms. The other package hotel here; pool. *Oasis* (M), on the beach (tel. 33 30 70). 48 rooms. Simple. *Cigueña Playa* (M–I), Cala Portinatx (tel. 33 30 44). 84 rooms. A simple establishment with pool and right on the beach. *Portinatx* (I), Playa de Portinatx (tel. 33 30 43). 10 rooms.

San Antonio Abad. Unattractive and brash resort, with poor beaches—though there is plenty of transport to better ones nearby. On the plus side, there's an interesting yacht harbor, a pleasant esplanade, and a lively nightlife. Souvenir shops abound. *Hotel Pike* (E), Carretera Sa Vorera (tel. 34 22 22). Outside the town, in unspoiled country setting. Small but exclusive, superbly decorated, and with a good restaurant; pool and tennis. No children. *Nautilus* (E), Bahía de San Antonio, Ctra. Port Torrent (tel. 34 04 00). 168 rooms. Excellent hotel; pool. AE, MC, V. *Palmyra* (E), Dr. Fleming (tel. 34 03 54). 160 rooms. On the beach, with pool, gardens.

Arenal (M), Dr. Fleming (tel. 34 01 12). 131 rooms. Pool. *Bergatín* (M), on Playa S'Estanyol, San Agustin (tel. 34 09 50). 205 rooms. Pool, tennis. *Els Pins* (M), Bahía de San Antonio, San Agustin (tel. 34 05 50). 170 rooms. Pool, tennis, garden. Good value. *Hawaii* (M), Isaac Peral 5 (tel. 34 05 62). 210 rooms. Pool and garden. *Riviera* (M), Bahía de San Antonio, San Agustin (tel. 34 08 12). 168 rooms. Pool and garden. *Tanit Sol* (M), Cala Gracio (tel. 34 13 00). 386 rooms. Two restaurants. V. *Ses Savines* (M), Playa San Antonio (tel. 34 00 66). 133 rooms. Tennis, pool and garden.

Gran Sol (M), Es Calo del Moro (tel. 34 11 08). 138 rooms. Pool. *Hostal Maricel* (I), Avda. Dr. Fleming (tel. 34 09 77).

Restaurants. *El Yate* (E), Paseo Marítimo 22 (tel. 34 00 99). Near the port, with rustic décor. *Celler El Refugio* (M), Bartolomé Vincente Ramón 5 (tel. 34 01 29). Atmospheric. *Sa Capella* (M), Capella de C'an Bassora, Ctra. Ca'n Germa, km.115 (tel. 34 00 57). In an old house which should once have been a church. Nouvelle cuisine with Spanish recipes. *S'Olivar* (M), San Mateo 9 (tel. 34 00 10). Spanish cuisine; pleasant, with a garden.

Santa Eulalia Del Río. A sizeable resort and a pleasant town, but the local beaches are not too good. However, there are ferries to better beaches nearby. *Fenicia* (E), Ca'n Fita (tel. 33 01 01). 191 rooms. Just across the river from the town. Pool, tennis, garden and nightclub. AE, DC, MC, V. *Los Loros* (E), Cas Capita (tel. 33 07 61). 262 rooms. In a lovely, quiet setting, with pool and garden. AE, DC, MC, V. *La Cala* (M), San Jaime 76 (tel. 33 00 09). 74 rooms. Pool and garden—and a matchless view. *Miami* (M), Playa Es Caná (tel. 33 02 01). 370 rooms. Pool, garden and nightclub. *S'Argamasa* (E), Urb. Sargamasa (tel. 33 00 75). 159 rooms. Located ten km. (six miles) north of town in a peaceful setting, with private beach; also pool, tennis and garden. AE, DC, MC, V. *Tres Torres* (M), Ses Estaques (tel. 33 03 26). 112 rooms. Pool and nightclub.

Restaurants. *El Vergel* (M), Camino de la Iglesia 8 (tel. 33 08 94). Menu shows Hispano–Suizza influences, reflecting the two owners' nationalities. Has a lovely patio. *Cami del Rey* (E–M), Ctra. Es Cana-Sta. Eulalia (tel. 33 04 73). International menu, very good. *Sa Punta* (E–M), Isodoro Macabich 36 (tel. 33 00 33). Excellent nouvelle cuisine.

San Jaun Bautista. *Hacienda Na Xamena* (E), Apartado 423 (tel. 33 30 46). 54 rooms. A very good hotel, but the rates are extremely high— above those of many luxury establishments. With pool, tennis and nightclub.

San Rafael. Restaurant. *Grill San Rafael* (M), Carretera de San Antonio (tel. 31 44 75). Not far from Ibiza. Spanish and Ibizencan dishes served in rustic Spanish setting. AE, DC, MC, V.

San Vicente. At the north end of the island. *Imperio Playa* (M), Cala San Vicente (tel. 33 30 55). 210 rooms. Pool and nightclub.

MALLORCA

Mallorca has plenty of good beaches and many activities for both day and nighttime. It also offers fine, varied scenery around the coasts and in the hills and farmlands of the interior.

El Arenal. A noisy, brash package resort just to the east of Palma. There is a good sandy beach but the town is unpleasant and untypical except of the worst kind of resort. Discos, souvenir shops and snack bars abound. All in all, the town is best avoided in the height of the season. It does, however, have all the facilities for a good family holiday, if small children are involved, with a good safe beach and various entertainments. There is an openair market every Tuesday.

Garonda Palace (E), Carretera del Arenal (tel. 26 22 00). 110 rooms. About six km. (nearly four miles) from Palma. Pool. *Playa de Palma-Sol* (E), Avda. Nacional (tel. 26 29 00). 113 rooms. Pool and garden. *Acapulco Playa* (M), Ctra. Arenal 10 km. (six miles) (tel. 26 18 00). Away from the center, but by beach, and with pool, garden and nightclub. *Copacabana* (M), Berlin 65 (tel. 26 16 34). 112 rooms. Set in a garden a short way from the sea, pool and tennis. *Riviera Sol* (M), Avda. Nacional (tel. 26 06 00). 74 rooms. Pool, and near beach.

Restaurant. *Cas Cotxer* (E), Carr. Arenal 31 (tel. 26 20 49). One of the few stars of this resort, a veritable gourmet restaurant, mainly for seafood.

Bañalbufar. This village is about 26 km. (16 miles) northwest of Palma, near some of the most beautiful scenery in all Mallorca. *Mar y Vent* (M), José Antonio 49 (tel. 61 00 25). A three-star hostel with 19 rooms, tennis and a pool. *Hostal La Baronia,* General Goded 16 (tel. 61 01 21). 39 rooms. High on a hill overlooking town.

Ca'n Pastilla. Adjacent to Arenal. A very noisy resort, six km. (nearly four miles) from busy Palma airport. Has a very crowded summertime beach. *Alexandra-Sol* (E), Calle Pinda 15 (tel. 26 23 50). 164 rooms. Pool, garden and nightclub. *Gran Hotel El Cid Sol* (M), Ctra. El Arenal eight km.(five miles) (tel. 26 08 50). 216 rooms. Pool, mini golf and tennis. *Linda* (M), Torre Redona (tel. 26 29 82). 189 rooms. Pool, tennis and mini golf.

Ca'n Picafort. An ugly resort town on the northern coast, full of concrete hotels, souvenir shops and snack bars, but there is a good long sandy beach. *Exagón* (M), Ronda de la Pieta 46 (tel. 52 70 75). 285 rooms. Pool, tennis, mini golf and nightclub. *Gran Vista* (M), Ctra. Artá-Alcudia (tel. 52 73 46). 277 rooms. Two pools, mini golf, garden, nightclub and huge recreational area. *Janeiro* (M), Via Diagonal 41 (tel. 52 71 25). 211 rooms. Good facilities. *Tonga Sol* (M), Ctra. Artá-Alcudia (tel. 52 70 00). 308 rooms. Pool, mini golf, tennis and garden and nightclub. One redeeming feature of the resort is its horse-riding facilities.

Cala Bona. Once an unspoiled fishing village, but now overwhelmed by neighboring Cala Millor. Mixed rocky and excellent sandy beach. *Gran Sol* (M), Paseo Marítimo (tel. 56 72 75). 58 rooms. Near beach; with pool, mini golf, tennis and garden. *Levante* (M), Calabona (tel. 56 71 75). 200 rooms. Pool and garden, tennis.

Cala D'or. 70 km. (about 43 miles) from Palma on the east coast, this is a pleasant resort with an attractive, indented coastline, sandy beach, good bistros, cosmopolitan atmosphere and horse-riding. *Iberotel Cala Esmeralda* (E), Urb. Cala Esmeralda (tel. 65 71 11). 151 rooms. Pool, tennis and garden. *Cala Gran* (M), on the beach (tel. 65 71 00). 72 rooms. Pool and garden. AE, MC, V. *Corfu Marina* (M), Urb. Cala Egos (tel. 65 76 00). 214 rooms. Garden and nightclub. *Gran Hotel Tucán* (M), Bulevard (tel. 65 72 00). 155 rooms. *Rocador* (M), Marqués de Comillas 3 (tel. 65 70 76). 95 rooms. Near beach; garden. AE, V. *Rocamarina* (M), Urb. Es Forti (tel. 65 78 32). 207 rooms. Pool and garden. *Skorpios Marina* (M), Cala Egos (tel. 65 71 51). 163 rooms. Pool and garden. *Oasis D'Or* (I), Es Revells 30 (tel. 65 74 27). 22 rooms.

Cala Fornells. A beautiful small bay, on the west coast close to Andraitx, 25 km. (15 miles) from Palma. Bathing from rocks. *Coronado* (E–M), on the beach (tel. 68 68 00). *Cala Fornells* (M), (tel. 68 69 50). 85 rooms.

Cala Gamba. Restaurant. *Club Nautico* (M), Paseo Cala Gamba (tel. 26 10 45). Waterside location, excellent fish.

Cala Mayor. Just east of Palma and, unless you like it noisy, not recommended. *Nixe Palace* (E), Avda. Pintor Joan Miro (tel. 40 38 11). 132 rooms. Pool and nightclub. *Santa Ana* (M), Gaviota 9 (tel. 40 15 12). 190 rooms. Pool.

Cala Millor. A big, purpose-built resort with a large sandy beach and good hotels, situated between the Caves of Drach and those of Artá, not far from Son Servera. *Iberotel Borneo* (E–M), Urb. Sa Maniga (tel. 58 53 61). 200 rooms. On the beach; pool and mini golf. *Iberotel Flamenco* (E–M), Sa Maniga (tel. 58 53 12). 220 rooms. On the beach. *Iberotel Playa*

Cala Millor (E–M), Urb. Sa Maniga (tel. 58 52 12). 242 rooms. By the beach; pool and garden. *Biniamar* (M), Urb. Son Moro (tel. 58 55 13). 108 rooms. *Don Juan* (M), (tel. 58 57 63). 134 rooms. On the beach; pool and tennis. *Osiris* (M), Na Peñal (tel. 56 73 25). 213 rooms. By the beach; pool and garden. *El Mundo* (I), Alondra 1 Urb. Son Moro. 15 rooms.

Cala Moreya. Pleasant small beach. *Colombo* (M), (tel. 57 09 49). 130 rooms. *Perla de S'Llot* (M), Sillot (tel. 57 08 50). 180 rooms. Pool and tennis.

Cala Murada. Good beach located near the picturesque villages of Porto Colón and Porto Cristo on the east coast. *Cala Murada* (M), (tel. 57 31 00). 77 rooms. Five minutes from the sandy beach in this well-planned villa development. *Valparaiso* (M), Solar F, Urb. Cala Murada (tel. 57 30 55). 39 rooms. Pool and gardens.

Cala Ratjada. In the extreme northeast, with easy access to picturesque Capdepera with its castle, and to the Caves of Artá. A fairly pleasant resort with two beaches and attractive harbor. *Aguait* (M), Avda. de los Pinos (tel. 56 34 08). 188 rooms. Pool, garden and rocky bathing. AE, DC, V. *Bella Playa* (M), Cala Guya 125 (tel. 56 30 50). 213 rooms. Close to the beach; pool and garden. *Serrano* (M), Son Moll (tel. 56 33 50). 52 rooms. Pool, and an Andalusian-style wine cellar. *Son Moll* (M), Tritón (tel. 56 31 00). 125 rooms. By the beach; garden. DC, V. *Cala Gat* (I), Ctra. del Faro (tel. 56 31 66). 44 rooms. Near a rocky beach, peacefully surrounded by pines. Pool and garden.

Restaurants. *Restaurante Lorenzo* (E), Leonor Servera 7 (tel. 56 39 39). Fish specialties with a French touch. AE, MC, V. *Ses Rotges* (E), Alcedo (tel. 56 31 08). French cuisine; one of the island's best.

Cala Santañy. Picturesque and peaceful. *Pinos Playa* (M), Costa D'En Nofre (tel. 65 39 00). 104 rooms. Near a good beach.

Cala San Vicente. A small resort on the rugged northwest coast. There are two pretty coves, and bathing is from rocky beaches—but there are underwater currents. *Cala San Vicente* (M), Capitán Juergens (tel. 53 02 50). 44 rooms. Tennis and garden. *Don Pedro* (M), on the beach (tel. 53 00 50). The largest hotel here, with 136 rooms. Pool and garden. *Molins* (E–M), on the beach (tel. 53 02 00). 90 rooms. Tennis and garden. *Simar* (M), Capitán Juergens (tel. 53 03 00). 107 rooms. Pool and nightclub.

Restaurants. For good seafood, try *Ca'l Patro* (M) or *Mar y Pi* (M).

Calas De Mallorca. A badly planned urban development on a rocky head amid scrubland, with possibly the tiniest beach in Mallorca. Many of the hotels are some way from the beach. *Los Chihuahuas Sol* (E), (tel. 57 32 50). 216 rooms. Pool, tennis, bowling, nightclub and many other amenities. *Los Mastines Sol* (E), (tel. 57 31 25). 261 rooms. Pool, tennis, mini golf and nightclub. *Balmoral Sol* (M), (tel. 57 31 02). 102 rooms. Pool, garden, mini golf and nightclub. *Los Canarios Sol* (M), (tel. 57 32 00). 215 rooms. Pool and garden. *Samoa* (M), (tel. 57 30 00). 331 rooms. Pool, tennis, mini golf, bowling and nightclub.

Restaurant. *Los Almendros* (M), Direction Porto Colón (tel. 57 30 11). Renowned for its fish dishes and excellent.

La Calobra. A beautiful spot in the north of the island which can also be reached by boat from Puerto Sóller. *La Calobra* (I), on the beach (tel. 51 70 16). 55 rooms. Garden.

Camp De Mar. A small resort 26 km. (16 miles) from Palma. There is a small, sandy beach surrounded by pinewoods. *Lido* (M), (tel. 67 11 00). 116 rooms. By the beach; garden. *Playa* (M), (tel. 67 10 25). 286 rooms. Pool, garden, tennis and nightclub. *Villa Real* (M), Ctra. del Puerto (tel. 67 10 50). 52 rooms. By the beach.

Canyamel-Capdepera. A charming resort, free from the usual commercialization, with an excellent beach. Located near the town of Capdepera, in the east of the island. *Caballito Blanco* (M), Via Melesigeni (tel. 56 38 50). 90 rooms. *Castell Royal* (M), Avda. Costa y Llobera (tel. 56 33 00). 112 rooms. Good amenities.
Restaurant. The *Porxada de sa Torre,* Carr. Canyamel (tel. 56 30 44), housed in an ancient tower, serves up Mallorcan grilled specialties.

Costa De Los Pinos. A small and stylish villa development with just one hotel, and a small, narrow beach surrounded by pinewoods and orchards. *Eurotel Golf Punta Rotja* (E), (tel. 56 76 00). 240 rooms. Extensive sports facilities include a nine-hole golf course.

Deya. A small village atop a hill and surrounded by mountains. Some 32 km. (20 miles) from Palma, it is a famous artist center. Sea bathing is from rocks, a few kilometers away. *Es Moli* (E), Ctra. Valldemossa a Deyá (tel. 63 90 00). 77 rooms. Set in delightful grounds and with beautiful views. Excellent food. Pool. *La Residencia* (E), Son Moragues (tel. 63 90 11). Old building, beautifully restored and furnished with antiques. Only 31 rooms. Good restaurant, pool. *Costa D'Or* (I), Lluch Alcari (tel. 63 90 25). 41 rooms. A villa set among pines and olives; very cheap but delightful.
Restaurants. *La Tablita* (M), Calle Archiduque Luis Salvador 26 (tel. 63 90 21). Delicious French cuisine. Book in summer. *El Olivo* (E), Son Canals (tel. 63 90 11). Excellent nouvelle cuisine, one of the best on the island.

Felanitx. A village in the interior, to the east of the island, that makes a pleasant center for touring. *Ponent* (M), on Cala Ferrera beach (tel. 65 77 34). 104 rooms. Pool. *Robinson Club Cala Serena* (E), Cala Serena Cala D'Or (tel. 65 78 00). 210 rooms. On the beach; pool and nightclub. *Tamarix* (M), Cala Ferrera (tel. 65 78 51). 40 rooms. Garden.

Formentor. At almost the northeast tip of Mallorca, 68 km. (42 miles) from Palma, a long, rugged peninsular with a long, narrow, sandy beach. *Formentor* (L), (tel. 53 13 00). 127 rooms. A luxury hotel wonderfully located among exquisite gardens, with magnificent views of the sea and mountains—plus one of the most attractive beaches in the Mediterranean.

Excellent restaurant; mini golf and tennis. Closed Nov. through Mar. AE, DC, MC, V.

Illetas. About eight km. (five miles) west of Palma, with excellent views of the bay but a very limited beach. *De Mar-Sol* (L), Pso. del Mar (tel. 40 25 11). 136 rooms. All amenities. Kosher food available. AE, DC, MC, V. *Bonanza Park* (E), Carretera del Illetas (tel. 40 11 12). 138 rooms. Pool and tennis. AE, DC, MC, V. *Bon Sol* (E), Pso. Illetas 4 (tel. 40 21 11). 73 rooms. Good views and genuine Spanish décor. Pool, tennis, mini golf and garden. *Illetas* (E), Carretera de Illetas (tel. 40 23 50). 67 rooms. Built on a series of rock terraces above the sea. Good food. Pool and garden. *Belmonte* (I), Pso. Adelfas (tel. 23 14 49).

Restaurant. *Bon Aire* (E), Avda. de las Adelfas (tel. 40 00 48). A real treat and well worth the money. Fish specialties. AE, DC, MC, V.

Inca. Mallorca's second-largest town, a center for the leather industry but not much for sightseers. No worthwhile hotel, either. **Restaurant.** *Celler Ca'n Amer* (M), Miguel Durán 35 (tel. 50 12 61). One of Mallorca's most famous restaurants, set in an attractive wine cellar. Try the roast suckling pig or fried artichokes.

Magalluf. A synthetic highrise resort of little merit, on Palma bay some 18 km. (11 miles) west of Palma. *Barbados-Sol* (E), Notario Alemany (tel. 68 05 50). Enormous hotel (428 rooms) with pool, tennis, mini golf and nightclub. *Playa Sol Magalluf* (E), Notario Alemany (tel. 68 10 50). 242 rooms. Pool and garden. *Atlantic* (M), Punta Ballena (tel. 68 02 08). 80 rooms. By the beach and surrounded by palm trees. *El Caribe* (M), Punta Ballena (tel. 68 08 08). 53 rooms. Pleasantly traditional for the area. Garden.

Orient. *L'Hermitage* (M), Ctra. de Sollerich (tel. 61 33 00). Lovely old building in country surroundings. 20 rooms, pool, tennis, good restaurant.

Paguera. A large resort 24 km. (15 miles) west of Palma, with a reasonable beach and some older buildings set among the usual concrete blocks. *Gran Hotel Sunna Park* (E), Gaviotas 25 (tel. 68 67 50). 75 rooms. Pool and garden. *Villamil* (E), Ctra. Andraitx (tel. 68 60 50). 103 rooms. Set amid pines above the sea. Pool and tennis. Very expensive. *Bahía Club* (M), Avda. de Paguera 81 (tel. 68 61 00). 55 rooms. Attractive gardens. *Carabela* (M), Ctra. Andraitx (tel. 68 64 08). 44 rooms. An older hotel. *Cormorán* (M), Puchet y Camino Capdella (tel. 68 66 50). 112 rooms. Pool and garden. *Gaya* (M), Calle Niza (tel. 68 68 50). 45 rooms. By the beach; a three-star hotel with pool and garden.

Restaurants. *La Gran Tortuga* (E), Urb. Aldea Cala Fornells I (tel. 68 60 20). International-class buffet with over 800 specialties. *La Gritta* (E), Aldea Cala Fornells 11 (tel. 68 61 66). Mediterranean specialties in beautiful setting. *Tristan* (E), Pto. Punta Portals, Potals Nous, near Paguera (tel. 68 25 00). Nouvelle cuisine here in one of the island's best eateries.

Palma De Mallorca. The capital city, port and tourist center. There is no beach, but it is nevertheless a fascinating, colorful place that has managed to retain its Spanish flavor—see the ancient buildings and narrow streets—despite the attentions of tourism. There is a vibrant nightlife and good shopping possibilities. The best place to stay if you are taking a winter vacation.

Valparaíso Palace (L), Francisco Vidal (tel. 40 04 11). 138 rooms. In the residential quarter, with pool, tennis, impressive garden and superb views of the bay. Rates are super-high. AE, DC, MC, V. *Victoria-Sol* (L), Joan Miró 21 (tel. 23 43 42). 171 rooms. Fabulous views. Renowned for its cuisine. Pool. AE, DC, MC, V.

Bellver-Sol (E), Paseo Ingeniero Gabriel Roca 11 (tel. 23 80 08). 393 rooms. Pool and nightclub. AE, DC, MC, V. *Palas Atenea-Sol* (E), Paseo Ingeniero Gabriel Roca (tel. 28 14 00). 370 rooms. Pool, beautiful views over bay.

Almudaina (M), Avda. Jaime III (tel. 72 73 40). 80 rooms. Central location. AE, DC, MC, V. *Bonanova* (M), Francisco Vidal 5 (tel. 23 59 48). 80 rooms. A comfortable place near El Terreno. Pool. *Costa Azul* (M), Paseo Ingeniero Gabriel Roca 7 (tel. 23 19 40). 140 rooms. Pool and garden. *Madrid* (M), Garita 28 (tel. 40 01 11). 84 rooms. A two-star hotel with pool and garden. *Saratoga* (M), Paseo de Mallorca 6 (tel. 72 72 40). 123 rooms. Pool and garden.

Restaurants. Palma is very well supplied with good restaurants, ranging from Spanish and Mallorquín, through Italian, French, international, to even Chinese. Fish, predictably, is a specialty of the island, but so too are pork and rabbit, and there is a wide range of local vegetables.

El Gallo (E), Teniente Torres 17 (tel. 23 74 11). Excellent international menu. *Porto Pi* (E), Joan Miró 174 (tel. 40 00 87). Not only French but also Basque dishes, one of the best. *Saridakis* (E), Fco. Vidal Sureda 115 (tel. 40 59 73). International cuisine. *L'Arcada* (E–M), Avda. Son Rigo 2 (tel. 26 24 50). A huge menu of delicious Italian food. AE, DC, V.

Amaro's Ca'n Barbara (M), (tel. 40 11 61). Located by the Club de Mar, Paseo Maritimo. Nouvelle cuisine. *Celler Payes* (M), Felipe Bauza 2 (tel. 72 60 36). Very good Mallorquín food. *Chez Sophie* (M), Apuntadores 24 (tel. 72 60 86). For good French cooking. AE, DC, MC, V. *Don Peppone* (M), Bayarte 14 (tel. 45 42 42). For amazing pastas and pizzas. *El Duende* (M), Cecilio Metelo 3 (tel. 71 50 35). Bistro with a small but excellent menu. *Mario's La Pizzeria* (M), Bellver 12 (tel. 28 18 14). For topnotch Italian food; there's a large garden with trees and a fountain for alfresco dining. *Portixol* (M), Avda. Nacional (tel. 27 18 00). Two km. (just over a mile) east of Palma, by the sea. Famous all over the island for its fish specialties.

La Casita (I), Joan Miró 68 (tel. 23 75 57). Top French-American food in a simple setting. *Cellar Payes* (I), on Bauza. Excellent Mallorquín food. *Cellèr Sa Premsa* (I), Plaza Obispo de Palou. One of the oldest—and still one of the best—budget bargains, with simple Spanish fare served in congenial surroundings.

Nightlife. Among the most popular discos in Palma is the one in the *Club de Mar,* Paseo Marítimo. *Tito's,* Playa Gomila, is also highly recommended. And worth a try are *Abaco,* Calle San Juan I, music bar with Fellini-style décor, and *Rikis,* Teniente Mulet García 8, an in-place with a sing-along atmosphere.

Eighteen km. (11 miles) west of Palma, in Magalluf, is an elegant casino which has a 1,000-seat supper club.

For the latest on the disco scene, as well as details of current events, artistic and cultural, consult the local English-language newspaper, *The Bulletin.*

Palma Nova. Another brash resort, 13 km. (eight miles) west of Palma, crammed with concrete tower hotels and tawdry souvenir shops. There is a good sandy beach, if you don't mind the crowded bodies and blaring music. It is near the Marineland oceanarium. *Cala Blanca-Sol* (E), Paseo Duque de Estremera 16 (tel. 68 01 50). 171 rooms. Elegant; with pool. *Comodoro Sol* (E), Paseo Calablanca (tel. 68 02 00). 83 rooms. Close to good bathing; pool, garden and nightclub. *Punta Negra* (E), Carretera Andraitx (tel. 68 07 62). 58 rooms. Beside a cove. Pool. Especially recommended. *Hawaii* (M), Urb. Torre Nova (tel. 68 11 50). 230 rooms. By the beach. Pool and nightclub. *Honolulu* (M), Pineda (tel. 68 04 50). 230 rooms. Pool. *Palma Nova* (M), Miguel Santos Oliver (tel. 68 14 50). 209 rooms. Pool, mini golf and nightclub. *Torrenova Marina* (M), Avda. de los Pinos (tel. 68 16 16). 254 rooms. Pool and gardens.

Porto Cristo. The fishing village ambience is almost wrecked by dozens of daily tourist coachloads, but the sidestreets offer some respite. There is a small beach and a pleasant harbor. Nightlife is limited, but it is close to the Caves of Drach. *Castell dels Hams* (M), Ctra. Manacor (tel. 57 00 07). Pool, tennis, garden. *Drach* (M), Ctra. de Cuevas (tel. 57 00 25). 70 rooms. Pool. *Estrella* (M), Currican 16 (tel. 57 00 82). 41 rooms. Pool and garden. *Perelló* (M), San Jorge 30 (tel. 57 00 04). 95 rooms.

Restaurants. *El Bosque* (M), Carretera de Felanitx. Typical Mallorquín inn serving giant-sized portions. *El Patio* (M), Burdils 45, specializes in fish dishes and international cuisine. AE, MC, V.

Puerto de Alcudia. Now becoming a major resort, with a superb beach and good facilities, but tends to be overcrowded in the high season. The yacht harbor is surrounded by cafes and restaurants. *Nuevas Palmeras* (E), Avda. Minerva (tel. 54 54 50). 114 rooms. Apartment hotel close to the beach. *Princesa* (E), Avda. Minerva (tel. 54 69 50). 102 rooms. Another apartment hotel. All rooms with TV. Pool. *Jupiter* (M), Dr. Davison (tel. 54 56 00). 463 rooms. Pool, mini golf and bowling garden. *Royal Fortuna Playa* (M), Urb. Las Gaviotas (tel. 54 59 94). 210 rooms. Pool and garden. *Saturno* (M), Dr. Davison (tel. 54 57 00). Pool, tennis and garden.

Restaurants. *Hermitage de la Victoria* (M). High in the hills beyond Bon Aire, with superb views out over the bay. Mallorquin specialties. *Mesón Los Patos* (M), for Mallorquín cooking. *Miramar* (M), overlooking the harbor, is a good place for fish. *S'Albufera* (M), Ctra. Alcudia-Arta, does excellent grills and vast portions. *Los Troncos* (M), (tel. 54 59 43). On the main road towards Can Picafort. Delightful wooded setting by beach; seafood specialties.

Puerto de Andraitx. *Mini-Folies* (E–M), Urb. Costa de Andraitx. 42 pleasant rooms; pool, tennis, gardens. *Brismar* (M), Avda. Mateo Bosch (tel. 67 16 00). Pleasant old hotel by the harbor, with a good restaurant. AE, DC, MC, V. *Catalina Vera* (M), Isaac Peral 68 (tel. 67 19 18). Small.

Restaurants. *Andraitx* (E–M), Avda. Mateo Bosch 35 (tel. 67 16 48). Overlooking harbor; excellent seafood. *Foc y Fum* (E), Carretera Andraitx (tel. 67 20 13). Two km. (just over a mile) to the north of Andraitx. The romantic atmosphere includes a flare-lit patio. International cuisine. *Miramar* (M), Avda. Mateo Bosch 22 (tel. 67 16 17). Fish specialties.

Puerto de Pollensa. A delightful fishing port-cum-resort with busy yachting marina and small hotels around a pleasant bay. *Daina* (E), Atilio Boveri 2 (tel. 53 12 50). 60 rooms. Pool. *Illa D'Or* (M), Colón (tel. 53 11 00). 119 rooms. In a quiet location by the beach. Tennis. *Miramar* (M), Anclada Camarasa 39 (tel. 53 14 00). 69 rooms. Tennis and garden. AE, V. *Pollensa Park* (M), Urb. Uyal (tel. 53 13 50). 316 rooms. The only really big hotel here. Pool, tennis, mini golf, garden and nightclub. *Raf* (M), Paseo Saralegui 84 (tel. 53 11 95). 40 rooms. Close to the beach. MC, V. *Sis Pins* (M), Anclada Camarasa 229 (tel. 53 10 50). 55 rooms. Close to the beach. *Uyal* (M), Paseo de Londres (tel. 53 15 00). Pool and gardens.

Restaurants. *Ca'n Pacienci* (E), (tel. 53 07 87). Between Pollensa and Puerto Pollensa. *Es Montelin* (E), Casa Bote (tel. 53 12 64). *La Lonja* (E), (tel. 53 00 23). Right on the marina. Good for seafood. *Bec Fi* (M), Anglada Camarasa 91 (tel. 53 10 40). Recommended for grills. *Cellar Ca Vostra* (M), on bay, between Pollensa and Alcudia, Mallorquín food. *El Cano* (M), Calle Elcano. Swiss specialties. *El Pozo* (M), Juan XXIII 25. Delightful atmosphere and food.

Puerto de Sóller. A small fishing port in the north of the island boasting a natural harbor. Day-trippers from Palma tend to crowd the small beach. *Edén* (M), Es Traves (tel. 63 16 00). 152 rooms. Overlooking the harbor. Pool, garden and bowling. AE, MC, V. *Es Port* (M), Antonio Montis (tel. 63 16 50). 96 rooms. In a converted medieval manor house, three minutes from the beach. Pool and garden. *Espléndido* (M), Marina Es Traves (tel. 63 18 50). 104 rooms. Two terraces for dining. AE, DC, MC, V. *Mare Nostrum* (I), Marina (tel. 63 14 12). 58 rooms. Garden.

Restaurants. *Ca's Carrette* (M), Cetre 4. In the main town of Sóller, away from the harbor; Mallorquín cuisine. *El Guia* (M), Castâner 1, for fish and local dishes. *Es Canyis* (M), Paseo La Playa d'en Repic. Charcoal-grilled specialties. AE, V.

Santa Ponsa. A brash resort within easy reach of Palma, and with a good, though small, beach. *Golf Santa Ponsa* (E), (tel. 69 02 11). 18 rooms. Amenities include pool and 18-hole golf course. *Iberotel Santa Ponsa Park* (E), Puig del Teix (tel. 69 01 11). 269 rooms. By the beach. Pool and garden. *Iberotel Bahía del Sol* (M), Avda. Jaime I (tel. 69 11 50). 162 rooms. By the beach. *Casablanca* (M), Via Rey Sancho 6 (tel. 69 03 61). 87 rooms. By the beach. Pool and garden. MC. *Isabela* (M), Puig del Teix (tel. 68 06 58). 156 rooms. Pool, garden and nightclub.

Restaurant. *Las Velas* (M), Puig de Galatxo, for international food. AE, DC, MC, V.

Son Vida. An attractive development in the hills behind Palma with good views toward Palma bay. *Sheraton Son Vida* (L), Castillo de Son Vida (tel. 45 10 11). 171 rooms. About 30 km. (18 miles) from Palma, located in an old castle. Some of the rooms have the original period furniture. Extensive grounds, pool, restaurant, tennis and golf course. *Racquet*

Club (E), (tel. 28 00 50). 51 rooms. Eight km. (five miles) from Palma in a beautiful setting. Pool, tennis and garden.

Valldemossa. A characterful old town set amidst spectacular mountain scenery. Famous for the visit paid it by Chopin and George Sand. Only one small hostel, *Ca'n Mario,* Vetam 8 (tel. 61 21 22), a nevertheless worthwhile touring destination.

Restaurants. *Ca'n Pedro* (M), Archiduque Luis Salvador (tel. 61 21 70). Typical mesón with good-value dining as, also, are *Ca'n Costa, Ses Epigues,* and *Marques de Vivot.*

MENORCA

A much quieter island than Mallorca. There are some good beaches—but many of them at the end of dirt paths. Though there has been quite a lot of development on the island recently, it has not been on such a large scale as on Mallorca. Villas tend to be more popular than hotels, and there are fewer package-tour travelers.

Cala Galdana-Ferrerias. Lovely beach near the town of Ferrerias. *Audax* (E), (tel. 37 31 25). 244 rooms. Facing the beach, but in a secluded position. Pool, tennis. *Los Gavilanes Sol* (E), (tel. 37 31 75). 375 rooms. Pool and nightclub.

Cala'n Porter. *Playa Azul* (M), Apartado 130 (tel. 36 70 67). 126 rooms. By the beach. Pool and garden.

Restaurants. *Cueva d'en Xoroi* (E), cave restaurant with a wonderful view, extraordinary setting—and excellent fish. *La Paletta* (M), at the end of town, overlooking the sea, in lovely gardens. Grilled specialties.

Ciudadela. *Cala Blanca* (M), Urb. Cala Blanca (tel. 38 04 50). 147 rooms. Near small, sandy beach. Pool and garden. *Calan Blanes* (M), (tel. 38 24 97). 103 rooms. Pool, garden, and tennis. *Esmeralda* (M), Paseo San Nicolás (tel. 38 02 50). 132 rooms. In the town itself. Pool, tennis and garden. *Iberotel Almirante Farragut* (M), but with some (I) rooms, Avda. de los Delfines (tel. 38 28 00). 472 rooms. Near the beach. Pool, tennis and nightclub. *Ses Voltes* (M), Cala de Santandria (tel. 38 04 00).

Restaurants. The best places are at the port. *Casa Manolo* (M), Marina 117 (tel. 38 17 28), is the pick of the bunch. AE, DC, MC, V. *El Gran Comilón* (M), Paseo Colón 48. Wide choice of menu and pleasant interior patio. MC, V. *La Payesa* (M), Marina 67 (tel. 38 00 21), is also good. *C'as Quinto* (I), Alfonso III, is simple and popular. *Es Pou* (M), San Rafael 10 (tel. 38 41 97). Very good Basque dishes.

Fornells. A delightful small fishing port on the north of the island, renowned for its fish restaurants specializing in lobster dishes. **Restaurants.** *Es Plá* and *Es Port* are both (M), by the port, and worth visiting.

Mahón. 4 km. (2½ miles) inland from the open sea, with a perfect natural harbor. Not many people actually stay here, but it is usually crowded with visitors in the daytime. A far quieter place than either Palma or Ibiza towns. *Port Mahón* (E), Paseo Marítimo (tel. 36 26 00). 60 rooms. Stands on a cliff directly above the yacht club, and has a good view over the harbor. Very comfortable, with pool, garden and nightclub. *Capri* (M), San Esteban 8 (tel. 36 14 00). 75 rooms. One of the only two hotels in town (there are about half-a-dozen hostels).

Restaurants. There is a whole host of good eating places at the port. *L'Arpo* (M), 2 Teniente Mártires del Atlante 124. On two floors—view of the sea from the upper. Catalan and Menorquín dishes. *De Nit* (M), Camino Ferranda 3 (tel. 36 30 30). Two km. (just over a mile) south, at Llumesanas. Possibly the best on the island. *El Greco* (M), Dr. Orfila 49 (tel. 36 43 67). AE, DC, MC, V. *Rocamar* (M), Cala Fonduco 16 (tel. 36 56 01). One km. (just over half-a-mile) out, in Cala Fonduco, with lovely views. Good for fish. AE, DC, MC, V. *Rosa de los Vientos* (M), 2 Teniente Mártires del Atlante 10 (tel. 36 41 76). Seafood specialties. *Pilar* (M), Cardona y Orfila 61 (tel. 36 68 17). Local Specialties.

Punta Prima/San Luis. Quite a well-established resort near the town of San Luis, with lots of villas, and a medium-sized shady beach which gets rather crowded. *Pueblo Menorca* (M), (tel. 36 18 50). 538 rooms. One-star hotel with pool, tennis, garden and nightclub. *Xaloc* (M), (tel. 36 19 22). 58 rooms. Pool, mini golf and garden.

S'Algar/San Luis. A modern development; mainly villas, only a few hotels. Rocky bathing. *S'Algar* (M), Urb. S'Algar (tel. 36 17 00). 106 rooms. Pool, garden and nightclub.

Santo Tomás/San Cristóbal. A very quiet development near the town of San Cristóbal, with a large sandy beach. *Los Condores Sol* (E), (tel. 37 00 50). 184 rooms. By the beach. Pool, garden and nightclub. *Santo Tomás* (E), (tel. 37 00 25). 60 rooms. By the beach. Pool, mini golf and garden among the many amenities.

Son Bou. Good beach area located near the town of Alayor. *Los Milanos* (M), Playa Son Bou Alayor (tel. 37 11 75), and *Los Pinguinos* (M), (tel. 37 10 75), are two large, modern, soulless hotels at the end of the beautiful beach.

Villa-Carlos. Stands on the cliffs above the inlet between Mahón and the sea. *Agamenon* (M), Paraje Fontanillas (tel. 36 21 50). 75 rooms. By the beach. Pool. *Hamilton* (M), Paseo de Santa Agueda 6 (tel. 36 20 50). 132 rooms. By far the biggest hotel here. Pool and nightclub. *Hotel del Almirante* (M), Fonduco Puerto de Mahón, Ctra. Villacarlos (tel. 36 27 00). 38 rooms. In an 18th-century house on the road to Mahón. *Rey Carlos III* (M), Miranda de Cala Corp (tel. 36 31 00). 87 rooms. By the beach. Pool.

Restaurants. There are many delightful places at the harbor; best for evening dining only. *Magatzems* (M), Cuevas de Pescadores. For good fish.

CAMPING. There are a number of authorized camping sites on the three main islands, with facilities for both tents and caravans. Independent camping is generally not allowed. The best-equipped camps are, in northern Mallorca, a large site on the coast road between Alcudia and Ca'n

Picafort, and in Ibiza at San Antonio Abad (two major sites), Santa Eulalia and San José.

Hitchhiking is possible on both Menorca and Ibiza, but less successful on Mallorca.

PLACES OF INTEREST. Although most visitors to the Balearics are intent on spending as much time in the sea and sun as they possibly can, when these pleasures begin to pall there are a surprising number of museums and historical sites that are well worth a visit. Don't forget that all opening hours are prone to sudden changes.

IBIZA

La Ciudad. Museo Arqueológico Dalt Vila, Plaza de la Catedral. Open Mon. to Sat. 10–1; closed Sun.

Museo de Arte Contemporáneo, Plaza de la Catedral. Small.

Museo de la Catedral, Plaza de la Catedral. Small collection of ecclesiastical artifacts displayed within the Cathedral. Open Mon. to Sat. 10–1; closed Sun.

Museo Monográfico Puig des Molins (Punic Museum), Necrópolis Púnica. Underground tombs that formed an extensive Punic burial ground which was used by the Carthaginians and as late as the Roman era. The most important Punic museum in the world, with a collection of funerary urns, ritual vessels, ceramics, terracotta masks, etc. Open Mon. to Sat. 4–7; closed Sun.

MALLORCA

Palma. Baños Arabes (Arab Baths), Calle de Serra 13. Dating from the Moorish period. Open 10–1.30, 4–6 daily.

La Lonja, Paseo de Sagrera. Originally the Exchange, now houses changing exhibitions. Excellent example of Gothic Spanish building, dating from the 15th century. Open 10–1, 5–9. Sun. 10–1.30 only during exhibitions.

Marineland, Costa d'en Blanes, eight km. (five miles) southwest of Palma. Performing dolphins, seals and other animals, and various entertainment and recreational activities.

Museo Catedral, in the Cathedral. Collections of relics and church plate, ornaments, tapestries and paintings. Open Mon. to Fri. 10–12.30 and 4–6.30, Sat. 10–1.30; closed Sun.

Museo de Arte Contemporáneo, Palau Sollerich, San Cayetano. Contemporary art displays in a superbly restored old palace. Open Tues. to Fri. 11–1.30, 5–8.30, Sat. 11–1.30; closed Sun. and Mon.

Museo de Mallorca, Calle Portella 5. Medieval paintings, ceramics and furniture. Open Tues. to Sat. 10–2 and 4–7, Sun. 10–2; closed Mon.

Museo Iglesia de Mallorca, in the Episcopal Palace, Calle Mirador 7. Medieval Mallorcan paintings, jewelry, ceramics and archeological finds. Open Mon. to Sat. 10–8; closed Sun.

Museo Municipal, Bellver Castle. Archeological and prehistoric exhibits, Roman remains, numismatic collection. The Castle itself is also of considerable interest—see preceding general text. Open daily 8 A.M.-sunset.

Palau Almudaina, Almudaina Palace, Plaza de la Catedral. Collections of furniture and tapestries, paintings, armor and ceramics. Open Tues. to Sat. 9.30–1.30 and 4–6.30 Sun. and Mon.

Pueblo Espanol, Capitan Mesquida Veny 39. Model village with buildings of many styles, representations of the cities of Spain, narrow streets and small squares. Open daily 9–8.

San Francisco Basilica and Monastery, Plaza San Francisco. Superb Gothic cloisters and chapel. Open daily 9.30–1, 3.30–7; closed Sun.

Town Hall, Plaza de Cort. An impressive 16th/17th-century public building.

Outside Palma. Alaro, to the north of Palma. Remains of a Moorish castle spectacularly set atop a mountain. You can drive up bad roads to near the summit, completing the journey with a 20-minute walk. Refreshments available at the summit. Simple, rustic restaurant half way up.

Alfabia, Carretera de Soller, km. 17. Moorish-period gardens. Open Nov.–Mar. Mon. to Sat. 9.30–5; Apr.–Oct. Mon. to Sat. 9.60–6.30; closed Sun.

Artá. Famous and spectacular caves. Open daily 9.30–6 (til 5 in winter).

Cala Figuera. Picturesque natural fishing harbor.

Campanet. Interesting caves, less crowded than Artá. Open 10–7.30 (til 6 in winter).

Capdepera. Picturesque small town with a castle, near Cala Ratjada resort.

Deyá. Well-restored old village, home now of many artists, in a beautiful mountain setting.

Formentor, Cape Formentor, at the northernmost tip of the island. Fantastic views and rugged scenery.

Lluch. Monastery, with miraculous statue of the Virgin in a small church. Interesting folk and crafts museum also. Open daily 10–7.

Muro, *Museo Etnológico.* Small, but interesting, collection of folk and craft items. Open Tues. to Sat. 10–2, 4–7, Sun. 10–2 only; closed Mon.

Orient. Charming small village in spectacular setting, with a beautiful, tiny Baroque church.

Petra. Birthplace of Father Junipero Serra, founder of San Francisco. Monastery and a small museum. Open daily 9–8.

Pollensa. Medieval town in the north. Calvario steps to small, hilltop chapel with lovely views. A stiff one-hour climb takes you to Puig Maria, an old hilltop monastery offering even finer views, as well as welcome refreshments.

Porto Cristo. Picturesque fishing harbor. Nearby are the spectacular Caves of Drach, with a huge underground lake, and a drive-through, African-style Safari Park containing various types of wild game. Open daily 9–7. Concerts at 10, 11, 12, 2, 3, 4, and 5 during the summer. In winter last concert at 3.

Valldemossa. Beautiful mountain village with a famous Carthusian monastery, church and cloister. Also, the *Museo Chopin-Sand* (Real Cartija) plus an unusual reconstruction of an antique apothecary's shop. Open Mon. to Sat. 9.30–1, 3–6.30 during summer; closed Sun.

SPORTS. The Balearics provide splendid opportunities for indulging in various sporting and other recreational activities. **Watersports** are among the more obvious attractions. Almost every hotel has its own swimming pool, and sea bathing is excellent at the many, generally unpolluted, beaches. Sailing, waterskiing, scuba diving and windsurfing are all available in the major resorts, with lessons/instruction easy to arrange for beginners.

Golf. There are seven courses on Mallorca, two on Menorca, and one on Ibiza. Pick of the bunch are Mallorca's 18-hole courses at Son Vida and Santa Ponsa. Clubs can be hired.

Tennis. Many hotels throughout the islands list tennis courts among their available facilities, and there are various specialist clubs in leading resort areas.

Horse-riding. This is easily available, by arrangement through your hotel. In Mallorca, the open landscapes of the north coast offer excellent riding excursions.

Walking. The islands' beautiful rural areas and rugged scenery provide spectacular walking opportunities. The local tourist office in Mallorca publishes a good brochure outlining 20 routes in all parts of the island.

SHOPPING. Mallorca has a number of specialties that provide charming, delightful, and even useful **souvenirs** and gifts to take home with you. Among them are the artificial Mallorcan pearls, in soft colors, made into necklaces, bracelets, brooches and earrings—they are manufactured by *Majorica,* in Manacor; also **ceramics,** tiles, cups and plates, all brightly colored, with blue and red prevailing; embroidery; and wrought-iron articles of all kinds, from lamps to flower bowls. Wrought-ironwork is done with great taste and skill here, and extremely cheaply. Local handmade glassware is also popular.

Perhaps the best buys of all are in **leather.** Shoes, made largely in Inca, gloves, extremely reasonable and very soft, jackets and so on, are all easily available in most parts of the island, but choice and prices are usually better in Palma. Palma also boasts many antique shops.

The two main areas to explore are the myriad of winding streets and staircases around the Plaza Mayor, crammed with tiny shops each vying for the visitor's attention, and the smart Avenida Jaime III which is packed from end to end with chic, attractive shops with special concentration on shoes and fashion.

Markets are always great fun to visit, even if you're not buying. Palma is well supplied with them. Mercado Pedro Garau in the Plaza Pedro Garau is a riot of animals and food. The Flea Market held in Avenida Mexico on Saturday mornings is a maze of everything from wood and leather to cast-off clothes and furniture. A lesser version is the Baratillo on Gran Vía. The main city market, selling almost everything, everyday, is located on Plaza Olivar.

The rest of the island is well supplied with interesting markets, held in the mornings. One of the biggest is at Inca on Thursdays; here you can find almost anything. Alcudia's is on Sun. and Tues.; Artá, Tues.; Felanitx, Sun.; Lluchmayor, Wed. and Sun.; Pollensa, Sun.; La Puebla, Sun.; and Sóller, Sat.

The other islands have less to offer in the way of shops. Leather, again, is a good buy usually, but less so than in Mallorca. The main thing is to shop around, look long and carefully, and haggle whenever you can. All the islands have tourist traps that would make Long John Silver turn in his grave. If you are after typical souvenirs, go to the small shops that sell groceries or kitchen utensils. Locally produced spices or woodware can be cheap and excellent, but you will have to thread your way through a wilderness of plastic. Best buys on Ibiza are trendy fashions.

USEFUL ADDRESSES. Tourist Offices. **Palma de Mallorca:** Avda. Jaime III 10 (tel. 71 22 16), and at the airport. **Mahón** (Menorca): Plaza Explanada 40 (tel. 36 37 90). **Ibiza:** Vara del Rey 15 (tel. 30 19 00).

British Consulates. **Palma:** Plaza Mayor 3D (tel. 71 24 45). **Ibiza:** Avda. Isidoro Macabich 45 (tel. 30 18 18). U.S. Consulate. **Palma:** Avda. Jaime III 26 (tel. 72 26 60).

For boats to the mainland and between the islands, go to the *Trasmediterránea* office on the quay in Palma; or ask at any travel agent.

In Palma the Police Emergency number is: 092.

For day-to-day information on events and local cultural activities throughout Mallorca consult the English-language daily newspaper, *The Bulletin*.

ENGLISH–SPANISH TOURIST VOCABULARY

Pronunciation. The important thing to remember with Spanish pronunciation is that the vowels are emphasized much more than the consonants.

Spanish pronunciation is always regular—once you have mastered the basic rules there are no exceptions to them. It is a very easy language to read and speak.

The Spanish alphabet has 27 letters; most are the same as the English ones, except there is no "k" and no "w." The Spanish alphabet has three letters that do not exist in English—"ch," "ll," and "ñ." When looking anything up in a Spanish sequence, "ch" comes after "c," "ll" follows "l," and "ñ" comes after "n."

Of the tricky sounds to pronounce the most difficult can be:

c   Can be hard as in "cat" or "cut"—casa (house); color (color) or soft and lisped, like "th" in "thanks." This happens before an "e" or an "i"—cielo (thee-ay-lo), celoso (thay-lo-soh).

d   Said as in English when it starts a word—data and delta; otherwise a hard "th" sound (like "this")—moda (mo-tha) meaning fashion or style; dado (dah-tho) meaning given.

j   A hard gutteral sound, harsher than the English "h" and made in the throat. There is no equivalent. Examples are—jamón (ha-mon) ham; jabón (ha-bón) soap; Jijona (Hee-hon-a) a town name; juro (hoo-row) I swear. If you have trouble with this sound, say it like an English "h" and you won't be far wrong.

ll   Almost the English "y." Llamar (ye-am-ar) to call; billete (beeyey-tay) ticket.

ñ   Nasal twang to an "n." Same kind of sound as in English "gnu" or the Italian "gnocchi."

z   The same as the lisped "c." "Z" is always lisped before *all* vowels. Zamora (Tha-mo-ra) a town name; zebra (thay-bra) zebra; zumo (thoo-mo) juice.

Basics

yes	sí
no	no
please	por favor
thank you	gracias
thank you very much	muchas gracias
excuse me	perdóneme, perdon
sorry	lo siento
good morning	buenos días
good afternoon	buenas tardes
good night	buenas noches
goodbye	adiós /hasta la vista
see you soon	hasta pronto
be seeing you	hasta luego
goodbye (literally "until tomorrow")	hasta mañana

Numbers

1	uno, una	16	dieciséis
2	dos	17	diecisiete
3	tres	18	dieciocho
4	cuatro	19	diecinueve
5	cinco	20	veinte
6	seis	21	veintiuno
7	siete	30	treinta
8	ocho	40	cuarenta
9	nueve	50	cincuenta
10	diez	60	sesenta
11	once	70	setenta
12	doce	80	ochenta
13	trece	90	noventa
14	catorce	100	ciento, cien
15	quince	1000	mil

Days of the Week

Monday	el lunes
Tuesday	el martes
Wednesday	el miércoles
Thursday	el jueves
Friday	el viernes
Saturday	el sábado
Sunday	el domingo

Months

January	enero	July	julio
February	febrero	August	agosto
March	marzo	September	setiembre
April	abril	October	octubre
May	mayo	November	noviembre
June	junio	December	diciembre

Useful Phrases

Do you speak English?	Habla Usted inglés?
What time is it?	Qué hora es?
Is this seat free?	Esta plaza está libre, por favor?
How much does it cost?	Cuanto vale?
Would you please direct me to. . . the bullring?	Por favor, para ir a. . . la plaza de toros?
Where is the station? the museum?	Donde está la estación? el museo?
I am American, British.	Soy americano/americana, inglés/inglesa.
It's very kind of you.	Es Usted muy amable.
I don't understand.	No entiendo.

I don't know.	No sé.
Please speak more slowly.	Hable más despacio, por favor.
Please sit down.	Siéntese, por favor.

Everyday Needs

cigar, cigarette	puro, cigarillo
matches	cerillas, fósforos
dictionary	diccionario
key	llave
razor blades	hojas de afeitar
shaving cream	crema de afeitar
soap	jabón
city plan	plano de la ciudad
road map	mapa de carreteras
country map	mapa del país
newspaper	periódico
magazine	revista
telephone	teléfono
telegram	telegrama
envelopes	sobres
writing paper	papel de escribir
airmail writing paper	papel de avión
postcard	tarjeta postal
stamp	sello

Services and Stores

bakery	panadería
bookshop	librería
butcher's	carnicería
dry cleaner's	tintorería
grocery	tienda de comestibles
hairdresser, barber	peluquería
laundry	lavandería
laundromat	lavandería automática
shoemaker	zapatero (man), zapatería (shop)
stationery store	papelería
supermarket	supermercado

Emergencies

ill, sick	enfermo, enferma
I am ill.	Estoy enfermo.
My wife/husband/child is ill.	Mi esposa/marido/hijo (hija) está enfermo./enferma.
doctor	médico
nurse	enfermera
prescription	receta
pharmacist/chemist	farmacia
Please fetch/call a doctor.	Llame al médico, por favor.

accident	accidente
road accident	accidente de carretera
hospital	hospital/clínica
dentist	dentista
X-ray	rayos X, radiografía

Pharmacist's

pain-killer	calmante, analgésico
bandage	venda
sticking plaster	tiritas
scissors	tijeras
hot-water bottle	bolsa de agua caliente
sanitary towels	compresas higiénicas
tampons	tampones
ointment for stings	pomada para picaduras
coughdrops	pastillas para la tos
laxative	laxante

Traveling

plane	avión
hovercraft	aero deslizador
hydrofoil	hidrofoil
train	tren
boat, small boat	barco, barca
ferry	ferry
taxi	taxi
car	coche
truck	camión
bus, long-distance bus	autobus, autocar
seat	asiento
reservation	reservación/reserva
smoking/non-smoking compartment	compartimiento de fumadores/ de non fumadores
rail station	estación de ferrocarril
subway station	estación de metro
bus station	estación de autobuses
airport	aeropuerto
harbor	puerto
town terminal	terminal
sleeper	coche cama
couchette	litera
porter	mozo
luggage	equipaje
luggage trolley	carretilla, carro
single ticket	billete de ida
return ticket	billete de ida y vuelta
first class	primera clase
second class	segunda clase

When does the train leave?	A qué hora sale el tren?
What time does the train arrive at. . . ?	A qué hora llega el tren a. . . ?
When does the first/last train leave?	A qué hora sale el primero/ último tren?

Hotels

room	habitación
bed	cama
bathroom	cuarto de baño
bathtub	bañera
shower	ducha
toilet	aseo, servicio, retrete; lavabo (in a train)
toilet paper	papel higiénico
pillow	almohada
blanket	manta
sheet	sábana
chambermaid	camarera
breakfast	desayuno
lunch	comida (de mediodia)
dinner	cena

Do you have a single/double/ twin-bedded room?	Tiene Usted una habitación individual/con cama de matrimonio/con dos camas?
I'd like a quiet room.	Quiero una habitación tranquila.
I'd like some pillows.	Quiero unas almohadas.
What time is breakfast?	A qué hora sirven el desayuno?
Come in!	Pase!
Are there any messages for me?	Hay recados para mi?
Would you please call me a taxi?	Me llama un taxi, por favor?
Please take our bags to our room.	Nos lleva las maletas a la habitación, por favor.

Restaurants

menu	lista (de platos), carta, menú
fixed-price menu	menú del dia, menú turístico
wine list	la lista de vinos
waiter	camarero
head waiter	maitre
bill/check	cuenta

ON THE MENU

Starters

aguacate con gambas	avocado and prawns
caldo	thick soup
champiñones al ajillo	mushrooms in garlic
consomé	clear soup
gazpacho	iced soup made with tomatoes, onions, peppers, cucumber and oil
huevos flamencos	eggs with spicy sausage and tomato
judías con tomate/jamón	green beans with tomato/ham
sopa	soup
sopa de ajo	garlic soup
sopa de garbanzos	chick-pea soup
sopa de lentejas	lentil soup
sopa de mariscos	shellfish soup
sopa sevillana	soup made with mayonnaise, shellfish, asparagus and peas

Omelets (Tortillas)

tortilla de champiñones	mushroom omelet
tortilla de gambas	prawn omelet
tortilla de mariscos	seafood omelet
tortilla de patatas, tortilla española	Spanish potato omelet
tortilla francesa	plain omelet
tortilla sacromonte (in Granada)	omelet with ham, sausage and peas

Meats (Carnes)

cerdo	pork	cordero	lamb
chorizo	seasoned sausage	filete	beef steak
chuleta	chop, cutlet	jamón	ham
cochinillo	suckling pig	salchichón	salami
		ternera	veal

Poultry (Aves) and Game (Caza)

cordonices	quail	pato	duck
conejo	rabbit	pato salvaje	wild duck
faisán	pheasant	pavo	turkey
jabalí	wild boar	perdiz	partridge
oca, ganso	goose	pollo	chicken

Variety Meats, Offal

callos	tripe	hígado	liver
criadillas	literally, bull's testicles (shown on Spanish menus as "unmentionables")	lengua	tongue
		mollejas	sweetbreads
		riñones	kidneys
		sesos	brains

Fish (Pescados)

ahumados	smoked fish (i.e. trout, eel, salmon)	besugo	sea bream
		lenguado	sole
		lubina	sea bass
anchoa	anchovy	merluza	hake, white fish
anguila	eel		
angulas	elver (baby eel)	mero	grouper fish
		pez espada, emperador	sword fish
atún, bonito	tuna		
bacalao	cod	rape	angler fish
salmón	salmon	sardina	sardine
salmonete	red mullet	trucha	trout

Shellfish and Seafood (Mariscos)

almeja	clam	ostra	oyster
boquerones	whitebait	percebes	barnacles
calamares	squid	pulpo	octopus
cangrejo	crab	sepia	cattlefish
centolla	spider crab	vieiras	scallop (in Galicia)
gambas	prawns, shrimp		
langosta	lobster	zarzuela de mariscos	shellfish casserole
langostino	crayfish		
mejillones	mussels		

Vegetables (Verduras)

aceituna	olive	espárragos	asparagus
aguacate	avocado	espinacas	spinach
ajo	garlic	espinacas a la catalana	spinach with garlic, raisins, and pine kernels
alcachofa	artichoke		
apio	celery		
berenjena	egg plant		
cebolla	onion	guisantes	peas
calabaza	pumpkin	haba	broad bean
champiñon	mushroom	judía verde	green bean
col	cabbage	lechuga	lettuce
coliflor	cauliflower	lenteja	lentil
endivia	endive, chicory	palmitos	palm hearts
escarola	chicory	pepino	cucumber
ensalada	salad	pepinos	zucchine
ensaladilla rusa	potato salad	pimiento	green pepper
		patata	potato

puerro	leak	tomate	tomato
seta	chanterelle mushroom	zanahoria	carrot

Fruit (Frutas)

albaricoque	apricot	limón	lemon
ananás	pineapple	manzana	apple
cereza	cherry	melocotón	peach
ciruela	plum	melón	melon
frambuesa	raspberry	naranja	orange
fresa	strawberry	pera	pear
fresón	large strawberry	plátano	banana
		sandía	water melon
grosella negra	blackcurrant	uvas	grapes
		zarzamora	blackberry

Desserts (Postres)

cuajada	thick yogurt with honey	pastel	cake
		flan	caramel custard
ensalada de frutas, macedonia	fruit salad	fresas con nata	strawberries and cream
helado de vainilla, fresa, café, chocolate	vanilla, strawberry, coffee, chocolate ice cream	pera en almibar	canned pear
		piña en almibar	canned pineapple
		tarta helada	ice-cream cake
melocotón en almibar	canned peach	yogur	yogurt

Miscellaneous

a la brasa	barbecued	guisado	stewed
a la parrilla	grilled	mahonesa	mayonnaise
al horno	roast/baked	mostaza	mustard
arroz	rice	pan	bread
asado	roasted	pasta	pasta
carbonade	pot-roasted	pimienta	pepper
espaguettis	spaghetti	sal	salt
fideos	noodles	salsa de tomate	catsup, ketchup
frito	fried		

Drinks (Bebidas)

agua	water	agua sin gas	still mineral water
agua con gas	carbonated mineral water		

blanco y negro	cold black coffee with vanilla ice cream	jerez	sherry
		leche	milk
		limonada	lemon-flavored lemonade
café con leche	coffee with cream	manzanilla	very dry sherry/ camomile tea
café solo	black coffee (expresso)	té	tea
caliente	hot	con limón	with lemon
caña	small draught beer	con leche	with milk
		vaso	glass
cava, champán	champagne	un vaso de agua	a glass of water
cerveza	beer	vermut	vermouth
chocolate	hot chocolate		
cuba libre	rum and coke	vino	wine
fino	very dry sherry	vino añejo	vintage wine
frío/fría	cold	vino blanco	white wine
gaseosa	English lemonade	vino dulce	sweet wine
granizado de limón (de café)	lemon (or coffee) on crushed ice	vino espumoso	sparkling wine
		vino rosado	rosé wine
		vino seco	dry wine
horchata	cold summer drink made from ground nuts	vino tinto	red wine
		zumo de naranja	orange juice

Index

The letter H indicates Hotels and other accommodations.
The letter R indicates Restaurants.

General Information

Air travel
  from the U.K., 15–16
  from the U.S., 14
  in Spain, 31–32
Alcázares, 31
Auto travel
  from the U.K., 16
  in Spain, 34–35
  rentals, 35–36

Bars and cafes
  Barcelona, 307–309
  Córdoba, 391–392
  Granada, 405
  Madrid, 124–126
  Salamanca, 180–181
  Seville, 378
  Toledo, 155
  Valencia, 343
Bullfights, 30–31, 86–93
  Barcelona, 315
  Madrid, 134
Bus travel
  from the U.K., 18
  in Madrid, 113, 114–115
  in Spain, 34

Camping, 22
Castles and walled cities, 31, 173–174
Cathedrals and churches, 31
Climate, 4
Clothing, 8
Costs, 9
Credit cards, 10
Culture and People, 38–46
Currency, 8–9
  exchange, 19
Customs
  on arrival, 18
  on leaving, 36–37

Electricity, 26–27

Fairs and fiestas, 28–30
Flamenco
  Granada, 407
  Madrid, 127
Food, 45–46, 79–85
  breakfast and snacks, 84–85
  regional specialties, 81–84

Geography, 40–41

Handicapped travelers, 13
History and Art, 41–44, 47–69
Hotels, 19–20
  Andalusia, 418–431
  Asturias, Leon, and Galicia, 218–224
  Barcelona, 300–303
  Basque country and Cantabria, 237–241
  Catalonia, 272–279
  Córdoba, 389–390
  Costa Brava, 326–332
  Extremadura, 441–443
  Gibraltar, 448–449
  Granada, 402–404
  Madrid, 115–118
  Navarre and Aragón, 256–261
  New Castile, 160–164
  Old Castile, 193–200
  paradores, 20–21
  Salamanca, 179
  Seville, 373–375
  Southeast Spain, 353–359
  Toledo, 153–154
  Valencia, 341–342
Hours of business, 26

Information sources
  Andalusia, 416–417
  Asturias, Leon, and Galicia, 216–217
  Barcelona, 296–297
  Basque country and Cantabria,
    235–236
  in Canada, 1
  Catalonia, 271
  Córdoba, 389
  Costa Brava, 325
  Extremadura, 440
  Granada, 402–407
  Madrid, 112, 138–139
  Navarre and Aragón, 254
  New Castile, 159
  Old Castile, 192
  Salamanca, 178–179
  Seville, 372
  Southeast Spain, 350–351
  in Spain, 1
  Toledo, 153
  in the U.K., 1
  in the U.S., 1
  Valencia, 340
Insurance, travel, 11–12

Fodor's Travel Guides

U.S. Guides

Alaska
American Cities
The American South
Arizona
Atlantic City & the
  New Jersey Shore
Boston
California
Cape Cod
Carolinas & the
  Georgia Coast
Chesapeake
Chicago
Colorado
Dallas & Fort Worth
Disney World & the
  Orlando Area

The Far West
Florida
Greater Miami,
  Fort Lauderdale,
  Palm Beach
Hawaii
Hawaii (Great Travel
  Values)
Houston & Galveston
I-10: California to
  Florida
I-55: Chicago to New
  Orleans
I-75: Michigan to
  Florida
I-80: San Francisco to
  New York

I-95: Maine to Miami
Las Vegas
Los Angeles, Orange
  County, Palm Springs
Maui
New England
New Mexico
New Orleans
New Orleans (Pocket
  Guide)
New York City
New York City (Pocket
  Guide)
New York State
Pacific North Coast
Philadelphia
Puerto Rico (Fun in)

Rockies
San Diego
San Francisco
San Francisco (Pocket
  Guide)
Texas
United States of
  America
Virgin Islands
  (U.S. & British)
Virginia
Waikiki
Washington, DC
Williamsburg,
  Jamestown &
  Yorktown

Foreign Guides

Acapulco
Amsterdam
Australia, New Zealand
  & the South Pacific
Austria
The Bahamas
The Bahamas (Pocket
  Guide)
Barbados (Fun in)
Beijing, Guangzhou &
  Shanghai
Belgium & Luxembourg
Bermuda
Brazil
Britain (Great Travel
  Values)
Canada
Canada (Great Travel
  Values)
Canada's Maritime
  Provinces
Cancún, Cozumel,
  Mérida, The
  Yucatán
Caribbean
Caribbean (Great
  Travel Values)

Central America
Copenhagen,
  Stockholm, Oslo,
  Helsinki, Reykjavik
Eastern Europe
Egypt
Europe
Europe (Budget)
Florence & Venice
France
France (Great Travel
  Values)
Germany
Germany (Great Travel
  Values)
Great Britain
Greece
Holland
Hong Kong & Macau
Hungary
India
Ireland
Israel
Italy
Italy (Great Travel
  Values)
Jamaica (Fun in)

Japan
Japan (Great Travel
  Values)
Jordan & the Holy Land
Kenya
Korea
Lisbon
Loire Valley
London
London (Pocket Guide)
London (Great Travel
  Values)
Madrid
Mexico
Mexico (Great Travel
  Values)
Mexico City & Acapulco
Mexico's Baja & Puerto
  Vallarta, Mazatlán,
  Manzanillo, Copper
  Canyon
Montreal
Munich
New Zealand
North Africa
Paris
Paris (Pocket Guide)

People's Republic of
  China
Portugal
Province of Quebec
Rio de Janeiro
The Riviera (Fun on)
Rome
St. Martin/St. Maarten
Scandinavia
Scotland
Singapore
South America
South Pacific
Southeast Asia
Soviet Union
Spain
Spain (Great Travel
  Values)
Sweden
Switzerland
Sydney
Tokyo
Toronto
Turkey
Vienna
Yugoslavia

Special-Interest Guides

Bed & Breakfast
  Guide: North America
  1936...On the
  Continent

Royalty Watching
Selected Hotels of
  Europe

Selected Resorts
  and Hotels of the U.S.
Ski Resorts of North
  America

Views to Dine by
  around the World